The Prentice Hall Reader

Eighth Edition

George Miller

www.prenhall.com/miller

The PRENTICE HALL *Reader*

EIGHTH EDITION

GEORGE MILLER

University of Delaware

PEARSON

Prentice
Hall

Upper Saddle River, New Jersey 07458

Library of Congress Cataloging-in-Publication Data

The Prentice Hall reader / [compiled by] George Miller—8th ed.
    p. cm.
  Includes index.
  ISBN 0-13-195571-3 (student book)
  1. College readers. 2. English language—Rhetoric—Problems, exercises, etc.
I. Miller, George
PE1417.P74 2007
808' .0427—dc22

2006001612

Editorial Director: Leah Jewell
Senior Acquisitions Editor: Brad Potthoff
Editorial Assistant: Tara Culliney
Production Liaison: Joanne Hakim
Director of Marketing: Brandy Dawson
Marketing Manager: Emily Cleary
Marketing Assistant: Kara Pottle
Assistant Manufacturing Manager: Mary Ann Gloriande
Cover Art Director: Jayne Conte
Cover Design: Kiwi Design
Cover Image: Richard T. Nowitz / CORBIS
Director, Image Resource Center: Melinda Reo
Manager, Rights and Permissions: Zina Arabia
Manager, Visual Research: Beth Brenzel
Manager, Cover Visual Research & Permissions: Karen Sanatar
Photo Coordinator: Nancy Seise
Full-Service Project Management: Patty Donovan/Pine Tree Composition, Inc.
Composition: Laserwords Private Limited
Printer/Binder: RR Donnelley & Sons Company
Cover Printer: Coral Graphics

Credits and acknowledgments borrowed from other sources and reproduced, with permission,
in this textbook appear on appropriate page within text on page 630.

Pearson Education Ltd., London
Pearson Education Singapore, Pte. Ltd
Pearson Education, Canada, Ltd
Pearson Education–Japan
Pearson Education Australia PTY, Limited

Pearson Education North Asia Ltd
Pearson Educación de Mexico, S.A. de C.V.
Pearson Education Malaysia, Pte. Ltd
Pearson Education, Upper Saddle River,
    New Jersey

10 9 8 7 6 5 4 3
ISBN 0-13-195571-3

For Evan, Adam, and Nathan, their book

CONTENTS

CHAPTER 2

NARRATION   110

CHAPTER 3

DESCRIPTION   161

CHAPTER 4

CHAPTER 5

CHAPTER 6

PROCESS   319

CHAPTER 7

CAUSE AND EFFECT   375

CHAPTER 8

DEFINITION   427

CHAPTER 9

ARGUMENT AND PERSUASION 473

CHAPTER 10

APPENDIX

THEMATIC CONTENTS

CHILDREN AND FAMILY

VIOLENCE AND PUNISHMENT

MEDIA AND COMPUTERS

STEREOTYPES, PREJUDICE, AND THE STRUGGLE FOR EQUALITY

WOMEN'S ROLES, WOMEN'S RIGHTS

GROWING OLDER

HUMOR AND SATIRE

READING, WRITING, AND LANGUAGE

SCHOOL AND COLLEGE

SELF-DISCOVERY

PREFACE

The Prentice Hall Reader is predicated on two premises: that reading plays a vital role in learning how to write and that writing and reading can best be organized around the traditional division of discourse into a number of structural patterns. Such a division is not the only way that the forms of writing can be classified, but it does have several advantages.

First, practice in these structural patterns encourages students to organize knowledge and to see the ways in which information can be conveyed. How else does the mind know except by classifying, comparing, defining, or seeking cause-and-effect relationships? Second, the most common use of these patterns occurs in writing done in academic courses. There students are asked to narrate a chain of events, to describe an artistic style, to classify plant forms, to compare two political systems, to tell how a laboratory experiment was performed, to analyze why famine occurs in Africa, to define a philosophical concept, or to argue for or against building a space station. Learning how to structure papers using these patterns is an exercise that has immediate application in students' other academic work. Finally, because the readings use these patterns as structural devices, they offer an excellent way in which to integrate reading into a writing course. Students can see the patterns at work and learn how to use them to become more effective writers and better, more efficient readers.

WHAT IS NEW IN THE EIGHTH EDITION?

The eighth edition of *The Prentice Hall Reader* features sixty essays, seventeen of which are new, eleven papers written by student writers, and nine poems or short, short stories that show the organizational strategies at work. New to this edition are nine selections that allow the students to see how writing and reading complement each other. As in the previous editions, the readings are chosen on the basis of several criteria: how well they demonstrate a particular pattern of organization, appeal to a freshman audience, and promote interesting and appropriate discussion and writing activities.

The eighth edition of *The Prentice Hall Reader* includes a number of new features:

- Detailed treatment of the writing process in three opening chapters
  How to Read an Essay
  How to Write an Essay
  How to Revise an Essay
- New "Writers at Work," which includes two examples of writing—one student and one professional—from the prewriting stage through drafting and then revision.
- New introductions to each of the nine chapters treating the organizational modes subdivided now into prewriting, writing, and revising. Each offers clear and succinct advice on how to write that particular type of paragraph or essay. The introductions anticipate questions, provide answers, and include checklists of the major concerns students should have when writing.
- New quick-reference checklists for writers in each chapter.
- New section "For Further Study" after each reading that includes activities focusing on grammar and writing, on working together, on seeing other modes at work, on finding connections, and on exploring the Web.
- New "Reading for————," an example of how learning to write in each of the modes or strategies helps you in reading a section that uses that mode or strategy.
- New "Responding to a Visual" and "Reading and Writing about Images" in each chapter that invite analysis of and writing about a visual image.
- New "Visiting the Web" in each chapter that invites students to pursue a Web-based problem and to write about it.
- New "Writing Suggestions" in each chapter. The text includes hundreds of possible writing topics.
- New Chapter 10, "Combinations at Work," a mini-anthology of classic essays that show a mixture of strategies at work.
- New student research paper on cell phone use.
- New section explaining and illustrating plagiarism.
- New "Ready Reference" section keyed to instructor's proofreading and grading symbols and keyed to grammar and writing activities included within the text.
- New larger, easier-to-read format.

What Is Distinctive About the Prentice Hall Reader?

The eighth edition retains and improves upon some of the popular student features from earlier editions:

- **Literary examples of each organizational strategy.** A poem or short, short story is included in each of the nine chapters. These creative examples show how the strategies can be used to structure not just essays but poetry and fiction as well. Each selection has discussion questions and writing suggestions.

- **Prereading questions.** Each essay is preceded by two questions that invite students to connect the reading to their own experience and to focus their attention on a close reading of the essay.

- **Writers on writing.** A paragraph in which writers share their observations on the process of finding a subject, composing, and revising.

- **Finding, using, and documenting sources.** An extensive appendix offers detailed advice on locating and evaluating sources of information—from printed texts to Web-based material. Also included are "Web Searching Tips," which help students narrow Web and database searches for more effective searching.

- **Detailed and extensive writing suggestions.** Each reading is followed by four writing suggestions: the first is a journal writing suggestion; the second calls for a paragraph-length response; the third, an essay; and the fourth, an essay involving research. Each of the suggestions is related to the content of the reading, and each calls for a response in the particular pattern or mode being studied. The material in the Annotated Instructor's Edition includes a fifth writing suggestion for each reading; additional suggestions can be found at the end of each chapter, and even more can be found at *The Prentice Hall Reader* Website at http://www.prenhall.com/miller. In all, the *Reader* has over 600 writing suggestions.

- **Selections arranged by difficulty.** *The Prentice Hall Reader* offers instructors flexibility in choosing readings. No chapter has fewer than five selections, and most have six or more. The readings are scaled in terms of length and sophistication. The selections in each chapter begin with a student essay, and the selections from professional writers are arranged so that they increase in length and in difficulty and sophistication.

- **Links to the Website.** *The Prentice Hall Reader* has a massive site at http://www.prenhall.com/miller. Additional materials for discussion, background information and reading suggestions, additional writing suggestions, and a group of hyperlinks are available for every reading in every chapter. Each chapter also has Web-based writing tasks, asking students to visit a site or a series of sites, gather information, and respond to a writing prompt. Students can use the *Reader* as they learn how to navigate the Web to find sources of information for their papers.

- **Commitment to exploring the links between grammar and writing and between reading and writing.** In addition to the three opening sections on reading, writing, and revising an essay, each chapter has an example of how learning to write in a particular mode contributes to learning to read selections using the mode. Further, each essay has an "Focusing on Grammar and Writing" activity and a new "Ready Reference" section included with the Glossary that explains and illustrates common problems with grammar and writing, tying these explanations back to activities included in the text. The links help build bridges between the content of the essays and the writing skills they reveal.

WHAT ARE THE ADDITIONAL RESOURCES AVAILABLE TO THE INSTRUCTOR?

ANNOTATED INSTRUCTOR'S EDITION

An annotated edition of *The Prentice Hall Reader* is available to instructors. Each of the selections in the text is annotated with

- a "Teaching Strategy" that suggests ways in which to teach the reading and to keep attention focused on how the selection works as a piece of writing
- appropriate background information that explains allusions or historical contexts
- specific class and collaborative learning activities that can be used with the reading
- a critical reading activity
- possible responses to all of the discussion questions included within the text
- an additional writing suggestion

Instructors Quiz Booklet   A separate *Instructor's Quiz Booklet* for *The Prentice Hall Reader* is available from your Prentice Hall representative. The booklet contains two quizzes for each selection in the *Reader*, one on content and the other on vocabulary. Each quiz has five multiple-choice questions. The quizzes are intended to be administered and graded quickly. They provide the instructor with a brief and efficient means of testing the students' ability to extract significant ideas from the readings and of demonstrating their understanding of certain vocabulary words as they are used in the essays. Keys to both content and vocabulary quizzes are included at the back of the *Quiz Booklet*.

Teaching Writing with *The Prentice Hall Reader* A separate manual on planning the writing and the reading in a composition course is available from your Prentice Hall representative. Primarily addressed to the new graduate teaching assistant or the adjunct instructor, the manual includes sections on teaching the writing process, including how to use prewriting activities, to conference, to design and implement collaborative learning activities, and to grade. In addition, it provides advice on how to plan a class discussion of a reading and how to avoid pointless discussions. An appendix contains an index to all of the activities and questions in *The Prentice Hall Reader* that involve grammatical, mechanical, sentence- or paragraph-level subjects, three additional sample syllabi, and a variety of sample course materials including self-assessment sheets, peer editing worksheets, and directions for small group activities.

The Prentice Hall Reader *Website* The *Reader* has an extensive Website at www.prenhall.com/miller that includes additional resources for both the student and the instructor for every essay in the *Reader.* The Website is divided into sections on Related Readings (print or online documents that are related to the topic under discussion or to the author), Background Information, Web Resources (with hyperlinked sites so that the students can immediately access these sites), and Additional Writing Suggestions. Each chapter also has writing tasks that involve examining Websites and documents. The Website adds a new dimension to the *Reader* and allows instructors to integrate the Web into their freshman English courses. Additional student essays are also available there, and you can submit the best of your students' work for inclusion as well!

Writer's OneKey Use *Writer's OneKey* to enhance your composition classes. Everything in one place on the Web for students and instructors, including:

- Personal tutoring available to students
- Paper review tool and research tools, including *The New York Times* archive
- Visual analysis exercises
- Mini-handbook
- And much more . . .

A subscription to *Writer's OneKey* can be packaged with each copy of this text by specifying ISBN 0-13-230171-7. See www.prenhall.com/writersonekey for details.

Prentice Hall Pocket Readers Each reading in our pocket readers has withstood the test of time and teaching, making each the perfect companion for any writing course.

To order the student edition packaged with . . .

> *ARGUMENT: A Prentice Hall Pocket Reader,* by Christy Desmet, Deborah Miller, and Kathy Houff, specify package ISBN 0-13-199440-9.
>
> *LITERATURE: A Prentice Hall Pocket Reader,* by Mary Balkun, specify package ISBN 0-13-238378-0.

PATTERNS: A Prentice Hall Pocket Reader, by Dorothy Minor, specify package ISBN 0-13-199441-7.
THEMES: A Prentice Hall Pocket Reader, by Clyde Moneyhun, specify package ISBN 0-13-230172-5.
WRITING ACROSS THE CURRICULUM: A Prentice Hall Pocket Reader, by Stephen Brown and *PAPERS ACROSS THE CURRICULUM,* by Judith Ferster, specify package ISBN 0-13-222573-5.
PURPOSES: A Prentice Hall Pocket Reader, by Stephen Reid, specify package ISBN 0-13-174626-X.

The New American Webster Handy College Dictionary   To order the student edition with a dictionary, specify package ISBN 0-13-228833-8.

The New American Roget's College Thesaurus   To order the student edition with a thesaurus, specify package ISBN 0-13-228797-8.

ACKNOWLEDGMENTS

Although writing is a solitary activity, no one can publish without the assistance of others. This text owes much to many people. To the staff at Prentice Hall who over the years have continued to play a large role in shaping and developing this text: Brad Potthoff, Senior Editor; Leah Jewell, Editorial Director; Emily Cleary, Marketing Manager; Brandy Dawson, Director of Marketing; and Tara Culliney, Editorial Assistant.

To my reviewers, who wrote extensive critiques of the previous edition and made many helpful suggestions: Sean Nighbert, St. Philip's College; Patricia A. Smith, Fitchburg State College; Clair Berry, Tennessee Community College; Betty Freeland, University of Arkansas at Little Rock; Justin Watson, Holy Cross College; Curtis Currie, Roane State Community College; Don S. Lawson, Lander University.

To the writing program staff at the University of Delaware, especially John Jebb. To my former students—both graduate and undergraduate—who tested materials, offered suggestions, and contributed essays to the introductions. To the University of Delaware Library and its staff, especially Shirley Brandon.

To my wife, Vicki, who encourages and sustains my work. To my son Eric, a freshman himself, who wrote the student research paper. And to my other children, Lisa, Jon, Craig, Valerie, Evan, Adam, and Nathan, and my stepchildren Alicia and Eric, who have learned over the years to live with a father who writes.
G.M.

George Miller
University of Delaware

How to
Read an Essay

Linking Reading and Writing

When your grade in most writing courses is determined by the papers that you write rather than by examinations based on the essays that you read in the course, you might wonder why any instructor would assign "readings" in a writing course. How do these two seemingly very different activities fit together?

How Does Reading Help You Write?

You read in a writing course for three purposes: First, the essays are a source of information: you learn by reading, and what you learn can then, in turn, be used in your writing. Any paper that involves research, for example, requires selective, critical reading on your part as you search for and evaluate sources. Second, readings offer a perspective on a particular subject, one with which you might agree or disagree. In this sense readings can serve as catalysts to spark writing. Many of the writing suggestions in this text grow out of the readings, asking you to explore some aspect of the subject more fully, to reply to a writer's position, or to expand on or refine that position. Finally, readings offer models to a writer; they show you how another writer dealt with a particular subject or a particular writing problem, and they demonstrate writing strategies. Other writing suggestions in this text ask you to employ the same strategy used in a reading with a different subject in an essay of your own.

    The first two purposes—readings as a source of information or as a stimulus to writing—are fairly obvious, but the third purpose might seem confusing. Exactly how are you, as a student writer, to use an essay written by a professional writer as an example or model? Are you supposed to sound like Margaret Atwood or Bob Greene or Maya Angelou? Are you to imitate their styles or the structures that they use in their essays?

To model, in the sense that the word is used here, does not mean to produce an imitation. You are not expected to use the same organizational structure or to imitate someone else's style, tone, or approach. Rather, what you can learn from these writers is how to handle information; how to adapt writing to a particular audience; how to structure the body of an essay; how to begin, make transitions, and end; how to construct effective paragraphs and achieve sentence variety. In short, the readings represent an album of performances, examples that you can use to study writing techniques.

Models or examples are important to you as a writer because you learn to write effectively in the same way that you learn to do any other activity. You study the rules or advice on how it is done; you practice, especially under the watchful eye of an instructor or a coach; and you study how others have mastered similar problems and techniques. A young musician learns how to read music and play an instrument, practices daily, studies with a teacher, and listens to and watches how other musicians play. A baseball player learns the proper offensive and defensive techniques, practices daily, is supervised by a coach, and listens to the advice and watches the performance of other players. As a writer in a writing class, you do the same thing: follow the advice offered by your instructor and textbooks, practice by writing and revising, listen to the advice and suggestions of your fellow students, and study the work of other writers.

How Does Writing Help You Read?

Reading and writing actually benefit each other: being a good reader will help you become a more effective writer, and being a good writer will help you become a more effective reader. As a writer, you learn how to plan an essay, how to use examples to support a thesis, how to structure an argument, how to make an effective transition from one point to another. You learn how to write beginnings, middles, and ends, and most especially you learn how essays can be organized. For example, through reading you learn that comparison and contrast essays can be organized in either the subject-by-subject or the point-by-point pattern, that narratives are structured chronologically, and that cause-and-effect analyses are linear and sequential. When you read other essays, you look for structure and pattern, realizing that such devices are not only creative tools you use in writing but also analytical ones that can be used in reading. By revealing to you an underlying organizational pattern, such devices help you understand what the essay says. To become an efficient reader, however, you need to exercise the same care and attention that you do when you write. You do that by becoming an active rather than a passive reader.

USING THE ACTIVE READING PROCESS

WHAT IS THE DIFFERENCE BETWEEN AN ACTIVE AND A PASSIVE READER?

Every reader first reads a piece of writing for plot or subject matter. On that level, the reader wants to know what happens, what is the subject, whether it is new or interesting. Generally that first reading is done quickly, even, in a sense, superficially. The reader is a spectator waiting passively to be entertained or informed. Then, if it is important for the reader to use that piece of writing in some way, to understand it in detail and in depth, the next stage of active reading begins. On this level, the reader asks questions, seeks answers, looks for organizational structures, and concentrates on themes and images or on the thesis and the quality of evidence presented. Careful reading requires this active participation of the reader. Writing and reading are, after all, social acts, and as such they involve an implied contract between writer and audience. A writer's job is to communicate clearly and effectively; a reader's job is to read attentively and critically.

Because as a reader you need to become an active participant in this process of communication, you should always read any piece of writing you are using in a course or on your job more than once. Rereading an essay or a textbook involves the same types of critical activities that you use when rereading a poem, a novel, or a play and demands your attention and your active involvement as a reader. You must examine how the author embodies meaning or purpose in prose. You must seek answers to a variety of questions: How does the author structure the essay? How does the author select, organize, and present information? To whom is the author writing? How does that audience influence the essay?

You can increase your effectiveness as an active and critical reader by following the same three-stage model that you use as a writer: divide your time into prereading, reading, and rereading activities.

WHAT IS THE ACTIVE READING PROCESS?

PREREADING

Before you begin reading an essay in this text, look first at the biographical headnote that describes the author and her or his work and that identifies where and when the essay was originally published, including any special conditions or circumstances that surrounded or influenced its publication. The headnote ends with two "Before Reading" questions that encourage you to connect aspects of the reading to your experiences and to anticipate the writer's thought. A careful reading of this material can help prepare you to read the essay.

Look next at the text of the essay itself. What does the title tell you about the subject or the tone? A serious, dignified title such as "The Value of Children:

A Taxonomical Essay" (Chapter 4) sets up a very different set of expectations than a playful title such as "When I Was Young an A Was an A" (See Chapter 9). Page through the essay—are there any obvious subdivisions in the text (extra spaces, sequence markers, subheadings) that signal an organizational pattern? Does the paragraphing suggest a particular structure? You might also read the first sentence in every paragraph to get a general sense of what the essay is about and where the author is going.

Finally, look at the series of questions that follow each selection. These questions always ask about subject and purpose, structure and audience, and vocabulary and style. Read through them so that you know what to look for when you read the essay. Before you begin to read, make sure that you have a pen or pencil, some paper on which to take notes, and a dictionary in which to check the meanings of unfamiliar words.

READING

When you begin to read a selection in this book, you already have an important piece of information about its structure. Each selection was chosen to demonstrate a particular type of writing (narration, description, exposition, and argumentation) and a particular pattern of organization (chronological, spatial, division and classification, comparison and contrast, process, cause and effect, definition, induction or deduction). As you read, think about how the author organized the essay. On a separate sheet of paper, construct a brief outline to help you focus your attention on how the whole essay is put together.

Remember that an essay typically expresses a particular idea or assertion **(thesis)** about a **subject** to an **audience** for a particular reason **(purpose)**. Probably one reading of an essay will be enough for you to answer questions about subject, but you may have to reread the essay several times to identify the author's thesis and purpose. Keep these three elements separate and clear in your own mind. It will help to answer each of the following questions as you read and reread:

1. **Subject:** What is this essay about?
2. **Thesis:** What particular point is the author trying to make about this subject?
3. **Audience:** To whom is the author writing? Where did the essay first appear? How does its intended audience help shape the essay and influence its language and style?
4. **Purpose:** Why is the author writing this? Is the intention to entertain? To inform? To persuade?

Effective writing contains specific, relevant details and examples. Look carefully at the writer's choice of examples. Remember that the author made a conscious decision to include each of these details. Ideally, each is appropriate to the subject and contributes to the thesis and purpose.

REREADING

Rereading, like rewriting, is not always a discrete stage in a linear process. Just as you might pause after writing several sentences and then go back and make some immediate changes, so as a reader, you might stop at the end of a paragraph and then go back and reread what you have just read. Depending on the difficulty of the essay, it might take several rereadings for you to be able to answer the questions posed about the writer's thesis and purpose. Even if you feel certain about your understanding of the essay, a final rereading is important.

In that rereading, focus on the essay as an example of a writer's craft. Look carefully at the paragraphing. How effective is the introduction to the essay? The conclusion? Have you ever used a similar strategy to begin or end an essay? How do both reflect the writer's purpose? Audience? Pay attention to the writer's sentence structures. How do these sentences differ from the ones that you typically write? Does the author employ a variety of sentence types and lengths? Is there anything unusual about the author's word choices? Do you use a similar range of vocabulary when you write? Remember that the writer of essays is just as conscious of craft as the poet, the novelist, or the playwright.

PRACTICING ACTIVE READING: AN ANNOTATED SAMPLE

Before you begin reading in the eighth edition of *The Prentice Hall Reader,* you can see how to use these techniques of prereading, reading, and rereading in the following essay, which has been annotated over the course of several readings. Following the essay are the reader's prereading, reading, and rereading notes.

ON CLONING A HUMAN BEING

Lewis Thomas

Lewis Thomas (1913–1993) was born in Flushing, New York, and received his M.D. from Harvard University. He served on the medical faculty at Johns Hopkins, Tulane, Cornell, and Yale before assuming the position of chancellor of the Memorial Sloan-Kettering Cancer Center in New York. Thomas published widely in his research specialty, pathology, the study of diseases and their causes.

In 1971 he began contributing a 1,200-word monthly column, focusing on current topics related to medicine and biological science, to the New England Journal of Medicine. *Titled "Notes of a Biology Watcher," the column proved highly popular with professionals who subscribed to the journal as well as nonspecialists. Several collections of these essays have been published, including* The Lives of a Cell: Notes of a Biology Watcher *(1974),* The Medusa and the Snail *(1979),* Late Night Thoughts on Listening to Mahler's Ninth Symphony *(1983), and* Fragile Species *(1992).*

In "On Cloning a Human Being," originally published in the New England Journal of Medicine, *Thomas sets out to analyze the effect that an experiment to clone a human being would have on the rest of the world.*

BEFORE READING

Connecting: What do you know about cloning, both in fact and from science fiction? Do you find cloning a positive technological development or a frightening one?

Anticipating: What seems to be Thomas's attitude toward cloning? As a scientist, does he express the opinion you expect?

Definition of cloning

1   It is now theoretically possible to recreate an identical creature from any animal or plant, from the DNA contained in the nucleus of any somatic cell. A single plant root-tip cell can be teased and seduced into conceiving a perfect copy of the whole plant; a frog's intestinal epithelial cell possesses the complete instructions needed for a new, same frog. If the technology were further advanced, you could do this with a human being, and there are now startling predictions all over the place that this will in fact be done, someday, in order to provide a version of immortality for carefully selected, especially valuable people.

2   The cloning of humans is on most of the lists of things to worry about from Science, along with behavior control,

genetic engineering, <u>transplanted heads, computer poetry,</u> and the <u>unrestrained growth of plastic flowers.</u>

Cloning is the most dismaying of prospects, mandating as it does the elimination of sex with only a metaphoric elimination of death as compensation. It is almost no comfort to know that one's cloned, identical surrogate lives on, especially when the living will very likely involve edging one's real, now aging self off to the side, sooner or later. It is hard to imagine anything like filial affection or respect for a single, unmated nucleus; harder still to think of one's new, self-generated self as anything but an absolute, desolate orphan. Not to mention the complex interpersonal relationship involved in raising one's self from infancy, teaching the language, enforcing discipline, instilling good manners, and the like. How would you feel if you became an incorrigible juvenile delinquent by (proxy,) at the age of fifty-five?

The public questions are obvious. Who is to be selected, and on what qualifications? How to handle the risks of misused technology, such as self-determined cloning by the rich and powerful but socially objectionable, or the cloning by governments of dumb, docile masses for the world's work? What will be the effect on all the uncloned rest of us of human sameness? After all, we've accustomed ourselves through hundreds of millennia to the continual exhilaration of uniqueness; each of us is totally different, in a fundamental sense, from all the other four billion. Selfness is an essential fact of life. The thought of human nonselfness, precise sameness, is terrifying, when you think about it.

Well, don't think about it, because it isn't a probable possibility, not even as a long shot for the distant future, in my opinion. I agree that you might clone some people who would look amazingly like their parental cell donors, but the odds are that they'd be almost as different as you or me, and certainly more different than any of today's identical twins.

The time required for the experiment is only one of the problems, but a formidable one. Suppose you wanted to clone a <u>prominent, spectacularly successful diplomat, to look after the Middle East problems of the distant future</u>. You'd have to catch him and persuade him, probably not very hard to do, and extirpate a cell. But then you'd have to wait for him to grow up through embryonic life and then for at least forty years more, and you'd have to be sure all observers remained patient and unmeddlesome through his unpromising, ambiguous childhood and adolescence.

Joking here.

3
Two versions of the same person living at once—the original and the clone. Wild idea.

proxy: person acting for another person

4

4-paragraph introduction sets up negatives about cloning

5   Thesis: Cloning human beings is not really possible.

6   Reason 1: Time involved

"valuable person"

7 Reason 2: Environment would have to be created

Moreover, you'd have to be sure of recreating his environment, perhaps down to the last detail. "Environment" is a word which really means people, so you'd have to do a lot more cloning than just the diplomat himself.

8
To be the same, the clone would have to have the same environment

This is a very important part of the cloning problem, largely overlooked in our excitement about the cloned individual himself. You don't have to agree all the way with B. F. Skinner to acknowledge that the environment does make a difference, and when you examine what we really mean by the word "environment" it comes down to other human beings. We use euphemisms and jargon for this, like "social forces," "cultural influences," even Skinner's "verbal community," but what is meant is the dense crowd of nearby people who talk to, listen to, smile or frown at, give to, withhold from, nudge, push, caress, or flail out at the individual.

genome: genetic organism

No matter what the genome says, these people have a lot to do with shaping a character. Indeed, if all you had was the genome, and no people around, you'd grow a sort of vertebrate plant, nothing more.

9
Casual chain: clone parents, grandparents, family, people outside the family who came in contact with the individual, the whole world.

So, to start with, you will undoubtedly need to clone the parents. No question about this. This means the diplomat is out, even in theory, since you couldn't have gotten cells from both his parents at the time when he was himself just recognizable as an early social treasure. You'd have to limit the list of clones to people already certified as sufficiently valuable for the effort, with both parents still alive. The parents would need cloning and, for consistency, their parents as well. I suppose you'd also need the usual informed-consent forms, filled out and signed, not easy to get if I know parents, even harder for grandparents.

10

But this is only the beginning. It is the whole family that really influences the way a person turns out, not just the parents, according to current psychiatric thinking. Clone the family.

11

Then what? The way each member of the family develops has already been determined by the environment set around him, and this environment is more people, people outside the family, schoolmates, acquaintances, lovers, enemies, carpool partners, even, in special circumstances, peculiar strangers across the aisle on the subway. Find them, and clone them.

12
Isn't this an exaggeration?

But there is no end to the protocol. Each of the outer contacts has his own surrounding family, and his and their outer contacts. Clone them all.

13

To do the thing properly, with any hope of ending up with a genuine duplicate of a single person, you really have no choice. You must clone the world, no less.

We are not ready for an experiment of this size, nor, I should think, are we willing. <u>For one thing, it would mean replacing today's world by an entirely identical world to follow immediately, and this means no new, natural, spontaneous, random, chancy children. No children at all, except for the manufactured doubles of those now on the scene. Plus all those identical adults, including all of today's politicians, all seen double. It is too much to contemplate</u>.

14
He's really joking here

Moreover, when the whole experiment is finally finished, fifty years or so from now, how could you get a responsible scientific reading on the outcome? Somewhere in there would be the original clonee, probably lost and overworked, now well into middle age, but everyone around him would be precise duplicates of today's everyone. <u>It would be today's same world, filled to overflowing with duplicates of today's people and their same, duplicated problems, probably all resentful at having had to go through our whole thing all over</u>, sore enough at the clone to make endless trouble for him, if they found him.

15

With the world cloned, everything would be the same, leading to dissatisfaction

And obviously, if the whole thing were done precisely right, they would still be casting about for ways to solve the <u>problem of universal dissatisfaction</u>, and sooner or later they'd surely begin to look around at each other, wondering who should be cloned for his special value to society, to get us out of all this. And so it would go, in regular cycles, perhaps forever.

16

I once lived through a period when I wondered what Hell could be like, and I stretched my imagination to try to think of a perpetual sort of damnation. I have to confess, I never thought of anything like this.

17

I have an alternative suggestion, if you're looking for a way out. Set cloning aside, and don't try it. Instead, go in the other direction. Look for ways to get mutations more quickly, new variety, different songs. <u>Fiddle around, if you must fiddle, but never with ways to keep things the same, no matter who, not even yourself. Heaven, somewhere ahead, has got to be a change</u>.

18

The author's real purpose comes out here; ties to paragraph 4.

Prereading Notes

The headnote indicates that the author, Lewis Thomas, was a physician and medical researcher and that most of his essays—including this one—were written for the New England Journal of Medicine. These facts and the title "On Cloning a Human Being" initially suggest that this will be a pretty serious, probably dry essay and that it may be full of a lot of technical information. However, scanning the essay by looking at the first sentence in each paragraph shows the tone to be fairly informal: paragraph 5, for example, begins, "Well, don't think about it. . . ." It is also clear from a quick scan of the essay that it is really on not cloning a human being. Thomas is focusing on the problems involved in cloning human beings and seems to say that it will never happen.

Reading Notes

Outline:
par. 1 Introduction to cloning and predictions that "especially valuable people" will be cloned
pars. 2–4 Worries about cloning
par. 5 Thomas says cloning "isn't a probable possibility"
par. 6 Reason 1: Too much time involved in any experiment with human cloning
pars. 7–15 Reason 2: Since individuals are shaped by their environments, to clone a person would require cloning his or her parents, grandparents, the whole family, "the world, no less." People are not ready to replace today's world with "an entirely identical world to follow immediately," so everyone would hate the original clonee for causing all the trouble.
par. 16 The cloning cycle would have to start again to duplicate someone who could "solve the problem of universal dissatisfaction" with the original cloning experiment.
par. 17 To Thomas, this would be worse than Hell.
par. 18 Instead of cloning, it would be better to experiment with "ways to get mutations more quickly, new variety, different songs."

After an initial reading, it is clear that Thomas's subject is cloning and predictions that "valuable people" will be cloned experimentally in the future. He states his thesis explicitly in paragraph 5: cloning "isn't a probable possibility, not even as a long shot for the distant future. . . ." Even though the essay was written for the New England Journal of Medicine, it would seem that Thomas intended to reach a general educated audience; for example, he includes very little specialized terminology and doesn't assume any particular medical or scientific expertise. His purpose seems to be basically to inform, to explain to his audience why cloning of human beings isn't likely to happen in the future.

But in explaining why human beings aren't likely to be cloned, Thomas gives reasons that seem exaggerated. Could it really be necessary to clone the whole world, as he says? Why would he want to suggest that the effects of cloning a single human being would be so drastic?

Rereading Notes

Rereading the essay reveals that Thomas is deliberately pushing the idea of cloning a human being to the point of absurdity. His tone is humorous from the beginning: in paragraph 2, for example, he lists as some of our worries about science—"transplanted heads, computer poetry, and the unrestrained growth of plastic flowers." When he describes the effects of an experiment in cloning an important diplomat and what would really be required to clone a human being (pars. 10–13), he builds each paragraph up to its logical—and increasingly absurd—conclusion: "Clone the family." "Find them, and clone them." "Clone them all." "You must clone the world, no less." In paragraph 14 he pushes the absurdity one step further, imagining a world where there are no longer unique children who grow up to be unique adults but only identical doubles of those who already exist— "including all of today's politicians. . . . It is too much to contemplate." The next two paragraphs continue in this vein, ending with the most absurd idea of all: that another cloning would have to take place of the person who could get everyone out of this mess. "And so it would go," Thomas says, "in regular cycles, perhaps forever."

Thomas is saying that it is absurd to imagine that an exact replica of another human being could ever be cloned; given the fact that the clone would necessarily grow up under different influences, the two might look alike, but "they'd be almost as different as you and me, and certainly more different than any of today's identical twins" (par. 5). Moreover, an even more substantial point emerges on rereading: there can be no benefit from cloning human beings to begin with. "Precise sameness," Thomas says, "is terrifying" (par. 4), an idea that he returns to in his conclusion, where he suggests that it is better for humans to experiment with "mutations," "variety," and "change" than with clones.

Thomas's purpose, therefore, seems to be more than simply informing readers about the impossibility of creating a human clone; at the core, he is arguing for a view of human nature that recognizes the value of "variety" over some standard of "perfection," and his method is to do so in an entertainingly humorous way.

Each of the essays in the eighth edition of *The Prentice Hall Reader* will repay you for the time and effort you put into reading it carefully and critically. Each essay shows an artful craftsperson at work, solving the problems inherent in communicating experiences, feelings, ideas, and opinions to an audience. Each writer is someone from whom you, as a reader and as a thinker, can learn. So when your instructor assigns a selection from the text, remember that as a reader you must assume an active role. Don't assume that reading an essay once—to see what it is "about"—will mean that you are prepared to write about it or that you have learned all that you can learn from the essay. Ask questions, seek answers to those questions, analyze, and reread.

SOME THINGS TO REMEMBER

1. Read the headnote to the selection. How does this information help you understand the writer and the context in which the selection was written?

2. Look at the questions that precede and follow each reading. They will help focus your attention on the important aspects of the selection. After you read, write out answers to each question.

3. Read through the selection first to see what happens and to satisfy your curiosity.

4. Reread the selection several times, taking notes or underlining as you go.

5. Write or locate in the essay a thesis statement. Remember that the thesis is the particular point that the writer is trying to make about the subject.

6. Define a purpose for the essay. Why is the writer writing? Does the author make that purpose explicit?

7. Imagine the audience for such an essay. Who is the likely reader? What does that reader already know about the subject? Is the reader likely to have any preconceptions or prejudices about the subject?

8. Isolate a structure in the selection. How is it put together? Into how many parts can it be divided? How do those parts work together? Outline the essay.

9. Be sure that you understand every sentence. How does the writer vary the sentence structures?

10. Look up every word that you cannot define with some degree of certainty. Remember that you might misinterpret what the author is saying if you simply skip over the unfamiliar words.

11. Reread the essay one final time, reassembling its parts into the artful whole that it was intended to be.

HOW TO WRITE
AN ESSAY

WRITING: AN OVERVIEW

Watching a performance, whether it is athletic or artistic, our attention is focused on the achievement displayed in that moment. In concentrating on the performance, however, we might forget about the extensive practice that lies behind that achievement. Writing is no different. Typically, writers rely on perspiration, not inspiration. An effective final product depends on careful preliminary work.

CHOOSING A SUBJECT

The first step in writing is to determine a subject, what a piece of writing is about. The majority of writing tasks that you face either in school or on the job require you to write in response to a specific assignment. Your instructor, for example, might ask you to use the specific writing suggestions that follow each reading in this book. Before you begin work on any writing assignment, take time to study what is being asked. What limits have already been placed on the assignment? What are the key words (for example, *compare*, *analyze*, *define*) used in the assignment?

Once you have a subject, the next step is to restrict, focus, or narrow that subject into a workable topic. Although the words *subject* and *topic* are sometimes used interchangeably, think of *subject* as the broader, more general word. You move from a subject to a *topic* by limiting or restricting what you will include or cover. The shift from subject to topic is a gradual one that is not marked by a clearly definable line. Just remember that a topic is a more restricted version of a larger subject.

HAVING A PURPOSE

A writer writes to fulfill three fundamental purposes: *to entertain*, *to inform*, and *to persuade*. Obviously, those purposes are not necessarily separate: an interesting, maybe even humorous, essay that documents the health hazards caused by smoking can, at the same time, attempt to persuade the reader to give up smoking. In this case the main purpose is still persuasion; entertainment and information play subordinate roles in catching the reader's interest and in providing appropriate evidence for the argument being advanced.

These three purposes are generally associated with the traditional division of writing into four forms—narration, description, exposition (including classification, comparison and contrast, process, cause and effect, and definition), and argumentation. *Narrative* or *descriptive essays* typically tell a story or describe a person, object, or place in order to entertain a reader and re-create the experience. *Expository essays* primarily provide information for a reader. *Argumentative* or *persuasive essays* seek to move a reader, to gain support, to advocate a particular type of action.

DEFINING AN AUDIENCE

Audience is a key factor in every writing situation. Writing is, after all, a form of communication and as such implies audience. In many writing situations, your audience is a controlling factor that affects both the content of your paper and the style in which it is written. An effective writer learns to adjust to an audience and to write for that audience, for a writer, like a performer, needs and wants an audience.

Writers adjust their style and tone on a spectrum ranging from informal to formal. Articles that appear in popular, wide-circulation magazines often are written in the first person, use contractions, favor popular and colloquial words, and contain relatively short sentences and paragraphs. Articles in more scholarly journals exhibit a formal style that involves an objective and serious tone, a more advanced vocabulary, and longer and more complicated sentence and paragraph constructions. In the informal style, the writer injects his or her personality into the prose; in the formal style, the writer remains detached and impersonal. A writer adopts whatever style seems appropriate for a particular audience or context. An effective writer does not have just one style or voice but many.

PREWRITING

Most people are reluctant writers who procrastinate as long as possible. Putting words on a page or a computer screen can be intimidating, especially when we know that they must be the right words in the right order and that we will be graded on the product that we produce. As professional writers will testify, however, much of the process of writing actually takes place before we ever put pen to paper or fingers to keyboard. Writing involves thinking and planning, looking for ideas, thinking about catchy opening sentences or arresting details or examples. The preparation stage is called *prewriting* to indicate that it begins before we commit our thoughts and ideas in actual words.

Writing on an Assigned Topic

In most college courses, you will be writing papers in response to a specific assignment that you have been given. That assignment will contain a set of clues or instructions about what you are to do in the paper. Before you begin to write, before you even begin to gather information for the paper, spend some time analyzing the assignment and the directions you have been given.

- **How long is the paper to be?** If your instructor specifies length (a certain number of pages or an approximate number of words), you have an idea of how detailed your paper must be. If the subject or topic seems fairly large and the length modest, then clearly you must focus your paper on the key or significant issues. If your instructor wants a longer paper or a research paper, then you must respond to the assignment with extended detail or evidence. The length is a key to how much detail you need in order to respond adequately to the assignment.

- **Who is your audience?** In most writing situations outside of school, you will have a very specific audience—your supervisors, your customers, people with technical knowledge about the subject, people who know very little about the subject. In contrast, many writing assignments that you get in school assume that you are writing to the instructor and/or a peer audience. Even then, though, you need to think about how much the audience knows about the subject. Are you going to be using words or concepts that might be unfamiliar to your readers? Will you have to find analogies that will help your audience understand? Will you have to define technical words or phrases? Is your audience likely to know everything that you are writing about? Why then would they be interested in reading your essay? If you are asked to argue for something, how deeply does your audience feel about the topic? Does the topic, for example, challenge the audience's deeply held beliefs?

- **What does the assignment suggest about the purpose and structure of the paper?** A vital key here is to look at the verbs or descriptive phrases used in the assignment. An essay that says "compare" and "contrast" two economic theories or two essays is signaling both a purpose and a structure to you. Look at the following chart for help in "reading" the purpose, structure, or approach suggested by how the assignment is worded.

- **Does the assignment suggest possible sources of information that you might use in your paper?** Are you expected to draw from the assigned reading that might be a part of the assignment? From class lectures or discussions? Are you to use your own personal experiences?

Are you to do some research? Interview people? Search the Web? Locate books and articles on the topic?

Looking for Key Word	Usually Means	Likely Organizational Pattern
Narrate **Tell**	to tell a story; to describe how something works	chronological; can use flashbacks; first step to last
Summarize	to rehearse the key points	follows structure of what is being summarized
Describe	to tell how something was perceived by the senses	spatial patterns—top to bottom, side to side, front to back, prominent to background
Classify	to place similar items into categories or groups	largest to smallest; most important to least
Divide	to separate a whole into its parts	largest to smallest; most important to least
Analyze	to show component parts; to assess correctness	how something works; what are its component parts; assess strengths and weaknesses
Compare	to show similarities between two or more items	subject-by-subject (A, B) point-by-point (A1/B1, A2/B2)
Contrast	to show differences between two or more items	subject-by-subject (A, B) point-by-point (A1/B1, A2/B2)
Explain	to clarify an idea, a process; to make clear	step-by-step
Identify **Causes and** **Effects**	to identify causes of a certain event; to identify effects that arise from a certain event	forward or backward; causes to event; event and its effects
Define	to provide an explanation for a word, concept, or event	place in a class and add distinguishing features; definition followed by examples
Argue or **Persuade**	to get a reader to agree with your position	inductive; deductive; logical (argument); emotional (persuasion)

Let's look at two sample writing assignments. The first follows Scott Russell Sanders's essay "The Inheritance of Tools" (Chapter 3). In the essay, Sanders is building a wall when he learns that his father has died. He has inherited from his father both the physical tools he is using and the knowledge of how to use them. In the essay, he reflects on that "inheritance" and what it means to him. Here is one of the writing assignments that follows that essay:

Topic

Think about a skill, talent, or habit that you have learned from or share with a family member. In addition to the ability or trait, what else have you "inherited"? How does it affect your life? In an essay, describe the inheritance and its effect on you.

Analysis

Key words: "*describe* the inheritance and its *effects* on you." You are asked to do two things. First, you are to select a "skill, trait, or talent" that you have "inherited" from or "share" with a family member and describe it. So the first portion of the topic will involve description, focusing on something and explaining or describing what it is. Second, you are to explain or describe the "effect" that "inheritance" has had on you. The key words not only signal your purpose in the essay but also suggest that the essay will have two parts—a description followed by an analysis of effect.

Length: An essay, typically defined as three to four pages
Audience: Not specified, but an audience of peers could be assumed
Source of information: Personal experience and reflection

The second assignment follows Malcolm Gladwell's "The Trouble with Fries" (Chapter 7).

Topic

Choose a single, risky behavior that is commonly engaged in by your peers—things such as cigarette smoking, binge drinking, purging, unprotected sex, recreational drug use, criminal acts. In an essay, explore through a cause-and-effect analysis why such behavior has an appeal. Knowing that such things are risky or dangerous, or even life threatening, why do people in your peer group engage in them? Remember that interviewing peers might prove to be an excellent source of information.

Analysis

Key words: "*single . . . cause-and-effect analysis.*" You are asked to identify a single behavior and then to suggest reasons why your peers might find it appealing. First, you are to identify the behavior by describing it. Second, you are to suggest reasons why might people indulge in it. Cause and effect moves in one direction or another—either from the causes to the effects or from the effects to the causes.

Behavior ➔ causes	or causes ➔ Behavior
Behavior ➔ effects	or effects ➔ Behavior

Length: An essay, typically defined as three to four pages
Audience: Peers
Sources of information: Personal experience, reflection, interviews with peers

CREATING YOUR OWN TOPIC

Writing from an assigned topic can seem frustrating and confining at times. Probably every writer at some point has resented being told what to write, has felt confined to a topic in which she or he has little to no interest. Devising your own topic can be more difficult but also more rewarding. You might be either excited or terrified about a completely open-ended assignment that simply says, "Write an essay on a topic of your choice." Either way, the key is to define for yourself the set of parameters within which you will write. That is, you need to answer—either before you start writing or while you are writing—each of the following questions:

How long will my paper be? What level of detail do I need?
Who is my audience? What can I assume about that audience?
What is my purpose in this paper? What am I trying to do? What are the
    key words or phrases that shape my response?
What are my possible sources of information?

GATHERING INFORMATION

What makes writing entertaining, informative, or persuasive is information—specific, relevant detail. If you try to write without gathering information, you end up skimming the surface of your subject, even if you "know" something about it.

How you go about gathering information on your topic depends on your subject and your purpose for writing. Some topics, such as those involving a personal experience, require a memory search; other assignments, such as describing a particular place, require careful observation. Essays that convey information or argue particular positions often require gathering information through research. Some possible strategies for gathering information and ideas about your topic are listed here. Before you start this step in your prewriting, remember three things.

First, remember that *different tactics work for different topics and for different writers.* You might find that freewriting is great for some assignments but not for others. As a writer, explore your options. Don't rule out any strategy until you have tried it. Second, remember that *prewriting activities sometimes produce information and sometimes just produce questions that you will then need to answer.* In other words, prewriting often involves learning what you don't know, what you need to find out. Learning to ask the right questions is just as important as knowing the right answers. Third, remember that *these prewriting activities are an excellent way in which to find a focus, to narrow a subject, or to suggest a working plan for your essay.* As you begin to explore a subject or topic, the possibilities spread out before you. Try not to be wedded to a particular topic or thesis until you have explored a subject through prewriting activities.

Listing Details from Personal Experience or Observation   Even your most unforgettable experience has probably been forgotten in part. If you are going to re-create it for a reader, you will have to do some active searching among your memories. By focusing your attention, you can slowly recall more details. Ask yourself a series of questions about the chronology of the experience. For example, start with a particular detail and then try to stimulate your memory: What happened just before? Just after? Who was there? Where did the experience take place? Why did it happen? When did it happen? How did it happen?

Sense impressions, like factual details, fade from memory. In the height of the summer, it is not easy to recall a crisp fall day. Furthermore, sensory details are not always noticed, let alone recorded. How many times have you passed by a particular location without really seeing it?

Descriptions, like every other form of writing, demand specific information, and the easiest way to gather that detail is to observe. Before you try to describe a person, place, or object, take some time to list specific details on a piece of paper. At first record everything you notice. Do not worry about having too much, for you can always edit later. At this stage it is better to have too much than to have too little.

The next step is to decide what to include in your description and what to exclude. As a general principle, an effective written description does not try to record everything. The selection of detail should be governed by your purpose in the description. Ask yourself what you are trying to show or reveal. For what reason? What is particularly important about this person, place, or object? A description is not the verbal equivalent of a photograph or a tape recording.

Freewriting   Putting words down on a page or a computer screen can be very intimidating. Your editing instincts immediately want to take over—are the words spelled correctly? Are the sentences complete? Do they contain any mechanical or grammatical errors? Not only must you express your ideas in words, but suddenly those words must be the correct words.

When you translate thoughts into written words and edit those words at the same time, writing can seem impossible. Instead of allowing ideas to take shape in words or allowing the writing to stimulate your thinking, you become fearful of committing anything to paper.

Writing, however, can stimulate thought. Every writer has experienced times when an idea became clear because it was written down. If those editing instincts can be turned off, you can use writing as a way of generating ideas about a paper.

Freewriting is an effective way to deal with this dilemma. Write without stopping for a fixed period of time—a period as short as ten minutes or as long as an hour. Do not stop; do not edit; do not worry about mistakes. If you find yourself stuck for something to write, repeat the last word or phrase you wrote until a new thought comes to mind. You are looking for a focus point—an idea or a subject for a paper. You are trying to externalize your thinking into writing. What emerges is a free association of ideas. Some are relevant; some are worthless. After you have ideas on paper, you can then decide what is worth saving, developing, or simply throwing away.

You can also do freewriting on a computer. One technique many writers find effective is to use the contrast control to darken the screen until it is completely black. Then as you write you won't be distracted by errors and typos or be tempted to stop and read what you have already written. Freewriting in this way provides an opportunity to free-associate almost as you might when you are speaking.

Journaling   A daily journal can be an effective seedbed of ideas for writing projects. Such a journal should not be a daily log of your activities (got up, went to class, had lunch) but rather a place where you record ideas, observations, memories, and feelings. Set aside a specific notebook or a pad of paper in which to keep your journal. Try to write for at least ten minutes every day. Over a period of time—such as a semester—you will be surprised how many ideas for papers or projects you will accumulate. When you are working on a paper, you might want to confine part of your daily journal entries to that particular subject.

Brainstorming and Mapping   Brainstorming is oral freewriting among a group of people jointly trying to solve a problem by spontaneously contributing ideas. Whatever comes to mind, no matter how obvious or unusual, gets said. The hope is that out of the jumble of ideas that surface, some possible solutions to the problem will be found.

Although brainstorming is by definition a group activity, it can also be done by the individual writer. In the center of a blank sheet of paper, write down a key word or phrase referring to your subject. Then in the space around your subject, quickly jot down any ideas that come to mind. Do not write in sentences—just key words and phrases. Because you are not filling consecutive lines with words and because you have space in which the ideas can be arranged, this form of brainstorming often suggests structural relationships. You can increase the usefulness of such an idea generator by adding graphic devices such as circles, arrows, or connecting lines to indicate the possible relationships among ideas. These devices can be added to your brainstorming sheet later, and they become a map to the points you might want to cover in your essay.

Formal Questioning   One particularly effective way to gather information on any topic is to ask yourself questions about it. This allows you to explore the subject from a variety of angles. After all, the secret to finding answers always lies in knowing the right questions to ask. A good place to start is with the list of questions presented here. Remember, though, that not every question is appropriate for every topic.

Illustration
1. What examples of _____ can be found?
2. In what ways are these things examples of _____?
3. What details about _____ seem the most important?

Comparison and Contrast

1. To what is _____ similar? List the points of similarity.
2. From what is _____ different? List the points of difference.
3. Which points of similarity or difference seem most important?
4. What does the comparison or contrast tell the reader about _____?

Division and Classification

1. Into how many parts can _____ be divided?
2. How many parts is _____ composed of?
3. What other category of things is _____ most like?
4. How does _____ work?
5. What are _____'s component parts?

Process

1. How many steps or stages are involved in _____?
2. In what order do those steps or stages occur?

Cause and Effect

1. What precedes _____?
2. Is that a cause of _____?
3. What follows _____?
4. Is that an effect of _____?
5. How many causes of _____ can you find?
6. How many effects of _____ can you find?
7. Why does _____ happen?

Definition

1. How is _____ defined in a dictionary?
2. Does everyone agree about the meaning of _____?
3. Does _____ have any connotations? What are they?
4. Has the meaning of _____ changed over time?
5. What words are synonymous with _____?

Argument and Persuasion

1. How do your readers feel about _____?
2. How do you feel about _____?
3. What are the arguments in favor of _____? List those arguments in order of strength.
4. What are the arguments against _____? List those arguments in order of strength.

Interviewing   Typically you gather information for college papers by locating printed or electronic sources—books, articles, reports, e-texts. Depending on your topic, however, printed or electronic sources are not always available. In that case, people often represent a great source of information for a writer. Obviously you should choose someone who has special credentials or knowledge about the subject.

Interviewing requires some special skills and tact. When you first contact someone to request an interview, always explain who you are, what you want to know, and how you will use the information. Remember that specific questions will produce more useful information than general ones. Take notes that you can expand later, or use a tape recorder. Keep attention focused on the information that you need, and do not be afraid to ask questions to keep your informant on the subject. If you plan to use direct quotations, make sure that the wording is accurate. If possible, check the quotations with your source one final time.

DEFINING A THESIS STATEMENT

The information-gathering stage of the writing process is the time in which to sharpen your general subject into a narrower topic. Your subject is a broad, general idea—for example, "violence on television." That subject is simply too large for an essay. Just think of a few possible approaches that the subject suggests:

- A history of violence on television
- A vivid description of televised violence
- A classification of the types of televised violence
- A comparison of the role of violence in the earliest days of television compared with today; or violence on European versus American television
- How parents might monitor televised violence
- An analysis of why violence is so prevalent on American television
- A definition of televised violence with examples
- An argument for or against the censorship of violence on television

You need to narrow the *subject* into what is called a *topic*, a more focused, more detailed, limiting idea. A topic limits the subject by narrowing its scope, by suggesting a specific approach to the subject, by defining a particular purpose for the essay. A topic is the first step in making a subject into something more manageable.

Subject: Violence on television
Topic: The impact that viewing televised violence has on young children

The final step in the process is to move from a topic to a *thesis*. Thesis is derived from a Greek word that means "placing," "position," or "proposition."

When you formulate a thesis, you are defining your position on the subject. A thesis lets your reader know exactly where you stand. Because it represents your "final" position, a thesis is typically something that you develop and refine as you move through the prewriting stage, testing your ideas and gathering information. Don't try to start with a final thesis, begin with a tentative thesis (also called a hypothesis, from the Greek for "supposition"). Allow your final position to emerge based on what you have discovered in the prewriting stage.

Before you write a thesis statement, you need to consider the factors that will control or influence the form that your thesis will take. For example, a thesis is a reflection of your purpose in writing. If your purpose is to persuade your audience to do or to believe something, your thesis will urge the reader to accept that position. If your purpose is to convey information to your reader, your thesis will forecast your main points and indicate how your paper will be organized.

Your thesis will also be shaped by the scope and length of your paper. Your topic and your thesis must be manageable within the space that you have available; otherwise, you end up skimming the surface. A short paper requires a more precise focus than a longer one. As a result, when you move from subject to topic to thesis, make sure that each step is more specific and has an increasingly sharper focus. To check that focusing process, ask yourself the following questions:

What is my general subject?

What is my specific topic within that general subject?

What do I intend to do in the paper? What is my purpose?

What is my position on that specific topic?

WRITING A THESIS STATEMENT

When you have answered the question about your purpose, when you have sharpened your general subject into a topic, when you have defined your position on that topic, you are ready to write a thesis statement. The process is simple. You write a thesis statement by linking together your topic and your position on that topic:

Subject:	Violence on television
Topic:	The impact that televised violence has on young children
Thesis:	Televised violence makes young children numb to violence in the real world, distorts their perceptions of how people behave, and teaches them how to be violent.

Notice that this thesis not only limits the scope of the paper and defines a precise position and purpose but also signals the structure that the body of the essay will have.

Introduction

Body (will consist of three blocks)

    A. Make them numb to violence in the real world

    B. Distorts perceptions of how people behave

    C. Teaches them how to be violent.

Conclusion

Characteristics of an Effective Thesis

A thesis should

1. clearly signal the purpose of the paper.
2. state or take a definite position. It tells the reader what will be covered in the paper.
3. express a definite purpose in precise, familiar terms. Avoid vague, abstract, or complicated technical terms.
4. offer a focused, specific position that can be explored or expanded within the scope of the paper.
5. often signal the structure that will follow in the essay.

WRITING A DRAFT

Once you have answered your key questions about the assignment or your proposed topic, once you have thought about what the essay should do, once you have gathered the information that you will use in the paper, once you have written a working thesis, it is time to write. Do not expect that this initial version of the essay will be the final, ready-to-be-handed-in paper, but rather consider it a work in progress—a draft of what will eventually become the final, polished version of the paper.

ORGANIZING YOUR ESSAY

Structuring the Body   No matter what their length, papers come in three parts: an introduction, a body, and a conclusion. Depending on the total length of the paper, the introduction generally ranges from one to two, or at most, three paragraphs. Conclusions rarely are longer than one paragraph. The body of an essay is obviously the longest section of any paper. Since it is difficult or even impossible to write an introduction or a conclusion until you know what it is that you are introducing or summarizing, the place to start with most essays is with the body. To make sure, however, that you have a controlling idea that helps you to decide how the body of your paper will be structured and what information is relevant, you should keep in mind your working thesis.

If you are working with the rhetorical strategies that are covered in this text, you have some clear suggestions for possible ways in which the middle of your paper might be arranged.

Strategy	Typical Body Arrangement
Narration	To tell a story or narrate an event or action • Chronological, from first to last • Flashbacks can be used to rearrange time
Description	To record sense impressions • Visual–spatial, from side to side, front to back • Most obvious or important to least
Division	To break a whole into its component parts • Largest to smallest • Most important to least
Classification	To place similar items in categories or groups • Largest to smallest • Most important to least
Comparison	To find similarities between two or more items • Compare subject-by-subject (all of A–all of B) • Compare point-by-point (A point 1–B point 1)
Contrast	To find difference between two or more items • Contrast subject-by-subject (all of A–all of B) • Contrast point-by-point (A point 1–B point 1)
Process	To tell how to do something • First step, next step • Chronological order
Cause and Effect	To explain what caused something or what the effects of that something are • Forward and backward, lineal order • Causes or effects arranged in order of time or importance
Definition	To offer an explanation of a word, concept, or event • Placing item in a class and adding distinguishing features • Extended examples, explanation of how it works, comparison to something familiar
Argumentation	To offer logical reasons for a particular course of action or conclusion • Inductive • Deductive
Persuasion	To offer emotional reasons for a particular course of action or conclusion • Strongest to weakest • Weakest to strongest

Beginning and Ending

Introductions   Do you always finish everything that you start to read? Every newspaper or magazine article? Every piece of mail? Every book? The truth is that readers are far more likely to stop reading than they are to continue. You stop because you get distracted; you stop because you are bored by the subject or already know the information; you stop because you completely disagree with the position being argued. Only in school where you must read what is assigned in order to be prepared for the examination do you force yourself to keep going (in most cases!). Only in school do you have a reader who will read every word that you write—a teacher.

As a writer, you need to remember that your readers are more likely to quit reading than to continue. No one thing is the key to keeping a reader interested. All of the elements of good writing contribute: an interesting subject, valuable and accurate information, insightful analyses, a clear organizational pattern, grammatically correct and varied sentences, careful proofreading. Beginnings or introductions to essays are, however, especially important. Every paper needs a strong and effective introduction that will catch your readers' attention and pull them into your paper. Introductions are typically divided into two categories, reflecting the two goals that every introduction should have:

Hook, intended to "hook" readers and "pull" them into the body of the paper
Thesis, intended to state clearly and concisely what the thesis or controlling
    idea of the paper is

Introductions can vary in length depending on the length of the paper that follows. They can be a single paragraph long or several paragraphs long. An effective introduction can consist of both a hook and a thesis—perhaps the first sentence or even paragraph is a hook; the later sentences or the last paragraph in a multiparagraphed introduction might be the thesis. You see the fundamental differences between the two types in two of the student essay examples in this text.

The *hook* paragraph is from an essay that contrasts two different search strategies to be used in a library's online catalogue. It appeals to the reader's self-interest (also students at the school) and arouses curiosity: most of us probably never realized that it takes two different approaches to locate books on any particular subject.

Hook   The Cecil County Community Library has twenty books dealing with the death penalty, but unless you pay attention to the next couple of pages, you will never find all of them. Why? Because no single search strategy will lead you to all twenty books.

The *thesis* introduction is from an essay on the American "hobo," which explains where the term came from and what the factors were in American society that led to the creation of this huge group of people. The paragraph does not start with a vivid example or a startling statistic; instead it gets right to its thesis.

Thesis   Although homelessness and vagrancy might seem to be a distinctively modern phenomenon, the problem is probably less acute today (in terms of percentage of our total population) than it was at the turn of the twentieth century. At that time, a series of factors combined to create a large migratory population comprised almost exclusively of young males.

An introduction is an extremely important part of your paper. Spend time in planning and polishing it. For specific suggestions on types of introductions that you might try, check the glossary at the back of this text.

Conclusions   Generally the conclusion is the last thing that you write in a paper. Because it comes last and time is sometimes running short, a conclusion often gets the least amount of attention. You might revise your introduction a couple of times, trying to get it to reflect what is happening in the middle of the paper, but you only have time to write one draft of your conclusion. Worse yet, sometimes we just stop: the paper comes to an abrupt end instead of achieving a sense of an ending, a closure. If an introduction is the "first" impression that a reader gets of your paper, its conclusion is the "last" impression. Every paper should have a planned conclusion. Do not just stop.

   Conclusions can employ a variety of strategies depending upon the length and nature of the paper. Using the traditional division between the various purposes for writing, conclusions typically do use three general strategies:

Purpose	Types of Conclusions
Entertain	End with the climatic moment or realization—the "end" of the story, the reason for telling the story or for describing something
Inform	End with a summary of the key points
Argue/Persuade	End with a call to action or for agreement on an issue

Langston Hughes in the narrative "Salvation" (Chapter 2) recounts an experience he had at a church revival meeting when he was twelve. The narrative ends at a climatic moment, the "last" moment in the story. Hughes concludes by reflecting on the significance of that experience.

> That night, for the last time in my life but one—I was a big boy twelve years old—I cried, I cried, in bed alone, and couldn't stop. I buried my head under the quilts, but my aunt heard me. She woke up and told my uncle I was crying because the Holy Ghost had come into my life, and because I had seen Jesus. But I was really crying because I couldn't bear to tell her that I had lied, that I had deceived everybody in the church, that I hadn't seen Jesus, and that now I didn't believe there was a Jesus any more, since he didn't come to help me.

David Bodanis in "What's in Your Toothpaste" (Chapter 4), a humorous, informational essay that identifies the ingredients in a typical tube of toothpaste, ends with a summary of the ingredients:

> So it's chalk, water, paint, seaweed, antifreeze, paraffin oil, detergent, peppermint, formaldehyde, and fluoride (which can go some way towards preserving children's teeth)—that's the usual mixture raised to the mouth on the toothbrush for a fresh morning's clean. If it sounds too unfortunate, take heart. Studies show that thoroughly brushing with just plain water will often do as good a job.

David Gelernter in "What Do Murderers Deserve?" (Chapter 9) argues for the death penalty. It is a position on which people disagree. Some states, for example, have outlawed the penalty. Gelernter's purpose in the essay is to win over his audience, to get them to understand and support his position. He ends with an appeal for their support:

> In executing murderers, we declare that deliberate murder is absolutely evil and absolutely intolerable. This is a painfully difficult proclamation for a self-doubting community to make. But we dare not stop trying. Communities in which capital punishment is no longer the necessary response to deliberate murder may exist: America today is not one of them.

Plan a conclusion to your essay and try out different strategies. For additional advice on writing conclusions, consult the glossary in the back of this text.

CHECKING YOUR ESSAY'S STRUCTURE

The body of your essay needs to be coherently and logically organized. It typically needs to be organized in units that are phrased in parallel form and in a hierarchical structure in which paragraphs and sentences are related in either coordinate or subordinate form. To be coordinate means to be on the same level of hierarchy and to be phrased in parallel structures; to be subordinate means that the idea or point stems from the one immediately above it.

Outlining   The logical organization of your essay can be checked in several ways, but one of the easier means is to construct an outline. An outline is a visual display of your paper in which your paragraphs and sentences are arranged on levels that reveal the relationships among them. The basic idea is to display the coordinate and subordinate structures. An abbreviated model looks something like this:

  A. Topic Sentence for Paragraph 1 (coordinate with B)
      1. Support/detail (subordinate to A but coordinate to 2 and 3)
      2. Support/detail
      3. Support/detail
  B. Topic Sentence for Paragraph 2

The full form of an outline consists of coordinate and subordinate items that are designated using Roman numbers, alphabet letters, and Arabic numbers:

I.
  A.
    1.
      a.
        (1).
          (a).

Sometimes teachers and texts will tell you to outline your paper before you begin drafting. It is a rare writer who can do so. Typically, if asked to submit an outline for a paper, nearly every writer prepares the outline after a draft is complete.

A carefully done outline will reveal problems with the structure of both the paper as a whole and individual body paragraphs. Taking the time to outline your first draft before you begin to revise is an excellent way to check your paper's structure.

Cutting and Moving   One of the great advantages of word processors is that they allow you to block and move sections of your paper—to try out different possible orders for the body paragraphs. If you are uncomfortable doing so electronically, you can always print out your paper, cut the body paragraphs apart, and then try rearranging those paragraphs in other possible orders. First instincts are not always the best. Sometimes if you try other possible arrangements, you might find another order that seems to work better. In some writing situations, the order of the paper's body is flexible. For example, if you are citing reasons why someone ought to agree with your position, you might decide to start either with your most persuasive reason or end with it. Do you want to create a strong initial impression, or do you want your reader to be left with your strongest point?

Placing a Thesis in Your Paper   In the process of drafting your essay, you might have sharpened or modified your thesis statement—remember, it should accurately reflect what your paper is about, its purpose, and even how it is structured. At this point in drafting, you need to make two final decisions about your thesis sentence. First, you have to decide whether to include that explicit statement in your paper or to allow your paper's structure to imply the thesis. Second, if you decide to include a thesis statement, you must determine where to place it in your paper. For example, should it appear in the first paragraph or at some point later in the paper?

If you look carefully at examples of professional writing, you will discover that neither question has a single answer. Writers make those decisions based on the type of paper they are writing. As a student, however, you can follow several guidelines. Most pieces of writing done in college—either papers or essay examinations—should have explicit thesis statements. Typically, these statements should be placed early in the paper (although the thesis for a narrative or descriptive essay may come at the end). The thesis will not always be in the first paragraph, since your introduction might be designed first to attract your reader's attention. Nevertheless, placing a thesis statement early in your paper guarantees that the readers know exactly what to expect.

Every argumentative or persuasive paper should have an explicitly stated thesis. Where you place that thesis depends on whether the paper is structured deductively or inductively. A deductive argument begins with a general truth or principle and then moves to a specific application of that statement, so such an arrangement requires that the thesis be stated early. Conversely, an inductive argument moves in the opposite direction, starting with the specific evidence and then moving to a conclusion, an arrangement that requires that the thesis be withheld until near the end of the paper.

Similarly, when your strategy in a paper is to build to a conclusion, a realization or a discovery, you can withhold an explicit statement of your thesis until late in the paper. An early statement would spoil the suspense.

Some Things to Remember

1. Do not start writing before you have spent some time studying the assigned topic or defining a topic of your choice.

2. Think about the number of pages you are to write. Is this a three- to four-page essay or a fifteen-page research paper? Can you write about this subject in that amount of space? You might need either to narrow your subject or make it larger.

3. Plan a timeline for writing the paper. Allow sufficient time to move through the prewriting and writing stages. Try to avoid starting a paper the night before it is due. Ideally, try to have it finished at least a day early so that you will be able to revise it.

4. Locate or create key words in the topic. What is it that you are to do? Key words are verbs such as *narrate, describe, explain, compare, contrast, analyze, argue.*

5. Consider what those key words imply about the structure of your essay. How will the body of your essay be structured?

6. Define a thesis or key idea for your paper. Write it out in a sentence and keep it before you as you begin to draft.

7. Define your audience. How much do they already know about the subject? What will be the appropriate level of detail or explanation that you will need to provide?

8. Gather information before you start to write. Once you begin writing, you may need to gather more, but do not start writing without having a sense of what will go into your paper.

9. Plan a structure for the body of your essay. Outline it as you write to make sure that it is logically structured and developed.

10. Write an introduction for your essay. If you start by writing an introduction before you write the body of the paper, go back once you have a complete draft and see if the introduction needs to be sharpened or focused.

11. Allow time to write an effective conclusion for your paper. Do not just stop. Find a way in which to signal to your reader that the paper has closure.

12. Make sure that your essay has a real title. No paper should ever be titled "Essay 1" or "Persuasive Essay."

How to Revise
an Essay

The idea of revising a paper may not sound appealing in the least. By the time you have finished the paper, often the last thing you want to do is revise it. Nevertheless, revising is a crucial step in the writing process, one you cannot afford to skip. Not even the best professional writers produce only perfect sentences and paragraphs. Good writing almost always results from rewriting or revising.

What Does Revising Involve?

The word *revision* literally means "to see again." You do not revise a paper just by proofreading it for mechanical and grammatical errors, although that is the expected final step in the writing process. A revision is a re-seeing of what you have written. In its broadest sense, this re-seeing is a complete rethinking of a paper from idea through execution.

Revision takes place after a draft of the whole paper or a part of it has been completed, and ideally after a period of time has elapsed and you have had a chance to get some advice or criticism on what you wrote. Revision is quite different from proofreading. When you proofread, you mostly look for small things—misspellings or typographical errors, incorrect punctuation, awkwardly constructed sentences, undeveloped paragraphs. Revision, on the other hand, looks at everything—from the larger issues (subject, thesis, purpose, audience), to the structure of paragraphs and sentences, to smaller issues such as word choices and title. Everything in a paper should be actively and carefully scrutinized.

Revising does not occur only after you have written a complete draft of a paper. In fact, many writers revise as they draft. They may write a sentence, then stop to change its structure, even erase it and start over; they may shift the positions of sentences and paragraphs or delete them altogether. In their search for the right words, the graceful sentence, the clear paragraph, writers revise constantly. The revising that writers do while composing usually focuses on the sentence or paragraph being composed. When you are struggling to find the right word or the right sentence structure, you are probably not thinking much about the larger whole.

Consequently, allowing some time to elapse between drafts of your paper is important. You need to put the completed draft aside for a while if you are to get a perspective on what you have written and read your paper objectively. For this reason, it is important to finish a complete draft at least one day before you hand in the paper. If circumstances prevent you from finishing a paper until an hour or two before class, you will not have a chance to revise. You will only be able to proofread.

ANALYZING YOUR OWN WRITING

The key to improving your writing is self-awareness. You have to look carefully and critically at what you have written, focus on areas that caused you the most problems, and then work to correct them. Most writers can, in fact, identify the key problems that they faced in a particular paper or in writing in general, even though they might not know how to solve those problems. Knowing what causes you problems is the essential first step toward solving them.

RETHINKING THE LARGER ISSUES

When you analyze the first draft of a paper, begin by asking a series of specific questions, starting with the larger issues and working toward the smaller ones. Ideally, you should write out your answers—doing so will force you to have a specific response. Consider each of the following groups of questions.

Subject   What is your subject? Was it too large for the length of your paper? Did you have to skim over the subject because it was complex? Was your subject too small or simple? Did you have to stretch your essay to reach the appropriate length? Is the subject interesting? Does it tell readers something that they already know?

Directions   If the paper responds to an assigned topic, did you do what the assignment asked? Look again at the assignment and circle the key words, verbs such as *analyze, argue, classify, compare, criticize, define, evaluate, narrate, describe, summarize, recommend.* Did you do what was asked?

Thesis   What is the thesis of your paper? Can you find a single sentence in your essay that states the position you have taken on your subject? If so, underline it. If not, write a one-sentence thesis statement. If you are unsure what a thesis is, review the material in the glossary.

Purpose   Why did you write this paper? What is it intended to demonstrate or prove other than showing that you can write? If the topic was assigned, look back at the assignment. Does it suggest what your purpose should have been? Words such as *recommend, argue for, analyze, explain* all signal a purpose. Is that purpose clear in your paper?

Audience   Whom do you imagine as your audience? Who will read this paper, and why? In one sense, the answer is always your instructor, but papers should be written with a broader audience in mind. Did the assignment specify an audience—peers, people who need this information, people trying to make some decision? What does this audience already know about the subject? How much previous knowledge or experience do you assume your reader will have? If you find that your paper has serious problems related to these larger issues, you need to rethink what you have written. Cleaning up minor grammatical and writing problems will not "save" a paper that does not address the assignment, lacks a thesis, has an unclear purpose, or ignores its audience.

JUDGING LENGTH

After you finish a draft of a paper, look carefully at how your response measures up to your instructor's guidelines about the length of the paper. Such guidelines are important in that they give you some idea of the amount of space that you will need to develop and illustrate your thesis sufficiently. If your papers are consistently short, you have probably not included enough examples or illustrating details. Writing the suggested number of words does not, of course, guarantee a good essay, but writing only half of the suggested number because you fail to develop and illustrate your thesis can result in a lower grade.

Similarly, if your papers consistently exceed your instructor's guidelines, you have probably not sufficiently narrowed your subject or you have included too many details and examples. Of the material available to support, develop, and illustrate a thesis, some is more significant and relevant than the rest. Never try to include everything—select the best, the most appropriate, the most convincing.

ANALYZING THE STRUCTURE OF YOUR PAPER

Your paper must have a beginning (introduction), a middle (a series of body paragraphs), and an ending (conclusion). The introduction both states the subject and thesis of the paper and tries to catch the readers' interest. The middle or body of the paper needs to have a coherent, logical structure that is revealed through how the middle of the paper is paragraphed. The conclusion must bring a sense of an ending to the reader—endings typically summarize, reinforce the thesis, or appeal to the reader. A paper should never just stop.

You can check the structure of your essay by looking first at how you have paragraphed it. Remember that paragraphs reveal the structure of the essay and also provide readers with places at which to rest. If you have only several paragraphs in a three-page essay, you have not clearly indicated the structure of your essay to your reader, or your essay does not have a clear, logical organization. Likewise, a paper full of very short paragraphs probably is poorly developed. You might be shifting ideas too quickly and failing to provide supporting evidence and details. A good paragraph is meaty; a good essay is not a string of undeveloped ideas or bare generalizations.

A good analytical tool for checking structure is to outline the body of your paper. An outline is organized hierarchally—that is, it reveals the main points and the relationships among those points. Ideas, as an outline reveals, are either coordinate or subordinate.

A. (Coordinate, or equal in structure, with B)
   1. (Subordinate to A, but coordinate with 2 and 3)
   2.
   3.
      a. (Subordinate to 3, but coordinate with b)
      b.
B.

Once you have looked carefully at the structure of the whole essay, then examine each paragraph.

Paragraph Structure   Is each paragraph structured around a single idea? Is there an explicit statement of that idea—often called a topic sentence? If so, underline it. If not, jot down in the margin the key word or words in that paragraph. Should that idea be specifically stated in the paragraph? Consider adding a sentence that signals what the paragraph is about. Typically, such a sentence appears early in the paragraph—either the first sentence or the second sentence if the first sentence serves as a transition from the material in the previous paragraph.

Paragraph Development   Are body paragraphs well developed with a series of sentences that provide details, support, and examples for the topic sentence? Can you outline each paragraph to reveal the coordinate and subordinate patterns? Does the outline reveal that anything is out of place?

Introduction   Does the introduction indicate both the subject and thesis of the essay? Does it attempt to catch its readers' interest? Remember that an introduction can consist of more than one paragraph, especially in a longer essay. The first paragraph might be designed to "hook" the reader's interest, and the second then might contain the thesis statement. Is the introduction proportional to the rest of the paper—that is, a three-page paper should not contain a page-long introduction. For some suggestions on how to introduce a paper, consult "How to Write an Essay" and the glossary at the back of this text.

Conclusion   Does the paper really conclude, or does it just stop? Conclusions are sometimes difficult to write because they are the sections typically written last when time is often short. For suggestions on how to conclude a paper, consult "How to Write an Essay" and the glossary at the back of this text.

Transitions   If a paper is logically structured, it will have coherence, but the use of transitional expressions or transitional sentences—see the glossary—will help your reader by providing "signposts" that direct the reader from one point to another. Such devices promote both unity and coherence between paragraphs.

Title   Writing a title for your paper is not always easy. Sometimes it is tempting to omit a title completely or to use a descriptive phrase such as "Essay," "Essay 1," or "Argument Essay." Every essay needs a title, a real title, and not just a descriptive phrase. An interesting, descriptive title is part of the attraction of your paper for readers. After all, no company ever sold its product with no name on the box or with a title such as "Cereal" or "Automobile." Brainstorm some ideas; check them out with potential readers, ask them for suggestions, consult the glossary at the back of this text for some title writing strategies. Just make sure that you give your paper—and every paper—a title.

LOOKING AT SENTENCES AND WORD CHOICES

Only after you have asked and answered questions about the larger elements of your paper should you move to questions dealing with style, grammar, and mechanics.

Sentence or Fragment?   Is everything that you punctuated as a sentence—that is, with a beginning capital letter and an end mark such as a period—truly a sentence? Are any of these in fact fragments? If you are not sure of the difference, check the glossary. If you have written an intentional fragment for effect, check with your instructor to see if that is acceptable.

Sentence Variety   Have you used a variety of sentence types and lengths? Check the glossary for an explanation. Ideally, your paper should have a mix of sentence types and a variety of lengths. Be particularly careful that you do not write strings of short, simple sentences, which make you sound either like a young and immature writer or like you are writing to an elementary school audience.

Punctuation   Look carefully at every mark of punctuation that you have used. Is it the right choice for this place in the sentence? A quick review of the major uses of each punctuation mark can be found in the glossary.

Word Choice   Check your choice of words. Are you certain what each word means? Are there any words that might be too informal or too colloquial (words that might be appropriate in a conversation with friends but not in academic writing)? Is every word spelled correctly? If you have any doubts about a word's spelling or meaning, be sure to check the word in a dictionary.

KEEPING A REVISION LOG

Keeping a log of writing problems you most often encounter is an excellent way of promoting self-awareness. Your log should include subdivisions for a wide range of writing problems, not just grammatical and mechanical errors. The log will help you keep track of the areas with which you know you have trouble and those your instructor, peer readers, or writing tutors point out as needing improvement. Do you have a tendency to over-paragraph? To stop rather than conclude? To have trouble with parallelism? Each time you discover a problem or one is pointed out to you, list it in your log. Then, as you revise your papers, look back through your revision log to remind yourself of these frequent problems and look closely for them in your current draft.

If a revision log seems a lot of trouble, remember that only you can improve your own writing. Improvement, in turn, comes with recognizing your weaknesses and working to correct them.

USING PEER READERS

Most of the writing you do in college is aimed toward only one reader—an instructor. Writing just for the instructor has both advantages and disadvantages. A teacher is a critical reader who evaluates your paper by a set of standards, but a teacher can also be a sympathetic reader, one who understands the difficulties of writing and is patient with the problems that writers have. Classmates, colleagues, or supervisors can be just as critical as teachers, but less sympathetic.

Only in school, however, do you have someone who will read everything that you write and offer constructive comments. After you graduate, your letters and reports will be read by many different readers, but you will no longer have a teacher to offer advice or a tutor to conference with you. Instead, you will have to rely on your own analysis of your writing and on the advice of fellow workers. For this reason, learning to use a peer reader as a resource in your revising process is extremely important. At first, you might feel a little uncomfortable asking someone other than your instructor to read your papers, but after some experience, you will feel better about sharing. Remember that every reader is potentially a valuable resource for suggestions.

It is often difficult to accept criticism, but if you want to improve your writing skills, you need someone to say, "Why not do this?" After all, you expect that an athletic coach or a music or dance teacher will offer criticism. Your writing instructor and your other readers play the same role, and the advice and criticism they offer is meant to make your writing more effective. It is not intended as a personal criticism of you or your abilities.

PEER EDITING

Many college writing courses use peer editing as a regular classroom activity. On a peer editing day, students swap papers with their classmates and then critique one another's work, typically using a list of peer editing guidelines. But you don't have to do peer editing in class to reap the benefits of such an arrangement. If your instructor approves, you can arrange to swap papers with a classmate outside of class, or you can ask a roommate or a friend to do a peer reading for you.

From the start, though, several ground rules are important. First, when you ask a peer to edit your paper, you are asking for criticism. You want advice; you want reaction. You cannot expect that your reader will love everything that you have written.

Second, peer editing is not proofreading. You should not ask your reader to look for misspelled words and missing commas. Rather, you want your reader to react to the whole paper. Is the thesis clear? Does the structure seem appropriate? Are there enough examples or details? Does the introduction catch the reader's attention and make him or her want to keep reading? You need to keep your reader's attention focused on these larger, significant issues. One good way to do so is to give your reader a checklist or a set of questions that reflect the criteria appropriate for evaluating this kind of paper.

Third, you want a peer reader to offer specific and constructive criticism. To get that type of response, you must ask questions that invite—or even require—a reader to comment in more than yes and no answers. For example, do not ask your reader, "Is the thesis clear?"; instead ask, "What is the thesis of this paper?" If your reader has trouble answering that question or if the answer differs from your own, you know that this aspect of your paper needs more work.

GROUP EDITING

Sharing your writing in a small group is another good way to get reader reaction to your papers. Such an editing activity can take place either inside or outside of the classroom. In either case, you can prepare for a group editing session in the same way. Plan to form a group of four or five students, and make a copy of your paper for each group member. If possible, distribute those copies prior to the group editing session so that each member will have a chance to read and prepare some comments for the discussion. Then follow these guidelines:

Before the Group Editing Session

1. Read each paper carefully, marking or underlining the writer's main idea and key supporting points. Make any other notes about the paper that seem appropriate.
2. On a separate sheet, comment specifically on one or two aspects of the paper that most need improvement.

At the Group Editing Session

1. When it is your turn, read your own paper aloud to the group. Since you might hear problems as you read, keep a pen or pencil handy to jot down notes.
2. When you are finished, tell the group members what you would like them to comment on.
3. Listen to their remarks, and make notes. Feel free to ask group members to explain or expand on their observations. Remember, you want as much advice as you can get.
4. Collect the copies of your paper and the sheets on which the group members have commented on specific areas that need improvement.

After the Group Editing Session

1. Carefully consider both the oral and written comments of your group. You may not agree with everything that was said, but you need to weigh each comment.

2. Revise your paper. Remember that you are responsible for your own work. No one else—not your instructor, your peer editors, or your group readers—can or should tell you *everything* that you need to change.

USING YOUR SCHOOL'S WRITING CENTER OR A WRITING TUTOR

Most colleges operate writing centers, writing labs, or writing tutor programs. Their purpose is to provide individual assistance to any student who has a question about writing. They are staffed by trained tutors who want to help you. In part, such services are intended to supplement the instruction that you receive in a writing class, since most writing teachers have too many students to be able to offer extensive help outside of class to everyone. These services also exist to provide advice to students writing papers for courses in other disciplines where writing might be required but not discussed.

If you are having trouble with grammar or mechanics, if you consistently have problems with beginnings or middles or ends of papers, if you are baffled by a particular assignment, do not be afraid to ask for help. After all, every writer can benefit from constructive advice or additional explanations, and writing centers and tutors exist to provide that help. Remember, though, that a writing tutor is a teacher whose job is to explain and to instruct. You do not drop off your paper at the writing center like you drop off your automobile at the service station. Your tutor will suggest ways that *you* can improve your paper or follow a particular convention. A tutor will not do the work for you.

Come to your appointment with a specific set of questions or problems. Why are you there? What do you want to discuss? What don't you understand? After all, when you have a medical problem, you make an appointment with a doctor to discuss a specific set of symptoms. A conference with a writing tutor should work in a similar way.

Finally, make sure that you keep some form of written record of your conference. Jot down the tutor's advice and explanations. Those notes will serve as a valuable reminder of what to do when you are revising your paper.

USING AN OWL

For students who have access to the Internet and the World Wide Web—either from home or from school—another source of help in revising is an online writing lab, or OWL. Most OWLs are operated by traditional writing centers at colleges and universities. Although most provide help predominantly to students enrolled at those schools, many have services also available to students from anywhere who access the site through the Internet.

The services that OWLs provide range widely. Some offer e-mail tutoring; some provide access to MOOs (multiple user dimensions, object-oriented), where you can hold conversations with other writers. Most provide access to writing reference materials and extensive links to other related sites. One of the oldest OWLs is Purdue University's. Purdue's site offers information about writing based on reference materials and also maintains a listing of other OWLs and their e-mail addresses. A good place to start in a search for online revising help is the National Writing Centers Association List of Online Writing Labs and Centers. Visit the *Reader*'s Website (www.prenhall.com/miller) for a list of hot-linked resources for revision.

CONFERENCING WITH YOUR INSTRUCTOR

Your instructor in a writing class is always willing to talk with you about your writing. You can, of course, visit your instructor during scheduled office hours. In addition, many instructors, if their teaching schedule permits it, will schedule a set of regular conference times spaced throughout the semester. Whatever the arrangement, such a conference is an opportunity for you to ask questions about your writing in general or about a particular paper.

Whether you have asked for the conference or the instructor has scheduled it as a part of the class requirements, several ground rules apply. As with a tutoring session, you should always come to an instructor conference with a definite agenda in mind and a specific set of questions to ask. Writing these questions out is an excellent way to prepare for a conference. Generally, a conference is intended to be a dialogue, and so your active participation is expected. Do not be surprised, for example, if your instructor begins by asking you what you want to talk about. Since time is always limited (remember that your instructor might have to see dozens of students), you will not be able to ask about everything. Try to concentrate on the issues that trouble you the most.

Instructors like to use conferences as opportunities to discuss the larger issues of a paper: Is the thesis well defined? Is the structure as clear as it might be? Are there adequate transitions? Although your instructor will be happy to explain a troublesome grammatical or mechanical problem, do not expect your instructor to find and fix every mistake in your paper. A conference is not a proofreading session.

A conference is also not an oral grading of your paper. Grading a paper is a complicated task and one that frequently involves seeing your essay in the context of the other papers from the class. As a result, your instructor cannot make a quick judgment. Do not ask what grade the paper might receive.

As the conference proceeds, make notes for yourself about what is said. Do not rely on your memory. Those notes will constitute a plan for revising your paper.

PROOFREADING YOUR PAPER

At one point or another, virtually everyone has had the injunction "proof-read!" written on a paper. (*Proofreading* comes from printing terminology: a printer reads and corrects "proofs"—trial impressions made of the pages of set type—before printing a job.) You probably stared in dismay at those obvious slips that somehow managed to escape your eye. Why, you may have asked yourself, was I penalized for what were obviously just careless mistakes? In response, you could ask another question: Why do businesses and industries spend so much money making sure that their final written products are as free from errors as possible?

Basically, the answer is related to an audience's perception of the writer (or the business). If a paper, letter, report, or advertisement contains even minor mistakes, they act as a form of "static" that interferes with the communication process. The reader's attention is shifted away from the message to some fundamental questions about the writer. A reader might wonder why you did not have enough pride in your work to check it before handing it in. Even worse, a reader might question your basic competence as a writer and researcher. As the number of errors in proportion to the total number of words rises, the reader's distraction grows. In college such static can have serious consequences. Studies conducted in New York City colleges, for example, revealed that readers would tolerate on the average only five to six basic errors in a three-hundred-word passage before assigning a student to a remedial English course. The point is that careless mistakes are rhetorically damaging to you as a writer; they undermine your voice and authority.

Once you have revised your paper thoroughly—considering the effectiveness of the thesis, the clarity of the organization, the strength of the opening and the conclusion, and any other problems in previous papers that you have listed in your revision log—you are ready to proofread. The secret of proofreading is to make sure that you read each word as you have written it. If you read too quickly, your mind often "corrects" or skips over problems. Force yourself to read each word exactly by moving a ruler or a piece of paper slowly down the page, reading aloud as you go. When you combine looking at the page with listening to the words, you increase your chances of catching mistakes that are visual (such as misspellings) and those that are aural (such as awkward phrasings).

Misspellings are so common that they need special attention. Everyone misspells some words; even the most experienced writer, teacher, or editor has to check a dictionary for correct spellings of certain words. English is a particularly tricky language, for words are not always spelled the way in which they are pronounced. English has silent *e*'s as in *live; ph*'s and *gh*'s that sound like *f*'s as in *phone* and *tough*; silent *ough*'s and *gh*'s as in *through* and *bright*. It is easy to get confused about when to double consonants before adding–*ed* to the end of a word or when to drop the final *e* before adding–*able*. All of these difficulties are perfectly natural and common. No one expects you to remember how to spell every word in your speaking vocabulary, but people do expect that you will check your writing for misspelled words.

Most misspellings can be eliminated if you do two things. First, recognize the kinds of words you are likely to misspell; learn when not to trust your instinct, particularly with words that sound alike, such as *there* and *their* and *its* and *it's*. Second, once you have finished your paper, go back and check your spelling. If you have written your paper on a word processor that has a spell-check function, be sure to run it. However, do not rely on that type of checking alone; for example, spell checkers won't show you that you've used *there* when you mean *their*. Always have a dictionary at hand. Go through your essay and look up every word that might be a problem. Doing these two things will go a long way toward eliminating misspellings in your papers.

IS AN ERROR-FREE PAPER AN "A" PAPER?

Although good, effective writing is mechanically and grammatically correct, you cannot reverse the equation. It is perfectly possible to write a paper that has no "errors" but is still a poor paper. An effective paper fulfills the requirements of the assignment, has something interesting or meaningful to say, and provides specific evidence and examples rather than vague generalizations. Effective writing is a combination of many factors: appropriate content, focused purpose, clear organization, and fluent expression.

Although perfect grammar and mechanics do not make a perfect paper, such things are important. Minor errors are like static in your writing. Too many of them distract your reader and focus the reader's attention not on your message but on your apparent carelessness. Minor errors can undermine your reader's confidence in you as a qualified authority. If you make errors in spelling or punctuation, for example, your reader might assume that you made similar errors in reporting information. So while revision is not just proofreading, proofreading should be a part of the revision process.

When you draft using a computer, always print out a hard-copy version of your paper for proofreading. Most writers find that they miss more errors when they proofread only on screen. Also keep in mind that while your word processor's spell-check function will catch many spelling errors, it won't identify mistakes that occur because two words sound alike but are spelled differently (*its* and *it's*, for example) or typos that result in a correctly spelled word (such as *the* for *they*). You need to proofread carefully yourself for mistakes like these.

SOME THINGS TO REMEMBER

1. Put your paper aside for a period of time before you attempt to revise it.
2. Seek the advice of your instructor or a writing center tutor or the help of classmates.

3. Reconsider your choice of topic. Were you able to treat it adequately in the space you had available?

4. State your thesis in a sentence as a way of checking your content. Is everything in the paper relevant to that thesis?

5. Check to make sure that you have given enough examples to clarify your topic, to support your argument, or to make your thesis clear. Relevant specifics convince and interest a reader.

6. Look through the advice given in each of the introductions to this text. Have you organized your paper carefully? Is its structure clear?

7. Define your audience. To whom are you writing? What assumptions have you made about your audience? What changes are necessary to make your paper clear and interesting to that audience?

8. Check the guidelines your instructor provided. Have you done what was asked? Is your paper too short or too long?

9. Examine each sentence to make sure that it is complete and grammatically correct. Try for a variety of sentence structures and lengths.

10. Look carefully at each paragraph. Does it obey the rules for effective paragraph construction? Do your paragraphs clearly indicate the structure of your essay?

11. Check your word choice. Have you avoided slang, jargon, and clichés? Have you used specific words? Have you used appropriate words for your intended audience?

12. Proofread one final time.

WRITERS AT WORK

When you have the time in which to plan, draft, and then revise an essay, the result will be considerably better than when you start and finish a paper the night before it is due. The key is time—you need to begin planning and gathering information before you put words on paper or screen; you need to allow some time between your first draft and the final; you will benefit from the advice of other writers who respond to your drafts. This process of prewriting, writing a draft, and then revising can be seen in the work of the two writers reproduced here. Tina Burton is a student writer producing a paper for a course; Gordon Grice is a professional writer who worked on his essay intermittently for over two years. Despite those differences, both essays show how the writing process ideally works.

A STUDENT WRITER: TINA BURTON'S "THE WATERMELON WOOER"

FINDING A TOPIC AND PREWRITING

The planning, writing, and revising process can be seen in the evolution of Tina Burton's essay, "The Watermelon Wooer." Tina's essay was written in response to a totally open assignment: she was asked to write an essay using examples. The paper was due in three weeks. The openness of the assignment proved initially frustrating to Tina. When she first began work on the essay, she started with a completely different topic than the one she eventually decided on. That weekend, however, she went home to visit her parents. Her grandfather had died a few months before, and the family was sorting through some photographs and reminiscing about him. Suddenly she had the idea she wanted. She would write about her grandfather and her ambivalent feelings toward him. Once she had settled on this specific topic, she also determined her purpose (to inform readers about her grandfather and her mixed feelings, as well as to entertain through a vivid description of this unusual old man) and her audience (her instructor and peers). When

Tina filled out answers to the questions her instructor had posed, she noted:

Subject: My grandfather, a character sketch
Topic: My ambivalent feelings about my grandfather—love and embarrassment
Purpose: To inform my reader and to entertain
Audience: My peers—we all have grandparents, and we often have ambivalent feelings toward them

Tina's first written work on the assignment came when she made a list of about thirty things that she remembered about her grandfather. "The list had to be cut," Tina said, "so I marked off things that were too bawdy or too unbelievable. I wanted to portray him as sympathetic, but I was really afraid that the whole piece would come off as too sentimental or drippy."

At the next class meeting, the instructor set aside some time for prewriting activities. The teacher recommended that the students try either a freewriting or a brainstorming exercise. Tina did the brainstorming that appears next.

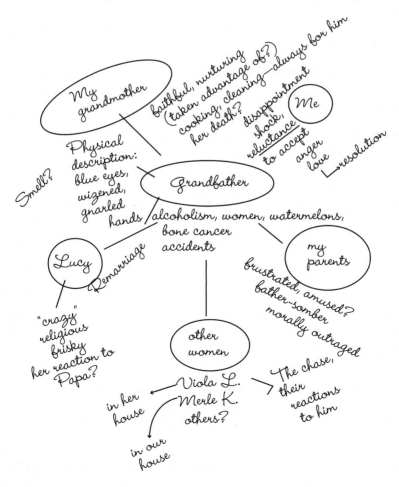

DRAFTING

From here, Tina wrote a complete draft of her essay in one sitting. She had the most difficulty with the beginning of the essay. "I kept trying to describe him, but I found that I was including too much," she commented. The breakthrough came with the advice of two other students in the class. The first page of the first draft of Tina's essay follows. The handwritten comments were provided by Kathrine Varnes, a classmate.

EARLIER DRAFT

THE WATERMELON WOOER

When someone you love dearly behaves in a manner that offends you, do you stop loving that person? Do you lose all respect for that person because you cannot forget ~~repulsive [?]~~ *Eventually,?* *
the act (that you judged as repulsive?) (On the contrary), you might (eventually) fondly recall the once offensive behavior. (Perhaps,) In time, you might even understand *so?* why you found the behavior loathesome. Maybe, you will reach a point in time when you will be unable to think of your loved one without thinking of the once questionable behavior. Such is the case with my grandfather.

*I have a personal dislike for this 3-word transition

some way to condense?

Before I tell the story of how my grandfather behaved in ways that I could neither understand nor tolerate, I must *introduce?* first (give some background information on) him. A wizened little man with dancing blue eyes and hands gnarled from years of carpentry work, "Papa" was a notorious womanizer and an alcoholic. Born and raised in Halifax County, Virginia, he spent most of his life building houses, distilling and selling corn liquor, and chasing women. After he and my grandmother had been married for thirty years or so, he decided to <u>curtail some of his wild behavior and treat her with more respect</u>. Actually, he remained faithful to her only after he discovered that she was ill and probably wouldn't be around to feed and nurture him for much longer. ~~So, as~~

both of these things? or respect by curtailing?

Use alternative diction to soften tone?

didn't

~~you can see~~, <u>m</u>y grandfather (does not) have a <u>spot</u>less, or

reputation

even a remotely commendable (record of personal

achievements.)

REVISING

Second Draft "Kathrine wanted me to condense and to find a way in which to jump right into the story," Tina noted. "She also said, 'You're trying to tell too much. Let the story tell itself. Try to think of one thing that might capture something essential or important about him.'" In a second peer edit, Tina sought the advice of Stephen Palley, another classmate. Stephen offered these comments on the first page of the Tina's second draft.

THE WATERMELON WOOER

characterize an essential part of his eccentricity Intro?

my grandfather never really (settled down)

Let me tell you a story about my grandfather ~~and, I~~

~~guess, me too. I don't pretend to know whether my story~~

~~will shock, offend, amuse, or bore.~~ I only know that I feel

it

the need to tell ~~the story.~~

For a time he   but eventually

~~Before I tell the story of how my grandfather~~ behaved

in ways that I could neither understand nor tolerate, I must

(I see him now)   Let me introduce

first introduce him. A wizened little man with ~~dancing blue~~

~~eyes~~ and hands ~~gnarled from years of carpentry work,~~

It's funny but when I think of my grandfather I think 1st of the way he smelled

Miller ponies, fertilizer

smell?

"Papa" was a notorious womanizer and an alcoholic. Born

and raised in Halifax County, Virginia, he spent most of his

life building houses, distilling and selling corn liquor, and

chasing women. After he and my grandmother had been

married for thirty years or so, he decided to show her some

respect by curtailing his wild behavior. Actually, he

remained faithful to her only after he discovered that she

was ill and probably wouldn't be around to feed and nurture

him for much longer. Papa didn't have a spotless reputation.

"Stephen offered me quite a few helpful suggestions," Tina recalled, "but he also suggested something that I just didn't quite feel comfortable with." As you can see in the revised draft, Tina had queried Stephen about including her memories of scent. In a conversation, Stephen urged Tina to substitute memories of smells for memories of sights. In the end, though, Tina observed, "I just couldn't do what Stephen suggested."

Final Draft   Before the three weeks were over, Tina actually wrote five separate drafts of her essay. "Everything here is true," she said, "but I worried so much about what was included because I didn't want to embarrass anyone in my family."

"Throughout the process," she added, "I was also worried about my tone. I wanted it to be funny; I wanted my readers to like my grandfather and his watermelon adventures." As she moved toward her final draft, Tina was also able to write a thesis statement for her essay. Even though the essay is a humorous character sketch using narration and description, it still has a clearly stated thesis. Notice, however, that the thesis is placed not at the beginning of the essay but at the very end.

Thesis: The acts that troubled me eventually allowed me to glimpse the frail side of my grandfather, to see him as a human being possessed of fears and flaws rather than a cardboard ideal.

Reproduced here is Tina's final draft of her essay.

THE WATERMELON WOOER
Tina M. Burton

I see him now, sprawled on our couch, clutching a frayed afghan, one brown toenail escaping his sock. His darting eyes are betraying his withered body.

Born and raised in backwoods Virginia, my grandfather spent most of his life building houses, distilling and selling corn liquor, and chasing women. After he and my grandmother had been married for thirty years or so, he decided to show her some respect by curtailing his wild behavior. Actually, he remained faithful to her only after he discovered that she was ill and probably wouldn't be around to feed and nurture him much longer. Papa didn't have a spotless reputation.

Because he'd been on the wagon for several years and hadn't had any affairs for the last ten years, my family thought that Papa would continue to behave in a "respectable" manner even after my grandmother died. I guess we were hoping for some sort of miracle. After my grandmother died in 1983, Papa became a rogue again: he insisted on reveling in wild abandon. When my father found out that Papa was drinking heavily again and crashing his car into mailboxes, houses, and other large obstacles, he asked Papa to move into our house. The fact that three of Papa's female neighbors had complained to the police about Papa's exposing himself probably had something to do with my father's decision.

The year that Papa lived with us rivaled the agony of Hell.

I was always Papa's favorite grandchild, his "gal," and I worshipped him from the time that I was old enough to spend summers with him on his farm. Until I saw him every day, witnessed for myself his sometimes lewd behavior and his odd personality quirks, I never really believed the stories about him that I had heard from my mother and father. Every morning, he baited my mother with comments like "the gravy's too thick," "my room's too cold," "your kids are too loud," and "the phone rings too often." Against my mother's wishes, he smoked in the house. In mixed company, he gleefully explained how to have sex in an inner tube in the ocean without getting caught and gave detailed physical descriptions of the women he'd had sex with. It surprised me how much my opinion of Papa changed in one year.

During this one year, Papa did many things that I thought were embarrassing and inexcusable. I came face-to-face with the "dark" side of his personality. One week after moving into my parents' home, Papa began to sneak the orange juice from the refrigerator and doctor it with Smirnoff's vodka. I knew he'd been pickling his brain with alcohol for years and that this was part of the disease, but he'd said that he'd gone dry. Besides, he was violating my father's most important rule: no alcohol in the house. I didn't know that his drinking was only the first of a long line of incredible acts.

The behaviors that ultimately endeared Papa to me, that made me forgive him his shortcomings, are also those which I recall with a great deal of sadness. These are the memories of him that I treasure, the stories that I will tell to my grandchildren when they are old enough to deal with graphic material. A year ago, I never would have believed that I could fondly remember, much less write about, these episodes.

For about a year, Papa engaged in what I refer to as the "watermelon affairs." Perhaps because he had lived on a vegetable farm for the majority of his life Papa had a special affinity for a wide variety of fruits and vegetables. Especially dear to him were watermelons. So, he assumed that other elderly people, particularly women, shared his proclivity for produce. One week after he moved into my parent's house, he embarked upon his mission—to woo with watermelons as many women as he could.

A shrewd man, possessed of a generous supply of common sense and watermelons, Papa decided to seduce a woman who lived very close to him. This woman happened to be my maternal grandmother who also lived in our house. Unaware of his lascivious intentions and bent on helping him assuage his grief over the loss of his wife, Grandmother Merle prepared special meals for Papa and spent long hours conversing with him about farming, grandchildren, and life in the "Old South." Merle assumed that the watermelons Papa brought to her were nothing more than a token of his appreciation for her kindness. When Papa grabbed a part of Merle that she preferred to remain untouched, these conversations came to an abrupt halt. Of course, we were mortified by his inappropriate behavior, but I suspect that my parents secretly were amused. While Papa's indiscretion with Merle was upsetting, at least no one other than members of my immediate family knew about the incident. His next romantic adventure earned him immediate notoriety in the neighborhood. One afternoon, huge watermelon in hand, he trotted over to visit Viola Lampson, a decrepit and cranky elderly woman with whom my family had been friendly for twenty years. Twenty minutes after Papa entered her house, the police came. Poor Viola was in a state of disrepair because my grandfather had been chasing her around her kitchen table demanding kisses. Fortunately, the policeman who arrived at the scene of the crime was quite understanding and polite; he advised my father to keep a careful watch on Papa at all times. My somber father was very embarrassed. Finally, we were all beginning to see the relationship between watermelons and women. He'd disappear with a watermelon and return with the police.

I was mortified by Papa's lecherous desire for other women. After all, wasn't he supposed to be grieving over the death of my grandmother, his wife of fifty years? I resigned myself to the fact that I never would love him or respect him in the manner that I once had. For a while, I avoided his company and refused to answer his frequent questions about why I was avoiding him. I didn't think about why he was behaving the way he was; I simply cast judgment on his behavior and shut myself off from him. Not until Papa remarried did I even try to understand his needs or his behavior.

Approximately one year after his wife died, Papa remarried. Finally, he found a woman who not only loved watermelon but also loved him and his frisky behavior. Lucy, often referred to as "crazy Lucy" by her neighbors who had heard her speak of miracle healings and visions of Christ, wed Papa and took him into her already jam-packed home. Amazingly, she convinced him to stop drinking and to refrain from molesting other women. She could not, however, convince Papa to "get the religion" as she called it. My family was nonplussed both by Papa's decision to remarry at age 77 and to stop drinking after all these years. We all were annoyed by the fact that Lucy convinced him to do in several months what we had been trying to get him to do for many years.

Not until I learned that Papa was dying of bone cancer did I try to understand why he needed to remarry and why I found that fact unbearable. Until this time, I harbored the feeling that Papa somehow was degrading the memory of my grandmother by remarrying. His attempted seductions of women disturbed me, but his decision to marry Lucy saddened me. Only after

I spent many afternoons with Papa and Lucy did I realize that they truly loved each other. More importantly, I realized that Papa, devastated by his wife's death, was afraid to be alone in his old age. Perhaps sensing his illness, even though he knew nothing of its development at this time, he wanted to recapture some of his stamina, some of his youth. He really wasn't searching for someone to replace my grandmother: he simply wanted to have a companion to comfort him, to distract him from his grief.

Fortunately, I accepted Papa's actions and resolved my conflict with him before he died. Once again, I was his "gal" in spirit, and I even came to love and respect Lucy. Now, I find that I cannot conjure images of Papa without thinking of watermelons and his romantic escapades. The acts that once troubled me eventually allowed me to glimpse the frail side of my grandfather, to see him as a human being possessed of fears and flaws rather than a cardboard ideal.

A Professional Writer: Gordon Grice's "Caught in the Widow's Web"

Finding a Topic and Prewriting

Gordon Grice began work on the essay "Caught in the Widow's Web" in a journal. He wrote a series of consecutive entries over a two-month period. This is not his usual way of working. He commented, "I rarely use this technique. I don't use it when I have a good idea of where I am going. Keeping a journal helps me when I don't really have a good subject in mind." He continued, "I kept this one while I was taking a nonfiction writing workshop, because I had to turn in pieces on deadline and didn't really know how to start."

Reproduced here are some of the original journal entries for the essay. Grice printed his entries in ink in a spiral-bound notebook. His revisions of those entries—made while he was keeping the journal—are preserved here. Crossed-out words are indicated by a line running through the word. Additions placed above or to the side of the cross-outs are reproduced here in brackets. As the entries show, writers often revise even as they first begin work on an essay.

Entry 1

1/16/93
Idea for essay: What people have nightmares about. Paul dreamed of people vomiting up human flesh, knew he was in hell.

1/16/93
The black widow has the ugliest web of any spider. The orb weavers ~~have~~ make those seemingly delicate nets that poets have ~~turned~~ traditionally used as symbols of imagination (~~Dickinson~~), order (~~Shakespeare~~), [and] perfection.

The sheet-web weavers make spiders weave crisp linens for the lawn [~~on the lawn~~] ~~—some of these have impressive-looking underlayers and tunnels~~. But the widow makes messy-looking tangles in the corners and bends of things and under logs and debris. Often the web ~~has~~ is littered with leaves. Beneath ~~the web~~ it lie the ~~corpses~~ husks of insect prey, [their antenna stiff as gargoyle horns], cut loose and dropped; on them and the surrounding ground are splashes of the spider's white ~~dung~~ [urine], which looks like bird ~~urine~~ [guano] and smells of ammonia even at a distance of several feet. ~~If these spiders this ground is biolog~~ This fetid material draws scavengers—ants, sow bugs, crickets, roaches, and so on—which ~~walk into~~ become tangled in vertical strands of ~~web~~ [silk] reaching from the ground up into the web. The widow comes down and, with a bicycling ~~motion~~ of the hind [pair of] legs, throws [gummy] ~~liquid~~ silk onto this new prey.

> *Point of Comparison: Compare this entry with paragraphs 2 and 3 in "Caught in the Widow's Web."*

ENTRY 2

1/20/93

3   When the prey is seriously tangled but still struggling, the widow cautiously descends and bites the creature, usually on a leg joint. This is ~~the~~ a killing bite. ~~She will~~; it pumps neurotoxin into the victim. She will deliver a series of bites as the creature dies; these later bites inject substances that liquify the organs. And finally she will settle down to suck the liquified innards out of the prey, changing her ~~position~~ [place] two or three times to get [it] all.

> *Point of Comparison: Compare this entry with paragraph 3 in "Caught in the Widow's Web."*

ENTRY 3

4   The [architectural] complexity[ities] of the widow-web ~~are beyond us. As a home~~ do not particularly impress the widow. ~~She~~ They move around in these webs ~~essentially~~ [almost] blind, yet they never snare themselves, misstep, or ~~lose their wa~~ get lost. In fact, a widow forcibly removed from her web and put back at a different point does not seem confused; she will quickly return to her habitual resting place. ~~All this~~

> *Point of Comparison: This material does not appear in "Caught in the Widow's Web."*

ENTRY 4

2/3/93

5   The first thing people ask when they [hear] about my fascination with the widow is why ~~I'm~~ [am] not afraid. The truth is that my fascination is rooted in fear.

6   I know a man who as a child was frightened by ~~the~~ his preacher's ~~claim that~~ invitation to eat the flesh of Jesus. The man's [worst] nightmares are about

~~cannibals. His hobby~~ vomiting up human meat. The thing he likes best to watch [horror] ~~movies~~ [films] about cannibals.

Point of Comparison: Compare this entry with paragraph 6 in "Caught in the Widow's Web."

ENTRY 5

2/4/93

There is, of course, one pragmatic reason for fearing the widow. 7

These markings include a pair of triangles on the ventral side of the abdomen—the infamous "hourglass." 8

The widow's venom is, of course, a soundly pragmatic reason for fear. 9
The venom contains a neurotoxin that produces chills, [sweats], vomiting, ~~and~~ fiery pain, ~~sometimes~~ [and] convulsions and death. ~~Death It is [And]~~ Occasionally ~~a person~~ [people] dies from ~~the~~ widow bites ~~but less than the~~ Some researchers ~~have theorized~~ [hypothesized] that the virulence of the venom was necessary for killing ~~scarab~~ beetles of the scarab family. This family contains thousands of ~~beetles~~ [species], including the june bug and the famous ~~Egyptian~~ dung beetle the Egyptians thought immortal. All the scarabs have thick, strong bodies and [unusually] tough exoskeletons, and ~~these~~ many of them are common prey for the widow.

Point of Comparison: Compare this entry with paragraphs 11 and 12 in "Caught in the Widow's Web."

ENTRY 6

2/9/93

The widow, it was proposed, needs a strong venom to kill such thick-hided 10
creatures. But this idea is yet another that owes more to ~~the widow's~~ dark romance ~~than~~ with the widow than to hard evidence. The venom is thousands of times too virulent ~~for this than~~ [for] this purpose. ~~We see~~ An emblem of immortality ~~trapped~~, killed by a creature ~~thing~~ whose most distinctive [blood-colored] markings people invariably describe as an hourglass: scientists, being human, want to see a deep causality.

But no one has ever offered a sufficient explanation for the <u>widow's</u> 11
[dangerous] venom. It ~~has no~~ provides no evolutionary advantages: all of ~~its~~ [the widow's] prey items ~~are~~ would find lesser toxins fatal, and there is no particular ~~advantage to~~ benefit in harming or killing larger animals. A widow biting a human or other large animal is almost certain to be killed. Evolution does occasionally produce such flowers of [natural] evil—traits that are not functional, but vestiges of lost functions, but ~~pure~~ utterly pointless. ~~This~~ Such ~~things~~ [traits] come about because natural selection merely ~~works against~~ [favors] the inheritance of useful ~~traits~~ [characteristics] that arise from random mutation and extinguishes disadvantageous characteristics. All other characteristics, the ones that neither help nor hinder survival, are preserved [or not] (almost) randomly; when mutation links a useless but harmless trait to a useful

one, both are preserved. Many people—even many scientists—assume that every animal is elegantly engineered for its ecological niche, that every bit of an animal's anatomy and behavior ~~can be~~ has a functional explanation. This assumption is false. Nothing in evolutionary theory sanctions it; fact refutes it. ~~It is in fact a lapse into magical thinking. But we want to order and explain things. But We all want order and order in the world and in the room of order In the ordered rooms~~

12   We want the world to be an ordered room, but in a corner of that room there hangs an untidy web ~~that says~~. Here the analytic mind finds an irreducible mystery, a motiveless evil in nature; [and] the scientist's vision of evil comes to match the vision of a religious woman with a ten-foot pole. No picture of the cosmos as elegant design accounts for the widow. No picture of a benevolent God explains the widow. She hangs in her haphazard web (that marvel of design) defying teleology.

> *Point of Comparison: Compare the entry with paragraphs 12–15 of "Caught in the Widow's Web."*

QUESTIONS FOR DISCUSSION

1. What thought or idea appears to trigger Grice's essay? Does he ever return to that idea in the sections of the journal reproduced here?

2. How does the black widow's web differ from those of most spiders?

3. What is puzzling about the widow's venom?

4. What associations do we have with the hourglass (paragraph 10)?

5. In what sense does the widow's web "defy teleology" (paragraph 12)? What is teleology?

6. What are the most common types of revisions that Grice makes in these journal entries?

7. Be prepared to define the following words: *gargoyle* (paragraph 2), *scavengers* (2), *neurotoxin* (3), *innards* (3), *habitual* (4), *pragmatic* (9), *exoskeletons* (9), *causality* (10), *vestiges* (11), *benevolent* (12).

DRAFTING

Grice moved from his journal entries to a first draft of the essay. In a conversation, Grice commented extensively on how the essay was revised.

> When I started revising the black widow piece, I went to a junkyard with an empty mayonnaise jar and caught a widow. I kept her on my desk as I wrote. I kept observing interesting things I had never thought of putting in the piece before. If I'm writing about something I can't catch in a jar, I find some other way to research it. I hit the library or interview people. This helps me find interesting details that will fire up a boring draft.

I try to figure out what's working in a draft and what's not. I put it away for a while so I can get some distance on it. I get other people to criticize it. I don't trust anybody who likes everything I write or anybody who hates everything I write.

I analyze a draft like this: I want something interesting in the first sentence. Usually my first draft begins badly, so my job on revision is to decapitate the essay. I cut until I hit something interesting. Or I may find an interesting part somewhere else in the draft and move it to the beginning. I move things around a lot. If I get frustrated trying to keep it all straight on the computer, I print it out and sit on the floor with scissors rearranging things.

I look for long sections of exposition or summary and try to break these up with vivid examples or details. If some part is boring, I try to think of ways to make it into a story.

I fiddle with the sentences as I go. I try to cut all the passive voice verbs and all the *be* verbs. I strike filler words like *very*. If it doesn't sound right without the filler, I take that as a clue that something's wrong with the ideas themselves. I aim for the prose to sound simple, even if the ideas are complex.

He tried to get the revised draft published but with no success. He reflected: "I wasn't having any luck. I theorized that the opening wasn't catchy enough. I also thought that the piece didn't fit any magazine I could think of—it was too arty for a science magazine, and most of the essays I saw in literary journals had more personal material than I used."

A considerable amount of time elapsed: "I carried the piece around with me until I got the chance to work on it. I was substitute teaching a middle school shop class when I scribbled down a new opening." In the new opening, Grice describes having young widow spiders crawl all over his arms: "I thought the danger made it interesting." Grice sent off the essay—with its new opening—and it was immediately published in the *High Plains Literary Review* under the title "The Black Widow."

Final Draft   Grice's essay actually has three "final" forms. After the essay appeared in *High Plains Literary Review*, it was rewritten and reprinted in the large-circulation monthly magazine *Harper's*. Ironically, the new, more personal opening that Grice had written was cut and some other minor changes were made. Revision did not stop there, though, for the essay was later included in a collection of Grice's essays titled *The Red Hourglass: Inner Lives of the Predators* (1998). Commenting on that revision, he said, "It's five or six times longer, so I covered a lot of new material. For example, I developed the section about the widow's venom with some case studies. I added details and changed the overall shape of the essay. I changed word choices and sentence structures as well."

The draft reproduced here is the one that originally appeared in *Harper's* magazine.

CAUGHT IN THE WIDOW'S WEB

Gordon Grice

Gordon Grice earned his B.A. at Oklahoma State University and his M.F.A. at the University of Arkansas. Grice has published essays and poems in a wide range of literary magazines. His first collection of essays was The Red Hourglass: Lives of the Predators *(1998). The following essay, originally titled "The Black Widow," first appeared in the* High Plains Literary Review. *Grice reworked it for its appearance in* Harper's *magazine and then again for* The Red Hourglass. *The version reproduced here appeared in* Harper's.

On Writing: *Widely praised for his precise and detailed attention to the "microworld," Grice has said, "Personal observation and experience are part of my approach to writing as a whole. I like to delve into the details and give my readers the feeling of being there and having their own hands in it."*

BEFORE READING

Connecting: How do you feel about spiders? To what do you attribute your reaction?

Anticipating: As you read, think about what the black widow symbolizes for Grice.

1   I hunt black widows. When I find one, I capture it. I have found them in discarded wheels and tires and under railroad ties. I have found them in house foundations and cellars, in automotive shops and toolsheds, in water meters and rock gardens, against fences and in cinder-block walls.

2   Black widows have the ugliest webs of any spider, messylooking tangles in the corners and bends of things and under logs and debris. Often the widow's web is littered with leaves. Beneath it lie the husks of consumed insects, their antennae stiff as gargoyle horns; on them and the surrounding ground are splashes of the spider's white urine, which looks like bird guano and smells of ammonia even at a distance of several feet.

3   This fetid material draws scavengers—ants, sow bugs, crickets, roaches, and so on—which become tangled in vertical strands of silk reaching from the ground up into the web. The widow climbs down and throws gummy silk onto this new prey. When the insect is seriously tangled but still struggling, the widow cautiously descends and bites it, usually on a leg joint. This is a killing bite; it pumps poison into the victim. As the creature dies, the widow delivers still more bites, injecting substances that liquefy the organs. Finally it settles down to suck the liquefied innards out of the prey, changing position two or three times to get it all.

Widows reportedly eat mice, toads, tarantulas—anything that wanders   4
into that remarkable web. I have never witnessed a widow performing a gustatory act of that magnitude, but I have seen them eat scarab beetles heavy as
pecans, carabid beetles strong enough to prey on wolf spiders, cockroaches
more than an inch long, and hundreds of other arthropods of various sizes.

Many widows will eat as much as opportunity allows. One aggressive fe-   5
male I raised had an abdomen a little bigger than a pea. She snared a huge
cockroach and spent several hours subduing it, then three days consuming it.
Her abdomen swelled to the size of a largish marble, its glossy black stretch-
ing to a tight red-brown. With a different widow, I decided to see whether that
appetite really was insatiable. I collected dozens of large crickets and
grasshoppers and began to drop them into her web at a rate of one every three
or four hours. After catching and devouring her tenth victim, this bloated
widow fell from her web, landing on her back. She remained in this position
for hours, making only feeble attempts to move. Then she died.

The first thing people ask when they hear about my fascination with the   6
widow is why I am not afraid. The truth is that my fascination is rooted in fear.

I have childhood memories that partly account for this. When I was six   7
my mother took my sister and me into the cellar of our farmhouse and told us
to watch as she killed a widow. With great ceremony she produced a long stick
(I am tempted to say a ten-foot pole) and, narrating her technique in exactly
the hushed voice she used for discussing religion or sex, went to work. Her
flashlight beam found a point halfway up the cement wall where two marbles
hung together—one a crisp white, the other a shiny black. My mother ran her
stick through the dirty silver web around them. As it tore it sounded like the
crackling of paper in fire. The black marble rose on thin legs to fight off the
intruder. My mother smashed the widow onto the stick and carried it up into
the light. It was still kicking its remaining legs. Mom scraped it against the
floor, grinding it into a paste. Then she returned for the white marble—the
widow's egg sac. This, too, came to an abrasive end.

My mother's stated purpose was to teach us how to recognize and deal   8
with a dangerous creature that we would probably encounter on the farm. But,
of course, we also took away the understanding that widows were actively
malevolent, that they waited in dark places to ambush us, that they were worthy of ritual disposition, like an enemy whose death is not sufficient but must
be followed by the murder of his children and the salting of his land and whose
unclean remains must not touch our hands.

The odd thing is that so *many* people, some of whom presumably did not   9
first encounter the widow in such an atmosphere of mystic reverence, hold the
widow in awe. Various friends have told me that the widow's bite is always fatal to humans—in fact, it almost never is. I have heard told for truth that goods
imported from the Orient are likely to be infested with widows and that
women with bouffant hairdos have died of widow infestation. Any contradiction of such tales is received as if it were a proclamation of atheism.

We project our archetypal terrors onto the widow. It is black; it avoids   10
the light; it is a voracious carnivore. Its red markings suggest blood. The female's

habit of eating her lovers invites a strangely sexual discomfort; the widow becomes an emblem for a man's fear of extending himself into the blood and darkness of a woman, something like the legendary Eskimo vampire that takes the form of a fanged vagina.

11   The widow's venom is, of course, a sound reason for fear. The venom contains a neurotoxin that can produce sweats, vomiting, swelling, convulsions, and dozens of other symptoms. The variation in symptoms from one person to the next is remarkable. The constant is pain. A useful question for a doctor trying to diagnose an uncertain case: "Is this the worst pain you've ever felt?" A "yes" suggests a diagnosis of a black widow bite. Occasionally people die from widow bites. The very young and the very old are especially vulnerable. Some people seem to die not from the venom but from the infection that may follow: because of its habitat, the widow carries dangerous microbes.

12   Researchers once hypothesized that the virulence of the venom was necessary for killing beetles of the scarabaeidae family. This family contains thousands of species, including the June beetle and the famous dung beetle that the Egyptians thought immortal. All the scarabs have thick, strong bodies and unusually tough exoskeletons, and many of them are common prey for the widow. The tough hide was supposed to require a particularly nasty venom. As it turns out, the venom is thousands of times more virulent than necessary for this purpose.

13   No one has ever offered a sufficient explanation for the dangerous venom. It provides no evolutionary advantages: all of the widow's prey would find lesser toxins fatal, and there is no particular benefit in killing or harming larger animals. A widow that bites a human being or other large animal is likely to be killed.

14   Natural selection favors the inheritance of useful characteristics that arise from random mutation and tends to extinguish disadvantageous traits. All other characteristics, the ones that neither help nor hinder survival, are preserved or extinguished at random as mutation links them with useful or harmful traits. Many people—even many scientists—assume that every animal is elegantly engineered for its ecological niche, that every bit of an animal's anatomy and behavior has a functional explanation. This assumption is false. Evolution sometimes produces flowers of natural evil—traits that are neither functional nor vestigial but utterly pointless.

15   We want the world to be an ordered room, but in a corner of that room there hangs an untidy web. Here the analytical mind finds an irreducible mystery, a motiveless evil in nature; here the scientist's vision of evil comes to match the vision of a God-fearing country woman with a ten-foot pole. No idea of the cosmos as elegant design accounts for the widow. No idea of a benevolent God is comfortable in a world with the widow. She hangs in her web, that marvel of design, and defies reason.

QUESTIONS ON SUBJECT AND PURPOSE

1. Why is Grice so fascinated by black widow spiders? To what does he trace his fascination?

2. What particular aspects of the black widow spider does Grice focus on?
3. What does the spider symbolize to Grice?

QUESTIONS ON STRATEGY AND AUDIENCE

1. Explain why Grice begins with the simple sentence "I hunt black widows." What is the effect of that sentence?
2. Grice divides his essay into three sections through the use of additional white space (after paragraphs 5 and 10). How does that division reflect the structure of the essay?
3. What assumptions could Grice make about his audience and their attitudes toward spiders?

QUESTIONS ON VOCABULARY AND STYLE

1. In describing how his mother killed the spider, Grice writes, "With great ceremony she produced a long stick (I am tempted to say a ten-foot pole)" (paragraph 7). Why does he add the material in the parentheses?
2. What is the effect of labeling the spider a "voracious carnivore"? To what extent is that an accurate phrase?
3. Be prepared to define the following words: *fetid* (paragraph 3), *gustatory* (4), *malevolent* (8), *bouffant* (9), *voracious* (10), *carnivore* (10), *virulence* (12), *niche* (14), *vestigial* (14).

WRITING SUGGESTIONS

1. **For Your Journal.** We tend to ignore the natural details that surround us. Try looking closely, even minutely, at the things around you. For example, take a magnifying glass and carefully examine an insect or a plant leaf. Take a walk and sit down with your journal. Study the landscape around you. Make journal entries about what you are suddenly able to see.
2. **For a Paragraph.** Select one of your journal entries and expand the entry into a descriptive paragraph. Try to make your reader see with you.
3. **For an Essay.** Nature can be seen and interpreted in many ways. Look back over your journal entries, look around you, select some natural thing—a living creature, a plant or leaf, an event, or even a landscape. In an essay, describe it to your reader in such a way as to reveal a significance. You are not writing an encyclopedia article or a guide book for tourists; you are seeing a meaning.
4. **For Research.** Grice does not attempt to tell the "full" story of the black widow. Research the black widow (or any other poisonous insect or reptile) using traditional library resources. You could also explore resources on the World Wide Web and various other online electronic

information sources. Your object is not to present an informational report—"here is everything about the subject." Rather, try to formulate a thesis about your subject. For example, you might explore the myths and symbols that have attached themselves to your subject or the role of the creature in our environment or the "lethalness" of its venom.

FOR FURTHER STUDY

Focusing on Grammar and Writing. Look closely at the first five paragraphs in Grice's essay. How does he create vivid images? To what extent does he use precise nouns, vivid verbs, and arresting details? What can writers learn from Grice's descriptive techniques?

Working Together. Divide into small groups. Check the glossary for the definitions of *simile* and *metaphor*. Each group should then take a block of paragraphs and locate all the similes and metaphors that Grice uses. Report your findings to the class as a whole.

Seeing Other Modes at Work. The essay makes extensive use of narration and of process narrative in its description of how the black widow kills its prey and how Grice's mother went black widow hunting.

Finding Connections. For a discussion of how each writer sees nature, Grice's essay can be paired with N. Scott Momaday's "The Way to Rainy Mountain" (Chapter 3).

Exploring the Web. Want to know more about the black widow spider and how its name came to represent a murderous woman? You can start at the Website www.prenhall.com/miller.

1

GATHERING AND USING
EXAMPLES

PREPARING TO WRITE

WHAT ROLE DO EXAMPLES PLAY IN WRITING?

Settling into your seat, you look at the midterm essay question that your professor has just handed out in your Introduction to Sociology course:

> Part II. Essay (25%). Identify the advantages or disadvantages of a "voucher" or "choice" system in providing education from public funds. Be sure to provide specific examples drawn from the assigned readings.

The success of your answer depends upon gathering and organizing appropriate examples from the course readings. A good answer will have specifics, not just generalizations and personal opinions. That realization about effective, successful writing applies to all types of writing: Effective writing in any form depends on details and examples. Relevant details and examples make writing interesting, informative, and persuasive. If you try to write without having gathered these essential specifics, you are forced to skim the surface of your subject, relying on generalizations, incomplete and sometimes inaccurate details, and unsubstantiated opinions. Without specifics, even a paper with a strong, clearly stated thesis becomes superficial. For example, how convinced would you be by the following argument?

> In their quest for big-time football programs, American universities have lost sight of their educational responsibilities. Eager for the revenues and alumni support that come with winning teams, universities exploit their football players. They do not care if the players get an education. They care only that they remain academically eligible to play for four seasons. At many schools only a small percentage of these athletes graduate. Throughout their college careers, they are encouraged to take easy courses and to put athletics first. It does not matter how they perform in the classroom as long as they distinguish themselves every Saturday afternoon. This exploitation should not be allowed to continue. Universities have a responsibility to educate their students, not to use them to gain publicity and to raise money.

Even if you agree with the writer's thesis, the paragraph does not go beyond the obvious. The writer generalizes—and probably distorts as a result. What the reader gets is an opinion unsupported by any evidence. For example, you might reasonably ask questions about the statement "At many schools only a small percentage of these athletes graduate."

> How many schools?
> How small a percentage?
> How does this percentage compare with that of nonathletes? After all, not everyone who starts college ends up graduating.

To persuade your reader—even just to interest your reader—you need specific information, details, and examples that illustrate the points you are trying to make.

WHERE CAN YOU FIND DETAILS AND EXAMPLES?

You gather details and examples either from your own experiences and observations or from research. Your sources vary, depending on what you are writing about. For example, *Life* magazine once asked writer Malcolm Cowley for an essay on what it was like to turn eighty. Cowley was already eighty years old, so he had a wealth of firsthand experiences from which to draw. Since nearly all of Cowley's readers were younger than eighty, he decided to show his readers what it was like to be old by providing a simple list of the occasions on which his body reminds him that he is old:

- When it becomes an achievement to do thoughtfully, step by step, what he once did instinctively
- When his bones ache
- When there are more and more little bottles in the medicine cabinet, with instructions for taking four times a day
- When he fumbles and drops his toothbrush (butterfingers)
- When his face has bumps and wrinkles, so that he cuts himself while shaving (blood on the towel)
- When year by year his feet seem farther from his hands
- When he can't stand on one leg and has trouble pulling on his pants
- When he hesitates on the landing before walking down a flight of stairs
- When he spends more time looking for things misplaced than he spends using them after he (or more often his wife) has found them
- When he falls asleep in the afternoon
- When it becomes harder to bear in mind two things at once
- When a pretty girl passes him in the street and he doesn't turn his head

Much of what you might be writing about, however, lies outside of your own experiences and observations. David Guterson, for example, set out to write a magazine article for *Harper's* about the Mall of America in Minneapolis. He chose to begin his essay with a series of facts:

> Last April, on a visit to the new Mall of America near Minneapolis, I carried with me the public-relations press kit provided for the benefit of reporters. It included an assortment of "fun facts" about the mall: 140,000 hot dogs sold each week, 10,000 permanent jobs, 44 escalators and 17 elevators, 12,750 parking places, 13,300 short tons of steel, $1 million in cash disbursed weekly from 8 automatic-teller machines. Opened in the summer of 1992, the mall was built on the 78-acre site of the former Metropolitan Stadium, a five-minute drive from the Minneapolis–St. Paul International Airport. With 4.2 million square feet of floor space—including twenty-two times the retail footage of the average American shopping center—the Mall of America was "the largest fully enclosed combination retail and family entertainment center in the United States."

The accumulation of facts—taken from the press kit—becomes a way of catching the reader's attention. In a nation impressed by size, what better way to "capture" the country's largest mall than by heaping up facts and statistics.

As the examples in this chapter show, writers sometimes draw exclusively on their personal experiences, as do Anna Quindlen in "The Name Is Mine," Edwidge Danticat in "Westbury Court," and George Orwell in "Shooting an Elephant." At other times, though, writers mix examples drawn from their personal experiences with information gathered from outside sources. Leslie Heywood in "One of the Girls" draws upon her own experiences as a Division I track and cross-country runner, but then adds the examples of the athletic achievements of Gertrude Ederle and Kathrine Switzer. Heywood also reflects on the impact that Title IX has had on women's athletics and on the dangers that young women athletes still face—from themselves and from society. Remember that regardless of where you find them, specific, relevant details and examples are very important in everything you write. They add life and interest to your writing, and they support or illustrate the points you are trying to make.

HOW DO YOU GATHER DETAILS AND EXAMPLES FROM YOUR EXPERIENCES?

Even when you are narrating an experience that happened to you or describing something that you saw, you will have to spend some time remembering the event, sorting out the details of the experience, and deciding which examples best support the point that you are trying to make. The best place to start in your memory and observation search is with the advice offered in "How to Write an Essay" and by considering the resources available to you. Exploring a personal experience, as the following diagram suggests, can involve a number of different activities:

Probing memory

Looking for photographs

FROM PERSONAL EXPERIENCE   **Revisiting places**

Reexperiencing sense impressions

Talking with people who were also there

Looking for material evidence (scrapbooks, letters, journals)

Many of the essays in this and later chapters begin with the writer's memories, experiences, and observations. Anna Quindlen, for example, draws only on a series of experiences in her married life to write "The Name Is Mine." Edwidge Danticat recalls an experience that occurred nearly twenty years earlier, one which she has never forgotten. Similarly, Bob Greene's "Cut" begins with his own experience. Even when writers add information from sources outside of their personal experiences—as Leslie Heywood does in "One of the Girls"—observation and personal experience might still play a significant role in shaping the essay.

How Do you Gather Information from Outside Sources?

When you think about researching a subject, you might only think of going to a library to look up your topic in the online catalog or a database or logging on to the World Wide Web to search for appropriate sites. As varied as these search methods are, you can also find information in many other ways, as the following diagram suggests:

Locating books

Visiting a library   **Using databases**

Finding other media resources

FROM RESEARCH   **Interviewing knowledgeable people**

Searching the Web

**Gathering documentation provided
by other knowledgeable sources**

The experiences of other people can also be excellent sources of information. Bob Greene, for example, recounts the experiences of four men who were also cut from athletic teams when they were young. Leslie Heywood has written extensively about women athletes and modern culture; she has spent years not only directly experiencing what it is to be a competitive athlete and a woman but also studying, researching, and publishing in these areas. Her essay reflects a complex mix of sources.

When you use information gathered from outside sources—whether those sources are written texts, electronic media, or interviews—it is important that you document those sources. Though it is true that articles in newspapers and magazines do not provide the type of documentation that you find in a paper written for a college course, recognize that you are a student and not a reporter. Be sure to ask your instructor how you are to document quotations and paraphrases—is it all right just to mention the sources in the text, or do you need to provide formal parenthetical documentation? Additional advice and a sample paper can be found in the appendix, "Finding, Using, and Documenting Sources." Be sure to read that material before you hand in a paper that uses outside sources.

Prewriting Suggestions

1. Don't try to rush the example-gathering stage of your prewriting. Good writing depends on good examples—quality is more important than quantity. Before sitting down to write, try to spend a day just jotting down examples.

2. Depending on your topic, examples can come from personal experience, from interviews with sources, or from information gathered in printed or online sources. Think about where you might find the best examples and remember that finding examples often requires research on your part.

3. Remember that the examples you select are chosen for a reason: to support a point or a thesis that you are making. On a separate sheet of paper, jot down each example and then next to it explain in a sentence how the example supports the larger point you are trying to make.

4. Think about possible ways in which the examples in your essay can be ordered or organized. If you are narrating an event, do you use a chronological order or a flashback? If you are using examples to support an argument, do you start with your strongest example or end with it? Make an organizational strategy for your essay.

5. Plan an opening strategy for your essay—maybe you will start with a vivid example or maybe with a statement of your thesis. Your opening paragraph is really important because that is where you will either catch your readers or lose them.

WRITING

How Many Examples Are Enough?

It would make every writer's job much easier if there were a single, simple answer to the question of how many examples to use. Instead, the answer is "enough to interest or convince your reader." Sometimes one fully developed example might be enough. Advertisements for organizations such as Save the Children and the Christian Children's Fund often tell the story of a specific child in need of food and shelter. The single example, accompanied by a photograph, is enough to persuade many people to sponsor a child.

Readers aren't going to respond to a statement like "Millions of people are starving throughout the world." Not only is the statement too general, most of us would throw up our hands in frustration. What can I do about millions? On the other hand, I can help one child on a monthly basis. Anna Quindlen in "The Name Is Mine" focuses on a single example drawn from her own experience—using that example as a way to make her point about the significance and the consequences of keeping your own name.

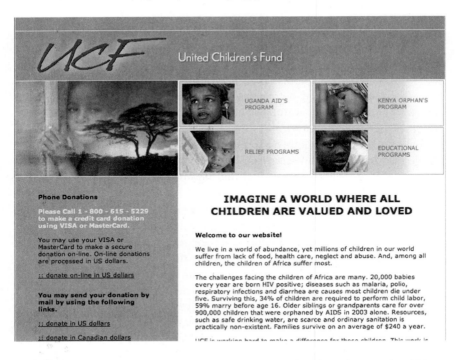

At other times you might need to use many details and examples. These need to be appropriate, accurate, and convincing. If you are actively involved in a national political party on your college campus, your chances of persuading your classmates to vote for members of your party for Congress will probably depend on providing them specific examples of what your candidate stands for and how she or he has voted in the past. Responsible voters are not swayed by vague general statements such as "I support public prayer, or environmental responsibility, or a strong national defense."

On the other hand, when you write from personal experience, your readers might not demand the same level of detail and accuracy in your examples. In "Cut," Bob Greene writes about how being cut from the junior high school basketball team changed his life. To support his thesis and extend it beyond his own personal experience, Greene includes the stories of four other men who had similar experiences. But why give five examples of the same experience? Why not three or seven? There is nothing magical about the number five—Greene might have used five because he had that much column space in the magazine—but the five give authority to Greene's assertion, or at least they create the illusion of authority. To prove the validity of Greene's thesis would require a proper statistical sample. Only then could it be said with some certainty that the experience of being cut makes men superachievers later in life. In most writing situations, however, thoroughness is not needed. If the details and examples are well chosen and relevant, the reader is likely to accept your assertions.

How Do You Fit Examples into the Structure of an Essay?

Whether you use one example or many, examples alone do not make an essay. There is no such thing as an "exemplification essay." Examples are always subordinated to a thesis, an assertion, an argument. Examples fill out the framework of an essay; they are the supporting evidence and details that justify that thesis, assertion, or argument. Every essay—whether structured using narration, description, comparison and contrast, or any of the other rhetorical strategies used to organize information—every essay uses examples. Without examples, an essay is just a bare framework of statements, opinions, and generalizations.

That framework in turn is derived from one of the strategies or patterns that you are using. In a narrative, details and examples are inserted into a chronological timeline; in a description, details and examples are added to a spatial pattern as the eye and ear move over the person, place, or landscape that is being described. The same procedure applies to each of the other rhetorical structures. A classification scheme is fleshed out with examples; a comparison demands that specific shared or differing examples or details be cited. Finally, in argument and persuasion, examples are used to show that your position is the right and logical one to take.

Examples are inserted into essays in three possible places. An essay might begin with a particularly arresting example that is intended to catch the readers' attention and draw them into the essay. If you are using an example as a "hook" for your introduction, you begin with the example and then place the essay's thesis or assertion either at the end of the opening paragraph or at the beginning of the next paragraph.

Examples make up a substantial part of the body of most essays. An extended example might occupy a whole body paragraph; smaller, shorter examples might be grouped into a single paragraph. Remember, though, that there is no reward for providing the greatest number of examples. The guiding principle is always quality and relevance of example over quantity of example. Depending on the purpose of your essay, you must decide how to order your examples. Examples can always be ranked on the basis of their prominence or importance. Generally, your examples will be arranged in that order, either beginning or ending with the strongest and best example.

Sometimes you might end an essay with a relevant or emotional example. Since the end of an essay is a strong place—that is, it is what the reader encounters last and is left with—a well-chosen example can be quite powerful.

Drafting Suggestions

1. Look carefully at each example that you plan to use. Is it completely relevant—does it really prove the point that you want to make or support? Is it accurate and fair, or is it distorted? In college writing, you are not trying to be a propagandist.

2. Do you have enough examples? Too many? A single example is rarely enough to convince a reader of anything. On the other hand, a long list of examples can overwhelm your reader with unnecessary detail.

3. Are your examples specific? Or are they really just generalizations or unsubstantiated opinions? Do you provide facts? Statistics? Quotations? Or do you just assume that your readers will agree with you? Go through your draft and color-code or label each example.

4. Are your examples subordinated to the larger point that you are trying to make? Giving examples is not a goal in itself—the examples are there to support or justify a larger goal. Examples must be proportional to the essay. Check to see if any of your examples are too long or too detailed. Do they obscure the real reason for their use?

5. Have you provided clear transitional statements or markers as you move from one example to another? Your examples need to be connected together in ways that make your essay flow smoothly.

REVISING

How Do You Revise when Using Examples?

Remember that revising is not just proofreading your draft for misspellings and mechanical/grammatical errors. Revising requires a re-seeing of what you have written. Ideally, after you have a draft of the entire essay, you should do two things. First, allow a little time to pass between the writing and the revising. You need to get some distance from what you have written so that you can read it in a more critical way. That detachment is very difficult to get if you have just finished writing the draft. Second, always try to get someone else to read your draft and comment on it. Advice on finding readers can be found in "How to Revise an Essay".

Typically, the potential problem areas when using examples in an essay come in three areas.

- Choosing examples
- Ordering or arranging examples
- Making transitions from example to example

Choosing Examples   Your examples must meet a series of tests, depending on the type of essay you are writing. In informational or persuasive writing, your examples must be accurate and unbiased. We are bombarded, for instance, by misleading, inaccurate examples in advertisements and in political rhetoric, but such techniques are not appropriate for college writing. Look carefully at your examples. Are they fair, accurate? Examples must also be relevant or important. Do they really support or clarify your assertion or thesis? Look at the examples you are using and number or grade them in terms of their importance. Forget about those that are weak. Use only your strongest examples. The number of examples you need varies with how long your paper is. A short paper, several pages in length, typically will not have or require as many examples as a many-paged research paper. Finally, examples often need to be interesting or attention-getting. This is particularly true if you are starting or ending your essay with an example.

Ordering or Arranging Examples   If you have numbered or graded your examples in terms of their relevance and importance, look at how you have arranged them in your paper. Remembering that you are only using the best examples, you should then have arranged them in either descending order (the best comes first) or ascending order (the best comes last). That choice is yours to make: one order is not necessarily better or more correct than the other. The greatest danger in arranging examples in an essay comes when you start with a thesis or assertion and follow that with a series of short examples that trail off into insignificance. Because each example is different and therefore is put into its own paragraph, you can sometimes end up with a string of short, thin, poorly developed paragraphs. Look carefully at your essay. Count the number of paragraphs you have written. A three-page paper that has twenty short paragraphs needs to be revised—some examples can be deleted; other examples might be expanded.

Do not assume that each example must be in a separate paragraph. Long, developed examples must be set off, but shorter examples, if they are related in some way, can often be grouped under a topic sentence that signals what follows.

Making Transitions from Example to Example   Check to see if you have provided clear transition markers in your essay as you move from example to example. Transitional markers include words and phrases such as *for example, first, next, finally, also, on the other hand, in addition.* The glossary provides a fuller explanation and a more complete listing of such devices. Transitional devices, however, are no substitute for logical order and a clear sense of purpose. Still, you need to help your reader see how all of these examples fit into the essay. A logical arrangement and transitional markers are like highway signs that signal to the reader what is coming and how it connects with what has already been covered in the essay.

Revising Suggestions

1. If you are writing about yourself, it is especially important to keep your readers interested. They need to feel how significant this experience was. They need to become involved in the situation—to sympathize or empathize with what happened. Do not just tell them: show them. One way to do this is to dramatize the experience, to tell it as if it were happening at that moment. Did you do that?

2. Print a copy of your paper, cut it apart, and try different arrangements of the examples, sentences, and even paragraphs. Which order seems to work best? Consider other alternatives. Do not just assume that your essay can be assembled in only one way.

3. How effective is your conclusion? Do you stop abruptly? Do you just repeat in slightly altered words what you said in your introduction? Remember that the end of your essay—especially if you are arguing for something—is what will stay in your readers' minds.

4. If you interviewed people in your research or used information from printed or online sources, make sure you punctuated your quotations properly and documented those sources (check the appendix for guidelines on both).

5. Find someone to read your essay—a friend, roommate, classmate, or tutor in a writing center. Ask your reader for some constructive criticism, and listen to what you hear.

SAMPLE STUDENT ESSAY

FIRST DRAFT

Frank Smite, recently divorced and recently returned to college, chose to work on an essay about the difficulties that older single or newly single people have in meeting people they can date. "Young college kids have it easy," Frank complained. "You are constantly surrounded by eligible people your own age. Try meeting someone when you're thirty-five, slightly balding, just divorced, and working all day." His first draft of the opening of his essay appears here:

My Search for Love

My wife and I separated and then quickly divorced a year ago. I figured that I would be able to forget some of the pain by returning to dating. At first, I was excited about the prospect of meeting new people. It made me feel young again. Besides, this time I'd be able to avoid the problems that led to my divorce. While I'm not exactly a male movie star—I'm thirty-five, a little overweight, kind of thin on the top, and have one daughter who I desperately miss seeing every day—I figured that romance was just around the corner.

It wasn't until I started to look for people to ask out that I realized how far away that corner was. Frankly, in my immediate world, there seemed to be no one who was roughly my age and unmarried. That's when I began to look at the various ways that people in my situation can meet people. I attended several meetings of the local Parents Without Partners group, but that didn't seem promising; I joined a computerized dating service; and, believe it or not, I started reading the "personals" in the newspaper.

COMMENTS

When Frank came to revise his essay, he had his instructor's comments and the reactions of several classmates. Everyone agreed that he had an excellent subject and some good detail, but several readers were a little troubled by Frank's overuse of "I." One reader asked Frank if he could make his essay focus a little less on his own immediate experience and a little more on what anyone in his position might do. His instructor suggested that with the right type of revision, Frank might be able to publish his essay in the local newspaper—after all, she noted, many people are in the same situation. His instructor also suggested that Frank might eliminate the reference to his daughter and how much he misses her. Although those feelings are important, that is not where Frank wanted to center the essay. Frank liked the idea of sharing his experiences with a wider audience. His revised introduction—complete with a new title—follows.

REVISED DRAFT

Looking for Love

Ask any single or divorced adult about the problems of meeting "prospective partners" and you are likely to get a litany of complaints and horrifying experiences. No longer can people rely on introductions from well-meaning friends. After all, most of those friends are also looking for love. Matchmaking has become big business—even, in fact, a franchised business.

Today the search for love takes many forms, from bar hopping, to organizations such as Parents Without Partners, to computerized and videotaped "search services," to singles groups organized around a shared concern (for example, those who are concerned about the environment or who love books). A little more desperate (and risky and certainly tacky) is the newspaper classified. Titled "Getting Personal" in my local newspaper, advertisements typically read like this one running today: "Single white female, pretty, petite blond, 40's ISO [in search of] WM [white male] for a perfect relationship (it does exist!)."

SOME THINGS TO REMEMBER

1. Use details and examples—effective writing depends on them.
2. For some subjects you can find the illustrations you need from your own experiences and observations. You will, however, probably need to work at remembering and gathering those specifics.
3. For some subjects you will need to do some type of research—interviewing people, looking up material in your school's library, using the Internet and the World Wide Web to locate relevant documents and sites. Remember as well that you are always connecting your observations with knowledge that you have acquired in other courses and other experiences.
4. Choose examples that are relevant and accurate. Quality is more important than quantity. Make sure your examples support your argument or illustrate the points you are trying to make. If you use an outside authority—an interview, a printed text, an electronic source—make sure that the source is knowledgeable and accurate. Remember also to document those sources.
5. The number of details and examples you need necessarily varies. Sometimes one will do; sometimes you will need many. If you want your readers to do or to believe something, you must supply some evidence to gain their support or confidence.

EXAMPLE AS A LITERARY STRATEGY

We could find examples in any literary work, but Bret Lott's very short story "Night" uses a single example to capture a continuing painful reality. A father wakes up to hear what he thinks is his child breathing. It seems at first like an ordinary experience, but we quickly discover what that single example reveals.

NIGHT

Bret Lott

He woke up. He thought he could hear their child's breathing in the next room, the near-silent, smooth sound of air in and out.

He touched his wife. The room was too dark to let him see her, but he felt her movement, the shift of blanket and sheet.

"Listen," he whispered.

"Yesterday," she mumbled. "Why not yesterday," and she moved back into sleep.

He listened harder, though he could hear his wife's breath, thick and heavy next to him, there was beneath this the thin frost of his child's breathing.

The hardwood floor was cold beneath his feet. He held out a hand in front of him, and when he touched the doorjamb, he paused, listened again, heard the life of his child.

His fingertips led him along the hall and to the next room. Then he was in the doorway of a room as dark, as hollow as his own. He cut on the light.

The room, of course, was empty. They had left the bed just as their child had made it, the spread merely thrown over bunched and wrinkled sheets, the pillow crooked at the head. The small blue desk was littered with colored pencils and scraps of construction paper, a bottle of white glue.

He turned off the light and listened. He heard nothing, then backed out of the room and moved down the hall, back to his room, his hands at his sides, his fingertips helpless.

This happened each night, like a dream, but not.

DISCUSSION QUESTIONS

1. What does this experience reveal to the reader? Is the single example sufficient to capture the emotion that the father feels? Would more examples, more experiences, be necessary?
2. Who narrates the experience? How does that point of view contribute to the story? What would the story be like if it were told by the father?
3. At what point in the story do you realize what is happening? Why might the author not reveal what has happened earlier?
4. Which of the descriptive details in the story seem most effective? Why?
5. What effect does the final sentence have?

WRITING SUGGESTIONS

Lott does not tell us how the parents felt; he allows the single example to reveal the loss that the father feels. It is simple and sparse, but extremely effective. Think about an emotion that you have had and then try to capture and convey that feeling in a single example. You might think about the following as possible starting points for your essay:

   a. A life-changing event—something that has forever changed your life or your expectations

   b. A loss—of a person, a pet, a personal possession

   c. A discovery or a realization—a moment of insight into life, your identity, your future

READING FOR EXAMPLES

Examples are essential to all types of writing—you explain, entertain, analyze, persuade by citing specific, relevant examples. Examples make writing vivid and interesting. Without examples, you just have a framework, a skeletal outline of an essay. When we read, we should notice certain things about the examples and about the role they play in effective writing. The paragraph below is taken from Steven Pinker's *The Language Instinct: How the Mind Creates Language.* As you read, remember what you have learned about how to write with examples—that knowledge can help you as a reader.

   • Examples do not provide a structure for an essay. They are inserted into essays in order to fill out a predetermined rhetorical strategy or organizational pattern. Consequently, if you outlined the essay or the paragraph in which they occur, you would find that the examples support the assertions. They are subordinated to the frame of the essay and to the structure of the paragraph.

   • Examples are organized—that is, the writer has planned the arrangement of the examples in the essay or the paragraph. In an argument essay, for example, the strongest and best example might be placed first.

   • Examples are taken from personal experience or observation, from research such as interviews with people, from printed sources such as articles or books, or from online research.

   • Examples must be accurate, relevant, and interesting. Each example should be judged by those tests.

Topic sentence—the frame into which the examples will fit	For centuries people have been terrified that their programmed creations might outsmart them, overpower them, or put them out of work. The fear has been played out in fiction, from the medieval Jewish legend of the Golem, a clay automaton animated by an inscription of the name of God placed in its mouth, to

Two examples—Golem and HAL support the initial assertion "for centuries"

Examples of what computers can do supporting the fears people have. Number tasks are understandable; thinking tasks scary to people.

Examples arranged chronologically (growth of problem solving)

Familiar examples from popular films. Example of what experts thought might be possible

Topic sentence—frame

Example—what a four-year-old can do that a computer cannot

Example—seemingly smart robots are dumb

Examples—questions that computers cannot answer (and a four-year-old probably could)

Examples—jobs that might be done by computers and jobs that cannot; ties back to the topic sentence of the previous paragraph

HAL, the mutinous computer of *2001: A Space Odyssey*. But when the branch of engineering called "artificial intelligence" (AI) was born in the 1950s, it looked as though fiction was about to turn into frightening fact. It is easy to accept a computer calculating pi to a million decimal places or keeping track of a company's payroll, but suddenly computers were also proving theorems in logic and playing respectable chess. In the years following there came computers that could beat anyone but a grand master and programs that outperformed most experts at recommending treatments for bacterial infections and investing pension funds. With computers solving such brainy tasks, it seemed like only a matter of time before a C3P0 or a Terminator would be available from the mail-order catalogues; only the easy tasks remained to be programmed. According to legend, in the 1970s, Marvin Minsky, one of the founders of AI, assigned "vision" to a graduate student as a seminar project.

But household robots are still confined to science fiction. The main lesson of thirty-five years of AI research is that the hard problems are easy and the easy problems are hard. The mental abilities of a four-year-old that we take for granted—recognizing a face, lifting a pencil, walking across a room, answering a question—in fact solve some of the hardest engineering problems ever conceived. Do not be fooled by the assembly-line robots in the automobile commercials; all they do is weld and spray paint, tasks that do not require these clumsy Mr. Magoos to see or hold or place anything. And if you want to stump an artificial intelligence system, ask it questions like, Which is bigger, Chicago or a breadbox? Do zebras wear underwear? Is the floor likely to rise up and bite you? If Susan goes to the store, does her head go with her? Most fears of automation are misplaced. As the new generation of intelligent devices appears, it will be the stock analysts and petrochemical engineers and parole board members who are in danger of being replaced by machines. The gardeners, receptionists, and cooks are secure in their jobs for decades to come.

RESPONDING TO A VISUAL

Visuals—tables, photographs, charts, diagrams—are also forms of examples. Information can often be displayed more efficiently and effectively through visuals than through words. Many of your textbooks, for example, make extensive use of visual elements to help you understand complex information. Advertisements use photographs to catch our attention. If you are planning a vacation or renting a hotel room, you want to see photographs before you make your reservations.

During your junior and senior years of high school, when you were trying to make a decision about which college to attend, you probably received
many catalogs and admission folders that were full of color photographs of the
campus, the students, and the college's facilities. Those visual examples might
have been influential in your final decision. Following are four photographs
that appear in one college's admission materials. Study each photograph.
What "thesis" or purpose might have been behind choosing these photographs? How do these examples support that thesis? What do they suggest
about the school? In what ways might these photographs persuade a student
to apply?

READING AND WRITING ABOUT IMAGES

Given your college experiences so far, think about a group of photographs that
you might include in an "insider's guide to college life at——." Write an essay
that describes what you are trying to capture and describe the content of each
photograph that you would include. You can ask your instructor if you may include the photographs as part of your essay.

Visiting the Web

The companion Website, **www.prenhall.com/miller**, contains additional information about using examples and about the writers and essays in this chapter. You will also find a number of hyperlinks to other sources of information about the subjects of the essays included in this chapter.

Exploring on Your Own

Create an appealing advertisement for your dorm room, apartment, or home. Depending on what you are describing, you have one of several possible goals and audiences.

- Dorm room—try to convince new students to request this dorm on their housing request
- Apartment—try to persuade someone to sublet the apartment from you
- Home—try to rent or sell your home to prospective buyers

Use the Web to explore sample real estate advertisement and to locate ideas about how to write the advertisement. If you plan on using photographs or sketches, you can find advice on the Web on how to choose and use the visuals.

Google.com is a good starting place to search for examples and advice. Particularly helpful is the National Association of Realtors' Website (**www.realtor.org**). Check out the Field Guide to Creating Effective Classified Advertisement located there (**www.realtor.org/libweb.nsf/pages/fg206**).

Looking for Writing Suggestions

Examples are typically used in essays to explain a concept or an assertion, to make a point vivid or interesting, or to support a thesis or argument. Remember that examples can come from your own personal experiences or the experiences of others; from authorities or experts you interview; from newspaper, magazine, or online articles; or from books. Using a range of examples, write an essay in which you use examples to achieve one of the following purposes. Remember that you will have to narrow the topics and define a stance or thesis for your paper.

Explain a Concept or Assertion:

1. The "language" of text messaging
2. Patriotism
3. Courage
4. Conservative values
5. Liberal values
6. Fundamentalism
7. Success

8. A well-rounded education
9. Function/purpose of a college education
10. Celibacy

MAKE A POINT VIVID OR INTERESTING:

1. Dormitory life
2. Campus parking
3. The perfect course schedule
4. Parenthood
5. The date from hell
6. Highlight of my life
7. Being an only child
8. An embarrassing moment
9. Part-time job
10. Saying no

SUPPORT A THESIS OR ARGUMENT:

1. Bans on cigarette smoking in public restaurants/bars or at public events such as concerts and sports events
2. Use of a cell phone while driving
3. Changes in the age by which young drivers can drive alone or at night
4. Prohibition of prayer in public schools
5. Performance-enhancing drugs for athletes
6. Importance of high grades in college
7. Required courses or distribution requirements for college students
8. Popularity of reality-based TV shows
9. Values promoted by TV advertisements
10. Popularity of instant messaging

THE NAME IS MINE
Anna Quindlen

Born in 1953, Anna Quindlen attended Barnard College in New York City. She enjoyed a successful career at The New York Times, *where she wrote three different weekly columns, including her syndicated column, "Public and Private," for which she won the 1992 Pulitzer Prize for commentary. Her most recent books are* Loud and Clear *(2004), a collection of her columns, and* Being Perfect *(2005).*

This essay first appeared in "Life in the 30's," a weekly column that Quindlen wrote for the Times *from 1986 to 1988. Based on her own experiences as a mother, a wife, and a journalist, the column attracted millions of readers and was syndicated in some sixty other newspapers. She ended the column because of its personal nature: "It wasn't just that I was in the spotlight; it was like I was in the spotlight naked. . . . I became public property."*

On Writing: *Quindlen writes on a laptop computer and observes, "I listen to all those authors who say they write longhand in diaries they buy in London, and I say, 'Get a life.'" A perfectionist who "wants every sentence to be the best it can be," Quindlen notes, "I don't want anything to be loose or sloppy."*

BEFORE READING

Connecting: Can you remember times when your "identity" was defined not by yourself but by your association with someone else, when you were the child *of*, the sibling *of*, the spouse *of*, the parent *of*, the employee *of*? How did these occasions make you feel?

Anticipating: Every decision we make has consequences—some of which we are immediately aware of and some of which only emerge later. What are the consequences of Quindlen's decision not to take her husband's name?

I am on the telephone to the emergency room of the local hospital. My elder son is getting stitches in his palm, and I have called to make myself feel better, because I am at home, waiting, and my husband is there, holding him. I am 34 years old, and I am crying like a child, making a slippery mess of my face. "Mrs. Krovatin?" says the nurse, and for the first time in my life I answer "Yes." 1

This is a story about a name. The name is mine. I was given it at birth, and I have never changed it, although I married. I could come up with lots of reasons why. It was a political decision, a simple statement that I was somebody and not an adjunct of anybody, especially a husband. As a friend of mine told her horrified mother, "He didn't adopt me, he married me." 2

It was a professional and a personal decision, too. I grew up with an ugly dog of a name, one I came to love because I thought it was weird and unlovable. 3

Amid the Debbies and Kathys of my childhood, I had a first name only my grandmothers had and a last name that began with a strange letter. "Sorry, the letters, I, O, Q, U, V, X, Y and Z are not available," the catalogues said about monogrammed key rings and cocktail napkins. Seeing my name in black on white at the top of a good story, suddenly it wasn't an ugly dog anymore.

4   But neither of these are honest reasons, because they assume rational consideration, and it so happens that when it came to changing my name, there was no consideration, rational or otherwise. It was mine. It belonged to me. I don't even share a checking account with my husband. Damned if I was going to be hidden beneath the umbrella of his identity.

5   It seemed like a simple decision. But nowadays I think the only simple decisions are whether to have grilled cheese or tuna fish for lunch. Last week, my older child wanted an explanation of why he, his dad and his brother have one name, and I have another.

6   My answer was long, philosophical and rambling—that is to say, unsatisfactory. What's in a name? I could have said disingenuously. But I was talking to a person who had just spent three torturous, exhilarating years learning names for things, and I wanted to communicate to him that mine meant something quite special to me, had seemed as form-fitting as my skin, and as painful to remove. Personal identity and independence, however, were not what he was looking for; he just wanted to make sure I was one of them. And I am— and then again, I am not. When I made this decision, I was part of a couple. Now, there are two me's, the me who is the individual and the me who is part of a family of four, a family of four in which, in a small way, I am left out.

7   A wise friend who finds herself in the same fix says she never wants to change her name, only to have a slightly different identity as a family member, an identity for pediatricians' offices and parent-teacher conferences. She also says that the entire situation reminds her of the women's movement as a whole. We did these things as individuals, made these decisions about ourselves and what we wanted to be and do. And they were good decisions, the right decisions. But we based them on individual choice, not on group dynamics. We thought in terms of our sense of ourselves, not our relationships with others.

8   Some people found alternative solutions: hyphenated names, merged names, matriarchal names for the girls and patriarchal ones for the boys, one name at work and another at home. I did not like those choices; I thought they were middle grounds, and I didn't live much in the middle ground at the time. I was once slightly disdainful of women who went all the way and changed their names. But I now know too many smart, independent, terrific women who have the same last names as their husbands to be disdainful anymore. (Besides, if I made this decision as part of a feminist world view, it seems dishonest to turn around and trash other women for deciding as they did.)

9   I made my choice. I haven't changed my mind. I've just changed my life. Sometimes I feel like one of those worms I used to hear about in biology, the ones that, chopped in half, walked off in different directions. My name works fine for one half, not quite as well for the other. I would never give it up. Except

for that one morning when I talked to the nurse at the hospital, I always answer the question "Mrs. Krovatin?" with "No, this is Mr. Krovatin's wife." It's just that I understand the down side now.

When I decided not to disappear beneath my husband's umbrella, it did not occur to me that I would be the only one left outside. It did not occur to me that I would ever care—not enough to change, just enough to think about the things we do on our own and what they mean when we aren't on our own anymore. 10

QUESTIONS ON SUBJECT AND PURPOSE

1. Why did Quindlen not change her last name when she married?
2. How does she feel about her decision now?
3. Since Quindlen does not plan to change her name, what purpose might she have in writing the essay?

QUESTIONS ON STRATEGY AND AUDIENCE

1. The essay could begin at the second paragraph. Why might Quindlen have chosen to begin the essay with the telephone call experience?
2. In paragraph 9, Quindlen returns to the incident at the hospital. How does this device help hold the essay together?
3. The essay appeared in a column headed "Life in the 30's." How might that affect the nature of the audience who might read the essay?

QUESTIONS ON VOCABULARY AND STYLE

1. At the beginning of paragraphs 2 and 9, Quindlen uses three very short simple sentences in a row. Why?
2. Twice in the essay (paragraphs 4 and 10), Quindlen refers to coming under her husband's "umbrella." What is the effect of such an image?
3. Be able to define the following words: *disingenuously* (paragraph 6) and *disdainful* (8).

WRITING SUGGESTIONS

1. **For Your Journal.** Do you have any desire to change your name? If so, why? If not, why not? In your journal, explore what changing or not changing your name might mean. Would "you" be any different?
2. **For a Paragraph.** In a paragraph, explore the meaning that you find in your last name. How does that name define you?
3. **For an Essay.** In paragraph 6, Quindlen remarks, "There are two me's, the me who is the individual and the me who is part of a family of four." Everyone experiences such moments of awareness. Think about

those times when you have been "two," and in an essay, explore the dilemma posed by being an individual and, at the same time, a part of a larger whole.

4. **For Research.** How widespread and recent is the phenomenon of women not taking their husbands' names? Research the phenomenon through the various databases that your library has. A crucial problem will be identifying the subject headings and keywords to use in your search. If you have problems, ask a reference librarian for some guidance. Remember as well that people make excellent sources of information. Then, using that research, write an essay for one of the following audiences:

   a. An article intended for a male audience

   b. An article intended for an audience of unmarried women who might be considering such a decision

   c. A traditional research paper for a college course

FOR FURTHER STUDY

Focusing on Grammar and Writing. Quindlen uses a number of words and phrases that are colloquial and perhaps too informal. Make a list of these. Why might she mix levels of diction in the essay? What does that suggest about your own writing?

Working Together. Divide into small groups. Each group should choose a detail or example that Quindlen uses in the essay (for instance, the opening example in the emergency room, the catalog of monogrammed goods, her name at the top of a new story, the umbrella image, the older child's questions about her different name). How effective is each example or detail?

Seeing Other Modes at Work. Quindlen makes use of cause and effect in explaining how she decided to keep her own name and what the effects of that decision proved to be.

Finding Connections. On the basis of their essays, how might Judy Brady ("I Want a Wife") and Margaret Atwood ("The Female Body"), both in Chapter 8, feel about Quindlen's decision?

Exploring the Web. What percentage of women in the United States choose not to take their husband's last name? What factors—for example, socioeconomic, age, education—influence that decision? Explore the Web for answers to these questions. Check **www.prenhall.com/miller** for some suggestions on how to begin your search.

CUT

Bob Greene

Bob Greene was born in Columbus, Ohio, in 1947 and received a B.J. from North-western University in 1969. A columnist and essayist, Greene's most recent books are Duty: A Father, His Son, and the Man Who Won the War *(2000) and* Once Upon a Town: The Miracle of the North Platte Canteen *(2002).*

On Writing: *Greene is, in many ways, a reporter of everyday events. He rarely tries to be profound but concentrates instead on human interest stories, the experiences that we all share. "Beyond entertaining or informing [my readers]," he has said, "the only responsibility I feel is . . . to make sure that they get to the last period of the last sentence of the last paragraph of the story . . . I feel I have a responsibility to make the story interesting enough for them to read all the way through." In this essay from* Esquire, *a magazine aimed at a male audience, Greene relates the stories of five successful men who shared the experience of being "cut from the team." Does being cut, Greene wonders, make you a superachiever later in life?*

BEFORE READING

Connecting: Was there ever a time when you realized that you were not going to be allowed to participate in something that you wanted very much? Did someone tell you, "You're not good enough," or did you realize it yourself?

Anticipating: Writers recount personal experiences for some reason, and that reason is never just "here is what happened to me"; instead, writers focus on the significance of the experience. What significance does Greene see in these narratives?

I remember vividly the last time I cried. I was twelve years old, in the seventh   1
grade, and I had tried out for the junior high school basketball team. I walked into the gymnasium; there was a piece of paper tacked to the bulletin board.

It was a cut list. The seventh-grade coach had put it up on the board.   2
The boys whose names were on the list were still on the team; they were welcome to keep coming to practices. The boys whose names were not on the list had been cut; their presence was no longer desired. My name was not on the list.

I had not known the cut was coming that day. I stood and stared at the   3
list. The coach had not composed it with a great deal of subtlety; the names of the very best athletes were at the top of the sheet of paper, and the other members of the squad were listed in what appeared to be a descending order of talent. I kept looking at the bottom of the list, hoping against hope that my name would miraculously appear there if I looked hard enough.

4   I held myself together as I walked out of the gym and out of the school, but when I got home I began to sob. I couldn't stop. For the first time in my life, I had been told officially that I wasn't good enough. Athletics meant everything to boys that age; if you were on the team, even a substitute, it put you in the desirable group. If you weren't on the team, you might as well not be alive.

5   I had tried desperately in practice, but the coach never seemed to notice. It didn't matter how hard I was willing to work; he didn't want me there. I knew that when I went to school the next morning I would have to face the boys who had not been cut—the boys whose names were on the list, who were still on the team, who had been judged worthy while I had been judged unworthy.

6   All these years later, I remember it as if I were still standing right there in the gym. And a curious thing has happened: in traveling around the country, I have found that an inordinately large proportion of successful men share that same memory—the memory of being cut from a sports team as a boy.

7   I don't know how the mind works in matters like this; I don't know what went on in my head following that day when I was cut. But I know that my ambition has been enormous ever since then; I know that for all of my life since that day, I have done more work than I had to be doing, taken more assignments than I had to be taking, put in more hours than I had to be spending. I don't know if all of that came from a determination never to allow myself to be cut again—never to allow someone to tell me that I'm not good enough again—but I know it's there. And apparently it's there in a lot of other men, too.

8   Bob Graham, thirty-six, is a partner with the Jenner & Block law firm in Chicago. "When I was sixteen, baseball was my whole life," he said. "I had gone to a relatively small high school, and I had been on the team. But then my family moved, and I was going to a much bigger high school. All during the winter months I told everyone that I was a ballplayer. When spring came, of course I went out for the team.

9   "The cut list went up. I did not make the team. Reading that cut list is one of the clearest things I have in my memory. I wanted not to believe it, but there it was.

10   "I went home and told my father about it. He suggested that maybe I should talk to the coach. So I did. I pleaded to be put back on the team. He said there was nothing he could do; he said he didn't have enough room.

11   "I know for a fact that it altered my perception of myself. My view of myself was knocked down; my self-esteem was lowered. I felt so embarrassed; my whole life up to that point had revolved around sports, and particularly around playing baseball. That was the group I wanted to be in—the guys on the baseball team. And I was told that I wasn't good enough to be one of them.

12   "I know now that it changed me. I found out, even though I couldn't articulate it at the time, that there would be times in my life when certain people would be in a position to say 'You're not good enough' to me. I did not want that to happen ever again.

"It seems obvious to me now that being cut was what started me in determining that my success would always be based on my own abilities, and not on someone else's perceptions. Since then I've always been something of an overachiever; when I came to the law firm I was very aggressive in trying to run my own cases right away, to be the lead lawyer in the cases with which I was involved. I made partner at thirty-one; I never wanted to be left behind. 13

"Looking back, maybe it shouldn't have been that important. It was only 14 baseball. You pass that by. Here I am. That coach is probably still there, still a high school baseball coach, still cutting boys off the baseball team every year. I wonder how many hundreds of boys he's cut in his life?"

Maurice McGrath is senior vice-president of Genstar Mortgage Corporation, 15 a mortgage banking firm in Glendale, California. "I'm forty-seven years old, and I was fourteen when it happened to me, and I still feel something when I think about it," he said.

"I was in the eighth grade. I went to St. Philip's School in Pasadena. I 16 went out for the baseball team, and one day at practice the coach came over to me. He was an Occidental College student who had been hired as the eighth-grade coach.

"He said, 'You're no good.' Those were his words. I asked him why he 17 was saying that. He said, 'You can't hit the ball. I don't want you here.' I didn't know what to do, so I went over and sat off to the side, watching the others practice. The coach said I should leave the practice field. He said that I wasn't on the team, and that I didn't belong there anymore.

"I was outwardly stoic about it. I didn't want anyone to see how I felt. I 18 didn't want to show that it hurt. But oh, did it hurt. All my friends played baseball after school every day. My best friend was the pitcher on the team. After I got whittled down by the coach, I would hear the other boys talking in class about what they were going to do at practice after school. I knew that I'd just have to go home.

"I guess you make your mind up never to allow yourself to be hurt like 19 that again. In some way I must have been saying to myself, 'I'll play the game better.' Not the sports game, but anything I tried. I must have been saying, 'If I have to, I'll sit on the bench, but I'll be part of the team.'

"I try to make my own kids believe that, too. I try to tell them that they 20 should show that they're a little bit better than the rest. I tell them to think of themselves as better. Who cares what anyone else thinks? You know, I can almost hear that coach saying the words. 'You're no good.' "

Author Malcolm MacPherson (*The Blood of His Servants*), forty, lives in New 21 York. "It happened to me in the ninth grade, at the Yalesville School in Yalesville, Connecticut," he said. "Both of my parents had just been killed in a car crash, and as you can imagine, it was a very difficult time in my life. I went out for the baseball team, and I did pretty well in practice.

"But in the first game I clutched. I was playing second base; the batter 22 hit a pop-up, and I moved back to catch it. I can see it now. I felt dizzy as I looked up at the ball. It was like I was moving in slow motion, but the ball was going at regular speed. I couldn't get out of the way of my own feet. The ball dropped to the ground. I didn't catch it.

23   "The next day at practice, the coach read off the lineup. I wasn't on it. I was off the squad.

24   "I remember what I did: I walked. It was a cold spring afternoon, and the ground was wet, and I just walked. I was living with an aunt and uncle, and I didn't want to go home. I just wanted to walk forever.

25   "It drove my opinion of myself right into a tunnel. Right into a cave. And when I came out of the cave, something inside of me wanted to make sure in one manner or another that I would never again be told I wasn't good enough.

26   "I will confess that my ambition, to this day, is out of control. It's like a fire. I think the fire would have pretty much stayed in control if I hadn't been cut from that team. But that got it going. You don't slice ambition two ways; it's either there or it isn't. Those of us who went through something like that always know that we have to catch the ball. We'd rather die than have the ball fall at our feet.

27   "Once that fire is started in us, it never gets extinguished, until we die or have heart attacks or something. Sometimes I wonder about the home-run hitters; the guys who never even had to worry about being cut. They may have gotten the applause and the attention back then, but I wonder if they ever got the fire. I doubt it. I think maybe you have to get kicked in the teeth to get the fire started.

28   "You can tell the effect of something like that by examining the trail you've left in your life, and tracing it backward. It's almost like being a junkie with a need for success. You get attention and applause and you like it, but you never quite trust it. Because you know that back then you were good enough if only they would have given you a chance. You don't trust what you achieve, because you're afraid that someone will take it away from you. You know that it can happen; it already did.

29   "So you try to show people how good you are. Maybe you don't go out and become Dan Rather; maybe you just end up owning the Pontiac dealership in your town. But it's your dealership, and you're the top man, and every day you're showing people that you're good enough."

30   Dan Rather, fifty-two, is anchor of the CBS *Evening News.* "When I was thirteen, I had rheumatic fever," he said. "I became extremely skinny and extremely weak, but I still went out for the seventh-grade baseball team at Alexander Hamilton Junior High School in Houston.

31   "The school was small enough that there was no cut as such; you were supposed to figure out that you weren't good enough, and quit. Game after game I sat at the end of the bench, hoping that maybe this was the time I would get in. The coach never even looked at me; I might as well have been invisible.

32   "I told my mother about it. Her advice was not to quit. So I went to practice every day, and I tried to do well so that the coach would be impressed. He never even knew I was there. At home in my room I would fantasize that there

was a big game, and the three guys in front of me would all get hurt, and the coach would turn to me and put me in, and I would make the winning hit. But then there'd be another game, and the late innings would come, and if we were way ahead I'd keep hoping that this was the game when the coach would put me in. He never did.

"When you're that age, you're looking for someone to tell you you're 33 okay. Your sense of self-esteem is just being formed. And what that experience that baseball season did was make me think that perhaps I wasn't okay.

"In the last game of the season something terrible happened. It was the 34 last of the ninth inning, there were two outs, and there were two strikes on the batter. And the coach turned to me and told me to go out to right field.

"It was a totally humiliating thing for him to do. For him to put me in 35 for one pitch, the last pitch of the season, in front of all the other boys on the team . . . I stood out there for that one pitch, and I just wanted to sink into the ground and disappear. Looking back on it, it was an extremely unkind thing for him to have done. That was nearly forty years ago, and I don't know why the memory should be so vivid now; I've never known if the coach was purposely making fun of me—and if he was, why a grown man would do that to a thirteen-year-old boy.

"I'm not a psychologist. I don't know if a man can point to one event in 36 his life and say that that's the thing that made him the way he is. But when you're that age, and you're searching for your own identity, and all you want is to be told that you're all right . . . I wish I understood it better, but I know the feeling is still there."

QUESTIONS ON SUBJECT AND PURPOSE

1. Greene's "cuts" all refer to not making an athletic team. What other kinds of "cuts" can you experience?

2. It is always risky to speculate on an author's purpose, but why would Greene write about this? Why reveal to everyone something that hurt so much?

3. How might Greene have gone about gathering examples of other men's similar experiences? Why would they be willing to contribute? Would everyone who has been cut be so candid?

4. What can be said in the coaches' defense? Should everyone who tries out be automatically guaranteed a place on the team?

QUESTIONS ON STRATEGY AND AUDIENCE

1. Greene structures his essay in an unusual way. How can the essay be divided? Why give a series of examples of other men who were "cut"?

2. How many examples are enough? What if Greene had used two examples? Eight examples? How would either extreme have influenced your reaction as a reader?

3. Greene does not provide a final concluding paragraph. Why?

4. Are you skeptical after you have finished the essay? Does everyone react to being cut in the same way? What would it take to convince you that these reactions are typical?

QUESTIONS ON VOCABULARY AND STYLE

1. How would you characterize the tone of Greene's essay? How is it achieved? Through language? Sentence structure? Paragraphing?

2. Why does Greene allow each man to tell his own story? Why not just summarize their experiences? Each story is enclosed in quotation marks. Do you think that these were the exact words of each man? Why?

3. What do *inordinately* (paragraph 6) and *stoic* (18) mean?

WRITING SUGGESTIONS

1. **For Your Journal.** Greene attributes enormous significance to a single experience; he feels that it literally changed his entire life. Try to remember some occasions when a disappointment seemed to change your life by changing your expectations for yourself. In your journal, list some possible instances, and then explore one.

2. **For a Paragraph.** As children, we imagine ourselves doing or being anything we want. As we grow older, however, we discover that our choices become increasingly limited; in fact, each choice we make seems to cut off whole paths of alternative choices. We cannot be or do everything that we once thought we could. Choose a time in your life when you realized that a particular expectation or dream would never come true. In a paragraph, narrate that experience. Be sure to make the significance of your realization clear to your reader.

3. **For an Essay.** Describe an experience similar to the one that Greene narrates. It might have happened in an academic course during your school years, in a school or community activity, in athletics, or on the job: we can be "cut," "released," or "fired" from almost anything. Remember to make your narrative vivid through the use of detail and to make the significance of your narrative clear to the reader.

4. **For Research.** Check the validity of Greene's argument. Is there any evidence from research studies about the psychological effects of such vivid rejections? Using print and on-line sources (if they are available), see what you can find. A reference librarian can help you start your search for information. Use that research in an essay about the positive or negative effects of such experiences. Remember to document all

sources. You might write your paper in one of the following forms (each has a slightly different audience):

a. A conventional research paper for a college course

b. An article for a popular magazine (for example, *Esquire, Working Woman, Parents'*)

c. A feature article for your school's newspaper

FOR FURTHER STUDY

Focusing on Grammar and Writing. Greene uses *ands* and *buts* to connect many sentences in his essay. We use both words more frequently in oral than in written speech. Why might Greene use them in his essay? What cautions might be offered in using such words to link sentences together?

Working Together. Working in small groups, discuss what evidence Greene would need in order to "prove" his assertion that being cut makes you an overachiever in life. What is the strength and the weakness of the type of example that Green uses as evidence?

Seeing Other Modes at Work. Each example is a narrative. How does Greene tell each story? To what extent are the narratives similar in structure? To what extent different?

Finding Connections. For a discussion of how a personal experience can be the springboard for a more general comment on human experience, read Scott Russell Sanders, "The Inheritance of Tools" (Chapter 3).

Exploring the Web. Greene's essay originally appeared in *Esquire*, not a sports magazine such as *Sports Illustrated* or *Sporting News*. Why? You can compare the magazines electronically to see how their target audiences shape their content. Visit **www.prenhall.com/miller** for suggestions on how to start.

WESTBURY COURT
Edwidge Danticat

Edwidge Danticat (1969–) was born in Port-au-Prince, Haiti. At the age of twelve she came to New York City to join her parents who had emigrated some years earlier. She earned a degree in French literature from Barnard College and an M.F.A. from Brown University. At twenty-six she was a finalist for a National Book Award for her collection of short stories Krik? Krak! *Her other books include* The Farming of Bones *(1998),* Behind the Mountains *(2002), and* The Dew Breaker *(2004).*

On Writing: *Danticat's native languages were Haitian Creole and French. She comments, "My writing in English is a consequence of my migration, in the same way that immigrant children speaking to each other in English is a consequence of their migration." She continues, "When I first started writing, I wasn't thinking about publishing it. I was working at writing. . . . Writing in any language is difficult. . . . I like to walk and think things out. . . . I prefer silence when writing. That was hard to come by when growing up with three [brothers]."*

BEFORE READING

Connecting: Danticat writes of a tragic experience that occurred when she was fourteen and living in Brooklyn. Do you have a particular sad or joyful experience that you connect with a place that you lived?

Anticipating: The core experience about which Danticat writes in the essay occurred almost twenty years ago. Why does she remember it now? What significance does it still have for her?

1   When I was fourteen years old, we lived in a six-story brick building in a cul-de-sac off of Flatbush Avenue, in Brooklyn, called Westbury Court. Beneath the building ran a subway station through which rattled the D, M, and Q trains every fifteen minutes or so. Though there was graffiti on most of the walls of Westbury Court, and hills of trash piled up outside, and though the elevator wasn't always there when we opened the door to step inside and the heat and hot water weren't always on, I never dreamed of leaving Westbury Court until the year of the fire.

2   I was watching television one afternoon when the fire began. I loved television then, especially the afternoon soap operas, my favorite of which was *General Hospital*. I would bolt out of my last high school class every day, pick up my youngest brother, Karl, from day care, and watch *General Hospital* with him on my lap while doing my homework during the commercials. My other two brothers, André and Kelly, would later join us in the apartment, but they preferred to watch cartoons in the back bedroom.

One afternoon while *General Hospital* and afternoon cartoons were on, a   3
fire started in apartment 6E, across the hall. There in that apartment lived our
new neighbors, an African-American mother and her two boys. We didn't
know the name of the mother, or the names and ages of her boys, but I ven-
ture to guess that they were around five and ten years old.

I didn't know a fire had started until two masked, burly firemen came   4
knocking on our door. My brothers and I rushed out into the hallway filled
with smoke and were quickly escorted down to the first floor by some other
firemen already on our floor. While we ran by, the door to apartment 6E had
already been knocked over by the fire squad and inside was filled with bright
flames and murky smoke.

All of the tenants of the building who were home at that time were   5
crowded on the sidewalk outside. My brothers and I, it seemed, were the last
to be evacuated. Clutching my brothers' hands, I wondered if I had remembered to lock our apartment door. Was there anything valuable we could have
taken?

An ambulance screeched to a stop in front of the building, and the two   6
firemen who had knocked on our door came out carrying the pliant and
lifeless bodies of the two children from across the hall. Their mother
jumped out of the crowd and ran toward them, screaming, "My babies—not
my babies," as the children were lowered into the back of the ambulance
and transferred into the arms of the emergency medical personnel. The fire
was started by the two boys, after their mother had stepped out to pick up
some groceries at the supermarket down the street. They had been playing
with matches.

(Later my mother would tell us, "See, this is what happens to children   7
who play with matches. Sometimes it is too late to say, 'I shouldn't have.' "
My brother Kelly, who was fascinated with fire and liked to hold up a match
to the middle of his palm until the light fizzled out, gave up this party trick
after the fire.)

We were quiet that afternoon when both our parents came home. We   8
were the closest to the fire in the building, and the most religious of our
parents' friends saw it as a miracle that we had escaped safe and sound.
When my mother asked how come I, the oldest one, hadn't heard the children scream or hadn't smelled the smoke coming from across the hall, I
confessed that I had been watching *General Hospital* and was too consumed
in the intricate plot.

(After the fire, my mother had us stay with a family on the second floor   9
for a few months, after school. I felt better not having to be wholly responsible for myself and my brothers, in case something like that fire should ever
happen again.)

The apartment across the hall stayed empty for a long time, and   10
whenever I walked past it, a piece of its inner skeleton would squeak, and
occasionally burnt wood that might have been hanging by a fragile singed
thread would crash down and cause a domino effect of further ruptures, un-
leashed like those children's last cries, which I had not heard because I had

been so wrapped up in the made-up drama of a world where, even though the adults' lives were often in turmoil, the children came home to the welcoming arms of waiting mommies and nannies who served them freshly baked cookies on porcelain plates and helped them to remove their mud-soaked boots, if it was raining, lest they soil the lily-white carpets. But should their boots accidentally sully the carpet, or should their bright yellow raincoats inadvertently drip on the sparkling linoleum, there would be a remedy for that as well. And if their house should ever catch fire, a smart dog or a good neighbor would rescue them just in time, and the fire trucks would come right quick because some attentive neighbor would call them.

11   Through the trail of voices that came up to comfort us, I heard that the children's mother would be prosecuted for negligence and child abandonment. I couldn't help but wonder, would our parents have suffered the same fate had it been my brothers and me who were killed in the fire?

12   When they began to repair the apartment across the hall, I would occasionally sneak out to watch the workmen. They were shelling the inside of the apartment and replacing everything from the bedroom closets to the kitchen floors. I never saw the mother of the dead boys again and never heard anything of her fate.

13   A year later, after the apartment was well polished and painted, two blind Haitian brothers and their sister moved in. They were all musicians and were part of a group called les Frères Parent, the Parent Brothers. Once my parents allowed my brothers and me to come home from school to our apartment, I would always listen carefully for our new tenants, so I'd be the first to know if anything went awry.

14   What I heard coming from the apartment soon after they moved in was music, "engagé" music, which the brothers were composing to protest against the dictatorship in Haiti, from which they had fled. The Parent Brothers and their sister, Lydie, did nothing but rehearse a cappella most days when they were not receiving religious and political leaders from Haiti and from the Haitian community in New York.

15   The same year after the fire, a cabdriver who lived down the hall in 6J was killed on a night shift in Manhattan; a good friend of my father's, a man who gave great Sunday afternoon parties in 6F, died of cirrhosis of the liver. One day while my brothers and I were at school and my parents were at work, someone came into our apartment through our fire escape and stole my father's expensive camera. That same year a Nigerian immigrant was shot and killed in front of the building across the street. To appease us, my mother said, "Nothing like that ever happens out of the blue. He was in a fight with someone." It was too troublesome for her to acknowledge that people could die randomly, senselessly, at Westbury Court or anywhere else.

16   Every day on my way back from school, I hurried past the flowers and candles piled in front of the spot where the Nigerian, whose name I didn't know, had been murdered. Still I never thought I was living in a violent place.

It was an elevated castle above a clattering train tunnel, a blind alley where children from our building and the building across the street had erected a common basketball court for hot summer afternoon games, an urban yellow brick road where hopscotch squares dotted the sidewalk next to burned-out, abandoned cars. It was home.

My family and I moved out of Westbury Court three years after the fire. 17 Every once in a while, though, the place came up in conversation, linked to either a joyous or a painful memory. One of the girls who had scalded her legs while boiling a pot of water for her bath during one of those no-heat days got married last year. After the burglar had broken into the house and taken my father's camera, my father—an amateur photography buff—never took another picture.

My family and I often reminisce about the Parent Brothers when we see 18 them in Haitian newspapers or on television; we brag that we knew them when, before one of the brothers became a senator in Haiti and the sister, Lydie, became mayor of one of the better-off Haitian suburbs, Pétion-Ville. We never talk about the lost children.

Even now, I question what I remember about the children. Did they re- 19 ally die? Or did their mother simply move away with them after the fire? Maybe they were not even boys at all. Maybe they were two girls. Or one boy and one girl. Or maybe I am struggling to phase them out of my memory altogether. Not just them, but the fear that their destiny could have so easily been mine and my brothers'.

A few months ago, I asked my mother, "Do you remember the children 20 and the fire at Westbury Court?"

Without missing a flutter of my breath, my mother replied, "Oh those 21 children, those poor children, their poor mother. Sometimes it is too late to say, 'I shouldn't have.' "

QUESTIONS ON SUBJECT AND PURPOSE

1. How long ago did the fire take place? What details in the story allow you to arrive at an approximate answer?
2. How many examples of life at Westbury Court does Danticat include?
3. Why might the essay be titled "Westbury Court"? What does that suggest about the essay? How appropriate would a title such as "Sometimes It Is Too Late" have been?

QUESTIONS ON STRATEGY AND AUDIENCE

1. In paragraphs 7 and 21, Danticat repeats her mother's observation: "Sometimes it is too late to say, 'I shouldn't have.' " Why?
2. Danticat encloses paragraphs 7 and 9 within parentheses. Why?
3. What is it about the essay and the experiences that it relates that might appeal to a reader?

QUESTIONS ON VOCABULARY AND STYLE

1. What is the effect of the typical televised depiction of children returning home in paragraph 10?
2. In paragraph 16, Danticat describes Westbury Court as an "elevated castle," "a blind alley," "an urban yellow brick road." What are these figures of speech called?
3. Be prepared to define the following words: *pliant* (paragraph 6), *sully* (10), *appease* (15).

WRITING SUGGESTIONS

1. **For Your Journal.** Everyone has had scary experiences, but sometimes an experience will forever change the way we think or act. In your journal brainstorm about some past experiences that altered your later life. Jot down both a short account of what happened and a sentence or two about the significance of that single experience.
2. **For a Paragraph.** Expand your journal entry into a paragraph. Concentrate on a single event, focusing especially on its significance.
3. **For an Essay.** "Sometimes it is too late to say, 'I shouldn't have.'" Use the mother's observation for the basis of an essay in which you explore an example or series of related examples or experiences that taught you the truth (or the falseness) of such a claim.
4. **For Research.** When children suddenly and unexpectedly die, schools (elementary, secondary, colleges, and universities) often have grief counselors available for their peers. What do we know about the impact that the sudden death of a friend or a classmate might have on a peer? Research the topic—or an aspect of the topic—and present your findings in a longer essay. If you recall a similar experience from your life, you might use that as a departure point for your paper.

FOR FURTHER STUDY

Focusing on Grammar and Writing. Select one or more of Danticat's paragraphs (1–3, 7–8, or 1–14 would be good choices) and explain why she uses each comma. A grammar handbook will give you a list of rules for comma usage. Remember that we use marks of punctuation to help our readers see the structures of our sentences.

Working Together. Divide into small groups. Each group should choose a group of paragraphs (there are 21 in all) and list the details or examples that Danticat uses. How effective is each example or detail?

Seeing Other Modes at Work. Where can you see both narration and description at work in the essay?

Finding Connections. Bob Greene's "Cut" offers another example of how a personal experience changes our perceptions, as does Terry Tempest Williams' "The Village Watchman" (Chapter 3).

Exploring the Web. What do we know about the impact that a sudden death of a friend or classmate might have on a peer? Use the Web to gather information and examples. You can start your search at **www.prenhall.com/miller**.

ONE OF THE GIRLS

Leslie Heywood

Leslie Heywood (1964–), a former Division I track and cross-country runner and currently a competitive powerlifter, is professor of English and Cultural Studies at the State University of New York, Binghamton. She has an M.F.A. in poetry from the University of Arizona and a Ph.D. in English and Critical Theory from the University of California, Irvine. Her books include Pretty Good for a Girl: A Memoir *(1998), from which this selection is taken, and* Built to Win: The Rise of the Female Athlete as Cultural Icon *(2003).*

The Preamble to Title IX of the Education Amendments of 1972 reads: "No person in the United States shall, on the basis of sex, be excluded from participation in, be denied the benefits of, or be subject to discrimination under any educational programs or activity receiving financial assistance." Among the many areas of gender inequality that Title IX has addressed are the opportunities for young women to participate in scholastic sports.

On Writing: *Asked about her writing habits, Heywood replied: "Some of my very best writing ideas come during a long run. Titles, an elusive piece of an argument, even a compelling voice often emerge in the cadence of my steps on a trail through the woods where there is nothing but quiet, deer, and wild turkeys. Something about physical movement, a steady heartbeat, the endorphin buzz, seems to catalyze my thinking."*

BEFORE READING

Connecting: The title of the book from which this essay is taken is *Pretty Good for a Girl.* Have you ever heard that phrase used in conversation? In what context might that expression be used? What does it seem to imply?

Anticipating: For Heywood, has it been enough just to provide equal opportunities for young women to participate in sports? Is anything more necessary?

1   When Gertrude Ederle swam the English Channel in 1926, two hours faster than any of the men who had preceded her, people began to think that women might not be so weak. Imagine her there, her hair cropped short like a flapper, looking into the water and saying *I will.* Imagine the pull of the water that day, the fierceness of the currents, her fearlessness as she greased up. For her, unlike the world that followed her swim, it wasn't a question of whether she could but how fast she would do it. Not wavering a bit, she coats herself from head to foot and heads out. As her face touches water and she takes her first stroke, what she feels is how a wolf feels setting in for an all-day run: she feels right. Her hand passes high above the water with precision and

she feels the currents, rolling her over the way they would rough up a boat. Her heart opens with joy, it will be a fight, her muscles pulling the water for hours while exhaustion sets in and she keeps moving. Nothing can stop her, not the manta rays whose tentacles leave a blistering kiss around her throat, not the weather so bad there is an advisory for boats. Twelve hours in, nervous to see the waver in her stroke, the way her arms dip and weave, the way she floats in the seconds in between, her companions pace the deck, lean over the water, cupping their hands in a shout. Gertrude, they say, you should stop. But they're speaking another language, live different lives in which a body doesn't ask itself to dig itself in, to rally, to find an energy that simply doesn't exist, to explode from that gray space of silence and dread into a muscle that is supple, feeling blood beginning to tingle again, ready to bear itself on, to the limit, to the limit, to feel what *is*. No, she says, I have to go.

Forty-one years later, Kathrine Switzer knew she could go the 26.2 miles 2 it took to run the Boston Marathon, knew the feel of the hills and the wind on her skin, knew where she had to dig to scale that inevitable wall, rising at mile 18, when her muscles start to sag and her back is tight far beyond the pounding of her heart stabbing like scabby birch bark. From training runs, she knew the breathing it takes to soar over that wall, the way she had to close her mind to the creeping exhaustion contracting her back, the ache that spreads and spreads like shooting stars of blood rushing through a limb too long compressed, iron spikes between the shoulders. She knew she was up to it. Every day she rose in the morning longing for that ache and the strength that would break in lemon waves, electric. Many times her feet kept moving, still in stride, the air sharp through her lungs past startled pines and leafless maples, through snow and ice, then rain and glittering sleeves of summer green. And every time she scaled that wall and ran beyond those pressing hands along her spine, she opened up. Legs firm and sure, lungs silver-tanked, her strides taking the ground like a monster breathing. *I can do this. Here I am. Watch me run.* And Switzer wants to run like this in an official race, to see it, feel it measured. One for the girls, for the books.

But in 1967, women are not allowed to run. Still she needs to do it. She 3 covers her body and her tracks. She enters the Boston Marathon, K. Switzer, number 261, and goes to the starting line thickened by sweats. A hooded head. No face. The gun goes off and she takes off with the pack, her training partners around her. They start at a decent pace, and breathing, settle in. The hood gathering her face and the top of her head makes her hot. Hothead. Sweat. Two miles in, she pushes it back, her chin-length hair falling free. She looks at her training partner and smiles. Her arms pump, her legs are steady.

But rushing at her from the corner is the race director, midsixties heavy 4 in a long dark coat, stabbing his arms toward the number on her chest. *No girls allowed.* Her partner steps between them, and she pulls away, still running. They leave the race director behind. But then comes another, hips spread wide, rushing at her in heavy boots. Look at his lips curling back from his teeth, *a woman will not compete in this race, not ever, not if it is up to me.* His coat flies up as he grabs at her, his eyes narrowed to a slit. Her partner rushes between them again as Kathrine turns and slips away. For 24.2 more miles. Her heart beats even heavier, adrenaline strong. *I will do this.* And this time there is no wall rising at mile 18. This time, the four hours and twenty minutes it takes her to finish are a lime-long breeze. Pain in her ankles, ball joints of her hips, steel clamps on her neck, she breathes easy. Heart steadier than ever. When the newspapers mob the race director and ask him to speak, he says that he is "hurt to think that an American girl would go where she is not wanted. If that girl were my daughter I would spank her." So they turn to Switzer. Ask her why she runs. Because running makes her "strong, all there." It is another five years, 1972, before women are allowed to run, pound out the long roads laid by the still-grown trees. Stronger than strong. All there. They come. They run.

5   This is where I begin. Title IX of the Education Act of 1972, that law that made gender discrimination illegal, made athletes of millions of girls like me. No more female incompetence and physical weakness, *you throw like a girl, no girls allowed, why don't you just go home.* Not now, excuse me. Stepping out.

6   So now she is everywhere around us, staring back at you from the television screen, from women's magazines: a fierce babe with biceps, straight shoulders, a proud look, claiming the planet for her own. Gabby Reece. Lisa Leslie. Rebecca Lobo. Mia Hamm. She's given to us in blacks and in whites: you can see the stark beauty of her body like straight-line cords. She's no one you would mess with. She's someone you might like to become. She's beautiful. She's strong. She's proud. She's doing it for herself: you project on her all the strength you've never felt, all the invulnerability you've never mustered, all the desire for self-sufficiency and completion you've never owned. She has it. You want it. Look closer.

7   Are you the one she's looking at when she asks if you'll let her play sports? Are you the one who'll prepare her to win? Are you the one who follows, looks, watches her step out and stride? If she lets you touch her, is it because she wants to be touched? What if she turned from her chiseled silhouette, poised, and looked you in the face? What if she could speak? What if she could tell you a story you haven't heard, not yet, what if the image of perfection took on some blood and began to tell you? Would you listen? Would you follow her voice like a glistening chime? Would her story take you over, overcome where you need her to stay—way up there pedestaled, just out of reach, an image of hope and a goal that you can become—sometime soon, next month or next week? But who is she? How does she live? What does she think about, what does she eat? Who touches her, who does she touch? Her muscles, her body, her pillars of strength—what's inside her? Is her life like yours, like your best friend's? Look closer.

8   There are some great Nike ads out there that are a gateway to my vanished world, where I used to win races and everyone knew. In the black-and-white images, dreams, possibilities beckon to girls, welcome them into the world. Sports can give us that place, but a lot of work needs to be done before we've finished that race. Female athletes fight the same unrealistic images everyone fights, and researchers are only beginning to understand the relationship between those images and the "female athlete triad"—eating disorders

and exercise compulsion, amenorrhea—that had me training until my bones fractured, my tendons ripped, and I stuck my fingers down my throat or simply didn't eat to stay lean. Nobody's been quite loud enough in saying that the female athlete triad is almost surely connected to all the old negative ideas about girls—girls trying to prove beyond a shadow of a doubt that they are not what those ideas say they are: weak, mild, meek, meant to serve others instead of achieving for themselves. The ideas that made the race directors chase Kathrine Switzer away.

Are those ideas really gone? Let's face it—many of the images of female　9 athletes out there are more about having a great butt or a great set of pecs than they are about winning races and feeling confident. If we really want a society where, as one of the young girls in the Nike ads says, "I can be anything I want to be," each of us will have to do everything we can to make this dream more than words sliding easily out of the mouth. We need to make sure Title IX is enforced so that as many girls as possible have the opportunity to play sports. We need to make sure girls are treated as athletes, not just pretty girls. We need to continue the research that's been started on all the different aspects of girls' and women's lives, which shows sports' potential to give us a sense of competence and power—like that feeling deep in my lungs as, running by, I dared the very cacti not to see me.

Because national attention has turned to female athletes, because we are　10 no longer disparaged or scorned, or seen as exceptions to the woman-as-weakness rule, I know some things now I didn't know then. I belonged to the first wave of women in sports after Title IX, part of the gathering wave that ballooned the stats from 300,000 girls in interscholastic athletics to the 2.25 million who play today. Is it really safe now? Can we begin to try out some of the new ideas about competing, ideas I was struggling with competing against Sheila in the gym? Can we smile at each other without being fake? Can we find ways to get out there, still swallowing the world, still roaring like Tarzan swinging mightily on his vines, and not have to knock everyone else off the vines just so it looks like we're the one who soars best? Can we move toward what, in her new book, *Embracing Victory*, Mariah Burton Nelson names "the Champion" model of competition, which "respects all contestants, including the self"?

The old competitive model—what I did—led many of us from an earlier　11 generation to the female athlete triad, and we missed out on the true benefits of sports. Can we revise people's ideas about girls enough so that my ghost will give up having to prove herself, and the other girls running in her place won't have to erase whole worlds inside themselves just so someone will notice them, just so they can stand out and win?

In spite of everything that happened I continued in sport. I knew in-　12 stinctively what research is proving now: sports, if not played in the way I did, where everyone around you had to be stomped out with boots to their face because there was only one winner and it had to be you—if played a little differently than this, sports help with depression. They help with what the books call self-esteem: feeling the sun on your warm face, walking across the field like a giant, feeling that just for a moment, the world belongs to you.

13   Running and lifting are as much a part of my life as is the quiet in-and-out of my steady chest. I write this book with hopes that other girls will have some support I didn't have and won't make the same mistakes. So here's to many, many more women's hockey teams and Picabo Streets—and to the women and men who'll work hard to make it possible for every young girl to burn bright as the sun without paying the price of self-destruction. And then when there are girls all around who are stronger and with better biceps than me, well, I just might be able to deal with it.

QUESTIONS ON SUBJECT AND PURPOSE

1. For Heywood, what benefits do sports hold for women?
2. Did Heywood herself only experience benefits from competing in sports? Were there any drawbacks or problems?
3. This essay forms the final chapter or epilogue to Heywood's memoir. What final thoughts does she want to leave with her reader?

QUESTIONS ON STRATEGY AND AUDIENCE

1. Why might Heywood have titled the essay "One of the Girls"?
2. Paragraph 7 is composed entirely of rhetorical questions—questions that provoke thought rather than require response. Specifically, to whom are those questions addressed? Define that "you."
3. As the headnote explains, this essay appeared in her memoir, not a magazine. What assumptions might Heywood have made about a book-reading audience rather than a magazine-reading audience?

QUESTIONS ON VOCABULARY AND STYLE

1. When Heywood writes of the "blistering kiss" (paragraph 1) of the manta ray or the "ache that spreads . . . like shooting stars of blood" (2), what type of language is she using?
2. In narrating Ederle's swim and Switzer's run, Heywood shifts to the present tense (for example, "she takes her first stroke" or "she takes off with the pack") rather than the past tense ("took"), even though the events occurred in the past. Why tell the story in this way?
3. Be prepared to define the following words: *flapper* (1), *supple* (1), *glistening* (7), *amenorrhea* (8), *disparaged* (10).

WRITING SUGGESTIONS

1. **For Your Journal.** How do you view women athletes? Are your images only positive? Do you stereotype women athletes? In your journal explore that idea—with reference to yourself (if you are a woman athlete) or to others.

2. **For a Paragraph.** How does our society seem to view women athletes? Look for advertisements, for example, that depict women athletes. Are they depicted in the same way as male athletes are? For a paragraph writing, pick a particular advertisement and explore the image that is projected.

3. **For an Essay.** Extend your analysis of the depiction of women athletes in our culture into an essay. If you are using advertisements, make sure that you gather them from a range of magazines. You might also use other visual examples—film, television, photographs, or drawings illustrating articles.

4. **For Research.** How did Title IX influence the women's athletic program at your school? Visit the athletic department and your school's library and archives and research the development of women's athletics since 1972. Then, using that research—with specific facts and appropriate quotations—write an essay in which you trace that impact. Be sure to document your sources. You might want to submit your final paper to your school's newspaper for possible publication.

FOR FURTHER STUDY

Focusing on Grammar and Writing. What is the difference between a sentence fragment and a sentence? How many fragments can you find in Heywood's essay? Do they appear to be intentional or unintentional? Why might she use them if she knows that they are fragments? What is the danger in using sentence fragments in your writing?

Working Together. Working in small groups, discuss other types of examples that might be used in an essay that analyzes the impact of Title IX on secondary education in the United States. Do you have any personal experience examples? For instance, are there now new opportunities for college athletic scholarships?

Seeing Other Modes at Work. The two extended examples—the stories of Ederle and Switzer—are narratives with extensive descriptions.

Finding Connections. Interesting pairings can be made with Bob Greene's "Cut" (Chapter 1) and Margaret Atwood's "The Female Body" (Chapter 8).

Exploring the Web. What impact has Title IX of the Educational Amendment had on the education (not just sports participation) of young women in the United States? It's pretty amazing. See for yourself. You can start your search at **www.prenhall.com/miller.**

SHOOTING AN ELEPHANT
George Orwell

George Orwell, the pen name of Eric Arthur Blair (1903–1950), was born in Moti-hari, Bengal, India, the son of an English colonial administrator. After studying at Eton in England, Orwell served for five years as a police official in Rangoon, Burma. In 1928, he embarked on a three-year investigation of poverty in London's East End—experiences recorded in his first book, Down and Out in Paris and London *(1933). In 1936, he joined the Loyalists in Spain and was severely wounded during the Spanish Civil War. In addition to his best-known books* Animal Farm *(1945) and* 1984 *(1949), Orwell produced a vast amount of journalism as well as numerous es-says and reviews. His writing is marked by an independence of mind, a hatred of op-pression, and a sympathy for the underdog.*

"Shooting an Elephant" grows out of Orwell's experiences with the Indian Im-perial Police from 1922 to 1927, although the essay was not written until 1936.

On Writing: *In his essay "Why I Write," Orwell talks about his "political" purpose for writing: "My starting point is always a feeling of partisanship, a sense of injustice. When I sit down to write a book, I do not say to myself, 'I am going to pro-duce a work of art.' I write it because there is some lie that I want to expose, some fact to which I want to draw attention, and my initial concern is to get a hearing."*

BEFORE READING

Connecting: Can you think of any time in your life when you were forced to act in a certain way because people expected you to? As an older child? As a leader? As a representative of an organization? Perhaps even as a soldier, vol-unteer, or student in another country?

Anticipating: Orwell uses a single example to prove a point. As you read the essay, try to find a sentence that might serve as a thesis—a statement that the example is intended to illustrate and support.

1   In Moulmein, in Lower Burma, I was hated by large numbers of people—the only time in my life that I have been important enough for this to happen to me. I was subdivisional police officer of the town, and in an aimless, petty kind of way anti-European feeling was very bitter. No one had the guts to raise a riot, but if a European woman went through the bazaars alone somebody would probably spit betel juice over her dress. As a police officer I was an ob-vious target and was baited whenever it seemed safe to do so. When a nimble Burman tripped me up on the football field and the referee (another Burman) looked the other way, the crowd yelled with hideous laughter. This happened more than once. In the end the sneering yellow faces of young men that met

me everywhere, the insults hooted after me when I was at a safe distance, got badly on my nerves. The young Buddhist priests were the worst of all. There were several thousands of them in the town and none of them seemed to have anything to do except stand on street corners and jeer at Europeans.

All this was perplexing and upsetting. For at that time I had already 2 made up my mind that imperialism was an evil thing and the sooner I chucked up my job and got out of it the better. Theoretically—and secretly, of course— I was all for the Burmese and all against the oppressors, the British. As for the job I was doing, I hated it more bitterly than I can perhaps make clear. In a job like that you see the dirty work of Empire at close quarters. The wretched prisoners huddling in the stinking cages of the lockups, the grey, cowed faces of the long-term convicts, the scarred buttocks of the men who had been flogged with bamboos—all these oppressed me with an intolerable sense of guilt. But I could get nothing into perspective. I was young and ill-educated and I had had to think out my problems in the utter silence that is imposed on every Englishman in the East. I did not even know that the British Empire is dying, still less did I know that it is a great deal better than the younger empires that are going to supplant it. All I knew was that I was stuck between my hatred of the empire I served and my rage against the evil-spirited little beasts who tried to make my job impossible. With one part of my mind I thought of the British Raj as an unbreakable tyranny, as something clamped down, in *saecula saeculorum*, upon the will of prostrate peoples; with another part I thought that the greatest joy in the world would be to drive a bayonet into a Buddhist priest's guts. Feelings like these are the normal by-products of imperialism; ask any Anglo-Indian official, if you can catch him off duty.

One day something happened which in a roundabout way was enlight- 3 ening. It was a tiny incident in itself, but it gave me a better glimpse than I had had before of the real nature of imperialism—the real motives for which despotic governments act. Early one morning the subinspector at a police station the other end of town rang me up on the phone and said that an elephant was ravaging the bazaar. Would I please come and do something about it? I did not know what I could do, but I wanted to see what was happening and I got on to a pony and started out. I took my rifle, an old .44 Winchester and much too small to kill an elephant, but I thought the noise might be useful *in terrorem*. Various Burmans stopped me on the way and told me about the elephant's doings. It was not, of course, a wild elephant, but a tame one which had gone "must." It had been chained up, as tame elephants always are when their attack of "must" is due, but on the previous night it had broken its chain and escaped. Its mahout, the only person who could manage it when it was in that state, had set out in pursuit, but had taken the wrong direction and was now twelve hours' journey away, and in the morning the elephant had suddenly reappeared in the town. The Burmese population had no weapons and were quite helpless against it. It had already destroyed somebody's bamboo hut, killed a cow and raided some fruit stalls and devoured the stock; also it had met the municipal rubbish van and, when the driver jumped out and took to his heels, had turned the van over and inflicted violences upon it.

4   The Burmese subinspector and some Indian constables were waiting for me in the quarter where the elephant had been seen. It was a very poor quarter, a labyrinth of squalid bamboo huts, thatched with palmleaf, winding all over a steep hillside. I remember that it was a cloudy, stuffy morning at the beginning of the rains. We began questioning the people as to where the elephant had gone and, as usual, failed to get any definite information. That is invariably the case in the East; a story always sounds clear enough at a distance, but the nearer you get to the scene of events the vaguer it becomes. Some of the people said that the elephant had gone in one direction, some said that he had gone in another, some professed not even to have heard of any elephant. I had almost made up my mind that the whole story was a pack of lies, when we heard yells a little distance away. There was a loud, scandalized cry of "Go away, child! Go away this instant!" and an old woman with a switch in her hand came round the corner of a hut, violently shooing away a crowd of naked children. Some more women followed, clicking their tongues and exclaiming; evidently there was something that the children ought not to have seen. I rounded the hut and saw a man's dead body sprawling in the mud. He was an Indian, a black Dravidian coolie, almost naked, and he could not have been dead many minutes. The people said that the elephant had come suddenly upon him round the corner of the hut, caught him with its trunk, put its foot on his back and ground him into the earth. This was the rainy season and the ground was soft, and his face had scored a trench a foot deep and a couple of yards long. He was lying on his belly with arms crucified and head sharply twisted to one side. His face was coated with mud, the eyes wide open, the teeth bared and grinning with an expression of unendurable agony. (Never tell me, by the way, that the dead look peaceful. Most of the corpses I have seen looked devilish.) The friction of the great beast's foot had stripped the skin from his back as neatly as one skins a rabbit. As soon as I saw the dead man I sent an orderly to a friend's house nearby to borrow an elephant rifle. I had already sent back the pony, not wanting it to go mad with fright and throw me if it smelled the elephant.

5   The orderly came back in a few minutes with a rifle and five cartridges, and meanwhile some Burmans had arrived and told us that the elephant was in the paddy fields below, only a few hundred yards away. As I started forward practically the whole population of the quarter flocked out of the houses and followed me. They had seen the rifle and were all shouting excitedly that I was going to shoot the elephant. They had not shown much interest in the elephant when he was merely ravaging their homes, but it was different now that he was going to be shot. It was a bit of fun to them, as it would be to an English crowd; besides they wanted the meat. It made me vaguely uneasy. I had no intention of shooting the elephant—I had merely sent for the rifle to defend myself if necessary—and it is always unnerving to have a crowd following you. I marched down the hill, looking and feeling a fool, with the rifle over my shoulder and an ever-growing army of people jostling at my heels. At the bottom, when you got away from the huts, there was a metalled road and beyond that a miry waste of paddy fields a thousand yards across, not yet ploughed but soggy from the

first rains and dotted with coarse grass. The elephant was standing eight yards from the road, his left side towards us. He took not the slightest notice of the crowd's approach. He was tearing up bunches of grass, beating them against his knees to clean them and stuffing them into his mouth.

I had halted on the road. As soon as I saw the elephant I knew with per- 6 fect certainty that I ought not to shoot him. It is a serious matter to shoot a working elephant—it is comparable to destroying a huge and costly piece of machinery—and obviously one ought not to do it if it can possibly be avoided. And at that distance, peacefully eating, the elephant looked no more dangerous than a cow. I thought then and I think now that his attack of "must" was already passing off; in which case he would merely wander harmlessly about until the mahout came back and caught him. Moreover, I did not in the least want to shoot him. I decided that I would watch him for a little while to make sure that he did not turn savage again, and then go home.

But at that moment, I glanced round at the crowd that had followed me. 7 It was an immense crowd, two thousand at the least and growing every minute. It blocked the road for a long distance on either side. I looked at the sea of yellow faces above the garish clothes—faces all happy and excited over this bit of fun, all certain that the elephant was going to be shot. They were watching me as they would watch a conjuror about to perform a trick. They did not like me, but with the magical rifle in my hands I was momentarily worth watching. And suddenly I realized that I should have to shoot the elephant after all. The people expected it of me and I had got to do it; I could feel their two thousand wills pressing me forward, irresistibly. And it was at this moment, as I stood there with the rifle in my hands, that I first grasped the hollowness, the futility of the white man's dominion in the East. Here was I, the white man with his gun, standing in front of the unarmed native crowd—seemingly the leading actor of the piece; but in reality I was only an absurd puppet pushed to and fro by the will of those yellow faces behind. I perceived in this moment that when the white man turns tyrant it is his own freedom that he destroys. He becomes a sort of hollow, posing dummy, the conventionalized figure of a sahib. For it is the condition of his rule that he shall spend his life in trying to impress the "natives," and so in every crisis he has got to do what the "natives" expect of him. He wears a mask, and his face grows to fit it. I had got to shoot the elephant. I had committed myself to doing it when I sent for the rifle. A sahib has got to act like a sahib; he has got to appear resolute, to know his own mind and do definite things. To come all that way, rifle in hand, with two thousand people marching at my heels, and then to trail feebly away, having done nothing—no, that was impossible. The crowd would laugh at me. And my whole life, every white man's life in the East, was one long struggle not to be laughed at.

But I did not want to shoot the elephant. I watched him beating his 8 bunch of grass against his knees, with that preoccupied grandmotherly air that elephants have. It seemed to me that it would be murder to shoot him. At that age I was not squeamish about killing animals, but I had never shot an elephant and never wanted to. (Somehow it always seems worse to kill a *large* animal.)

Besides, there was the beast's owner to be considered. Alive, the elephant was worth at least a hundred pounds; dead, he would only be worth the value of his tusks, five pounds, possibly. But I had got to act quickly. I turned to some experienced-looking Burmans who had been there when we arrived, and asked them how the elephant had been behaving. They all said the same thing: He took no notice of you if you left him alone, but he might charge if you went too close to him.

9   It was perfectly clear to me what I ought to do. I ought to walk up to within, say, twenty-five yards of the elephant and test his behavior. If he charged, I could shoot; if he took no notice of me, it would be safe to leave him until the mahout came back. But also I knew that I was going to do no such thing. I was a poor shot with a rifle and the ground was soft mud into which one would sink at every step. If the elephant charged and I missed him, I should have about as much chance as a toad under a steamroller. But even then I was not thinking particularly of my own skin, only of the watchful yellow faces behind. For at that moment, with the crowd watching me, I was not afraid in the ordinary sense, as I would have been if I had been alone. A white man mustn't be frightened in front of "natives"; and so, in general, he isn't frightened. The sole thought in my mind was that if anything went wrong those two thousand Burmans would see me pursued, caught, trampled on, and reduced to a grinning corpse like that Indian up the hill. And if that happened it was quite probable that some of them would laugh. That would never do. There was only one alternative. I shoved the cartridges into the magazine and lay down on the road to get a better aim.

10   The crowd grew very still, and a deep, low, happy sigh, as of people who see the theater curtain go up at last, breathed from innumerable throats. They were going to have their bit of fun after all. The rifle was a beautiful German thing with cross-hair sights. I did not then know that in shooting an elephant one would shoot to cut an imaginary bar running from ear-hole to ear-hole. I ought, therefore, as the elephant was sideways on, to have aimed straight at his ear-hole; actually I aimed several inches in front of this, thinking the brain would be further forward.

11   When I pulled the trigger I did not hear the bang or feel the kick—one never does when a shot goes home—but I heard the devilish roar of glee that went up from the crowd. In that instant, in too short a time, one would have thought, even for the bullet to get there, a mysterious, terrible change had come over the elephant. He neither stirred nor fell, but every line of his body had altered. He looked suddenly stricken, shrunken, immensely old, as though the frightful impact of the bullet had paralyzed him without knocking him down. At last, after what seemed a long time—it might have been five seconds, I dare say—he sagged flabbily to his knees. His mouth slobbered. An enormous senility seemed to have settled upon him. One could have imagined him thousands of years old. I fired again into the same spot. At the second shot he did not collapse but climbed with desperate slowness to his feet and stood weakly upright, with legs sagging and head drooping. I fired a third

time. That was the shot that did for him. You could see the agony of it jolt his whole body and knock the last remnant of strength from his legs. But in falling he seemed for a moment to rise, for as his hind legs collapsed beneath him he seemed to tower upward like a huge rock toppling, his trunk reaching sky-wards like a tree. He trumpeted, for the first and only time. And then down he came, his belly towards me, with a crash that seemed to shake the ground even where I lay.

I got up. The Burmans were already racing past me across the mud. It 12 was obvious that the elephant would never rise again, but he was not dead. He was breathing very rhythmically with long rattling gasps, his great mound of a side painfully rising and falling. His mouth was wide open. I could see far down into caverns of pale pink throat. I waited a long time for him to die, but his breathing did not weaken. Finally I fired my two remaining shots into the spot where I thought his heart must be. The thick blood welled out of him like red velvet, but still he did not die. His body did not even jerk when the shots hit him, the tortured breathing continued without a pause. He was dying, very slowly and in great agony, but in some world remote from me where not even a bullet could damage him further. I felt I had got to put an end to that dreadful noise. It seemed dreadful to see the great beast lying there, powerless to move and yet powerless to die, and not even to be able to finish him. I sent back for my small rifle and poured shot after shot into his heart and down his throat. They seemed to make no impression. The tortured gasps continued as steadily as the ticking of a clock.

In the end I could not stand it any longer and went away. I heard later 13 that it took him half an hour to die. Burmans were bringing dahs and baskets even before I left, and I was told they had stripped his body almost to the bones by the afternoon.

Afterwards, of course, there were endless discussions about the shooting 14 of the elephant. The owner was furious, but he was only an Indian and could do nothing. Besides, legally I had done the right thing, for a mad elephant has to be killed, like a mad dog, if its owner fails to control it. Among the Europeans opinion was divided. The older men said I was right, the younger men said it was a damn shame to shoot an elephant for killing a coolie, because the elephant was worth more than any damn Coringhee coolie. And afterwards I was very glad that the coolie had been killed; it put me legally in the right and it gave me sufficient pretext for shooting the elephant. I often wondered whether any of the others grasped that I had done it solely to avoid looking a fool.

QUESTIONS ON SUBJECT AND PURPOSE

1. What is imperialism?
2. How does Orwell view the Burmese people?
3. What possible purpose might Orwell have for writing the essay? Does he seek to entertain? To persuade? To inform? A mixture of all three?

QUESTIONS ON STRATEGY AND AUDIENCE

1. What is the effect of Orwell's opening sentence: "I was hated by a large number of people"?
2. What is the effect of Orwell's final sentence: "I often wondered whether any of the others grasped that I had done it solely to avoid looking a fool"?
3. Based just on your reading experience, who is Orwell's audience? What evidence in the essay supports your definition of his audience?

QUESTIONS ON VOCABULARY AND STYLE

1. Why might Orwell have titled the essay "Shooting an Elephant"? Why not something like "The Death of an Elephant"?
2. Orwell uses two Latin phrases in his essay: *saecula saeculorum* ("world with end," paragraph 2) and *in terrorem* ("to give warning," paragraph 3). What does the use of these phrases suggest about Orwell's sense of his audience?
3. Be prepared to define the following words: *despotic* (paragraph 3), *miry* (5), *garish* (7), *resolute* (7).

WRITING SUGGESTIONS

1. **For Your Journal.** How do you react to the killing of the elephant? What would you have done in Orwell's situation? Do you agree with his action? Explore in your journal some possible responses that you might have made. What would have been the motivations for your different response?
2. **For a Paragraph.** Can you think of a time when, because of the position that you held, you were forced to act in a certain way because that is what others expected of you? In a paragraph, re-create that moment and comment on how it made you feel.
3. **For an Essay.** Expand your paragraph writing from exercise 2 into a full-length essay. Alternatively, write an essay in which you describe a moment in your past when you, like Orwell, came to a sudden realization. Something happened, you reacted in a certain way, and suddenly you had a new understanding of the significance of that event or moment.
4. **For Research.** As a nation, we too began as a colony—a number of European countries, including Great Britain, France, and Spain, saw us as a part of their colonial empire. How did our ancestors react to the imperialistic designs of these other nations? For example, could an English official stationed in New England have had an experience and realization similar to Orwell's? In what way did our country react to the colonial expectations of other nations?

FOR FURTHER STUDY

Focusing on Grammar and Writing. Throughout the essay, Orwell uses dashes to insert material into his sentences or to add material at the end of his sentences. Make a list of each use of the dash and, on the basis of these examples, write a set of rules that govern the use of the dash in writing.

Working Together. Divide into small groups. Each group should take one of the following topics, discuss how it fits into the essay as a whole, and then present their findings to the larger class:

a. The examples that Orwell uses in paragraph 1

b. The description of the man killed by the elephant (4)

c. The image of the puppet (7)

d. The description of the dying elephant (11–13)

e. The "endless discussions" of the outcome (14)

Seeing Other Modes at Work. The essay is a narrative—in this case, the story or narrative serves as a single example. The essay also reveals a cause-and-effect pattern as well.

Finding Connections. The strategy of using a personal experience to make a larger point is a common writing strategy—compare, for example, Richard Rodriguez's "None of This Is Fair" (Chapter 9). Other essays with similar content are David Brooks's "The Culture of Martyrdom" (Chapter 6) and Peter Singer's "The Singer Solution to World Poverty" (Chapter 10).

Exploring the Web. The Web has a number of sites devoted to George Orwell that include e-texts of his essays. You might also look for additional information about and maps of Burma. The CIA Fact Book has maps and background information that are helpful. Check **www.prenhall.com/miller** for some places at which to start your search.

2

NARRATION

PREPARING TO WRITE

WHAT IS NARRATION AND WHAT ARE ITS ELEMENTS?

> Once upon a time . . .
> Did you hear the one about?
> What did you two do last night?
> Well, officer, it was like this . . .
> What happened at the Battle of Gettysburg?

What follows each of those lines is a story or a narrative. All stories, whether they are personal experiences, jokes, novels, histories, films, or television serials, have the same essential ingredients: a series of events arranged in a chosen order and told by a narrator for some particular purpose.

On the simplest level, all stories are made up of three elements:

beginning (the initiating action)	
middle	**PLOT**
end (the concluding action)	

As these terms suggest, stories are told in time—the fundamental arrangement of those events is chronological. But stories do not always begin at the beginning. The time order of events can be rearranged by using flashbacks. Stories can begin with the last event in the chronological sequence or with any event that falls into the middle.

Stories also involve tellers, or narrators, who relate the story. The narrators of stories almost always either tell the story themselves ("I"—a first-person point of view) or tell the story as an observer (a third-person point of view).

First person ("I was saved from sin when I was going on thirteen.")	**POINT**
Third person ("One of the captains of the high school football team had something big he wanted to tell the other players.")	**OF** **VIEW**

Finally, stories have a purpose, a reason for being told, and that purpose controls the narrative and its selection of detail. As you start to write your narrative, always ask yourself what point you are trying to make. Force yourself to finish the following statement:

I am telling this story because _____.   **PURPOSE**

Any type of writing can use narration; it is not something found only in personal experience essays or in fiction. Narration can also be used as examples to support a thesis, as Bob Greene does in "Cut" (Chapter 1) by providing five personal narratives to support his assertion that being cut from an athletic team can make a person a superachiever later in life. Narration can also be found mixed with description in William Least Heat Moon's "Nameless, Tennessee" (Chapter 3) or underlying a persuasive argument in Richard Rodriguez's "None of This Is Fair" (Chapter 9). In fact, you can find examples of narration in readings throughout this text.

WHAT ARE THE COMMON FORMS OF NARRATIVE WRITING?

In writing courses, the narratives that you produce tend to come in several forms. Most common are personal experience narratives: you recount an experience that happened to you. You are the narrator; the event is more or less true (that is, you might add a few minor details or rearrange some things to make the story more interesting or more artful). You typically recount the experience in order to share with your reader an insight. It might be funny or serious, but either way, it must connect with your readers' experiences: it should be about something that is universal—a realization, a sudden understanding, an awareness the experience brought you. Most of the essays in this chapter are personal experience narratives.

Less common in freshman writing courses are "here-is-what-happened" narratives. Stories in newspapers and histories are good examples of this type of narrative. Writing such a narrative generally requires that you do some research—just as a newspaper reporter cannot write any news story without first gathering the facts. Factual or historical narratives are typically told by an omniscient narrator who is not a part of the story; they are intended to inform a reader, to provide information. This type of narrative also occurs in process writing (see Chapter 6) when you are describing how something happens or works.

The third common form for narratives in writing courses is the story designed to entertain. It might be what we call a short story, a joke, or a tall tale. It might be intended to scare us, to puzzle us, or to get us to think about a situation or a course of action. Typically, such narratives are fictionalized—that is, the author invents the characters and plot.

WHAT DO YOU WRITE ABOUT IF NOTHING EVER HAPPENED TO YOU?

Writing a personal narrative can pose some specific prewriting problems. It is easy to assume that the only things worth writing about are once-in-a-lifetime experiences—a heroic or death-defying act, a personal tragedy, an Olympic medal–winning performance. It is likely that few readers have been in a lockdown in a prison, and probably not many have heard a tale like that of Marina and Kiki; but a good personal narrative does not need to be based on an extraordinary experience. In fact, ordinary experiences, because they are about things familiar to every reader, are often the best sources for personal narratives. There is nothing extraordinary, for example, about the events Langston Hughes relates in "Salvation," even though Hughes's experience was a turning point in his life. Bob Greene in "Cut" (Chapter 1) narrates the kind of story—about being "cut" from a team—that is all too familiar to most readers; in one way or another, probably everyone has experienced a similar rejection and subsequent disappointment.

The secret to writing an effective personal narrative is twofold. First, you must tell your story artfully, following the advice outlined in this chapter's introduction. Simply relating what happened is not enough, however, for you must do a second, equally important thing: you must reveal a purpose in your tale. Purposes can be many. You might offer insight into human behavior or motivation; you might mark a significant moment in your life; you might reveal an awareness of what it is to be young and to have dreams; you might reflect on the precariousness of life and inevitability of change and decay; you might even use your experience to argue, as Evans Hopkins does, for a change in social attitudes. However you use your narrative, what is important is that your story have a point, a reason for being, and that you make that reason clear to your reader.

WHAT DO YOU INCLUDE IN A NARRATIVE?

> Just tell me what happened!
> Get to the punch line!

No one, probably not even your mother, wants to hear everything you did today. Readers, like listeners, want you to be selective, for some things are more important or interesting than others. Historians have to select out of a mass of data what they will include and emphasize; they have to choose a place to begin and a place to end. Even in relating personal experiences, you must condense and select. Generally, you need to pare away, to cut out the unnecessary and the uninteresting. What you include depends, of course, on what happened and, more important, on the purpose or meaning that you are trying to convey.

Maya Angelou's story of "Sister Monroe" actually blends two experiences, widely separated in time, into a single story. The story opens on a Sunday morning in church, but Sister Monroe's comic performance does not occur on that morning. Once the initial story is underway, Angelou shifts to an earlier point in time, on a morning when Sister Monroe seized Reverend Taylor ("once she [Sister Monroe] hadn't been to church for a few months . . . she got the spirit and started shouting"). Angelou focuses our attention on the significant action—she doesn't relate every event that occurred.

Prewriting Suggestions

1. Before you start writing, set aside some time to brainstorm about your paper. If you are writing about a personal experience, you will discover that, with time, you will slowly remember more and more details. Do you need to do some research for your essay? Do the gathering and the note-taking before you start to write.

2. Complete the following sentence: "I am narrating this story because. . . ." As you gather information, use your purpose statement to decide what to include and what to exclude.

3. Choose a point of view from which to tell the story. Personal narratives tend to be told in the first person ("I"); historical narratives and journalistic stories tend to be told in the third person ("they," "he," "she").

4. Remember that your narrative must have a beginning, a middle, and an end, but stories do not have to be told in straight chronological order. You can flashback or forward in your narrative.

5. Look at the narratives in this chapter. Think about how each is organized. Do you see any strategies that might work in your essay?

WRITING

HOW DO YOU STRUCTURE A NARRATIVE?

Time structures all narratives, although events need not always be arranged in chronological order. A narrative can begin at one point in time and then "flash back" to an earlier action or event. Langston Hughes's "Salvation" begins with a narrator looking back at an experience that occurred when he was thirteen, although the story itself is told in the order in which it happened. The most typical inversion is to begin at the end of the narrative and then to move backward in time to explain how that end was reached. More complex narratives may shift several times back and forth between incidents in the past or between the past and the present. Two cautions are obvious: first, do not switch time too frequently, especially in short papers; second, make sure that any switches you make are clearly marked for your readers.

Remember as well that you control where your narrative begins and ends. For example, Evans Hopkins begins "Lockdown" with a predawn visit from two prison guards in armored vests and riot helmets; he does not begin with an account of the events that led to the lockdown or with the events that led to his imprisonment. Those details Hopkins fills in later, for they are not as dramatic or central to the points that he is trying to make. In a similar way, you might want to build your narrative to a climactic moment of insight that concludes the story. A formal, summary conclusion tacked on to a narrative essay sometimes actually obscures the significance of the experience.

Writers frequently change or modify an actual personal experience in order to tell the story more effectively, heighten the tension, or make their purpose clearer. In her essay "On Keeping a Notebook," essayist and novelist Joan Didion remarks:

> I tell what some would call lies. "That's simply not true," the members of my family frequently tell me when they come up against my memory of a shared event. "The party was *not* for you, the spider was *not* a black widow, *it wasn't that way at all.*" Very likely they are right, for not only have I always had trouble distinguishing between what happened and what merely might have happened, but I remain unconvinced that the distinction, for my purposes, matters.

Whenever you recall an experience, even if it happened last week, you do not necessarily remember it exactly as it occurred. The value of a personal narrative does not rest on relating the original experience with absolute accuracy. It does not matter, for example, whether the scene with Sister Monroe in the Christian Methodist Episcopal Church occurred exactly as Maya Angelou describes it years later. What does matter is that it could have happened as she describes it and that it is faithful to Angelou's purpose.

"It's plotted out. I just have to write it."

Keep your plots simple. Do not approach your construction of plot like this writer.
© *The New Yorker Collection 1996 Charles Barsotti from* **cartoonbank.com.** *All Rights Reserved.*

HOW ARE NARRATIVES TOLD?

Two things are especially important in relating your narrative. First, you need to choose a point of view from which to tell the story. Personal experience narratives, such as those by Hughes, Angelou, and Hopkins, are generally told in the first person: the narrator is an actor in the story. Historical narratives and narratives used as illustrations in a larger piece of writing are generally told in the third person. The historian or the reporter, for example, stands outside the narrative and provides an objective view of the actions described. In "Marina" Judith Ortiz Cofer mixes first-person and third-person narration. The essay begins with a first-person account of how she and her mother went for a walk after an argument. They encounter a distinguished older gentleman with a little girl, and that meeting leads to the "story within the story," the tale of Marina and Kiki, which Cofer narrates in the third person. Once that story is finished, Cofer returns to the first person as she and her mother ponder the significance of the tale. Point of view can vary in one other way. The narrator can reveal only his or her own thoughts (using what is known as the limited point of view), or the narrator can reveal what anyone else in the narrative thinks or feels (using the omniscient, or all-knowing, point of view).

Second, you need to decide whether you are going to "show" or "tell" or mix the two. You "show" in a narrative by dramatizing a scene and creating dialogue. Hughes re-creates his experience for the reader by showing what happened and by recording some of the conversation that took place the night he was "saved from sin." Telling, by contrast, is summarizing what happened. For example, the story of Marina and Kiki in Cofer's "Marina" is told to the reader by the narrator. Marina and Kiki never talk; the story within the story contains no dialogue. Showing makes a narrative more vivid, for it allows the reader to experience the scene directly. Telling allows you to include a greater number of events and details. Either way, selectivity is necessary. Even when the experience being narrated took place over a short period of time—such as Hughes's experiences one evening at church—a writer cannot dramatize everything that happened. When an experience lasts four-and-a-half months, as does the lockdown Hopkins describes, a writer could never summarize events on a day-to-day basis. Each writer selects the moments that best give shape and significance to the experience.

HOW DO YOU WRITE DIALOGUE?

Dialogue creates the illusion of speech, of verbal interaction among the characters in the narrative. It is an illusion because real conversation is longer, slower, and much more boring than written dialogue. You use dialogue when you create scenes in which your characters talk to one another. Dialogue is a way of dramatizing. It reveals characters; your readers can "hear" the characters and get a sense of their personalities from how they react and what they say. Creating small scenes in your narrative increases its vividness. Instead of just telling the reader what happened, dialogue allows you to "show" what happened.

Writing effective dialogue in a narrative involves recognizing when it can play an important role in your story. Dialogue should be used sparingly. Dialogue slows down the action of a story, and too much dialogue can bring a narrative to a crawl. The point to dialogue is to reveal character or to generate tension, not to have characters summarize the events that are happening in the plot. In "Salvation," Hughes creates tension in his narrative by including four tiny scenes with dialogue—two are the appeals that the minister makes to him, one is his aunt's appeal, and one voices Westley's decision to fake being "saved." Hughes might have written, "My aunt begged me to be saved," a simple summary statement. Instead, he generates tension and makes the scene more vivid by having his aunt say, "Langston, why don't you come? Why don't you come and be saved? Oh, Lamb of God! Why don't you come?"

Short exchanges of dialogue are typically set off as if they were separate paragraphs and are "tagged" with something like "he said" or "she replied." Do not get too clever in the verbs that you use in the tags; they are only likely to distract the reader. Notice how Cofer handles these two lines of dialogue:

> "Do you think he made a good husband?" I asked my mother.
>
> "He would know what it takes to make a woman happy," she said as she turned to face me, and winked in camaraderie.

The assumption behind dialogue is that speakers take turns. In an exchange of short lines of dialogue, you can omit the tags and even the quotation marks that typically are used to mark speech. Toward the end of his essay, Haines records a conversation in which he tries to find the right English words to convey the feelings that the famine generates in those who suffer through it:

> Misery?
>
> Yes, Berhanu said calmly, that is a part of it.
>
> Emptiness? Yes, he said, that too.
>
> Anguish? Despair?
>
> His eyes sparkled at the connection.
>
> Anger? Yes.
>
> Frustration? Yes.
>
> Fear?
>
> Fear, Berhanu said, like sorry, was too light a word.
>
> Terror?
>
> Yes, Berhanu said, "terror" is a good word.

Drafting Suggestions

1. Outline your narrative. Is the plot line clear? Are there any places in which your readers might have difficulty in following the sequence of events?
2. Look carefully at any moment that you have dramatized. Does it add to the tension of your story? Does it reveal something about the characters and their reactions or feelings? Write a one-line justification for any scene you have included.
3. Check your use of point of view. Are you consistent throughout the essay—or do you switch from first-person to third?
4. Have you signaled the structure of your narrative to your reader? Do you need to introduce some type of typographical device (such as white space or numbering) to indicate to your reader that the story comes in sections?
5. Recruit readers for your draft, ask them questions, and then follow their advice.

REVISING

HOW DO YOU REVISE A NARRATIVE?

Once you have a complete draft of your essay—not just a series of notes—always try to get some feedback from peer readers, from your instructor, or from a writing center tutor. Listen carefully to what your readers say. If several readers see problems in your essay, they are right, even if you do not agree with them. Reconsider every choice that you made in your essay—do not limit your revising to correcting obvious errors and changing an occasional word. Typically, your revision should be directed at three concerns:

- Pruning out unnecessary detail
- Making your essay's structure clear
- Looking again at showing and telling

Pruning Out Unnecessary Detail   Remember that your narrative has a purpose, a reason you are telling this story. Your purpose might be to entertain, to inform, to persuade, or a mixture of purposes. Write down on a separate sheet of paper your purpose statement, and use that statement to test every incident and detail that you have included in your narrative. Think about how frustrated you get when someone tries to tell a joke and obscures the punch line. Think about how often you get impatient when people are telling you what happened and include lots of unnecessary details. Prune away details in your narrative that do not support or illustrate your purpose.

Making Your Essay's Structure Clear   Narratives are told in time—they can be organized in a straightforward, chronological order, or they can manipulate time by flashing back or even forward. Remember that time changes can be puzzling to your reader unless you clearly signal them. Sometimes changing verb tenses—moving from past tense to present or present to future—is enough of a marker. More often, writers use a variety of typographical devices to mark such shifts: setting off a section in a different time by using extra white space before and after, numbering sections of the essay, or italicizing a section set in a different time. When you get advice from your readers as you are revising your essay, make sure to ask them if they are ever confused by the sequence of events in the story. A good test, for example, is to ask them to construct a chronological timeline for what happens in the essay. If they have problems or if they make mistakes, you know that you must revise the time changes in your essay.

Looking Again at Showing and Telling   Most narratives benefit from having a mixture of showing (dramatizing) and telling (summarizing). Dramatizing a scene involves having the characters verbally interact through dialogue. Remember, though, to keep these scenes short and to choose only appropriate moments. Such scenes can add tension to a story, or reveal a conflict between the characters, or show how characters interact. Ask yourself if there are moments in your narrative in which dramatization might be particularly effective. Do not have your characters speak unless there is a clear and important reason for including that scene. Do not try to summarize what is happening in the story by having one character narrate events to another: "And so, Maria, you remember that I told you yesterday that John took me out for dinner last night and we went to the restaurant where we saw his former girlfriend who dumped him three years ago."

Revising Suggestions

1. Look again at your title. An informative, even catchy, title is a tremendous asset to an essay. If yours seems a little boring, brainstorm some other possibilities. Never title your essay "Narrative Essay."

2. Remember to catch your reader's attention in the opening paragraphs. Look closely at your introduction. Ask a friend or classmate to read it. Does your reader want to continue reading?

3. Ask a reader to construct a timeline for what happens in your story. Is the plot line clear and unambiguous? Do you ever shift time in the story? If so, is the shift clearly marked or signaled?

4. Look carefully at the dialogue you have written. Does it sound plausible that characters might speak like this? Is it too long? Too wordy? Too formal or too colloquial? Remember that you are creating the illusion of speech rather than recording actual speech.

5. Look at your conclusion. How did you end? Did you lead up to a climactic moment, or did you just end with a flat conclusion ("And so you can see why this experience was important to me")? Compare how the writers in this chapter end their narratives. You might be able to use a similar strategy.

SAMPLE STUDENT ESSAY

FIRST DRAFT

Hope Zucker decided to write about a powerful childhood memory—a pair of red shoes that became her "ruby slippers" and the key to the Land of Oz.

MY NEW SHOES

When you are four years old anything longer than five minutes feels like eternity, so when the clerk told me and my mom that it would take three to four weeks for my new shoes to arrive, I was almost in tears. Since seeing *The Wizard of Oz*, I had thought of little else other than owning a pair of ruby slippers. My dreams were full of spinning houses, little munchkins, flying monkeys, and talking lions. All I wanted was to be Dorothy, and the shoe store had made a promise to find me a pair of red mary-janes which would hopefully take me to Munchkin Land and Oz.

For the next three weeks I made all the preparations I could think of in order to become Dorothy. It did not matter how convincing Judy Garland was because I knew in my heart that I was the true Dorothy. I sang "Somewhere Over the Rainbow" day and night, and I played dress up with an old light blue checked dress of my mother's. I even went as far as to carry my dog in a basket, but that did not work out too well. I had my mom braid my long brown hair, and after I insisted, she tied a light blue ribbon around each braid. I skipped wherever I went, and I even went as far as coloring part of our driveway with chalk to create my very own yellow brick road.

The only thing missing to my new persona was my ruby slippers. After my mother explained to me that three weeks really was not that far off in the future, I decided to help the store in their search for my red mary-janes. For a month I called the store everyday when I got home from preschool. Mr. Rogers and Big Bird could wait because there was nothing in the whole wide world that was more important than my red patent leather shoes. By the end of the month, the nice little old ladies at the store knew me by name and thought that I was the cutest child. Lucky for them, they did not have to put up with me.

Finally, after what seemed like years, the lady on the other side of the phone said that yes, my shiny red shoes had arrived. Now I had only to plead with my mother to get her to make a special trip into the city. After a few days of delay and a great deal of futile temper tantrums, my mom took me to the store. I could hardly contain my excitement. During the ride, I practiced the one and only line that only the real Dorothy could say, "There's no place like home." And of course, I clicked my beat up boondockers three times each time I recited my part. It was all practice for the real thing.

As we pulled into the parking lot, all the little old ladies inside the store waved to me as if they had been expecting me for days. I finally got to see my shoes, and they were as perfect as I knew they'd be. I was practically jumping out of my seat when she began to remove the stiff tissue paper surrounding my shoes, so rather than wait for her to fit my little feet into my slippers, I grabbed them from her and did it myself. They were the prettiest pair of shoes any girl could have!

For the next few weeks I was Dorothy and I'd stop everyone I'd see in order to prove it by tapping my heels together and saying, "There's no place like home." But soon my feet grew too big for my ruby slippers, and as I graduated into the next larger size, I no longer wanted to be Dorothy. As I grew up, so did my dreams. Cinderella, now she was someone to be! Yet, once again that phase, like the phases I am going through now, passed fairly quickly.

COMMENTS

Hope made enough copies of her essay so that the whole class could read and then discuss it. After reading her essay to the class, Hope asked her classmates for their reactions. Several students suggested that she tighten her narrative, eliminating details that were not essential to the story. Most of their suggestions were centered in paragraphs 4 and 5. "Why mention Mr. Rogers and Big Bird?" someone asked. "I didn't want you to have to wait several days to pick them up, and I didn't want to be reminded of your temper," commented another. When Hope came to revise her draft, she used this advice. She also eliminated a number of clichés and made a significant change in the ending of the paper. Notice how much more effective the final version is as the result of these minor revisions.

FINAL DRAFT

THE RUBY SLIPPERS

To a four-year old, anything longer than five minutes feels like eternity, so when the clerk told me and my mom that it would take three to four weeks for my new shoes to arrive, I was almost in tears. Since seeing *The Wizard of Oz*, I had thought of little else other than owning a pair of ruby slippers. My dreams were full of spinning houses, little munchkins, flying monkeys, and talking lions. All I wanted was to be Dorothy, and the shoe store had made a promise to find me a pair of red mary-janes which would hopefully take me to Munchkin Land and Oz.

For the next three weeks I made all the preparations I could think of in order to become Dorothy. It did not matter how convincing Judy Garland was because I knew in my heart that I was the true Dorothy. I sang "Somewhere Over the Rainbow" day and night, and I played dress up with an old light blue checked dress of my mother's. I even went as far as to carry my dog in a basket. My mom braided my long brown hair, and after I insisted, she tied a light blue ribbon around each braid. I skipped everywhere I went and colored part of our driveway with chalk to create my very own yellow brick road.

The only thing missing was my ruby slippers. After my mother explained that three weeks really was not that far off, I decided to help the store in their search for my red mary-janes. For a month I called the store everyday when I got home from preschool. By the end of the month, the ladies at the store knew me by name.

Finally, the woman on the other end of the phone said that yes, my shiny red shoes had arrived. I could hardly contain my excitement. During the ride, I practiced the one line that only the real Dorothy could say, "There's no place like home." And of course, I clicked my beat up loafers three times each time I recited that line. It was all practice for the real thing.

As we pulled into the parking lot, all the ladies inside the store waved to me as if they had been expecting me. I finally got to see my shoes, and they were as perfect as I had imagined. I was practically jumping out of my seat when she began to remove the stiff tissue paper surrounding my shoes, so rather than wait for her to fit my little feet into my slippers, I grabbed them from her and did it myself. They were the prettiest pair of shoes any girl could have!

For the next few weeks I was Dorothy and I'd stop everyone I'd see in order to prove it by tapping my heels together and saying, "There's no place like home." But soon my feet grew too big for my ruby slippers, and as I graduated into the next larger size, I no longer wanted to be Dorothy. As I grew up, so did my dreams.

SOME THINGS TO REMEMBER

1. Decide first why you are telling the reader *this* story. You must have a purpose clearly in mind.
2. Choose an illustration, event, or experience that can be covered adequately within the space limitations you face. Do not try to narrate the history of your life in an essay!
3. Decide on which point of view you will use. Do you want to be a part of the narrative or an objective observer? Which is more appropriate for your purpose?
4. Keeping your purpose in mind, select the details or events that seem the most important or the most revealing.
5. Arrange those details in an order—either a strict chronological one or one that employs a flashback. Remember to keep your verb tenses consistent and to signal any switches in time.
6. Remember the differences between showing and telling. Which method will be better for your narrative?

NARRATION AS A LITERARY STRATEGY

All stories—whether they are personal essays, imaginative fictions, journalistic reports, or histories—contain the same essential ingredients: a series of events arranged in an order structured through time recounted by a "narrator" for some particular purpose. Narratives can range from hundreds, even thousands, of pages to only a single paragraph. Peggy McNally's short story "Waiting" is an example of what is called "microfiction," a genre that is limited to a maximum of 250 words.

WAITING

Peggy McNally

Five days a week the lowest-paid substitute teacher in the district drives her father's used Mercury to Hough and 79th, where she eases it, mud flaps and all, down the ramp into the garage of Patrick Henry Junior High, a school where she'll teach back-to-back classes without so much as a coffee break and all of this depressing her until she remembers her date last night, and hopes it might lead to bigger things, maybe love, so she quickens her pace towards the main office to pick up her class lists with the names of students she'll never know as well as she has come to know the specials in the cafeteria, where she hopes the coffee will be perking and someone will have brought in those donuts she has come to love so much, loves more than the idea of teaching seventh-graders the meaning of a poem, because after all she's a sub who'll finish her day, head south to her father's house, and at dinner, he'll ask her how her job is going, and she'll say okay, and he'll remind her that it might lead to a full-position with benefits but she knows what teaching in that school is like, and her date from last night calls to ask if she's busy and she says yes because she's promised her father she'd wash his car and promises to her father are sacred since her mother died, besides it is the least she can do now that he lets her drive his car five days a week towards the big lake, to the NE corner of Hough and 79th and you know the rest.

DISCUSSION QUESTIONS

1. McNally composes her story as a single sentence. Why might she have chosen to do this? How does the story's form (as a single sentence) relate to what is occurring in the story?
2. The story contains a number of details, yet the woman is never named. Why is she nameless?
3. Who narrates the story? Why might this point of view be used? What would happen if the point of view were changed?
4. Stories have beginnings, middles, and ends. Is there an end to McNally's story? What shape does the story seem to take and why? How is that shape appropriate to what happens in the story?
5. What central impression does the story leave in your mind?

WRITING SUGGESTIONS

Often we find ourselves locked into repetitive patterns, small daily or weekly cycles that define us. Think about a pattern that you see in your own life. In a short personal essay, narrate that cycle for your readers. You don't need to use McNally's story as a structural model; you can narrate the story from the first person, and you can include dialogue if you wish. Remember, though, to have a purpose for your narrative. What does the pattern reveal about you? As a possible starting point, you might consider the following:

   a. A bad (or good) habit or behavior
   b. Situations in which you know how you will always react
   c. An endless quarrel or disagreement

READING NARRATION

Every state has a nickname, and the origins of those nicknames are frequently related in a folktale, a short narrative that explains how the state or the people from the state acquired that name. Delaware has an unusual name—the Blue Hen State—and here S.E. Schlosser recounts the folktale that explains how that name came about.

As you read this short narrative, remember what you have learned about how to write a narrative—that knowledge can help you as a reader.

- Narratives (stories) are told for a reason or purpose: they might be purely informational (here is what happened or how it happened); they might be entertaining (jokes, for example, are mini-narratives); they might be persuasive (a vivid story of what happened to someone can move you to action or empathy). As you read a narrative, ask yourself why the writer is telling this story. Is there a thesis or obvious reason for the story?

- Narratives are structured in time—they might open with the first event in the chronological sequence or they might use flashbacks, but you can always construct a timeline for a narrative.

- Narratives are always told by someone. It might be an objective, omniscient narrator (as in a history text or a newspaper story); it might be a person involved in the story. A guide to types of narration can be found in the Glossary and Ready Reference. Always ask yourself as you read a narrative, Who is telling this story, and why might the writer be using this type of narration?

- Narratives are economical—that is, they do not tell everything. Ask yourself as you read, What has the writer not told me in this narrative? What is left out is just as revealing as what is included.

- Narratives frequently dramatize scenes within the story by using dialogue. Although dialogue can make the characters come alive for the reader, dialogue also slows down the pace of the story. Does the narrative you are reading use dialogue? Why might the writer choose to render part of a scene in dialogue rather than just describe or summarize what happens?

BLUE HEN'S CHICKS

Opening sentence places the the story in time and place	<u>A Delaware man went to war during the American Revolution</u>. For entertainment, he brought with him two fighting cocks. When

Character introduced, single sentence of dialogue—an exaggeration; they are only the "babies" of the hen at home

Story told chronologically

Application of story to the men

Final explanation of the nickname

asked about these chickens, the soldier said slyly, "They are the chicks of a blue hen that I have at home."

Well, those cocks could fight. They were so fierce, they caused quite a stir among the men. It did not take long for the Delaware troops to begin boasting among the troops from the other states that they could outfight anyone, just like those famous fighting cocks. "We're the Blue Hen's Chickens. We will fight to the end!" became the theme of the Delaware troops. The other troops took to calling the men from Delaware "The Blue Hen's Chicks," and to this day, Delaware is known as the Blue Hen State.

RESPONDING TO A VISUAL

Every photograph is a part of a story—something was happening before it was taken; something happened afterwards. A photograph is a frozen moment in time. Looking through a family photograph album, you can relive events from your life. The photographs become single frames in a movie that your memory re-creates. Because they trigger memories, we take photographs of the good and memorable times of our lives, not of the sad or depressing times. Following are two photographs of people crying—one of a young woman and one of a young man.

We do not know what triggered these responses, but we can easily imagine a set of circumstances that might have preceded the photographs. Imagine some possibilities—what have they experienced? Why are they reacting in this way?

READING AND WRITING ABOUT IMAGES

Write a narrative essay that could accompany one of the photographs. The photograph could be either the end point of your story (you narrate the events that led up to this moment) or it might be the beginning point (you tell what happened after the photograph was taken). As you begin to think about your response, you might consider how the gender differences influence your story. Can the same scenarios in your mind make both the young woman and the young man cry? Or do you expect differences in the circumstances that have triggered this reaction?

VISITING THE WEB

The companion Website, **www.prenhall.com/miller**, contains additional information about narratives and about the writers and essays in this chapter. You will also find a number of hyperlinks to other sources of information about the subjects of the essays included in this chapter.

EXPLORING ON YOUR OWN

What is the nickname of your home state? Of your high school or college's mascot? Write a folktale that explains how that name came about. It can be a serious or a comic explanation and should be several paragraphs in length. You can use dialogue in your folktale if it seems appropriate.

Print sources might be helpful, as might the local historical society or your school's special collections in the library. Online, Google.com is a good starting place to search for examples of American folktales and the characteristics that they share as mini-narratives. Some specific starting places can be found on the Reader's Website at **www.prenhall.com/miller**.

LOOKING FOR WRITING SUGGESTIONS

Remember that your readers must find your experiences important, interesting, universal. Always test your topic by asking, Who would care? If you answer "my parents," you had better choose another subject.

DRAWING ON PERSONAL EXPERIENCES

1. A day in the life of; the first day of
2. A moment of terror (fear, heartbreak, joy, triumph, embarrassment)
3. Hardest (best, worst, stupidest) decision I ever made
4. My greatest regret
5. I will never forget when
6. I knew I was growing up (getting old) when

PLAYING REPORTER OR HISTORIAN

1. A local hero (villain); an act of heroism (a criminal act)
2. The events leading up to (coming after)
3. A local (campus) moment in history
4. You have to meet——to believe——
5. The stupidest (cleverest, kindest, most selfish) person I know
6. How——got its name

SALVATION

Langston Hughes

Born in Joplin, Missouri, Langston Hughes (1902—1967) was an important figure in the Harlem Renaissance. He is best known for his jazz- and blues-inspired poetry, though he was also a talented prose writer and playwright. Among his writings are Simple Speaks His Mind *(1950), the first of four volumes of some of his best-loved stories, and* Ask Your Mama: 12 Moods for Jazz *(1961), one of his later, angry collections of poetry fueled by emotions surrounding the civil rights movements.*

The Big Sea: An Autobiography (1940), published when Hughes was thirty-eight years old, is a memoir of his early years, consisting of a series of short narratives focusing on events and people. After the death of his grandmother, Hughes was raised by Auntie Reed, one of his grandmother's friends. Uncle Reed, Auntie's husband, was, as Hughes notes in The Big Sea, *"a sinner and never went to church as long as he lived . . . but both of them were very good and kind. . . . And no doubt from them I learned to like both Christians and sinners equally well."*

On Writing: *Hughes once noted that, to him, the prime function of creative writing is "to affirm life, to yeah-say the excitement of living in relation to the vast rhythms of the universe of which we are a part, to untie the riddles of the gutter in order to closer tie the knot between man and God."*

BEFORE READING

Connecting: Was there a time in your teenage years when you were disappointed by someone or something?

Anticipating: No narrative recounts every minute of an experience. Writers must leave out far more than they include. What events connected with this experience does Hughes leave out of his narrative? Why?

1   I was saved from sin when I was going on thirteen. But not really saved. It happened like this. There was a big revival at my Auntie Reed's church. Every night for weeks there had been much preaching, singing, praying, and shouting, and some very hardened sinners had been brought to Christ, and the membership of the church had grown by leaps and bounds. Then just before the revival ended, they held a special meeting for children, "to bring the young lambs to the fold." My aunt spoke of it for days ahead. That night I was escorted to the front row and placed on the mourners' bench with all the other young sinners, who had not yet been brought to Jesus.

2   My aunt told me that when you were saved you saw a light, and something happened to you inside! And Jesus came into your life! And God was with you from then on! She said you could see and hear and feel Jesus in your soul. I believed her. I had heard a great many old people say the same thing

and it seemed to me they ought to know. So I sat there calmly in the hot, crowded church, waiting for Jesus to come to me.

The preacher preached a wonderful rhythmical sermon, all moans and 3 shouts and lonely cries and dire pictures of hell, and then he sang a song about the ninety and nine safe in the fold, but one little lamb was left out in the cold. Then he said: "Won't you come? Won't you come to Jesus? Young lambs, won't you come?" And he held out his arms to all us young sinners there on the mourners' bench. And the little girls cried. And some of them jumped up and went to Jesus right away. But most of us just sat there.

A great many old people came and knelt around us and prayed, old 4 women with jet-black faces and braided hair, old men with work-gnarled hands. And the church sang a song about the lower lights are burning, some poor sinners to be saved. And the whole building rocked with prayer and song.

Still I kept waiting to *see* Jesus. 5

Finally all the young people had gone to the altar and were saved, but 6 one boy and me. He was a rounder's son named Westley. Westley and I were surrounded by sisters and deacons praying. It was very hot in the church, and getting late now. Finally Westley said to me in a whisper: "God damn! I'm tired o' sitting here. Let's get up and be saved." So he got up and was saved.

Then I was left all alone on the mourner's bench. My aunt came and 7 knelt at my knees and cried, while prayers and song swirled all around me in the little church. The whole congregation prayed for me alone, in a mighty wail of moans and voices. And I kept waiting serenely for Jesus, waiting, waiting— but he didn't come. I wanted to see him, but nothing happened to me. Nothing! I wanted something to happen to me, but nothing happened.

I heard the songs and the minister saying: "Why don't you come? My 8 dear child, why don't you come to Jesus? Jesus is waiting for you. He wants you. Why don't you come? Sister Reed, what is this child's name?"

"Langston," my aunt sobbed. 9

"Langston, why don't you come? Why don't you come and be saved? 10 Oh, Lamb of God! Why don't you come?"

Now it was really getting late. I began to be ashamed of myself, holding 11 everything up so long. I began to wonder what God thought about Westley, who certainly hadn't seen Jesus either, but who was now sitting proudly on the platform, swinging his knickerbockered legs and grinning down at me, surrounded by deacons and old women on their knees praying. God had not struck Westley dead for taking his name in vain or for lying in the temple. So I decided that maybe to save further trouble, I'd better lie, too, and say that Jesus had come, and get up and be saved.

So I got up. 12

Suddenly the whole room broke into a sea of shouting, as they saw me rise. 13 Waves of rejoicing swept the place. Women leaped in the air. My aunt threw her arms around me. The minister took me by the hand and led me to the platform.

When things quieted down, in a hushed silence, punctuated by a few ec- 14 static "Amens," all the new young lambs were blessed in the name of God. Then joyous singing filled the room.

15   That night, for the last time in my life but one—for I was a big boy twelve years old—I cried. I cried, in bed alone, and couldn't stop. I buried my head under the quilts, but my aunt heard me. She woke up and told my uncle I was crying because the Holy Ghost had come into my life, and because I had seen Jesus. But I was really crying because I couldn't bear to tell her that I had lied, that I had deceived everybody in the church, that I hadn't seen Jesus, and that now I didn't believe there was a Jesus any more, since he didn't come to help me.

QUESTIONS ON SUBJECT AND PURPOSE

1. Who narrates the story? From what point in time is it told?
2. What does the narrator expect to happen when he is to be saved? What does happen?
3. Why does the narrator cry at the end of the story?
4. What was Hughes's attitude toward his experience when it first happened? At the time he originally wrote this selection? How does the opening sentence reflect that change in attitude?

QUESTIONS ON STRATEGY AND AUDIENCE

1. Why did Hughes not tell the story in the present tense? How would doing so change the story?
2. How much dialogue is used in the narration? Why does Hughes not use more?
3. Why does Hughes blend telling with showing in the story?
4. How much time is represented by the events in the story? Where does Hughes compress the time in his narrative? Why does he do so?

QUESTIONS ON VOCABULARY AND STYLE

1. What is the effect of the short paragraphs (5, 9, and 12)? How does Hughes use paragraphing to help shape his story?
2. How much description does Hughes include in his narrative? What types of details does he single out?
3. What is the effect of the exclamation marks used in paragraph 2?
4. Try to identify or explain the following phrases: *the ninety and nine safe in the fold* (paragraph 3), *the lower lights are burning* (4), *a rounder's son* (6), *knickerbockered legs* (11).

WRITING SUGGESTIONS

1. **For Your Journal.** What can you remember from your early teenage years? In your journal, first make a list of significant moments—both high and low points—and then re-create one moment in prose.

2. **For a Paragraph.** We have all been disappointed by someone or something in our life. Single out a particular moment from your past. After spending some time remembering what happened and how you felt, narrate that experience for a general reader in a paragraph. Remember that your paragraph must reveal what the experience meant to you. Try using some dialogue.

3. **For an Essay.** Have you ever experienced anything that changed your life? It does not need to be a dramatic change—perhaps just a conviction that you will never do that again or that you will *always* be sure to do that again. In an essay, narrate for a reader that experience. Remember that your narrative should illustrate or prove the experience's significance to you.

4. **For Research.** Does Hughes seem to be serious about his experience—did he "lose" his faith as a result of what happened? Find other examples of Hughes's writing (check your college's library catalog for books by Hughes and perhaps also some of the on-line databases). Then, in an essay, analyze the significance (or insignificance) of this event in Hughes's writing. Be sure to formulate an explicit thesis about the importance of the event in Hughes's work. Be sure to document any direct quotations or information taken from other sources.

FOR FURTHER STUDY

Focusing on Grammar and Writing. First, be sure that you can identify adjectives and adverbs (see glossary). Then go through Hughes's narrative and make a list of all the adjectives and adverbs that you can find. Are there as many as you expected? Sometimes we assume that vividness in writing comes from using many adjectives and adverbs. Is that true here? What parts of speech make Hughes's narrative vivid? What does that suggest about writing narration and description?

Working Together. Divide into small groups. The focus of your collaboration is on how Hughes creates tension in his narrative. What devices does he use to keep the reader in suspense, wondering what the outcome can possibly be? How does the ending fit with the tension that Hughes has generated throughout the narrative? Once your group has finished its analysis, choose someone to report to the class as a whole.

Seeing Other Modes at Work. Hughes uses description to create a vivid sense of the place in which the experience occurs.

Finding Connections. For a similar handling of point of view, try Maya Angelou's "Sister Monroe" also in this chapter. Joan Didion's "On Keeping a Notebook" (Chapter 10) is also relevant in a discussion of writing and memory.

Exploring the Web. Do you think that the episode Hughes narrates in the essay actually happened? Do you think it really did become a memory he never forgot? Use the Web to check out the biographical background for the essay. Some starting points can be found at **www.prenhall.com/miller**.

SISTER MONROE

Maya Angelou

Maya Angelou was born Marguerita Johnson in St. Louis, Missouri, in 1928. A talented performing artist as well as a poet and autobiographer, Angelou has used much of her writing to explore the American black female identity. Her most significant writings have been her six volumes of autobiography (1970–2002).

The following selection is from the first of Angelou's memoirs, I Know Why the Caged Bird Sings *(1970), a work that describes her early years in Stamps, Arkansas. One critic called that work a "revealing portrait of the customs and harsh circumstances of black life in the segregated South." Here in a brilliantly comic moment, Angelou recalls how Sister Monroe "got the spirit" one Sunday morning at church.*

On Writing: *In an interview about her goals as a writer, Angelou observed: "When I'm writing, I am trying to find out who I am, who we are, what we're capable of, how we feel, how we lose and stand up. . . . But I'm also trying for the language. I'm trying to see how it can really sound. I really love language. I love it for what it does for us, how it allows us to explain the pain and the glory, the nuances and delicacies of our existence. And then it allows us to laugh. . . . We need language."*

BEFORE READING

Connecting: As a spectator, when do you find a physical mishap, such as a fight or fall, comic? What is necessary for us to laugh at "slapstick comedy" and not be concerned about the welfare of the people involved?

Anticipating: How does Angelou create humor in this narrative? What makes it funny?

In the Christian Methodist Episcopal Church the children's section was on the right, cater-cornered from the pew that held those ominous women called the Mothers of the Church. In the young people's section the benches were placed close together, and when a child's legs no longer comfortably fitted in the narrow space, it was an indication to the elders that that person could now move into the intermediate area (center church). Bailey and I were allowed to sit with the other children only when there were informal meetings, church socials or the like. But on the Sundays when Reverend Thomas preached, it was ordained that we occupy the first row, called the mourners' bench. I thought we were placed in front because Momma was proud of us, but Bailey assured me that she just wanted to keep her grandchildren under her thumb and eye.

Reverend Thomas took his text from Deuteronomy. And I was stretched between loathing his voice and wanting to listen to the sermon. Deuteronomy was my favorite book in the Bible. The laws were so absolute, so clearly set down, that I knew if a person truly wanted to avoid hell and brimstone, and being roasted forever in the devil's fire, all she had to do was memorize Deuteronomy and follow its teaching, word for word. I also liked the way the word rolled off the tongue.

3   Bailey and I sat alone on the front bench, the wooden slats pressing hard on our behinds and the backs of our thighs. I would have wriggled just a bit, but each time I looked over at Momma, she seemed to threaten, "Move and I'll tear you up," so, obedient to the unvoiced command, I sat still. The church ladies were warming up behind me with a few hallelujahs and praise the Lords and Amens, and the preacher hadn't really moved into the meat of the sermon.

4   It was going to be a hot service.

5   On my way into church, I saw Sister Monroe, her open-faced gold crown glinting when she opened her mouth to return a neighborly greeting. She lived in the country and couldn't get to church every Sunday, so she made up for her absences by shouting so hard when she did make it that she shook the whole church. As soon as she took her seat, all the ushers would move to her side of the church because it took three women and sometimes a man or two to hold her.

6   Once she hadn't been to church for a few months (she had taken off to have a child), she got the spirit and started shouting, throwing her arms around and jerking her body, so that the ushers went over to hold her down, but she tore herself away from them and ran up to the pulpit. She stood in front of the altar, shaking like a freshly caught trout. She screamed at Reverend Taylor. "Preach it. I say, preach it." Naturally he kept on preaching as if she wasn't standing there telling him what to do. Then she screamed an extremely fierce "I said, preach it" and stepped up on the altar. The Reverend kept on throwing out phrases like home-run balls and Sister Monroe made a quick break and grasped for him. For just a second, everything and everyone in the church except Reverend Taylor and Sister Monroe hung loose like stockings on a washline. Then she caught the minister by the sleeve of his jacket and his coattail, then she rocked him from side to side.

7   I have to say this for our minister, he never stopped giving us the lesson. The usher board made its way to the pulpit, going up both aisles with a little more haste than is customarily seen in church. Truth to tell, they fairly ran to the minister's aid. Then two of the deacons, in their shiny Sunday suits, joined the ladies in white on the pulpit, and each time they pried Sister Monroe loose from the preacher he took another deep breath and kept on preaching, and Sister Monroe grabbed him in another place, and more firmly. Reverend Taylor was helping his rescuers as much as possible by jumping around when he got a chance. His voice at one point got so low it sounded like a roll of thunder, then Sister Monroe's "Preach it" cut through the roar, and we all wondered (I did, in any case) if it would ever end. Would they go on forever, or get tired out at last like a game of blindman's bluff that lasted too long, with nobody caring who was "it"?

I'll never know what might have happened, because magically the pan- 8
demonium spread. The spirit infused Deacon Jackson and Sister Willson, the
chairman of the usher board, at the same time. Deacon Jackson, a tall, thin,
quiet man, who was also a part-time Sunday school teacher, gave a scream like
a falling tree, leaned back on thin air and punched Reverend Taylor on the arm.
It must have hurt as much as it caught the Reverend unawares. There was a
moment's break in the rolling sounds and Reverend Taylor jerked around surprised, and hauled off and punched Deacon Jackson. In the same second Sister
Willson caught his tie, looped it over her fist a few times, and pressed down on
him. There wasn't time to laugh or cry before all three of them were down on
the floor behind the altar. Their legs spiked out like kindling wood.

Sister Monroe, who had been the cause of all the excitement, walked off 9
the dais, cool and spent, and raised her flinty voice in the hymn, "I came to Jesus, as I was, worried, wounded, and sad, I found in Him a resting place and
He has made me glad."

The minister took advantage of already being on the floor and asked in 10
a choky little voice if the church would kneel with him to offer a prayer of
thanksgiving. He said we had been visited with a mighty spirit, and let the
whole church say Amen.

On the next Sunday, he took his text from the eighteenth chapter of the 11
Gospel according to St. Luke, and talked quietly but seriously about the Phar-
isees, who prayed in the streets so that the public would be impressed with
their religious devotion. I doubt that anyone got the message—certainly not
those to whom it was directed. The deacon board, however, did appropriate
funds for him to buy a new suit. The other was a total loss.

QUESTIONS ON SUBJECT AND PURPOSE

1. Who is the narrator? How old does she seem to be? How do you know?
2. Why does Sister Monroe behave as she does?
3. How does the section on the narrator and Bailey act as a preface to the
   story of Sister Monroe? Is it relevant, for example, that the narrator's
   favorite book of the Bible is Deuteronomy?

QUESTIONS ON STRATEGY AND AUDIENCE

1. Part of the art of narration is knowing what events to select. Look
   carefully at Angelou's story of Sister Monroe (paragraphs 5–9). What
   events does she choose to include in her narrative?
2. How is Sister Monroe described? Make a list of all of the physical
   particulars we are given about her. How, other than direct description,
   is Sister Monroe revealed to the reader?
3. What shift occurs between paragraphs 5 and 6? Did you notice it the
   first time you read the selection?

QUESTIONS ON VOCABULARY AND STYLE

1. Other than a few words uttered by Sister Monroe, Angelou uses no other dialogue in the selection. How, then, is the story told? What advantage does this method have?

2. Writing humor is never easy. Having a funny situation is essential, but in addition, the story must be told in the right way. (Remember how people can ruin a good joke?) How does Angelou's language and style contribute to the humor in the selection?

3. How effective are the following images:
   a. "She stood in front of the altar, shaking like a freshly caught trout" (paragraph 6).
   b. "The Reverend kept on throwing out phrases like home-run balls" (6).
   c. "Everyone in the church . . . hung loose like stockings on a washline" (6).
   d. "Their legs spiked out like kindling wood" (8).

WRITING SUGGESTIONS

1. **For Your Journal.** Observe people for a day. In your journal, make a list of the funny or comic moments that you notice. Select one of those moments and first describe the situation you witnessed, then analyze why it seemed funny to you.

2. **For a Paragraph.** Everyone has experienced a funny, embarrassing moment—maybe it happened to you or maybe you just witnessed it. In a paragraph, narrate that incident for your reader. Remember to keep the narrative focused.

3. **For an Essay.** Select a "first" from your experience—your first day in junior high school, your first date, your first time driving a car, your first day on a job or at college. Re-create that first for your reader. Remember to shape your narrative, and select only important contributing details. Focus your narrative around a significant aspect of that first experience, whether it was funny or serious.

4. **For Research.** What is an autobiography? Is it always a factual account of events in the writer's life? Is it ever "made up" or fictional? Is it ever propagandistic? What purposes do autobiographies have? Select an autobiography written by someone who interests you—check your college's library catalog for possibilities. Then analyze that work as an autobiography. Do not summarize. Instead, formulate a thesis about what you see as the writer's sense of purpose in the book. Support your argument with evidence from the text, and be sure to document your quotations.

FOR FURTHER STUDY

Focusing on Grammar and Writing. First, be sure that you can identify figurative language, especially simile and metaphor (see glossary). Then go through Angelou's narrative and make a list of all the similes and metaphors you can find. What effect do these devices have on the narrative? Why does she use them? Have you tried creating similes and metaphors in your own narrative writing? What cautions should you be aware of when you use these devices?

Working Together. Working in small groups, look closely at how Angelou manipulates time in the narrative. Does the story take place on one day? If there are time shifts, where do they come and how does Angelou make sure that readers are not confused? Once your group has finished work, choose someone to report your findings to the class as a whole.

Seeing Other Modes at Work. Angelou is equally skillful in her use of description to create a sense of both place and character.

Finding Connections. For a good comparison of both context and narrative technique, read Langston Hughes's "Salvation," also in this chapter. For some insights on memory and autobiographical narrative, try Joan Didion's "On Keeping a Notebook" (Chapter 10).

Exploring the Web. The Web has many sites with extensive information about Maya Angelou, including interviews and even audio and video clips. You can find some suggested sites by visiting **www.prenhall.com/miller**.

FACING FAMINE

Tom Haines

Tom Haines grew up in the suburbs of Pittsburgh, Pennsylvania, and worked as a computer programmer in a bank after college. He took three months off to travel and never returned to his old job. He went to Berkeley for a journalism degree and spent the next ten years as a news reporter. After a period as a freelance writer, he accepted his current position as staff travel writer at the Boston Globe. *Haines has accumulated a number of awards for his travel writing, including Travel Journalist of the Year by the Society of Travel Writers. "Facing Famine" originally appeared in the* Boston Globe *in 2003.*

On Writing: *Commenting on the role of the writer as a narrator in an essay such as this, Haines remarked: "If you have something to say compelling about yourself, fine, but it better be pretty compelling. . . . I think that the standard has to be pretty high when you introduce yourself into the story—not necessarily if you're doing this as a part of the narrative, such as 'I went there . . . ; we went there . . .' in order to move the plot along, but more if you are making a point about your perceptions."*

BEFORE READING

Connecting: American media regularly carry stories about famine in Africa. Famine, of course, is something that Americans have never experienced. Does Haines's essay make the famine "more real" to you as a reader than what you have seen or read elsewhere? If so, why? If not, why?

Anticipating: As you read, think about why Haines might be telling this story in this way. What might he want his readers to feel or to do after reading the essay? Can you find any evidence in the essay to support your conclusion?

1   BURTUKAN ABE braces against the hard mud wall as Osman, her two-year-old son, wails and wobbles on stick legs.

2   Are there others? I ask.

3   Yes, one, she says. A boy, one month old. He is inside.

4   There is no turning back. Through the low, narrow doorway, in the darkness that guards cool by day, heat by night, lies little Nurhusein.

5   May I see him?

6   This journey began weeks earlier, when yet another report described widespread drought and the threat of famine across much of Africa.

7   What can that life be like?

8   Travel often approaches boundaries of wealth and health. But what does it feel like to cross those boundaries and enter a place that is, everywhere, collapsing? What comes from knowing people who, with an empty grain basket or a thinning goat, edge closer to death?

The route led first to Addis Ababa, a highland capital, then east and 9
south, down into rolling stretches of the Great Rift Valley. In the tattered town
of Ogolcho, Berhanu Muse, a local irrigation specialist, agreed to serve as
translator and guide.

A narrow road of rock headed south, through one village, then another, 10
for one hour, then two.

In late afternoon, before evening wind lifted dirt from north to south, 11
east to west, we stopped and parked near a hilltop. A man and woman collected
grain from a tall stick bin on the corner of their rectangular plot of land.

Gebi Egato offered his hand from his perch inside the bin. Halima, his 12
wife, smiled warmly, then carried a half-filled sack toward the family's low,
round hut. Abdo, a three-year-old with determined eyes, barreled out the door.

I asked if we could stay. 13

"Welcome," Gebi said. 14

For four nights, a photographer and I would sleep here, beneath open 15
sky, then wake to wander this village of one thousand people. We would step
into a schoolhouse, a clinic, and other thatch-roofed huts, including the one
that held Nurhusein.

But that first afternoon, the village came to us. They were mostly old, all 16
men, a group of perhaps two dozen. Many held walking sticks, one a long
spear. One man said he would like to show us something: a hole, not too far,
that used to hold water. The hole was shallow and wide, perhaps the size of a
Boston backyard. It was empty, nothing but hard earth.

The men calmly debated how many months it had been since water 17
filled the hole. Flies buzzed and jumped from eyelids to lips.

A young schoolteacher, a specialist in math and science, sat at my side, 18
his legs crossed, hands in his lap.

"Thirst is thirst, hunger is hunger," he said. 19

Hours later, I awoke to a setting moon and could imagine this land as it 20
long had been: Beneath my cot, wheat, barley, and teff shot from the ground.
Birds swarmed tree branches, trading throaty, bubbling calls. Water pooled in
ditches and holes. Thick green hedges framed the farmyard.

Gebi would describe to me what this can feel like. The land offers so 21
much bounty, so much comfort, he said, that even when the sun is high and
hot, you want to lie down on the earth, close your eyes, and sleep.

In the hut's outer room there is a low wooden bench, but little else. The 22
food, furniture, even a grandmother and three uncles have gone.

Now five people remain: Burtukan, the mother, age nineteen; Ab- 23
durkedir Beriso, her husband, twenty-seven; Abduraman Beriso, his brother,
sixteen. And the children, Osman and Nurhusein.

They have no animals, no money. Neighbors share hard bread and flour. 24

"I have nowhere to go," Abdurkedir told me. "I will die here." 25

From behind a curtain, in the hut's back room, I hear the rustle of blankets, 26
a whimper, a soothing voice: sounds of a mother gathering a baby in her arms.

***

27   On our first morning, as nighttime hilltop sounds—a howling hyena, a barking dog, a farting donkey—gave way to those of dawn, we were outsiders, in the cool air, listening.

28   Beneath Gebi and Halima's thatch roof, Abdo squealed and pouted. Bontu, barely a year old, cried for breakfast.

29   Soon, with the fire made, the children fed, Halima strapped plastic canisters on the back of the family donkey and began to walk. Gebi followed with the ox.

30   Halima sauntered gracefully, as though out for a stroll. She crossed a parched soccer field to a footpath lined with huts. She greeted a woman walking toward her. They held hands and talked.

31   Farther along, in an empty cradle of land set back from the trail, a stack of branches and twigs covered a hole roughly twelve inches in diameter. Three times, the government had tried to dig a well in this village, which sits far from any river. The last time, a powerful machine made the narrow hole and bore in search of water. Villagers gathered and watched as earth spit upward. Then the drill bit broke, 820 feet underground. It was there still.

32   Halima walked on for more than an hour, then stopped in a spot of shade. She untied the canisters and knelt by a wide pond of muddy water. The pond teemed with salmonella, the root of typhoid fever, and parasites that thrive in intestines, infecting 70 percent of Adere Lepho's children.

33   Another young woman leaned at the pond's edge and filled every last ounce of space in her canister. She stuffed the spout with a plug of withered grass.

34   Hundreds of people came each day to this pond, the only water source for Adere Lepho and two neighboring villages, and carted home water to quench the thirst of thousands.

35   A month earlier, this pond, too, had been nearly empty. Then two days of heavy February rain filled it. How long would it last? Even village elders, men and women forty, forty-five, and fifty years old, had never seen this kind of drought.

36   Two years earlier, and two years before that, meager rains had fallen. Families had to sell animals, eat thinner harvests, and spend precious savings just to survive. But this was worse: the February downpour was the first time it had rained in nearly a year.

37   Late the next afternoon, rain fell. As the drops landed thick and heavy, men, women, and children took shelter in the low, open building that houses the village's grain mill. After three, maybe four minutes, the rain stopped.

38   Women heaved sacks of grain, some of them holding well-rationed harvests from years past, others gifts from farmland half a world away, onto a scale. Across the room, the mill owner sat alongside a conveyor belt spun by a howling generator, the only power in the village. The owner opened sacks into the mouth of a grinder that turned kernel to flour. Dust filled the air, sticking to hair and eyelashes.

39   Outside, dozens of men gathered beneath the branches of a wide tree.

40   Gebi Tola, elected leader of a local farmers' group, explained that the government had offered land for ten volunteers to move to another region.

The government owns all land in Ethiopia. This resettlement program provided a rare chance.

The men, sitting on the ground in orderly rows, faced Tola. He explained that some plots of land were north, in a neighboring district. Most would be farther, three hundred miles to the west. 41

Voices rose. How can we know this land is good? one man asked. How can we trust that life will be better there? 42

Kedir Husein, a young father who had stood to ask many questions, stepped away from the group. He told me he had decided not to volunteer to leave. 43

"I am afraid," he said. 44

Nurhusein emerges, his head resting in the crook of his mother's left elbow. 45

A soft cotton blanket opens to shocks of slick, curly hair. Tiny fingers spread in the air. I touch Nurhusein's forehead, cool and smooth. 46

"He is beautiful," I say. 47

Nurhusein bleats softly. His lips often latch on to a dry breast. He has a small stomachache, Burtukan tells me. 48

The bleating rises then falls, just beyond the blanket's edge. 49

Nurhusein is already too wise. It is as if he knows. 50

Morning inside Gebi Egato's hut. Glowing coals. Boisterous children. Hearty porridge. A calf, head low, softly chewed its cud. 51

Shilla, the oldest at five, licked her fingers and pondered her favorite foods as Abdo crammed both hands full of porridge. 52

"Milk," she said. She raised her head and smiled. "And sugar." 53

Finished, Shilla and Abdo scrambled to waiting friends. Gebi and Halima took turns digging a wooden scoop deep into a jug decorated with shells. 54

Each bite brought more peril. 55

Gebi's tired cow and thirsty goats were giving little milk. The porridge was made from wheat that had been meant as seed for planting if the spring rains came. Neighbors with less were already selling cows and goats, driving prices down. 56

As the coals darkened, I asked how long the family could last. 57

Gebi told me that in two weeks the family's wheat would be gone. He would then sell his goats, then the cow. Then the ox and, finally, the donkey. He paused. 58

"Five months," he said. 59

Gebi, like most villagers a Muslim, said he was confident rain would come. Then he could partner his ox with that of a neighbor and together they could churn the dark, moist earth. 60

"We have seen so much hardship already, God will not add more," Gebi said. "I hope." 61

After breakfast, Gebi took the donkey and walked beneath the high sun for three hours. He crested three low ridges and crossed three shallow valleys. The first was carpeted in six inches of dust. The second traced the steep gorge 62 of a dry creek. The third, staggered with acacia trees, opened widely toward the village of Cheffe Jilla.

63   A group of men, women, children, and donkeys swayed in the village's main square. White sacks of grain sat in lopsided piles. Gebi joined the hopeful and registered his name in a government office.

64   I saw Gebi Tola, the leader of Adere Lepho's farmers' association, standing beneath a tree. He told me families from his village would take home five hundred sacks of grain. But they could use a thousand. How do you judge the needy when a whole village is staggering?

65   He spoke quickly. A crowd of dozens, young, old, pressed in around us.

66   I asked Gebi how he felt.

67   "I feel sorry," he said.

68   I had grown used to stoicism. But sorry? I stepped aside with Berhanu, our translator. "Sorry" does not feel like the right word, I said.

69   In English, I explained, "sorry" often has a light sense. Sorry I stepped on your toe. Sorry I'm late for dinner. It is not something felt by someone watching his friends and neighbors beginning to starve.

70   Berhanu is a compassionate, intimate man. He raised his hand to his chin.

71   He told me that, in that case, "sorry" was not the word he meant.

72   The crowd moved in again and curious eyes followed our exchange.

73   I asked Berhanu to choose another English word that more closely matched the Oromigna word Tola had used.

74   He could not find an exact translation. I asked him to describe the feeling.

75   "Well," Berhanu said, "it is the feeling you have when something bad happens. Say, for example, when you lose your lovely brother. Is there a word in English for that?"

76   Misery?

77   Yes, Berhanu said calmly, that is part of it.

78   Emptiness? Yes, he said, that too.

79   Anguish, despair?

80   His eyes sparked at the connection.

81   Anger? Yes.

82   Frustration? Yes.

83   Fear? No.

84   Fear, Berhanu said, like sorry, was too light a word.

85   Terror?

86   Yes, Berhanu said, "terror" is a good word.

87   I stand before Nurhusein and start to cry.

88   Is it empathy? I have a ten-month-old son, a spirited boy with muscles across his back and a quick laugh.

89   Or am I crying from fear?

90   In the hot sun, looking from hut to hut, from face to face, the problem was always too vast.

91   I stare at Nurhusein. I cannot look again into his mother's eyes.

QUESTIONS ON SUBJECT AND PURPOSE

1. Haines is a travel writer and the story appeared in the travel section of a newspaper. Is this the type of essay that you would expect to find in this section of a newspaper? Why or why not?
2. Where is this story taking place? In what part of the world?
3. Based on your reading experience, what purpose might Haines have had in writing the essay?

QUESTIONS ON STRATEGY AND AUDIENCE

1. Look carefully at the essay. In five places in the essay, Haines uses extra white space to mark divisions within the text. Locate those places.
2. Why is Haines so moved by the sight of the infant Nurhusein?
3. Who is Haines's audience? How does that audience influence the essay?

QUESTIONS ON VOCABULARY AND STYLE

1. How does its place of original publication (a newspaper) influence the paragraphing of the essay?
2. What is the effect of the passage in which Haines tries to find English words to describe the emotions that Gebi Tola felt (paragraphs 66–86)?
3. Be prepared to define the following words: *sauntered* (paragraph 30), *teemed* (32), *stoicism* (68), *empathy* (88).

WRITING SUGGESTIONS

1. **For Your Journal.** How do you react to the story that Haines narrates? Do you have any emotional reaction? Do you feel indifferent or that it is not your problem? Is the problem simply too large or too distant for you to worry about? Do you want to do something, but do not know what? In your journal, explore your reaction to Haines's essay.
2. **For a Paragraph.** Assume that you have been hired as a writer for an international agency that tries to find sponsors for children in need. Using the material from the essay, write a paragraph in which you attempt to get donors to support the infant Nurhusein.
3. **For an Essay.** A single narrative (story) can be extremely effective in helping people to understand a situation or in persuading people to do something about it. The single example makes it easier to empathize— it puts a human face on the situation that can never be achieved with

just facts and statistics. Pick a painful social issue—for example, poverty, homelessness, chronic illness, disability, hate crimes, drug addiction, sexual abuse—and put a human face on the problem. You might want to interview a victim or create a fictional victim, then look for stories that victims have told, explore stories on the Web, and talk with professionals who counsel such victims. Using your research, construct a narrative in which you use this one story to create empathy and understanding in your readers.

4. **For Research.** What are things like in Ethiopia today? Is there still a famine? Has anything improved? Using print and online sources, gather information about living conditions there. You might want to use a mix of data—photographs, statistics, examples—to make your essay more vivid and informative.

FOR FURTHER STUDY

Focusing on Grammar and Writing. In the essay, Haines uses a number of sentence fragments. See how many you can locate. Check the glossary if you need a definition of a fragment. Why might Haines have used the fragments that he does? What effect is he trying to achieve? Would it make any difference if the fragments were rewritten as complete sentences?

Working Together. Haines's essay originally appeared in the narrow columns of a newspaper. That is why it contains so many paragraphs. How easily could the essay be re-paragraphed to reduce the total number of paragraphs? Divide into small groups. Each group should take one of the six sections of the essay and discuss how small, often one-sentence paragraphs might be combined into larger units. What changes, if any, would need to be made?

Seeing Other Modes at Work. The essay includes description, cause and effect, and even elements of definition (how a famine makes you feel) and persuasion.

Finding Connections. An interesting pairing would be Peter Singer's "The Singer Solution" (Chapter 10).

Exploring the Web. You can read other travel articles by Haines at the *Boston Globe* Website. You might also look for additional information about and maps of Ethiopia and the famine in parts of Africa. The CIA Fact Book has maps and background information that are helpful. Check **www.prenhall.com/miller** for some places at which to start your search.

MARINA

Judith Ortiz Cofer

Judith Ortiz Cofer was born in Puerto Rico in 1952. Her family settled in Patterson, New Jersey, in 1954, but frequently returned to the Island. She is currently a professor of English and creative writing at the University of Georgia. Her recent books include Woman in Front of the Sun: On Becoming a Writer *(2000). "Marina" is taken from Cofer's collection of her essays* Silent Dancing: A Partial Remembrance of a Puerto Rican Childhood *(1990).*

On Writing: *Cofer observes, "Much of my writing begins as a meditation on past events. But memory for me is the 'jumping off' point; I am not, in my poetry and fiction writing, a slave to memory. I like to believe that the poem or story contains the 'truth' of art rather than the factual, historical truth that the journalist, sociologist, scientist—most of the rest of the world—must adhere to."*

BEFORE READING

Connecting: How would you define the word *woman?* What does that word mean to you?

Anticipating: What does the story of Marina have to do with Cofer and her mother? Or is Cofer merely setting the scene in which the story of Marina is told?

Again it happened between my mother and me. Since her return to Puerto   1
Rico after my father's death ten years before, she had gone totally "native," regressing into the comfortable traditions of her extended family and questioning all of my decisions. Each year we spoke more formally to each other, and each June, at the end of my teaching year, she would invite me to visit her on the Island—so I could see for myself how much I was missing out on.

These yearly pilgrimages to my mother's town where I had been born   2
also, but which I had left at an early age, were for me symbolic of the clash of cultures and generations that she and I represent. But I looked forward to arriving at this lovely place, my mother's lifetime dream of home, now endangered by encroaching "progress."

Located on the west coast, our pueblo is a place of contrasts: the origi-   3
nal town remains as a tiny core of ancient houses circling the church, which sits on a hill, the very same where the woodcutter claimed to have been saved from a charging bull by a lovely dark Lady who appeared floating over a treetop. There my mother lives, at the foot of this hill; but surrounding this postcard scene there are shopping malls, a Burger King, a cinema. And where the sugar cane fields once extended like a green sea as far as the eye

could see: condominiums, cement blocks in rows, all the same shape and color. My mother tries not to see this part of her world. The church bells drown the noise of traffic, and when she sits on her back porch and looks up at the old church built by the hands of generations of men whose last names she would not recognize, she feels safe—under the shelter of the past.

4   During the twenty years she spent in "exile" in the U.S. often alone with two children, waiting for my father, she dedicated her time and energy to creating a "reasonable facsimile" of a Puerto Rican home, which for my brother and me meant that we led a dual existence: speaking Spanish at home with her, acting out our parts in her traditional play, while also daily pretending assimilation in the classroom, where in the early sixties, there was no such thing as bilingual education. But, to be fair, we were not the only Puerto Rican children leading a double life, and I have always been grateful to have kept my Spanish. My trouble with Mother comes when she and I try to define and translate key words for both of us, words such as "woman" and "mother." I have a daughter too, as well as a demanding profession as a teacher and writer. My mother got married as a teenager and led a life of isolation and total devotion to her duties as mother. As a Penelope-like wife, she was always waiting, waiting, waiting, for the return of her sailor, for the return to her native land.

5   In the meantime, I grew up in the social flux of the sixties in New Jersey, and although I was kept on a steady diet of fantasies about life in the tropics, I liberated myself from her plans for me, got a scholarship to college, married a man who supported my need to work, to create, to travel and to experience life as an individual. My mother rejoices at my successes, but is often anxious at how much time I have to spend away from home, although I keep assuring her that my husband is as good a parent as I am, and a much better cook. Her concern about my familial duties is sometimes a source of friction in our relationship, the basis for most of our arguments. But, in spite of our differences, I miss her, and as June approaches, I yearn to be with her in her tiny house filled with her vibrant presence. So I pack up and go to meet my loving adversary in her corner of the rapidly disappearing "paradise" that she waited so long to go home to.

6   It was after a heated argument one afternoon that I sought reconciliation with my mother by asking her to go with me for a walk down the main street of the pueblo. I planned to request stories about the town and its old people, something that we both enjoy for different reasons: she likes recalling the old days, and I have an insatiable curiosity about the history and the people of the Island which have become prominent features in my work.

7   We had been walking around the church when we saw a distinguished looking old man strolling hand-in-hand with a little girl. My mother touched my arm and pointed to them. I admired the pair as the old man, svelte and graceful as a ballet dancer, lifted the tiny figure dressed up in pink lace onto a stool at an outdoor cafe.

8   "Who is he?" I asked my mother, trying not to stare as we pretended to examine the menu taped on the window.

9   "You have heard his story at your grandmother's house."

She took my elbow and led me to a table at the far end of the cafe. "I will 10 tell it to you again, but first I will give you a hint about who he is: he has not always been the man he is today."

Though her "hint" was no help, I suddenly recalled the story I had heard 11 many years earlier as told by my grandmother, who had started the tale with similar words, "People are not always what they seem to be, that is something we have all heard, but have you heard about the one who ended up being what he was but did not appear to be?" Or something like that. Mamá could turn any story—it did not have to be as strange and fascinating as this one—into an event. I told my guess to my mother.

"Yes," she nodded, "he came home to retire. You know he has lived in 12 Nueva York since before you were born. Do you remember the story?"

As we continued our walk, my mother recounted for me her mother's 13 dramatic tale of a famous incident that had shaken the town in Mamá's youth. I had heard it once as a child, sitting enthralled at my grandmother's knee.

In the days when Mamá was a young girl, our pueblo had not yet been 14 touched by progress. The cult of the Black Virgin had grown strong as pilgrims traveled from all over the island to visit the shrine, and the Church preached chastity and modesty as the prime virtues for the town's daughters. Adolescent girls were not allowed to go anywhere without their mothers or *dueñas*—except to a certain river that no man was allowed to approach.

Río Rojo, the river that ran its course around the sacred mountain where 15 the Virgin had appeared, was reserved for the maidens of the pueblo. It was nothing but a stream, really, but crystalline, and it was bordered by thick woods where the most fragrant flowers and herbs could be found. This was a female place, a pastoral setting where no true *macho* would want to be caught swimming or fishing.

Nature had decorated the spot like a boudoir—royal poincianas ex- 16 tended their low branches for the girls to hang their clothes, and the mossy grass grew like a plush green carpet all the way down to the smooth stepping-stones where they could sun themselves like *favoritas* in a virginal harem.

As a "grown" girl of fifteen, Mamá had led her sisters and other girls of 17 the pueblo to bathe there on hot summer afternoons. It was a place of secret talk and rowdy play, of freedom from mothers and chaperones, a place where they could talk about boys, and where they could luxuriate in their bodies. At the río, the young women felt free to hypothesize about the secret connection between their two concerns: their changing bodies and boys.

Sex was the forbidden topic in their lives, yet these were the same girls 18 who would be given to strangers in marriage before they were scarcely out of childhood. In a sense, they were betrayed by their own protective parents who could bring themselves to explain neither the delights, nor the consequences of sex to their beloved daughters. The prevailing practice was to get them safely married as soon after puberty as possible—because nature would take its course one way or another. Scandal was to be avoided at all costs.

At the río, the group of girls Mamá grew up with would squeal and splash 19 away their last few precious days as children. They would also wash each other's hair while sitting like brown nyads upon the smooth rocks in the shallow water. They had the freedom to bathe nude, but some of them could not break through a lifetime of training in modesty and would keep their chemises and bloomers on. One of the shyest girls was Marina. She was everyone's pet.

20   Marina was a lovely young girl with her *café-con-leche* skin and green eyes. Her body was willowy and her thick black Indian hair hung down to her waist. Her voice was so soft that you had to come very close to hear what she was saying during the rare times when she did speak. Everyone treated Marina with special consideration, since she had already known much tragedy by the time she reached adolescence. It was due to the traumatic circumstances of her birth, as well as her difficult life with a reclusive mother, all the girls believed, that Marina was so withdrawn and melancholy as she ended her fifteenth year. She was surely destined for convent life, they all whispered when Marina left their company, as she often did, to go sit by herself on the bank, and to watch them with her large, wet, melancholy eyes.

21   Marina had fine hands and all the girls liked for her to braid their hair at the end of the day. They argued over the privilege of sitting between her legs while Marina ran her long fingers through their hair like a cellist playing a soothing melody. It caused much jealousy that last summer before Mamá's betrothal (which meant it was the last summer she could play at the río with her friends) when Marina chose to keep company only with Kiki, the mayor's fourteen year old daughter who had finally won permission from her strict parents to bathe with the pueblo's girls at the river.

22   Kiki would be a pale fish among the golden tadpoles in the water. She came from a Spanish family who believed in keeping the bloodlines pure, and she had spent all of her childhood in the cool shade of mansions and convent schools. She had come to the pueblo to prepare for her debut into society, her *quinceañera*, a fifteenth birthday party where she would be dressed like a princess and displayed before the Island's eligible bachelors as a potential bride.

23   Lonely for the company of girls her age, and tired of the modulated tones of afternoons on the verandah with her refined mother, Kiki had pressured her father to give her a final holiday with the other girls, whom she would see going by the mansion, singing and laughing on their way to the río. Her father began to see the wisdom of her idea when she mentioned how democratic it would seem to the girls' parents for the mayor's daughter to join them at the river. Finally, he agreed. The mother took to her bed with a sick headache when she thought of her lovely daughter removing her clothes in front of the uncouth spawn of her husband's constituents: rough farmers and their sun-darkened wives.

24   Kiki removed all her clothes with glee as soon as the group arrived at the river. She ran to the water tossing lace, satin, and silk over her head. She behaved like a bird whose cage door had been opened for the first time. The girls giggled at the sight of the freckles on her shoulders, her little pink nipples, like rosebuds, her golden hair. But since she was the mayor's daughter, they dared not get too close. They acted more like her attendants than her friends. Kiki would have ended up alone again if it had not been for Marina.

Marina was awestruck by the exuberant Kiki; and Kiki was drawn to the   25
quiet girl who watched the others at play with such yearning. Soon the two
girls were inseparable. Marina would take Kiki's wet hair, like molten gold,
into her brown hands and weave it into two perfect plaits which she would pin
to the girl's head like a crown. It was fascinating to watch how the two came
together wordlessly, like partners in a *pas de deux*.

It was an idyllic time, until one afternoon Marina and Kiki did not return   26
to the river from an excursion into the woods where they had ostensibly gone
to gather flowers. Mamá and her friends searched for them until nearly dark,
but did not find them. The mayor went in person to notify Marina's mother of
the situation. What he found was a woman who had fallen permanently into
silence: secluded in a secret place of shadows where she wished to remain.

It was the events of one night long ago that had made her abandon the   27
world.

Marina's mother had lost her young husband and delivered her child   28
prematurely on the same night. The news that her man had been drowned in
a fishing accident had brought on an agonizing labor. She had had a son, a tiny
little boy, perfect in his parts, but sickly. The new mother, weakened in body
and mind by so much pain, had decided that she preferred a daughter for company. Hysterically, she had begged the anxious midwife to keep her secret. And
as soon as she was able to walk to church, she had the child dressed in a flowing gown of lace and had her christened Marina. Living the life a recluse, to
which she was entitled as a widow, and attended by her loyal nurse, and later,
by her quiet obedient Marina, the woman had slipped easily out of reality.

By the time Marina was old enough to discover the difference between   29
her body and the bodies of her girlfriends, her mother had forgotten all about
having borne a son. In fact, the poor soul would have been horrified to discover a man under her roof. And so Marina kept up appearances, waiting out
her body's dictates year by year. The summer that Kiki joined the bathers at
the río, Marina had made up her mind to run away from home. She had been
in torment until the blonde girl had appeared like an angel, bringing Marina
the balm of her presence and the soothing touch of her hands.

The mayor found the woman sitting calmly in a rocking chair. She looked   30
like a wax figure dressed in widow's weeds. Only her elegant hands moved as
she crocheted a collar for a little girl's dress. And although she smiled deferen-
tially at the men speaking loudly in her parlor, she remained silent. Silence was
the place she had inhabited for years, and no one could draw her out now.

Furious, the mayor threatened to have her arrested. Finally it was the old   31
nurse who confessed the whole sad tale—to the horror of the mayor and his
men. She handed him an envelope with *Papá y Mamá* written on its face in
Kiki's hand. In a last show of control, the mayor took the sealed letter home to
read in the privacy of the family mansion where his wife was waiting, still under the impression that the two girls had been kidnapped for political reasons.

Kiki's letter explained briefly that she and *Marino* had eloped. They had   32
fallen in love and nothing and no one could change their minds about getting
married. She had sold her pearl necklace—the family heirloom given to her by

33   her parents to wear at her quinceañera, and they were using the money for passage on the next steamship out of San Juan to New York.

34   The mayor did not finish his term in office. He and his wife, now a recluse, exiled themselves to Spain.

35   "And Marina and Kiki?" I had asked Mamá, eager for more details about Kiki and Marino. "What happened to them?"

36   "What happens to *any* married couple?" Mamá had replied, putting an end to her story. "They had several children, they worked, they got old . . ." She chuckled gently at my naiveté.

37   On our way back through town from our walk, Mother and I again saw Marino with his pretty granddaughter. This time he was lifting her to smell a white rose that grew from a vine entangled on a tree branch. The child brought the flower carefully to her nose and smelled it. Then the old man placed the child gently back on the ground and they continued their promenade, stopping to examine anything that caught the child's eye.

38   "Do you think he made a good husband?" I asked my mother.

39   "He would know what it takes to make a woman happy," she said as she turned to face me, and winked in camaraderie.

40   As I watched the gentle old man and the little girl, I imagined Marina sitting alone on the banks of a river, his heart breaking with pain and wild yearnings, listening to the girls asking questions he could have answered; remaining silent; learning patience, until love would give him the right to reclaim his original body and destiny. Yet he would never forget the lessons she learned at the río—or how to handle fragile things. I looked at my mother and she smiled at me; we now had a new place to begin our search for the meaning of the word *woman*.

QUESTIONS ON SUBJECT AND PURPOSE

1. In what way is the essay about "the clash of cultures and generations" (paragraph 2)?
2. Why does Marina not reveal his identity before?
3. Why might Cofer want to retell the story of Marina?

QUESTIONS ON STRATEGY AND AUDIENCE

1. How many narratives are there in the essay?
2. What is the effect of the riddles—"He has not always been the man he is today" (paragraph 10) and "Have you heard about the one who ended up being what he was but did not appear to be?" (11)?
3. Although it really does not matter one way or another, as you read the story of Marina and Kiki, did you think it might have actually happened?

QUESTIONS ON VOCABULARY AND STYLE

1. How is the story of Marina narrated?
2. What is the effect of the mother's reply to Cofer's question "What happened to them?" (paragraph 34)?
3. Be prepared to define the following words: *encroaching* (paragraph 2), *insatiable* (6), *svelte* (7), *boudoir* (16), *traumatic* (20), *uncouth* (23), *ostensibly* (26).

WRITING SUGGESTIONS

1. **For Your Journal.** Make a list of the characteristics that you associate with the word *woman* or the word *man*.
2. **For a Paragraph.** Use the list of characteristics that you made for your journal to write a paragraph in which you narrate an event or an action that demonstrates or reveals someone as being either a man or a woman.
3. **For an Essay.** "Clashes of cultures and generations" are inevitable. Choose a time in which you were aware that your behavior or values were in conflict with those of your parents or grandparents. Narrate the event, but at the same time explore why you did what you did and how it made you feel. Were you right, or do you now see that they were right and you were wrong?
4. **For Research.** To what extent does Cofer explore similar themes in her other work? Find other examples of her writing (see the headnote and check the catalog and databases available at your library). Another good source of information is interviews that Cofer has granted. A number of these have appeared in print, and the full text of some is available through electronic databases. Once you have gathered your information, write an essay analyzing her writing to isolate her central concerns. Be sure to formulate a thesis about the themes that occur in her writing; do not just summarize what you have read. Be sure to document your sources.

FOR FURTHER STUDY

Focusing on Grammar and Writing. What is the mark of punctuation called the *colon*? How do you use that mark in your writing? Cofer uses the colon a number of times in her essay (for example, paragraphs 3, 6, 10, 17, and 26). Study how she uses them. Can you write a rule or two for their use working just from Cofer's essay?

Working Together. Divide into small groups. Each group should choose one of the following to examine:

1. The pueblo in Puerto Rico (paragraph 3)
2. Cofer's description of the old man (7 and 36)

3. The river setting (15 and 16)

4. The description of Marina (20)

5. Kiki's parents (23)

6. The revelation of Marina's identity (28–31)

How does each of these details fit into the larger whole? What is the significance of each in the narrative?

Seeing Other Modes at Work. In addition to elements of description, Cofer uses comparison and contrast when she describes the differences between herself and her mother.

Finding Connections. A good pairing is Judy Brady's "I Want a Wife" (Chapter 8).

Exploring the Web. Several extensive interviews with Cofer are available on the Web, as are other sites with information about her life and writing. Places to start can be found at **www.prenhall.com/miller.**

LOCKDOWN

Evans D. Hopkins

A former inmate at Nottoway Correctional Center in Virginia and writer for the Black Panther Party, Evans Hopkins was paroled in 1997 after serving sixteen years for armed robbery. He has published essays in the Washington Post, Nerve, *and* The New Yorker, *where this essay first appeared. His memoir,* Life After Life: A Story of Rage and Redemption, *was published in 2005.*

BEFORE READING

Connecting: What associations do you have with the words *prison* and *prisoner*?

Anticipating: Before you start to read, write down in a sentence or two how you feel about people sentenced to prison. For example, how should they be treated while they are in jail? Then read the essay.

I know something serious has happened when I wake up well before dawn to discover two guards wearing armored vests and riot helmets taking a head count. I'd gone to bed early this August evening, so that I might write in the early morning, as is my custom, before the prison clamor begins. So when I wake up I have no idea what was going down while I slept. But it's apparent that the prison is on "full lockdown status." At the minimum, we will be locked in our cells twenty-four hours a day for the next several days.

While lockdowns at Nottoway Correctional Center in Virginia are never announced in advance, I'm not altogether surprised by this one. The buzz among the eleven-hundred-man prison population was that a lockdown was imminent. The experienced prisoner knows to be prepared for a few weeks of complete isolation.

But I'm hardly prepared for the news I receive later in the day from a local TV station: two corrections officers and two nurses were taken hostage by three prisoners, following what authorities are calling "a terribly botched escape attempt" that included a fourth man. The incident was ended around 5:30 A.M. by a Department of Corrections strike-force team, with the hostages unharmed. However, according to authorities, eight of the rescuers, including the warden, were slightly wounded when a shotgun was discharged accidentally.

Oh, God, I think. Forget a few weeks. No telling how long we'll be on lock *now*. I try to take heart by telling myself, "It's nothing you haven't seen before, might as well take the opportunity to get the old typewriter pumpin', maybe even finish your book."

The idea that most people have of prison life consists of images from worst-case-scenario movies, or from news footage of local jails. Visitors to prison often comment on how surprised they are to see men moving around, without apparent restraint, having believed that prisoners are kept in their cells most of the time. In modern prisons, however, there is usually lots of orderly movement, as inmates go about the activities of normal life: working, eating, education, recreation, etc.

6   In a well-run institution, long lockdowns—where all inmate movement stops—are aberrations. Yet major institutions lock down regularly, for short periods, so that the prison can be searched for weapons and other contraband. Lockdowns are also called for emergencies, as this one has been at Nottoway, or, in fact, for any reason deemed necessary for security.

7   By the second week of the lockdown, one of our hot meals has been replaced with a bag lunch—four slices of bread, two slices of either cheese or a luncheon meat, and a small piece of plain cake or, more rarely, fruit. Since counsellors or administrative personnel must do most of the cooking, the lockdown menu usually consists of meals that require minimal culinary skills. Today we have chili-mac (an ungodly concoction of macaroni and ground beef), along with three tablespoons of anemic mixed vegetables and a piece of plain cake—all served on a disposable aluminum tray the size of a hard-cover book.

8   We have not yet been allowed out to shower, so I lay newspaper on the concrete floor and bathe at the sink. There is a hot water tap, in contrast to the cells at the now demolished State Penitentiary, in Richmond, where I served the first several years of my life sentence for armed robbery, and where I went through many very long lockdowns.

9   I have endured lockdowns in buildings with little or no heat; lockdowns during which authorities cut off the plumbing completely, so contraband couldn't be flushed away; and lockdowns where we weren't allowed out to shower for more than a month. I have been in prison since 1981, and my attitude has had to be "I can do time on the moon," if that is what's called for. So I'm not about to let this lockdown faze me. (Besides, I am in what is known as the "honor building," where conditions are marginally better.)

10   Around one o'clock in the morning, the three guards of the "shower squad" finally get around to our building. They have full riot gear on, and a Rottweiler in tow. One by one, we are handcuffed and escorted to the shower stalls at the center of the dayroom area. As I walk past the huge dog, I turn my head to keep an eye on it. The beast suddenly lunges against the handler's leash and barks at me with such ferocity that I actually feel the force of air on my face. I walk to the shower with feigned insouciance, but my heart is pumping furiously. I can forget sleeping for a while.

11   Back in the cell, I contemplate what's happening to this place. Information about the hostage incident has been trickling in. While the show of force seems absurd to those of us here in the honor building, I have heard reports of assaults on guards in the cell houses of the main compound, where the treatment of the inmates is said to have been more severe. On the night of the original incident, some men in a section of one building refused to return to their cells, and in at least one section there was open rebellion—destruction and burning.

***

Today a memorandum from the warden is passed out, and the warden 12
himself appears on a video broadcast on the prison's TV system. He announces that there will be no visitation until some time in October—about
two months from now.

Other restrictions are to be imposed, he says, including immediate im- 13
plementation of a new Department of Corrections guideline, stripping all
prisoners of most personal property: televisions with screens larger than five
and a half inches; any tape player other than a Walkman; nearly all personal
clothing (jeans, nongray sweatsuits, colored underwear, etc.); and—most devastating for me—*all typewriters.*

I find this news disquieting, to say the least, and I decide to lie down, 14
to try to get some sleep. This is difficult, as men are yelling back and forth
from their cells, upset about this latest development. Many of them have
done ten or fifteen years, like me, obeying all the rules and saving the meagre pay from prison jobs to buy a few personal items—items that we must
now surrender.

I awaken in the night, sweating and feverish in the humid summer air. 15
Sitting on the edge of my bed while considering my plight, I look at photographs of my family. My eyes rest on the school portrait of my son, taken
shortly before he died from heart disease ten years ago, at age twelve. Sorrow overwhelms me, and I find myself giving in to grief, then to great, mourn-
ful sobs.

The tears stop as suddenly as they began. It has been years since I've 16
wept so, and I realize that the grief has been only a trigger—that I am, by and
large, really feeling sorry for myself. This is no good, if I'm to survive with my
mind and spirit intact. I can't afford to succumb to self-pity.

This new day begins shortly after 8 A.M., when three guards come to my 17
cell door. One of them says, "We're here to escort you to Personal Property.
You have to pack up everything in your cell, and they will sort out what you
have to send out, and what you can keep, over there."

He looks through the long, narrow vertical slot in the steel door and— 18
seeing all the books, magazines, journal notebooks, and piles of papers I have
stacked around the cell—shakes his head in disbelief. "Looks like you're gonna
need a lot of boxes," he says. I have the accumulated papers, magazines, and
books of a practicing freelance writer. The only problem is that my "office" is
about as big as your average bathroom—complete with toilet and sink, but
with a steel cot where your bathtub would be.

Now the new rules say twelve books, twelve magazines, twelve audio- 19
tapes. Period. And "a reasonable number of personal and legal papers." I wonder how much of all this stuff they will say is reasonable, when sometimes even
I question the sanity of holding on to so much. But who knows *when* I'll be
able to get to any files, manuscripts, books, and notes that I send home? I finish packing after three hours, ending up with twelve full boxes. I sit and smoke
a cigarette while waiting for the guards to return, and contemplate the stacked
boxes filling the eight feet between the cot and the door. *Where are all the books,
plays, and film scripts I dreamed of producing?*

20   As I walk to the property building, on the far side of the compound, the sun is bright, the sky is cloudless, and the air of the Virginia countryside is refreshing. I look away from the fortress-gray concrete buildings of the prison, and out through the twin perimeter fences and the gleaming rolls of razor wire, to note that the leaves of a distant maple have gone to orange. I realize that the season has changed since I was last out of the building.

21   I am accompanied by three guards. Two push a cart laden with my boxes, grumbling; the third, an older man I know, walks beside me, making small talk.

22   "Man, things are really changing here," this guard says. Lowering his voice so that the other two cannot hear him, he tells me that he considered transferring to work at another institution, but that the entire system is now going through similar changes.

23   Back in my cell, I don't have the energy to unpack the four boxes I've returned with. I am glad to have at least salvaged the part of the manuscripts I've worked on over the years.

24   I lie upon the bed like a mummy, feet crossed at the ankle and hands folded over my chest, and try to meditate. However, with my tape player gone (along with my television), I have no music to drown out the sounds coming from the cell house. A wave of defeat settles over me.

25   I think of what I've often told people who ask about my crime—that I got life for a robbery in which no one was hurt. I'll have to rephrase that from now on. If robbery can be said to be theft by force, I can't help but feel like I've just been robbed. And I've most certainly been *hurt*. Maybe that's the whole idea, I think—to injure us, eye for an eye.

26   Perhaps I should acknowledge that the lockdown—and, indeed, all these years—have damaged me more than I want to believe. But self-pity is anathema to the prisoner, and self-doubt is deadly to the writer.

27   I get up quickly, pull out a yellow pad and ballpoint from one of the boxes, and stuff spongy plugs in my ears to block out the noise. I know that if I don't go back to work immediately—on *something*—the loss of my typewriter may throw up a block that I'll never overcome.

28   Just before Christmas, the lockdown officially ends. The four and a half months have taken their toll on everyone. There have been reports of two or three suicides. Some inmates have become unhinged, and can be seen shuffling around, on Thorazine or something.

29   Things are far from being back to "normal operations." There is now the strictest control of *all* movement; attack dogs are everywhere and officers escort you wherever you go. The gym is closed, and recreation and visitation privileges have been drastically curtailed. At least the educational programs, which were once touted as among the best in the state's prison system, are to resume again in the new year.

30   On Christmas Eve, the first baked "real chicken on the bone" since summer is served. But the cafeteria-style serving line has been replaced with a wall of concrete blocks. Now the prisoner gets a standard tray served through a small slot at the end of the wall.

As I hasten to finish my food in the allotted fifteen minutes, I look at the   31
men from another building in the serving line. There is a drab sameness to the
men, all dressed in the required ill-fitting uniform of denim jeans, blue work
shirts, and prison jackets.

I spot a friend of more than fifteen years, whom I haven't seen in months.   32
I can only wave and call out a greeting, for as we are seated separately, "mingling"
with men from another building is nearly impossible in the chow hall. "I'm a
grandfather now," he shouts to me, beaming. "I've got some pictures to show
you, when we get a chance." Then he remembers the strict segregation by building now, and his smile fades. He knows that I may never get a chance to see them.

I notice a large number of new faces among the men in line. Most of them   33
are black. Many are quite young, with a few appearing to be still in their teens.

Such young men are a primary reason for the new lockdown policies,   34
which are calculated largely to contain the "eighty-five-per-centers"—those
now entering Virginia's growing prison system, who must serve eighty-five
per cent of their sentences, under new, no-parole laws.

Virginia, like most states and the federal government, has passed puni-   35
tive sentencing laws in recent years. This has led to an unprecedented United
States prison/jail population of more than a million six hundred thousand—
about three times what it was when I entered prison, sixteen years ago. In the
resulting expansion of the nation's prison systems, authorities have tended to
dispense with much of the rehabilitative programming once prevalent in
America's penal institutions.

When I was sent to the State Penitentiary, in 1981, I was twenty-six—the   36
quintessential angry young black male. However, there was a very different attitude toward rehabilitation at that time, particularly as regards education. I
was able to take college courses for a number of years on a Pell grant. Vocational training was available, and literacy (or at least enrollment in school) was
encouraged and increased one's chances for making parole.

In the late seventies, there was a growing recognition that rehabilitation   37
programs paid off in lower rates of recidivism. But things began to change a few
years later. First, the highly publicized violence of the crack epidemic encouraged mandatory minimum sentencing. The throw-away-the-key fever really
took off in 1988, when George Bush's Presidential campaign hit the Willie Hor-
ton hot button, and sparked the tough-on-crime political climate that continues
to this day. The transformation was nearly complete when President Clinton
endorsed the concept of "three strikes you're out" in his 1994 State of the Union
address. And when Congress outlawed Pell grants for prisoners later that year
the message became clear: We really don't give a damn if you change or not.

Although the men are glad, after more than four months, to be out of   38
their cells, there is little holiday spirit; it's just another day. Several watch
whatever banality is on the dayroom TV screen. Most sit on the stainless-steel
tables and listlessly play cards to kill time, while others wait for a place at the
table. Some wait to use one of two telephones, while others, standing around
in bathrobes or towels, wait for a shower stall to become available.

39   Most of the men in this section of the building are in their forties or fifties, with a few elderly. It strikes me that for most of them prison has become a life of waiting: waiting in line to eat, for a phone call, the mail, or a visit. Or just waiting for tomorrow—for parole and freedom. For the older ones, with no hope of release, I suppose that they wait for the deliverance of death.

40   As I record the day in my notebook, I find myself thinking about my aunt's grandnephew—her adopted son. He was rumored to have been dealing drugs, and he was shot dead in the doorway of her home on Thanksgiving Day, just over a month ago; my father, who is seventy-five, was called to comfort her. With violence affecting so many lives, one can understand the desire—driven by fear—to lock away young male offenders. But considering their impoverished, danger-filled lives, I wonder whether the threat of being locked up for decades can really deter them from crime.

41   I understand the philosophy behind the increased use of long sentences and harsh incarceration. The idea is to make prison a secular hell on earth—a place where the young potential felon will fear to go, where the ex-con will fear to return. But an underlying theme is that "these people" are irredeemable "predators" (i.e., "animals"), who are without worth. Why, then, provide them with the opportunity to rehabilitate—or give them any hope?

42   Still, what really bothers me is knowing that many thousands of the young men entering prison now may *never* get the "last chance to change," which I was able to put to good use—in an era that, I'm afraid, is now in the past. And more disturbing, to my mind, are the long "no hope" sentences given to so many young men now—they can be given even to people as young as thirteen and fourteen. Although I personally remain eligible for parole—and in all likelihood will be released eventually—I can't help thinking of all the young lives that are now being thrown away. I know that if I had been born in another time I might very well have suffered the same fate.

QUESTIONS ON SUBJECT AND PURPOSE

1. How long does the lockdown last? How many specific days during that period does Hopkins write about?
2. At what point in the essay does Hopkins move away from his narrative account of the lockdown? What does Hopkins then do in the essay?
3. What objectives might Hopkins have in writing his essay?

QUESTIONS ON STRATEGY AND AUDIENCE

1. At times, Hopkins seems to talk to himself—even using quotation marks around his words, as in paragraph 4. Why? What is the effect of this strategy?
2. Hopkins uses white space to separate sections of the essay. How many divisions are there?
3. Who might Hopkins imagine as his readers? To whom is he writing? How do you know?

QUESTIONS ON VOCABULARY AND STYLE

1. When the Rottweiler lunges at him, Hopkins writes, "I walk to the shower with feigned insouciance" (paragraph 10). What is the effect of his word choice?
2. Hopkins chooses to quote a few remarks that the guards make when he is asked to pack up his possessions (paragraphs 17, 18, and 22). Why?
3. Be prepared to define the following words: *clamor* (paragraph 1), *aberrations* (6), *insouciance* (10), *anathema* (26), *punitive* (35), *quintessential* (36), *recidivism* (37), *banality* (38).

WRITING SUGGESTIONS

1. **For Your Journal.** Spend some time thinking about instances in which a personal experience that you had might be used to argue for a change in society's attitudes. For example, were you ever discriminated against for any reason? Were you ever needlessly embarrassed or ridiculed for something? Make a list of some possible experiences.
2. **For a Paragraph.** Look at the list of personal experiences that you made for your journal. Select one of those experiences and in a paragraph narrate what happened and then reflect on the significance of that experience. Try to make your reader see the injustice that was done.
3. **For an Essay.** If you have written the paragraph in suggestion 2, treat that as a draft for a longer, fuller narrative. Write an essay in which you narrate a personal experience for a specific purpose. If you are having trouble finding a suitable experience from your own life, you might want to narrate the experience of someone else.
4. **For Research.** What evidence is there to support or to refute the idea that prison can be a place for rehabilitation, can offer a "last chance to change"? Research the problem using your library's resources. Some online or CD-ROM databases would also be good places to start. You might want to talk to a reference librarian for search strategy suggestions. Use your findings to argue for or against providing educational or vocational opportunities to people in prison.

FOR FURTHER STUDY:

Focusing on Grammar and Writing. What is the mark of punctuation called the *dash*? How do you use it in your writing? How does a dash differ from parentheses or a comma? When might you use one and not the others? Hopkins uses dashes throughout his essay. Could you write a rule for the use of the dash using Hopkins's sentences as examples?

Working Together. Working in small groups, choose one substantial paragraph from the essay. What does Hopkins focus on in that paragraph? How does that one paragraph fit into the whole? Some good examples would be the lockdown meals (paragraph 7), the walk to the shower (10), the walk to the property building (20), the encounter with a friend (32), the waiting (39), and the death of his aunt's grandnephew (40).

Seeing Other Modes at Work. In the latter third of the essay, Hopkins abandons narration for reflection and then persuasion, trying to make his audience realize the implications of denying prisoners opportunities for rehabilitation.

Finding Connections: Interesting pairings can be made with Sister Helen Prejean, "Memories of a Dead Man Walking" (Chapter 9) and with Joseph Epstein, "What Are You Afraid Of?" (4).

Exploring the Web. Additional essays by Hopkins can be found online, as can a number of sources that debate the value and appropriateness of educational programs in prison. You can start your search at **www.prenhall.com/miller**.

3

DESCRIPTION

PREPARING TO WRITE

WHAT IS DESCRIPTION?

Description, like narration, is an everyday activity. You describe to a friend what cooked snails really taste like, how your favorite perfume smells, how your body feels when you have a fever, how a local band sounded last night, what your date for the evening looked like. Description records and re-creates sense impressions by translating them into words.

Consider, for example, Darcy Frey's description of Russell Thomas, a star basketball player at a Brooklyn, New York, high school, as he practices on a playground on an August evening:

> At this hour Russell usually has the court to himself; most of the other players won't come out until after dark, when the thick humid air begins to stir with night breezes and the court lights come on. But this evening is turning out to be a fine one—cool and foggy. The low, slanting sun sheds a feeble pink light over the silvery Atlantic a block away, and milky sheets of fog roll off the oceans and drift in tatters along the project walkways. The air smells of sewage and saltwater. At the far end of the court, where someone has torn a hole in the chicken wire fence, other players climb through and begin warming up.

Frey uses descriptive words and phrases to record sense impressions—sights and smells. Sensory details make it easy for the reader to create mentally a feeling for what it must have been like that evening on the basketball court at the project.

Translating sense impressions into words is not always easy. For one thing, when you have a firsthand experience, all of your senses are working at the same time: you see, taste, smell, feel, hear; you experience feelings and have thoughts about the experience. When you convey that experience to a reader or a listener, you can record only one sense impression at a time. Furthermore, sometimes it is difficult to find an adequate translation for a particular sense impression—how do you describe the smell of musk perfume or the taste of freshly squeezed orange juice?

Descriptions occur in all forms of writing. When you write a narrative, you include passages of description; when you compare and contrast two things, you describe both as part of that process; when you try to persuade an audience that strip mining destroys the landscape, you describe the abandoned mine site. Scientists write descriptions; writers create descriptions. Sometimes descriptions are a sentence long, sometimes a paragraph; sometimes an entire essay is composed of description.

IF RECORDING SENSE IMPRESSIONS IN WORDS IS DIFFICULT, WHY BOTHER?

Many types of sense impressions—smells, tastes, textures—cannot really be captured in any way except in words or in a physical re-creation of the original experiences. Sights and sounds, on the other hand, can be recorded in photographs and audio and video recordings. Indeed, there are times when a photograph or a video works much better than a verbal description. As the cliché says, a picture is worth a thousand words. We cannot deny the power of the visual. Look, for example, at the following photograph of a sod house, probably taken in the midwest in the 1880s. If we wanted to know what a settler's life was like on the Great Plains, if we wanted to see the physical reality of that life, what better way than to study a group of photographs?

Nebraska State Historical Society Photograph

At the same time, though, words can do something that photographs never can. Photographs are static—a visual but unchanging moment captured in time. What were the people in the photograph thinking? What were they feeling? What impression did the landscape leave on their minds and lives? What was it like to go to bed and wake up each morning in a sod house? How cold did it get in the winter? How wet and damp in the spring? What did it smell like? Descriptions in words should never attempt to capture a photographic reality. Instead, images are filtered through the mind of the writer—the writer evokes our feelings, our senses, our memories and emotions. The writer makes us feel that we are there. The writer of description records what she or he saw as important in the scene. For example, three of the writers in this chapter write about people important in their lives. Would their descriptions have been more effective—or even unnecessary—if they had included a photograph of the person about whom they were writing? Of course not. In each case, what is important about the person is not that static external appearance, but rather what the person being described meant to the writer and how that person is revealed in action and in speech.

Translating sense impressions into words offers two distinct advantages. First, ideally, it isolates the most important aspects of the experience, ruling out anything else that might distract your reader's attention. Many things can be seen in a scene, but what are the important ones on which the reader is to focus? Second, it makes those experiences more permanent. Sensory impressions decay in seconds, but written descriptions survive indefinitely and can be re-accessed each time they are reread.

WHAT IS THE DIFFERENCE BETWEEN OBJECTIVE AND SUBJECTIVE DESCRIPTION?

Traditionally, descriptions are divided into two categories: objective and subjective. In objective description, you record details without making any personal evaluation or reaction. For example, Roger Angell offers this purely objective description of a baseball, recording weight, dimensions, colors, and material:

> It weighs just five ounces and measures between 2.86 and 2.94 inches in diameter. It is made of a composition-cork nucleus encased in two thin layers of rubber, one black and one red, surrounded by 121 yards of tightly wrapped blue-gray wool yarn, 45 yards of white wool yarn, 53 more yards of blue-gray wool yarn, 150 yards of fine cotton yarn, a coat of rubber cement, and a cowhide (formerly horsehide) exterior, which is held together with 216 slightly raised red cotton stitches.

Few descriptions outside of science writing, however, are completely objective. Instead of trying to include every detail, writers choose a few details carefully. That process of selection is determined by the writer's purpose and by the impression that the writer wants to create. Consider this example from Eric Liu. Visiting his grandmother, he goes to wash his hands in the bathroom. As he looks around the bathroom, he records a selection of details:

> In the small bath were the accessories of her everyday life: a frayed toothbrush in a plastic Star Wars mug I'd given her in 1979, stiff washrags and aged pantyhose hanging from a clothesline, medicine bottles and hair dye cluttered the sinktop.

Liu captures a loneliness and a sadness through those few details. Nothing else in the bathroom is described. Liu is not interested in visually describing the bathroom, in capturing it photographically in words; he is creating an emotion, an impression. Obviously, not everyone who saw the bathroom would have "seen" what Liu did.

In subjective description, you are free to interpret details for your reader; your choice of words and images can be suggestive, emotional, and value-loaded. Subjective descriptions frequently make use of figurative language—similes and metaphors that forge connections in the reader's mind. When Gordon Grice, in "Caught in the Widow's Web" (another descriptive essay found in Writers at Work), sees the debris that litters the ground under the spider's web, he uses a **simile** (a comparison that uses "like" or "as") when he writes, "the husks of consumed insects, their antennae stiff as gargoyle horns." When Scott Russell Sanders, in "The Inheritance of Tools" (in this chapter), looks at his smashed thumbnail, he creates a **metaphor** (an analogy that directly identifies one thing with another) when he describes the wound as a "crescent moon" that "month by month . . . rose across the pink sky of my thumbnail."

WHAT DO YOU INCLUDE IN AND WHAT DO YOU EXCLUDE FROM A DESCRIPTION?

Writing a description, like writing a narrative, involves selection. If your mother asks you what happened today, she does not expect you to report the events minute by minute. Much as she might be interested in you, she still wants just the high points, the significant moments of your day. When you write a narrative, you have a purpose, a shaping focus, for the story. You strip away the unnecessary details and focus on the points or details that relate to that focus. The same principle holds true for writing a description. You cannot record every detail about a person, or an object or place, or a landscape. How could you capture every aspect of anything? How could you include all that could be seen, or smelled, or heard, or felt? Like your mother, your reader wants to know the main points and is distracted by unnecessary details. As you write description, stay focused on your purpose and be selective about the details you include.

Descriptions can serve a variety of purposes, but in every case it is important to make that purpose clear to your reader. Some description is done solely to record the facts, as in Angell's description of a baseball, or to evoke an atmosphere, as in Frey's description of an August evening at a basketball court in Brooklyn. More often, description is used to support subjective purposes. Gordon Grice, in describing the black widow, is not trying to describe the spider as a scientist might. He uses description to emphasize the evil or malevolence that he sees embodied in the "flower of natural evil." The spider is more than just a physical thing; it becomes a symbol.

Ask yourself, What am I trying to describe and why? Write a purpose statement for your descriptive essay or even for a passage of description. Then use that purpose statement as a tool by which to measure the relevance or irrelevance of every detail that you are thinking about including.

Prewriting Suggestions

1. Decide what you are going to describe in your essay—a person, a place, an object. Decide as well about length—will this be a paragraph? A full-length essay?

2. Make a list of the details that best describe your subject. Consider all of the senses. Which of the details are objective and which are subjective?

3. If possible, re-experience the place, person, or subject of your paper. Go and visit. Take notes. Listen. Look. Jot down details.

4. Once you have gathered details, write a purpose statement for your description. What are you trying to do? Create an emotion? Set a mood? Verbally photograph or record an event? Use that purpose statement to test each detail that you plan to include. Do all of your details contribute to the purpose?

5. Remember that extended descriptions are static and can potentially bore a reader. Be careful that you do not record too much detail. You are not describing everything about your subject; you are being selective.

WRITING

HOW DO YOU DESCRIBE AN OBJECT OR A PLACE?

The first task in writing a description is to decide what you want to describe. As in every other writing task, making a good choice means that the act of writing will be easier and probably more successful. Before you begin, keep two things in mind. First, there is rarely any point in describing a common object or place—something every reader has seen—unless you do it in a fresh and perceptive way. Roger Angell describes a baseball, but he does so by dissecting it, giving a series of facts about its composition. Probably most of Frey's readers had at least seen pictures of a project playground, but after reading his description, what they are left with is a sense of vividness—this passage evokes or re-creates in our minds a mental picture of that evening.

Second, remember that your description must create a focused impression. To do so, you need to select details that contribute to your purpose. This will give you a way of deciding which details out of the many available are relevant. Details in a description must be carefully chosen and arranged; otherwise, your reader will be overwhelmed or bored by the accumulation of detail.

HOW DO YOU DESCRIBE A PERSON?

Before you begin to describe a person, remember an experience that everyone has had. You have read a novel and then seen a film or a made-for-television version, and the two experiences did not mesh. The characters, you are convinced, just did not look like the actors and actresses: "She was thinner and blond" or "He was all wrong—not big enough, not rugged enough." Any time you read a narrative that contains a character—either real or fictional—you form a mental picture of the person, and that picture is generally not based on any physical description that the author has provided. In fact, in many narratives, authors provide only minimal description of the people involved. For example, if you look closely at the Thurmond Watts family in William Least Heat Moon's "Nameless, Tennessee," you will find almost no physical description of the people. Thurmond, we are told, is "tall" and "thin"—those are the only adjectives used to describe him. The rest of the family—his wife, Miss Ginny; his sister-in-law, Marilyn; and his daughter, Hilda—are not physically described at all. Nevertheless, we get a vivid sense of all four as people.

Fictional characters or real people are created or revealed primarily through ways other than direct physical description. What a person does or says, for example, also reveals personality. The reader "sees" Alan in Terry Tempest Williams's "The Village Watchman" in part through what he does (for example, his behavior at the bowling alley) and through what he says. The Wattses, in Least Heat Moon's description, are revealed by how they react, what they say, how their speech sounds, what they consider to be important. These are the key factors in re-creating Least Heat Moon's experience for the reader.

In fact, descriptions of people should not try to be verbal portraits recording physical attributes in photographic detail. Words finally are never as efficient in doing that as photographs. If the objective in describing a person is not photographic accuracy, what then is it? Go back to the advice offered earlier in this introduction: decide first what impression you want to create in your reader. Why are you describing this person? What is it about this person that is worth describing? In all likelihood the answer will be something other than physical attributes. Once you know what that something is, you can then choose the details that best reveal or display the person.

How Do You Organize a Description?

You have found a subject; you have studied it—either firsthand or in memory; you have decided on a reason for describing this particular subject; you have selected details that contribute to that reason or purpose. Now you need to organize your paragraph or essay. Descriptions, like narratives, have principles of order, although the principles vary depending on what sensory impressions are involved. When the primary descriptive emphasis is on seeing, the most obvious organization is spatial—moving from front to back, side to side, outside to inside, top to bottom, general to specific. The description moves as a camera would. Roger Angell's description of a baseball moves outward from the cork nucleus through the layers of rubber, wool yarn, and rubber cement to the cowhide exterior.

Other sensory experiences might be arranged in order of importance, from the most obvious to the least—the loudest noise at the concert, the most pervasive odor in the restaurant—or even in chronological order. Eric Liu's description of his visit to his grandmother is structured chronologically—from his arrival at her apartment building to their farewell embrace.

Drafting Suggestions

1. Plan a structure for your essay. Does your description move spatially? From the most obvious detail to the least obvious? Does time underlie the structure of your description? Remember, you need an organizational pattern to control the details of your description.
2. Look again at your purpose statement. Go through your essay and check each detail against that purpose. Do the details in your description fit with your intended purpose?
3. Have you included too many details? Are there parts of the paper that seem too long, too crowded, too detailed? Because description is static, it tends to be blended with narration; relatively few essays contain only description.
4. Plan an opening for your paper. Try to think of at least three possible ways in which to begin. Write out sample openings on cards and ask friends to rate them.
5. Plan an ending for your paper. Try to think of several different ways to end your essay. How do you know when you are finished? How does your reader know? Do you end with a summary? What will bring closure to your essay?

REVISING

HOW DO YOU REVISE A DESCRIPTION?

Always try to finish a complete draft of your paper prior to its due date. That will allow you to put it aside for awhile so that when you come back to it, you have a fresh perspective on what you have written. Sometimes when you look again at the paper, you will be pleased with how good it seems; sometimes you will realize that more work needs to be done. Always also try to get some feedback from other readers. Ask for constructive advice; do not settle for empty responses such as "it's pretty good" or "I liked it." In writing descriptive passages or essays, problems tend to cluster around several key areas.

Overusing Adjective and Adverbs   You can create an image without providing a mountain of adjectives and adverbs—just as you imagine what a character looks like without being told. When Terry Tempest Williams describes Alan's behavior at the bowling alley, the scene and Alan come alive for the reader: "When it was Alan's turn, it was an event. Nothing subtle. His style was Herculean. Big man. Big ball. Big roll. Big bang. Whether it was a strike or a gutter ball, he clapped his hands, spun around on the floor, clapped his thighs, and cried, 'Goddamn! Did you see that one? Send me another ball, sweet Jesus!' " One of the greatest dangers in writing a description lies in trying to describe too much, trying to qualify every noun with at least one adjective and every verb with an adverb. Precise, vivid nouns and verbs will do most of the work for you.

Overusing Figurative Language   Similes and metaphors can be powerful descriptive tools, but as in the case of adjectives and adverbs, such figurative devices can present problems. Remember that while similes and metaphors can add freshness and vividness to your writing, while they can help your reader understand the unfamiliar by linking it to the familiar, they are still artificial language constructs that tend to call attention to themselves. The point to a description should not be to display your cleverness as a writer. You are describing something for a reason, a purpose (whatever that might be), not to show off your verbal skills. Do not try to be too clever, but on the other hand, do not be too obvious and end up with similes and metaphors that are nothing more than clichés. If a character in your essay does things in an unconventional way, do not write that she "marches to a different drummer"; if someone has no hair, do not write, he "was as bald as a billiard ball." Finally, do not write strings of similes and metaphors; use them sparingly. Resist the temptation to sprinkle your paper with lots of figurative language.

Keeping Focused   An effective description is focused and tight. Never try to describe everything about a person, a scene, an object; never feel compelled to include every possible sense impression. Descriptions can sprawl out of control, and because they are static, readers can easily get bored by the accumulation of descriptive detail. If you are describing a person, for example, do not give your reader several paragraphs of description—what the person looks like, what the person is wearing, what the person is thinking or feeling. Instead, put that person in motion: have the person do something, interact with someone, say lines of dialogue. Intermix the descriptive details with action.

Revising Suggestions

1. Check that you have used vivid nouns and verbs to carry most of the descriptive burden.
2. Have you been too heavy-handed in emphasizing the significance or importance that you see in the object of your description? Remember, you are trying to reveal significance; you are not lecturing your reader on the "meaning" of your description.

3. Go through your essay and underline every descriptive detail. Are there too many? Are you trying to make the reader experience too much? Compare your descriptive technique with those of writers in this chapter.

4. Find readers for your draft—a roommate, a classmate, a writing center tutor. Ask your readers for honest advice. What did they like about your paper? What did they find tedious? What do they think your purpose was in writing this paper? Are they right?

5. Look at your title again. Does it arouse interest? Will it attract a reader or scare one away? Remember that "Descriptive Essay" is not a title for your paper.

SAMPLE STUDENT ESSAY

Nadine Resnick chose to describe her favorite childhood toy, a stuffed doll she had named Natalie.

FIRST DRAFT

PRETTY IN PINK

Standing in the middle of the aisle, staring up at the world as most children in nursery school do, something pink caught my eye. Just like Rapunzel in her high tower, there was a girl inside a cardboard and plastic prison atop a high shelf that smiled down at me. I pointed to the doll and brought her home with me that same day. Somehow I knew that she was special.

She was named Natalie. I do not know why, but the name just seemed perfect, like the rest of her. Natalie was less than twelve inches tall and wore a pink outfit. Her hands and grimacing face were made of plastic while the rest of her body was stuffed with love. She had brown eyes and brown hair, just like me, which peeked through her burgundy and pink-flowered bonnet. Perhaps the most unusual feature about her was that my mom had tattooed my name on her large bottom so that if Natalie ever strayed from me at nursery school or at the supermarket, she would be able to find me.

There was some kind of magic about Natalie's face. I think it was her grin from ear to ear. Even if I had played with her until she was so dirty that most of her facial features were hidden, Natalie's never-ending smile usually shown through. When I neglected her for days to play with some new toy and then later returned, her friendly smirk was still there. When I was left home alone for a few hours, her smile assured me that I need not be afraid. Natalie's bright smile also cheered me up when I was sick or had a bad day. And she always had enough hugs for me.

As I was growing up, Natalie and her beaming face could usually be found somewhere in my room—on my bed, in her carriage, hiding under a pile of junk, and later piled in my closet with the rest of my other dolls and stuffed animals. When I got older, I foolishly decided that I no longer needed such childish toys. So I put Natalie and the rest of my stuffed animals in a large black plastic bag in a dark corner of the basement. I now realize that the basement really is not an honorable place for someone who has meant so much to me. But, I will bet that she is still smiling anyway.

COMMENTS

Nadine had a chance to read her essay to a small group of classmates during a collaborative editing session. Everyone liked the essay and most of their suggested changes were fairly minor. For example, several people objected to her choice of the words *grimaced* and *smirk*, feeling that such words were not appropriate choices for a lovable doll. Another student, however, suggested a revision in the final paragraph. "It seems like you put her farther and farther away from you as you got older. Why don't you emphasize that distancing by having it occur in stages?" he commented. When Nadine rewrote her essay, she made a number of minor changes in the first three paragraphs and then followed her classmate's idea in the fourth paragraph.

REVISED DRAFT

NATALIE

Standing in the store's aisle, staring up at the world as most preschool children do, something pink caught my eye. Just like Rapunzel in her high tower, a girl trapped inside a cardboard and plastic prison atop a high shelf smiled down at me. I pointed to the doll and brought her home with me that same day. Somehow I knew that she was special.

She was named Natalie. I do not know why, but the name just seemed perfect, like the rest of her. Natalie was less than twelve inches tall and wore a pink outfit. Her hands and smiling face were made of plastic while the rest of her body was plumply stuffed. Just like me, she had brown eyes and brown hair which peeked through her burgundy and pink-flowered bonnet. Perhaps her most unusual feature was my name tattooed on her bottom so that if Natalie ever strayed from me at nursery school or at the supermarket, she would be able to find me.

Natalie's face had a certain glow, some kind of magic. I think it was her grin from ear to ear. After I had played with her, no matter how dirty her face was, Natalie's never-ending smile still beamed through. When I neglected her for days to play with some new toy and then later returned, her friendly grin was still there. Years later, when I was old enough to be left home alone for a few hours, her smile assured me that I need not be afraid. Natalie's bright smile also cheered me up when I was sick or had a bad day. And she always had enough hugs for me.

As I was growing up, Natalie and her beaming face could usually be found somewhere in my room. However, she seemed to move further away from me as I got older. Natalie no longer slept with me; she slept in her own carriage. Then she rested on a high shelf across my room. Later she made her way into my closet with the rest of the dolls and stuffed animals that I had outgrown. Eventually, I decided that I no longer needed such childish toys, so I put Natalie and my other stuffed animals in a large black plastic bag in a dark cellar corner. Even though I abandoned her, I am sure that Natalie is still smiling at me today.

SOME THINGS TO REMEMBER

1. Choose your subject carefully, making sure that you have a specific reason or purpose in mind for whatever you describe.
2. Study or observe your subject—try to see it or experience it in a fresh way. Gather details; make a list; use all your senses.
3. Use your purpose as a way of deciding which details ought to be included and which excluded.
4. Choose a pattern of organization to focus your reader's attention.
5. Use precise, vivid nouns and verbs, as well as adjectives and adverbs, to create your descriptions.

DESCRIPTION AS A LITERARY STRATEGY

Description is often intertwined with narration as it is in "Traveling to Town," a poem by Duane BigEagle that recalls a regular experience that occurred during his childhood near the Osage Reservation in Oklahoma. As he explains in a note to the poem, "Monkey Ward" was the name many people used to refer to catalog merchandiser Montgomery Ward—once a competitor of Sears. As you read the poem, think about how sparse, but effective, the use of description is here.

TRAVELING TO TOWN

Duane BigEagle

When I was very young,
we always went to town
in the flatbed wagon.
We'd leave as soon as the day's first heat
had stopped the mare's breath
from forming a cloud
in the air.
Kids sprawled in the back
among the dusty bushels
of corn and beans.
As we rode down main street,
the town revealed itself
backwards
for my sister and me to see.
We loved the brick and sandstone buildings
and the farmer's market
with its sawdust floor.
Best of all
was Monkey Ward
with its large wood paneled center room
and little wires
with paper messages
that flew back and forth
like trained birds.
We finally got to Safeway
where Grandma did the shopping
and Grandpa sat outside
on the brick steps in the sunlight
watching all the grandkids.
From a shady coolness
on the other side of the street
the ice cream store
would call to us
with its banging screen door.
Grandpa always had money for ice cream
and we'd ride home down main street
licking ice cream
watching the town reveal itself
backwards again
in afternoon sun.

DISCUSSION QUESTIONS

1. Probably few readers have ridden to town in a horse-drawn wagon. Despite the lack of similar experiences, can you visualize the scene that BigEagle is describing? Why or why not?

2. The trip presumably takes an entire day. Out of the whole experience, what does BigEagle describe? Why these things?

3. Description doesn't always mean surrounding nouns with clusters of adjectives and verbs with adverbs. Focus on a detail or two in the poem that adds to the description. What does BigEagle do to make the detail seem vivid? What does that suggest about writing effective descriptions?

4. What is the overall impression that BigEagle seems to be trying to convey to his readers? How do the individual details contribute to that impression?

5. How is the description organized in the poem?

WRITING SUGGESTIONS

Describe an experience out of your childhood or adolescence. Notice that description often works best when it is sparsely done. Some possible places to start could include the following prompts:

a. An experience you had with your grandparents or parents

b. A place that you (or you and your family) regularly visited

c. A trip—a ride, for example, in a car, train, bus, subway, or airplane

READING DESCRIPTION

One of the most famous examples of subjective description comes from the opening paragraphs of Charles Dickens's *Bleak House* (1853). The novel is set in London, a city with muddy streets and polluted air from the coal-burning stoves, a city enveloped in fog. While London in the 1850s might have been somewhat like that, Dickens is not just describing a place, he is creating a symbolic landscape. The mud, mire, and suffocating fog of the city reflect the London legal system and the eternally unsettled litigation of the Jarndyce estate case, which is as murky and miserable as the weather Dickens describes in these paragraphs.

As you read these paragraphs, remember what you have learned about how to write a description—and see how that knowledge can help you as a reader.

- Descriptions are written with a purpose in mind, and the details are cho-sen to reinforce that purpose. What the author includes and excludes are both important, and both choices are made with an eye to purpose.
- Descriptions can be either objective or subjective. A scientist attempt-ing to describe something precisely produces an objective description. A writer trying to evoke an emotion in you through the description (or a real estate agent trying to sell you a property) relies on subjective description.
- Descriptions are organized so that the reader can sense an order to the material. Sometimes that order follows a chronological pattern; some-times it moves from the most obvious to the least obvious. Whatever the pattern, the organizational scheme allows the reader to orient within the description.
- Descriptions frequently use figurative language, especially simile and metaphor, and capture a range of sense impressions.

Opening sentence places the scene in the legal district; season is winter	London, Michaelmas Term lately over, and the Lord Chancellor sitting in Lincoln's Inn Hall. Implacable November weather. As much mud in the streets, as if the waters had but newly retired from the face of the earth, and it would not be wonderful to meet Megalosaurus, forty
Extended similes	feet long or so, waddling like an elephantine lizard up Holborn Hill. Smoke lowering down from chimney pots, making a soft black drizzle,
Metaphor	with flakes of soot in it as big as full-grown snow-flakes—gone into mourning, one might imagine, for the death of the sun. Dogs, undistinguishable in mire. Horses, scarcely better, splashed to their very blinkers. Foot passengers, jostling one another's umbrellas, in a general infection of ill-temper, and losing their foothold at street-corners, where tens of thousands of other foot passengers have been slipping and sliding since the day broke (if this day ever broke), adding new deposits to the crust upon crust of mud, sticking at these points tenaciously in the pavement, and
Metaphor	accumulating at compound interest.

RESPONDING TO A VISUAL

Photographs can transport us backward in time. We can see ourselves as chil-dren and relive what our childhood home was like and where we went to ele-mentary school. We can see our parents as children, our grandparents as young men and women. We can experience a world that was very different from what we see around us now. The following photograph is of Mulberry Street in New York City, taken about 1900. The passage from Dickens's *Bleak*

House is a subjective, symbolic description; the photograph is an objective, visual record of exactly what this street looked like on the day when the photograph was taken.

READING AND WRITING ABOUT IMAGES

Using the photograph as a departure point, write one of two possible essays. Try to render the scene in the photograph as an objective description. Suppose the photograph could not be reproduced, but you want to describe for your reader what urban street life was like at the turn of the last century. Or write a subjective description in which you evoke in your reader an emotional reaction to the scene. Either way, make sure that you use a variety of sense impressions in your description.

VISITING THE WEB

The companion Website, **www.prenhall.com/miller,** contains additional information about descriptions and about the writers in this chapter. You will also find a number of links to other sources of information about the subjects of the essays found in this chapter.

EXPLORING ON YOUR OWN

Can you imagine yourself living in an earlier time in America?. What might it have been like to live in a sod house on the northern Great Plains in the 1800s? To be a suffragette campaigning for women's right to vote at the turn of the century? To live in Chicago between 1902 and 1933? American Memory at the Library of Congress in Washington, D.C., has spectacular online collections and exhibitions covering a broad range of topics, timeframes, and geographical regions of the United States. For an overview of the exhibits and for writing topics that invite you to describe what you see in your virtual experience, go to the **www.prenhall.com/miller**.

Looking for Writing Suggestions

Persons

1. A living/historical person whom you admire
2. A person who has made a difference in your life
3. Someone extraordinary/ordinary who catches your attention
4. A best friend/roommate/partner
5. A great/horrible teacher/coach

Places

1. A favorite place from your past
2. A summer/fall/winter memory
3. A campus/community location
4. A destination
5. A place described so as to evoke a powerful emotion (such as fear or terror)

Objects

1. Your favorite possession
2. A sentimental possession
3. Something unusual/of great value/of cultural significance
4. Something ordinary seen a new and different way
5. A scary thing (for example, a snake, a spider, a coffin) described objectively or scientifically

A PEN BY THE PHONE

Debra Anne Davis

Debra Anne Davis was born in southern California. She received her B.A. in American Studies from the University of California at Santa Cruz and an M.F.A. from the Nonfiction Writing Program at the University of Iowa. She has published essays in literary journals; her published work is online at **www.debraannedavis.com**. *Davis is currently working on a memoir. "A Pen by the Phone" first appeared in the* Redwood Coast Review *in 2004.*

On Writing: *Davis observes: "I love to write. Some of the happiest moments and hours of my life have been spent with a pen in hand, with my fingers curved over a keyboard. I'm actually a pretty lazy person, so I don't think I would bother writing (it is a lot of hard work and does take a lot of time and energy) if I didn't enjoy it. The hard part, though, is rejection. Writing is one thing; publishing, or trying to publish, is another. I would say I have "stacks" of rejection slips from journals, agents, and editors— but I tend to throw them away, so there are no physical stacks. The mental ones, though, do weigh on one. I think this is probably true of all authors. And this is why I chose to write about this here, because I want to send a message to the reader of this anthology. You've probably heard it before, but I'll say it again anyway—and maybe it will stick: Trust yourself. If you want to be a writer, write, and send your writing out knowing that much of it will be rejected. It is not you who is being rejected when this happens. What has happened is this. You have joined a club, largely anonymous, physically disconnected but bound by the long traditions of civilizations, by the love of literature. You are a writer now; enjoy your moments and hours."*

BEFORE READING

Connecting: Think about one of your parents or grandparents. If you had to isolate one quality about one of them, something that you will always remember about him or her, what would it be?

Anticipating: What has Davis's father come to represent to her? How is that trait or quality described in the essay?

My father was an avid reader. And a quiet person. But not an especially solitary soul. And he was a fairly large man. So, through much of my youth, there was this comforting sight: Dad reading. Lying flat on his back on the family couch, a book or folded-back magazine held straight over his head by an arm bent 30 degrees at the elbow, his belly a small hill against the tapestry landscape. Noise and commotion did not faze him. He read science books mostly, books about the planets or earthquakes or nutrition, *Psychology Today* and *Scientific American* (though we'd tried a couple of times, my sister Lisa and I could not understand a single word of that publication; the pictures weren't even all that interesting—yet it could absorb Dad's attention for hours). That's how he read the evening newspaper and *Newsweek*, too. That was where he felt comfortable, reading amidst the mild chaos of his family.

2   There's a family story about Dad's reading. Though I don't remember it happening, I do play a key role in the story. My sister Beth is 13 years older than I am. One night she was at her part-time job as an usher at a movie theater. I was at home playing with, presumably, my stuffed animals and dolls. Dad was, of course, reading. I guess at some point I decided it would be fun to brush his hair. I got a brush and some of my little plastic barrettes, green, pink, yellow. I brushed and styled Dad's hair. He continued reading. Mom (as the story goes) came in and reminded him that he needed to pick Beth up at work. So he left to go get her. Poor Beth. Sixteen years old and completely mortified when her father drove up with a rainbow of barrettes covering his tangled hair.

3   This story is told as such stories are, because it contains that humorous central image: a grown man wearing little girl hair accessories. But the central part of it is, I think, not that Dad had gone out in public like that but that he didn't even realize what he looked like. That he was so unselfconscious, so satisfied with each moment he was living that he could become absolutely absorbed in an article about telescopes or moon rockets—and not even notice a 3-year-old pulling on his hair, snapping barrettes into place, patting her handiwork into perfection. My yanking on his hair didn't bother him because he was completely content in that place at that time. He was there, I was there, his reading lamp was on, the house was warm, and all was right with the universe. (It's too bad, I suppose, that Beth wasn't able to have quite the same perspective on things that night.)

4   My father did have one request in life. All he ever wanted was *a pen by the phone*. A simple demand, as demands of patriarchs go, yes—but one we couldn't seem to honor. It would even cause him to raise his voice. He'd answer the phone in the kitchen; it would be for someone else and he'd want to take a message. Yet this quick task, this basic courtesy was impossible for him to perform. For there was No Pen By the Phone! Never a pen, right there by the phone. He would complain of this, loudly.

5   He'd pick up a bag of one dozen pens the next time he was at the drugstore buying aspirin, staples, chocolate bars. He'd put several of the pens in a cup by the phone. And, slowly or quickly, they'd disappear. We, his children and his wife, would take them. We weren't intentional thieves, just thoughtless kleptomaniacs. Frankly, though I do remember his harangues about the incredible and constant dearth of pens-by-the-phone, I have no recollection of ever having taken one. No memory of that whatsoever. Perhaps they got up and walked off on their own? Or perhaps I was too busy with the million other things I was doing at the moment to notice that I was also stealing the Pen that should stay By the Phone. And that I was not honoring the one clear and uncomplicated plea he had, a basic plan that would have made life better for all of us.

6   My father taught me simplicity, to live well in the ordinary moments of life—but he didn't know he taught me this. He taught this lesson purely by example, not by design, and so I learned it better than most lessons I've learned.

He read and looked so serene, so at home with the time and space he was inhabiting; It didn't take much: a soft sofa, a monthly magazine.

My father was one of the few truly content people I have ever known. 7
He had the same basic needs we all have—food, shelter, love—but few wants.
He required only a space to himself, intellectual stimulation, entertainment—
and he got these in such a gentle way. The rest of us, living our busy, full,
often disappointing and sometimes devastating lives required so much more.
Or felt that we did.

Looking back on all this, I wonder if I might be able to live more as my 8
father did. He has been gone now seven years, and we all miss him, his presence, his wisdom, his stacks of incomprehensible books and magazines next to
the couch. I learned from watching him that we need not search for serenity,
that peace comes unbidden if we prepare a small space and a little time to receive it. Perhaps now I will be able not just to appreciate the way he lived his
life but also to follow his example, to find my own precious and quiet bliss in
the life I already have. To read and read and read on my couch at home and to
wish only for a simple pen by the phone.

QUESTIONS ON SUBJECT AND PURPOSE

1. What quality or characteristic of her father does Davis focus on in the
   essay?
2. What might be appealing about those characteristics of her father in
   the twenty-first century?
3. Why might Davis have chosen to write the essay?

QUESTIONS ON STRATEGY AND AUDIENCE

1. How much of a description of her father does Davis give?
2. How does Davis structure her essay?
3. What could Davis assume about her audience?

QUESTIONS ON VOCABULARY AND STYLE

1. At three points in the essay (paragraphs 1, 2, and 3), Davis introduces
   material that is enclosed within parentheses. Why use parentheses?
   How would you describe the information that is contained with them?
2. Why "a pen by the phone"? What is the significance of that demand?
3. Be prepared to define the following words: *avid* (paragraph 1),
   mortified (2), *patriarch* (4), *kleptomaniac* (5), *harangue* (5), *dearth* (5).

WRITING SUGGESTIONS

1. **For Your Journal.** Make a list of your relatives or friends and jot
   down next to their names an activity, an emotion, or a behavior that
   you instinctively connect with each one.

2. **For a Paragraph.** Look back through your journal writing. Do you see one person who might be the focus of a descriptive paragraph? You might focus on a physical attribute, a characteristic expression or behavior, an obsession, a mannerism, whatever. You can treat the subject sympathetically, comically, critically, lovingly. Write a descriptive paragraph about this person capturing that particular quality.

3. **For an Essay.** Davis sees in her father a trait or quality that is probably not common among most parents today—simplicity and contentment. Those might or might not be words that would you apply to own parents or stepparents. Write a descriptive essay in which you describe a relative or friend in terms of his or her distinctive quality. If you have difficulty writing about a family member, perhaps you could choose a public figure or even a teacher. The goal, however, is not only to describe this person through the characteristic or quality, but also to connect the person's personality to our culture today. Maybe, for example, the person is highly competitive, materialistic, always multitasking.

4. **For Research.** Scholars debate the impact of work on Americans' leisure time. In a recent book, for example, one author notes that Americans average only 16 hours of leisure a week, and they are working longer hours than people did 40 years ago. Other studies, such as the U.S. government's "America Time-Use Survey" seem to dispute some of those claims. Research the problem through print and online sources, and present your conclusions in a researched essay. You can use personal examples or descriptions of people you know in your essay as well.

FOR FURTHER STUDY

Focusing on Grammar and Writing. Davis uses some sentence fragments in her essay. See how many you can find. Why is each a fragment and not a complete sentence? Rewrite each fragment, making it into a complete sentence.

Working Together. Divide into two large groups and then into smaller teams within each group. One set of teams will work with the scene in paragraph 2; the other, the scene in 4. Both scenes are summaries. Dramatize each scene to include characters interacting with some dialogue. The teams should then compare their results. What happens to the essay when these changes are made?

Seeing Other Modes at Work. The essay also involves narration.

Finding Connections. The essay could be effectively paired with any of the essays in Chapter 2: Narration for another example of a narrative strategy. Another excellent pairing involving a memory of a father is Scott Russell Sanders' "The Inheritance of Tools," in this chapter.

Exploring the Web. Davis maintains her own Website on which you can read a number of her essays. Start at **www.prenhall.com/miller.**

THE WAY TO RAINY MOUNTAIN
N. Scott Momaday

Navarre Scott Momaday was born in Lawton, Oklahoma, in 1934. He earned a B.A. from the University of New Mexico and a Ph.D. in English from Stanford University. Professor of English, artist, editor, poet, and novelist, Momaday is above all a storyteller committed to preserving and interpreting the rich oral history of the Kiowa Indians. His work includes a book of Kiowa folktales, The Journey of Tai-me *(1967), which he revised as* The Way to Rainy Mountain *(1969), and the Pulitzer Prize-winning novel* House Made of Dawn *(1968). His most recent book is* The Man Made of Words *(1997), a collection of essays, stories, and "passages."*

This essay originally appeared in the magazine The Reporter *in 1967, but Momaday revised it and used it as the introduction to* The Way to Rainy Mountain.

On Writing: *Momaday commented: "There's a lot of frustration in writing. I heard an interview with a writer not long ago in which the interviewer said, tell me, is writing difficult? And the writer said, oh, no . . . no, of course not. He said, 'All you do is sit down at a typewriter, you put a page in it, and then you look at it until beads of blood appear on your forehead. That's all there is to it.' There are days like that."*

BEFORE READING

Connecting: In what way does one of your relatives, perhaps a grandparent or a great-grandparent, connect you to a part of your family's past?

Anticipating: How and why does Momaday interlink descriptions of the landscape with descriptions of his grandmother?

A single knoll rises out of the plain in Oklahoma, north and west of the Wichita Range. For my people, the Kiowas, it is an old landmark, and they gave it the name Rainy Mountain. The hardest weather in the world is there. Winter brings blizzards, hot tornadic winds arise in the spring, and in summer the prairie is an anvil's edge. The grass turns brittle and brown, and it cracks beneath your feet. There are green belts along the rivers and creeks, linear groves of hickory and pecan, willow and witch hazel. At a distance in July or August the steaming foliage seems almost to writhe in fire. Great green and yellow grasshoppers are everywhere in the tall grass, popping up like corn to sting the flesh, and tortoises crawl about on the red earth, going nowhere in the plenty of time. Loneliness is an aspect of the land. All things in the plain are isolate; there is no confusion of objects in the eye, but one hill or one tree or one man. To look upon that landscape in the early morning, with the sun at your back, is to lose the sense of proportion. Your imagination comes to life, and this, you think, is where Creation was begun.

2   I returned to Rainy Mountain in July. My grandmother had died in the spring, and I wanted to be at her grave. She had lived to be very old and at last infirm. Her only living daughter was with her when she died, and I was told that in death her face was that of a child.

3   I like to think of her as a child. When she was born, the Kiowas were living the last great moment of their history. For more than a hundred years they had controlled the open range from the Smoky Hill River to the Red, from the headwaters of the Canadian to the fork of the Arkansas and Cimarron. In alliance with the Comanches, they had ruled the whole of the southern Plains. War was their sacred business, and they were among the finest horsemen the world has ever known. But warfare for the Kiowas was preeminently a matter of disposition rather than of survival, and they never understood the grim, unrelenting advance of the U.S. Cavalry. When at last, divided and ill-provisioned, they were driven onto the Staked Plains in the cold rains of autumn, they fell into panic. In Palo Duro Canyon they abandoned their crucial stores to pillage and had nothing then but their lives. In order to save themselves, they surrendered to the soldiers at Fort Sill and were imprisoned in the old stone corral that now stands as a military museum. My grandmother was spared the humiliation of those high gray walls by eight or ten years, but she must have known from birth the affliction of defeat, the dark brooding of old warriors.

4   Her name was Aho, and she belonged to the last culture to evolve in North America. Her forebears came down from the high country in western Montana nearly three centuries ago. They were a mountain people, a mysterious tribe of hunters whose language has never been positively classified in any major group. In the late seventeenth century they began a long migration to the south and east. It was a journey toward the dawn, and it led to a golden age. Along the way the Kiowas were befriended by the Crows, who gave them the culture and religion of the Plains. They acquired horses, and their ancient nomadic spirit was suddenly free of the ground. They acquired Tai-me, the sacred Sun Dance doll, from that moment the object and symbol of their worship, and so shared in the divinity of the sun. Not least, they acquired the sense of destiny, therefore courage and pride. When they entered upon the southern Plains they had been transformed. No longer were they slaves to the simple necessity of survival; they were a lordly and dangerous society of fighters and thieves, hunters and priests of the sun. According to their origin myth, they entered the world through a hollow log. From one point of view, their migration was the fruit of an old prophecy, for indeed they emerged from a sunless world.

5   Although my grandmother lived out her long life in the shadow of Rainy Mountain, the immense landscape of the continental interior lay like memory in her blood. She could tell of the Crows, whom she had never seen, and of the Black Hills, where she had never been. I wanted to see in reality what she had seen more perfectly in the mind's eye, and traveled fifteen hundred miles to begin my pilgrimage.

6   Yellowstone, it seemed to me, was the top of the world, a region of deep lakes and dark timber, canyons and waterfalls. But, beautiful as it is, one might have the sense of confinement there. The skyline in all directions is close at

hand, the high wall of the woods and deep cleavages of shade. There is a perfect freedom in the mountains, but it belongs to the eagle and the elk, the badger and the bear. The Kiowas reckoned their stature by the distance they could see, and they were bent and blind in the wilderness.

Descending eastward, the highland meadows are a stairway to the plain.   7
In July the inland slope of the Rockies is luxuriant with flax and buckwheat, stonecrop and larkspur. The earth unfolds and the limit of the land recedes. Clusters of trees, and animals grazing far in the distance, cause the vision to reach away and wonder to build upon the mind. The sun follows a longer course in the day, and the sky is immense beyond all comparison. The great billowing clouds that sail upon it are shadows that move upon the grain like water, dividing light. Farther down, in the land of the Crows and Blackfeet, the plain is yellow. Sweet clover takes hold of the hills and bends upon itself to cover and seal the soil. There the Kiowas paused on their way; they had come to the place where they must change their lives. The sun is at home on the plains. Precisely there does it have the certain character of a god. When the Kiowas came to the land of the Crows, they could see the dark lees of the hills at dawn across the Bighorn River, the profusion of light on the grain shelves, the oldest deity ranging after the solstices. Not yet would they veer southward to the caldron of the land that lay below; they must wean their blood from the northern winter and hold the mountains a while longer in their view. They bore Tai-me in procession to the east.

A dark mist lay over the Black Hills, and the land was like iron. At the   8
top of a ridge I caught sight of Devil's Tower up-thrust against the gray sky as if in the birth of time the core of the earth had broken through its crust and the motion of the world was begun. There are things in nature that engender an awful quiet in the heart of man; Devil's Tower is one of them. Two centuries ago, because they could not do otherwise, the Kiowas made a legend at the base of the rock. My grandmother said:

> Eight children were there at play, seven sisters and their brother. Suddenly the boy was struck dumb; he trembled and began to run upon his hands and feet. His fingers became claws, and his body was covered with fur. Directly there was a bear where the boy had been. The sisters were terrified; they ran, and the bear after them. They came to the stump of a great tree, and the tree spoke to them. It bade them climb upon it, and as they did so it began to rise into the air. The bear came to kill them, but they were just beyond its reach. It reared against the tree and scored the bark all around with its claws. The seven sisters were borne into the sky, and they became the stars of the Big Dipper.

From that moment, and so long as the legend lives, the Kiowas have kinsmen in the night sky. Whatever they were in the mountains, they could be no more. However tenuous their well-being, however much they had suffered and would suffer again, they had found a way out of the wilderness.

My grandmother had a reverence for the sun, a holy regard that now   9
is all but gone out of mankind. There was a wariness in her, and an ancient awe. She was a Christian in her later years, but she had come a long way

about, and she never forgot her birthright. As a child she had been to the Sun Dances; she had taken part in those annual rites, and by them she had learned the restoration of her people in the presence of Tai-me. She was about seven when the last Kiowa Sun Dance was held in 1887 on the Washita River above Rainy Mountain Creek. The buffalo were gone. In order to consummate the ancient sacrifice—to impale the head of a buffalo bull upon the medicine tree—a delegation of old men journeyed into Texas, there to beg and barter for an animal from the Goodnight herd. She was ten when the Kiowas came together for the last time as a living Sun Dance culture. They could find no buffalo; they had to hang an old hide from the sacred tree. Before the dance could begin, a company of soldiers rode out from Fort Sill under orders to disperse the tribe. Forbidden without cause the essential act of their faith, having seen the wild herds slaughtered and left to rot upon the ground, the Kiowas backed away forever from the medicine tree. That was July 20, 1890, at the great bend of the Washita. My grandmother was there. Without bitterness, and for as long as she lived, she bore a vision of deicide.

10   Now that I can have her only in memory, I see my grandmother in the several postures that were peculiar to her: standing at the wood stove on a winter morning and turning meat in a great iron skillet; sitting at the south window, bent above her beadwork, and afterwards, when her vision failed, looking down for a long time into the fold of her hands; going out upon a cane, very slowly as she did when the weight of age came upon her; praying. I remember her most often at prayer. She made long, rambling prayers out of suffering and hope, having seen many things. I was never sure that I had the right to hear, so exclusive were they of all mere custom and company. The last time I saw her she prayed standing by the side of her bed at night, naked to the waist, the light of a kerosene lamp moving upon her dark skin. Her long, black hair, always drawn and braided in the day, lay upon her shoulders and against her breasts like a shawl. I do not speak Kiowa, and I never understood her prayers, but there was something inherently sad in the sound, some merest hesitation upon the syllables of sorrow. She began in a high and descending pitch, exhausting her breath to silence; then again and again—and always the same intensity of effort, of something that is, and is not, like urgency in the human voice. Transported so in the dancing light among the shadows of her room, she seemed beyond the reach of time. But that was illusion; I think I knew then that I should not see her again.

11   Houses are like sentinels in the plain, old keepers of the weather watch. There, in a very little while, wood takes on the appearance of great age. All colors wear soon away in the wind and rain, and then the wood is burned gray and the grain appears and the nails turn red with rust. The windowpanes are black and opaque; you imagine there is nothing within, and indeed there are many ghosts, bones given up to the land. They stand here and there against the sky, and you approach them for a longer time than you expect. They belong in the distance; it is their domain.

12   Once there was a lot of sound in my grandmother's house, a lot of coming and going, feasting and talk. The summers there were full of excitement

and reunion. The Kiowas are a summer people; they abide the cold and keep to themselves, but when the season turns and the land becomes warm and vital they cannot hold still; an old love of going returns upon them. The aged visitors who came to my grandmother's house when I was a child were made of lean and leather, and they bore themselves upright. They wore great black hats and bright ample shirts that shook in the wind. They rubbed fat upon their hair and wound their braids with strips of colored cloth. Some of them painted their faces and carried the scars of old and cherished enmities. They were an old council of warlords, come to remind and be reminded of who they were. Their wives and daughters served them well. The women might indulge themselves; gossip was at once the mark and compensation of their servitude. They made loud and elaborate talk among themselves, full of jest and gesture, fright and false alarm. They went abroad in fringed and flowered shawls, bright beadwork and German silver. They were at home in the kitchen, and they prepared meals that were banquets.

There were frequent prayer meetings, and great nocturnal feasts. When I   13
was a child I played with my cousins outside, where the lamplight fell upon the ground and the singing of the old people rose up around us and carried away into the darkness. There were a lot of good things to eat, a lot of laughter and surprise. And afterwards, when the quiet returned, I lay down with my grandmother and could hear the frogs away by the river and feel the motion of the air.

Now there is a funeral silence in the rooms, the endless wake of some fi-   14
nal word. The walls have closed in upon my grandmother's house. When I returned to it in mourning, I saw for the first time in my life how small it was. It was late at night, and there was a white moon, nearly full. I sat for a long time on the stone steps by the kitchen door. From there I could see out across the land; I could see the long row of trees by the creek, the low light upon the rolling plains, and the stars of the Big Dipper. Once I looked at the moon and caught sight of a strange thing. A cricket had perched upon the handrail, only a few inches away from me. My line of vision was such that the creature filled the moon like a fossil. It had gone there, I thought, to live and die, for there, of all places, was its small definition made whole and eternal. A warm wind rose up and purled like the longing within me.

The next morning I awoke at dawn and went out on the dirt road to   15
Rainy Mountain. It was already hot, and the grasshoppers began to fill the air. Still, it was early in the morning, and the birds sang out of the shadows. The long yellow grass on the mountain shone in the bright light, and a scissortail hied above the land. There, where it ought to be, at the end of a long and legendary way, was my grandmother's grave. Here and there on the dark stones were ancestral names. Looking back once, I saw the mountain and came away.

QUESTIONS ON SUBJECT AND PURPOSE

1. What event triggers Momaday's essay?
2. How many "journeys" are involved in Momaday's story?

3. Why might Momaday have titled the essay "The Way to Rainy Mountain"? Why not, for example, refer more specifically to the event that has brought him back?

QUESTIONS ON STRATEGY AND AUDIENCE

1. Why might Momaday retell the legend of the "seven sisters" (paragraph 8)? How does that fit into his essay?
2. How much descriptive detail does Momaday give of his grandmother? Go through the essay, and isolate each physical detail the reader is given.
3. What expectations might Momaday have of his audience? How might those expectations affect the essay?

QUESTIONS ON VOCABULARY AND STYLE

1. Identify the figure of speech used in each of these descriptions:
   a. "in summer the prairie is an anvil's edge" (paragraph 1)
   b. "the highland meadows are a stairway to the plain" (7)
   c. "the land was like iron" (8)
   d. "houses are like sentinels in the plain" (11)
2. Between the essay's first appearance in a magazine and its inclusion in a book of essays two years later, Momaday added two new paragraphs, now 6 and 7. What do these paragraphs add to the essay?
3. Be prepared to define the following words: *knoll* (paragraph 1), *writhe* (1), *pillage* (3), *nomadic* (4), *luxuriant* (7), *lees* (7), *solstices* (7), *veer* (7), *tenuous* (8), *deicide* (9), *enmities* (12), *purled* (14), *hied* (15).

WRITING SUGGESTIONS

1. **For Your Journal.** What memories do you have of a grandparent or a great-grandparent? When you think of that person, what comes to mind? In your journal, make a list of those memories—sights, sounds, smells, associations of any sort.
2. **For a Paragraph.** In a substantial paragraph, analyze the effects that Momaday achieved by adding paragraphs 6 and 7 to the essay.
3. **For an Essay.** Momaday once told an interviewer, "I believe that the Indian has an understanding of the physical world and of the earth as a spiritual entity that is his, very much his own. The non-Indian can benefit a good deal by having that perception revealed to him." What do such perceptions reveal to the non-Indian?
4. **For Research.** What part have geography and other aspects of the natural world played in determining who you are? If you had to undertake a "pilgrimage" to a place or a geographical location or to

retrace a migration, where would you go? What were the stages on the journey? Research part of your own family history, and write a research paper in which you trace out that journey for a reader. You might want to start by talking with your relatives. Then use research—in the library, in archives, in electronic databases, in atlases, in talks with people—to fill out the story for your reader. Be sure to acknowledge all of your sources.

FOR FURTHER STUDY

Focusing on Grammar and Writing. Teachers often urge students to explore a variety of sentence types, not to rely, for example, on writing strings of simple sentences. Look at paragraph 10 in Momaday's essay. The long first sentence, a complex series of parallel clauses introduced by a colon and separated by semicolons, ends with a single participle, *praying*. That seven-line sentence is followed a simple sentence that grows out of that participle. The remainder of the paragraph shows other patterns at work—long, compound sentences held together with coordinating conjunctions and complex sentences containing dependent clauses. How do the sentences' structures reflect their meaning? What does Momaday gain by varying his sentence structures? What does this suggest about your own writing?

Working Together. Divide into small groups; each group should take a block of paragraphs to examine. Go through that block and locate all the uses of simile and metaphor (see glossary). Are there sections of the essay in which such devices do not occur at all? Where do the similes and metaphors tend to congregate? Why in those places and not others? Present your findings to the class as a whole.

Seeing Other Modes at Work. Momaday's essay involves a cause-and-effect strategy as well, explaining how the Kiowa people moved from the mountains to the Plains, how their gods changed, and how they suffered.

Finding Connections. Good pairings are with Debra Anne Davis's "A Pen by the Phone" and Scott Russell Sanders's "The Inheritance of Tools" (both in this chapter).

Exploring the Web. Among the many Web resources for Momaday is a long, detailed interview with him that includes extensive audio clips. You can find the link at **www.prenhall.com/miller.**

NAMELESS, TENNESSEE
William Least Heat Moon

William Least Heat Moon was born William Trogdon in Missouri in 1939 and earned a Ph.D. in English from the University of Missouri in 1973. Trogdon's father created his pen name in memory of their Sioux forefather. His books include Blue Highways: A Journey into America *(1982),* PrairyErth *(1991), and* River-Horse: A Voyage Across America *(1999), an account of his five-thousand mile journey across America's waterways from New York harbor to the Pacific Ocean. The following essay is from* Blue Highways, *an account of Least Heat Moon's 14,000-mile journey through American backroads in a converted van called Ghost Dancing. Its title refers to the blue ink used by map publisher Rand McNally to indicate smaller, or secondary, roads.*

On Writing: *Asked about his writing, Least Heat Moon observed: "Woody Allen once said the hardest thing in writing is going from nothing to something. And I think he's right. I struggle so much getting that first draft down. My writing draws so much upon every bit that I am, that I feel drained when I finish a book, and it's years before I'm ready to write again."*

BEFORE READING

Connecting: If you could get in an automobile and drive off, and time, money, and responsibilities posed no obstacles, where would you go?

Anticipating: "Nameless, Tennessee" does more than just faithfully record everything Least Heat Moon saw while visiting the Wattses. The narrative has a central focus that controls the selection of detail. What is that focus?

1 Nameless, Tennessee, was a town of maybe ninety people if you pushed it, a dozen houses along the road, a couple of barns, same number of churches, a general merchandise store selling Fire Chief gasoline, and a community center with a lighted volleyball court. Behind the center was an open-roof, rusting metal privy with PAINT ME on the door, in the hollow of a nearby oak lay a full pint of Jack Daniel's Black Label. From the houses, the odor of coal smoke.

2 Next to a red tobacco barn stood the general merchandise with a poster of Senator Albert Gore, Jr., smiling from the window. I knocked. The door opened partway. A tall, thin man said, "Closed up. For good," and started to shut the door.

3 "Don't want to buy anything. Just a question for Mr. Thurmond Watts."

4 The man peered through the slight opening. He looked me over. "What question would that be?"

"If this is Nameless, Tennessee, could he tell me how it got that name?"   5

The man turned back into the store and called out, "Miss Ginny! Some-   6
body here wants to know how Nameless come to be Nameless."

Miss Ginny edged to the door and looked me and my truck over.   7
Clearly, she didn't approve. She said, "You know as well as I do, Thurmond.
Don't keep him on the stoop in the damp to tell him." Miss Ginny, I found
out, was Mrs. Virginia Watts, Thurmond's wife.

I stepped in and they both began telling the story, adding a detail here,   8
the other correcting a fact there, both smiling at the foolishness of it all. It
seems the hilltop settlement went for years without a name. Then one day the
Post Office Department told the people if they wanted mail up on the mountain they would have to give the place a name you could properly address a letter to. The community met; there were only a handful, but they commenced
debating. Some wanted patriotic names, some names from nature, one man
recommended in all seriousness his own name. They couldn't agree, and they
ran out of names to argue about. Finally, a fellow tired of the talk; he didn't like
the mail he received anyway. "Forget the durn Post Office," he said. "This
here's a nameless place if I ever seen one, so leave it be." And that's just what
they did.

Watts pointed out the window. "We used to have signs on the road, but   9
the Halloween boys keep tearin' them down."

"You think Nameless is a funny name," Miss Ginny said. "I see it plain   10
in your eyes. Well, you take yourself up north a piece to Difficult or Defeated
or Shake Rag. Now them are silly names."

The old store, lighted only by three fifty-watt bulbs, smelled of coal oil   11
and baking bread. In the middle of the rectangular room, where the oak floor
sagged a little, stood an iron stove. To the right was a wooden table with an
unfinished game of checkers and a stool made from an apple-tree stump. On
shelves around the walls sat earthen jugs with corncob stoppers, a few canned
goods, and some of the two thousand old clocks and clockworks Thurmond
Watts owned. Only one was ticking, the others he just looked at. I asked how
long he'd been in the store.

"Thirty-five years, but we closed the first day of the year. We're hopin'   12
to sell it to a churchly couple. Upright people. No athians."

"Did you build this store?"   13

"I built this one, but it's the third general store on the ground. I fear it'll   14
be the last. I take no pleasure in that. Once you could come in here for a gallon of paint, a pickle, a pair of shoes, and a can of corn."

"Or horehound candy," Miss Ginny said. "Or corsets and salves. We had   15
cough syrups and all that for the body. In season, we'd buy and sell blackberries and walnuts and chestnuts, before the blight got them. And outside, Thurmond milled corn and sharpened plows. Even shoed a horse sometimes."

"We could fix up a horse or a man or a baby," Watts said.   16

"Thurmond, tell him we had a doctor on the ridge in them days."   17

"We had a doctor on the ridge in them days. As good as any doctor   18
alivin'. He'd cut a crooked toenail or deliver a woman. Dead these last years."

19   "I got some bad ham meat one day," Miss Ginny said, "and took to vomitin'. All day, all night. Hangin' on the drop edge of yonder. I said to Thurmond, 'Thurmond, unless you want shut of me, call the doctor.'"

20   "I studied on it," Watts said.

21   "You never did. You got him right now. He come over and put three drops of iodeen in half a glass of well water. I drank it down and the vomitin' stopped with the last swallow. Would you think iodeen could do that?"

22   "He put Miss Ginny on one teaspoon of spirits of ammonia in well water for her nerves. Ain't nothin' works better for her to this day."

23   "Calms me like the hand of the Lord."

24   Hilda, the Wattses' daughter, came out of the backroom. "I remember him," she said. "I was just a baby. Y'all were talkin' to him, and he lifted me up on the counter and gave me a stick of Juicy Fruit and a piece of cheese."

25   "Knew the old medicines," Watts said. "Only drugstore he needed was a good kitchen cabinet. None of them anteebeeotics that hit you worsen your ailment. Forgotten lore now, the old medicines, because they ain't profit in iodeen."

26   Miss Ginny started back to the side room where she and her sister Marilyn were taking apart a duck-down mattress to make bolsters. She stopped at the window for another look at Ghost Dancing. "How do you sleep in that thing? Ain't you all cramped and cold?"

27   "How does the clam sleep in his shell?" Watts said in my defense.

28   "Thurmond, get the boy a piece of buttermilk pie afore he goes on."

29   "Hilda, get some buttermilk pie." He looked at me. "You like good music?" I said I did. He cranked up an old Edison phonograph, the kind with the big morning-glory blossom for a speaker, and put on a wax cylinder. "This will be 'My Mother's Prayer,'" he said.

30   While I ate buttermilk pie, Watts served as disc jockey of Nameless, Tennessee. "Here's 'Mountain Rose.'" It was one of those moments that you know at the time will stay with you to the grave: the sweet pie, the gaunt man playing the old music, the coals in the stove glowing orange, the scent of kerosene and hot bread. "Here's 'Evening Rhapsody.'" The music was so heavily romantic we both laughed. I thought: It is for this I have come.

31   Feathered over and giggling, Miss Ginny stepped from the side room. She knew she was a sight. "Thurmond, give him some lunch. Still looks hungry."

32   Hilda pulled food off the woodstove in the backroom: home-butchered and canned whole-hog sausage, home-canned June apples, turnip greens, cole slaw, potatoes, stuffing, hot cornbread. All delicious.

33   Watts and Hilda sat and talked while I ate. "Wish you would join me."

34   "We've ate," Watts said. "Cain't beat a woodstove for flavorful cookin'."

35   He told me he was raised in a one-hundred-fifty-year-old cabin still standing in one of the hollows. "How many's left," he said, "that grew up in a log cabin? I ain't the last surely, but I must be climbin' on the list."

36   Hilda cleared the table. "You Watts ladies know how to cook."

37   "She's in nursin' school at Tennessee Tech. I went over for one of them football games last year there at Coevul." To say *Cookeville*, you let the word collapse in upon itself so that it comes out "Coevul."

"Do you like football?" I asked. 38

"Don't know. I was so high up in that stadium, I never opened my eyes." 39

Watts went to the back and returned with a fat spiral notebook that he 40
set on the table. His expression had changed. "Miss Ginny's *Deathbook*."

The thing startled me. Was it something I was supposed to sign? He 41
opened it but said nothing. There were scads of names written in a tidy hand
over pages incised to crinkliness by a ball-point. Chronologically, the names
had piled up: Wives, grandparents, a stillborn infant, relatives, friends close
and distant. Names, names. After each, the date of the unknown finally known
and transcribed. The last entry bore yesterday's date.

"She's wrote out twenty years' worth. Ever day she listens to the hospi- 42
tal report on the radio and puts the names in. Folks come by to check a date.
Or they just turn through the books. Read them like a scrapbook."

Hilda said, "Like Saint Peter at the gates inscribin' the names." 43

Watts took my arm. "Come along." He led me to the fruit cellar under 44
the store. As we went down, he said, "Always take a newborn baby upstairs
afore you take him downstairs, otherwise you'll incline him downwards."

The cellar was dry and full of cobwebs and jar after jar of home-canned 45
food, the bottles organized as a shopkeeper would: sausage, pumpkin, sweet
pickles, tomatoes, corn relish, blackberries, peppers, squash, jellies. He held a
hand out toward the dusty bottles. "Our tomorrows."

Upstairs again, he said, "Hope to sell the store to the right folk. I see 46
now, though, it'll be somebody offen the ridge. I've studied on it, and maybe
it's the end of our place." He stirred the coals. "This store could give a comfortable livin', but not likely get you rich. But just gettin' by is dice rollin' to
people nowadays. I never did see my day guaranteed."

When it was time to go, Watts said, "If you find anyone along your ways 47
wants a good store—on the road to Cordell Hull Lake—tell them about us."

I said I would. Miss Ginny and Hilda and Marilyn came out to say good- 48
bye. It was cold and drizzling again. "Weather to give a man the weary dismals," Watts grumbled. "Where you headed from here?"

"I don't know." 49

"Cain't get lost then." 50

Miss Ginny looked again at my rig. It had worried her from the first as 51
it had my mother. "I hope you don't get yourself kilt in that durn thing gallivantin' around the country."

"Come back when the hills dry off," Watts said. "We'll go lookin' for 52
some of them round rocks all sparkly inside."

I thought a moment. "Geodes?" 53

"Them's the ones. The country's properly full of them." 54

QUESTIONS ON SUBJECT AND PURPOSE

1. At one point in the narrative (paragraph 30), Least Heat Moon
   remarks, "I thought: It is for this I have come." What does he seem to
   be suggesting? What is the "this" that he finds in Nameless?

2. Why do "Miss Ginny's *Deathbook*" (paragraph 40) and the "fruit cellar" (44) seem appropriate details?
3. What might have attracted Least Heat Moon to this place and these people? What does he want you to sense? Is there anything in his description and narrative that suggests how he feels about Nameless?

QUESTIONS ON STRATEGY AND AUDIENCE

1. After you have read the selection, describe each member of the Watts family. Describe the exterior and interior of their store. Then carefully go through the selection and see how many specific descriptive details the author uses. List them.
2. What devices other than direct description does Least Heat Moon use to create the sense of place and personality? Make a list, and be prepared to tell how those devices work.
3. How is the narrative arranged? Is the order just spatial and chronological?
4. This selection is taken from *Blue Highways: A Journey into America,* a bestseller for nearly a year. Why would a travel narrative full of stories such as this be so appealing to an American audience?

QUESTIONS ON VOCABULARY AND STYLE

1. Least Heat Moon attempts to reproduce the pronunciation of some words—for example, *athians* (paragraph 12), *iodeen* (21), and *anteebeeotics* (25). Make a list of all such phonetic spellings. Why does Least Heat Moon do this? Do you think he captures all of the Wattses' accent or just some part of it? Is the device effective?
2. Examine how Least Heat Moon uses dialogue in his description. How are the Wattses revealed by what they say? How much of what was actually said during the visit is recorded? Can you find specific points in the story where Least Heat Moon obviously omits dialogue?
3. Try to define or explain the following words and phrases: *horehound candy* (paragraph 15), *bolsters* (26), *buttermilk pie* (28), *incised to crinkliness by a ballpoint* (41), *weary dismals* (48), *gallivantin' around* (51).

WRITING SUGGESTIONS

1. **For Your Journal.** Have you ever encountered or experienced a person, a place, or an event that seemed cut off from the modern world? In your journal, try to recall a few such experiences.
2. **For a Paragraph.** Virtually every campus has a building or a location that has acquired a strange or vivid name (for example, the cafeteria in

the Student Center known as "The Scrounge"). In a paragraph, describe such a place to a friend who has never seen it. Remember to keep a central focus—you want to convey an atmosphere more than a verbal photograph.

3. **For an Essay.** Look for an unusual business in your town or city (a barber shop, a food co-op, a delicatessen or diner, a secondhand clothing store, a specialized boutique). In an essay, describe the place. Your essay will need to have a focus—a central impression or thesis—that will govern your selection of details. It will probably work best if you also include some descriptions of people and dialogue.

4. **For Research.** Least Heat Moon is fascinated by unusual names and often drives considerable distances to visit towns with names such as Dime Box, Hungry Horse, Liberty Bond, Ninety-Six, and Tuba City. Choose an unusual place name (town, river, subdivision, topographical feature) from your home state and research the origin of the name. A reference librarian can show you how to locate source materials. If possible, contact your local historical society or public library for help or interview some knowledgeable local residents. Using your research, write an essay about how that name was chosen. Remember to document your sources.

FOR FURTHER STUDY

Focusing on Grammar and Writing. Writing dialogue is never easy, but there are times when dialogue is extremely effective. Select a group of paragraphs from the essay and rewrite them using no dialogue. You could simply have your narrator indirectly report what was said. What is lost when the dialogue is removed? What does this suggest about the effectiveness of dialogue? Study the dialogue that Least Heat Moon writes. What can you learn from him?

Working Together. Working in small groups, divide the essay into blocks of paragraphs. Take turns reading the story aloud and time it as you do. Presumably, Least Heat Moon's visit lasted several hours. How much time elapses in the dialogue? As you read, look for places in the narrative where time is abridged or when actions are clearly omitted. What does that reveal about artfully telling a story?

Seeing Other Modes at Work. The essay is also a narrative. How does Least Heat Moon structure his narrative?

Finding Connections. An interesting comparison in creating character is with Debra Anne Davis's "A Pen by the Phone" (this chapter). Davis, for example, uses no dialogue at all.

Exploring the Web. Want to read an excerpt from Least Heat Moon's *River-Horse*, an account of a 5,000-mile water voyage across America in a small boat named *Nikawa?* Is there really a Nameless, Tennessee? Visit **www.prenhall.com/miller.**

THE VILLAGE WATCHMAN
Terry Tempest Williams

Terry Tempest Williams (1955–), a fifth-generation Mormon, grew up within sight of Great Salt Lake. Williams has written and edited a number of books including the recent Red: Passion and Patience in the Desert *(2001) and* The Open Space of Democracy *(2004).*

"The Village Watchman" first appeared in Between Friends *(1994), a collection of essays; it was reprinted in her collection of essays titled* An Unspoken Hunger *(1994).*

On Writing: *A writer deeply concerned about environmental issues, Williams has observed that she writes "through my biases of gender, geography, and culture, that I am a woman whose ideas have been shaped by the Colorado Plateau and the Great Basin, that these ideas are then sorted out through the prism of my culture—and my culture is Mormon. Those tenets of family and community that I see at the heart of that culture are then articulated through story."*

BEFORE READING

Connecting: In her essay, Williams writes of our attitude toward people who are "mentally disabled or challenged": "We see them for who they are not, rather than for who they are." What does that sentence mean to you?

Anticipating: Williams is writing about her memories of her uncle. Out of the many that she has, why might she select the ones that she does? How does each included detail or incident affect our sense of Alan?

Stories carved in cedar rise from the deep woods of Sitka. These totem   1
poles are foreign to me, this vertical lineage of clans: Eagle, Raven, Wolf, and Salmon. The Tlingit craftsmen create a genealogy of the earth, a reminder of mentors, a reminder that we come into this world in need of proper instruction. I sit on the soft floor of this Alaskan forest and feel the presence of Other. The totem before me is called "Wolf Pole" by locals. The Village Watchman sits on top of Wolf's head with his knees drawn to his chest, his hands holding them tight against his body. He wears a red and black striped hat. His eyes are direct, deep set, painted blue.

The expression on his face reminds me of a man I loved, a man who was   2
born into this world feet first. "Breech," my mother told me of her brother's birth. "Alan was born feet first. As a result, his brain was denied oxygen. He is special." As a child, I was impressed by this information. I remember thinking that fish live underwater. Maybe Alan had gills, maybe he didn't need a face-first gulp of air like the rest of us. The amniotic sea he had floated in for nine months delivered him with a fluid memory. He knew something. Other.

3   There is a story of a boy who was kidnapped from his village by the Salmon People. He was taken from his family to learn the ways of water. When he returned many years later to his home, he was recognized by his own as a holy man privy to the mysteries of the unseen world. Twenty years after my uncle's death, I wonder if Alan could have been that boy.

4   But our culture tells a different story, more alien. My culture calls people of such births retarded, handicapped, mentally disabled or challenged. We see them for who they are not, rather than for who they are.

5   My grandmother, Lettie Romney Dixon, wrote in her journal, "It wasn't until Alan was 16 months old that a busy doctor cruelly broke the news to us. Others may have suspected our son's limitations but to those of us who loved him so unquestionably, lightning struck without warning. I hugged my sorrow to myself. I felt abandoned and lost. I wouldn't accept the verdict. Then we started the trips to a multitude of doctors. Most of them were kind and explained that our child was like a car without brakes, like an electric wire without insulation. They gave us no hope for a normal life."

6   Normal. Latin: *normalis; norma*, a rule: conforming with or constituting an accepted standard, model, or pattern, especially corresponding to the median or average of a large group in type, appearance, achievement, function, or development.

7   Alan was not normal. He was unique; one and only; single; sole; unusual; extraordinary; rare. His emotions were not measured, his curiosity not bridled. In a sense, he was wild like a mustang in the desert, and like most wild horses, he was eventually rounded up.

8   He was unpredictable. He created his own rules and they changed from moment to moment. Alan was 12 years old, hyperactive, mischievous, easily frustrated, and unable to learn in traditional ways. The situation was intensified by his seizures. Suddenly, without warning, he would stiffen like a rake, fall forward, and crash to the ground, hitting his head. My grandparents could not keep him home any longer. They needed professional guidance and help. In 1957, they reluctantly placed their youngest child in an institution for handicapped children called the American Fork Training School. My grandmother's heart broke for the second time.

9   Once again, from her journal: "Many a night my pillow is wet from tears of sorrow and senseless dreamings of 'if things had only been different,' or wondering if he is tucked in snug and warm, if he is well and happy, if the wind still bothers him. . . ."

10   The wind may have continued to bother Alan: certainly the conditions he was living under were less than ideal, but there was much about his private life his family never knew. What we did know was that Alan had an enormous capacity for adaptation. We had no choice but to follow him.

11   I followed him for years.

12   Alan was ten years my senior. In my mind, he was mythic. Everything I was taught not to do, Alan did. We were taught to be polite, to not express displeasure or anger in public. Alan was sheer, physical expression. Whatever was on his mind he vocalized and usually punctuated with colorful speech. We

would go bowling as a family on Sundays. Each of us would take our turn, hold the black ball to our chest, take a few steps, swing our arm back, forward, glide, and release. The ball would roll down the alley, hit a few pins; we would wait for the ball to return, and then take our second run. Little emotion was shown. When it was Alan's turn, it was an event. Nothing subtle. His style was Herculean. Big man. Big ball. Big roll. Big bang. Whether it was a strike or a gutter ball, he clapped his hands, spun around on the floor, slapped his thighs, and cried, "Goddamn! Did you see that one? Send me another ball, sweet Jesus!" And the ball was always returned.

I could count on my uncle for a straight answer. He taught me that one   13
of the remarkable aspects of being human was to hold opposing views in our mind at once.

"How are you doing?" I would ask.   14

"Ask me how I am feeling?" he answered.   15

"Okay, how are you feeling?"   16

"Today? Right now?"   17

"Yes."   18

"I am very happy and very sad."   19

"How can you be both at the same time?" I asked in all seriousness, a girl   20
of nine or ten.

"Because both require each other's company. They live in the same   21
house. Didn't you know?"

We would laugh and then go on to another topic. Talking to my uncle   22
was always like entering a maze of riddles. Ask a question. Answer with a question and see where it leads you.

My younger brother Steve and I spent a lot of time with Alan. He of-   23
fered us shelter from the conventionality of a Mormon family. At our home during Christmas, he would direct us in his own nativity plays. "More—" he would say to us, making wide gestures with his hands. "Give me more of yourself." He was not like anyone we knew. In a culture where we were taught to be seen and not heard. Alan was our mirror.

We could be different, too. His unquestioning belief in us as children, as   24
human beings, was in startling contrast to the way we saw the public react to him. It hurt us. We could never tell if it hurt him.

Each week, Steve and I would accompany our grandparents south to   25
visit Alan. It was an hour's drive to the school from Salt Lake City, mostly through farmlands. We would enter the grounds, pull into the parking lot to a playground filled with huge papier-mâché storybook figures (a 20-foot pied piper, a pumpkin carriage with Cinderella inside, the old woman who lived in a shoe), and nine times out of ten, Alan would be standing outside his dormitory waiting for us. We would get out of the car and he would run toward us and throw his powerful arms around us. His hugs cracked my back and at times I had to fight for my breath. My grandfather would calm him down by simply saying, "We're here, son. You can relax now."

Alan was a formidable man, now in his early twenties, stocky and strong. His   26
head was large, with a protruding forehead that bore many scars, a line-by-line

history of seizures. He always had on someone else's clothes—a tweed jacket too small, brown pants too big, a striped golf shirt that didn't match. He showed us that appearances didn't matter, personality did. If you didn't know him, he could look frightening. It was an unspoken rule in our family that the character of others was gauged by how they treated Alan. The only consistent thing about his attire was that he always wore a silver football helmet from Olympus High School, where my grandfather was coach. It was a loving, practical solution to protect Alan when he fell.

27   "Part of the team," my grandfather would say as he slapped Alan affectionally on the back, "You're a Titan, son, and I love you."

28   The windows to the dormitory were dark, reflecting Mount Timpanogos to the east. It was hard to see inside, but I knew what the interior held. It looked like an abandoned gymnasium without bleachers, filled with hospital beds. The stained white walls and yellow-waxed floors offered no warmth. The stench was nauseating: sweat and urine trapped in the oppression of stale air. I recall the dirty sheets, the lack of privacy, and the almond-eyed children who never rose from their beds. And then I would turn around and face Alan's cheerfulness, the open and loving manner in which he would introduce me to his friends, the pride he exhibited as he showed me around his home. I kept thinking, "Doesn't he see how bad this is, how poorly they are being treated?" His words would return to me: "I am very happy and very sad."

29   For my brother and me, Alan was guide, elder. He was fearless. But neither one of us will ever be able to escape the image of Alan kissing his parents good-bye after an afternoon with family and slowly walking back to his dormitory. Before we drove away, he would turn toward us, take off his silver helmet, and wave. The look on his face haunts me still.

30   Alan liked to talk about God. Perhaps it was in these private conversations that our real friendship was forged.

31   "I know Him," he would say when all the adults were gone.

32   "You do?" I asked.

33   "I talk to Him every day."

34   "How?"

35   "I talk to Him in my prayers. I listen and then I hear His voice."

36   "What does He tell you?"

37   "He tells me to be patient. He tells me to be kind. He tells me that He loves me."

38   In Mormon culture, children are baptized as members of the Church of Jesus Christ of Latter-day Saints when they turn 8 years old. Alan had never been baptized because my grandparents believed it should be his choice, not something simply taken for granted. When he turned 22, he expressed a sincere desire to join the church. A date was set immediately.

39   The entire Dixon clan convened in the Lehi chapel, a few miles north of the group home where Alan was then living. We were there to support and witness his conversion. As we walked toward the meetinghouse where this sacred rite was to be performed, Alan had a violent seizure. My grandfather and uncle Don, Alan's elder brother, dropped down with him, holding his head and body as every muscle thrashed on the pavement like a school of netted fish

brought on deck. I didn't want to look, but to walk away would have been worse. We stayed with him, all of us.

"Talk to God,—" I heard myself saying under my breath. "I love you, Alan." 40

"Can you hear me, darling?" It was my grandmother, holding her son's hand. 41

By now, many of us were gathered on our knees around him, our trembling hands on his rigid body. 42

Alan opened his eyes. "I want to be baptized," he said. The men helped him to his feet. The gash on his left temple was deep. Blood dripped down the side of his face. My mother had her arm around my grandmother's waist. Shaken, we all followed him inside. 43

Alan's father and brother stopped the bleeding and bandaged the pressure wound, then helped him change into the designated white garments for baptism. He entered the room with great dignity and sat on the front pew with a dozen or more 8-year-old children seated on either side. Row after row of family sat behind him. 44

"Alan Romney Dixon." His name was called by the presiding bishop. Alan rose from the pew and met his brother Don, also dressed in white, who took his hand and led him down the blue-tiled stairs into the baptismal font filled with water. They faced the congregation. Don raised his right arm to the square in the gesture of a holy oath as Alan placed his hands on his brother's left forearm. The sacred prayer was offered in the name of the Father, the Son, and the Holy Ghost, after which my uncle put his right hand behind Alan's shoulder and gently lowered him into the water for a baptism by complete immersion. 45

Alan emerged from the holy waters like an angel. 46

Six years later, I found myself sitting with my uncle at a hospital where he was being treated for a severe ear infection. I was 18. He was 28. 47

"Alan," I asked, "what is it really like to live inside your body?" 48

He crossed his legs and placed both hands on the arms of the chair. His brown eyes were piercing. 49

"I can't tell you what it's like except to say I feel pain for not being seen as the person I am." 50

A few days later, Alan died—alone, unique, one and only, single—in American Fork, Utah. 51

The Village Watchman sits on top of his totem with Wolf and Salmon. It is beginning to rain in the forest. I find it curious that this spot in southeast Alaska has brought me back into relation with my uncle, this man who came into the world feet first. He reminds me of what it means to live and love with a broken heart; how nothing is sacred, how everything is sacred. He was a weather vane, at once a storm and a clearing. 52

Shortly after his death, Alan appeared to me in a dream. We were standing in my grandmother's kitchen. He was leaning against the white stove with his arms folded. 53

"Look at me now, Terry," he said, smiling. "I'm normal—perfectly normal." And then he laughed. We both laughed. 54

55   He handed me his silver football helmet, which was resting on the counter, kissed me, and opened the back door.

56   "Do you recognize who I am?"

57   On this day in Sitka, I remember.

QUESTIONS ON SUBJECT AND PURPOSE

1. What associations do you have with the word *normal?* Does Williams's definition (paragraph 6) challenge those associations?
2. In two places (paragraphs 5 and 9), Williams quotes from her grandmother's journal. What is the effect of these quotations?
3. Why would a reader be interested in a tribute to her uncle? Do you find the story moving?

QUESTIONS ON STRATEGY AND AUDIENCE

1. Why does Williams begin and end with the references to the totem poles in Alaska?
2. At several places, Williams reproduces—or rather re-creates—conversations she had with Alan (for example, paragraphs 14–21, 31–37, and 48–50). Why? What is the effect of these sections?
3. What expectations might Williams have about her audience and their reaction to Alan?

QUESTIONS ON VOCABULARY AND STYLE

1. At a number of points in the essay, Williams quotes Alan. What do these quotations add to her description?
2. What is the effect of Alan's question, "Do you recognize who I am?"
3. Be prepared to define the following words: *privy* (paragraph 3) and *convened* (39).

WRITING SUGGESTIONS

1. **For Your Journal.** Select a vivid memory that involves a family member or a close friend who touched your life. In your journal, describe for yourself what you remember. Do not worry about trying to be too focused. Concentrate on recovering memories.
2. **For a Paragraph.** In a paragraph, try to "capture" that person. Remember that your description needs a central focus or purpose. Why are you writing about this person? What is important for the reader to know about this person? Select details to reveal the person to your reader rather than simply telling the reader what to think.

3. **For an Essay.** In writing about Alan, Williams achieves two purposes: she memorializes her uncle, and she comments on society's perceptions of persons who are "mentally disabled or challenged." Try for a similar effect in an essay about someone who has touched your life.
   Remember that your essay needs to have a duel purpose or thesis.

4. **For Research.** Explore our society's reactions to people who are, to use Williams's words, "retarded, handicapped, mentally disabled or challenged." How does society see such people? How are they treated or portrayed? This is a large subject, so you will need to find a way to focus your research and writing. You could concentrate on changes in reaction over time (early twentieth century versus late in the century), portrayals (or their lack) in the popular media, family attitudes versus outsiders' attitudes, or reactions to a specific disability (such as Down's syndrome). Textbooks might be one place to start. You will need to establish a list of possible subject headings and keywords before you start searching library resources, online databases, and the World Wide Web. Remember to document your sources, including any information that you obtain through interviews.

FOR FURTHER STUDY

Focusing on Grammar and Writing. Select some of the longer paragraphs in Williams's essay. Look carefully at the first sentence in each paragraph. How does that sentence serve to control the details that follow? Even though many of Williams's paragraphs are narrative in nature, she still forecasts their structure through those first sentences. What does this suggest about your own paragraphs in your essay?

Working Together. Divide into small groups. Each group should choose one of the following to examine:

1. The story of the boy kidnapped by the Salmon People (paragraph 3)
2. The scene in the bowling alley (12)
3. The papier-mâché storybook figures (25)
4. The dormitory (28)
5. Alan's conversations with God (30–37)
6. Williams's dream after Alan's death (53–56)

What does each section or detail contribute to the essay? What does each add to the story of Alan?

Seeing Other Modes at Work. The essay employs a range of other strategies or modes, including narration (throughout), definition (paragraph 6), comparison and contrast (5, 7, 12), and persuasion (throughout).

Finding Connections. The essay can be paired with William Least Heat Moon's "Nameless Tennessee" for a comparison on creating and revealing character, or with Scott Russell Sanders's "The Inheritance of Tools" for a comparison on how the death of a loved one is handled. Both essays are in this chapter.

Exploring the Web. A listing of sites dealing with Williams and her writing and with specific genetic or birth conditions can be found at **www.prenhall.com/miller.**

THE INHERITANCE OF TOOLS

Scott Russell Sanders

Born in Memphis, Tennessee, in 1945, Scott Russell Sanders received a Ph.D. from Cambridge University. Currently a professor of English at Indiana University, Sanders is a novelist, an essayist, and a science fiction writer. He has contributed fiction and essays to many journals and magazines and has published numerous books, including the recent collection of essays The Force of Spirit *(2000).*

Sanders writes often about his childhood and his efforts to "ground" himself. In another of his collections of essays, Secrets of the Universe *(1991), Sanders describes growing up with an alcoholic father, noting that he "wants to drag into the light what eats at me—the fear, the guilt, the shame—so that my own children may be spared."*

On Writing: *Commenting on the development of his writing style from academic prose to creative writing and essays, Sanders observed: "I flouted the rules I learned about writing in school. I played with sound, strung images together line after line, flung out metaphors by the handful. Sin of sins, I even mixed metaphors, the way any fertile field will sprout dozens of species of grass and flower and fern. I let my feelings and opinions show. . . . I drew shamelessly on my own life. I swore off jargon and muddle and much. I wrote in the active voice."*

BEFORE READING

Connecting: Can you think of something that you learned how to do from a family member or friend?

Anticipating: In what ways is "The Inheritance of Tools" an appropriate title for the essay? What is the essay about?

At just about the hour when my father died, soon after dawn one February   1
morning when ice coated the windows like cataracts, I banged my thumb with a hammer. Naturally I swore at the hammer, the reckless thing, and in the moment of swearing I thought of what my father would say: "If you'd try hitting the nail it would go in a whole lot faster. Don't you know your thumb's not as hard as that hammer?" We both were doing carpentry that day, but far apart. He was building cupboards at my brother's place in Oklahoma; I was at home in Indiana putting up a wall in the basement to make a bedroom for my daughter. By the time my mother called with news of his death—the long distance wires whittling her voice until it seemed too thin to bear the weight of what she had to say—my thumb was swollen. A week or so later a white scar in the shape of a crescent moon began to show above the cuticle, and month by month it rose across the pink sky of my thumbnail. It took the better part of a year for the scar to disappear, and every time I noticed it I thought of my father.

2   The hammer had belonged to him, and to his father before him. The three of us have used it to build houses and barns and chicken coops, to upholster chairs and crack walnuts, to make doll furniture and book shelves and jewelry boxes. The head is scratched and pockmarked, like an old plowshare that has been working rocky fields, and it gives off the sort of dull sheen you see on fast creek water in the shade. It is a finishing hammer, about the weight of a bread loaf, too light, really, for framing walls, too heavy for cabinetwork, with a curved claw for pulling nails, a rounded head for pounding, a fluted neck for looks, and a hickory handle for strength.

3   The present handle is my third one, bought from a lumberyard in Tennessee down the road from where my brother and I were helping my father build his retirement house. I broke the previous one by trying to pull sixteen-penny nails out of floor joists—a foolish thing to do with a finishing hammer, as my father pointed out. "You ever hear of a crowbar?" he said. No telling how many handles he and my grandfather had gone through before me. My grandfather used to cut down hickory trees on his farm, saw them into slabs, cure the planks in his hayloft, and carve handles with a drawknife. The grain in hickory is crooked and knotty, and therefore rough, hard to split, like the grain in the two men who owned this hammer before me.

4   After proposing marriage to a neighbor girl, my grandfather used this hammer to build a house for his bride on a stretch of river bottom in northern Mississippi. The lumber for the place, like the hickory for the handle, was cut on his own land. By the day of the wedding he had not quite finished the house, and so right after the ceremony he took his wife home and put her to work. My grandmother had worn her Sunday dress for the wedding, with a fringe of lace tacked on around the hem in honor of the occasion. She removed this lace and folded it away before going out to help my grandfather nail siding on the house. "There she was in her good dress," he told me some fifty-odd years after that wedding day, "holding up them long pieces of clapboard while I hammered, and together we got the place covered up before dark." As the family grew to four, six, eight, and eventually thirteen, my grandfather used this hammer to enlarge his house room by room, like a chambered nautilus expanding his shell.

5   By and by the hammer was passed along to my father. One day he was up on the roof of our pony barn nailing shingles with it, when I stepped out the kitchen door to call him for supper. Before I could yell, something about the sight of him straddling the spine of that roof and swinging the hammer caught my eye and made me hold my tongue. I was five or six years old, and the world's commonplaces were still news to me. He would pull a nail from the pouch at his waist, bring the hammer down, and a moment later the *thunk* of the blow would reach my ears. And that is what had stopped me in my tracks and stilled my tongue, that momentary gap between seeing and hearing the blow. Instead of yelling from the kitchen door, I ran to the barn and climbed two rungs up the ladder—as far as I was allowed to go—and spoke quietly to my father. On our walk to the house he explained that sound takes time to make its way through air. Suddenly the world seemed larger, the air more dense, if sound could be held back like any ordinary traveler.

By the time I started using this hammer, at about the age when I discov- 6
ered the speed of sound, it already contained houses and mysteries for me.
The smooth handle was one my grandfather had made. In those days I needed
both hands to swing it. My father would start a nail in a scrap of wood, and I
would pound away until I bent it over.

"Looks like you got ahold of some of those rubber nails," he would tell me. 7
"Here, let me see if I can find you some stiff ones." And he would rummage in
a drawer until he came up with a fistful of more cooperative nails. "Look at the
head," he would tell me. "Don't look at your hands, don't look at the hammer.
Just look at the head of that nail and pretty soon you'll learn to hit it square."

Pretty soon I did learn. While he worked in the garage cutting dovetail 8
joints for a drawer or skinning a deer or tuning an engine, I would hammer
nails. I made innocent blocks of wood look like porcupines. He did not talk
much in the midst of his tools, but he kept up a nearly ceaseless humming, slip-
ping in and out of a dozen tunes in an afternoon, often running back over the
same stretch of melody again and again, as if searching for a way out. When
the humming did cease, I knew he was faced with a task requiring great deli-
cacy or concentration, and I took care not to distract him.

He kept scraps of wood in a cardboard box—the ends of two-by-fours, 9
slabs of shelving and plywood, odd pieces of molding—and everything in it
was fair game. I nailed scraps together to fashion what I called boats or houses,
but the results usually bore only faint resemblance to the visions I carried in
my head. I would hold up these constructions to show my father, and he would
turn them over in his hands admiringly, speculating about what they might be.
My cobbled-together guitars might have been alien spaceships, my barns
might have been models of Aztec temples, each wooden contraption might
have been anything but what I had set out to make.

Now and again I would feel the need to have a chunk of wood shaped or 10
shortened before I riddled it with nails, and I would clamp it in a vise and
scrape at it with a handsaw. My father would let me lacerate the board until
my arm gave out, and then he would wrap his hand around mine and help
me finish the cut, showing me how to use my thumb to guide the blade, how
to pull back on the saw to keep it from binding, how to let my shoulder do
the work.

"Don't force it," he would say, "just drag it easy and give the teeth a 11
chance to bite."

As the saw teeth bit down, the wood released its smell, each kind with its 12
own fragrance, oak or walnut or cherry or pine—usually pine because it was
the softest, easiest for a child to work. No matter how weathered and gray the
board, no matter how warped and cracked, inside there was this smell waiting,
as of something freshly baked. I gathered every smidgen of sawdust and stored
it away in coffee cans, which I kept in a drawer of the workbench. When I did
not feel like hammering nails I would dump my sawdust on the concrete floor
of the garage and landscape it into highways and farms and towns, running
miniature cars and trucks along miniature roads. Looming as huge as a colos-
sus, my father worked over and around me, now and again bending down to

inspect my work, careful not to trample my creations. It was a landscape that smelled dizzyingly of wood. Even after a bath my skin would carry the smell, and so would my father's hair, when he lifted me for a bedtime hug.

13   I tell these things not only from memory but also from recent observation, because my own son now turns blocks of wood into nailed porcupines, dumps cans full of sawdust at my feet and sculpts highways on the floor. He learns how to swing a hammer from the elbow instead of the wrist, how to lay his thumb beside the blade to guide a saw, how to tap a chisel with a wooden mallet, how to mark a hole with an awl before starting a drill bit. My daughter did the same before him, and even now, on the brink of teenage aloofness, she will occasionally drag out my box of wood scraps and carpenter something. So I have seen my apprenticeship to wood and tools reenacted in each of my children, as my father saw his own apprenticeship renewed in me.

14   The saw I use belonged to him, as did my level and both of my squares, and all four tools had belonged to his father. The blade of the saw is the bluish color of gun barrels, and the maple handle, dark from the sweat of hands, is inscribed with curving leaf designs. The level is a shaft of walnut two feet long, edged with brass and pierced by three round windows in which air bubbles float in oil-filled tubes of glass. The middle window serves for testing if a surface is horizontal, the others for testing if a surface is plumb or vertical. My grandfather used to carry this level on the gun-rack behind the seat in his pickup, and when I rode with him I would turn around to watch the bubbles dance. The larger of the two squares is called a framing square, a flat steel elbow, so beat up and tarnished you can barely make out the rows of numbers that show how to figure the cuts on rafters. The smaller one is called a try square, for marking right angles, with a blued steel blade for the shank and a brass-faced block of cherry for the head.

15   I was taught early on that a saw is not to be used apart from a square: "If you're going to cut a piece of wood," my father insisted, "you owe it to the tree to cut it straight."

16   Long before studying geometry, I learned there is a mystical virtue in right angles. There is an unspoken morality in seeking the level and the plumb. A house will stand, a table will bear weight, the sides of a box will hold together only if the joints are square and the members upright. When the bubble is lined up between two marks etched in the glass tube of a level, you have aligned yourself with the forces that hold the universe together. When you miter the corners of a picture frame, each angle must be exactly forty-five degrees, as they are in the perfect triangles of Pythagoras, not a degree more or less. Otherwise the frame will hang crookedly, as if ashamed of itself and of its maker. No matter if the joints you are cutting do not show. Even if you are butting two pieces of wood together inside a cabinet, where no one except a wrecking crew will ever see them, you must take pains to insure that the ends are square and the studs are plumb.

17   I took pains over the wall I was building on the day my father died. Not long after that wall was finished—paneled with tongue-and-groove boards of yellow pine, the nail holes filled with putty and the wood all stained and sealed— I came close to wrecking it one afternoon when my daughter ran howling up the stairs to announce that her gerbils had escaped from their cage and were

hiding in my brand new wall. She could hear them scratching and squeaking behind her bed. Impossible! I said. How on earth could they get inside my drumtight wall? Through the heating vent, she answered. I went downstairs, pressed my ear to the honey-colored wood, and heard the *scritch scritch* of tiny feet.

"What can we do?" my daughter wailed. "They'll starve to death, they'll   18
die of thirst, they'll suffocate."

"Hold on," I shouted, "I'll think of something."   19

While I thought and she fretted, the radio on her bedside table delivered   20
us the headlines. Several thousand people had died in a city in India from a
poisonous cloud that had leaked overnight from a chemical plant. A nuclear-
powered submarine had been launched. Rioting continued in South Africa. An
airplane had been hijacked in the Mediterranean. Authorities calculated that
several thousand homeless people slept on the streets within sight of the
Washington Monument. I felt my usual helplessness in face of all these
calamities. But here was my daughter weeping because her gerbils were holed
up in a wall. This calamity I could handle.

"Don't worry," I told her. "We'll set food and water by the heating vent   21
and lure them out. And if that doesn't do the trick, I'll tear the wall apart
until we find them."

She stopped crying and gazed as me. "You'd really tear it apart? Just for   22
my gerbils? The *wall?*" Astonishment slowed her down only for a second,
however, before she ran to the workbench and began tugging at drawers, saying, "Let's see, what'll we need? Crowbar. Hammer. Chisels. I hope we don't
have to use them—but just in case."

We didn't need the wrecking tools. I never had to assault my handsome   23
wall, because the gerbils eventually came out to nibble at a dish of popcorn.
But for several hours I studied the tongue-and-groove skin I had nailed up on
the day of my father's death, considering where to begin prying. There were
no gaps in that wall, no crooked joints.

I had botched a great many pieces of wood before I mastered the right   24
angle with a saw, botched even more before I learned to miter a joint. The
knowledge of these things resides in my hands and eyes and the webwork of
muscles, not in the tools. There are machines for sale—powered miter boxes
and radial-arm saws, for instance—that will enable any casual soul to cut
proper angles in boards. The skill is invested in the gadget instead of the person who uses it, and this is what distinguishes a machine from a tool. If I had
to earn my keep by making furniture or building houses, I suppose I would buy
powered saws and pneumatic nailers; the need for speed would drive me to it.
But since I carpenter only for my own pleasure or to help neighbors or to re-
make the house around the ears of my family, I stick with hand tools. Most of
the ones I own were given to me by my father, who also taught me how to
wield them. The tools in my work-bench are a double inheritance, for each
hammer and level and saw is wrapped in a cloud of knowing.

All of these tools are a pleasure to look at and to hold. Merchants would   25
never paste NEW NEW NEW! signs on them in stores. Their designs are old
because they work, because they serve their purpose well. Like folksongs and
aphorisms and the grainy bits of language, these tools have been pared down

to essentials. I look at my claw hammer, the distillation of a hundred generations of carpenters, and consider that it holds up well beside those other classics—Greek vases, Gregorian chants, *Don Quixote*, barbed fish hooks, candles, spoons. Knowledge of hammering stretches back to the earliest humans who squatted beside fires chipping flints. Anthropologists have a lovely name for those unworked rocks that served as the earliest hammers. *Dawn stones*, they are called. Their only qualification for the work, aside from hardness, is that they fit the hand. Our ancestors used them for grinding corn, tapping awls, smashing bones. From dawn stones to this claw hammer is a great leap in time, but no great distance in design or imagination.

26   On that iced-over February morning when I smashed my thumb with the hammer, I was down in the basement framing the wall that my daughter's gerbils would later hide in. I was thinking of my father, as I always did whenever I built anything, thinking how he would have gone about the work, hearing in memory what he would have said about the wisdom of hitting the nail instead of my thumb. I had the studs and plates nailed together all square and trim, and was lifting the wall into place when the phone rang upstairs. My wife answered, and in a moment she came to the basement door and called down softly to me. The stillness in her voice made me drop the framed wall and hurry upstairs. She told me my father was dead. Then I heard the details over the phone from my mother. Building a set of cupboards for my brother in Oklahoma, he had knocked off work early the previous afternoon because of cramps in his stomach. Early this morning, on his way into the kitchen of my brother's trailer, maybe going for a glass of water, so early that no one else was awake, he slumped down on the linoleum and his heart quit.

27   For several hours I paced around inside my house, upstairs and down, in and out of every room, looking for the right door to open and knowing there was no such door. My wife and children followed me and wrapped me in arms and backed away again, circling and staring as if I were on fire. Where was the door, the door, the door? I kept wondering. My smashed thumb turned purple and throbbed, making me furious. I wanted to cut it off and rush outside and scrape away the snow and hack a hole in the frozen earth and bury the shameful thing.

28   I went down into the basement, opened a drawer in my workbench, and stared at the ranks of chisels and knives. Oiled and sharp, as my father would have kept them, they gleamed at me like teeth. I took up a clasp knife, pried out the longest blade and tested the edge on the hair of my forearm. A tuft came away cleanly, and I saw my father testing the sharpness of tools on his own skin, the blades of axes and knives and gouges and hoes, saw the red hair shaved off in patches from his arms and the backs of his hands. "That will cut bear," he would say. He never cut a bear with his blades, now my blades, but he cut deer, dirt, wood. I closed the knife and put it away. Then I took up the hammer and went back to work on my daughter's wall, snugging the bottom plate against a chalk line on the floor, shimming the top plate against the joists overhead, plumbing the studs with my level, making sure before I drove the first nail that every line was square and true.

QUESTIONS ON SUBJECT AND PURPOSE

1. What is the subject of Sanders's essay? Is it tools? His father's death?
2. Is Sanders's father or grandfather (or his children) ever described in the story? How are they revealed to the reader?
3. What "door" (paragraph 27) is Sanders searching for?
4. What exactly has Sanders inherited from his father?

QUESTIONS ON STRATEGY AND AUDIENCE

1. How does Sanders use time to structure his essay? Is the story told in chronological order?
2. What is the function of each of the following episodes or events in the essay?
   a. The sore thumb
   b. "A mystical virtue in right angles" (paragraph 16)
   c. The wall he was building
3. What expectations does Sanders seem to have about his audience?

QUESTIONS ON VOCABULARY AND STYLE

1. How much dialogue does Sanders use in the story? What does the dialogue contribute?
2. Throughout the essay, Sanders makes use of many effective similes and metaphors. Make a list of six such devices. What does each contribute to the essay? How fresh and arresting are these images?
3. Be able to define each of the following words or phrases: *plowshare* (paragraph 2), *sixteen-penny nails* (3), *chambered nautilus* (4), *rummage* (7), *lacerate* (10), *smidgen* (12), *plumb* (14), *miter* (24), *aphorisms* (25), *shimming* (28).

WRITING SUGGESTIONS

1. **For Your Journal.** The word *inheritance* may suggest money or property that is bequeathed to a descendent. But you can "inherit" many things that are far less tangible. In your journal, explore what you might have inherited from someone in your family—perhaps a talent, an interest, an ability, or an obsession.
2. **For a Paragraph.** Study the childhood scenes or episodes that Sanders includes in his essay—for example, calling his father to supper (paragraph 5), hammering nails (6–9), landscaping with sawdust (12). Notice how Sanders re-creates sensory experiences. Then in a paragraph, re-create a similar experience from your childhood. Remember to evoke sensory impressions for your reader—sight, sound, smell, touch.

3. **For an Essay.** Think about a skill, talent, or habit that you have learned from or share with a family member. In addition to the ability or trait, what else have you "inherited"? How does it affect your life? In an essay, describe the inheritance and its effect on you.

4. **For Research.** The passing on of traditional crafts or skills is an important part of cultural tradition. Choose a society that interests you, and find a particular craft that is preserved from one generation to another. It might also be something that has been preserved in your family's religious or ethnic heritage. In a research paper, document the nature of the craft and the methods by which the culture ensures its transmission. What is important about this craft? What does it represent to that society? Why bother to preserve it?

FOR FURTHER STUDY

Focusing on Grammar and Writing. Sanders often uses dashes to insert material into his sentences and to add material to the ends of sentences. Make a list of each use, and on the basis of that sample, write some "rules" for the use of the dash in writing. What other punctuation alternatives could Sanders have used in each case? Could he have used commas? Parentheses? What would have been the difference?

Working Together. Working in small groups, choose a block of paragraphs from the essay. Starting with a definition of simile and metaphor (see glossary), how many similes and metaphors can you find in the block you are analyzing? What do those images have in common? Discuss your findings with the class as a whole.

Seeing Other Modes at Work. In addition to narration, Sanders uses comparison and contrast, particularly to draw the relationship between two generations of fathers and children.

Finding Connections. The impact of a relative's death is also the subject of Terry Tempest Williams' "The Village Watchman" in this chapter.

Exploring the Web. Another view of Sanders's relationship with his father can be found in his essay "Under the Influence," which can be read online. The link is available at **www.prenhall.com/miller.**

DIVISION AND
CLASSIFICATION

PREPARING TO WRITE

Division and classification are closely related methods of analysis, but you can remember the difference by asking yourself whether you are analyzing a single thing by dividing it into its constituent parts, or analyzing two or more things by sorting them into related categories.

WHAT IS DIVISION?

Division occurs when a single subject is subdivided into its parts. To cut a pizza into slices, to list the ingredients in a can of soup or a box of cereal, or to create a pie chart is to perform a division. The key is that you start with a single thing.

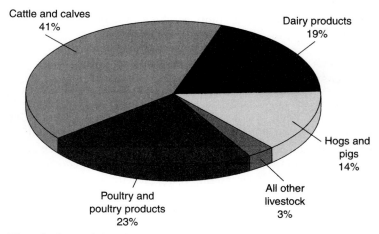

Cattle and calves
41%

Dairy products
19%

Hogs and
pigs
14%

All other
livestock
3%

Poultry and
poultry products
23%

The ideal visual for division is a pie chart. A whole is divided into parts. Here for example is a U.S. Department of Agriculture chart on the value of livestock and poultry sold in the United States.
U.S. Department of Agriculture, National Agricultural Statistics Services.

We can also divide a subject in writing. In the following excerpt from a "chemistry primer" for people interested in cooking, Harold McGee uses division twice—first to subdivide the atom into its smaller constituent particles and second to subdivide the "space" within the atom into two areas (nucleus and shell):

> An atom is the smallest particle into which an element can be subdivided without losing its characteristic properties. The atom too is divisible into smaller particles, electrons, protons, and neutrons, but these are the building blocks of all atoms, no matter of what element. The different properties of the elements are due to the varying combinations of subatomic particles contained in their atoms. The Periodic Table arranges the elements in order of the number of protons contained in one atom of each element. That number is called the atomic number.
>
> The atom is divided into two regions: the nucleus, or center in which the protons and neutrons are located, and a surrounding "orbit," or more accurately a "cloud" or "shell," in which the electrons move continuously. Both protons and neutrons weigh about 2000 times as much as electrons, so practically all of an atom's mass is concentrated in the nucleus.

Similarly, David Bodanis in an essay in this chapter uses division to structure a discussion of toothpaste; he analyzes its composition, offering some surprising insights into the "ingredients" we brush with every morning. Barbara Ehrenreich in "In Defense of Talk Shows" also uses division when she analyzes the distinctive features that a number of different television talk shows exhibit. She treats the shows—hosted by people such as Montel Williams, Sally Jessy Raphael, and Geraldo Rivera—as a single subject that can then be divided or analyzed into its component parts. Ehrenreich does not classify television talk shows; rather, she analyzes the common characteristics that such shows share.

Division, then, is used to show the components of a larger subject; it helps the reader understand a complex whole by considering it in smaller units.

WHAT IS CLASSIFICATION?

Classification, instead of starting with a single subject and then subdividing it into smaller units, begins with two or more items that are then grouped or classified into categories. Newspapers, for example, contain "classified" sections in which advertisements for the same type of goods or services are grouped or classified together. A classification must have at least two categories.

Depending on how many items you start with and how different they are, you can end up with quite a few categories. Consider the books in your school's library—they have to be arranged or classified in some way so that they can be easily found. Many schools use the Library of Congress Classification System, which organizes books by their subject matter. The sciences, especially the biological sciences, make extensive use of classification. You probably remember, in at least rough form, the taxonomic classification you learned in high school biology. It begins by setting up five kingdoms (animals,

- A — GENERAL WORKS
- B — PHILOSOPHY, PSYCHOLOGY, RELIGION
- C — AUXILIARY SCIENCES OF HISTORY
- D — HISTORY (GENERAL) AND HISTORY OF EUROPE
- E — HISTORY: AMERICA
- F — HISTORY: AMERICA
- G — GEOGRAPHY, ANTHROPOLOGY, RECREATION
- H — SOCIAL SCIENCES
- J — POLITICAL SCIENCE
- K — LAW
- L — EDUCATION
- M — MUSIC AND BOOKS ON MUSIC
- N — FINE ARTS
- P — LANGUAGE AND LITERATURE
- Q — SCIENCE
- R — MEDICINE
- S — AGRICULTURE
- T — TECHNOLOGY
- U — MILITARY SCIENCE
- V — NAVAL SCIENCE
- Z — BIBLIOGRAPHY, LIBRARY SCIENCE, INFORMATION RESOURCES (GENERAL)

> In the Library of Congress Classification System, books are first organized by "main classes" or by what we might call "subjects." Each class is assigned a letter of the alphabet. By knowing the Library of Congress's system, you can browse the sections knowing that books on these general headings will be grouped together.

plants, monera, fungi, and protista) and then moves downward to increasingly narrower categories (phylum or division, class, order, family, genus, species).

Most classifications outside of the sciences are not as precisely and hierarchically defined. For example, E. B. White uses classification to discuss the three different groups of people who make up New York City:

> There are roughly three New Yorks. There is, first, the New York of the man or woman who was born here, who takes the city for granted and accepts its size and its turbulence as natural and inevitable. Second, there is the New York of the commuter—the city that is devoured by locusts each day and spat out each night. Third, there is the New York of the person who was born somewhere else and came to New York in quest of something. Of these three trembling cities the greatest is the last—the city of final destination, the city that is a goal.

In this chapter, Bernard R. Berelson's classification of the reasons people want children is precisely and logically ordered—something we would expect in an essay that is titled "The Value of Children: A Taxonomical Essay" and that uses headings to display its organizational pattern clearly.

How Do You Choose a Subject?

Division and classification both are tools to help readers understand a subject. In that sense part of the purpose of both is to inform readers. To know how something is or can be divided, how it can be broken apart into smaller units, helps readers understand the whole. If the question is where our tax dollars go, a division into smaller units—such as can be found in a pie chart—makes a complex, huge whole seem a little more manageable. It also allows us to compare the relative size of each slice. Similarly, if readers are faced with many things, a classification scheme helps organize those things into more understandable and smaller categories. Just think about the classified advertisements in a newspaper. If there were no structure or order to the advertisements, you would have to look through page after page to find the advertisements that relate to the specific subject for which you are looking. Because both division and classification impose order, because their purpose is to make things clearer or more understandable, it is really important that they be clearly and logically structured.

That primary informative purpose also suggests that in choosing a topic, you need to consider how interesting or informative the subject might be to a reader. Avoid the obvious approach to the obvious topic. Every teacher has read at some point a classification essay placing teachers into groups based solely on the grade level at which they teach: elementary school teachers teach in elementary school, middle school teachers teach in middle school, and high school teachers teach in high school. Although such a classification scheme is complete and accurate, such a subject and approach are likely to lead you into writing that is boring and simply not worth your time or your reader's. No subject is inherently bad, but if you choose to write about something common or obvious, you need to find an interesting angle from which to approach it. Always ask yourself, will your reader learn something or be entertained by what you plan to write?

Prewriting Suggestions

1. Make a list of possible subjects for division and classification. Try each idea out on peer readers. Pay attention to their reactions to the possible subjects.
2. Consider what types of information you might need in order to divide or classify. Do you need to research the topic, or can it be done with just the information that you already have?
3. Jot down a purpose statement for each possible topic. Why are you writing about this? Is it purely informative? Does it also have a persuasive value? Test out your purpose statement on peer readers.
4. Think about your audience. What do they already know about this subject? Are you telling them something that is too obvious? Are you telling them about a subject that might be too complex or technical to handle in a short paper?
5. Brainstorm a tentative structure for the division or classification. That will help you as you gather and begin to organize the information.

WRITING

HOW DO YOU DIVIDE OR CLASSIFY A SUBJECT?

Since both division and classification involve separation into parts—either dividing a whole into pieces or sorting many things into related groups or categories—you have to find ways in which to divide or group. Those ways can be objective and formal, such as the classification schemes used by biologists or by Bernard R. Berelson in "The Value of Children: A Taxonomical Essay," or they can be subjective and informal, like Joseph Epstein in "What Are You Afraid Of?" Either way, several things are particularly important.

Have a Purpose   You subdivide or categorize for a reason or purpose, and your division or classification should be made with that end in mind. For example, Bernard R. Berelson in "The Value of Children" places people's reasons for wanting children into six categories: biological, cultural, political, economic, familial, and personal. His purpose is to explain the various factors that motivate people—all people, in all cultures, over all time—to want children. Berelson does not include, for example, a category labeled "accidental," for such a heading would be irrelevant to his stated purpose. There is a significant difference, after all, between why people *want* children and why people *have* children.

Make Your Classification or Division Complete   Your division or classification must be complete—you cannot omit pieces or leave items unclassified. How complete your classification will be depends on your purpose. Epstein's classification of fears in "What Are You Afraid Of" does not represent all the possible fears that people might have, but then, Epstein is not attempting to list everything. He is focusing on what he regards as the most significant fears—and the ones that he understands. Berelson, in contrast, sets out to be exhaustive, to isolate all the reasons people at any time and in every place have wanted children. As a result, he has to include some categories that are essentially irrelevant for most Americans. For example, probably few Americans want or have ever wanted children for political reasons—that is, because their government encourages them or forbids them to have children. But in some societies or in certain times, political reasons have been important. Therefore, Berelson must include that category as well.

Use Parallelism   The categories or subdivisions you establish need to be parallel in form. In mathematical terms, the categories should share a lowest common denominator. A simple and fairly effective test for parallelism is to see whether your categories are all phrased in similar grammatical terms. Berelson, for example, defines his categories (the reasons for wanting children) in exactly parallel form:

- Biological
- Cultural
- Political
- Economic

- Familial
- Personal
     Personal power
     Personal competence
     Personal status
     Personal extension
     Personal experience
     Personal pleasure

For this reason, you should not establish a catch-all category that you label something like "Other." When Berelson is finished with his classification scheme, no reasons for wanting children are left unaccounted for; everything fits into one of the six subdivisions. Finally, your categories or subdivisions should be mutually exclusive; that is, items should belong in only one category.

How Do You Structure a Division or Classification Essay?

The body of a division or classification essay will have as many parts as you have subdivisions or categories. Each subdivision or category will probably be treated in a single paragraph or in a group of related paragraphs. Aaron Copeland, for example, uses a very symmetrical form in his essay: he cites three different "planes" on which we listen to music, and he treats each in a parallel way. Not every essay will be so evenly and perfectly divided. Judith Ortiz Cofer's essay "The Myth of the Latin Woman" uses narrative examples to establish and explore the common stereotypes of the "Latin woman" that she has encountered. Though the essay has a clear, chronological structure, Cofer analyzes the myth in sections of varying length.

Once you have decided how many subdivisions or categories you will have and how long each one will be, you have to decide in what order to arrange those parts or categories. Sometimes you must devise your own order. Epstein, for example, could have arranged his fears in any order. Nothing in the material itself determines the sequence. However, not all divisions or classifications have the same flexibility in their arrangement. Some invite, imply, or even demand a particular order. For example, if you were classifying films using the ratings established by the motion picture industry, you would essentially have to follow the G, PG, PG-13, R, and NC-17 sequence; you could begin at either end, but it would not make sense to begin with one of the middle categories.

Having an order underlying your division or classification can be a great help for both you and your reader. It allows you to know where to place each section, dictating the order you will follow. It gives your reader a clear sense of direction. Berelson, for example, in "The Value of Children: A Taxonomical Essay," arranges the reasons that people have children in an order that "starts with chemistry and proceeds to spirit." That is, he deals first with the biological reasons for wanting children and moves finally to the most spiritual of reasons, love.

Drafting Suggestions

1. Are you using division or classification? Look again at your subject and make sure that your approach is one or the other.
2. Can your subject and your approach to it be handled in the amount of space that you have available? For example, it might be impossible to categorize all the types of fear in a few pages, but you could categorize your own fears within that space. Narrow your subject if necessary.
3. Remember that the number of parts or categories in your essay has to be manageable. You cannot subdivide into a dozen pieces or a dozen categories and keep your paper a reasonable length. As a rough rule, in a two- to four-page essay, you probably should not have more than six parts or categories. If you have more, see if they can be grouped under larger headings.
4. Remember that your essay needs a logical organizational pattern. Once you have selected your subdivisions or categories, write each one on a separate index card. Try moving around the order of the cards to see how many arrangements might be possible.
5. Remember that, depending on your subject, your subdivisions or categories need to account for all or most of your subject. This is especially important if your analysis is objective rather than subjective.

REVISING

HOW DO YOU REVISE A DIVISION OR CLASSIFICATION?

Since a primary purpose for both division and classification is to help the reader analyze or organize information about a single topic or about a number of related items, it is vital that the information be clearly and logically presented. When you have a draft of your essay and are beginning to revise, remember that the clarity and accuracy of your presentation is fundamental to an effective essay. Ask a peer reader, a writing fellow or tutor, or your instructor to look closely at those issues. Does your paper make the subject or topic easier to understand? If your reader does not think so, you must address that problem.

When revising a division or classification paper, pay particular attention to the following areas: purpose, structure, proportional development, and parallelism.

Having a Clear Purpose   Why have you chosen this particular subject? Check again to make sure that it is not so common or obvious that your readers are likely to be bored. Make sure that it is not so large and complicated a topic that you cannot treat it adequately in the space you have available. Ask yourself again what your audience is likely to know about the topic, and be wary of either end of the spectrum—too much or too little knowledge. As you revise, look back to your purpose statement and use it to test what you have written.

Keeping the Analysis Logically Structured   The order in which information is presented in a division or classification is important. Do you move from the largest unit or group to the smallest, or in the other direction? The subdivisions or categories must be presented in an order that makes logical sense for the subject. You cannot jump around without a clear rationale. What principle have you used as you move from section to section? Is that principle clearly stated and consistently followed?

If your paper is logically structured and ordered, it will need only a minimum of stage or step markers (for example, "first," "next") or transitional words or phrases ("the next category," "finally"). Coherence in a paper is best achieved by a clearly articulated, logical presentation of the material.

Making Sure the Categories or Parts Are Proportionally Developed
Obviously, some of the subdivisions represent a larger part of the whole than other subdivisions. Likewise, some of the categories in the classification might contain many more items than others. The principle of proportion does not mean that the parts must be equal in content. Rather, it means that you need to present each subdivision and each category in approximately the same amount of space. You should not have one category or subdivision that takes a page and a half of your paper and another that gets only three sentences.

Do not subdivide or classify in too great a detail. Your scheme needs to account for the whole subject—that is, you should not have things that do not fit into your division or your classification scheme. If you have 100 objects on the table that you are to place into categories, your scheme must accommodate all of them; you cannot have ten left over that do not fit into the scheme. Similarly, try to avoid catch-all categories—"other" or "miscellaneous."

Checking for Parallelism One Final Time   Subdivisions and categories need to be worded in parallel form—that is, they need to be cast into the same grammatical forms. Similar forms make it easy for the reader to see the relationships between the parts. Look back at the headings in this chapter, for example. Notice that the largest units in the chapter are phrased as single words: "prewriting," "writing," and "revising." The next level of headings are all written as questions ("How do you . . .?"). The third level of headings (where you are reading now) are identically structured clauses ("having a clear purpose," "keeping the analysis," "checking for parallelism.") Parallelism is an easy way to signal your paper's structure to your readers and an excellent way to promote clarity.

Revising Suggestions

1. Once you have a draft, write out a several-sentence summary of your essay. Ask some peers to read just that summary. Do they find your subject and approach potentially interesting? Remember, there are no bad subjects, just bad approaches to subjects. Do you need to reconsider your approach?

2. Look again at how you organized the body of your essay. Why did you begin and end where you did? Did you move from largest to smallest? Most important to least? What is your principle of order?

3. Have you accounted for everything in your division or classification? Make sure you have not omitted any classifications or divisions of your broader topic.

4. Can your reader clearly tell when you move from one division or category to another? Have you paragraphed to make that structure clear? Have you used parallelism?

5. Look again at your introduction. Have you tried to catch your reader's attention? Or have you written a standard thesis introduction? Try an alternate beginning.`

SAMPLE STUDENT ESSAY

Evan James chose to write his term paper for his introductory American studies course on the hobo in America. He read widely in the library about the phenomenon, so he had plenty of information, but he was having trouble getting started and getting organized. He took his draft to the Writing Center.

FIRST DRAFT

HOBOS

Among the many social problems that the United States faced at the turn of this past century was that of the "hobo." My interest in hobos came about because of the book <u>The Ways of the Hobo</u> that we read. The term <u>hobo</u>, the dictionary says, was probably derived from the greeting "Ho! Beau!" commonly used by vagrants to greet each other, although other possibilities have been suggested as well. The number of hobos in the United States at the turn of the century was large because of soldiers returning from the Civil War and because increasing mechanization had reduced the number of jobs in factories and businesses. In fact, the unemployment rate in the late 1800s ran as high as 40% of the workforce. We think that unemployment rates of 6% are unacceptable today!

Actually hobos were careful about how they referred to themselves. Today, for example, we might use the words <u>hobo</u>, <u>tramp</u>, and <u>bum</u> interchangeably. I was surprised to learn that among the hobos themselves, the distinctions were clear. A hobo was a migrant worker, a tramp was a migrant nonworker, and a bum was a nonmigrant nonworker.

COMMENTS

When the tutor asked about the problems Evan saw in his essay, Evan listed a couple: he thought the introduction was flat and boring and the essay didn't move smoothly from sentence to sentence ("I think I just jump around from idea to idea"). The tutor and Evan collaborated on a list of the qualities that make a good introduction. They also discussed how writers can group information and make transitions. In the process of revising, Evan found a stronger, more interesting way to begin, and he reparagraphed and developed his opening paragraphs to reflect an analysis both by division and by cause and effect.

REVISED DRAFT

RIDING THE RAILS: THE AMERICAN HOBO

Although homelessness and vagrancy might seem to be a distinctively modern phenomenon, the problem is probably less acute today (in terms of percentage of our total population) than it was at the turn of the twentieth century. At that time, a series of factors combined to create a large migratory population comprised almost exclusively of young males.

The Civil War was an uprooting experience for thousands of young men. Many left home in their teenage years, had acquired no job skills during their military service, and had grown accustomed to the nomadic life of the soldier—always on the move, living off the land, sleeping in the open. As the armies disbanded, many young men chose not to return home but to continue wandering the countryside.

Even if these former soldiers had wanted to work, few jobs were available to absorb the thousands of men who were mustered out. Increasingly, mechanization in the last decades of the 1800s brought the loss of jobs. In a world before unemployment benefits and social welfare, unemployment encouraged migration. The problem worsened in the 1870s when the country spiraled into a depression. Businesses failed, construction sagged, and the unemployment rate soared to an estimated 40%. Men, looking for work, took to the road.

Such men were called by a variety of names. One was <u>hobo</u>. The origin of that word is unknown. It has been suggested that <u>hobo</u> might be a shortened form of the Latin phrase <u>homo bonus</u> ("good man") or derived from the greeting "Ho! Beau!" commonly used among vagrants (dictionaries favor this suggestion). Other possibilities include a shortened form of the phrase "homeward bound" or "hoe boy," a term used in the eighteenth century for migrant farm workers.

Strictly speaking, not everyone who took to the road should be called a hobo. "Real" hobos were quick to insist on a series of distinctions. The words <u>hobo</u>, <u>tramp</u>, and <u>bum</u> were not interchangeable. By definition within the hobo community, the term <u>hobo</u> referred to a migrant worker, <u>tramp</u> to a migrant nonworker, and <u>bum</u> to a nonmigrant nonworker.

Obviously, the motives of the men traveling the road varied widely. Some were in search of work—migrant agricultural workers were an accepted fact by the turn of the century. Others were fleeing from the law, from family responsibilities, from themselves. Many were alcoholics; some were mentally impaired. All, though, were responding to a version of the American myth—the hope that a better future lay somewhere (geographically) ahead and that, meanwhile, the open road was the place to be.

SOME THINGS TO REMEMBER

1. In choosing a subject for division or classification, ask yourself, first, what is my purpose? and second, will my reader learn something or be entertained by my paper?
2. Remember that your subdivision or classification should reflect your purpose—that is, the number of categories or parts is related to what you are trying to do.
3. Make sure that your division or classification is complete. Do not omit any pieces or items. Everything should be accounted for.
4. Take care that the parts or categories are phrased in parallel form.
5. Avoid a category labeled something such as "Other" or "Miscellaneous."
6. Remember to make your categories or subdivisions mutually exclusive.
7. Once you have established your subdivisions, check to see whether there is an order implied or demanded by your subject.
8. As you move from one subdivision to another, provide markers for the reader so that the parts are clearly labeled.

DIVISION AND CLASSIFICATION AS A LITERARY STRATEGY

Victorian poet Elizabeth Barrett wrote a series of sonnets to poet Robert Browning during their courtship. She did not show him the sonnets until some months after they were married. She thought that the sonnets were too private to ever be published, but her husband disagreed. In Sonnet 43 in the series, Barrett "counted" the ways in which she loved Browning. Notice how she "divides" her love for him:

HOW DO I LOVE THEE?

Elizabeth Barrett

How do I love thee? Let me count the ways.
I love thee to the depth and breadth and height
My soul can reach, when feeling out of sight
For the ends of Being and ideal Grace.
I love thee to the level of everyday's
Most quiet need, by sun and candle-light.
I love thee freely, as men strive for Right;
I love thee purely, as they turn from Praise.
I love thee with the passion put to use
In my old griefs, and with my childhood's faith.
I love thee with a love I seemed to lose
With my lost saints,—I love thee with the breath,
Smiles, tears, of all my life!—and, if God choose,
I shall but love thee better after death.

DISCUSSION QUESTIONS

1. Barrett has one love, but it is a love that she sees as showing itself in many different ways. Using the punctuation of the poem as a clue, how many ways are "counted" in the poem?

2. Is there a sense of progression or movement in the ways in which Barrett loves? Is the division organized in any particular sequence? Could the ways be organized in different order?

3. What stylistic device(s) does Barrett use to help her reader "count" the ways?

4. How does Barrett vary the pattern in the final two lines of the poem?

5. How does Barrett bring the poem to an end? Judging simply from what is being said, how do we know that the poem is now finished?

WRITING SUGGESTIONS

The American greeting card industry flourishes because most of us have difficulty putting our feelings into words. It is much easier to buy a card with the appropriate preprinted sentiment. In a paragraph express your thanks, gratitude, love, affection, devotion, whatever, to someone important to you. Do so using division as an organizational pattern. Possible starting points might include the following:

   a. A note of thanks to the person or persons responsible for helping you through school

b. A note to a child (maybe your own child, your sibling, your niece or nephew)

c. A note to someone who is a model for you (such as a coach, a grandparent, a former teacher, a close friend)

READING DIVISION AND CLASSIFICATION

The following excerpt is taken from Mark Lester's *Grammar in the Classroom*, a college text intended for prospective teachers of grammar. Since the purpose of a textbook is to explain a subject to students, clarity of presentation is especially important. You do not demand to be entertained by a textbook; you expect to have material presented as clearly and simply as possible. Notice how Lester uses classification to explain how traditional grammar classifies sentences by purpose. Notice as well how Lester uses typographical devices and parallelism to promote the clarity and simplicity of the material.

As you read, remember what you have learned about how to write using division or classification—and how that knowledge can help you as a reader.

- Division and classification are used to present information in a clear and organized fashion. Their primary purpose is to inform and clarify, not to entertain or persuade.

- Division and classification involve either dividing a subject into its constituent parts or sorting things into related categories—making order where there appears to be chaos.

- The parts or categories in division and classification must allow for completeness. Nothing should be left over; you should be able to place every part within a division or classification of the broader subject.

- The parts or categories in division and classification must be arranged in a logical order.

- Division and classification make extensive use of parallelism (using the same grammatical structure for statements about related aspects of the parts or categories).

- Division and classification both lend themselves to visual displays and in fact might best be shown through a visual arrangement or device.

Classifying Sentences By Purpose

Topic sentence—announces how the subject will broken into categories

In traditional grammar, sentences are classified in a four-fold manner depending upon the purpose of the sentence. The following are the four types of sentences.

Typographical devices—spacing and numbering promote clarity

1. **Declarative:** A declarative sentence makes a statement. Declarative sentences are punctuated with a period.

John went away.

Parallelism

a. Spacing
b. Bold face
c. Numbering
d. Sentence structures
e. Order of sentences
f. Examples

Classification is complete

These are the only four ways in which sentences can be classified by purpose in traditional grammar

2. **Imperative:** An imperative sentence gives a command or makes a request. Imperative sentences must have an understood *you* as subject. Imperative sentences may be punctuated with either a period or an exclamation point.

> Go away.
> Come here!
> Stop it!

3. **Interrogative:** An interrogative sentence asks a question. Interrogative sentences must be punctuated with a question mark.

> Did John go away?
> Where are you?

4. **Exclamatory:** An exclamatory sentence expresses strong feeling. Exclamatory sentences are declarative sentences with an exclamation point. Remember that imperative sentences can have exclamation points too. The difference is that imperative sentences must always have an understood *you* as subject; exclamatory sentences can never have an understood *you* as subject. Exclamatory sentences *must* be punctuated with an exclamation point.

> John went away!
> Sally has no cavities!

RESPONDING TO A VISUAL

Division and classification are both strongly rooted in the visual. Division takes a single subject and breaks it into its parts. Typically, division might be represented by a list or table—here are the ingredients or the subdivisions of this subject. Pie charts are visual displays of division. The whole is a circle or a pie; the wedges in the pie show how the whole is divided into its constituent parts. On the other hand, classification takes many related items and imposes order on them, arranging or sorting them into groups that can clearly be differentiated. For example, scientists attempting to catalog plants, animals, and insects establish elaborate classification schemes or taxonomies to group and separate, seeing both similarities and differences among the related items. The following photograph shows an assortment of buttons—all have the same function (that is, all are buttons), but they come in a variety of shapes and sizes.

READING AND WRITING ABOUT IMAGES

Study the photograph, then devise a classification scheme for the buttons—that is, sort them into groups based on the characteristics that they share and

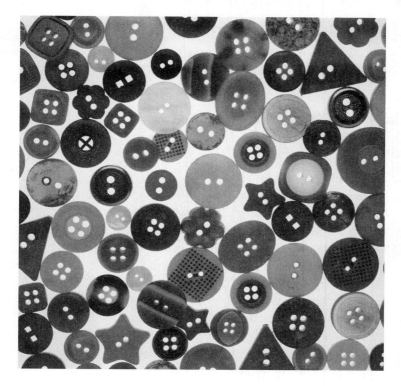

those that they do not. In an essay, first, explain how and why the buttons could be classified, and second, suggest the reasons why such a classification scheme might prove particularly helpful.

VISITING THE WEB

The companion Website **www.prenhall.com/miller** contains additional information about division and classification and about the writers in this chapter. You will also find a number of links to other sources of information about the subjects of the essays found in this chapter.

EXPLORING ON YOUR OWN

Classification systems rate both films and video games. The ratings are primarily to allow parents to judge whether or not their child should see a particular film or purchase a particular video game. In the case of film, the ratings go even further. For example, theaters cannot allow anyone under the age of 17 to buy a ticket to an R (unless accompanied by a parent) or an NC-17 film. All films are covered by the classification system; the categories are defined in such a way as to include every film that is made. You can find a full explanation of the current ratings system on the Web. For the link, visit **www.prenhall.com/miller**. Construct a classification scheme for a group of products or services. Possible subjects can be found under Looking for Writing Suggestions and on the *Reader*'s Website.

LOOKING FOR WRITING SUGGESTIONS

DIVISION

1. Freshman class at your college
2. Makeup of a band/musical group/sports team
3. Organizational structure of a club or business
4. A subject you are studying in another course
5. Distribution of tax dollars/money given to a particular charity
6. Breakdown of the costs associated with the sale of any item (for example, gasoline)
7. Costs for tuition/room and board at your school
8. Composition of a prepared food that you regularly consume
9. Responsibilities/rights within a relationship/family
10. Your stages in the writing process (as humor)

CLASSIFICATION

1. Magazines published for people interested in a particular subject
2. Prime-time network television shows
3. Television talk shows/reality shows
4. Friends/enemies
5. Music/CDs/books in your collection
6. Collectible objects
7. Things/items found in a drawer/pocket/bookbag/purse
8. Pets/plants
9. E-mails you receive each day
10. Excuses for bad behavior/lateness/missing class/not reading assignment

WHAT'S IN YOUR TOOTHPASTE
David Bodanis

Raised in Chicago, David Bodanis earned a degree in mathematics from the University of Chicago and did postgraduate work in theoretical biology and population genetics. He traveled to London and then to Paris, where he began his journalism career as a copyboy at the International Herald Tribune. *Bodanis has a special talent for explaining complex concepts in simple, yet entertaining, language. His most recent book is* Electric Universe: The Shocking True Story of Electricity *(2005).*

This essay is excerpted from The Secret House *(1986). One reviewer noted: "The book explores the gee-whiz science that sits unnoticed under every homeowner's nose." If you are appalled to discover what is in your toothpaste, you ought to read Bodanis's account of some mass-produced ice cream that contains "leftover cattle parts that no one else wants."*

On Writing: *Asked about the start of his writing career, Bodanis replied: "I failed my writing exam at the University of Chicago, but it was fair. I didn't know how to write, didn't know the basics of structure." Later, he got a job at the* Herald-Tribune *in Paris. "The people there taught practical writing. And I read books, and I felt that writing was a skill to learn, I never thought of it as a career."*

BEFORE READING

Connecting: Most of us are well aware of the toxic nature of some common products, but there are many others that we assume are safe and maybe even good for us. Think about the things that you use, eat, or drink every day. Which ones have you never worried about?

Anticipating: Is Bodanis being fair and objective in his essay? How can you judge?

I nto the bathroom goes our male resident, and after the most pressing need   1
is satisfied it's time to brush the teeth. The tube of toothpaste is squeezed, its pinched metal seams are splayed, pressure waves are generated inside, and the paste begins to flow. But what's in this toothpaste, so carefully being extruded out?

Water mostly, 30 to 45 percent in most brands: ordinary, everyday sim-   2
ple tap water. It's there because people like to have a big gob of toothpaste to spread on the brush, and water is the cheapest stuff there is when it comes to making big gobs. Dripping a bit from the tap onto your brush would cost virtually nothing; whipped in with the rest of the toothpaste the manufacturers can sell it at a neat and accountant-pleasing $2 per pound equivalent. Toothpaste manufacture is a very lucrative occupation.

3   Second to water in quantity is chalk: exactly the same material that schoolteachers use to write on blackboards. It is collected from the crushed remains of long-dead ocean creatures. In the Cretaceous seas chalk particles served as part of the wickedly sharp outer skeleton that these creatures had to wrap around themselves to keep from getting chomped by all the slightly larger other ocean creatures they met. Their massed graves are our present chalk deposits.

4   The individual chalk particles—the size of the smallest mud particles in your garden—have kept their toughness over the aeons, and now on the toothbrush they'll need it. The enamel outer coating of the tooth they'll have to face is the hardest substance in the body—tougher than skull, or bone, or nail. Only the chalk particles in toothpaste can successfully grind into the teeth during brushing, ripping off the surface layers like an abrading wheel grinding down a boulder in a quarry.

5   The craters, slashes, and channels that the chalk tears into the teeth will also remove a certain amount of build-up yellow in the carnage, and it is for that polishing function that it's there. A certain amount of unduly enlarged extra-abrasive chalk fragments tear such cavernous pits into the teeth that future decay bacteria will be able to bunker down there and thrive; the quality control people find it almost impossible to screen out these errant super-chalk pieces, and government regulations allow them to stay in.

6   In case even the gouging doesn't get all the yellow off, another substance is worked into the toothpaste cream. This is titanium dioxide. It comes in tiny spheres, and it's the stuff bobbing around in white wall paint to make it come out white. Splashed around onto your teeth during the brushing it coats much of the yellow that remains. Being water soluble it leaks off in the next few hours and is swallowed, but at least for the quick glance up in the mirror after finishing it will make the user think his teeth are truly white. Some manufacturers add optical whitening dyes—the stuff more commonly found in washing machine bleach—to make extra sure that that glance in the mirror shows reassuring white.

7   These ingredients alone would not make a very attractive concoction. They would stick in the tube like a sloppy white plastic lump, hard to squeeze out as well as revolting to the touch. Few consumers would savor rubbing in a mixture of water, ground-up blackboard chalk, and the whitener from latex paint first thing in the morning. To get around that finicky distaste the manufacturers have mixed in a host of other goodies.

8   To keep the glop from drying out, a mixture including glycerine glycol—related to the most common car antifreeze ingredient—is whipped in with the chalk and water, and to give *that* concoction a bit of substance (all we really have so far is wet colored chalk) a large helping is added of gummy molecules from the seaweed *Chondrus Crispus*. This seaweed ooze spreads in among the chalk, paint, and antifreeze, then stretches itself in all directions to hold the whole mass together. A bit of paraffin oil (the fuel that flickers in camping lamps) is pumped in with it to help the moss ooze keep the whole substance smooth.

With the glycol, ooze, and paraffin we're almost there. Only two major 9
chemicals are left to make the refreshing, cleansing substance we know as
toothpaste. The ingredients so far are fine for cleaning, but they wouldn't
make much of the satisfying foam we have come to expect in the morning
brushing.

To remedy that every toothpaste on the market has a big dollop of de- 10
tergent added too. You've seen the suds detergent will make in a washing machine. The same substance added here will duplicate that inside the mouth. It's
not particularly necessary, but it sells.

The only problem is that by itself this ingredient tastes, well, too like de- 11
tergent. It's horribly bitter and harsh. The chalk put in toothpaste is pretty
foul-tasting too for that matter. It's to get around that gustatory discomfort
that the manufacturers put in the ingredient they tout perhaps the most of all.
This is the flavoring, and it has to be strong. Double rectified peppermint oil
is used—a flavorer so powerful that chemists know better than to sniff it in the
raw state in the laboratory. Menthol crystals and saccharin or other sugar sim-
ulators are added to complete the camouflage operation.

Is that it? Chalk, water, paint, seaweed, antifreeze, paraffin oil, deter- 12
gent, and peppermint? Not quite. A mix like that would be irresistible to the
hundreds of thousands of individual bacteria lying on the surface of even an
immaculately cleaned bathroom sink. They would get in, float in the water
bubbles, ingest the ooze and paraffin, maybe even spray out enzymes to break
down the chalk. The result would be an uninviting mess. The way manufacturers avoid that final obstacle is by putting something in to kill the bacteria.
Something good and strong is needed, something that will zap any accidentally intrudant bacteria into oblivion. And that something is formaldehyde—
the disinfectant used in anatomy labs.

So it's chalk, water, paint, seaweed, antifreeze, paraffin oil, detergent, 13
peppermint, formaldehyde, and fluoride (which can go some way towards preserving children's teeth)—that's the usual mixture raised to the mouth on the
toothbrush for a fresh morning's clean. If it sounds too unfortunate, take
heart. Studies show that thorough brushing with just plain water will often do
as good a job.

QUESTIONS ON SUBJECT AND PURPOSE

1. Bodanis explains to the reader what toothpaste is composed of.
   Is his description objective? Could it appear, for example, in an
   encyclopedia?
2. After reading the essay, you might feel that Bodanis avoids certain
   crucial issues about the composition of toothpaste. Does he raise for
   you any questions that he does not answer?
3. What might Bodanis's purpose be? Is he arguing for something? Is he
   attacking something?

QUESTIONS ON STRATEGY AND AUDIENCE

1. How does Bodanis seem to arrange or order his division?
2. Bodanis gives the most space (three paragraphs) to chalk. Why? What is his focus in the section?
3. What could Bodanis expect about his audience?

QUESTIONS ON VOCABULARY AND STYLE

1. How would you characterize the tone of the essay?
2. Bodanis links most of the ingredients to their use in another product. Find these links, and be prepared to comment on the effect that these linkages have on the reader.
3. Be prepared to define the following words: *splayed* (paragraph 1), *extruded* (1), *lucrative* (2), *aeons* (4), *abrading* (4), *carnage* (5), *errant* (5), *finicky* (7), *dollop* (10), *gustatory* (11), *tout* (11), *intrudant* (12).

WRITING SUGGESTIONS

1. **For Your Journal.** Over a period of several days, keep a list of every product that you use or consume—everything from a lip balm to cosmetics to after-shave or cologne to mouthwash to chewing gum. When you really think about it, which ones would you like to know more about?

2. **For a Paragraph.** Select a common food or beverage, and subdivide it into its constituent parts. Use the contents label on the package as a place to start. You could use either the list of ingredients or the nutrition information. Present your division in a paragraph. Do not just describe what you find; rather, develop an attitude or thesis toward those findings. Bodanis, for example, certainly expresses (or implies) how he feels about what he finds in toothpaste.

3. **For an Essay.** Americans exhibit widely differing attitudes toward the food they eat, in large part because they have the greatest choice of any people in the world. In an essay, classify the American eater. You can approach your subject from a serious or a comic point of view. Do not just describe types; your essay should either state or imply your feelings or judgments about your findings. Try to establish four to six categories.

5. **For Research.** Americans have become increasingly concerned about the additives that are put into food. Research the nature of food additives. How many are there? In general, what do they do? Develop a classification scheme to explain the largest groups or subdivisions. Be sure to adopt a stand or thesis about the use of such additives; also be sure to document your sources.

FOR FURTHER STUDY

Focusing on Grammar and Writing. Bodanis uses summary sentences at times to repeat or reinforce the points that he has made so far—examples occur in paragraphs 7, 8, 9, 12, and 13. Why might he keep doing this? What is the effect of such summary or repetition? When might you use such a strategy in your own writing?

Working Together. Throughout the essay, Bodanis links the ingredients in toothpaste to other products in which they can be found. Divide into small groups and choose one of the following ingredients to examine: water (paragraph 1); chalk (2–5); titanium dioxide (6); glycerine, glycol, seaweed, and paraffin oil (8); detergent (10); peppermint oil (11), and formaldehyde (12). How does Bodanis, in listing the ingredients, manage at the same time to shock the reader? Pay attention to word choice and analogy.

Seeing Other Modes at Work. The essay could easily be turned into a persuasive essay. What elements of persuasion does the essay already contain? What would have to be added?

Finding Connections. An interesting pairing can be made on the basis of tone. In what ways, for example, are the tones of Bodanis's essay and Judy Brady's "I Want a Wife" (Chapter 8) similar?

Exploring the Web. Shocked to find out what is in your toothpaste? That is nothing compared to the ingredients in a jar of baby food! Read a description from Bodanis's *The Secret Family* at the *Reader's* Website, **www.prenhall.com/miller.** Links to additional information about Bodanis and his writing can also be found there.

IN DEFENSE OF TALK SHOWS

Barbara Ehrenreich

Born in Butte, Montana, in 1941, Barbara Ehrenreich earned her Ph.D. in biology at Rockefeller University. After a period of university teaching, Ehrenreich turned to writing full time. A prolific writer, Ehrenreich's most recent book is Bait and Switch: The (Futile) Pursuit of the American Dream *(2005).*

On Writing: *Ehrenreich writes regularly for* The Progressive *and a wide range of other magazines, including* Time, *where "In Defense of Talk Shows" first appeared. Commenting on writing essays for magazines, she observed: "I don't see myself as writing polemics where I'm just trying to beat something into people's heads. An essay is like a little story, a short story, and I will obsess about what is the real point, what are the real connections, a long time before I ever put finger to keyboard."*

BEFORE READING

Connecting: Do you ever watch talk shows such as the ones that Ehrenreich mentions? What attracts you to them?

Anticipating: To what extent is the essay a "defense" of talk shows?

1   Up until now, the targets of Bill *(The Book of Virtues)* Bennett's crusades have at least been plausible sources of evil. But the latest victim of his wrath—TV talk shows of the Sally Jessy Raphael variety—are in a whole different category from drugs and gangsta rap. As anyone who actually watches them knows, the talk shows are one of the most excruciatingly moralistic forums the culture has to offer. Disturbing and sometimes disgusting, yes, but their very business is to preach the middle-class virtues of responsibility, reason and self-control.

2   Take the case of Susan, recently featured on *Montel Williams* as an example of a woman being stalked by her ex-boyfriend. Turns out Susan is also stalking the boyfriend and—here's the sexual frisson—has slept with him only days ago. In fact Susan is neck deep in trouble without any help from the boyfriend: She's serving a yearlong stretch of home incarceration for assaulting another woman, and home is the tiny trailer she shares with her nine-year-old daughter.

3   But no one is applauding this life spun out of control. Montel scolds Susan roundly for neglecting her daughter and failing to confront her role in the mutual stalking. A therapist lectures her about this unhealthy "obsessive kind of love." The studio audience jeers at her every evasion. By the end Susan has lost her cocky charm and dissolved into tears of shame.

4   The plot is always the same. People with problems—"husband says she looks like a cow," "pressured to lose her virginity or else," "mate wants more

sex than I do"—are introduced to rational methods of problem solving. People with moral failings—"boy crazy," "dresses like a tramp," "a hundred sex partners"—are introduced to external standards of morality. The preaching— delivered alternately by the studio audience, the host and the ever present guest therapist—is relentless. "This is wrong to do this," Sally Jessy tells a cheating husband. "Feel bad?" Geraldo asks the girl who stole her best friend's boyfriend. "Any sense of remorse?" The expectation is that the sinner, so hectored, will see her way to reform. And indeed, a Sally Jessy update found "boy crazy," who'd been a guest only weeks ago, now dressed in schoolgirlish plaid and claiming her "attitude {had} changed"—thanks to the rough-and-ready therapy dispensed on the show.

All right, the subjects are often lurid and even bizarre. But there's no part 5 of the entertainment spectacle, from *Hard Copy* to *Jade*, that doesn't trade in the lurid and bizarre. At least in the talk shows, the moral is always loud and clear: Respect yourself, listen to others, stop beating on your wife. In fact it's hard to see how *The Bill Bennett Show*, if there were to be such a thing, could deliver a more pointed sermon. Or would he prefer to see the feckless Susan, for example, tarred and feathered by the studio audience instead of being merely booed and shamed?

There is something morally repulsive about the talks, but it's not any- 6 thing Bennett or his co-crusader Senator Joseph Lieberman has seen fit to mention. Watch for a few hours, and you get the claustrophobic sense of lives that have never seen the light of some external judgment, of people who have never before been listened to, and certainly never been taken seriously if they were. "What kind of people would let themselves be humiliated like this?" is often asked, sniffily, by the shows' detractors. And the answer, for the most part, is people who are so needy—of social support, of education, of material resources and self-esteem—that they mistake being the center of attention for being actually loved and respected.

What the talks are about, in large part, is poverty and the distortions it 7 visits on the human spirit. You'll never find investment bankers bickering on *Rolonda*, or the host of *Gabrielle* recommending therapy to sobbing professors. With few exceptions the guests are drawn from trailer parks and tenements, from bleak streets and narrow, crowded rooms. Listen long enough, and you hear references to unpaid bills, to welfare, to twelve-hour workdays and double shifts. And this is the real shame of the talks: that they take lives bent out of shape by poverty and hold them up as entertaining exhibits. An announcement appearing between segments of *Montel* says it all: The show is looking for "pregnant women who sell their bodies to make ends meet."

This is class exploitation, pure and simple. What next—"homeless peo- 8 ple so hungry they eat their own scabs"? Or would the next step be to pay people outright to submit to public humiliation? For $50 would you confess to adultery in your wife's presence? For $500 would you reveal your thirteen-year-old's girlish secrets on *Ricki Lake*? If you were poor enough, you might.

It is easy enough for those who can afford spacious homes and private 9 therapy to sneer at their financial inferiors and label their pathetic moments of stardom vulgar. But if I had a talk show, it would feature a whole different cast of characters and category of crimes than you'll ever find on the talks: "CEOs who rake in millions while their employees get downsized" would be an obvious theme, along with "Senators who voted for welfare and Medicaid cuts"—and, if he'll agree to appear, "well-fed Republicans who dithered about talk shows while trailer-park residents slipped into madness and despair."

QUESTIONS ON SUBJECT AND PURPOSE

1. Write a thesis statement—or find one—for the essay.
2. According to Ehrenreich, why would people agree to appear on these talk shows?
3. What makes such shows "morally repulsive" (paragraph 6)?

QUESTIONS ON STRATEGY AND AUDIENCE

1. How does Ehrenreich divide or analyze the distinctive common features of the talk shows?
2. Why are such shows popular?
3. What expectations does Ehrenreich seem to have about her audience?

QUESTIONS ON VOCABULARY AND STYLE

1. In paragraphs 4 and 5, Ehrenreich uses an extended metaphor to explain the pattern that the shows follow. What is that metaphor? (Check the glossary for a definition of *metaphor*.)
2. How would you characterize the tone of the rhetorical questions that Ehrenreich asks in paragraph 8? (Check the glossary for a definition of *tone*.)
3. Be prepared to define the following words: *excruciatingly* (paragraph 1), *frisson* (2), *hectored* (4), *lurid* (5), *feckless* (5), *dithered* (9).

WRITING SUGGESTIONS

1. **For Your Journal.** All forms of media—compact discs, software programs, magazines, books, television or radio shows, even Websites—try to mimic whatever has been successful. For example, if one television show about "friends" or a new primetime game show is popular, expect next season to see several other imitators. Select one medium, and make notes in your journal about the similarities that you see among the items that belong in that category.
2. **For a Paragraph.** Expand your observations from your journal into a paragraph. Try for the same type of analysis or division that Ehrenreich achieves. Focus your paragraph around a single shared element.

3. **For an Essay.** Expand your paragraph analysis or division into a full essay. You are analyzing the elements that a series of similar media products share—for example, the common elements of television cooking shows or of magazines intended for teenage girls. Remember that the choice of medium is yours—software programs, magazines, advertisements, Websites. You will probably want to analyze three or four shared elements. How do these shared elements work together? To what purpose or goal do all of these things contribute?

4. **For Research.** Test your analysis by checking research done on the subject. Using the resources of your library, and perhaps of online databases and the World Wide Web, see what other writers have said. Remember that information will appear in communication journals, marketing and business journals, trade papers for that particular medium, and scholarly and general journals and magazines. A keyword search might be a good place to begin. If you are having trouble gathering information, ask a reference librarian.

FOR FURTHER STUDY

Focusing on Grammar and Writing. Assuming a spectrum from formal to informal, where would you place Ehrenreich's essay on the scale? Identify those features in her prose (such as word choice and sentence structure) that support your opinion. Under what circumstances do you want your writing to be formal? When can it be informal?

Working Together. Working in small groups, examine one of the following paragraphs: 2, 4, 5, and 7. Each group should then report on how Ehrenreich uses language, detail, and sentence structure in the paragraph.

Seeing Other Modes at Work. In paragraph 9 Ehrenreich uses comparison and contrast to introduce the types of guests she would invite to her talk show. The essay also exhibits persuasion.

Finding Connections. An interesting pairing is Lars Eighner's "My Daily Dives into the Dumpster" (Chapter 6).

Exploring the Web. Did you know that most talk shows have extensive Websites where you can see additional photographs, watch video clips, and explore other special features. For some places to start, visit **www.prenhall.com/miller.**

HOW WE LISTEN TO MUSIC

Aaron Copeland

Aaron Copeland (1900–1990) was an American composer particularly known for his ballet scores (such as Billy the Kid *and* Appalachian Spring*) and his film scores (such as* Of Mice and Men *and* Our Town*). In addition to his many music compositions, Copeland wrote three books on music, the most famous of which is* What to Listen for in Music *(1938, revised 1957), from which this selection comes.*

On Writing: *On the links between writing and music, Copeland observed: "The more I live the life of music, the more I am convinced that it is the freely imaginative mind that is at the core of all vital music making and music listening. When Coleridge put down his famous phrase, 'the sense of musical delight with the power of producing it is a gift of the imagination,' he was referring, of course, to the musical delight of poetry. But it seems to me even more true when applied to the musical delights of music. An imaginative mind is essential to the creation of art in any medium."*

BEFORE READING

Connecting: If someone asked you, "How do you listen to music?" (and the question did not mean on an iPod or an MP3 player!), what might you say? Have you ever thought about that question?

Anticipating: Copeland argues that we listen to music on three levels. What are those levels?

1   We all listen to music according to our separate capacities. But, for the sake of analysis, the whole listening process may become clearer if we break it up into its component parts, so to speak. In a certain sense we all listen to music on three separate planes. For lack of a better terminology, one might name these: (1) the sensuous plane, (2) the expressive plane, (3) the sheerly musical plane. The only advantage to be gained from mechanically splitting up the listening process into these hypothetical planes is the clearer view to be had of the way in which we listen.

2   The simplest way of listening to music is to listen for the sheer pleasure of the musical sound itself. That is the sensuous plane. It is the plane on which we hear music without thinking, without considering it in any way. One turns on the radio while doing something else and absent-mindedly bathes in the sound. A kind of brainless but attractive state of mind is engendered by the mere sound appeal of the music.

3   You may be sitting in a room reading this book. Imagine one note struck on the piano. Immediately that one note is enough to change the atmosphere of the room—providing that the sound element in music is a powerful and mysterious agent, which it would be foolish to deride or belittle.

The surprising thing is that many people who consider themselves qual-   4
ified music lovers abuse that plane in listening. They go to concerts in order
to lose themselves. They use music as a consolation or an escape. They enter
an ideal world where one doesn't have to think of the realities of everyday life.
Of course they aren't thinking about the music either. Music allows them to
leave it, and they go off to a place to dream, dreaming because of and apropos
of the music yet never quite listening to it.

Yes, the sound appeal of music is a potent and primitive force, but you   5
must not allow it to usurp a disproportionate share of your interest. The sensuous plane is an important one in music, a very important one, but it does not
constitute the whole story.

There is no need to digress further on the sensuous plane. Its appeal to   6
every normal human being is self-evident. There is, however, such a thing as
becoming more sensitive to the different kinds of sound stuff as used by various composers. For all composers do not use that sound stuff in the same way.
Don't get the idea that the value of music is commensurate with its sensuous
appeal or that the loveliest sounding music is made by the greatest composer.
If that were so, Ravel would be a greater creator than Beethoven. The point is
that the sound element varies with each composer, that his usage of sound
forms an integral part of his style and must be taken into account when listening. The reader can see, therefore, that a more conscious approach is valuable even on this primary plane of music listening.

The second plane on which music exists is what I have called the ex-   7
pressive one. Here, immediately, we tread on controversial ground. Composers have a way of shying away from any discussion of music's expressive
side. Did not Stravinsky himself proclaim that his music was an "object," a
"thing," with a life of its own, and with no other meaning than its own purely
musical existence? This intransigent attitude of Stravinsky's may be due to the
fact that so many people have tried to read different meanings into so many
pieces. Heaven knows it is difficult enough to say precisely what it is that a
piece of music means, to say it definitely, to say it finally so that everyone is
satisfied with your explanation. But that should not lead one to the other extreme of denying to music the right to be "expressive."

My own belief is that all music has an expressive power, some more and   8
some less, but that all music has a certain meaning behind the notes and that
the meaning behind the notes constitutes, after all, what the piece is saying,
what the piece is about. The whole problem can be stated quite simply by asking, "Is there a meaning to music?" My answer to that would be, "Yes." And
"Can you state in so many words what the meaning is?" My answer to that
would be, "No." Therein lies the difficulty.

Simple-minded souls will never be satisfied with the answer to the sec-   9
ond of these questions. They always want music to have a meaning, and the
more concrete it is the better they like it. The more the music reminds them
of a train, a storm, a funeral, or any other familiar conception the more expressive it appears to be to them. This popular idea of music's meaning—
stimulated and abetted by the usual run of musical commentator—should be
discouraged wherever and whenever it is met. One timid lady once confessed

to me that she suspected something seriously lacking in her appreciation of music because of her inability to connect it with anything definite. That is getting the whole thing backward, of course.

10   Still, the question remains, How close should the intelligent music lover wish to come to pinning a definite meaning to any particular work? No closer than a general concept, I should say. Music expresses, at different moments, serenity or exuberance, regrets or triumph, fury or delight. It expresses each of these moods, and many others, in a numberless variety of subtle shadings and differences. It may even express a state of meaning for which there exists no adequate word in any language. In that case, musicians often like to say that it has only a purely musical meaning. They sometimes go further and say that *all* music has only a purely musical meaning. What they really mean is that no appropriate word can be found to express the music's meaning and that, even if it could, they do not feel the need of finding it.

11   But whatever the professional musician may hold, most musical novices still search for specific words with which to pin down their musical reactions. That is why they always find Tschaikovsky easier to "understand" than Beethoven. In the first place, it is easier to pin a meaning-word on a Tschaikovsky piece than on a Beethoven one. Much easier. Moreover, with the Russian composer, every time you come back to a piece of his it almost always says the same thing to you, whereas with Beethoven it is often quite difficult to put your finger right on what he is saying. And any musician will tell you that that is why Beethoven is the greater composer. Because music which always says the same thing to you will necessarily soon become dull music, but music whose meaning is slightly different with each hearing has a greater chance of remaining alive.

12   Listen, if you can, to the forty-eight fugue themes of Bach's *Well Tempered Clavichord*. Listen to each theme, one after another. You will soon realize that each theme mirrors a different world of feeling. You will also soon realize that the more beautiful a theme seems to you the harder it is to find any word that will describe it to your complete satisfaction. Yes, you will certainly know whether it is a gay theme or a sad one. You will be able, in other words, in your own mind, to draw a frame of emotional feeling around your theme. Now study the sad one a little closer. Try to pin down the exact quality of its sadness. Is it pessimistically sad or resignedly sad; is it fatefully sad or smilingly sad?

13   Let us suppose that you are fortunate and can describe to your own satisfaction in so many words the exact meaning of your chosen theme. There is still no guarantee that anyone else will be satisfied. Nor need they be. The important thing is that each one feel for himself the specific expressive quality of a theme or, similarly, an entire piece of music. And if it is a great work of art, don't expect it to mean exactly the same thing to you each time you return to it.

14   Themes or pieces need not express only one emotion, of course. Take such a theme as the first main one of the *Ninth Symphony*, for example. It is clearly made up of different elements. It does not say only one thing. Yet anyone hearing it immediately gets a feeling of strength, a feeling of power. It isn't a power that comes simply because the theme is played loudly. It is a power inherent in the theme itself. The extraordinary strength and vigor of the

theme results in the listener's receiving an impression that a forceful statement has been made. But one should never try to boil it down to "the fateful hammer of life," etc. That is where the trouble begins. The musician, in his exasperation, says it means nothing but the notes themselves, whereas the nonprofessional is only too anxious to hang on to any explanation that gives him the illusion of getting close to the music's meaning.

Now, perhaps, the reader will know better what I mean when I say that music does have an expressive meaning but that we cannot say in so many words what that meaning is. 15

The third plane on which music exists is the sheerly musical plane. Besides the pleasurable sound of music and the expressive feeling that it gives off, music does exist in terms of the notes themselves and of their manipulation. Most listeners are not sufficiently conscious of this third plane. . . . 16

Professional musicians, on the other hand, are, if anything, too conscious of the mere notes themselves. They often fall into the error of becoming so engrossed with their arpeggios and staccatos that they forget the deeper aspects of the music they are performing. But from the layman's standpoint, it is not so much a matter of getting over bad habits on the sheerly musical plane as of increasing one's awareness of what is going on, in so far as the notes are concerned. 17

When the man in the street listens to the "notes themselves" with any degree of concentration, he is most likely to make some mention of the melody. Either he hears a pretty melody or he does not, and he generally lets it go at that. Rhythm is likely to gain his attention next, particularly if it seems exciting. But harmony and tone color are generally taken for granted, if they are thought of consciously at all. As for music's having a definite form of some kind, that idea seems never to have occurred to him. 18

It is very important for all of us to become more alive to music on its sheerly musical plane. After all, an actual musical material is being used. The intelligent listener must be prepared to increase his awareness of the musical material and what happens to it. He must hear the melodies, the rhythms, the harmonies, the tone colors in a more conscious fashion. But above all he must, in order to follow the line of the composer's thought, know something of the principles of musical form. Listening to all of these elements is listening on the sheerly musical plane. 19

Let me repeat that I have split up mechanically the three separate planes on which we listen merely for the sake of greater clarity. Actually, we never listen on one or the other of these planes. What we do is to correlate them—listening in all three ways at the same time. It takes no mental effort, for we do it instinctively. 20

Perhaps an analogy with what happens to us when we visit the theater will make this instinctive correlation clearer. In the theater, you are aware of the actors and actresses, costumes and sets, sounds and movements. All these give one the sense that the theater is a pleasant place to be in. They constitute the sensuous plane in our theatrical reactions. 21

The expressive plane in the theater would be derived from the feeling that you get from what is happening on the stage. You are moved to pity, 22 excitement, or gayety. It is this general feeling, generated aside from the particular words being spoken, a certain emotional something which exists on the stage, that is analogous to the expressive quality in music.

23   The plot and plot development is equivalent to our sheerly musical plane. The playwright creates and develops a character in just the same way that a composer creates and develops a theme. According to the degree of your awareness of the way in which the artist in either field handles his material you will become a more intelligent listener.

24   It is easy enough to see that the theatergoer never is conscious of any of these elements separately. He is aware of them all at the same time. The same is true of music listening. We simultaneously and without thinking listen on all three planes.

25   In a sense, the ideal listener is both inside and outside the music at the same moment, judging it and enjoying it, wishing it would go one way and watching it go another—almost like the composer at the moment he composes it; because in order to write his music, the composer must also be inside and outside his music, carried away by it and yet coldly critical of it. A subjective and objective attitude is implied in both creating and listening to music.

26   What the reader should strive for, then, is a more *active* kind of listening. Whether you listen to Mozart or Duke Ellington, you can deepen your understanding of music only by being a more conscious and aware listener—not someone who is just listening, but someone who is listening *for* something.

QUESTIONS ON SUBJECT AND PURPOSE

1. Copeland does not explore the question, Why do we listen to music? but rather, How do we listen to music? What might be the difference between the two questions?
2. How does Copeland divide the listening process?
3. In the essay, does Copeland suggest a reason why he might be writing about this topic?

QUESTIONS ON STRATEGY AND AUDIENCE

1. What do Copeland's examples in the essay have in common?
2. What does Copeland mean by the "sheerly musical plane"?
3. What expectations does Copeland seem to have of his audience?

QUESTIONS ON VOCABULARY AND STYLE

1. What is an analogy?
2. Does the analogy in paragraphs 21 through 24 work for you? That is, do you understand any more clearly the points that Copeland is making about music?

3. Be prepared to define the following words: *engendered* (paragraph 2), *deride* (3), *apropos* (4), *usurp* (5), *commensurate* (6), *intransigent* (7), *abetted* (9), *arpeggios* (17).

WRITING SUGGESTIONS

1. **For Your Journal.** In what ways do you listen to music? Select a particular time or situation in which you normally listen to music— any kind of music. Can you identify your experience in that situation with any of the three ways that Copeland suggests? Explore the idea.

2. **For a Paragraph.** Read again through the section on "What is the Difference Between on Active and a Passive Reader" _____ (in "How to Read an Essay"). What similarities do you see between that concept as it applies to reading and Copeland's active listening (paragraph 26)? In a paragraph, explore the similarities.

3. **For an Essay.** Think about the type or types of music that you listen to. Do Copeland's planes fit the music you favor? In an essay, explore how you listen to music. What are the "planes" that you can distinguish in your listening? You might also explore the extent to which your experience might differ if you can play music yourself. Do people who play or compose experience music in a different way?

4. **For Research.** Copeland notes, "We all listen to music on three separate planes" (paragraph 1). Is there widespread agreement that there are three (and only three) planes on which we listen? What do other music critics or composers say? Are they in agreement with Copeland? Are there competing theories of listening? Other systems for dividing the "listening process"? Using print and online sources, research the issue and present your findings in an paper with appropriate documentation.

FOR FURTHER STUDY

Focusing on Grammar and Writing. Look carefully at Copeland's essay. Can you identify a thesis statement? Can you identify topic sentences in the main paragraphs? Does Copeland repeat his thesis in his conclusion? What do these things contribute to the essay?

Working Together. Divide into small groups. Within the group, each member should write down a set of circumstances under which he or she listens to music. Is the music a form of distraction or something that is consciously or intently listened to? Concentrate on coming up with a spectrum of situations in which you as a group listen to music and reasons why you listen.

Seeing Other Modes at Work. In each of the three sections on the planes of listening, Copeland uses definition to explain the characteristics of each plane and to show the differences among the planes.

Finding Connections. Copeland's essay will work nicely with essays that explore definition, such as John Hollander's "Mess" (Chapter 8).

Exploring the Web. Many Websites contain information about Aaron Copeland and his music, including some audio clips, photographs, and interviews. Check **www.prenhall.com/miller** for some starting places.

THE MYTH OF THE LATIN WOMAN: I JUST MET A GIRL NAMED MARIA

Judith Ortiz Cofer

Judith Ortiz Cofer's "Marina" is one of the readings in Chapter 2, and biographical information about her can be found in that headnote.

    On Writing: *Cofer comments about living in and writing about two cultures: "The very term 'bilingual' tells you I have two worlds. At least now, they're very strictly separated, but when I was growing up it was a constant shift back and forth. I think my brain developed a sense of my world and my reality as being composed of two halves. But I'm not divided in them. I accept them, and I think they have basically been the difference that has allowed me to write things that are not like anybody else's."*

BEFORE READING

Connecting: Have you ever been treated as a stereotype? Have people ever expected certain things of you (good or bad) because of how you were classified in their eyes?

Anticipating: What expectations would you have of a "Latin woman"? Or a "Latin man"? Do those expectations coincide with those about which Cofer writes?

On a bus trip to London from Oxford University where I was earning some   1
graduate credits one summer, a young man, obviously fresh from a pub, spotted me and as if struck by inspiration went down on his knees in the aisle. With both hands over his heart he broke into an Irish tenor's rendition of "Maria" from *West Side Story*. My politely amused fellow passengers gave his lovely voice the round of gentle applause it deserved. Though I was not quite as amused, I managed my version of an English smile: no show of teeth, no extreme contortions of the facial muscles—I was at this time of my life practicing reserve and cool. Oh, that British control, how I coveted it. But "Maria" had followed me to London, reminding me of a prime fact of my life: you can leave the island, master the English language, and travel as far as you can, but if you are a Latina, especially one like me who so obviously belongs to Rita Moreno's gene pool, the island travels with you.

    This is sometimes a very good thing—it may win you that extra minute   2
of someone's attention. But with some people, the same things can make *you* an island—not a tropical paradise but an Alcatraz, a place nobody wants to visit. As a Puerto Rican girl living in the United States and wanting like most children to "belong," I resented the stereotype that my Hispanic appearance called forth from many people I met.

3   Growing up in a large urban center in New Jersey during the 1960s, I suffered from what I think of as "cultural schizophrenia." Our life was designed by my parents as a microcosm of their *casas* on the island. We spoke in Spanish, ate Puerto Rican food bought at the *bodega*, and practiced strict Catholicism at a church that allotted us a one-hour slot each week for mass, performed in Spanish by a Chinese priest trained as a missionary for Latin America.

4   As a girl I was kept under strict surveillance by my parents, since my virtue and modesty were, by their cultural equation, the same as their honor. As a teenager I was lectured constantly on how to behave as a proper *señorita*. But it was a conflicting message I received, since the Puerto Rican mothers also encouraged their daughters to look and act like women and to dress in clothes our Anglo friends and their mothers found too "mature" and flashy. The difference was, and is, cultural; yet I often felt humiliated when I appeared at an American friend's party wearing a dress more suitable to a semi-formal than to a playroom birthday celebration. At Puerto Rican festivities, neither the music nor the colors we wore could be too loud.

5   I remember Career Day in our high school, when teachers told us to come dressed as if for a job interview. It quickly became obvious that to the Puerto Rican girls "dressing up" meant wearing their mother's ornate jewelry and clothing, more appropriate (by mainstream standards) for the company Christmas party than as daily office attire. That morning I had agonized in front of my closet, trying to figure out what a "career girl" would wear. I knew how to dress for school (at the Catholic school I attended, we all wore uniforms), I knew how to dress for Sunday mass, and I knew what dresses to wear for parties at my relatives' homes. Though I do not recall the precise details of my Career Day outfit, it must have been a composite of these choices. But I remember a comment my friend (an Italian American) made in later years that coalesced my impressions of that day. She said that at the business school she was attending, the Puerto Rican girls always stood out for wearing "everything at once." She meant, of course, too much jewelry, too many accessories. On that day at school we were simply made the negative models by the nuns, who were themselves not credible fashion experts to any of us. But it was painfully obvious to me that to the others, in their tailored skirts and silk blouses, we must have seemed "hopeless" and "vulgar." Though I now know that most adolescents feel out of step much of the time, I also know that for the Puerto Rican girls of my generation that sense was intensified. The way our teachers and classmates looked at us that day in school was just a taste of the cultural clash that awaited us in the real world, where prospective employers and men on the street would often misinterpret our tight skirts and jingling bracelets as a "come-on."

6   Mixed cultural signals have perpetuated certain stereotypes—for example, that of the Hispanic woman as the "hot tamale" or sexual firebrand. It is a one-dimensional view that the media have found easy to promote. In their special vocabulary, advertisers have designated "sizzling" and "smoldering" as the adjectives of choice for describing not only the foods but also the women of Latin America. From conversations in my house I recall hearing about the

harassment that Puerto Rican women endured in factories where the "boss-men" talked to them as if sexual innuendo was all they understood, and worse, often gave them the choice of submitting to their advances or being fired.

It is custom, however, not chromosomes, that leads us to choose scarlet over pale pink. As young girls, it was our mothers who influenced our decisions about clothes and colors—mothers who had grown up on a tropical island where the natural environment was a riot of primary colors, where showing your skin was one way to keep cool as well as to look sexy. Most important of all, on the island, women perhaps felt freer to dress and move more provocatively since, in most cases, they were protected by the traditions, mores, and laws of a Spanish/Catholic system of morality and machismo whose main rule was: *You may look at my sister, but if you touch her I will kill you.* The extended family and church structure could provide a young woman with a circle of safety in her small pueblo on the island; if a man "wronged" a girl, everyone would close in to save her family honor.

My mother has told me about dressing in her best party clothes on Saturday nights and going to the town's plaza to promenade with her girlfriends in front of the boys they liked. The males were thus given an opportunity to admire the women and to express their admiration in the form of *piropos:* erotically charged street poems they composed on the spot. (I have myself been subjected to a few *piropos* while visiting the island, and they can be outrageous, although custom dictates that they must never cross into obscenity.) This ritual, as I understand it, also entails a show of studied indifference on the woman's part; if she is "decent," she must not acknowledge the man's impassioned words. So I do understand how things can be lost in translation. When a Puerto Rican girl dressed in her idea of what is attractive meets a man from the mainstream culture who has been trained to react to certain types of clothing as a sexual signal, a clash is likely to take place. I remember the boy who took me to my first formal dance leaning over to plant a sloppy, over-eager kiss painfully on my mouth; when I didn't respond with sufficient passion, he remarked resentfully: "I thought you Latin girls were supposed to mature early," as if I were expected to *ripen* like a fruit or vegetable, not just grow into womanhood like other girls.

It is surprising to my professional friends that even today some people, including those who should know better, still put others "in their place." It happened to me most recently during a stay at a classy metropolitan hotel favored by young professional couples for weddings. Late one evening after the theater, as I walked toward my room with a colleague (a woman with whom I was coordinating an arts program), a middle-aged man in a tuxedo, with a young girl in satin and lace on his arm, stepped directly into our path. With his champagne glass extended toward me, he exclaimed "Evita!"

Our way blocked, my companion and I listened as the man half-recited, half-bellowed "Don't Cry for Me, Argentina." When he finished, the young girl said: "How about a round of applause for my daddy?" We complied, hoping this would bring the silly spectacle to a close. I was becoming aware that our little group was attracting the attention of the other guests. "Daddy" must have perceived this too, and he once more barred the way as we tried to walk past him. He began to shout-sing a ditty to the tune of "La Bamba"—except the lyrics were about a girl named Maria whose exploits rhymed with her name and gonorrhea. The girl kept saying "Oh, Daddy" and looking at me with pleading eyes. She wanted me to laugh along with the others. My companion and I stood silently waiting for the man to end his offensive song. When he finished, I looked not at him but at his daughter. I advised her calmly never to ask her father what he had done in the army. Then I walked between them and to my room. My friend complimented me on my cool handling of the situation, but I confessed that I had really wanted to push the jerk into the swimming pool. This same man—probably a corporate executive, well-educated, even worldly by most standards—would not have been likely to regale an Anglo woman with a dirty song in public. He might have checked his impulse by assuming that she could be somebody's wife or mother, or at least *somebody* who might take offense. But, to him, I was just an Evita or a Maria: merely a character in his cartoon-populated universe.

11   Another facet of the myth of the Latin woman in the United States is the menial, the domestic—Maria the housemaid or countergirl. It's true that work as domestics, as waitresses, and in factories is all that's available to women with little English and few skills. But the myth of the Hispanic menial—the funny maid, mispronouncing words and cooking up a spicy storm in a shiny California kitchen—has been perpetuated by the media in the same way that "Mammy" from *Gone with the Wind* became America's idea of the black woman for generations. Since I do not wear my diplomas around my neck for all to see, I have on occasion been sent to that "kitchen" where some think I obviously belong.

12   One incident has stayed with me, though I recognize it as a minor offense. My first public poetry reading took place in Miami, at a restaurant where a luncheon was being held before the event. I was nervous and excited as I walked in with notebook in hand. An older woman motioned me to her table, and thinking (foolish me) that she wanted me to autograph a copy of my newly published slender volume of verse, I went over. She ordered a cup of coffee from me, assuming I was the waitress. (Easy enough to mistake my poems for menus, I suppose.) I know it wasn't an intentional act of cruelty. Yet of all the good things that happened later, I remember that scene most clearly, because it reminded me of what I had to overcome before anyone would take me seriously. In retrospect I understand that my anger gave my reading fire. In fact, I have almost always taken any doubt in my abilities as a challenge, the result most often being the satisfaction of winning a convert, of seeing the cold, appraising eyes warm to my words, the body language change, the smile that indicates I have opened some avenue for communication. So that day as I read, I looked directly at that woman. Her lowered eyes told me she was embarrassed at her faux pas, and when I willed her to look up at me, she graciously allowed me to punish her with my full attention. We shook hands at the end of the reading and I never saw her again. She has probably forgotten the entire incident, but maybe not.

13   Yet I am one of the lucky ones. There are thousands of Latinas without the privilege of an education or the entrees into society that I have. For them

life is a constant struggle against the misconceptions perpetuated by the myth of the Latina. My goal is to try to replace the old stereotypes with a much more interesting set of realities. Every time I give a reading, I hope the stories I tell, the dreams and fears I examine in my work, can achieve some universal truth that will get my audience past the particulars of my skin color, my accent, or my clothes.

I once wrote a poem in which I called all Latinas "God's brown daugh-   14
ters." This poem is really a prayer of sorts, offered upward, but also, through the human-to-human channel of art, outward. It is a prayer for communication and for respect. In it, Latin women pray "in Spanish to an Anglo God / with a Jewish heritage," and they are "fervently hoping / that if not omnipotent, / at least He be bilingual."

QUESTIONS ON SUBJECT AND PURPOSE

1. What exactly is a stereotype? Where does the word *stereotype* come from?
2. What are the stereotypes or "myths" of the Latin woman that Cofer has experienced?
3. What is Cofer's announced goal in writing?

QUESTIONS ON STRATEGY AND AUDIENCE

1. At what point in time does the essay begin? Why does Cofer start with this example?
2. How does Cofer use time or chronology as a structural device in her essay?
3. Who does Cofer imagine as her reader? How can you tell?

QUESTIONS ON VOCABULARY AND STYLE

1. What does Cofer mean when she writes, "It is custom, however, not chromosomes, that leads us to choose scarlet over pale pink"?
2. What does *machismo* (paragraph 7) mean?
3. Be prepared to define the following words: *coveted* (paragraph 1), *microcosm* (3), *coalesced* (5), *innuendo* (6), *mores* (7), *regale* (10), *menial* (11), *faux pas* (12).

WRITING SUGGESTIONS

1. **For Your Journal.** Probably most people have in one way or another been stereotyped by someone else. Stereotyping is not reserved only for individuals from particular races or cultures. Think about the wide range of other stereotypes that exists in our culture, based on gender,

age, physical appearance, hair or clothing styles, language dialects, or geography. In your journal, make a list of such stereotypes, focusing on either those that have been applied to you or those that you have consciously or unconsciously applied to others.

2. **For a Paragraph.** Using your journal writing as a prewriting exercise, take one of the stereotypes and in a paragraph develop one aspect of that stereotype and how it is evidenced by others or by yourself.

3. **For an Essay.** Expand your paragraph into an essay. Remember now that you are fully exploring a stereotype that you yourself have encountered or that you apply to others. Stereotypes are everywhere—they are not encountered solely by people from different cultures, races, or religions. For example, has anyone ever considered you a "dumb blonde" or a "nerd" or a "jock"? What aspects of personality do people expect when they see you as a stereotype (or do you expect when you see someone else as a stereotype)? Classify these reactions.

4. **For Research.** Think about the stereotypes that Americans commonly hold about people from another culture. Cultural differences sometimes produce a great deal of misunderstanding. Select a culture (or some aspect of that culture) that seems to be widely misunderstood by most Americans. Research the cultural differences, and present your findings in an essay. One excellent source of information would be interviews with students from other countries and cultures. Where do they see those misunderstandings occurring most frequently? Your library, online databases, and the World Wide Web can also be good sources of information when you are able to narrow your search with appropriate specific subjects and keywords. Be sure to document all of your sources and to ask permission of any interviewees.

FOR FURTHER STUDY

Focusing on Grammar and Writing. Cofer uses a number of parentheses in her writing. What are the rules that govern the use of parentheses? How do they differ from a pair of commas or a pair of dashes? Look closely at how Cofer uses parentheses. Can you construct some rules or suggestions for their use based on her sentences? Under what circumstances might you enclose material within parentheses in your writing?

Working Together. Divide into small groups. Each group should choose one of the following assignments:

1. Explain why the men always break into song—"Maria," "Don't Cry for Me, Argentina," "La Bamba."
2. Analyze the Career Day experience.
3. Explain why the young men perform *piropos*.
4. Analyze the confrontation with the man and his daughter in the "classy" hotel (paragraphs 9 and 10).
5. Analyze the concluding paragraph.

What does each section or detail contribute to the essay?

Seeing Other Modes at Work. The essay uses narration to follow a Puerto Rican female from girlhood to adulthood.

Finding Connections. An interesting pairing is with Janice Mirikitani's "Recipe" (Chapter 6).

Exploring the Web. A listing of sites dealing with Cofer and her writing can be found at **www.prenhall.com/miller.**

THE VALUE OF CHILDREN: A
TAXONOMICAL ESSAY

Bernard R. Berelson

Bernard R. Berelson (1912–1979) was born in Spokane, Washington, and received a Ph.D. from the University of Chicago. He divided his time between the academic world and the world of international development assistance. In 1962, he joined the Population Council, eventually serving as its president until his retirement in 1974. Berelson published extensively on population policy and the prospects for fertility declines in developing countries.

Berelson's concern with population policy is obvious in this essay reprinted from the Annual Report *of the Population Council. Using a clear scheme of classification, Berelson analyzes the reasons why people want children.*

BEFORE READING

Connecting: The phrase "the value of children" might seem a little unusual. What, for example, was your "value" to your parents? If you have children, in what sense do they have "value" to you?

Anticipating: Despite the many reasons for having or wanting children, people in many societies today consciously choose to limit the number of children that they have. How might Berelson explain this phenomenon?

1   Why do people want children? It is a simple question to ask, perhaps an impossible one to answer.

2   Throughout most of human history, the question never seemed to need a reply. These years, however, the question has a new tone. It is being asked in a nonrhetorical way because of three revolutions in thought and behavior that characterize the latter decades of the twentieth century: the vital revolution in which lower death rates have given rise to the population problem and raise new issues about human fertility; the sexual revolution from reproduction; and the women's revolution, in which childbearing and -rearing no longer are being accepted as the only or even the primary roles of half the human race. Accordingly, for about the first time, the question of why people want children now can be asked, so to speak, with a straight face.

3   "Why" questions of this kind, with simple surfaces but profound depths, are not answered or settled; they are ventilated, explicated, clarified. Anything as complex as the motives for having children can be classified in various ways, and any such taxonomy has an arbitrary character to it. This one starts with chemistry and proceeds to spirit.

THE BIOLOGICAL

Do people innately want children for some built-in reason of physiology? Is   4
there anything to maternal instinct, or parental instinct? Or is biology satisfied
with the sex instinct as the way to assure continuity?

In psychoanalytic thought there is talk of the "child-wish," the "instinc-   5
tual drive of physiological cause," "the innate femaleness of the girl direct(ing)
her development toward motherhood," and the wanting of children as "the
essence of her self-realization," indicating normality. From the experimental literature, there is some evidence that man, like other animals, is innately attracted
to the quality of "babyishness."

> If the young and adults of several species are compared for differences in   6
> bodily and facial features, it will be seen readily that the nature of the
> difference is apparently the same almost throughout the phylogenetic scale.
> Limbs are shorter and much heavier in proportion to the torso in babies than
> in adults. Also, the head is proportionately much larger in relation to the
> body than is the case with adults. On the face itself, the forehead is more
> prominent and bulbous; the eyes large and perhaps located as far down as
> below the middle of the face, because of the large forehead. In addition, the
> cheeks may be round and protruding. In many species there is also a greater
> degree of overall fatness in contrast to normal adult bodies. . . . In man, as in
> other animals, social prescriptions and customs are not the sole or even
> primary factors that guarantee the rearing and protection of babies. This
> seems to indicate that the biologically rooted releaser of babyishness may
> have promoted infant care in primitive man before societies ever were
> formed, just as it appears to do in many animal species. Thus this releaser
> may have a high survival value for the species of man.*

In the human species the question of social and personal motivation dis-   7
tinctively arises, but that does not necessarily mean that the biology is completely obliterated. In animals the instinct to reproduce appears to be all; in
humans is it something?

THE CULTURAL

Whatever the biological answer, people do not want all the children they   8
physically can have—no society, hardly any woman. Everywhere social traditions and social pressures enforce a certain conformity to the approved childbearing pattern, whether large numbers of children in Africa or small numbers
in Eastern Europe. People want children because that is "the thing to do"—
culturally sanctioned and institutionally supported, hence about as natural as
any social behavior can be.

---

*Eckhard H. Hess, "Ethology and Developmental Psychology," in Paul H. Musser, ed.,
Carmichael's Manual of Child Psychology, Vol. 1 (New York: Wiley, 1970), pp. 20–21.

9   Such social expectations, expressed by everyone toward everyone, are extremely strong in influencing behavior even on such an important element in life as childbearing and on whether the outcome is two children or six. In most human societies, the thing to do gets done, for social rewards and punishments are among the most powerful. Whether they produce lots of children or few and whether the matter is fully conscious or not, the cultural norms are all the more effective if, as often, they are rationalized as the will of God or the hand of fate.

THE POLITICAL

10   The cultural shades off into political considerations: reproduction for the purposes of a higher authority. In a way, the human responsibility to perpetuate the species is the grandest such expression—the human family pitted politically against fauna and flora—and there always might be people who partly rationalize their own childbearing as a contribution to that lofty end. Beneath that, however, there are political units for whom collective childbearing is or has been explicitly encouraged as a demographic duty—countries concerned with national glory or competitive political position; governments concerned with the supply of workers and soldiers; churches concerned with propagation of the faith or their relative strength; ethnic minorities concerned with their political power; linguistic communities competing for position; clans and tribes concerned over their relative status within a larger setting. In ancient Rome, according to the Oxford English Dictionary, the proletariat—from the root *proles,* for progeny—were "the lowest class of the community, regarded as contributing nothing to the state but offspring": and a proletaire was "one who served the state not with his property but only with his offspring." The world has changed since then, but not all the way.

THE ECONOMIC

11   As the "new home economics" is reminding us in its current attention to the microeconomics of fertility, children are economically valuable. Not that that would come as a surprise to the poor peasant who consciously acts on the premise, but it is clear that some people want children or not for economic reasons.

12   Start with the obvious case of economic returns from children that appears to be characteristic of the rural poor. To some extent, that accounts for their generally higher fertility than that of their urban and wealthier counterparts: labor in the fields; hunting, fishing, animal care; help in the home and with the younger children; dowry and "bride-wealth"; support in later life (the individualized system of social security).

13   The economics of the case carries through on the negative side as well. It is not publicly comfortable to think of children as another consumer durable, but sometimes that is precisely the way parents do think of them, before conception: another child or a trip to Europe; a birth deferred in favor of a new car, the nth child requiring more expenditure on education or housing.

But observe the special characteristics of children viewed as consumer durables: they come only in whole units; they are not rentable or returnable or exchangeable or available on trial; they cannot be evaluated quickly; they do not come in several competing brands or products; their quality cannot be pretested before delivery; they usually are not available for appraisal in large numbers in one's personal experience; they themselves participate actively in the household's decisions. And in the broad view, both societies and families tend to choose standard of living over number of children when the opportunity presents itself.

THE FAMILIAL

In some societies people want children for what might be called familial reasons: to extend the family line or the family name; to propitiate the ancestors; to enable the proper functioning of religious rituals involving the family (e.g., the Hindu son needed to light the father's funeral pyre, the Jewish son needed to say Kaddish for the dead father). Such reasons may seem thin in the modern, secularized society but they have been and are powerful indeed in other places. 14

In addition, one class of family reasons shares a border with the following category, namely, having children in order to maintain or improve a marriage: to hold the husband or occupy the wife; to repair or rejuvenate their marriage; to increase the number of children on the assumption that family happiness lies that way. The point is underlined by its converse: in some societies the failure to bear children (or males) is a threat to the marriage and a ready cause for divorce. 15

Beyond all that is the profound significance of children to the very institution of the family itself. To many people, husband and wife alone do not seem a proper family—they need children to enrich the circle, to validate its family character, to gather the redemptive influence of offspring. Children need the family, but the family seems also to need children, as the social institution uniquely available, at least in principle, for security, comfort, assurance, and direction in a changing, often hostile, world. To most people, such a home base, in the literal sense, needs more than one person for sustenance and in generational extension. 16

THE PERSONAL

Up to here the reasons for wanting children primarily refer to instrumental benefits. Now we come to a variety of reasons for wanting children that are supposed to bring direct personal benefits. 17

Personal Power. As noted, having children sometimes gives one parent power over the other. More than that, it gives the parents power over the child(ren)—in many cases, perhaps most, about as much effective power as they ever will have the opportunity of exercising on an individual basis. They are looked up to by the child(ren), literally and figuratively, and rarely does 18 that happen otherwise. Beyond that, having children is involved in a wider circle of power:

19   In most simple societies the lines of kinship are the lines of political power, social prestige and economic aggrandizement. The more children a man has, the more successful marriage alliances he can arrange, increasing his own power and influence by linking himself to men of greater power or to men who will be his supporters. . . . In primitive and peasant societies, the man with few children is the man of minor influence and the childless man is virtually a social nonentity.*

20   *Personal Competence.* Becoming a parent demonstrates competence in an essential human role. Men and women who are closed off from other demonstrations of competence, through lack of talent or educational opportunity or social status, still have this central one. For males, parenthood is thought to show virility, potency, *machismo.* For females it demonstrates fecundity, itself so critical to an acceptable life in many societies.

21   *Personal Status.* Everywhere parenthood confers status. It is an accomplishment open to all, or virtually all, and realized by the overwhelming majority of adult humankind. Indeed, achieving parenthood surely must be one of the two most significant events in one's life—that and being born in the first place. In many societies, then and only then is one considered a real man or a real woman.

22   Childbearing is one of the few ways in which the poor can compete with the rich. Life cannot make the poor man prosperous in material goods and services but it easily can make him rich with children. He cannot have as much of anything else worth having, except sex, which itself typically means children in such societies. Even so, the poor still are deprived by the arithmetic; they have only two or three times as many children as the rich whereas the rich have at least forty times the income of the poor.

23   *Personal Extension.* Beyond the family line, wanting children is a way to reach for personal immortality—for most people, the only way available. It is a way to extend oneself indefinitely into the future. And short of that, there is simply the physical and psychological extension of oneself in the children, here and now—a kind of narcissism: there they are and they are mine (or like me).

24   *Look in thy glass and tell the face thou viewest,*
Now is the time that face should form another;
But if thou live, remember'd not to be,
Die single, and thine image dies with thee.

—Shakespeare's Sonnets, III

25   *Personal Experience.* Among all the activities of life, parenthood is a unique experience. It is a part of life, or personal growth, that simply cannot be experienced in any other way and hence is literally an indispensable element of the full life. The experience has many profound facets: the deep curiosity

*Burton Benedict, "Population Regulation in Primitive Societies," in Anthony Ellison, *Population Control* (London: Penguin, 1970), pp. 176–77.

as to how the child will turn out; the renewal of self in the second chance; the reliving of one's own childhood; the redemptive opportunity; the challenge to shape another human being; the sheer creativity and self-realization involved. For a large proportion of the world's women, there was and probably still is nothing else for the grown female to do with her time and energy, as society defines her role. And for many women, it might be the most emotional and spiritual experience they ever have and perhaps the most gratifying as well.

Personal Pleasure. Last, but one hopes not least, in the list of reasons for   26
wanting children is the altruistic pleasure of having them, caring for them, watching them grow, shaping them, being with them, enjoying them. This reason comes last on the list but it is typically the first one mentioned in the casual inquiry: "because I like children." Even this reason has its dark side, as with parents who live through their children, often to the latter's distaste and disadvantage. But that should not obscure a fundamental reason for wanting children: love.

There are, in short, many reasons for wanting children. Taken together,   27
they must be among the most compelling motivations in human behavior: culturally imposed, institutionally reinforced, psychologically welcome.

QUESTIONS ON SUBJECT AND PURPOSE

1. What is "the value of children"? How many different values does Berelson cite?
2. Berelson gives positive, negative, and neutral reasons for wanting children. Is the overall effect of the essay positive, negative, or neutral?
3. Which of Berelson's reasons seem most relevant in American society today? Which seem least relevant?

QUESTIONS ON STRATEGY AND AUDIENCE

1. How does Berelson organize his classification? Can you find an explicit statement of organization?
2. Could the classification have been organized in a different way? Would that have changed the essay in any way?
3. How effective is Berelson's introduction? His conclusion? Suggest other ways in which the essay could have begun or ended.

QUESTIONS ON VOCABULARY AND STYLE

1. Berelson asks a number of rhetorical questions (see the glossary). Why does he ask them? Does he answer them? Does he "ventilate," "explicate," and "clarify" them (paragraph 3)?
2. Describe the tone of Berelson's essay—what does he sound like? Be prepared to support your statement with some specific illustrations from the text.

3. Be able to define the following words: *taxonomy* (paragraph 3), *physiology* (4), *phylogenetic* (6), *bulbous* (6), *sanctioned* (8), *fauna and flora* (10), *demographic* (10), *consumer durable* (13), *propitiate* (14), *sustenance* (16), *aggrandizement* (19), *nonentity* (19), *machismo* (20), *fecundity* (20), *narcissism* (23).

WRITING SUGGESTIONS

1. **For Your Journal.** In your journal, explore the reasons why you do or do not want to have children. Would you choose to limit the number of children that you have? Why or why not?

2. **For a Paragraph.** Using your journal writing as a starting point, in a paragraph classify the reasons for your decision. Focus on two or three reasons at most, and be sure to have some logical order to your arrangement.

3. **For an Essay.** Few issues are so charged in American society today as abortion. In an essay, classify the reasons why people are either pro-choice or pro-life. Despite your personal feelings on the topic, try in your essay to be as objective as possible. Do not write an argument for or against abortion or a piece of propaganda.

4. **For Research.** Studies have shown that as countries become increasingly industrialized, their population growth approaches zero. For example, India's fertility rate has declined from six infants per female reproductive lifetime to four. In China, the rate is now 2.3 (zero growth is 2.1). In a research paper, explore how increasingly industrialized societies—such as India, China, Costa Rica, or Sri Lanka—have changed their views of the "value" of children. Be sure to document your sources wherever appropriate.

FOR FURTHER STUDY

Focusing on Grammar and Writing. Berelson uses several different typographical devices to signal the structure of his essay (spacing to separate subdivisions, centered headings, indented italic headings). Such devices are common in magazines and newspapers. What do such devices do? Are they helpful to you as a reader? In what ways? Under what circumstances? Might it be appropriate for you to use typographical devices in your writing?

Working Together. Finding the right order for categories within a classification scheme is important. Starting as a class, come up with some other possible choices for a classification—such as evening television shows, types of music, bottles or cans of drinks found in a convenience store cooler, newspapers, Hollywood films. Once you have generated some possible topics, divide into small groups. Each group should work on constructing a classification scheme for its topic and a rationale for the order in which the categories will be presented. Each group should then report to the class as a whole.

Seeing Other Modes at Work. Within each of the categories that he establishes, Berelson also uses cause and effect. How, for example, within the category "familial," would a cause-and-effect analysis be made?

Finding Connections. Judy Brady's "I Want a Wife" (Chapter 8) makes an effective pairing. How might Berelson rewrite Brady's essay? Brady's essay involves a classification scheme as well.

Exploring the Web. Is the world still facing a population explosion? Have birthrates stabilized? Declined? What type of population growth will the world see in the next millennium? For a variety of Web resources, visit **www.prenhall.com/miller**.

WHAT ARE YOU AFRAID OF?

Joseph Epstein

Joseph Epstein was born in Chicago and educated at the University of Chicago. He was a lecturer in English and writing at Northwestern University from 1974 to 2002. During most of that time, he was editor of American Scholar, *the magazine of Phi Beta Kappa, writing in each issue under the pen name Aristides. The author of many books, stories, and thousands of essays, Epstein's most recent collection of stories is* Fabulous Small Jews *(2003). "What Are You Afraid Of" first appeared in* Notre Dame Magazine *in 2001.*

On Writing: *Epstein comments: "Writing for discovery, to find out what one truly thinks of things, may be a bit riskier than writing knowing one's conclusions in advance, but it figures to be much more interesting, more surprising, and once one gets over one's early apprehension at the prospect of writing it, more fun."*

BEFORE READING

Connecting: Everyone has fears; not everyone's fears are exactly alike. What is it that you fear?

Anticipating: As you read, think about the relationship between courage and fear. Why does Epstein classify fears as a way of defining courage?

1   Courage isn't so easily defined. As splendid a mind as that of Socrates, in the early dialogue called *Laches*, is rather disappointing at the job. He tells us the kinds, or realms, of courage, which include courage in war, on sea, in disease and poverty, in politics, against pain, and—here's one you might have overlooked—in contending against desires and pleasures. He later tells us that we need to know a great deal about good and evil, to distinguish between what is and is not to be feared, if we are to know where the exercise of courage is required. Then, just when things begin to get interesting, the old boy knocks off for the afternoon, perhaps returning to his famously nagging wife, Xanthippe, which no doubt took a certain grim courage of its own.

2   Better perhaps to go at things the other way round, attempt to understand courage by taking up the subject of fear. Fears, taken at a fairly high level of generality, seem to me four: fear of death, of loss, of pain, and of humiliation. Over a respectable number of years, I have felt them all, in varying degrees of intensity, and am even now not through with them, with only the fear of humiliation having attenuated, or thinned out, a bit. I don't think of myself as perpetually living with fear. But, then, it occurs to me that I arranged a fair portion of my life in a way that has enabled me to play around these fears and fear generally.

If I am guilty of acts of outright cowardice, I do not remember them. I can say that I never backed out of a physical fight, but only when I add that one of the organizing principles of my quotidian life is not to look for fights. My last fight, at age eleven, was against a kid named David Netboy and ended in a dreary draw. I do not think myself, in the old playground word, a chicken, yet, as a boy playing baseball and football and (later) basketball, style not aggressiveness was my specialty, smooth moves not brutal strength on the playground gave me the keenest pleasure. 3

I might not have known about my want of physical aggressiveness but for the presence of a friend named Marty Summerfield, with whom I grew up and played on the same playgrounds. Marty didn't seem to mind pain. He would back into brick walls to catch fly balls, crash into the line without a helmet to pick up important short yardage. He was a catcher in hardball, a job that no one squeamish should ever consider, and in close plays at the plate would give up his body without a second thought. ("I'm glad my son is going into boxing," Rocky Marciano's mother, Pasqualina Marchegiano, is alleged to have said. "I didn't raise the boy to be a catcher.") In later life, when the occasion called for it, Marty would get into fights with guys fifty and seventy pounds heavier than he. In case you think Marty was a brute and a block-head into the bargain, I had better report that he is five feet nine inches tall, weighing maybe 150 pounds, and went on to teach university mathematics. 4

Possibly Marty had a little jingeroo: sometime early in life the fear button fell off his panel of emotions. We now know that there are people who not only are fearless but need to court danger, live on the rim, rev themselves up with such delightful pastimes as rock climbing, bungee jumping, and skydiving. Mention of the last reminds me that, when I was in the army, one morning our company was marched over to learn about going to jump school and becoming a paratrooper. As I sat listening to the youthful sergeant, in beret and ascot, recount all of the glories of being a paratrooper, including an additional $55 in "danger" pay, I thought, why not, let 'er rip, jumping out of a plane would at least expose me to a new experience. Before I got round to considering how I might spend the extra $55 in monthly salary, I said to myself, Yo, hold it there, kid, it's tough enough getting up in the morning as it is without the prospect of a sergeant screaming at you to jump out of a plane. Today, I shouldn't mind *having* jumped out of a plane; it is only the thought of doing it now that appalls me, using the word in its root sense of causing one to go pale. 5

I am no courage junky. I feel no regular need to prove myself, if only to myself. 6

I require absolutely no false fear stimulants. I watch no horror movies, ride no roller-coasters, answer no serious dares. I steer clear of all this in the firm belief that life, left to its own devices, is sufficiently fear laden on its own. No need to lay on extra ones. 7

I have no phobias, in the accepted psychological sense of irrational fears. I don't worry unduly about flying. Heights bring me no especial terrors. Close spaces, within reason, provide no problem. I think here of poor Kingsley Amis, the novelist, whose son reports that he "refused to drive and refused to 8 fly, couldn't easily be alone in a bus, a train, or a lift (or in a house, after dark), wasn't exactly keen on boats. . . ." I have a small terror about rats, one George Orwell seemed also to have had, but then I've read somewhere that humankind divides in its loathing for either rats or snakes. In short, I seem to be nearly nauseatingly normal.

9   Public speaking is said to be the second greatest fear among Americans (acquiring a fatal disease is first). I have known this fear, the extreme nervousness before standing up in front of a large crowd and, through one's intrinsic power to bore or through ill preparation or by dint of simple ignorance, making a great purple-bottomed baboon of oneself. But I have conquered this fear to the extent that I now do a fair amount of such speaking, ever ready to risk making a serious fool of myself for the right fee. Along with taking the check, I find myself also pleased that I have won through what was once a real fear, though I still feel a certain stomach churning, of a kind I prefer to think athletes feel before a big game begins, until I begin gassing away from the podium.

10   I have been lucky in that history has thus far seen fit to steer me clear of the larger fearful possibilities. Chief among these has been war. Born in 1937, I was a child during World War II, still too young for Korea, then too old for Vietnam. My army days—from 1958 to 1960—were spent in the Cold War. A part of me wishes I had gone to war. I suspect that most men who haven't feel themselves, in some fundamental way, untested. I haven't any longing for war, mind you, but because war has always seemed a test of manhood, I should have been pleased to have passed it, even while perhaps disapproving of it. As things stand, I shall never know if I would have come through. I have, meanwhile, admiration for those who have.

11   Between the efforts of my father—who regularly and I think rightly reminded me when a little boy "to be a man"—and the ethos of the playground and playing field, I was brought up on a program of courage. Boys don't cry. Don't back down before bullies. Don't let a little pain throw you; shake it off. Play on through. I seem to have passed most of these minor tests. But could I have conquered the terror of confronting other men with genuine homicide in their eyes? Under the horror, the squalor, the full terror of war, would my legs have come unstrung, my bowels held themselves in check, my mind retained some measure of its lucidity, my senses not become entirely deranged? I can only guess, and because I'm reduced to guessing, it is impossible not to have doubts. I shall never know—and it bothers me that I won't.

12   The only society on historical record that ever used courage as an organizing principle was that of the Spartans in the fifth century B.C. It was, in the nature of the case, male dominated, a military society through and through. Brawling, running, silently absorbing punishment, eliminating all traces of effeminacy, sleeping with one's shield and spear—in Sparta acculturation meant the inculcation of courage, at least physical courage.

13   In Steven Pressfield's excellent *Gates of Fire*, a historically accurate novel about the three hundred Spartans (all with living sons) who led a troop of roughly six thousand Greeks that held off tens of thousands of Persians at Thermopylae, one gets a clear view of how stern the training of Spartan youth could

be. In one scene, a Spartan knight and Olympic victor breaks the noses of all the youth under his training so that they learn the importance of their shields and of the seriousness of their training. Such tactics seem to work, but at what price?

How would a man with Spartan training have reacted the hot sunny af- 14
ternoon when, entering my car in the middle of a fairly empty supermarket parking lot, I was approached by a young, muscular man who looked to have no sense of humor whatsoever and who, with nothing of the supplicant in his voice, said, "Hey, man, I just got out of jail and could use some help. Let me have a buck?" My policy in the matter of begging is to give only to beggars who look to be in deep trouble or those whose stories are dramatically witty. This guy satisfied neither condition. Would a man with Spartan courage have come up with the dollar? I hope you find this an interesting theoretical question. At the time, I didn't even find it a question but instead forked over the dollar, relieved to enter my car without a knife protruding from my stomach.

We live in an age, I fear, when paranoia has become the better part of 15
valor. A writer in the *Wall Street Journal* not long ago wrote, "The American landscape of fear has been immutably changed by this era of success and affluence." Yet he allows that, despite this, the national anxiety level appears to have risen, judged by the increase in both the use of becalming drugs and the recourse to various psychotherapies, and he quotes a psychiatrist remarking that "anxiety is a condition of the privileged." Is this true? Do we really now have only to fear, as the man said, fear itself?

Statistically, true enough, there would appear to be less to fear in the 16
world: Crime rates continue to drop, job security in most places seems to have risen, nuclear holocaust isn't for the most part on the public consciousness. Yet statistics about safety, however overwhelming, are never finally reassuring. Tell someone the chances of dying in a plane crash are many times fewer than dying in an automobile and that does nothing to relieve the worry of the sound of a juddering engine when one is aloft during a thunderstorm. The battle against certain cancers may be showing great progress, but that doesn't much ease the mind of the man who discovers blood in his urine.

Most serious fears are at bottom fears of death. "The real world is sim- 17
ply too terrible to admit," writes Ernest Becker in *The Denial of Death*. "It tells man that he is a small trembling animal who will decay and die." For a peek into my own quavering consciousness, let me list the five forms of modern death I—at one time or another, for one reason or another—have found worth fearing and see if they check out with your own:

1. Though I am able to put it from my mind when flying, let me begin with air crash, for the obviousness of which I apologize. The classicist Mary Lefkowitz described not long ago (on the op-ed pages in the *New York Times*) the experience of surviving what looked to be a certain crash landing, when the plane she was flying in was reported to be unable to get its landing wheels to descend. She ends by writing, "Are the passengers on the planes that actually crash as uncannily calm

as we were—silent, unlamenting, bracing ourselves in the dark cabin? Do they, before the last moments, experience, as we did, a terror so anesthetizing that it could pass for courage?"

2. Arbitrary violence: a drive-by shooting, muggings that get out of hand, meeting up with a maniac. An acquaintance recently told me about a student of hers who made the mistake of getting caught staring at a young man in a Kalamazoo bus station who turned out to be a schizophrenic and pummeled him to death. In the backs of the minds of all of us who live in large cities is the figure of that terrified—and terrifying—wretch, the drug addict who holds us up or breaks into our homes and, out of control, goes too far. Oddly enough, I once had someone try to break into my home, waking me while doing so at three in the morning. I discovered myself going over to the window that he was attempting to pry loose and yelling at him in a voice rather deeper than I usually possess. I was not in the least afraid, but of all things furious at the nerve of the man attempting to violate my home.

3. Death in a hospital, through picking up some nutty infection, bad blood work, being given the wrong meds by an incompetent nurse or orderly. I continue to believe that hospitals are frightening places; too many people don't emerge from them. "To believe in medicine would be the height of folly," said Proust, "if not to believe in it were greater folly still." It's true, damn it, too true.

4. Death by modern appliance, not least an automobile driven by a drunk driver falling asleep at the wheel at just that moment when he is coming at you, passing you, crossing in front of you. But not by automobile alone. My friend Sonya Rudikoff, an excellent literary critic, came down one morning to turn up the gas under the kettle in her kitchen in Princeton, New Jersey, and was blown apart by an explosion. Too easy to imagine heating systems expelling gas into one's bedroom at night, being electrocuted by loose wires in one's refrigerator, and other delicious ways of going down in perfectly arbitrary, infuriatingly senseless death.

5. Death, finally, by that cause that I have already mentioned Americans fear even beyond public speaking: by an early, painful, and degrading disease. Lots of them out there, cause and cure unknown. I speak of "early" death, the way obituarists speak of "untimely" deaths, though few people seem to have died timely ones, unless quite aged or very ill.

18   Fears exist this side of death, of course. Tom Wolfe, who seems to me keenest among contemporary novelists in admiring physical courage and understanding fear, in his last novel, *A Man in Full*, neatly plays into the male heterosexual fear of homosexual rape in prison. I myself have always admired the physical courage of women who go through childbirth and, having done it once, are prepared to do it again. I hope I shan't be accused of male chauvinism when I say I am pleased that my masculinity has precluded my having to face that test in courage.

But I seem to have been talking almost entirely of fear and courage in the   19
physical realm. Physical courage not only has its limitations but needs qualifications. "Well," says the father of the hero of Mary Renault's fine novel *The Last
of the Wine*, "I am glad to see you not so wanting in courage as in sense. But
courage without conduct is the virtue of a robber, or a tyrant. Don't forget it."
There is a lot of foolish courage in the world. And lots in which people act on
instinct, which is still courage of a kind, but perhaps not of the highest kind.

Most of us, with a bit of luck, will go through life without having their   20
physical courage tested. But of course there is a courage greater than physical
courage. I myself know of no deeper courage than that required of parents
who raise a mentally damaged or emotionally deeply disturbed child. If heaven
be a football stadium—and I hope it isn't—theirs ought to be seats on the fifty.

It takes courage to die with serenity, especially if it means feigning seren-   21
ity to make your death easier for family and friends. I shall never forget the
death of my dearest friend, Edward Shils, who, when my wife went up to his
bedside for what both knew would be the final time, set *her* at ease by telling
her he wasn't frightened; reminded her of how much he valued her friendship
and all their time together; and, in short, did, as my wife said, all the work. To
die well not only requires the courage needed at the close of a life but also suggests that one has learned a vast amount, really learned courage, from much
that has gone before in life leading up to that close.

My friend Edward Shils also taught me to value intellectual courage,   22
though I only heard him use that exact phrase on one occasion. I was standing
near him after he gave the Jefferson Lecture in the Humanities at the University of Chicago, in which he dissected the various ways he thought the
modern university was becoming corrupted. A woman came up afterward to
congratulate him on his "intellectual courage" in saying the things he did. "Intellectual courage!" he exclaimed, genuinely surprised at the thought. "What
I said in that lecture took no intellectual courage. It takes intellectual courage
to speak one's mind in the Soviet Union or in South Africa. But here doing so
takes no courage whatsoever—only the absence of intellectual cowardice,
which isn't quite the same as intellectual courage."

And yet how few academics or intellectuals are willing to say what they   23
think? Not many, I have found. They fear what they think of as retaliation, a
greatly overdramatized word really meaning losing useful connections, chances
for promotion, minor raises, pathetically small lifts in their status in what is
called the profession. When a professor comes along who does show his hatred
for the false—a Sidney Hook, say, or a Paul Oskar Kristeller, or an Edward
Shils—the skies light up.

Courage also can be a quality of nations. In this realm, the United States   24
has not really been tested. How lucky we are since our founding never to have
been invaded. In the modern era one thinks, of course, of the English, who
came through World War II showing such admirable courage. "So let us drink
a toast," said Noel Coward of his countrymen's conduct in that war, "to the
courage and gallantry that made a strange heaven [of that time of courage] out
of a particular hell."

25   Would we Americans come through under such circumstances? Would our culture provide a figure of the courageousness of Winston Churchill? Would the great good fortune of our long prosperity leave us with sufficient inner strength to face sustained adversity? All have to be left as tantalizing, disturbing, yet finally unsettled questions.

26   On a less dramatic but not less significant plane, there is the courage that resides in doing one's duties, fulfilling one's obligations, day in and day out, without needing to be reminded by anyone else what those duties and obligations are. I speak here of the courage to carry on in the face of small but genuine setbacks, when one's dreams have been dashed, one's hopes rendered nugatory, all one's bets in life come up double zero. At such times who among us, man or woman, has not felt like chucking all life's onerous responsibilities, getting in the car, and driving away—for good? Courage of the most demanding kind can sometimes be required merely to hang in there.

27   In the words of Australian poet Adam Lindsey Gordon (1833–1870),

> *Life is mostly froth and bubble*
> *Two things stand like stone*
> KINDNESS *in another's trouble*
> COURAGE *in your own.*

28   Courage, then, consists in knowing—really knowing—what to fear, and in acting upon this knowledge. Saying this, I seem to have gotten no further with the subject of courage than Socrates, though, in my charming modesty, I suppose I am prepared to settle for that.

QUESTIONS ON SUBJECT AND PURPOSE

1. What is the relationship that Epstein sees between courage and fear?
2. Would you call Epstein's approach to his subject objective or subjective? What is the difference between the two?
3. Would "What Am I Afraid Of?" be a more appropriate title for the essay? Why or why not?

QUESTIONS ON STRATEGY AND AUDIENCE

1. What link exists between the opening and the closing paragraphs of the essay (1 and 28)?
2. What is the effect of the first-person ("I") in the story?
3. What expectations do you think Epstein has of his audience? Who might he imagine as his reader and on what basis do you reach that conclusion?

QUESTIONS ON VOCABULARY AND STYLE

1. How would you characterize the tone (see glossary) of the essay?
2. Epstein alludes to many different writers, literary works, and historical events throughout the essay. How do you as a reader react to these? Why might they be there? Do you find them annoying or distracting?

3. Be prepared to define the following words: *attenuated* (paragraph 2), *quotidian* (3), *intrinsic* (9), *dint* (9), *squalor* (11), *deranged* (11), *acculturation* (12), *inculcation* (12), *juddering* (16), *chauvinism* (18), *nugatory* (26), *onerous* (26),

WRITING SUGGESTIONS

1. **For Your Journal.** Make a list of things, actions, or situations that create fear in you. Can you organize or sort those fears into categories? Try to create a classification scheme that would organize those fears.
2. **For a Paragraph.** Using your journal notes as a starting point, write a paragraph in which you very briefly classify your major fears.
3. **For an Essay.** Reality television—and presumably the American viewing audience—is obsessed with the "fear factor." Yet, most of the fears addressed on these shows are physical in nature—they involve strong stomachs, a willingness to face traditional fears (heights, insects, snakes, tight places), and a significant amount of physical strength and endurance. Can you imagine another type of reality television that might draw on other types of fears? In an essay, explore other "fear" alternatives. You might want to suggest why other types of fears could prove either equally successful on such shows or absolutely unsatisfactory.
4. **For Research.** Amusement parks attract crowds each year and especially popular are the "thrill" rides, many of which have special names and are heavily advertised on television. Think about the types of rides that can be found in most parks. Use your own experience and knowledge, interview friends, visit Websites for the major parks with famous "thrill" rides. You should also examine print sources available online or through your school's library. Using that information, present in a research paper a classification system for thrill rides.

FOR FURTHER STUDY

Focusing on Grammar and Writing. Epstein's paragraphs nearly always have explicit topic sentences. Look at some of the longer paragraphs in the essay and notice how those topic sentences forecast the structure and content of the paragraph that follows. What does that suggest about the value of topic sentences in your writing?

Working Together. The essay contains 28 paragraphs. Divide into small groups. Each group should go through a block of paragraphs and make a list of every allusion (name, literary reference, quotation) that Epstein makes. Once the groups have finished, as a class construct a classification scheme for the types of allusions that Epstein makes in the essay. What does the list reveal about Epstein's style and his assumptions about his audience?

Seeing Other Modes at Work. The essay is also a definition of courage. Epstein argues that one way to understand courage is to analyze fear, since courage consists in "knowing . . . what to fear, and in acting upon this knowledge" (paragraph 28).

Finding Connections. For an interesting comparison of tone and approach, look at Bernard R. Berelson, "The Value of Children" (this chapter). Berelson's approach is objective, detached, and scientific; Epstein's is subjective, personal, and reflective. A good pairing on the question of courage is Ben Stein's "The Real Stars" (Chapter 8).

Exploring the Web. You can find an extensive number of sites on the Web dealing with Epstein's writing, including essays and reviews of his books. Particularly interesting is an essay published in 2004 titled, "Writing on the Brain." For some starting places, visit **www.prenhall. com/miller.**

5

COMPARISON AND CONTRAST

PREPARING TO WRITE

WHAT IS COMPARISON AND CONTRAST?

Whenever you decide between two alternatives, you engage in comparison and contrast. Which DVD player is the best value or has the most attractive set of features? Which professor's section of Introductory Sociology should you register for in the spring semester? In both cases, you make the decision by comparing alternatives on a series of relevant points and then deciding which has the greatest advantages.

In comparison and contrast, subjects are set in opposition in order to reveal their similarities and differences. Comparison involves finding similarities among two or more things, people, or ideas; contrast involves finding differences. Comparison and contrast writing tasks can involve, then, three activities: emphasizing similarities, emphasizing differences, or emphasizing both. Visually, comparison and contrast can be seen through a Venn diagram: the two or more subjects share some, but not all, things.

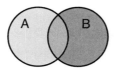

In a cartoon originally published in the *Utne Reader*, the Tour de France (the famous bicycle race) is compared with a Tour de America (which does not exist). By changing the background and the bikers' eyes, the artist creates a vivid contrast.

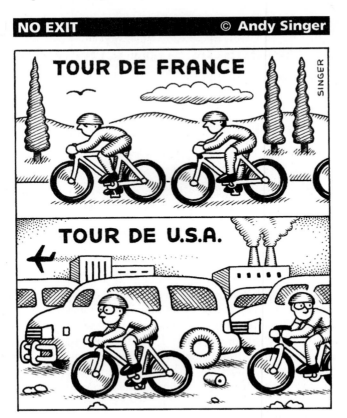

Biking is a popular recreation in the United States, but not always a safe sport in America's urbanized areas.
Andy Singer

Comparison and contrast often involves visual displays of the similarities and differences—things such as lists, tables, and charts—but it also occurs using just words. John Fischer uses comparison in this paragraph to emphasize the similarities between Ukrainians and Texans:

> The Ukrainians are the Texans of Russia. They believe they can fight, drink, ride, sing, and make love better than anybody else in the world, and if pressed will admit it. Their country, too, was a borderland—that's what Ukraine means—and like Texas it was originally settled by outlaws, horse thieves, land-hungry farmers, and people who hadn't made a go of it somewhere else. Some of these hard cases banded together, long ago, to raise hell and livestock. They called themselves Cossacks, and they would have felt right at home in any Western movie. Even today the Ukrainians cherish a wistful tradition of horsemanship, although most of them would feel as uncomfortable in a saddle as any Dallas banker. They still like to wear knee-high boots and big, furry hats, made of gray or Persian lamb, which are the local equivalent of the Stetson.

Fischer emphasizes only similarities. He tries to help his readers understand a foreign country by likening it to a place far more familiar to most Americans. Fischer concentrates on four similarities, which could be outlined:

Ukrainians and Texans

1. Believe that they are good at fighting, drinking, singing, making love
2. Are descended from people willing to take risks
3. Cherish a tradition of horsemanship
4. Wear high boots and big hats

Henry Petroski, in his essay "The Gleaming Silver Bird and the Rusty Iron Horse," contrasts air travel and train travel, emphasizing their differences.

> The airplane lets us fly and forget. We are as gods, even in coach class, attended by young, smiling stewards and stewardesses who bring us food, drink, and entertainment. From the window of the airplane we marvel at the cities far beneath us, at the great land formations and waterways, and at the clouds. Political boundaries are forgotten, and the world is one. Everything is possible.
>
> Nothing is forgotten on the train, however. The right of way is strewn with the detritus of technology, and technology's disruptiveness is everywhere apparent. Outside the once-clean picture window of the train, which has probably slowed down to pass over a deteriorating roadbed under repair, one sees not heaven in the clouds but the graveyards of people and machines. One cannot help but notice how technology has changed the land and the lives of those who live beside the rails. The factory abandoned is a blight not easily removed; the neglected homes of myriad factory (and railroad?) workers are not easily restored.

Petroski treats his two subjects in two separate paragraphs, emphasizing their differences. A simple outline of the paragraph would look like this:

Airplanes

1. We are as gods, passing over the earth—we see only the "big" picture, the world at a distance.
2. The view is an optimistic one—differences are eliminated.

Trains

1. We see out the dirty train windows all of the decay and deterioration that borders railroad tracks. We see the grimy details, not the "big" picture.
2. The view is a pessimistic one—we are constantly reminded of the "cost" of technology.

Like every writing task, comparison and contrast is done to achieve a particular purpose. In practical situations, you use it to help make a decision. You compare DVD players or professors in order to make an intelligent choice. In academic situations, comparison and contrast allows you to analyze two or more subjects carefully and thoroughly on the basis of a series of shared similarities or differences.

HOW DO YOU CHOOSE A SUBJECT?

Many times, especially on examinations in other academic courses, the subject for comparison and contrast is already chosen for you. On an economics examination you are asked, "What are the main differences between the public and private sectors?" In political science you are to "compare the political platforms of the Republican and Democratic parties in the last presidential election." At other times, however, you must choose the subject for comparison and contrast yourself.

The choice of subject is crucial. It is best to limit your paragraph or essay to subjects that have obvious similarities or differences. Esmeralda Santiago compares her experiences with guavas as a child and later in life; William Zinsser compares his writing process to Dr. Brock's; Mary Pipher contrasts the educational experiences and encouragements given to adolescent girls and boys; Suzanne Britt contrasts "sloppy" and "neat" people; Danzy Senna compares and contrasts herself with her grandmother; Meghan Daum is shocked to find that her "virtual love" Pete is much better than the "real" Pete.

Two other cautions are also important. First, be sure that you have a reason for making the comparison or contrast and that it will reveal something new or important to give your comparison or contrast an interesting thesis. Meghan Daum begins a "virtual," that is, an electronic, online relationship with an admirer named Pete. The romance flourishes until she meets the "real" Pete. Although the two have an electronic but "old-fashioned kind of courtship," although neither had lied or pretended to be someone else, although the two "real" people are the same as the two "virtual" people, the romance instantly dies when they meet each other in person. Daum uses comparison and contrast to make a point not just about this one relationship, but about our needs and our frustrations in trying to establish lasting relationships in contemporary society. She comments, "our need to worship somehow fuses with our need to be worshiped."

Second, limit your comparison and contrast to important points; do not try to cover everything. Mary Pipher, for example, focuses on how our educational system treats adolescent girls differently than adolescent boys. She does not write about parental expectations or other educational influences.

DO YOU ALWAYS FIND BOTH SIMILARITIES AND DIFFERENCES?

You can compare and contrast only if there is some basic similarity between the two subjects: John Fischer compares two groups of people—Ukrainians and Texans; Henry Petroski compares two modes of transportation—the airplane and the railroad. There is no point in comparing two totally unrelated subjects; for example, the mind could be compared to a computer since both process information, but there would be no reason to compare a computer to an airplane. Remember, too, that some similarities will be obvious and hence not worth writing about. It would be pointless for William Zinsser to observe that both he and Dr. Brock write on word processors, use dictionaries, or work best in a quiet study. This does not mean that similarities are not important or should not be mentioned. Danzy Senna sees a number of similarities between herself and her grandmother—both are writers, both are strong-willed and outspoken. At the same time, she is also struck by the differences in their backgrounds and their expectations.

Once you have chosen your subject, make a list of the possible points of comparison and contrast. Be sure that those points are shared. Zinsser, for example, organizes his comparison and contrast around six questions. To each of the six, Zinsser gives first Dr. Brock's response and then his own. The contrast depends on the two responses to each of the six questions. If Brock had answered one group of three and Zinsser a different group of three, the contrast would not have worked.

Be careful when you create analogies, similes, and metaphors. Do not try to be too clever, or your point will seem forced. But do not avoid such devices altogether. Used sparingly, these compressed comparisons can be evocative and effective.

Prewriting Suggestions

1. Jot down ideas on subjects that might be compared or contrasted. Remember that comparison involves finding similarities among two or more things—typically things that initially appear to be different. Contrast involves finding differences among things that seem quite similar.
2. Jot down under each possible subject a list of similarities or of differences. Do not worry about an order, just generate ideas.
3. Go back over your lists and make sure that the similarities or differences are important enough to write about. The idea is not to generate as many similarities or differences as possible but to find interesting and significant points.
4. Narrow down to a possible topic and then explain in one sentence (a thesis) why you are making this comparison or contrast.
5. Check your list to see that all of the items on it are phrased in parallel form—check the glossary for examples.

WRITING

HOW DO YOU STRUCTURE A COMPARISON AND CONTRAST ESSAY?

Comparison and contrast is not only an intellectual process but also a structural pattern that can be used to organize paragraphs and essays. In comparing and contrasting two subjects, three organizational models are available.

Subject by Subject (all of subject A and then all of subject B)

A.

   1.

   2.

   3.

B.

   1.

   2.

   3.

Esmeralda Santiago basically uses a subject-by-subject structure in her essay, treating the experience of eating ripe guavas in paragraphs 2 through 4 and unripe guavas in paragraphs 5 through 7. The subject-by-subject pattern for comparison and contrast works in paragraph units. If your comparison paper is fairly short, you could treat all of subject A in a paragraph or group of paragraphs and then all of subject B in a paragraph or group of paragraphs. If your paper is fairly long and the comparisons are fairly complicated, you might want to use either the point-by-point or mixed pattern.

Point by Point (point 1 in A, then point 1 in B)

A1/B1

A2/B2

A3/B3

William Zinsser's comparison of his writing process with that of Dr. Brock uses a point-by-point pattern of contrast. The two authors take turns responding to a series of six questions asked by students. The essay then follows a pattern that can be described as A1B1, A2B2, A3B3, A4B4, A5B5, A6B6. In replying to the fourth question, for example, about whether or not feeling "depressed or unhappy" will affect their writing, Brock and Zinsser reply:

> "Probably it will," Dr. Brock replied. "Go fishing. Take a walk."
> "Probably it won't," I said. "If your job is to write every day, you learn to do it like any other job."

The point-by-point, or alternating, pattern emphasizes the individual points of comparison or contrast rather than the subject as a whole. In college writing, this pattern most frequently devotes a sentence, a group of sentences, or a paragraph to each point, alternating between subject A and subject B. If you use the alternating pattern, you must decide how to order your points—for instance, by beginning or by ending with the strongest or most significant.

Mixed Sequence (includes both subject by subject and point by point)

A.

    1.

    2.

B.

    1.

    2.

A3/B3

etc.

In longer pieces of writing, writers typically mix the subject-by-subject and point-by-point patterns. Such an arrangement provides variety and can make the points of comparison and contrast much more vivid for the reader.

Much of the examination writing that you do in college probably should be organized either as subject by subject or point by point, since these are the clearest structures for short responses. Many of the essays that you encounter in magazines and newspapers will use a mixed pattern in order to achieve flexibility and variety.

HOW DO YOU USE ANALOGY, METAPHOR, AND SIMILE?

Writing a comparison often involves constructing an analogy, an extended comparison in which something complex or unfamiliar is likened to something simple or familiar. The reason for making the analogy is to help your reader more easily understand or visualize the more complex or unfamiliar subject. For example, if you are trying to explain how the hard disk on your computer is organized, you might use the analogy of a file cabinet. The hard disk, you write, is the file cabinet, which is partitioned off into directories (the file drawers), each of which contains subdirectories (the hanging folders), which in turn contain the individual files (the manila folders in which documents are stored). Think of the icons on your computer screen to display this relationship metaphorically.

Analogies are also used to provide a new way of seeing something. J. Anthony Lukas, for example, explains his attraction to the game of pinball by an analogy:

> Pinball is a metaphor for life, pitting man's skill, nerve, persistence, and luck against the perverse machinery of human existence. The playfield is rich with rewards: targets that bring huge scores, bright lights, chiming bells, free balls, and extra games. But is it replete with perils, too: culs-de-sac, traps, gutters, and gobble holes down which the ball may disappear forever.

Lukas's analogy does not seek to explain the unfamiliar. Probably every reader has seen a pinball game. Rather, the analogy invites the reader to see the game in a fresh way. The suggested similarity might help the reader understand why arcade games such as pinball have a particular significance or attraction.

Two common forms of analogy in writing are metaphor and simile. A metaphor directly identifies one thing with another. When Henry Petroski contrasts air travel and train travel, he uses metaphors—the airplane is a "silver bird" and the train is an "iron horse."

A simile, as its name suggests, is also a comparison based on a point or points of similarity. A simile differs from a metaphor by using the word *like* or *as* to link the two things being compared. In this sense, a simile suggests, rather than directly establishes, the comparison. On the February morning when his father died, Scott Russell Sanders (Chapter 3) saw that the ice "coated the windows like cataracts." Seventeenth-century poet Robert Herrick found a witty similarity: "Fain would I kiss my Julia's dainty leg, / Which is as white and hairless as an egg."

Drafting Suggestions

1. Decide on whether the best organizational strategy will be point by point, subject by subject, or a mix of the two. Plan the organization of your paper with an outline.

2. Decide on a rationale for the order of the points of comparison or contrast. What will go first and why? What will come last and why?

3. Rate each point of comparison or contrast. Is each one really significant or interesting? Eliminate any points that seem minor or trivial.

4. Check to see if your paragraphing in the essay reveals the structure of the essay. Can your reader clearly see your organizational plan?

5. Get a peer reader, writing tutor, or your instructor to read your draft. Ask him or her to make suggestions on how your paper might be improved. Weigh each suggestion.

REVISING

HOW DO YOU REVISE A COMPARISON AND CONTRAST ESSAY?

Comparison and contrast is intended to isolate similarities and differences between two or more objects. It is a fundamental process by which the mind understands things. Like all writing tasks, it is done for a purpose—in this instance, to help the reader make a choice or to help the reader clarify and understand the subject. Although comparison and contrast can be funny and entertaining, generally it has a serious, informative purpose. For that reason, it is important that a comparison and contrast essay be clearly and logically organized.

When revising a comparison and contrast essay, pay particular attention to the following areas: avoiding the obvious and keeping the analysis logically structured.

Avoiding the Obvious   Your paper needs to be both informative and interesting enough to hold your readers' attention. Do not compare or contrast the obvious. When John McPhee compares Florida and California oranges (under Reading Comparison and Contrast), he focuses only on the differences that are important, explaining why oranges from the two different parts of the country are so different. He contrasts them on the thickness of their skins, on their juiciness, and on the ease of peeling and separating. Readers tire easily of essays that offer only the obvious. Think again about what you have chosen to write. Ask a peer reader to assess its interest. Does it tell the reader only what he or she already knows? Are the points of contrast or comparison significant or trivial? If there is a problem, you will either need to change your points of similarity or contrast or find a new subject.

Keeping the Analysis Logically Structured   Comparison and contrast can be organized in three ways: subject by subject (all of A, all of B), point by point (A1/B1, A2/B2), or a mixture of the two. In order for the structure to be logical, it is essential that the points of comparison and contrast be identical in both subjects and that they be taken in exactly the same order. You guarantee a clear, easily followed organization if your points are logically organized.

If you are using a subject-by-subject model, it is fairly easy to signal to your reader when you have finished one subject and started another. Typically, the essay will be divided by paragraphs in such a way as to mark the switch from one subject to another. If you are using a point-by-point or a mixed method, you will need to provide clear step or sequence markers for your reader to signal when you are moving to the next point. Have you called out the points (for example, *first, second, next, then*) or used transitional words or phrases to signal the transition? Ask a peer reader if your essay is easy to follow and, if not, to identify those areas that are confusing.

Parallel structures—that is, items that are phrased in grammatically similar ways—are also important in comparison and contrast. Underline each of the points you are using. Have you cast those points in grammatical structures that are parallel in form?

Have you arranged the points of comparison and contrast in an order that makes sense? If the points are more or less of the same relative importance, their order might be flexible. If the points can be arranged from greater or lesser significance, then you need to arrange them in a descending or an ascending order. Look again at the order in which you have arranged the points of comparison or contrast.

Revising Suggestions

1. Assess the significance of your subject and your approach to it. Do not waste your readers' time on the obvious or trivial.

2. Experiment with the paper's organizational strategy. Could it be arranged in another way? Could the points be reordered? Print out your essay and cut it apart and experiment with different arrangements.
3. Look again at your introduction. Ask some friends to read it. On the basis of your introduction, do they want to keep reading? If not, rewrite your opening.
4. Honestly evaluate your conclusion. Did you just stop, or did you really write a conclusion? Does your final paragraph seem to emphasize the points that you are making in the essay? Does it reinforce your thesis?
5. Check your title. Every paper needs a real title—not something descriptive such as "Comparison and Contrast Essay." If necessary, force yourself to write several other titles before choosing a final one.

SAMPLE STUDENT ESSAY

As part of the library research paper unit in freshman English, Alicia Gray's class had been talking about searching their school's online library catalog for relevant books. The instructor had mentioned a number of times that card catalogs could be searched for both subjects and keywords since the software program allowed for both. To give the students practice in both kinds of searches, Meghan, their instructor, gave them a worksheet to do for homework. On the way out of class, Alicia stopped and remarked to her instructor, "I always just do a keyword search," she said, "and it always seems like I find plenty of material. Since we have the capability to do a keyword search, isn't doing a subject search just unnecessary and even old-fashioned?" "Do the worksheet," Meghan replied. "Maybe you could compare and contrast the two methods for your essay, which is due next week." A week later, Alicia brought to class the following rough draft of her essay comparing keyword and subject searches.

FIRST DRAFT

SUBJECT VS. KEYWORD SEARCHES

When it is time to start gathering information for your research paper in Freshman English, you will need to consult our Library's on-line catalog. The card catalog is a listing of the books that our library holds. Those books are catalogued, or listed, by author, title, subject, and keyword. Since normally we start by looking for books about our intended topic—rather than for specific titles by specific authors—we must start with either subject searches or keyword searches. What exactly is the difference between these two types of searches and how do you know when to use each?

When librarians refer to a "subject" search, they mean something quite specific and different from a "keyword." The term subject in library catalogs refers to a large listing of subject headings that are used by the Library of Congress to catalog a book. In fact, if you want to do a subject search in a library catalog, you don't start with the catalog itself. Instead you go to a multivolume series of books entitled the <u>Library of Congress Subject Headings</u>. Those books list alphabetically the various headings under which the Library of Congress files books. That listing is complete with cross-references, that is, with references to broader terms and to narrower, more specific terms. When catalogers at the Library of Congress look at new books, they do not just randomly assign a heading or a group of headings to the book, nor do they take the heading from a word in the book's title. Instead, they choose a heading or headings from the published list.

The principle behind the subject headings is to group related books under one heading. So instead of filing books about "the death penalty," "capital punishment," "death by lethal injection" under three separate subject headings, the Library of Congress uses a single subject heading ("capital punishment") and then provides cross-references from any other synonymous terms. The subject heading can also be followed by a whole series of other headings (for example, "capital punishment—history"). These other, more specific headings are very important because the Library of Congress always tries to assign the most specific subject heading to a book that it can. You never want to look under a large general heading if a more specific one is used. And how do you know if a more specific heading exists? You need to check the printed collection of headings currently in use. Subject headings impose a control on the vocabulary words used for headings.

In contrast, keyword searches look for words that are present somewhere in the book's record—typically in its title or subtitle, its author, its publisher. A keyword search retrieves information only when that word or group of words that you have entered appear in a record. That means there is no attempt at controlling the vocabulary. A book that had the phrase "the death penalty" somewhere in the title could be retrieved only if you typed in the keywords "death" and "penalty." A book on the same subject that used "capital punishment" would never appear—and keyword searches do not suggest related synonyms to you. Moreover, the presence of the key words would not necessarily mean that the book would be about the "death penalty" in the sense of "capital punishment." The words could appear in the title of novel or a collection of poems; they could refer to vastly different and unrelated circumstances—"the death penalty in ancient Rome." And, if you don't indicate the relationship (for example, immediately next to each other) that the two (or more) terms are to have, you'll end up retrieving a mountain of records that have the terms "death" and "penalty" somewhere in the record (for example, "The Penalty of Life: The Death of John Sayce").

Keyword searches have an advantage in that they can be used to find the very specific words for which you might be looking. Maybe those words haven't yet been added to the subject headings. Since subject headings depend on printed lists, subject headings are slow to react to new fields of study or new technologies.

COMMENTS

Alicia shared the opening paragraphs of her rough draft with a classmate during in-class peer editing. The instructor had asked the students to concentrate on the organizational pattern used in the body of the essay and on the introduction. After reading Alicia's paper, her partner Sara LaBarca offered some advice on revising the draft. "You have lots of information," she said, "but your main pattern of development is subject-by-subject except for the fifth paragraph where you switch to point-by-point. Maybe you should try doing more with the point-to-point; otherwise, by the time your readers come to the second half of your essay, they might forget the contrasts you established in the first half."

"I also think you need a strong introduction," she added. "You have a good thesis statement, but, well, frankly, I found the opening paragraph a little boring." Alicia tried to take Sara's advice and revised the opening of her essay and reorganized the body.

REVISED DRAFT

MINIMIZING THE GUESSWORK IN A LIBRARY SEARCH

The Cecil County Community College Library has twenty books dealing with the death penalty, but unless you pay attention to the next couple of pages, you will never find most of them. Why? Because no single search strategy will lead you to all twenty books.

Looking for book sources is more complicated than you might think. A successful search will require two different types of searches—a subject and a keyword search. They are very different kinds of searches with different rules and results. But to maximize your sources for a quality research paper, you will need to know how to do both.

In both subject and keyword searches, you are looking for single words or phrases that will lead you to the books you need. Those subject or keyword terms come from two different places. The term <u>subject</u> in library catalogs refers to a large alphabetized listing of subject headings that are assigned by the Library of Congress when cataloging a book. You find an appropriate heading not by guessing as you stand at a computer terminal, but by looking in a multivolume series of books entitled <u>Library of Congress Subject Headings</u>. When catalogers at the Library of Congress look at new books, they do not just randomly assign a heading or a group of headings to the book, nor do they necessarily take the heading from a word in the book's title. Instead, they choose a heading or headings from the published list. A <u>keyword</u>, on the other hand, is a significant word, generally a noun, that is typically in a book's title or subtitle. Unlike a subject search where the categories are "controlled" (that is, someone has predetermined what subject headings will be used), a keyword search is, in one sense, guesswork. You think of an important word or phrase that might describe the topic about which you want information and you try that. Just like any time you guess, though, there are risks. A keyword search retrieves information only when that word or group of words that you have entered appears in a record.

"If I have the choice of having to look things up in a set of books or of just guessing, I'll guess," you might reply. But before you reject subject searches, consider the problem of synonyms—that is, words or phrases that mean roughly the same thing. A controlled subject search groups related books under one heading. So instead of filing books about "the death penalty," "capital punishment," and "death by lethal injection" under three separate subject headings, the Library of Congress uses a single subject heading ("capital punishment") and then provides cross references from any other synonymous terms. In contrast, you can only retrieve a book in a keyword search if it has those specific words somewhere in its record. A book that had the phrase "the death penalty" somewhere in the title could be retrieved only if you typed in the keywords "death" and "penalty." A book on the same subject that used "capital punishment" would never appear, and keyword searches do not suggest related synonyms to you. Moreover, the presence of the key words would not necessarily mean that the book would be about the "death penalty" in the sense of "capital punishment." The words could appear in the title of a novel or a collection of poems; they could refer to vastly different and unrelated circumstances— "the death penalty in ancient Rome." And, if you don't indicate the relationship (for example, immediately next to each other) that the two (or more) terms are to have, you'll end up retrieving a mountain of records that have the terms "death" and "penalty" somewhere in the record (for example, "The Penalty of Life: The Death of John Sayce").

Keyword searches have some distinct advantages, however. Since subject searches are controlled, the Library of Congress tries to find existing appropriate terms under which to file books—even if they end up having to use more general terms. Although new subject headings are regularly added to the lists, emerging fields and technologies are rarely represented adequately in the subject headings. On the other hand, since keywords do not depend on any pre-existing published categories and since no one has tried to classify those keywords into categories, keywords can be the best way to look for books on new and emerging subjects. In that sense, a keyword can be far more precise (if you guess the right one!) than a subject heading.

Some Things to Remember

1. Limit your comparison and contrast to subjects that can be adequately developed in a paragraph or an essay.
2. Make sure that the subjects you are comparing and contrasting have some basic similarities. Make a list of similarities and differences before you begin to write.
3. Decide why the comparison or contrast is important. What does it reveal? Remember to make the reason clear to the reader.
4. Decide what points of comparison or contrast are the most important or the most revealing. In general, omit any points of comparison that would be obvious to anybody.
5. Decide which of the three patterns of comparison and contrast best fits your purpose: subject by subject, point by point, or mixed.
6. Remember to make clear to your reader when you are switching from one subject to another or from one point of comparison to another.

Comparison and Contrast as a Literary Strategy

Poet Martin Espada uses comparison and contrast to structure his poem "Coca-Cola and Coco Frío." As you read the poem, notice the points of comparison and contrast that Espada develops and think about what the comparison and contrast is intended to reveal.

COCA-COLA AND COCO FRIO
Martin Espada

On his first visit to Puerto Rico,
island of family folklore,
the fat boy wandered
from table to table
with his mouth open.
At every table, some great-aunt
would steer him with cool-spotted hands
to a glass of Coca-Cola.
One even sang to him, in all the English
she could remember, a Coca-Cola jingle
from the forties. He drank obediently, though
he was bored with this portion, familiar
from soda fountains in Brooklyn.

Then, at a roadside stand off the beach, the fat boy
opened his mouth to coco frio, a coconut
chilled, then scalped by a machete
so that a straw could inhale the clear milk.
The boy tilted the green shell overhead
and drooled coconut milk down his chin;
suddenly, Puerto Rico was not Coca-Cola
or Brooklyn, and neither was he.

For years afterwards, the boy marveled at an island
where the people drank Coca-Cola
and sang jingles from World War II
in a language they did not speak,
while so many coconuts in the trees
sagged heavy with milk, swollen
and unsuckled.

DISCUSSION QUESTIONS

1. How does Espada organize his comparison and contrast in the poem? In what ways are the two drinks similar? In what ways are they different?

2. What is it about the two drinks that catches Espada's attention? Why might he have written the poem? What is he trying to reveal?

3. What does the boy discover? How does the comparison and contrast lead to that discovery?

4. What image is developed in the final two lines of the poem? What is that image called? How is it also an example of comparison and contrast?

5. What is the significance of the word "unsuckled" in the final line? Who should consume the nourishment that the coconuts supply? Why?

WRITING SUGGESTIONS

Espada uses something from American popular culture to comment on the "island of [his] family folklore." Think about conflicts that you have experienced between how something is done in your culture in contrast to how it is done in another. The conflicts, for example, could result from differences in culture, in age, in religion, in values, in expectations, or in social or economic backgrounds. As a departure point, you might consider the following possible conflicts:

a. Between you and your parents
b. Between you and your grandparents
c. Between you and your siblings

READING COMPARISON AND CONTRAST

The following paragraph is taken from John McPhee's nonfiction book *Oranges*. McPhee is a writer fascinated by details, and *Oranges* contains just about everything you might ever want to know about the fruit. As McPhee indicates, domestically grown oranges typically come from either Florida or California. You might think first of the differences between seeded and unseeded (or navel) oranges, but as McPhee points out, the oranges grown in these two climates differ significantly.

As you read, remember what you have learned about how to write using comparison and contrast and how that knowledge might help you as a reader.

- Comparison finds similarities among things that appear to be different. An analogy—likening an unfamiliar thing to a familiar one—is a form of comparison.
- Contrast finds differences among things that appear to be similar. Any time we look at the features of a service or a product before we purchase it, we are making a contrast.
- The primary purpose of comparison and contrast is to explain or clarify.
- Comparison and contrast has three possible organizational patterns. The subjects are treated one at a time (subject by subject), or the points of similarity and difference between the subject are treated one at a time (point by point). In longer essays, a mixed pattern—a bit of both—is sometimes used.

- The points of comparison and contrast are typically arranged in an order that reflects their relative importance.
- The points of comparison and contrast are phrased in parallel form— identical grammatical forms.

The paragraph focuses on points of contrast—the similarities are obvious— both are oranges

Florida

1. Tight skin
2. Heavy with juice
3. Harder to peel

California

1. Thicker skin
2. Not as juicy
3. Easier to peel

Comparison of growing conditions

Florida—abundant rain
California—irrigation

Comparison of amount of oranges grown

An orange grown in Florida usually has a thin and tightly fitting skin and it is also heavy with juice. [Californians say that if you want to eat a Florida orange, you have to get into a bathtub first]. California oranges are light in weight and have thick skins that break easily and come off in chunks. The flesh inside is marvelously sweet, and the segments almost separate themselves. [In Florida, it is said that you can run over a California orange with a ten-ton truck and not even wet the pavement.] The differences from which these hyperboles arise will prevail in the two states even if the type of orange is the same. In arid climates, like California's, oranges develop a thick albedo, which is the white part of the skin. Florida is one of the two or three most rained-upon states in the United States. California uses the Colorado River and similarly impressive sources to irrigate its oranges, but of course irrigation can only do so much. The annual difference in rainfall between the Florida and California orange-growing areas is one million one hundred and forty-thousand gallons per acre. For years, California was the leading orange-growing state, but Florida surpassed California in 1942 and grows three times as many oranges now. California oranges, for their part, can safely be called three times as beautiful.

RESPONDING TO A VISUAL

Comparison and contrast frequently can be visually displayed. The "extreme makeovers" of people or houses popular on television are, at their core, comparison and contrast, more popularly phrased as "before and after." Comparison stresses similarities—despite the extreme physical makeovers, the people (their personalities, qualities, abilities, knowledge) have not changed. Even when the original house is torn down, the new house still is a house and fulfills the same function. In that sense, contrasts that highlight differences are what are visually emphasized. The following two photographs provoke painful memories for many Americans—the twin towers of the World Trade Center before and after the tragedy of 9/11.

READING AND WRITING ABOUT IMAGES

Study the two photographs. Then, using comparison and contrast, write an essay in which you focus on the similarities or differences between pre-9/11 America and post-9/11 America. What is similar? What has changed?

VISITING THE WEB

The companion Website, **www.prenhall.com/miller**, has additional information about comparison and contrast and about the writers in this chapter. You will also find a number of links to other sources of information about the subjects of the essays found in this chapter.

EXPLORING ON YOUR OWN

When you explore the resources of the Web, what search engine do you use? Google.com is so widely used and so well known that the verb "to google" (meaning to look up information on the Web using Google) is becoming a part of our language. But Google.com is not the only search engine. Reference librarians at research universities encourage searchers to use other "engines" to increase the number of results. Moreover, not everything on the Web is available through a search engine. The "invisible Web" (meaning it does not turn up in normal search) is an estimated two or three times bigger than the "visible Web." For a comparison of the major search engines and for tips on increasing your searching skills, visit the *Reader's* Website at **www.prenhall.com/miller.**

LOOKING FOR WRITING SUGGESTIONS

COMPARISON

1. Playing a sport/working for a company
2. Buffet/undergraduate course offerings
3. Similarities between fruits/vegetables/meats
4. Lessons learned in childhood/adult experiences
5. Shared characteristics of men and women
6. Similarities among different forms of government
7. Similarities among two different religions
8. An analogy between something technical (for example, hard drive) and something simple (a file cabinet)
9. An analogy between how a machine works and how the body or mind works
10. Past success or failure and future success or failure

CONTRAST

1. Pro-life/pro-choice
2. Meat eater/vegan
3. Science or engineering major/humanities major
4. Early riser/late sleeper
5. Instant messaging/talking on a phone
6. Street smarts/school smarts
7. E-mailing/letter writing
8. High school sports/college sports/professional sports
9. Men/women
10. Two diet plans

GUAVAS

Esmeralda Santiago

Esmeralda Santiago (1948–) was born in San Juan, Puerto Rico, and came to the United States at the age of thirteen. A Harvard graduate with an M.F.A. from Sarah Lawrence, Santiago is a founder of CantoMedia, a film and media production company. This essay appeared as the Prologue to When I Was Puerto Rican *(1993), an autobiographical memoir that Santiago continued in* Almost a Woman *(1998), and* The Turkish Lover *(2004).*

On Writing: *Santiago observes, "Writing memoir involves chipping away at things in small increments, like a sculptor does to a piece of marble, until the image inside emerges. The process of writing my memoirs involved solitary and painful self-examination."*

BEFORE READING

Connecting: Do you remember a particular food that you associate with childhood? Something that was special to you? Something that you particularly enjoyed?

Anticipating: Why does Santiago no longer eat guavas?

1   There are guavas at the Shop & Save. I pick one the size of a tennis ball and finger the prickly stem end. It feels familiarly bumpy and firm. The guava is not quite ripe; the skin is still a dark green. I smell it and imagine a pale pink center, the seeds tightly embedded in the flesh.

2   A ripe guava is yellow, although some varieties have a pink tinge. The skin is thick, firm, and sweet. Its heart is bright pink and almost solid with seeds. The most delicious part of the guava surrounds the tiny seeds. If you don't know how to eat a guava, the seeds end up in the crevices between your teeth.

3   When you bite into a ripe guava, your teeth must grip the bumpy surface and sink into the thick edible skin without hitting the center. It takes experience to do this, as it's quite tricky to determine how far beyond the skin the seeds begin.

4   Some years, when the rains have been plentiful and the nights cool, you can bite into a guava and not find many seeds. The guava bushes grow close to the ground, their branches laden with green then yellow fruit that seem to ripen overnight. These guavas are large and juicy, almost seedless, their roundness enticing you to have one more, just one more, because next year the rains may not come.

5   As children, we didn't always wait for the fruit to ripen. We raided the bushes as soon as the guavas were large enough to bend the branch.

A green guava is sour and hard. You bite into it at its widest point, be-   6
cause it's easier to grasp with your teeth. You hear the skin, meat, and seeds
crunching inside your head, while the inside of your mouth explodes in little
spurts of sour.

You grimace, your eyes water, and your cheeks disappear as your lips   7
purse into a tight O. But you have another and then another, enjoying the
crunchy sounds, the acid taste, the gritty texture of the unripe center. At night,
your mother makes you drink castor oil, which she says tastes better than a
green guava. That's when you know for sure that you're a child and she has
stopped being one.

I had my last guava the day we left Puerto Rico. It was large and juicy,   8
almost red in the center, and so fragrant that I didn't want to eat it because I
would lose the smell. All the way to the airport I scratched at it with my teeth,
making little dents in the skin, chewing small pieces with my front teeth, so
that I could feel the texture against my tongue, the tiny pink pellets of sweet.

Today, I stand before a stack of dark green guavas, each perfectly round   9
and hard, each $1.59. The one in my hand is tempting. It smells faintly of late
summer afternoons and hopscotch under the mango tree. But this is autumn
in New York, and I'm no longer a child.

The guava joins its sisters under the harsh fluorescent lights of the ex-   10
otic fruit display. I push my cart away, toward the apples and pears of my
adulthood, their nearly seedless ripeness predictable and bittersweet.

QUESTIONS ON SUBJECT AND PURPOSE

1. Where is Santiago at the start of the essay? What triggers her
   memory?
2. Santiago never buys the guava. Why not?
3. The essay appears at the start of Santiago's book *When I Was Puerto
   Rican* with the heading "Prologue: How to Eat a Guava." Can you
   think of other appropriate or suggestive titles for the essay?

QUESTIONS ON STRATEGY AND AUDIENCE

1. How does Santiago structure her comparison and contrast? Is it
   subject by subject or point by point or a mix of the two? What other
   structure underlies the essay?
2. Santiago's essay is taken from a memoir. What is a memoir? What do
   you expect in one?
3. What assumption about audience must the writer of a memoir make?

QUESTIONS ON VOCABULARY AND STYLE

1. In paragraph 7, how does Santiago suggest what happens to your
   mouth when you bite into a sour guava?

2. At the end of the essay, Santiago writes of apples and pears as being "bittersweet." What is "bittersweet"? In what ways might the apples and pears be "bittersweet"?

3. Be prepared to define the following word: *grimace* (paragraph 7).

WRITING SUGGESTIONS

1. **For Your Journal.** Sense impressions—sights, sounds, smells, touches—are a powerful stimulus to memory. Think back to your childhood. Do you associate a particular sense experience with that time? The perfume your mother wore? The sound of your father whistling? The texture or taste of your favorite cookie? Pick a period from your childhood and make a list of the sense impressions that you remember.

2. **For a Paragraph.** Using your journal as a prewriting exercise, select one of the remembered experiences and re-create it in a paragraph. Try to capture that sensual memory in words as Santiago does.

3. **For an Essay.** Santiago's essay contrasts, in part, a childhood experience with an adult experience—a "once I grew up I stopped doing . . ." theme. In an essay, make a similar comparison and contrast. Perhaps there was a climactic moment when you suddenly realized things had changed, that you had changed.

4. **For Research.** Santiago's memoir is about growing up and making the transition from the innocence of childhood to the experience of adulthood, but it is also about the problems of cultural identity—am I Puerto Rican or American? Research the problem of how people who immigrate to the United States (or to any other country) confront these issues. What does it mean to be a part of two cultures? Is it always problematic? Have you faced this problem? Do you know someone—a friend or classmate—who has? How can this contrast be made vivid to students for whom this is not an issue?

FOR FURTHER STUDY

Focusing on Grammar and Writing. Go through Santiago's essay and underline each use of the comma. Then explain why a comma was used there. You can check a grammar handbook for help or the short guide in the glossary of this book. How many different examples of comma use can you find in the essay?

Working Together. Divide into small groups. Each group should focus on two paragraphs in the essay and look closely at the descriptive details that Santiago provides. How effective is her description? How many senses does she draw on in each paragraph? The groups should report their findings to the class as a whole.

Seeing Other Modes at Work. The original title of this essay was "How to Eat a Guava." In what ways is the essay also a good example of process?

Finding Connections. A good pairing is Martin Espada's poem "Coca-Cola and Coco Frio" found in Comparison and Contrast as a Literary Strategy.

Exploring the Web. Visit Santiago's own Website, read an extensive interview with her, check out reviews of her work, and find out more about guavas—the links can be found at the *Reader's* Website at **www.prenhall.com/miller**.

THE TRANSACTION: TWO WRITING PROCESSES

William Zinsser

William Zinsser (1922–) has been an editor, critic, editorial writer, college teacher, and writing consultant. He is the author of many books including On Writing Well: An Informal Guide to Writing Nonfiction *(sixth edition, 1998), a textbook classic of which* The New York Times *wrote: "It belongs on any shelf of serious reference works for writers."*

    On Writing: *As someone who earns his living as a writer, Zinsser sees writing as hard work. "The only way to learn to write," he has observed, "is to force yourself to produce a certain number of words on a regular basis." In an interview, he once remarked: "I don't think writing is an art. I think sometimes it's raised to an art, but basically it's a craft, like cabinet making or carpentry."*

BEFORE READING

Connecting: If you had to describe your writing process to a group of younger students, what would you say?

Anticipating: Why should writing seem so easy to Brock and so difficult to Zinsser? If he finds it so difficult, why does Zinsser continue to write?

1   A school in Connecticut once held "a day devoted to the arts," and I was asked if I would come and talk about writing as a vocation. When I arrived I found that a second speaker had been invited—Dr. Brock (as I'll call him), a surgeon who had recently begun to write and had sold some stories to magazines. He was going to talk about writing as an avocation. That made us a panel, and we sat down to face a crowd of students and teachers and parents, all eager to learn the secrets of our glamorous work.

2   Dr. Brock was dressed in a bright red jacket, looking vaguely bohemian, as authors are supposed to look, and the first question went to him. What was it like to be a writer?

3   He said it was tremendous fun. Coming home from an arduous day at the hospital, he would go straight to his yellow pad and write his tensions away. The words just flowed. It was easy. I then said that writing wasn't easy and wasn't fun. It was hard and lonely, and the words seldom just flowed.

4   Next Dr. Brock was asked if it was important to rewrite. Absolutely not, he said. "Let it all hang out," he told us and whatever form the sentences take will reflect the writer at his most natural. I then said that rewriting is the essence of writing. I pointed out that professional writers rewrite their sentences repeatedly over and over and then rewrite what they have rewritten.

"What do you do on days when it isn't going well?" Dr. Brock was asked. 5
He said he just stopped writing and put the work aside for a day when it would
go better. I then said that the professional writer must establish a daily schedule and stick to it. I said that writing is a craft, not an art, and that the man who
runs away from his craft because he lacks inspiration is fooling himself. He is
also going broke.

"What if you're feeling depressed or unhappy?" a student asked. "Won't 6
that affect your writing?"

Probably it will, Dr. Brock replied. Go fishing. Take a walk. Probably 7
it won't, I said. If your job is to write every day, you learn to do it like any
other job.

A student asked if we found it useful to circulate in the literary world. 8
Dr. Brock said he was greatly enjoying his new life as a man of letters, and he
told several stories of being taken to lunch by his publisher and his agent at
Manhattan restaurants where writers and editors gather. I said that professional writers are solitary drudges who seldom see other writers.

"Do you put symbolism in your writing?" a student asked me. 9

"Not if I can help it," I replied. I have an unbroken record of missing the 10
deeper meaning in any story, play or movie, and as for dance and mime, I have
never had any idea of what is being conveyed.

"I *love* symbols!" Dr. Brock exclaimed, and he described with gusto the 11
joys of weaving them through his work.

So the morning went, and it was a revelation to all of us. At the end Dr. 12
Brock told me he was enormously interested in my answers—it had never occurred to him that writing could be hard. I told him I was just as interested in
his answers—it had never occurred to me that writing could be easy. Maybe I
should take up surgery on the side.

As for the students, anyone might think we left them bewildered. But 13
in fact we probably gave them a broader glimpse of the writing process than
if only one of us had talked. For there isn't any "right" way to do such personal work. There are all kinds of writers and all kinds of methods, and any
method that helps you to say what you want to say is the right method for
you. . . .

QUESTIONS ON SUBJECT AND PURPOSE

1. Zinsser uses contrast to make a point about how people write. What is
   that point?
2. How effective is the beginning? Would the effect have been lost if
   Zinsser had opened with a statement similar to his final sentence?
3. What process do you use when you write? Does it help in any way to
   know what other people do? Why? Why not?

QUESTIONS ON STRATEGY AND AUDIENCE

1. Which method of development does Zinsser use for his example? How
   many points of contrast does he make?

2. Would it have made any difference if he had used another pattern of development? Why?

3. How effective are the short paragraphs? Should they be longer?

QUESTIONS ON VOCABULARY AND STYLE

1. What makes Zinsser's story humorous? Try to isolate several aspects of humor.

2. Zinsser uses a number of parallel structures in his narrative. Make a list of them, and be prepared to show how they contribute to the narrative's effectiveness.

3. Be able to explain or define the following: *avocation* (paragraph 1), *bohemian* (2), *arduous* (3), *mime* (10), *gusto* (11), *drone* (12).

WRITING SUGGESTIONS

1. **For Your Journal.** How do you feel about writing? How do you feel about having other people read your writing? Is writing a source of great anxiety? Of pleasure? In your journal, explore those feelings.

2. **For a Paragraph.** Using the details provided by Zinsser, rewrite the narrative using a subject-by-subject pattern. Choose either writer, and put together his advice in a single paragraph. Be sure to formulate a topic sentence that will control the paragraph.

3. **For an Essay.** Let's be honest—writing instructors and textbooks offer one view of the writing process, but the practice of most writers can differ sharply. Prewriting and revising get squeezed out when a paper is due and only one night is available. In an essay, compare and contrast your typical behavior as a writer with the process outlined in this text. Do not be afraid to be truthful.

4. **For Research.** Compare the creative processes of two or more artists. You can choose painters, musicians, dancers, writers, actors—anyone involved in the creative arts. Check your library's catalog and the various periodical indexes and electronic databases for books and articles about the creative work of each person. Try to find interviews or statements in which the artists talk about how they work. If you are having trouble finding information, ask a reference librarian to help you. Be sure to document your sources.

FOR FURTHER STUDY

Focusing on Grammar and Writing. Rewrite paragraph 12 in the essay, casting it into simple sentences, each of which is followed by a period. What is the difference between the new paragraph and the one that Zinsser originally wrote? How does the punctuation of the original help reflect and emphasize Zinsser's meaning?

Working Together. What would be the result of a re-paragraphing of Zinsser's essay? Would it change it? Would it be more or less effective? Divide into small groups and re-paragraph the entire essay. Is there general agreement on where that new paragraphing could occur? Compare results.

Seeing Other Modes at Work. As the subtitle of the selection notes, Zinsser's piece is also a process narrative. How might either Zinsser or Dr. Brock describe his own writing process?

Finding Connections. A good pairing is with Nora Ephron's "Revision and Life" (Chapter 6).

Exploring the Web. Interested in finding some online help for your writing? Want to "blog" or want to know what that means? Some points of departure can be found at **www.prenhall.com/miller**.

ACADEMIC SELVES

Mary Pipher

Mary Pipher earned her B.A. in cultural anthropology from the University of California at Berkeley and a Ph.D. in psychology from the University of Nebraska. A clinical psychologist in private practice, she is the author of Reviving Ophelia: Saving the Selves of Adolescent Girls *(1994), which was on* The New York Times *bestseller list for 149 weeks. Her recent book is* Letters to a Young Therapist *(2003). This selection is taken from* Reviving Ophelia.

BEFORE READING

Connecting: In the years that you were in middle or high school, did you ever feel as if boys and girls were treated differently?

Anticipating: As you read Pipher's essay, try to decide which of the three patterns for comparison and contrast (point by point, subject by subject, or mixed) she uses.

1   Schools have always treated girls and boys differently. What is new in the nineties is that we have much more documentation of this phenomenon. Public awareness of the discrimination is increasing. This is due in part to the American Association of University Women (AAUW), which released a study in 1992 entitled "How Schools Shortchange Girls."

2   In classes, boys are twice as likely to be seen as role models, five times as likely to receive teachers' attention and twelve times as likely to speak up in class. In textbooks, one-seventh of all illustrations of children are of girls. Teachers chose many more classroom activities that appeal to boys than to girls. Girls are exposed to almost three times as many boy-centered stories as girl-centered stories. Boys tend to be portrayed as clever, brave, creative, and resourceful, while girls are depicted as kind, dependent and docile. Girls read six times as many biographies of males as of females. Even in animal stories, the animals are twice as likely to be males. (I know of one teacher who, when she reads to her classes, routinely changes the sex of the characters in the stories so that girls will have stronger role models.)

3   Analysis of classroom videos shows that boys receive more classroom attention and detailed instruction than girls. They are called on more often than girls and are asked more abstract, open-ended and complex questions. Boys are more likely to be praised for academics and intellectual work, while girls are more likely to be praised for their clothing, behaving properly and obeying rules. Boys are likely to be criticized for their behavior, while girls are criticized for intellectual inadequacy. The message to boys tends to be: "You're

smart, if you would just settle down and get to work." The message to girls is often: "Perhaps you're just not good at this. You've followed the rules and haven't succeeded."

Because with boys failure is attributed to external factors and success is   4
attributed to ability, they keep their confidence, even with failure. With girls it's just the opposite. Because their success is attributed to good luck or hard work and failure to lack of ability, with every failure, girls' confidence is eroded. All this works in subtle ways to stop girls from wanting to be astronauts and brain surgeons. Girls can't say why they ditch their dreams, they just "mysteriously" lose interest.

Some girls do well in math and continue to like it, but many who were   5
once good at math complain that they are stupid in math. Girl after girl tells me, "I'm not good in math." My observations suggest that girls have trouble with math because math requires exactly the qualities that many junior-high girls lack—confidence, trust in one's own judgment and the ability to tolerate frustration without becoming overwhelmed. Anxiety interferes with problem solving in math. A vicious circle develops—girls get anxious, which interferes with problem solving, and so they fail and are even more anxious and prone to self-doubt the next time around.

When boys have trouble with a math problem, they are more likely to   6
think the problem is hard but stay with it. When girls have trouble, they think they are stupid and tend to give up. This difference in attribution speaks to girls' precipitous decline in math. Girls need to be encouraged to persevere in the face of difficulty, to calm down and believe in themselves. They need permission to take their time and to make many mistakes before solving the problem. They need to learn relaxation skills to deal with the math anxiety so many experience.

The AAUW study found that as children go through school, boys do   7
better and feel better about themselves and girls' self-esteem, opinions of their sex and scores on standardized achievement tests all decline. Girls are more likely than boys to say that they are not smart enough for their dream careers. They emerge from adolescence with a diminished sense of their worth as individuals.

Gifted girls seem to suffer particularly with adolescence. Lois Murphy   8
found that they lose IQ points as they become feminized. In the 1920s Psychologist Louis Terman studied gifted children in California. Among the children, the seven best writers were girls and all the best artists were girls, but by adulthood all the eminent artists and writers were men.

Junior high is when girls begin to fade academically. Partly this comes   9
from the very structure of the schools, which tend to be large and impersonal. Girls, who tend to do better in relationship-based, cooperative learning situations, get lost academically in these settings. Partly it comes from a shift girls make at this time from a focus on achievement to a focus on affiliation. In junior high girls feel enormous pressure to be popular. They learn that good grades can even interfere with popularity. Lori learned to keep quiet about grades. She said, "Either way I lose. If I make a good grade, they are mad. If

I make a bad grade, they spread it around that even I can screw up." Another girl said, "When I started junior high I figured out that I'd have more friends if I focused on sports. Smart girls were nerds." Another, who almost flunked seventh grade, told me, "All I care about is my friends. Grades don't matter to me."

10   I saw a seventh-grader who was failing everything. I asked her why and she said, "My friends and I decided that making good grades wasn't cool." Her story has a happy ending, not because of my work, but because the next year, in eighth grade, she and her friends had another meeting and decided that it was now "cool" to make good grades. My client's academic situation improved enormously.

11   This tendency for girls to hide their academic accomplishments is an old one. Once on a date I was particularly untrue to myself. Denny and I went to the A&W Root Beer Drive-In on Highway 81, and he asked me what I would like. Even though I was famished I ordered only a small Coke. (Nice girls didn't eat too much.) Then he asked about my six-week grades. I had made As, but I said I had two Cs and was worried my parents would be mad. I can still remember his look of visible relief.

QUESTIONS ON SUBJECT AND PURPOSE

1. According to Pipher why do young girls "fade academically"?
2. Although Pipher cites a study done by the American Association of University Women (paragraph 1), she does not quote from the study or specifically document the "facts" that she provides. Does that affect your reading experience of the essay? Do you, for example, doubt anything that she says?
3. What purpose might Pipher have in her essay? Notice the title and subtitle of the book from which this is taken in the introductory information.

QUESTIONS ON STRATEGY AND AUDIENCE

1. In paragraphs 9 and 10, Pipher introduces examples of young girls reacting to peer pressure. How do these examples work in the essay?
2. In the final paragraph, Pipher relates a personal experience. What is the effect of telling that story about her own life?
3. To whom is Pipher writing? Would the imagined or intended audience be adolescent girls? Someone else?

QUESTIONS ON VOCABULARY AND STYLE

1. What effect does Pipher gain by quoting—rather than summarizing— the remarks of the girls in paragraphs 9 and 10?

2. Reread paragraph 11. Does it seem unusual that Pipher is able to recall such detailed information from her own past? Does it really matter whether or not each detail is accurate and truthful?

3. Be prepared to define the following words: *docile* (paragraph 2), *precipitous* (6), *persevere* (6).

WRITING SUGGESTIONS

1. **For Your Journal.** Pipher is writing about the educational and peer experiences that adolescent girls have. Do similar discrimination and pressure extend into the college years? Think about male and female students at your school. Do they behave differently in class? Do males talk more? Do professors call on males more often? Is peer pressure a factor in academic success or failure? For several days, just listen and watch what is going on in your classes and elsewhere on campus. Take notes in your journal.

2. **For a Paragraph.** Use your journal to provide the examples for a paragraph in which you explore gender differences in your college's classrooms.

3. **For an Essay.** Expand your paragraph writing into an essay. What differences do you see between male and female students, in the classroom, in the laboratory, in their expectations, in their assumptions?

4. **For Research.** Your essay dealt with your own experience and observation and the experiences and observations of fellow students. Does the body of scholarly research see any difference between how men and women are treated in college classrooms? Is there any perceived difference in peer pressure? In expectations? Is it suddenly acceptable to be a "brilliant" student in college if you are a woman? In an essay that includes research in printed or online sources, compare and contrast the educational experience for men and women in college. Be sure to document your sources.

FOR FURTHER STUDY

Focusing on Grammar and Writing. Throughout the essay, Pipher makes extensive use of parallelism in words, in sentences, and in groups of sentences. Review the concept of parallelism (see the glossary), and then see how many examples you can find in the essay. What effect does Pipher gain by using these types of structures?

Working Together. Divide into small groups. Each group should discuss the extent to which they have ever felt peer pressure about the grades that they earned or are earning in school. The pressure might be either to excel or to underachieve; it can be felt by both men and women. Where do those pressures come from and why?

Seeing Other Modes at Work. Although the essay is predominantly structured in a comparison and contrast pattern, it does make use as well of cause and effect.

Finding Connections. Good pairings could be made with Anna Quindlen's "The Name is Mine" (Chapter 1) and with Judy Brady's "I Want a Wife" (8).

Exploring the Web. A number of interviews with Pipher and additional information about the topic can be found online. Start with the suggestions found at **www.prenhall.com/miller.**

NEAT PEOPLE VS. SLOPPY PEOPLE

Suzanne Britt

Suzanne Britt was born in Winston-Salem, North Carolina, and currently teaches writing and literature courses at Meredith College in Raleigh, North Carolina. She has published essays in a number of newspapers and magazines and has published several collections of essays and a college writing textbook, A Writer's Rhetoric *(1988). "Neat People vs. Sloppy People" first appeared in her collection* Show and Tell *(1983).*

BEFORE READING

Connecting: Are you are a neat or a sloppy person ? Sometimes a little of both?

Anticipating: As you read, think about how Britt organizes her essay. What types of structures does she use?

I've finally figured out the difference between neat people and sloppy people. 1
The distinction is, as always, moral. Neat people are lazier and meaner than sloppy people.

Sloppy people, you see, are not really sloppy. Their sloppiness is merely 2
the unfortunate consequence of their extreme moral rectitude. Sloppy people carry in their mind's eye a heavenly vision, a precise plan, that is so stupendous, so perfect, it can't be achieved in this world or the next.

Sloppy people live in Never-Never Land. Someday is their métier. Some- 3
day they are planning to alphabetize all their books and set up home catalogs. Someday they will go through their wardrobes and mark certain items for tentative mending and certain items for passing on to relatives of similar shape and size. Someday sloppy people will make family scrapbooks into which they will put newspaper clippings, postcards, locks of hair, and the dried corsage from their senior prom. Someday they will file everything on the surface of their desks, including the cash receipts from coffee purchases at the snack shop. Someday they will sit down and read all the back issues of *The New Yorker*.

For all these noble reasons and more, sloppy people never get neat. 4
They aim too high and wide. They save everything, planning someday to file, order, and straighten out the world. But while these ambitious plans take clearer and clearer shape in their heads, the books spill from the shelves onto the floor, the clothes pile up in the hamper and closet, the family mementos accumulate in every drawer, the surface of the desk is buried under mounds of paper, and the unread magazines threaten to reach the ceiling.

Sloppy people can't bear to part with anything. They give loving atten- 5
tion to every detail. When sloppy people say they're going to tackle the surface

of a desk, they really mean it. Not a paper will go unturned; not a rubber band will go unboxed. Four hours or two weeks into the excavation, the desk looks exactly the same, primarily because the sloppy person is meticulously creating new piles of papers with new headings and scrupulously stopping to read all the old book catalogs before he throws them away. A neat person would just bull-doze the desk.

6   Neat people are bums and clods at heart. They have cavalier attitudes toward possessions, including family heirlooms. Everything is just another dust-catcher to them. If anything collects dust, it's got to go and that's that. Neat people will toy with the idea of throwing the children out of the house just to cut down on the clutter.

7   Neat people don't care about process. They like results. What they want to do is get the whole thing over with so they can sit down and watch the rasslin' on TV. Neat people operate on two unvarying principles: Never han-dle any item twice, and throw everything away.

8   The only thing messy in a neat person's house is the trash can. The minute something comes to a neat person's hand, he will look at it, try to de-cide if it has immediate use and, finding none, throw it in the trash.

9   Neat people are especially vicious with mail. They never go through their mail unless they are standing directly over a trash can. If the trash can is beside the mailbox, even better. All ads, catalogs, pleas for charitable contributions, church bulletins, and money-saving coupons go straight into the trash can without being opened. All letters from home, postcards from Europe, bills, and paychecks are opened, immediately responded to, then dropped in the trash can. Neat people keep their receipts only for tax purposes. That's it. No senti-mental salvaging of birthday cards or the last letter a dying relative ever wrote. Into the trash it goes.

10   Neat people place neatness above everything, even economics. They are incredibly wasteful. Neat people throw away several toys every time they walk through the den. I knew a neat person once who threw away a perfectly good dish drainer because it had mold on it. The drainer was too much trouble to wash. And neat people sell their furniture when they move. They will sell a La-Z-Boy recliner while you are reclining in it.

11   Neat people are no good to borrow from. Neat people buy everything in expensive little single portions. They get their flour and sugar in two-pound bags. They wouldn't consider clipping a coupon, saving a leftover, reusing plastic nondairy whipped cream containers, or rinsing off tin foil and draping it over the unmoldy dish drainer. You can never borrow a neat person's news-paper to see what's playing at the movies. Neat people have the paper all wadded up and in the trash by 7:05 A.M.

12   Neat people cut a clean swath through the organic as well as the inor-ganic world. People, animals, and things are all one to them. They are so in-sensitive. After they've finished with the pantry, the medicine cabinet, and the attic, they will throw out the red geranium (too many leaves), sell the dog (too many fleas), and send the children off to boarding school (too many scuff-marks on the hardwood floors).

QUESTIONS ON SUBJECT AND PURPOSE

1. Is Britt a neat or a sloppy person? How do you know?
2. If you are sloppy or neat, are you offended by anything in the essay? Do you regard this as an unfair criticism of you? Why or why not?
3. What might Britt's purpose be in writing the essay?

QUESTIONS ON STRATEGY AND AUDIENCE

1. How does Britt structure her essay? Is it subject by subject or point by point?
2. Is this comparison or contrast? Or both?
3. What can Britt assume about her audience? What does she expect of her audience?

QUESTIONS ON VOCABULARY AND STYLE

1. How would you describe the tone (see glossary) of the essay?
2. What is the effect of the repetition of the phrases "sloppy people" and "neat people" at the start of so many sentences in the essay?
3. Be prepared to define the following words: *rectitude* (paragraph 2), *metier* (3), *meticulously* (5), *scrupulously* (5), *cavalier* (6), *swath* (12).

WRITING SUGGESTIONS

1. **For Your Journal.** Brainstorm about some other possible pairings of people. Remember that you are not classifying people, so your pairings do not need to include all people. Consider both serious topics and humorous ones.
2. **For a Paragraph.** Choose one of the topics from your journal writing and explore it in an paragraph. Concentrate on a single point of comparison and contrast.
3. **For an Essay.** Expand your paragraph into an essay. Compare or contrast a pairing of people (for example, late people and early people; PC users/ MAC users; morning people/night people). Make sure that you compare or contrast on a number of points, not just a single one. You can try a humorous or serious approach.
4. **For Research.** What do we know about neatness or sloppiness? What makes a person one or the other? Is it just an attitude or behavior that could be changed, or is it more deeply ingrained in personality? What does research tell us? Using Web sources, interviews, and print sources, see what other evidence exists about why a person might be neat or sloppy.

FOR FURTHER STUDY

Focusing on Grammar and Writing. Look closely at the opening sentences of each of Britt's paragraphs. What role do these topic sentences play in the paragraph? How do such sentences help you as a reader?

Working Together. Divide into small groups. Each should consider whether it is possible to exhibit some of the characteristics of both groups. What would happen if a third group—a group that exhibited both sloppy and neat traits—were added to the essay? What might such a section look like, and what might it add or detract from the essay?

Seeing Other Modes at Work. Both sections of the essay show elements of definition as well. Sloppy and neat people are defined by the ways in which they react to certain situations.

Finding Connections. Good pairings on the nature of humor writing are Judy Brady's "I Want a Wife" (Chapter 8) and Jonathan Swift's "A Modest Proposal" (10). A similar subject is explored by John Hollander in "Mess" (8).

Exploring the Web. Tempted to send an electronic postcard to a "sloppy" friend? You can do so on the Web. Not everyone finds the essay funny. One reader replied, "The essay was painful to read, like a Klan pamphlet or a Homophobic newsletter." For starting points, go to **www.prenhall.com/miller.**

THE COLOR OF LOVE

Danzy Senna

Danzy Senna (1970–) is a graduate of Stanford University with an M.F.A. from the University of California, Irvine. She is currently teaching at the College of the Holy Cross in Worcester, Massachusetts. The daughter of a White mother and a Black father, Senna is particularly interested in multiracial identity in the United States, which she explores in her first novel, Caucasia *(1998). "The Color of Love" first appeared in* O, The Oprah Magazine.

On Writing: *In an interview, Senna commented: "I'm not interested in memoir, or purely autobiographical writing. I'm more interested in what might have happened than what really did."*

BEFORE READING

Connecting: "The Color of Love" focuses on the conflict between Senna and her grandmother. Are there some fundamental ways in which you and a grandparent are opposites?

Anticipating: Is the conflict between Senna and her grandmother ever resolved in the essay? Why or why not?

We had this much in common: We were both women, and we were both 1
writers. But we were as different as two people can be and still exist in the same family. She was ancient—as white and dusty as chalk—and spent her days seated in a velvet armchair, passing judgments on the world below. She still believed in noble bloodlines; my blood had been mixed at conception. I believed there was no such thing as nobility or class or lineage, only systems designed to keep some people up in the big house and others outside, in the cold.

She was my grandmother. She was Irish but from that country's Protes- 2
tant elite, which meant she seemed more British than anything. She was an actress, a writer of plays and novels and still unmarried in her thirties when she came to America to visit. One night while in Boston, she went to a dinner party, where she was seated next to a young lawyer with blood as blue as the ocean. Her pearl earring fell in his oyster soup—or so the story goes—and they fell in love. My grandmother married that lawyer and left her native Ireland for New England.

How she came to have black grandchildren is a story of opposites. It was 3
1968 in Boston when her daughter—my mother—a small, blonde Wasp poet, married my father, a tall and handsome black intellectual, in an act that was as rebellious as it was hopeful. The products of that unlikely union—my older sister, my younger brother and I—grew up in urban chaos, in a home filled

with artists and political activists. The old lady across the river in Cambridge seemed to me an endangered species. Her walls were covered with portraits of my ancestors, the pale and dead men who had conquered Africa and built Boston long before my time. When I visited, their eyes followed me from room to room with what I imagined to be an expression of scorn. Among the portraits sat my grandmother, a bird who had flown in to remind us all that there had indeed been a time when lineage and caste meant something. To me, young and dark and full of energy, she was the missing link between the living and the dead.

4   But her blood flowed through me, whether I liked it or not. I grew up to be a writer, just like her. And as I struggled to tell my own stories—about race and class and post–civil rights America—I wondered who my grandmother had been before, in Dublin, when she was friend and confidante to literary giants such as William Butler Yeats and Samuel Beckett. Once, while snooping in her bedroom, I discovered her novels, the ones that had been published in Ireland when she was my age. I stared at her photograph on the jacket and wondered about the young woman who wore a mischievous smile. Had she ever worried about becoming so powerful that no man would want her? Did she now feel that she had sacrificed her career and wild Irishwoman dreams to become a wife and mother and proper Bostonian?

5   I longed to know her—to love her. But the differences between us were real and alive, and they threatened to squelch our fragile connection. She was an alcoholic. In the evening, after a few glasses of gin, she could turn vicious. Though she held antiquated racist views, my grandmother would still have preferred to see my mother married and was saddened when my parents split in the seventies. She believed that a woman without a man was pitiable. The first question she always asked me when she saw me: "Do you have a man?" The second question: "What is he?" That was her way of finding out his race and background. She looked visibly pleased if he was a Wasp, neutral if he was Jewish and disappointed if he was black.

6   My mother ignored her hurtful comments but felt them just the same. She spent her visits to my grandmother's house slamming dishes in the kitchen, hissing her anger just out of hearing range, then raving, on the drive home, about what awful thing her mother had said this time. Like my mother, I knew the rule: I was not to disrespect elders. She was old and gray and would soon be gone. But I had inherited my grandmother's short temper. When I got angry, even as a child, I felt as if blood were rushing around in my head, red waves battering the shore. Words spilled from my mouth—cutting, vicious words that I regretted.

7   One autumn day in Cambridge, at my grandmother's place, I lost my temper. I was home from college for the holidays, staying in her guest room. I woke from a nap to the sound of her enraged voice shouting at what I could only imagine was the television.

8   "Idiot! You damn fool!" she bellowed. "You stupid, stupid woman!" It has to be *Jeopardy!*, I thought. She must be yelling at those tiny contestants on the screen. She knows the answers to those questions better than they do. But

when the shouting went on for a beat too long, I went to the top of the stairs and looked down into the living room. She was speaking to a real person: her cleaning lady, a Greek woman named Mary, who was on her hands and knees, nervously gathering the shards of a broken vase. My grandmother stood over her, hands on hips, cursing.

"You fool," my grandmother repeated. "How in bloody hell could you have done something so stupid?"   9

"Grandma." I didn't shout her name but said it loudly enough that she, though hard of hearing, glanced up.   10

"Oh, darling!" she piped, suddenly cheerful. "Would you like a cup of tea? You must be dreadfully tired."   11

Mary was on her feet again. She smiled nervously at me, then rushed into the kitchen with the pieces of the broken vase.   12

I told myself to be a good girl, to be polite. But something snapped. I marched down the stairs, and even she noticed something on my face that made her sit in her velvet chair.   13

"Don't you ever talk to her that way," I shouted. "Where do you think you are? Slavery was abolished long ago."   14

I stood over her, tall and long-limbed, daring her to speak. My grandmother shook her head. "It's about race, isn't it?"   15

"Race?" I said, baffled. "Mary's white. This is about respect—treating other human beings with respect."   16

She wasn't hearing me. All she saw was color. "The tragedy about you," she said soberly, "is that you are mixed." I felt those waves in my head: "Your tragedy is that you're old and ignorant," I spat. "You don't know the first thing about me."   17

She cried into her hands. She seemed diminished, a little old woman. She looked up only to say, "You are a cruel girl."   18

I left her apartment trembling yet feeling exhilarated by what I had done. But my elation soon turned to shame. I had taken on an old lady. And for what? Her intolerance was, at her age, deeply entrenched. My rebuttals couldn't change her.   19

Yet that fight marked the beginning of our relationship. I've since decided that when you cease to express anger toward those who have hurt you, you are essentially giving up on them. They are dead to you. But when you express anger, it is a sign that they still matter, that they are worth the fight.   20

After that argument, my grandmother and I began a conversation. She seemed to see me clearly for the first time, or perhaps she, a "cruel girl" herself, had simply met her match. And I no longer felt she was a relic. She was a living, breathing human being who deserved to be spoken to as an equal.   21

I began visiting her more. I would drive to Cambridge and sit with her, eating mixed nuts and sipping ginger ale, regaling her with tales of my latest love drama or writing project. In her presence, I was proudly black and young and political, and she was who she was: subtly racist, terribly elitist and awfully funny. She still said things that angered me: She bemoaned my mother's marriage to my father, she said that I should marry not for love but for money, and   22 she told me that I needn't identify as black, since I didn't look it. I snapped back at her. But she, with senility creeping in, didn't seem to hear me; each time I came, she said the same things.

23   Last summer I went into hiding to work on my second novel at a writers' retreat in New Hampshire. The place was a kind of paradise for creative souls, a hideaway where every writer had his or her own cabin in the woods with no phone or television—no distractions to speak of. But I was miserable. I could not write. Even the flies outside my window seemed to whisper, "Go out and play. Forget the novel. Leave it till tomorrow."

24   I woke one morning at four, the light outside my window still blue. I felt panic and sadness, though I didn't know why I got up, dressed and went outside for a walk through the forest. But the panic persisted, and I began to cry. I assumed that my writer's block had seized me suddenly.

25   That night I ate dinner in the main house and received a call on the pay phone from my mother. She told me my grandmother had fallen and broken her leg. But that wasn't all; she had subsequently suffered a heart attack. Her other organs were failing. I had to hurry if I wanted to say good-bye.

26   I drove to Boston that night, not believing that we could be losing her. She would make it. I was certain. Sure, she was ninety-two, frail, unable to walk steadily. But she was lucid, and her tongue was as sharp as ever. Somehow I had imagined her as indestructible, made immortal by power and cruelty and wit.

27   The woman I found in the hospital bed was barely recognizable. My grandmother had always been fussy about her appearance. She never showed her face without makeup. Even in the day, when it was just she and the cleaning lady, she dressed as if she were ready for a cocktail party. At night she usually had cocktail parties; doddering old men hovered around her, sipping Scotch and bantering about theater and politics.

28   My grandmother's face had swollen to twice its normal size, and tubes came out of her nose. She had struggled so hard to pull them out that the nurses had tied her wrists to the bed rails. Her hair was gray and thin. Her body was withered and bruised, barely covered by the green hospital gown.

29   Her hazel eyes were all that was still recognizable, but the expression in them was different from any I had ever seen on her—terror. She was terrified to die. She tried to rise when she saw me, and her eyes pleaded with me to help her, to save her, to get her out of this mess. I stood over her, and I felt only one thing: overwhelming love. Not a trace of anger. That dark gray rage I'd felt toward her was gone as I stroked her forehead and told her she would be okay, even knowing she would not.

30   For two days, my mother, her sisters and I stood beside my grandmother, singing Irish ballads and reading passages to her from the works of her favorite novelist, James Joyce. For the first time, she could not talk. At one point, she gestured wildly for pen and paper. I brought her the pen and the paper and held them up for her, but she was too weak for even that. What came out was only a faint, incomprehensible line.

In death we are each reduced to our essence: the spirit we are when we   31
are born. The trappings we hold on to our whole lives—our race, our money,
our sex, our age, our politics—become irrelevant. My grandmother became a
child in that hospital bed, a spirit about to embark on an unknown journey,
terrified and alone, no matter how many of us were crowded around her. In
the final hours, even her skin seemed to lose its wrinkles and take on a waxy
glow. Then, finally, the machines around us went silent as she left us behind
to squabble in the purgatory of the flesh.

QUESTIONS ON SUBJECT AND PURPOSE

1. In what sense is this a comparison and contrast essay? What is being
   compared and contrasted?
2. Why might Senna have titled the essay "The Color of Love"? Does
   love have a color?
3. Does the essay transcend the personal? That is, do you as a reader feel
   that Senna's experience is relevant to you?

QUESTIONS ON STRATEGY AND AUDIENCE

1. What shift occurs in the essay in paragraphs 7–19?
2. What is the significance of the scene that occurs in paragraphs 7–19?
3. In what way is the writing of the essay similar to the fight between
   Senna and her grandmother?

QUESTIONS ON VOCABULARY AND STYLE

1. What is your sense of the narrator? Do you find her sympathetic?
2. What is the effect of the use of dialogue in paragraphs 7–19?
3. Be prepared to define the following words: *antiquated* (paragraph 5),
   shards (8), *elation* (19), *regaling* (22), *lucid* (26), *doddering* (27).

WRITING SUGGESTIONS

1. **For Your Journal.** What generational conflicts have you experienced
   within your own family? Are there conflicts between you and your
   grandparents, between your parents and your grandparents, between
   you and your parents? Jot down some ideas and possible scenes in your
   journal. Try to think not only about an issue on which the two
   disagree, but also about a possible scene where that disagreement is
   clearly revealed.
2. **For a Paragraph.** Using your journal as a departure point, create for
   the reader that conflict in a paragraph. Try not just to tell the reader;
   try also to show how the two sides revealed their differences.

3. **For an Essay.** Expand your paragraph into an essay. Remember that the conflicts are likely to be rooted in a set of values or a particular expectation. Even if you feel that one side is completely wrong, it is at least possible to understand why the person feels the way that he or she does. Remember that your experience is probably not unique—that is, that most of your readers have experienced similar things. Like Senna, try to include at least one dramatized scene with some dialogue.

4. **For Research.** Select one or more significant differences or conflicts between generations. Look for a charged issue—such things as race relations, attitudes toward sex or money, views of gender roles, or work ethics. What are the significant factors or experiences that fuel those conflicts? What can you learn from research and interviews? What explains the differences between the two generations and their attitudes toward this subject?

FOR FURTHER STUDY

Focusing on Grammar and Writing. Choose one of the paragraphs in the essay (good choices include paragraphs 1, 3, 4, 5, 6, 29), and look closely at how Senna punctuates her sentences. Using a grammar handbook, try to find the reasons why each mark is appropriate in its particular context. When do you use a colon, a semicolon, a dash? What are the most common uses of the comma? What does the variety of Senna's punctuation suggest about your own writing? Do you use a variety of punctuation marks?

Working Together. Divide into small groups. Each group should choose one of the following details from the story. What does each detail contribute to the essay?

a. The portraits of her ancestors (paragraph 1)

b. The grandmother's sudden change of tone when Senna comes downstairs (11)

c. Senna's experience at the writers' retreat (23–24)

d. The physical appearance of her grandmother in the hospital (27–29)

e. The grandmother's unsuccessful attempt to write something down (30)

Seeing Other Modes at Work. Senna's essay depends upon a narrative structure and could be used as an example of narration.

Finding Connections. Scott Momaday's "The Way to Rainy Mountain" (Chapter 3) also deals with a relationship to a grandparent.

Exploring the Web. Read an interview with Senna, check out reviews of her book, and locate additional information—all at the *Reader's* Website **www.prenhall.com/miller.**

VIRTUAL LOVE
Meghan Daum

Meghan Daum graduated from Vassar College and earned an M.F.A. at Columbia University. Her essays and articles have appeared in The New Yorker, The New York Times Book Review, GQ, Vogue *and* Self, *among others, and have been collected in* My Misspent Youth *(2001). "Virtual Love" first appeared in* The New Yorker. *Her first novel,* The Quality of Life Report, *appeared in 2003.*

On Writing: *Asked about her writing, Daum commented: "The subjects that I find most fascinating concern ideas or events that have not only affected me personally but seem to resonate with the culture at large. Though I am often called a 'confessional' writer, I am less interested in 'confessing' than in using specific experiences as a tool for looking at more general or abstract phenomena in the world. The key to writing about yourself without falling into solipsism is to explore issues that transcend the merely personal and shed a new light on the experiences that many of us share. It also helps to have a sense of humor and respect for the absurdity of life by not taking yourself too seriously."*

BEFORE READING

Connecting: Do you think that it is possible to "fall in love" with someone that you have never met face to face?

Anticipating: What is it about this "virtual" relationship that attracts Daum?

I t was last November; fall was drifting away into an intolerable chill. I was at the end of my twenty-sixth year, and was living in New York City, trying to support myself as a writer, and taking part in the kind of urban life that might be construed as glamorous were it to appear in a memoir in the distant future. At the time, however, my days felt more like a grind than like an adventure: hours of work strung between the motions of waking up, getting the mail, watching TV with my roommates, and going to bed. One morning, I logged on to my America Online account to find a message under the heading "is this the real meghan daum?" It came from someone with the screen name PFSlider. The body of the message consisted of five sentences, written entirely in lower-case letters, of perfectly turned flattery: something about PFSlider's admiration of some newspaper and magazine articles I had published over the last year and a half, something about his resulting infatuation with me, and something about his being a sportswriter in California. 1

I was engaged for the thirty seconds that it took me to read the message and fashion a reply. Though it felt strange to be in the position of confirming that I was indeed "the real meghan daum," I managed to say, "Yes, it's me. 2

Thank you for writing." I clicked the "Send Now" icon, shot my words into the void, and forgot about PFSlider until the next day, when I received another message, this one headed "eureka."

3   "wow, it is you," he wrote, still in lower case. He chronicled the various conditions under which he'd read my few-and-far-between articles—a board-walk in Laguna Beach, the spring-training pressroom for a baseball team that he covered for a Los Angeles newspaper. He confessed to having a crush on me. He referred to me as "princess daum." He said he wanted to have lunch with me during one of his two annual trips to New York.

4   The letter was outrageous and endearingly pathetic, possibly the practi-cal joke of a friend trying to rouse me out of a temporary writer's block. But the kindness pouring forth from my computer screen was bizarrely exhilarat-ing, and I logged off and thought about it for a few hours before writing back to express how flattered and "touched"—this was probably the first time I had ever used that word in earnest—I was by his message.

5   I am not what most people would call a computer person. I have no in-terest in chat rooms, newsgroups, or most Websites. I derive a palpable thrill from sticking a letter in the United States mail. But I have a constant low-grade fear of the telephone, and I often call people with the intention of get-ting their answering machines. There is something about the live voice that I have come to find unnervingly organic, as volatile as live television. E-mail provides a useful antidote for my particular communication anxieties. Though I generally send and receive only a few messages a week, I take comfort in their silence and their boundaries.

6   PFSlider and I tossed a few innocuous, smart-assed notes back and forth over the week following his first message. Let's say his name was Pete. He was twenty-nine, and single. I revealed very little about myself, relying instead on the ironic commentary and forced witticisms that are the conceit of so many E-mail messages. But I quickly developed an oblique affection for PFSlider. I was excited when there was a message from him, mildly depressed when there wasn't. After a few weeks, he gave me his phone number. I did not give him mine, but he looked it up and called me one Friday night. I was home. I picked up the phone. His voice was jarring, yet not unpleasant. He held up more than his end of the conversation for an hour, and when he asked permission to call me again I granted it, as though we were of an earlier era.

7   Pete—I could never wrap my mind around his name, privately thinking of him as PFSlider, "E-mail guy," or even "baseball boy"—began phoning me two or three times a week. He asked if he could meet me, and I said that that would be O.K. Christmas was a few weeks away, and he told me that he would be coming back East to see his family. From there, he would take a short flight to New York and have lunch with me.

8   "It is my off-season mission to meet you," he said.

9   "There will probably be a snowstorm," I said.

10   "I'll take a team of sled dogs," he answered.

11   We talked about our work and our families, about baseball and Bill Clin-ton and Howard Stern and sex, about his hatred for Los Angeles and how

much he wanted a new job. Sometimes we'd find each other logged on simultaneously and type back and forth for hours.

I had previously considered cyber-communication an oxymoron, a fast road to the breakdown of humanity. But, curiously, the Internet—at least in the limited form in which I was using it—felt anything but dehumanizing. My interaction with PFSlider seemed more authentic than much of what I experienced in the daylight realm of living beings. I was certainly putting more energy into the relationship than I had put into many others. I also was giving Pete attention that was by definition undivided, and relishing the safety of the distance between us by opting to be truthful instead of doling out the white lies that have become the staple of real life. The outside world—the place where I walked around avoiding people I didn't want to deal with, peppering my casual conversations with half-truths, and applying my motto "Let the machine take it" to almost any scenario—was sliding into the periphery of my mind.

For me, the time on-line with Pete was far superior to the phone. There were no background noises, no interruptions from "call waiting," no long-distance charges. Through typos and misspellings, he flirted maniacally. "I have an absurd crush on you," he said. "If I like you in person, you must promise to marry me." I was coy and conceited, telling him to get a life, baiting him into complimenting me further, teasing him in a way I would never have dared to do in person, or even on the phone. I would stay up until 3 A.M. typing with him, smiling at the screen, getting so giddy that when I quit I couldn't fall asleep. I was having difficulty recalling what I used to do at night. It was as if he and I lived together in our own quiet space—a space made all the more intimate because of our conscious decision to block everyone else out. My phone was tied up for hours at a time. No one in the real world could reach me, and I didn't really care.

Since my last serious relationship, I'd had the requisite number of false starts and five-night stands, dates that I wasn't sure were dates, and emphatically casual affairs that buckled under their own inertia. With PFSlider, on the other hand, I may not have known my suitor, but, for the first time in my life, I knew the deal: I was a desired person, the object of a blind man's gaze. He called not only when he said he would call but unexpectedly, just to say hello. He was protected by the shield of the Internet; his guard was not merely down but nonexistent. He let his phone bill grow to towering proportions. He told me that he thought about me all the time, though we both knew that the "me" in his mind consisted largely of himself. He talked about me to his friends, and admitted it. He arranged his holiday schedule around our impending date. He managed to charm me with sports analogies. He didn't hesitate. He was unblinking and unapologetic, all nerviness and balls to the wall.

And so PFSlider became my everyday life. All the tangible stuff fell away. My body did not exist. I had no skin, no hair, no bones. All desire had converted itself into a cerebral current that reached nothing but my frontal lobe. There was no outdoors, no social life, no weather. There was only the computer screen and the phone, my chair, and maybe a glass of water. Most mornings, I would wake up to find a message from PFSlider, composed in Pacific time while I slept in the wee hours. "I had a date last night," he wrote. "And I am not ashamed to say it was doomed from the start because I couldn't stop thinking about you."

16   I fired back a message slapping his hand. "We must be careful where we tread," I said. This was true but not sincere. I wanted it, all of it. I wanted unfettered affection, soul-mating, true romance. In the weeks that had elapsed since I picked up "is this the real meghan daum?" the real me had undergone some kind of meltdown—a systemic rejection of all the savvy and independence I had worn for years, like a grownup Girl Scout badge.

17   Pete knew nothing of my scattered, juvenile self, and I did my best to keep it that way. Even though I was heading into my late twenties, I was still a child, ignorant of dance steps and health insurance, a prisoner of credit-card debt and student loans and the nagging feeling that I didn't want anyone to find me until I had pulled myself into some semblance of an adult. The fact that Pete had literally seemed to discover me, as if by turning over a rock, lent us an aura of fate which I actually took half-seriously. Though skepticism seemed like the obvious choice in this strange situation, I discarded it precisely because it was the obvious choice, because I wanted a more interesting narrative than cynicism would ever allow. I was a true believer in the urban dream: the dream of years of struggle, of getting a break, of making it. Like most of my friends, I wanted someone to love me, but I wasn't supposed to need it. To admit to loneliness was to smack the face of progress, to betray the times in which we lived. But PFSlider derailed me. He gave me all of what I'd never even realized I wanted.

18   My addiction to PFSlider's messages indicated a monstrous narcissism, but it also revealed a subtler desire, which I didn't fully understand at that time. My need to experience an old-fashioned kind of courtship was stronger than I had ever imagined. And the fact that technology was providing an avenue for such archaic discourse was a paradox that both fascinated and repelled me. Our relationship had an epistolary quality that put our communication closer to the eighteenth century than to the impending millennium. Thanks to the computer, I was involved in a well-defined courtship, a neat little space in which he and I were both safe to express the panic and the fascination of our mutual affection. Our interaction was refreshingly orderly, noble in its vigor, dignified despite its shamelessness. It was far removed from the randomness of real-life relationships. We had an intimacy that seemed custom-made for our strange, lonely times. It seemed custom-made for me.

19   The day of our date, a week before Christmas, was frigid and sunny. Pete was sitting at the bar of the restaurant when I arrived. We shook hands. For a split second, he leaned toward me with his chin, as if to kiss me. He was shorter than I had pictured, though he was not short. He struck me as clean-cut. He had very nice hands. He wore a very nice shirt. We were seated at a very nice table. I scanned the restaurant for people I knew, saw none, and couldn't decide how I felt about that.

He talked, and I heard nothing he said. I stared at his profile and tried   20
to figure out whether I liked him. He seemed to be saying nothing in particular, but he went on forever. Later, we went to the Museum of Natural History and watched a science film about storm chasers. We walked around
looking for the dinosaurs, and he talked so much that I wanted to cry. Outside,
walking along Central Park West at dusk, through the leaves, past the yellow
cabs and the splendid lights of Manhattan at Christmas, he grabbed my hand
to kiss me and I didn't let him. I felt as if my brain had been stuffed with cotton. Then, for some reason, I invited him back to my apartment. I gave him a
few beers and finally let him kiss me on the lumpy futon in my bedroom. The
radiator clanked. The phone rang and the machine picked up. A car alarm
blared outside. A key turned in the door as one of my roommates came home.
I had no sensation at all—only a clear conviction that I wanted Pete out of my
apartment. I wanted to hand him his coat, close the door behind him, and fight
the ensuing emptiness by turning on the computer and taking comfort in
PFSlider.

When Pete finally did leave, I berated myself from every angle: for not   21
kissing him on Central Part West, for letting him kiss me at all, for not liking
him, for wanting to like him more than I had wanted anything in such a long
time. I was horrified by the realization that I had invested so heavily in a made-
up character—a character in whose creation I'd had a greater hand than even
Pete himself. How could I, a person so self-congratulatingly reasonable, have
been sucked into a scenario that was more akin to a television talk show than
to the relatively full and sophisticated life I was so convinced I led? How could
I have received a fan letter and allowed it to go this far?

The next day, a huge bouquet of FTD flowers arrived from him. No   22
one had ever sent me flowers before. I forgave him. As human beings with actual flesh and hand gestures and Gap clothing, Pete and I were utterly in-
compatible, but I decided to pretend otherwise. He returned home and we
fell back into the computer and the phone, and I continued to keep the real
world safely away from the desk that held them. Instead of blaming him for
my disappointment, I blamed the earth itself, the invasion of roommates and
ringing phones into the immaculate communication that PFSlider and I had
created.

When I pictured him in the weeks that followed, I saw the image of a   23
plane lifting off over an overcast city. PFSlider was otherworldly, more a concept than a person. His romance lay in the notion of flight, the physics of grav-
ity defiance. So when he offered to send me a plane ticket to spend the weekend
with him in Los Angeles I took it as an extension of our blissful remoteness, a
three-dimensional E-mail message lasting an entire weekend.

The temperature of the runway at J.F.K. was seven degrees Fahrenheit.   24
Our DC-10 sat for three hours waiting for deicing. Finally, it took off over
the frozen city, and the ground below shrank into a drawing of itself. Phone
calls were made, laptop computers were plopped onto tray tables. The recir-
culating air dried out my contact lenses. I watched movies without the sound
and told myself that they were probably better that way. Something about the

plastic interior of the fuselage and the plastic forks and the din of the air and the engines was soothing and strangely sexy.

25   Then we descended into LAX. We hit the tarmac, and the seat-belt signs blinked off. I hadn't moved my body in eight hours, and now I was walking through the tunnel to the gate, my clothes wrinkled, my hair matted, my hands shaking. When I saw Pete in the terminal, his face seemed to me just as blank and easy to miss as it had the first time I'd met him. He kissed me chastely. On the way out to the parking lot, he told me that he was being seriously considered for a job in New York. He was flying back there next week. If he got the job, he'd be moving within the month. I looked at him in astonishment. Something silent and invisible seemed to fall on us. Outside, the wind was warm, and the Avis and Hertz buses ambled alongside the curb of Terminal 5. The palm trees shook, and the air seemed as heavy and palpable as Pete's hand, which held mine for a few seconds before dropping it to get his car keys out of his pocket. He stood before me, all flesh and preoccupation, and for this I could not forgive him.

26   Gone were the computer, the erotic darkness of the telephone, the clean, single dimension of Pete's voice at 1 A.M. It was nighttime, yet the combination of sight and sound was blinding. It scared me. It turned me off. We went to a restaurant and ate outside on the sidewalk. We strained for conversation, and I tried not to care that we had to. We drove to his apartment and stood under the ceiling light not really looking at each other. Something was happening that we needed to snap out of. Any moment now, I thought. Any moment and we'll be all right. These moments were crowded with elements, with carpet fibers and automobiles and the smells of everything that had a smell. It was all wrong. The physical world had invaded our space.

27   For three days, we crawled along the ground and tried to pull ourselves up. We talked about things that I can no longer remember. We read the Los Angeles *Times* over breakfast. We drove north past Santa Barbara to tour the wine country. I felt like an object that could not be lifted, something that secretly weighed more than the world itself. Everything and everyone around us seemed imbued with a California lightness. I stomped around the countryside, an idiot New Yorker in my clunky shoes and black leather jacket. Not until I studied myself in the bathroom mirror of a highway rest stop did I fully realize the preposterousness of my uniform. I was dressed for war. I was dressed for my regular life.

28   That night, in a tiny town called Solvang, we ate an expensive dinner. We checked into a Marriott and watched television. Pete talked at me and through me and past me. I tried to listen. I tried to talk. But I bored myself and irritated him. Our conversation was a needle that could not be threaded. Still, we played nice. We tried to care, and pretended to keep trying long after we had given up. In the car on the way home, he told me that I was cynical, and I didn't have the presence of mind to ask him just how many cynics he had met who would travel three thousand miles to see someone they barely knew.

29   Pete drove me to the airport at 7 A.M. so I could make my eight-o'clock flight home. He kissed me goodbye—another chaste peck that I recognized

from countless dinner parties and dud dates. He said that he'd call me in a few days when he got to New York for his job interview, which we had discussed only in passing and with no reference to the fact that New York was where I happened to live. I returned home to frozen January. A few days later, he came to New York, and we didn't see each other. He called me from the plane taking him back to Los Angeles to tell me, through the static, that he had got the job. He was moving to my city.

PFSlider was dead. There would be no meeting him in distant hotel lobbies during the baseball season. There would be no more phone calls or E-mail messages. In a single moment, Pete had completed his journey out of our mating dance and officially stepped into the regular world—the world that gnawed at me daily, the world that fostered those five-night stands, the world where romance could not be sustained, because so many of us simply did not know how to do it. Instead, we were all chitchat and leather jackets, bold proclaimers of all that we did not need. But what struck me most about this affair was the unpredictable nature of our demise. Unlike most cyberromances, which seem to come fully equipped with the inevitable set of misrepresentations and false expectations, PFSlider and I had played it fairly straight. Neither of us had lied. We'd done the best we could. Our affair had died from natural causes rather than virtual ones.

Within a two-week period after I returned from Los Angeles, at least seven people confessed to me the vagaries of their own E-mail affairs. This topic arose, unprompted, in the course of normal conversation. I heard most of these stories in the close confines of smoky bars and crowded restaurants, and we all shook our heads in bewilderment as we told our tales, our eyes focussed on some point in the distance. Four of these people had met their correspondents, by travelling from New Haven to Baltimore, from New York to Montana, from Texas to Virginia, and from New York to Johannesburg. These were normal people, writers and lawyers and scientists. They were all smart, attractive, and more than a little sheepish about admitting just how deeply they had been sucked in. Mostly, it was the courtship ritual that had seduced us. E-mail had become an electronic epistle, a yearned-for rule book. It allowed us to do what was necessary to experience love. The Internet was not responsible for our remote, fragmented lives. The problem was life itself.

The story of PFSlider still makes me sad, not so much because we no longer have anything to do with each other but because it forces me to see the limits and the perils of daily life with more clarity than I used to. After I realized that our relationship would never transcend the screen and the phone— that, in fact, our face-to-face knowledge of each other had permanently contaminated the screen and the phone—I hit the pavement again, went through the motions of everyday life, said hello and goodbye to people in the regular way. If Pete and I had met at a party, we probably wouldn't have spoken to each other for more than ten minutes, and that would have made life easier but also less interesting. At the same time, it terrifies me to admit to a firsthand understanding of the way the heart and the ego are snarled and entwined like diseased trees that have folded in on each other. Our need to worship somehow fuses with our need to be worshipped. It upsets me still further to see how inaccessibility can make this entanglement so much more intoxicating. But I'm also thankful that I was forced to unpack the raw truth of my need and stare at it for a while. It was a dare I wouldn't have taken in three dimensions.

33   The last time I saw Pete, he was in New York, three thousand miles away from what had been his home, and a million miles away from PFSlider. In a final gesture of decency, in what I later realized was the most ordinary kind of closure, he took me out to dinner. As the few remaining traces of affection turned into embarrassed regret, we talked about nothing. He paid the bill. He drove me home in a rental car that felt as arbitrary and impersonal as what we now were to each other.

34   Pete had known how to get me where I lived until he came to where I lived: then he became as unmysterious as anyone next door. The world had proved to be too cluttered and too fast for us, too polluted to allow the thing we'd attempted through technology ever to grow in the earth. PFSlider and I had joined the angry and exhausted living. Even if we met on the street, we wouldn't recognize each other, our particular version of intimacy now obscured by the branches and bodies and falling debris that make up the physical world.

QUESTIONS ON SUBJECT AND PURPOSE

1. What is a "virtual" love?
2. In paragraph 18, Daum writes, "My need to experience an old-fashioned kind of courtship was stronger than I had ever imagined." How could an Internet romance be old-fashioned?
3. What is Daum saying or implying about "real" relationships in our society?

QUESTIONS ON STRATEGY AND AUDIENCE

1. What is the central contrast in Daum's essay?
2. The essay can be roughly divided into half. Where does the second half of the essay begin? What is the event that begins the second half?
3. Realistically, how large is Daum's audience? That is, to whom is she writing? How did you react to her essay?

QUESTIONS ON VOCABULARY AND STYLE

1. In paragraph 12, Daum writes: "I had previously considered cyber-communication an oxymoron." What is an *oxymoron*? What does she mean by that sentence?
2. Pete accuses Daum of being "cynical" (paragraph 28). What does that mean?

3. Be prepared to define the following words: *construed* (paragraph 1), *palpable* (5), *volatile* (5), *innocuous* (6), *conceit* (6), *periphery* (12), *unfettered* (16), *archaic* (18), *epistolary* (18), *berated* (21), *imbued* (27), *demise* (30), *vagaries* (31).

WRITING SUGGESTIONS

1. **For Your Journal.** Think about the times in your relationships—with a family member, a close friend, someone you were dating, someone to whom you might have been engaged or even married—when you suddenly realized something about the other person that really changed the way in which you "saw" that person. It could be a change for the better or for the worse. What you are looking for basically is a contrast—a before and an after. In your journal, first, make a list of possible subjects and, second, write two sentences for each about the before and after experience.

2. **For a Paragraph.** Using your journal as a prewriting exercise, explore one of these before and after situations in a paragraph.

3. **For an Essay.** Expand your paragraph writing into an essay. Look back at the guidelines for the assignment above. Remember that you are basically working on a contrast—what you had thought or assumed before and the reality that you discovered after.

4. **For Research.** The remarkable thing about Daum's "virtual" relationship was that it was honest—neither person pretended to be different from whom they were; neither "doled out white lies." Why do people often change their identities or their personalities in cyberspace? Research the problem. What you are exploring are the contrasts that occur between people's real life identities and personalities and the virtual identities and personalities that they assume. What do we know about these contrasts? Why do they occur? You might find that databases of articles are better sources for information than your school's online library catalog. Check with a reference librarian for search strategy suggestions. Be sure to document any direct quotations, paraphrases, or ideas that you take from your sources.

FOR FURTHER STUDY

Focusing on Grammar and Writing. At several points in the essay, Daum intentionally repeats the same sentence structure—for example, the final three sentences in paragraph 3; the first three sentences in paragraph 5; the final nine sentences in paragraph 14. See if you can locate other examples. Specifically, what types of opening structures does Daum repeat and why? Usually, teachers caution students about repeating the same types of sentences. Are they effective here? If so, why? What does this suggest about your own writing?

Working Together. Divide into small groups choose one of the following details from the story. What does each detail contribute to the essay?

   a. The small bits of direct quotation that Daum uses (for example, paragraphs 2, 8–10)
   b. The huge bouquet of flowers that Pete sends (2)
   c. Daum's realization that she was "dressed for war" (27)
   d. Pete's move to New York City (concentrate on 30)
   e. Daum's final dinner with Pete (33)

Seeing Other Modes at Work. Daum's essay is also a personal experience narrative. It follows her relationship with Pete linearly from its beginning to its end.

Finding Connections. An interesting pairing could be made with Judy Brady's "I Want a Wife" (Chapter 8).

Exploring the Web. Read more about online romances and locate additional online essays by Daum by going to the *Reader's* Website, **www.prenhall.com/miller.**

6

PROCESS

PREPARING TO WRITE:

WHAT IS PROCESS?

What do each of the following have in common?

> A recipe in a cookbook
> A textbook discussion of how the body converts food into energy and fat
> Directions on how to install a CD changer in your car
> An on-line explanation of an earthquake

Each is a process analysis—either a set of directions for how to do something (make lasagna or install a CD changer) or a description of how something happens or is done (food is converted or the earth "quakes"). These two different types of process writing have two different purposes.

The function of a set of directions is to allow the reader to duplicate the process. For example, *The Amy Vanderbilt Complete Book of Etiquette* offers the following step-by-step advice to the young executive woman about how to handle paying for a business lunch or dinner.

> No one likes a man who is known never to pick up a check. In today's world, people are going to feel the same about a woman who is known never to pick up a tab. The woman executive is going to have to learn how to pay gracefully when it's her turn.
>
> In order to save embarrassment all around, who will pay for the next business lunch should be decided without question in advance. If it's a woman's turn, she should make it very clear over the telephone or face to face when the appointment is made that she will be paying. She has only to say with a smile that it really is her turn. She should name the time and the place, call the restaurant, and make the reservation in her name.
>
> At the end of lunch she should unobtrusively ask for the bill, add the waiter's tip to the total without an agonizing exercise in mathematics, and then use her credit card or sign her name and her company's address to the back of the check (if she has a charge account there). If she does this quietly, no one around them need be aware of her actions.

Several readings in this chapter similarly offer advice or instructions. Lars Eighner in "My Daily Dives in the Dumpster" describes both how to "dive" into dumpsters and what the process eventually taught him about life and human acquisitiveness. Diane Cole offers the reader suggestions on how to respond to distasteful and bigoted remarks. Charlie Drozdyk offers advice to soon-to-graduate college students on how to "get the job you want after graduation."

Not every example of process is a set of directions about how to do something. Process can also be used to tell the reader how something happens or is made. Harold McGee, for example, explains to his readers how chewing gum, the quintessential American product, is made. McGee's paragraph is not a recipe. Instead, its function is to provide a general view of the manufacturing process.

> Today, chewing gum is made mostly of synthetic polymers, especially styrene-butadiene rubber and polyvinyl acetate, though 10 to 20% of some brands is still accounted for by chicle or jelutong, a latex from the Far East. The crude gum base is first filtered, dried, and then cooked in water until syrupy. Powdered sugar and corn syrup are mixed in, then flavorings and softeners—vegetable oil derivatives that make the gum easier to chew—and the material is cooked, kneaded to an even, smooth texture, cut, rolled thin, and cut again into strips, and packaged. The final product is about 60% sugar, 20% corn syrup, and 20% gum materials.

Nora Ephron in "Revision and Life" describes her own revision process; David Brooks describes the process through which martyrdom has become an end rather than a means in the Arab–Israeli conflict; Jennifer Kahn describes the process through which organs are "harvested" from a dead donor for transplantation. None of these essays is meant to describe a process that we are to perform or imitate. Ephron describes her own process of revision as also a process of maturing or aging. Brooks attempts to explain a phenomena that many Americans do not understand. Kahn writes as an observer who has come to watch a procedure about which she, like the reader, knows very little.

How Do You Choose a Subject to Write About?

Choosing a subject is not a problem if you have been given a specific assignment—to describe how a congressional bill becomes a law, how a chemistry experiment was performed, how to write an A paper for your English course. Often, however, you have to choose your own subject. Several considerations are crucial in making that decision.

First, choose a subject that can be adequately described or analyzed in the space you have available. When Nora Ephron in "Revision and Life" traces her revision process, she isolates three decades in her life—her 20s, 30s, and 40s. She alternates paragraphs dealing with her evolving attitudes toward revision with paragraphs establishing links between revision and life. At 20, she revised nothing; at 40, she is increasingly drawn to revision. Ephron does not try to identify every change that occurred during those three decades. Instead, she confines her analysis to the major periods.

Second, in a process analysis, as in any other writing assignment, identify the audience to whom you are writing. What does that audience already know about your subject? Are you writing to a general audience, an audience of your fellow classmates, or a specialized audience? You do not want to bore your reader with the obvious, nor do you want to lose your reader in a tangle of unfamiliar terms and concepts. Your choice of subject and certainly your approach to it should be determined by your audience. Charlie Drozdyk's essay on job-seeking strategies for young college students appeared in *Rolling Stone* magazine; to appeal to readers of this publication, he focused on interviewing people who held relatively "glamorous" positions in publishing, on Wall Street, in advertising, in fashion design, in interior design, and in television. David Brooks's essay appeared in *Atlantic Monthly*, a literary magazine aimed at older, sophisticated readers. Brooks writes to an American audience, an audience who is puzzled by the suicide bombings in the Middle East, but also probably more sympathetic to the Israelis than to the Palestinians. Identifying your audience—what they might be interested in, what they already know—will help in both selecting a subject and deciding how or what to write about it.

Prewriting Suggestions

1. Brainstorm some possible topics that lend themselves to a process narrative—how something is done, how to make something, the stages in which something occurred, or your plan for handling a situation. Do not commit too quickly to a particular topic—allow a couple of days for just thinking about possibilities. Jot down ideas; take notes.

2. Answer the question, Why am I writing about this? What purpose do you have in mind? Are you trying to inform your reader? Entertain your reader? Explore your own past or your motivations? Persuade your reader? Remember that an essay needs a purpose.

3. Define your audience and think about what they might already know about the subject. If your audience is very familiar with the subject, they are likely to be bored. If the subject is too technical or requires much prior knowledge, the audience will not understand.

4. Think about the steps or stages in the process that you are describing. Remember that you probably need somewhere between three and six. If the process involves fewer than three, it might be too simple to justify an essay; if it has more than six, it might be too complicated. This is not an unbreakable rule; use it for guidance.

5. Consider how your steps or stages might be ordered. Is there an obvious place in which to start? To end? What about the middle of the process? If you do have options, experiment with some to see what you think might work best.

WRITING

HOW DO YOU STRUCTURE A PROCESS PAPER?

If you have ever tried to assemble something from a set of directions, you know how important it is that each step or stage in the process be clearly defined and properly placed in the sequence. Because process always involves a series of events or steps that must be done or must occur in proper order, the fundamental structure for a process paragraph or essay will be chronological.

"Some assembly required." Most of us have come to fear those words. Directions—the most common form of process writing—must be clear and correctly ordered. The success of a set of directions is always easy to measure—did they work?
www.CartoonStock.com

Since proper order is essential, begin your planning by making a list of the various steps in the process. Once your list seems complete, arrange the items in the order in which they are performed or in which they occur. Check to make sure that nothing has been omitted or misplaced. If your process is a description of how to do or make something, you should check your arranged list by performing the process according to the directions you have assembled so far. This ordered list will serve as the outline for your process paper.

Converting your list or outline into a paragraph or an essay is the next step. Be sure that all of the phrases on your outline have been turned into complete sentences and that any technical terms have been carefully explained for your reader. You will also need some way of signaling to your reader each step or stage in the process. On your list, you probably numbered the steps, but in your paragraph or essay you generally cannot use such a device. More commonly, process papers employ various types of step or time markers to indicate order. Step markers like *first, second,* and *third* can be used at the beginning of sentences or paragraphs devoted to each individual stage. Time markers like *begin, next, in three minutes,* or *while this is being done* remind the reader of the proper chronological sequence.

Drafting Suggestions

1. Be sure to include each step necessary to perform or understand the process. Are those steps or stages in a logical or chronological order? Could you construct a flowchart or a timeline outlining those steps?

2. Have you clearly marked the steps or stages? Have you used sequence markers ("first," "then")? Have you put each stage in a separate paragraph? Does the appearance of the text on the page help explain the process?

3. Have you used any words or phrases that your audience might not understand? Be sure to provide a parenthetical definition after that word or phrase (see glossary).

4. Check to see if your steps or stages are phrased in parallel form (see glossary). Use a marker to underline the start of each new step or stage. Look at the underlined sentences. Are they parallel in grammatical form?

5. Once you have a complete draft, find someone to read your essay and offer honest advice. Perhaps a classmate? Maybe you could visit your school's writing center? Perhaps even your instructor might have the time to read your essay before you hand it in. Look for readers and then listen to what they say.

REVISING

HOW DO YOU REVISE A PROCESS ESSAY?

Many writers revise as they write, but even if you do so, "re-see" your paper once again when you have a complete, finished draft. Ideally, you should allow some time to elapse between finishing the draft and looking again at what you have written. If you try to revise too soon, sometimes you see what you want to see and not what you actually wrote. As you look again at your finished draft, remember that process is written for an informative purpose. A "how-to-do-it" process essay is successful if the reader can reproduce the process you describe without error and with the same result. A "here-is-how-it-works" process narrative is intended to explain to a reader how something is done with no intention of having the reader reproduce the process. Either way, the key element in process writing is clarity.

When revising a process essay, play particular attention to the following areas: choosing an interesting and manageable subject, checking for logical organization, and writing an appropriate beginning and ending.

Choosing an Interesting and Manageable Subject   Revision should always begin by looking critically at the essay as a whole. First, ask yourself about your choice of subject. Was it too simple? Was it too complicated? Does your draft have just three very short body paragraphs or twelve long ones? Unless you have an unusual approach to a simple subject, your audience is likely to be bored. Writing a process essay on making a peanut butter and jelly sandwich or putting gasoline in your car are probably not good subject choices. On the other hand, a complex process is likely to be too long and too detailed for an essay in a writing class. Second, define again your imaginable reader. How much prior knowledge is the reader likely to have about this subject? Are you expecting too little or too much of your reader? If you have used technical words and concepts, make sure to provide definitions for them, enclosed in parentheses or set off with commas. Depending on your subject and what your instructor wants, you might want to use visuals in your essay. Often, pictures are more effective than words in showing how something is done. Third, assess again your purpose in the essay. Are you giving directions so the reader might be able to duplicate the process? Or are you trying to describe a process so the reader understands how it works?

Checking for Logical Organization   Because process essays are either directions on how to do something or descriptions of how something happens, they must be clearly organized into steps or stages. Think of the directions in a cookbook or a repair manual. The steps of the process must be arranged in a logical, and often chronological, order: first do this, then this, finally this. The steps in the process need to be clearly marked by the use of place or sequence markers (*first, next, finally*) or by numbering (*first* or *1*). Often, the steps are also set apart in separate sentences or paragraphs. The steps must be arranged in the right order or the process will not work and will not produce the same result. A good test of your logical ordering is to ask a friend to follow the directions that you have given is see if they are clear, comprehensive, and in the right order. Directions or process narratives that you encounter outside of the classroom are also likely to make extensive use of typographical devices to visually reinforce the sequence and are likely to include visuals as well.

Parallelism—that is, placing words, phrases, or clauses in the steps or sequence in a similar grammatical form—is also extremely important in process writing. The glossary explains and illustrates parallelism.

Beginning and Ending   Readers elect to read process essays when they need the information that the essay provides. If you are trying to add a double major or a minor, you are motivated to read how to do it. If you are learning about how a solar panel creates electricity, you are motivated to read the process description. Do not just assume, however, that your reader will read regardless of what you say or how you say it. An introduction to a process essay identifies the subject, but it should always try to catch the readers' attention as well. In a sense, you are trying to persuade your readers to read your essay. What is important or interesting about this process? How will your readers benefit from knowing this?

Conclusions also pose challenges in process writing. Typically, you do not want simply to summarize the steps or stages in the process. That repetition would be boring and unnecessary. You might try suggesting what is important about this material and why it might be useful for your readers.

Revising Suggestions

1. Use the feedback provided by a peer reader, your instructor, or a tutor to revise your essay. Pay attention to their criticisms or suggestions.

2. Answer the following questions: The purpose of this paper is to—. My readers are—. Why would my readers be interested in reading about this subject?

3. Look again at your introduction and conclusion. Do you catch your readers' attention in your introduction? Do you have a clear statement of purpose? Does your conclusion simply repeat the steps or stages in the process? Consider another type of ending—maybe you could point out the importance or value of the process; maybe you could end on a thought-provoking note.

4. Never underestimate the power of a good title. Try to write at least four different titles for your paper. Ask some friends or classmates to evaluate each one.

5. Remember to proofread your final draft. See the advice on proofreading a paper in "How to Revise an Essay."

SAMPLE STUDENT ESSAY

As part of her student-teaching assignment, Julie Anne Halbfish was asked by her cooperating teacher to write out a set of directions on how to play dreidel, a game associated with the Jewish holiday Hanukkah. Most of the students in the seventh-grade class in which Julie was student-teaching had never played the game.

HOW TO PLAY DREIDEL

A dreidel is a small top with four sides. On each side is a Hebrew letter. The letters correspond to the first letters in each word of the Hebrew phrase "Nes gadol haya sham," which means "A great miracle happened there." That phrase refers to the military victory of the Maccabees over the Greeks and the story of the small jug of olive oil that burned for eight days. The corresponding Hebrew letters on the dreidel are called nun [נ], gimel [ג], hay [ה], and shin [ש].

Many people have heard the Hanukkah song "Dreidel," but most are unfamiliar with how to play the traditional children's game of the same name. The rules are actually quite simple.

To start the game, every player receives ten pieces of "money" (usually peanuts, candies, pennies, or anything else the players choose to play for) and a dreidel. Each player puts two pieces of money into the "pot" and then spins the dreidel. When the dreidel stops spinning, the letter that is on the side facing up determines how many pieces the player takes from or adds to the pot. If the dreidel lands on nun, the player takes nothing. If it lands on gimel, the player takes all of the pot. If the dreidel lands on hay, the player receives half of the pot. Finally, if the dreidel lands on shin, the player must put two additional pieces into the pot. After as many rounds of play as the players want, the game ends, and whoever has the most goodies is declared the winner. However, the reason so many people love this game is that everyone ends up with treats to enjoy, so nobody loses.

COMMENTS

After Julie finished a draft of her essay, she showed her paper to Adam Helenic, a fellow classmate. At first, Adam simply praised the draft—"It's good; it's clear; it's fine, Julie." But Julie would not settle for simple approval. When pushed, Adam made several suggestions. Since many students have heard the dreidel song, he urged her somehow to work at least part of the song into the essay—maybe as an attention-getting introduction. He also suggested that she reorder paragraphs 1 and 2 and that she tighten up her prose in a number of places. When Julie revised her set of directions, she tried to incorporate all of the changes that Adam had suggested. Interestingly, when Julie set out to check her "facts" about the song and the game, she used the World Wide Web. She found a computerized dreidel game that you might like to try (you can play at www.jcn18.com/spinner.htm).

HOW TO PLAY DREIDEL

I have a little dreidel,
I made it out of clay.
And when it's dry and ready,
Oh, dreidel I shall play!
It has a lovely body,
With legs so short and thin.
And when it gets all tired,
It drops and then I win.

During Hanukkah, we often hear the "Dreidel" song, but most people have never actually played the traditional children's game to which the song refers. The game is quite simple, and since every player is sure to win something, dreidel is a popular Hanukkah game.

A dreidel is a small, four-sided top, traditionally made out of clay. On each side is a Hebrew letter. The letters correspond to the first letters in each word of the Hebrew phrase "Nes gadol haya sham," which means "A great miracle happened there." That phrase refers to the military victory of the Maccabees over the Greeks and the story of the small jug of olive oil that miraculously burned for eight days. The corresponding Hebrew letters on the dreidel are called nun [נ], gimel [ג], hay [ה], and shin [ש].

To start the game, every player receives ten pieces of "money" (usually peanuts, candies, pennies, or anything else the players choose to play for) and a dreidel. Each player puts two pieces of money into the "pot" and then spins the dreidel. When the dreidel is spinning, the players are encouraged to sing a Hanukkah song or to shout "Gimel!" When the dreidel stops spinning, the letter that is on the side facing up determines how many pieces the player takes from or adds to the pot. If the dreidel lands on nun, the player takes nothing. If it lands on gimel, the player takes all of the pot. If the dreidel lands on hay, the player receives half of the pot. Finally, if the dreidel lands on shin, the player must put two additional pieces into the pot.

After as many rounds of play as the players want, the game ends, and whoever has the most goodies is declared the winner. Whether you win or not, no one really loses since everyone ends up with treats to enjoy.

SOME THINGS TO REMEMBER

1. Choose a subject that can be analyzed and described within the space you have available.

2. Remember that process takes one of two forms, reflecting its purpose: either to tell the reader how to do something or to tell the reader how something happens. Make sure that you have a purpose clearly in mind before you start your paper.

3. Identify your audience and write to that audience. Ask yourself, Will my audience be interested in what I am writing about? and How much does my audience know about this subject?

4. Make a list of the steps or stages in the process.

5. Order or arrange a list, checking to make sure nothing is omitted or misplaced.

6. Convert the list into paragraphs using complete sentences. Remember to define any unfamiliar terms or concepts.

7. Use step or time markers to indicate the proper sequence in the process.

8. Check your process one final time to make sure that nothing has been omitted. If you are describing how to do something, use your paper as a guide to the process. If you are describing how something happens, ask a friend to read your process analysis to see whether it is clear.

PROCESS AS A LITERARY STRATEGY

Janice Mirikitani, a third-generation Japanese American, uses process in her poem "Recipe." As the title and its list of "ingredients" suggests, the poem might at first seem like a set of directions that you would find in a magazine—"how to create the illusion of having round eyes." As you read the poem, think first about how Mirikitani uses the elements of a process analysis to structure her poem.

RECIPE

Janice Mirikitani

Round Eyes
Ingredients: scissors, Scotch magic transparent tape.
eyeliner—water based, black.
Optional: false eyelashes.
Cleanse face thoroughly.
For best results, powder entire face, including eyelids.
(lighter shades suited to total effect desired)
With scissors, cut magic tape 1/16" wide, 1/4–1/2" long—depending on length of eyelid.
Stick firmly onto mid-upper eyelid area
(looking down into handmirror facilitates finding adequate surface)
If using false eyelashes, affix first on lid, folding any excess lid over the base of eyelash with glue.
Paint black eyeliner on tape and entire lid.
Do not cry.

DISCUSSION QUESTIONS

1. How do you think that Mirikitani feels about "round eyes"? Is she trying simply to describe how to create that illusion? Is her poem trying to be "helpful"?

2. How would you characterize the tone of the poem? What in the poem provides evidence for your viewpoint?

3. How does the process structure contribute to the poem's effect? For example, what initial expectation did you have about the poem? Did your expectations change as you read? Where?

4. Is there anything in the "steps" of the process that seems unusual?

5. What makes this a poem and not a helpful set of instructions?

WRITING SUGGESTIONS

As this poem suggests, process does not have to be used in a simple, expository way. Mirikitani uses it to make a comment about a social issue, about cultural pressure and values. Explore a similar issue using a process model—either a set of directions or a description of how something works. Some possibilities for topics might include:

a. Underage drinking or smoking

b. The desire to change your "looks" (for example, hair coloring, body piercing, hair straightening or curling, plastic surgery, purging)

c. The desire to conform to your peers (for example, behavior, dress, attitude)

READING PROCESS

Every set of directions, or "how-to-do-it," or "how-it-is-done-or-produced" is a process narrative or analysis. When we read a description of a process, we can expect to see several distinctive features:

- Process is always structured in time, from the first step to the last. In that sense, it is similar to a narrative or story, but unlike a narrative, process does not use flashbacks. That would only confuse the reader.

- The function of process is to allow a reader to duplicate the procedure or to understand the stages or steps. In that sense, process has a very practical goal. It is effective only if the reader can follow it.

- To promote clarity, process frequently uses step or stage markers—first do this; then this. Typically, the steps or stages are numbered, or separated by extra space, or divided into paragraphs. The structure and how it is revealed on the printed page clearly emphasizes the steps.

- Process typically uses parallel structures—headings, sentences, and paragraphs are written so that they are grammatically similar in structure. (See glossary for examples.)

- Process is always conscious of its audience. Who is the intended audience? How much do they already know about the subject? The intended audience for an introductory biology textbook is obviously every different from the audience for a research article published in a scientific journal.

Let's test our awareness of how process works by analyzing the following essay taken from the CareerWomen.com Website.

Note the reference to TV program	**"GETTING THE INTERVIEW EDGE 'APPRENTICE-STYLE' "**
Who is the imagined audience? Young women looking for a job	The popularity of reality TV phenomenon *The Apprentice* provides job seekers new insights on the importance of the interview. While most employers have less than a 15-week interview process, many lessons can
What is the purpose? To help them gain an "interview edge"	be learned from how all candidates were evaluated during "The Apprentice." CareerWomen.com asked leading employers and recruiters for their top tips on gaining the interview edge.
	1. Be prepared
Starts with preparation— before an interview	Familiarize yourself with the company as well as the position. Get up-to-date on current corporate issues so you can address any questions about direction and opportunity. Develop a list of
Steps are in separate numbered, titled paragraphs	questions prior to the interview to demonstrate your interest and curiosity about the company.

According to one recruiter, "I'm always stunned at how many times someone applies for a new job that they know nothing about or are unqualified for. Be prepared, professional and qualified if you want to go to the next step."

Each block is written in clear, nontechnical language

2. Be qualified
Highlight related experience, education and skills. Have solid references that will validate your qualifications. A leading recruiter comments, "Be good at what you do. Create great references by being the best you can at the job you already have."

Moved from preparing to the actual interview

3. Make a positive impact
Highlight your strengths and what you uniquely bring to the job opening. Show how you can make a positive impact. Demonstrate interest, insight, initiative and enthusiasm. Do you want the job? A CareerWomen.com employer suggests, "If you're applying for a marketing job, for example, bring in a sample campaign or ideas. Doing this would demonstrate an extraordinary candidate."

Each step uses a quotation to support the advice

4. Be professional
Common courtesies will take you a long way at setting the right professional impression. For example, be sure to turn off the cell phone before the interview. If your interview is over lunch, watch your manners. Most importantly, be on time!

The headings for each paragraph are parallel in structure—"be," "make."

5. Be a good communicator
Get to the point quickly and say what needs to be said. A leading employer suggests, "Don't be too talkative or try to act like you know it all." Practice and prepare by answering sample interview questions found at sites like CareerWomen.com, and create responses for different levels within the organization.

Each paragraph offers some specific examples of the skill or preparation being emphasized

6. Follow-up appropriately
E-mail a thank you note immediately that summarizes the interview and your ability to contribute to the organization. Be sure that your e-mail address is professional, not "hotchick@aol.com."

Final advice—the last step in the process

Additional resources to enhance professional development and advance women's careers can be found at CareerWomen.com, including career development tools, career and employment news, professional associations and employment opportunities across the US with some of the best women-friendly companies.

Process typically doesn't have a summary ending since it would not be necessary

Looking for Process

1. Look through your textbooks for this semester. Can you find examples of process narratives or analyses. Bring an example to share with the rest of the class.

2. Look for examples of process that you encounter every day. Make a list of situations in which you have had to read about a process before being able to do it—download music, play a new electronic game, operate a feature on your cell phone, fix something on your car or motorcycle.

RESPONDING TO A VISUAL

Because process involves a series of steps or stages, it is typically represented through or accompanied by a series of photographs or drawings. Instructions for "how to assemble" often are nothing more than a series of illustrations with only a minimal number of words. Even descriptions of how something works or occurs generally use visuals to display the stages of the process. Single illustrations, however, can also suggest a process. Consider the following photograph. The young woman looks at herself in a mirror that is distorted. She sees herself in a distorted way.

READING AND WRITING ABOUT IMAGES

The photograph should suggest several possible process analyses. Choose one of the following possibilities and, in an essay, describe the process through which it happens or develops:

a. Steps or stages of eating disorders

b. Process by which women (and men) become obsessed by an ideal body shape

c. Steps or stages in healthy weight loss or muscular development or fitness

d. Steps or stages in recovering from an eating disorder or growth hormone abuse

e. Steps or stages in developing a healthy body image

VISITING THE WEB

The companion Website, **www.prenhall.com/miller**, contains additional information about process and about the writers included in this chapter. You will also find a number of links to other sources of information about the subjects of the essays found in this chapter.

EXPLORING ON YOUR OWN

Searching for information on the Web or in your school's online library catalogue is more complicated than it might seem. Electronic databases can be manipulated in many ways. Simply typing a keyword into a search engine like Google or into your school's online library catalogue is often not the best or most effective search strategy. Learn how to narrow or "fine-tune" your searches in order to retrieve the best results. Searching tips for Web search engines and library catalogues can be found online at the search engine's or library catalogue's home page. In an essay intended for classmates, write a process explanation on how to conduct effective online searches for information.

LOOKING FOR WRITING SUGGESTIONS

HOW-TO-DO-IT

1. Choose a cell phone plan
2. Fail a course
3. Choose a major

4. Find a summer internship in your major
5. Break up with a partner
6. Change a tire
7. Write an "F" essay
8. List an item for sale on e-Bay
9. Train for a race
10. Buy a particular piece of sports equipment (the best skis, tennis racket, mountain bike, backpacking or running shoes, roller blades, skateboard)

HOW-IT-WORKS

1. Text messaging
2. Instant messaging
3. Ice rink/artificial snow on a ski slope
4. Earthquakes/hurricanes/tornados/hail
5. Computer chips/modems/wireless networks
6. Air bags in automobiles
7. Hybrid automobile (gasoline/electric)
8. "Spiders" on electronic search engines
9. Graduate or professional school admission
10. Cell phones

MY DAILY DIVES IN THE DUMPSTER
Lars Eighner

Born in 1948, Lars Eighner grew up in Houston, Texas. He attended the University of Texas at Austin but dropped out before graduation to do social work. In the mid-1980s, he lost his job as an attendant at a mental institution, which launched him on a three-year nightmare as a homeless person, with his dog, Lizbeth, as his companion. He later reworked these experiences as a book, Travels with Lizbeth *(1993), the final manuscript of which was written on a personal computer that Eighner found in a dumpster.*

On Writing: *Advice from Eighner's Website: "The best thing you can do for your writing is to learn to revise effectively. Sure, some natural geniuses may never have to revise a word, but the number of writers who consider themselves geniuses must outnumber the true geniuses by a factor of a thousand. And yes, some writers who practice revision for a long time eventually learn to avoid most mistakes so that their first drafts do not need much revision. But everyone else needs to* revise and revise and revise. *Putting a work through a spelling checker or a grammar checker is not revision. . . . Revision means changing words and phrases and sometimes changing whole sentences and paragraphs. Almost everyone's writing needs this kind of revision."*

BEFORE READING

Connecting: If you came across someone "diving" into a dumpster, what assumptions would you be likely to make about that person?

Anticipating: One would hope that few of Eighner's readers will ever have to dive into dumpsters to survive. What then can readers learn from his essay?

I began Dumpster diving about a year before I became homeless. 1

I prefer the term "scavenging" and use the word "scrounging" when I 2
mean to be obscure. I have heard people, evidently meaning to be polite, use
the word "foraging," but I prefer to reserve that word for gathering nuts and
berries and such, which I do also, according to the season and opportunity.

I like the frankness of the word "scavenging." I live from the refuse of 3
others. I am a scavenger. I think it a sound and honorable niche, although if I
could I would naturally prefer to live the comfortable consumer life, perhaps—and only perhaps—as a slightly less wasteful consumer owing to what I
have learned as a scavenger.

Except for jeans, all my clothes come from Dumpsters. Boom boxes, can- 4
dles, bedding, toilet paper, medicine, books, a typewriter, a virgin male love
doll, change sometimes amounting to many dollars: All came from Dumpsters.
And, yes, I eat from Dumpsters too.

5   There are a predictable series of stages that a person goes through in learning to scavenge. At first the new scavenger is filled with disgust and self-loathing. He is ashamed of being seen and may lurk around trying to duck behind things, or he may try to dive at night. (In fact, this is unnecessary, since most people instinctively look away from scavengers.)

6   Every grain of rice seems to be a maggot. Everything seems to stink. The scavenger can wipe the egg yolk off the found can, but he cannot erase the stigma of eating garbage from his mind.

7   This stage passes with experience. The scavenger finds a pair of running shoes that fit and look and smell brand-new. He finds a pocket calculator in perfect working order. He finds pristine ice cream, still frozen, more than he can eat or keep. He begins to understand: People do throw away perfectly good stuff, a lot of perfectly good stuff.

8   At this stage he may become lost and never recover. All the Dumpster divers I have known come to the point of trying to acquire everything they touch. Why not take it, they reason, it is all free. This is, of course, hopeless, and most divers come to realize that they must restrict themselves to items of relatively immediate utility.

9   The finding of objects is becoming something of an urban art. Even respectable, employed people will sometimes find something tempting sticking out of a Dumpster or standing beside one. Quite a number of people, not all of them of the bohemian type, are willing to brag that they found this or that piece in the trash.

10   But eating from Dumpsters is the thing that separates the dilettanti from the professionals. Eating safely involves three principles: using the senses and common sense to evaluate the condition of the found materials; knowing the Dumpsters of a given area and checking them regularly; and seeking always to answer the question, Why was this discarded?

11   Perhaps everyone who has a kitchen and a regular supply of groceries has, at one time or another, eaten half a sandwich before discovering mold on the bread, or has gotten a mouthful of milk before realizing the milk had turned. Nothing of the sort is likely to happen to a Dumpster diver because he is constantly reminded that most food is discarded for a reason.

12   Yet perfectly good food can be found in Dumpsters. Canned goods, for example, turn up fairly often in the Dumpsters I frequent. All except the most phobic people would be willing to eat from a can even if it came from a Dumpster. I have few qualms about dry foods such as crackers, cookies, cereal, chips, and pasta if they are free of visible contaminates and still dry and crisp. Raw fruits and vegetables with intact skins seem perfectly safe to me, excluding, of course, the obviously rotten. Many are discarded for minor imperfections that can be pared away. Chocolate is often discarded only because it has become discolored as the cocoa butter de-emulsified.

13   I began scavenging by pulling pizzas out of the Dumpster behind a pizza delivery shop. In general, prepared food requires caution, but in this case I knew what time the shop closed and went to the Dumpster as soon as the last of the help left.

Because the workers at these places are usually inexperienced, pizzas are 14 often made with the wrong topping, baked incorrectly, or refused on delivery for being cold. The products to be discarded are boxed up because inventory is kept by counting boxes: A boxed pizza can be written off; an unboxed pizza does not exist. So I had a steady supply of fresh, sometimes warm pizza.

The area I frequent is inhabited by many affluent college students. I am 15 not here by chance; the Dumpsters are very rich. Students throw out many good things, including food, particularly at the end of the semester and before and after breaks. I find it advantageous to keep an eye on the academic calendar.

A typical discard is a half jar of peanut butter—though nonorganic 16 peanut butter does not require refrigeration and is unlikely to spoil in any reasonable time. Occasionally I find a cheese with a spot of mold, which, of course, I just pare off, and because it is obvious why the cheese was discarded, I treat it with less suspicion than an apparently perfect cheese found in similar circumstances. One of my favorite finds is yogurt—often discarded, still sealed, when the expiration date has passed—because it will keep for several days, even in warm weather.

I avoid ethnic foods I am unfamiliar with. If I do not know what it is supposed to look or smell like when it is good, I cannot be certain I will be able 17 to tell if it is bad.

No matter how careful I am I still get dysentery at least once a month, of- 18 tener in warm weather. I do not want to paint too romantic a picture. Dumpster diving has serious drawbacks as a way of life.

Though I have a proprietary feeling about my Dumpsters, I don't mind 19 my direct competitors, other scavengers, as much as I hate the sodacan scroungers.

I have tried scrounging aluminum cans with an able-bodied companion, 20 and afoot we could make no more than a few dollars a day. I can extract the necessities of life from the Dumpsters directly with far less effort than would be required to accumulate the equivalent value in aluminum. Can scroungers, then, are people who *must* have small amounts of cash—mostly drug addicts and winos.

I do not begrudge them the cans, but can scroungers tend to tear up the 21 Dumpsters, littering the area and mixing the contents. There are precious few courtesies among scavengers, but it is a common practice to set aside surplus items: pairs of shoes, clothing, canned goods, and such. A true scavenger hates to see good stuff go to waste, and what he cannot use he leaves in good condition in plain sight. Can scroungers lay waste to everything in their path and will stir one of a pair of good shoes to the bottom of a Dumpster to be lost or ruined in the muck. They become so specialized that they can see only cans and earn my contempt by passing up change, canned goods, and readily hockable items.

Can scroungers will even go through individual garbage cans, some- 22 thing I have never seen a scavenger do. Going through individual garbage cans without spreading litter is almost impossible, and litter is likely to reduce the public's tolerance of scavenging. But my strongest reservation about going through individual garbage cans is that this seems to me a very personal kind of invasion, one to which I would object if I were a homeowner.

23   Though Dumpsters seem somehow less personal than garbage cans, they still contain bank statements, bills, correspondence, pill bottles, and other sensitive information. I avoid trying to draw conclusions about the people who dump in the Dumpsters I frequent. I think it would be unethical to do so, although I know many people will find the idea of scavenger ethics too funny for words.

24   Occasionally a find tells a story. I once found a small paper bag containing some unused condoms, several partial tubes of flavored sexual lubricant, a partially used compact of birth control pills, and the torn pieces of a picture of a young man. Clearly,the woman was through with him and planning to give up sex altogether.

25   Dumpster things are often sad—abandoned teddy bears, shredded wedding albums, despaired-of sales kits. I find diaries and journals. College students also discard their papers; I am horrified to discover the kind of paper that now merits an A in an undergraduate course.

26   Dumpster diving is outdoor work, often surprisingly pleasant. It is not entirely predictable; things of interest turn up every day, and some days there are finds of great value. I am always very pleased when I can turn up exactly the thing I most wanted to find. Yet in spite of the element of chance, scavenging, more than most other pursuits, tends to yield returns in some proportion to the effort and intelligence brought to bear.

27   I think of scavenging as a modern form of self-reliance. After ten years of government service, where everything is geared to the lowest common denominator, I find work that rewards initiative and effort refreshing. Certainly I would be happy to have a sinecure again, but I am not heart-broken to be without one.

28   I find from the experience of scavenging two rather deep lessons. The first is to take what I can use and let the rest go. I have come to think that there is no value in the abstract. A thing I cannot use or make useful, perhaps by trading, has no value, however fine or rare it may be. (I mean useful in the broad sense—some art, for example, I would think valuable.)

29   The second lesson is the transience of material being. I do not suppose that ideas are immortal, but certainly they are longer-lived than material objects.

30   The things I find in Dumpsters, the love letters and rag dolls of so many lives, remind me of this lesson. Many times in my travels I have lost everything but the clothes on my back. Now I hardly pick up a thing without envisioning the time I will cast it away. This, I think, is a healthy state of mind. Almost everything I have now has already been cast out at least once, proving that what I own is valueless to someone.

31   I find that my desire to grab for the gaudy bauble has been largely sated. I think this is an attitude I share with the very wealthy—we both know there is plenty more where whatever we have came from. Between us are the rat-race

millions who have confounded their selves with the objects they grasp and who nightly scavenge the cable channels looking for they know not what.

I am sorry for them.   32

QUESTIONS ON SUBJECT AND PURPOSE

1. Is the subject of Eighner's essay simply how to "dive" into a dumpster? What other points does he make?
2. A substantial part of the essay deals with scavenging for food. Why does Eighner devote so much space to this?
3. What larger or more general lesson or truth does Eighner see in his experiences? For example, for whom does Eighner say he feels sorry at the end of the essay?

QUESTIONS ON STRATEGY AND AUDIENCE

1. In what ways does the essay use process as a writing strategy?
2. What are the "predictable stages" that a scavenger goes through?
3. What assumptions does Eighner make about his audience?

QUESTIONS ON VOCABULARY AND STYLE

1. Why does Eighner prefer the term *scavenging* to a more ambiguous or better-sounding term?
2. In what way is Eighner's final sentence ironic? Why might he choose to make it a separate paragraph?
3. Be prepared to define the following words: *niche* (paragraph 3), *stigma* (6), *pristine* (7), *bohemian* (9), *dilettanti* (10), *phobic* (12), *qualms* (12), *de-emulsified* (12), *affluent* (15), *proprietary* (19), *sinecure* (27), *transience* (29), *gaudy* (31), *bauble* (31), *sated* (31).

WRITING SUGGESTIONS

1. **For Your Journal.** Suppose that suddenly you found yourself without a full-time job or financial support from your family. What would you do? Using an ordered sequence, plan out the steps that you would take in trying to deal with the situation.
2. **For a Paragraph.** In a world in which many Americans can find only low-paying jobs with no benefits, what advice could you offer to a young high school student today? In a paragraph organized according to a process structure, address that audience. Be sure to have a specific point or thesis to your paragraph. Try to avoid clichéd answers; just saying "go to college," for example, is not particularly good advice since many college students are not able to find well-paying, full-time jobs.

3. **For an Essay.** Where are you going in your life, and how do you plan to get there? What are your objectives, goals, or aspirations? Where do you hope to be in ten years? In twenty years? What are you doing now to try to achieve those goals? What should you be doing? In an essay, honestly examine your directions and your actions.

4. **For Research.** With corporate and business "downsizing," many Americans have suddenly found themselves out of work. As advice for those trapped in such a situation, write a guide to the resources available to the newly unemployed. Use a process strategy as a way of providing step-by-step advice to your audience. Contact local and state agencies to see what help is available and how one goes about making an application. Be sure to document your sources—including interviews—wherever appropriate.

FOR FURTHER STUDY

Focusing on Grammar and Writing. Locate each instance in which Eighner uses a colon or a semicolon. On the basis of these examples, write a series of rules that govern colon and semicolon usage. How often do you use either mark in your own writing? What does each mark do that cannot be done by another mark of punctuation?

Working Together. Working with classmates in small groups, brainstorm responses on how to furnish a dorm room or an apartment with "free" or very inexpensive items. What would the process entail? Make a list of the steps or stages and experiment with using a numbered list, with explicit sequence markers, or with extra white space or paragraphs.

Seeing Other Modes at Work. To what extent is Eighner's essay persuasive? If the essay were to be recast to persuade readers about the importance or unimportance of things in life, what could be used in the essay, and what would have to be deleted, changed, or expanded?

Finding Connections. Read E. M. Forster's "My Wood" (Chapter 7). In what ways is that essay similar to Eighner's. About what might the two writers agree? Disagree?

Exploring the Web. Eighner has a home page on the Web that includes a wide range of information about his books, his other publications, and a bibliography of articles about him and his work. Starting points can be found at **www.prenhall.com/miller.**

REVISION AND LIFE: TAKE IT FROM THE TOP—AGAIN

Nora Ephron

Nora Ephron (1941–) graduated from Wellesley College and worked as a journalist and columnist for the New York Post, New York *magazine, and* Esquire. *She is also a successful screenplay writer and director whose credits include* Sleepless in Seattle *(1993),* You've Got Mail *(1998), and* Hanging Up *(2000). "Revision and Life," written in response to an invitation to participate in this textbook, was originally published in* The New York Times Book Review.

On Writing: *When asked about the autobiographical influences of her first novel, Ephron replied: "I've always written about my life. That's how I grew up. 'Take notes. Everything is copy.' All that stuff my mother [also a writer] said to us."*

BEFORE READING

Connecting: When it comes to writing, what does the word *revision* suggest to you?

Anticipating: When Ephron observes, "A gift for revision may be a developmental stage," what does she mean?

I have been asked to write something for a textbook that is meant to teach   1
college students something about writing and revision. I am happy to do this because I believe in revision. I have also been asked to save the early drafts of whatever I write, presumably to show these students the actual process of revision. This too I am happy to do. On the other hand, I suspect that there is just so much you can teach college students about revision; a gift for revision may be a developmental stage—like a 2-year-old's sudden ability to place one block on top of another—that comes along somewhat later, in one's mid-20s, say; most people may not be particularly good at it, or even interested in it, until then.

When I was in college, I revised nothing. I wrote out my papers in long-   2
hand, typed them up and turned them in. It would never have crossed my mind that what I had produced was only a first draft and that I had more work to do; the idea was to get to the end, and once you had got to the end you were finished. The same thinking, I might add, applied in life: I went pell-mell through my four years in college without a thought about whether I ought to do anything differently; the idea was to get to the end—to get out of school and become a journalist.

3   Which I became, in fairly short order. I learned as a journalist to revise on deadline. I learned to write an article a paragraph at a time—and I arrived at the kind of writing and revising I do, which is basically a kind of typing and retyping. I am a great believer in this technique for the simple reason that I type faster than the wind. What I generally do is to start an article and get as far as I can—sometimes no farther in than a sentence or two—before running out of steam, ripping the piece of paper from the typewriter and starting all over again. I type over and over until I have got the beginning of the piece to the point where I am happy with it. I then am ready to plunge into the body of the article itself. This plunge usually requires something known as a transition. I approach a transition by completely retyping the opening of the article leading up to it in the hope that the ferocious speed of my typing will somehow catapult me into the next section of the piece. This does not work—what in fact catapults me into the next section is a concrete thought about what the next section ought to be about—but until I have the thought the typing keeps me busy, and keeps me from feeling something known as blocked.

4   Typing and retyping as if you know where you're going is a version of what therapists tell you to do when they suggest that you try changing from the outside in—that if you can't master the total commitment to whatever change you want to make, you can at least do all the extraneous things connected with it, which make it that much easier to get there. I was 25 years old the first time a therapist suggested that I try changing from the outside in. In those days, I used to spend quite a lot of time lying awake at night wondering what I should have said earlier in the evening and revising my lines. I mention this not just because it's a way of illustrating that a gift for revision is practically instinctive, but also (once again) because it's possible that a genuine ability at it doesn't really come into play until one is older—or at least older than 25, when it seemed to me that all that was required in my life and my work was the chance to change a few lines.

5   In my 30's, I began to write essays, one a month for *Esquire* magazine, and I am not exaggerating when I say that in the course of writing a short essay—1,500 words, that's only six double-spaced typewritten pages—I often used 300 or 400 pieces of typing paper, so often did I type and retype and catapult and recatapult myself, sometimes on each retyping moving not even a sentence farther from the spot I had reached the last time through. At the same time, though, I was polishing what I had already written: as I struggled with the middle of the article, I kept putting the beginning through the typewriter; as I approached the ending, the middle got its turn. (This is a kind of polishing that the word processor all but eliminates, which is why I don't use one. Word processors make it possible for a writer to change the sentences that clearly need changing without having to retype the rest, but I believe that you can't always tell whether a sentence needs work until it rises up in revolt against your fingers as you retype it.) By the time I had produced what you might call a first draft—an entire article with a beginning, middle and end— the beginning was in more like 45th draft, the middle in 20th, and the end was

almost newborn. For this reason, the beginnings of my essays are considerably better written than the ends, although I like to think no one ever notices this but me.

As I learned the essay form, writing became harder for me. I was finding a personal style, a voice if you will, a way of writing that looked chatty and informal. That wasn't the hard part—the hard part was that having found a voice, I had to work hard month to month not to seem as if I were repeating myself. At this point in this essay it will not surprise you to learn that the same sort of thing was operating in my life. I don't mean that my life had become harder—but that it was becoming clear that I had many more choices than had occurred to me when I was marching through my 20's. I no longer lost sleep over what I should have said. Not that I didn't care—it was just that I had moved to a new plane of late-night anxiety: I now wondered what I should have done. Whole areas of possible revision opened before me. What should I have done instead? What could I have done? What if I hadn't done it the way I did? What if I had a chance to do it over? What if I had a chance to do it over as a different person? These were the sorts of questions that kept me awake and led me into fiction, which at the very least (the level at which I practice it) is a chance to rework the events of your life so that you give the illusion of being the intelligence at the center of it, simultaneously managing to slip in all the lines that occurred to you later. Fiction, I suppose, is the ultimate shot at revision.

Now I am in my 40's and I write screenplays. Screenplays—if they are made into movies—are essentially collaborations, and movies are not a writer's medium, we all know this, and I don't want to dwell on the craft of screenwriting except insofar as it relates to revision. Because the moment you stop work on a script seems to be determined not by whether you think the draft is good but simply by whether shooting is about to begin: if it is, you get to call your script a final draft; and if it's not, you can always write another revision. This might seem to be a hateful way to live, but the odd thing is that it's somehow comforting; as long as you're revising, the project isn't dead. And by the same token, neither are you.

It was, as it happens, while thinking about all this one recent sleepless night that I figured out how to write this particular essay. I say "recent" in order to give a sense of immediacy and energy to the preceding sentence, but the truth is that I am finishing this article four months after the sleepless night in question, and the letter asking me to write it, from George Miller of the University of Delaware, arrived almost two years ago, so for all I know Mr. Miller has managed to assemble his textbook on revision without me.

Oh, well. That's how it goes when you start thinking about revision. That's the danger of it, in fact. You can spend so much time thinking about how to switch things around that the main event has passed you by. But it doesn't matter. Because by the time you reach middle age, you want more than anything for things not to come to an end; and as long as you're still revising, they don't.

I'm sorry to end so morbidly—dancing as I am around the subject of death—but there are advantages to it. For one thing, I have managed to move fairly effortlessly and logically from the beginning of this piece through the middle and to the end. And for another, I am able to close with an exhortation, something I rarely manage, which is this: Revise now, before it's too late.

QUESTIONS ON SUBJECT AND PURPOSE

1. For Ephron, how are revision and life connected?
2. Why is fiction the "ultimate shot at revision" (paragraph 6)?
3. Is the essay about how to revise or about something else?

QUESTIONS ON STRATEGY AND AUDIENCE

1. How does Ephron structure her essay? What principle of order does she follow?
2. What might Ephron mean by her final sentence ("Revise now, before it's too late")?
3. It would have been a simple matter for Ephron to omit the references to this textbook (paragraphs 1 and 8). The *New York Times* audience, for example, would not be interested in knowing these details. Why might she have chosen to include these references in her essay?

QUESTIONS ON VOCABULARY AND STYLE

1. Have you ever heard the phrase "take it from the top—again"? In what context is it usually used? What might such a figure of speech be called?
2. Ephron refers to her strategy of retyping as a way of "catapulting" herself into the next section. Where does the verb *catapult* come from? What does it suggest?
3. Be prepared to define the following words: *pell-mell* (paragraph 2), *extraneous* (4), *exhortation* (10).

WRITING SUGGESTIONS

1. **For Your Journal.** What obstacles do you face when you try to revise something that you have written? Make a list of the ones that immediately come to mind. Add to your list as you finish each paragraph and essay during this course.
2. **For a Paragraph.** Formulate a thesis about Ephron's process of revision based on this essay. In a paragraph, assert your thesis and support it with appropriate evidence from the essay.
3. **For an Essay.** On the basis of your own experience as a writer and as a student in this course, argue for or against *requiring* revision in a college writing course. Should a student be forced to do it? Does revision always produce a better paper?

4. **For Research.** What role does revision play in the writing process of faculty and staff at your college or university? Interview a range of people—faculty (especially professors in disciplines other than English) and other professional staff members who write as a regular part of their job (for example, librarians, information officers, and admissions officers). Using notes from your interviews, write an essay about the revision practices of these writers. Your essay could be a feature article in the campus newspaper.

FOR FURTHER STUDY

Focusing on Grammar and Writing. Information inserted into a sentence can be set off by commas, parentheses, or dashes. In paragraphs 5 and 6, Ephron uses all three marks. Study these paragraphs, and then offer an explanation for why Ephron chooses to punctuate each insertion or addition as she does.

Working Together. Working in small groups, discuss if and how each of you "revise" an essay. Probably no one works as Ephron did, but what other strategies do writers use? How many ask classmates, friends, or relatives to read their papers? How many are willing to really change the structure of a paper? How many regard revision as changing words and punctuation? Prepare to share your experiences with others in the class.

Seeing Other Modes at Work. Ephron uses division to structure the middle of her essay—what revision meant to her at each stage of her life, from her college years to her forties.

Finding Connections. A number of essays explore the "knowledge" or "recognition" that comes with age—possible comparisons include Anne Quindlen's "The Name is Mine" (Chapter 1), Scott Russell Sanders's "The Inheritance of Tools" (Chapter 3), and E. B. White's "Once More to the Lake" (Chapter 10).

Exploring the Web. Ephron is increasingly known as both a screenwriter and director. You can find detailed Web resources on all of her films, including stills, audio, and video clips starting from **www.prenhall.com/miller**. How does this essay explain her interest in filmmaking?

DON'T JUST STAND THERE

Diane Cole

Diane Cole was born in Baltimore, Maryland, in 1952. Educated at Radcliffe College (B.A.) and Johns Hopkins University (M.A.), she is a freelance journalist well versed in psychological issues. Her most recent book, co-authored with Scott Wetzler, is Is It You or Is It Me?: How We Turn Our Emotions Inside Out and Blame Each Other *(1998). "Don't Just Stand There" originally appeared as part of a national campaign against bigotry in a special supplement to* The New York Times *titled "A World of Difference" (April 16, 1989), sponsored by the Anti-Defamation League of B'nai B'rith.*

On Writing: *In an article about her life as a writer, Cole wrote: "I've been scribbling things down for as long as I can remember. . . . And when [my fourth-grade teacher] encouraged me to keep on writing I thought: Maybe it's possible, maybe I can become a writer one day. And there was also the desire—maybe the need—to leave my mark, by writing something that would somehow be of use to others, whether it entertained, gave solace, provided practical information, or simply made another person smile."*

BEFORE READING

Connecting: Can you remember a time when you were told a joke that maligned your national or ethnic origin, race, religion, gender, sexual orientation, or age? How did you respond?

Anticipating: According to Cole and the experts that she cites, what are improper responses to such distasteful or bigoted remarks?

1   It was my office farewell party, and colleagues at the job I was about to leave were wishing me well. My mood was one of ebullience tinged with regret, and it was in this spirit that I spoke to the office neighbor to whom I had waved hello every morning for the past two years. He smiled broadly as he launched into a long, rambling story, pausing only after he delivered the punch line. It was a very long pause because, although he laughed, I did not: This joke was unmistakably anti-Semitic.

2   I froze. Everyone in the office knew I was Jewish; what could he have possibly meant? Shaken and hurt, not knowing what else to do, I turned in stunned silence to the next well-wisher. Later, still angry, I wondered, what else should I—could I—have done?

3   Prejudice can make its presence felt in any setting, but hearing its nasty voice in this way can be particularly unnerving. We do not know what to do and often we feel another form of paralysis as well: We think, "Nothing I say or do will change this person's attitude, so why bother?"

But left unchecked, racial slurs and offensive ethnic jokes "can poison   4
the atmosphere," says Michael McQuillan, adviser for racial/ethnic affairs for
the Brooklyn borough president's office. "Hearing these remarks conditions
us to accept them; and if we accept these, we can become accepting of other
acts."

Speaking up may not magically change a biased attitude, but it can change   5
a person's behavior by putting a strong message across. And the more messages
there are, the more likely a person is to change that behavior, says Arnold Kahn,
professor of psychology at James Madison University, Harrisonburg, Va., who
makes this analogy: "You can't keep people from smoking in *their* house, but you
can ask them not to smoke in *your* house."

At the same time, "Even if the other party ignores or discounts what you   6
say, people always reflect on how others perceive them. Speaking up always
counts," says LeNorman Strong, director of campus life at George Washington University, Washington, D.C.

Finally, learning to respond effectively also helps people feel better   7
about themselves, asserts Cherie Brown, executive director of the National
Coalition Building Institute, a Boston-based training organization. "We've
found that, when people felt they could at least in this small way make a difference, that made them more eager to take on other activities on a larger
scale," she says. Although there is no "cookbook approach" to confronting
such remarks—every situation is different, experts stress—these are some
effective strategies.

When the "joke" turns on who you are—as a member of an ethnic or religious group,   8
a person of color, a woman, a gay or lesbian, an elderly person, or someone with a
physical handicap—shocked paralysis is often the first response. Then, wounded and
vulnerable, on some level you want to strike back.

Lashing out or responding in kind is seldom the most effective response,   9
however. "That can give you momentary satisfaction, but you also feel as if
you've lowered yourself to that other person's level," Mr. McQuillan explains.
Such a response may further label you in the speaker's mind as thin-skinned,
someone not to be taken seriously. Or it may up the ante, making the speaker,
and then you, reach for new insults—or physical blows.

"If you don't laugh at the joke, or fight, or respond in kind to the slur," says   10
Mr. McQuillan, "that will take the person by surprise, and that can give you more
control over the situation." Therefore, in situations like the one in which I found
myself—a private conversation in which I knew the person making the remark—
he suggests voicing your anger calmly but pointedly: "I don't know if you realize
what that sounded like to me. If that's what you meant, it really hurt me."

State how *you* feel, rather than making an abstract statement like, "Not   11
everyone who hears that joke might find it funny." Counsels Mr. Strong: "Per-
sonalize the sense of 'this is how I feel when you say this.' That makes it very
concrete"—and harder to dismiss.

Make sure you heard the words and their intent correctly by repeating   12
or rephrasing the statement: "This is what I heard you say. Is that what you

meant?" It's important to give the other person the benefit of the doubt because, in fact, he may *not* have realized that the comment was offensive and, if you had not spoken up, would have had no idea of its impact on you.

13   For instance, Professor Kahn relates that he used to include in his exams multiple-choice questions that occasionally contained "incorrect funny answers." After one exam, a student came up to him in private and said, "I don't think you intended this, but I found a number of those jokes offensive to me as a woman." She explained why. "What she said made immediate sense to me," he says. "I apologized at the next class, and I never did it again."

14   But what if the speaker dismisses your objection, saying, "Oh, you're just being sensitive. Can't you take a joke?" In that case, you might say, "I'm not so sure about that, let's talk about that a little more." The key, Mr. Strong says, is to continue the dialogue, hear the other person's concerns, and point out your own. "There are times when you're just going to have to admit defeat and end it," he adds, "but I have to feel that I did the best I could."

15   When the offending remark is made in the presence of others—at a staff meeting, for example—it can be even more distressing than an insult made privately.

16   "You have two options," says William Newlin, director of field services for the Community Relations division of the New York City Commission on Human Rights. "You can respond immediately at the meeting, or you can delay your response until afterward in private. But a response has to come."

17   Some remarks or actions may be so outrageous that they cannot go unnoted at the moment, regardless of the speaker or the setting. But in general, psychologists say, shaming a person in public may have the opposite effect of the one you want: The speaker will deny his offense all the more strongly in order to save face. Further, few people enjoy being put on the spot, and if the remark really was not intended to be offensive, publicly embarrassing the person who made it may cause an unnecessary rift or further misunderstanding. Finally, most people just don't react as well or thoughtfully under a public spotlight as they would in private.

18   Keeping that in mind, an excellent alternative is to take the offender aside afterward: "Could we talk for a minute in private?" Then use the strategies suggested above for calmly stating how you feel, giving the speaker the benefit of the doubt, and proceeding from there.

19   At a large meeting or public talk, you might consider passing the speaker a note, says David Wertheimer, executive director of the New York City Gay and Lesbian Anti-Violence Project: You could write, "You may not realize it, but your remarks were offensive because . . ."

20   "Think of your role as that of an educator," suggests James M. Jones, Ph.D., executive director for public interest at the American Psychological Association. "You have to be controlled."

21   Regardless of the setting or situation, speaking up always raises the risk of rocking the boat. If the person who made the offending remark is your boss, there may be an even bigger risk to consider: How will this affect my job? Several things can help minimize the risk, however. First, know what other

resources you may have at work, suggests Caryl Stern, director of the A World of Difference—New York City campaign: Does your personnel office handle discrimination complaints? Are other grievance procedures in place?

You won't necessarily need to use any of these procedures, Ms. Stern 22 stresses. In fact, she advises, "It's usually better to try a one-on-one approach first." But simply knowing a formal system exists can make you feel secure enough to set up that meeting.

You can also raise the issue with other colleagues who heard the remark: 23 Did they feel the same way you did? The more support you have, the less alone you will feel. Your point will also carry more validity and be more difficult to shrug off. Finally, give your boss credit—and the benefit of the doubt: "I know you've worked hard for the company's affirmative action programs, so I'm sure you didn't realize what those remarks sounded like to me as well as the others at the meeting last week. . . ."

If, even after this discussion, the problem persists, go back for another 24 meeting, Ms. Stern advises. And if that, too, fails, you'll know what other options are available to you.

It's a spirited dinner party, and everyone's having a good time, until one guest starts 25 *reciting a racist joke. Everyone at the table is white, including you. The others are still laughing, as you wonder what to say or do.*

No one likes being seen as a party-pooper, but before deciding that 26 you'd prefer not to take on this role, you might remember that the person who told the offensive joke has already ruined your good time.

If it's a group that you feel comfortable in—a family gathering, for in- 27 stance—you will feel freer to speak up. Still, shaming the person by shouting "You're wrong!" or "That's not funny!" probably won't get your point across as effectively as other strategies. "If you interrupt people to condemn them, it just makes it harder," says Cherie Brown. She suggests trying instead to get at the resentments that lie beneath the joke by asking open-ended questions: "Grandpa, I know you always treat everyone with such respect. Why do people in our family talk that way about black people?" The key, Ms. Brown says, "is to listen to them first, so they will be more likely to listen to you."

If you don't know your fellow guests well, before speaking up you could 28 turn discreetly to your neighbors (or excuse yourself to help the host or hostess in the kitchen) to get a reading on how they felt, and whether or not you'll find support for speaking up. The less alone you feel, the more comfortable you'll be speaking up: "I know you probably didn't mean anything by that joke, Jim, but it really offended me. . . ." It's important to say that *you* were offended—not state how the group that is the butt of the joke would feel. "Otherwise," LeNorman Strong says, "you risk coming off as a goody two-shoes."

If you yourself are the host, you can exercise more control; you are, after 29 all, the one who sets the rules and the tone of behavior in your home. Once, when Professor Kahn's party guests began singing offensive, racist songs, for instance, he kicked them all out, saying, "You don't sing songs like that in my house!" And, he adds, "they never did again."

30   *At school one day, a friend comes over and says, "Who do you think you are, hanging out with Joe? If you can be friends with those people, I'm through with you!"*

31   Peer pressure can weigh heavily on kids. They feel vulnerable and, because they are kids, they aren't as able to control the urge to fight. "But if you learn to handle these situations as kids, you'll be better able to handle them as an adult," William Newlin points out.

32   Begin by redefining to yourself what a friend is and examining what friendship means, advises Amy Lee, a human relations specialist at Panel of Americans, an intergroup-relations training and educational organization. If that person from a different group fits your requirement for a friend, ask, "Why shouldn't I be friends with Joe? We have a lot in common." Try to get more information about whatever stereotypes or resentments lie beneath your friend's statement. Ms. Lee suggests: "What makes you think they're so different from us? Where did you get that information?" She explains: "People are learning these stereotypes from somewhere, and they cannot be blamed for that. So examine where these ideas came from." Then talk about how your own experience rebuts them.

33   Kids, like adults, should also be aware of other resources to back them up: Does the school offer special programs for fighting prejudice? How supportive will the principal, the teachers, or other students be? If the school atmosphere is volatile, experts warn, make sure that taking a stand at that moment won't put you in physical danger. If that is the case, it's better to look for other alternatives.

34   These can include programs or organizations that bring kids from different backgrounds together. "When kids work together across race lines, that is how you break down the barriers and see that the stereotypes are not true," says Laurie Meadoff, president of CityKids Foundation, a nonprofit group whose programs attempt to do just that. Such programs can also provide what Cherie Brown calls a "safe place" to express the anger and pain that slurs and other offenses cause, whether the bigotry is directed against you or others.

35   In learning to speak up, everyone will develop a different style and a slightly different message to get across, experts agree. But it would be hard to do better than these two messages suggested by teenagers at CityKids: "Everyone on the face of the earth has the same intestines," said one. Another added, "Cross over the bridge. There's a lot of love on the streets."

QUESTIONS ON SUBJECT AND PURPOSE

1. According to Cole, why should we object to "racial slurs and offensive ethnic jokes"?
2. The body of Cole's essay (paragraphs 8–34) offers strategies to use when confronting offensive remarks or jokes. How does Cole divide or organize this part of her subject?
3. What purposes might Cole have had in writing the essay?

QUESTIONS ON STRATEGY AND AUDIENCE

1. Why does Cole begin the essay with a personal example (paragraphs 1 and 2)?
2. Cole quotes a number of authorities in her essay. Why? What do the quotations and the authorities contribute to the article?
3. Why might Cole include the final section—the advice to children about handling such situations among friends? What does this section suggest about her intended audience?

QUESTIONS ON VOCABULARY AND STYLE

1. Throughout the essay, Cole uses first- or second-person pronouns such as *I, you*, and *we*. Why? How would the essay differ if she used *one* or *he* or *she?*
2. At several points (in paragraph 23, for instance), Cole suggests a possible response to a situation, enclosing that remark within quotation marks. Why might she create these imagined sentences for her reader?
3. Be prepared to define the following words: *ebullience* (paragraph 1), *tinged* (1), *rift* (17), *volatile* (33).

WRITING SUGGESTIONS

1. **For Your Journal.** Would you honestly say that after reading Cole's essay you will respond as she suggests when you hear offensive remarks? Does it matter if they are directed at a group to which you belong or at another group? Start with a typical offensive remark that you have often heard, and plan a response to it. If you feel that you would still "just stand there," explain for yourself why you would choose not to react.
2. **For a Paragraph.** Studies from colleges and universities across the United States suggest that many students have cheated at some point during their college years. Typically, these students either plagiarized someone else's work in a paper or a laboratory report or copied answers on a quiz or an exam. Suppose that a friend asks to borrow your research paper or laboratory report, explaining that he or she wants to submit it as his or her own work, or that a friend tries to copy answers from your paper. How can you handle such a situation? In a process paragraph, explain a procedure for replying to that person.
3. **For an Essay.** Cole's essay describes a process—what to do when you encounter prejudice. Select another occasion when we might need advice on how to handle a similarly awkward situation, and write an essay offering advice on what to do.
4. **For Research.** Many colleges and universities have established policies for dealing with sexual harassment and discrimination. Research your

own institution's position on these issues. See if, for example, a policy statement is available. You might also wish to interview members of the administration and faculty. Then, using your research, write an essay in which you explain to students how to handle a case of sexual harassment or discrimination.

FOR FURTHER STUDY

Focusing on Grammar and Writing. Cole uses a variety of sentence structures in the essay. See if you can find examples of the following types of sentences: compound sentences linked with coordinating conjunctions; compound sentences linked with semicolons; sentences containing colons; short, simple sentences. (Check the glossary for examples and definitions.). What is the effect of this variety of sentences? Look at your own writing. Do you use a variety of sentence types?

Working Together. Working in small groups, explore how people react to being "dissed" or "disrespected." Cole assumes that people will react tactfully or not at all. That is certainly not how everyone reacts. What are the other possible responses? Is it ever appropriate to react more aggressively? What are the issues at stake in such a situation?

Seeing Other Modes at Work. Part of Cole's purpose in the essay is also persuasive. She explains not only how to react to such remarks but also why one should object. Identify those portions of the essay that are clearly persuasive in function.

Finding Connections. Cole's essay can be paired with any of the other essays dealing with prejudice or discrimination. Particularly good choices include Judith Ortiz Cofer's "The Myth of the Latin Woman" (Chapter 4), Brent Staples's "Black Men and Private Space" (Chapter 7), and Judy Brady's "I Want a Wife" (Chapter 8).

Exploring the Web. The Web has wonderful resources for dealing with discrimination. For example, check out the sites maintained by the Anti-Defamation League of B'nai B'rith, the National Organization for Women, and the National Association for Colored People. Links can be found at **www.prenhall.com/miller.**

THE CULTURE OF MARTYRDOM

David Brooks

David Brooks, a graduate of the University of Chicago, is a senior editor at The
Weekly Standard, *a contributing editor at* Newsweek, *a correspondent for* Atlantic
Monthly, *and a political analyst for* The NewsHour with Jim Lehrer. *His most
recent book is* On Paradise Drive: How We Live Now (And Always Have) in the
Future Tense *(2004). "The Culture of Martyrdom" appeared in the* Atlantic
Monthly *in the summer of 2002.*

   On Writing: *In the Acknowledgments to* Bobos in Paradise, *Brooks suggests
the importance to professional writers of peer readers and editors. He thanks numerous readers of his manuscript for their "valuable advice" and, in particular, his editor, who "seemed to ponder every word" and whose "comments improved it in ways
great and small."*

BEFORE READING

Connecting: What does the word *martyr* mean to you?

Anticipating: Throughout the essay Brooks suggests that suicide bombings
are an "addiction." Why does he make this analogy? In his mind, what justifies such a link?

Suicide bombing is the crack cocaine of warfare. It doesn't just inflict death   1
and terror on its victims; it intoxicates the people who sponsor it. It unleashes
the deepest and most addictive human passions—the thirst for vengeance, the
desire for religious purity, the longing for earthly glory and eternal salvation.
Suicide bombing isn't just a tactic in a larger war; it overwhelms the political
goals it is meant to serve. It creates its own logic and transforms the culture of
those who employ it. This is what has happened in the Arab-Israeli dispute.
Over the past year suicide bombing has dramatically changed the nature of the
conflict.

   Before 1983 there were few suicide bombings. The Koran forbids the   2
taking of one's own life, and this prohibition was still generally observed. But
when the United States stationed Marines in Beirut, the leaders of the Islamic
resistance movement Hizbollah began to discuss turning to this ultimate terrorist weapon. Religious authorities in Iran gave it their blessing, and a wave
of suicide bombings began, starting with the attacks that killed about sixty
U.S. embassy workers in April of 1983 and about 240 people in the Marine
compound at the airport in October. The bombings proved so successful at
driving the United States and, later, Israel out of Lebanon that most lingering
religious concerns were set aside.

3   The tactic was introduced into Palestinian areas only gradually. In 1988 Fathi Shiqaqi, the founder of the Palestinian Islamic Jihad, wrote a set of guidelines (aimed at countering religious objections to the truck bombings of the 1980s) for the use of explosives in individual bombings; nevertheless, he characterized operations calling for martyrdom as "exceptional." But by the mid-1990s the group Hamas was using suicide bombers as a way of derailing the Oslo peace process. The assassination of the master Palestinian bomb maker Yahya Ayyash, presumably by Israeli agents, in January of 1996, set off a series of suicide bombings in retaliation. Suicide bombings nonetheless remained relatively unusual until two years ago, after the Palestinian leader Yasir Arafat walked out of the peace conference at Camp David—a conference at which Israel's Prime Minister, Ehud Barak, had offered to return to the Palestinians parts of Jerusalem and almost all of the West Bank.

4   At that point the psychology shifted. We will not see peace soon, many Palestinians concluded, but when it eventually comes, we will get everything we want. We will endure, we will fight, and we will suffer for that final victory. From then on the struggle (at least from the Palestinian point of view) was no longer about negotiation and compromise—about who would get which piece of land, which road or river. The red passions of the bombers obliterated the grays of the peace process. Suicide bombing became the tactic of choice, even in circumstances where a terrorist could have planted a bomb and then escaped without injury. Martyrdom became not just a means but an end.

5   Suicide bombing is a highly communitarian enterprise. According to Ariel Merari, the director of the Political Violence Research Center, at Tel Aviv University, and a leading expert on the phenomenon, in not one instance has a lone, crazed Palestinian gotten hold of a bomb and gone off to kill Israelis. Suicide bombings are initiated by tightly run organizations that recruit, indoctrinate, train, and reward the bombers. Those organizations do not seek depressed or mentally unstable people for their missions. From 1996 to 1999 the Pakistani journalist Nasra Hassan interviewed almost 250 people who were either recruiting and training bombers or preparing to go on a suicide mission themselves. "None of the suicide bombers—they ranged in age from eighteen to thirty-eight—conformed to the typical profile of the suicidal personality," Hassan wrote in *The New Yorker*. "None of them were uneducated, desperately poor, simple-minded, or depressed." The Palestinian bombers tend to be devout, but religious fanaticism does not explain their motivation. Nor does lack of opportunity, because they also tend to be well educated.

6   Often a bomber believes that a close friend or a member of his family has been killed by Israeli troops, and this is part of his motivation. According to most experts, though, the crucial factor informing the behavior of suicide bombers is loyalty to the group. Suicide bombers go through indoctrination processes similar to the ones that were used by the leaders of the Jim Jones and Solar Temple cults. The bombers are organized into small cells and given countless hours of intense and intimate spiritual training. They are instructed

in the details of *jihad*, reminded of the need for revenge, and reassured about the rewards they can expect in the afterlife. They are told that their families will be guaranteed a place with God, and that there are also considerable rewards for their families in this life, including cash bonuses of several thousand dollars donated by the government of Iraq, some individual Saudis, and various groups sympathetic to the cause. Finally, the bombers are told that paradise lies just on the other side of the detonator, that death will feel like nothing more than a pinch.

Members of such groups re-enact past operations. Recruits are sometimes made to lie in empty graves, so that they can see how peaceful death will be; they are reminded that life will bring sickness, old age, and betrayal. "We were in a constant state of worship," one suicide bomber (who somehow managed to survive his mission) told Hassan. "We told each other that if the Israelis only knew how joyful we were they would whip us to death! Those were the happiest days of my life!"   7

The bombers are instructed to write or videotape final testimony. (A typical note, from 1995: "I am going to take revenge upon the sons of the monkeys and the pigs, the Zionist infidels and the enemies of humanity. I am going to meet my holy brother Hisham Hamed and all the other martyrs and saints in paradise.") Once a bomber has completed his declaration, it would be humiliating for him to back out of the mission. He undergoes a last round of cleansing and prayer and is sent off with his bomb to the appointed pizzeria, coffee shop, disco, or bus.   8

For many Israelis and Westerners, the strangest aspect of the phenomenon is the televised interview with a bomber's parents after a massacre. These people have just been told that their child has killed himself and others, and yet they seem happy, proud, and—should the opportunity present itself—ready to send another child off to the afterlife. There are two ways to look at this: One, the parents feel so wronged and humiliated by the Israelis that they would rather sacrifice their children than continue passively to endure. Two, the cult of suicide bombing has infected the broader culture to the point where large parts of society, including the bombers' parents, are addicted to the adrenaline rush of vengeance and murder. Both explanations may be true.   9

It is certainly the case that vast segments of Palestinian culture have been given over to the creation and nurturing of suicide bombers. Martyrdom has replaced Palestinian independence as the main focus of the Arab media. Suicide bombing is, after all, perfectly suited to the television age. The bombers' farewell videos provide compelling footage, as do the interviews with families. The bombings themselves produce graphic images of body parts and devastated buildings. Then there are the "weddings" between the martyrs and dark-eyed virgins in paradise (announcements that read like wedding invitations are printed in local newspapers so that friends and neighbors can join in the festivities), the marches and celebrations after each attack, and the displays of things bought with the cash rewards to the families. Woven together, these images make gripping packages that can be aired again and again.   10

11   Activities in support of the bombings are increasingly widespread. Last year the BBC shot a segment about so-called Paradise Camps—summer camps in which children as young as eight are trained in military drills and taught about suicide bombers. Rallies commonly feature children wearing bombers' belts. Fifth- and sixth-graders have studied poems that celebrate the bombers. At Al Najah University, in the West Bank, a student exhibition last September included a re-created scene of the Sbarro pizzeria in Jerusalem after the suicide bombing there last August: "blood" was splattered everywhere, and mock body parts hung from the ceiling as if blown through the air.

12   Thus suicide bombing has become phenomenally popular. According to polls, 70 to 80 percent of Palestinians now support it—making the act more popular than Hamas, the Palestinian Islamic Jihad, Fatah, or any of the other groups that sponsor it, and far more popular than the peace process ever was. In addition to satisfying visceral emotions, suicide bombing gives average Palestinians, not just PLO elites, a chance to play a glorified role in the fight against Israel.

13   Opponents of suicide bombings sometimes do raise their heads. Over the last couple of years educators have moderated the tone of textbooks to reduce and in many cases eliminate the rhetoric of holy war. After the BBC report aired, Palestinian officials vowed to close the Paradise Camps. Nonetheless, Palestinian children grow up in a culture in which suicide bombers are rock stars, sports heroes, and religious idols rolled into one. Reporters who speak with Palestinians about the bombers notice the fire and pride in their eyes.

14   "I'd be very happy if my daughter killed Sharon," one mother told a reporter from *The San Diego Union-Tribune* last November. "Even if she killed two or three Israelis, I would be happy." Last year I attended a dinner party in Amman at which six distinguished Jordanians—former cabinet ministers and supreme-court justices and a journalist—talked about the Tel Aviv disco bombing, which had occurred a few months earlier. They had some religious qualms about the suicide, but the moral aspect of killing teenage girls—future breeders of Israelis—was not even worth discussing. They spoke of the attack with a quiet sense of satisfaction.

15   It's hard to know how Israel, and the world, should respond to the rash of suicide bombings and to their embrace by the Palestinian people. To take any action that could be viewed as a concession would be to provoke further attacks, as the U.S. and Israeli withdrawals from Lebanon in the 1980s demonstrated. On the other hand, the Israeli raids on the refugee camps give the suicide bombers a propaganda victory. After Yasir Arafat walked out of the Camp David meetings, he became a pariah to most governments, for killing the peace process. Now, amid Israeli retaliation for the bombings, the global community rises to condemn Israel's actions.

16   Somehow conditions must be established that would allow the frenzy of suicide bombings to burn itself out. To begin with, the Palestinian and Israeli populations would have to be separated; contact between them inflames the passions that feed the attacks. That would mean shutting down the

vast majority of Israeli settlements in the West Bank and Gaza and creating a buffer zone between the two populations. Palestinian life would then no longer be dominated by checkpoints and celebrations of martyrdom; it would be dominated by quotidian issues such as commerce, administration, and garbage collection.

The idea of a buffer zone, which is gaining momentum in Israel, is not without problems. Where, exactly, would the buffer be? Terrorist groups could shoot missiles over it. But it's time to face the reality that the best resource the terrorists have is the culture of martyrdom. This culture is presently powerful, but it is potentially fragile. If it can be interrupted, if the passions can be made to recede, then the Palestinians and the Israelis might go back to hating each other in the normal way, and at a distance. As with many addictions, the solution is to go cold turkey. 17

QUESTIONS ON SUBJECT AND PURPOSE

1. What is a martyr?
2. What does the phrase "the culture of martyrdom" suggest to you?
3. What purpose or purposes might Brooks have in his essay?

QUESTIONS ON STRATEGY AND AUDIENCE

1. How effective is Brooks's introduction?
2. How does Brooks use process in his essay?
3. To whom is Brooks writing? What assumptions does he make about his audience? How can you tell?

QUESTIONS ON VOCABULARY AND STYLE

1. What does the expression "to go cold turkey" mean? From what context is it derived? What might we call such an expression?
2. How appropriate is Brooks's final sentence as a concluding statement for the essay?
3. Be prepared to define the following words: *obliterated* (paragraph 4), *infidels* (8), *visceral* (12), *pariah* (15), *quotidian* (16).

WRITING SUGGESTIONS

1. **For Your Journal.** In your journal, reflect on how you handle conflict—with parents, friends, authority figures, or people you perceive as "enemies." Be honest with yourself. Try to think of specific situations in which you were faced with a conflict. Make a list of several. What did you do in response to that conflict? What should you have done?

2. **For a Paragraph.** Conflict often provokes counterproductive reactions. Someone screams at us; we scream louder in response. Generally, we know how we ought to react, even if we rarely do so. Expand your journal writing into a paragraph. In the paragraph offer advice in a step-by-step process about how to handle a specific type of conflict. Possible situations might include a quarrel with your parents or with a sibling, a conflict with a teacher over a grade, resentment toward a friend who clearly takes advantage of you, or your response to someone who insults or demeans you.

3. **For an Essay.** "How to Negotiate Conflicts." Expand your paragraph into an essay offering advice to your contemporaries on how to handle a commonly encountered conflict. You might want to imagine that your essay will appear in your college or university newspaper. Remember that you can address serious conflicts such as sexual, racial, or ethnic discrimination, domestic abuse, or criminal and/or immoral behavior.

4. **For Research.** What proposals have been put forth for a settlement of the Arab-Israeli conflict? How have people suggested creating a peace? What are the key steps in such a process? Research the issue. Remember to treat both sides fairly—any resolution must be equally embraced by both sides.

FOR FURTHER STUDY

Focusing on Grammar and Writing. What is a topic sentence? Look carefully at Brooks's essay. Do his paragraphs always have topic sentences? Where are they placed in his paragraphs? Are they always the first sentences? How do they help you as a reader? What does Brooks's use of topic sentences suggest about your own writing?

Working Together. What is the difference between a *martyr* and a *terrorist*? Working in small groups, brainstorm about your understanding of those two terms. What about the term *insurgent*? What does that mean? If you have a dictionary available, check the dictionary definitions. Is a martyr to one culture or faith a terrorist or insurgent to another culture or faith? What is the impact on the audience of using each word?

Seeing Other Modes at Work. Identify those portions of Brooks's essay in which he uses a cause-and-effect structure.

Finding Connections. A good pairing is with Diana Cole's "Don't Just Stand There" (also in this chapter).

Exploring the Web. The Web offers a wide variety of sources for gathering information about the Arab–Israeli conflict and about suicide bombing. In addition, you can read interviews with Brooks and check out reviews of his most recent book. Starting points can be found at **www.prenhall.com/miller.**

INTO THE LOOP: HOW TO GET THE JOB YOU WANT AFTER GRADUATION

Charlie Drozdyk

Charlie Drozdyk has had a wide range of job experiences. He has worked for the Big Apple Circus and the Brooklyn Academy of Music. He has also been theater manager at the Criterion Center on Broadway, a researcher at CBS, a director of development for a film production company, a producer of videos, and a talent agent. He is the author of Hot Jobs Handbook *(1994) and* Jobs That Don't Suck *(1998). This essay originally appeared in* Rolling Stone *magazine.*

BEFORE READING

Connecting: At this point, what expectations do you have about your first job after college?

Anticipating: What seems like the most surprising piece of information or advice in the essay?

When Benjamin Braddock, Dustin Hoffman's bewildered twenty-something hero in *The Graduate*, finished college, he was hit with a mind-numbing barrage of good wishes from well-meaning friends. Who can forget that single depressing word of advice that sent Benjamin into catatonic shock— *plastics?* It was no wonder he wound up sleeping with his girlfriend's mother and hanging out all summer at the bottom of his parents' swimming pool.

In 1995, 1.38 million college graduates will find themselves in Benjamin's shoes. They might not share *all* of his summer adventures, but with the flip of a tassel, they will soon find themselves at the bottom of the employment pool. Whom are they going to listen to?

The truth is, Benjamin had it pretty good back in 1967. Not only were jobs being created as fast as the labor force would grow, but once a job seeker got a foot in the door at an IBM or a Grey Advertising, he or she could expect to stroll the halls for some 40 years while waiting for the gold watch. Unfortunately, the Fortune 500 companies that 20 years ago employed one in five of all Americans now employ fewer than one in 10.

It's called corporate downsizing, and it's not over yet. In 1994 the largest U.S. companies dropped around 700,000 employees. But in spite of that, unemployment numbers are actually shrinking. The big guys may be busy handing out pink slips, but small employers are even busier signing up new hires.

5   But beware of *under*employment. Among the 30 fastest-growing occupations, 21 require no college degree. In fact, the 10 occupations that will pour the greatest number of jobs into the economy, in order, are salespeople (retail), registered nurses, cashiers, general office clerks, truck drivers, waiters/waitresses, nursing aides, janitors/cleaners, food-preparation workers and systems analysts. It is the service industry that will contribute the bulk—approximately two-thirds—of all new jobs.

6   So the question is, How can the class of 1995 put to use the $140 billion it spent on higher education last year? The graduates didn't spend five years—the average amount of time it now takes to get a B.A.—to land a job that doesn't require a college degree. Or did they? Well, the sad truth is that 25 percent of the class of 1995 will be working at jobs that don't require a college diploma.

7   They could always stay on campus. If you're planning on getting a master's degree, the odds of not using your education in a career will drop to 10 percent. For Ph.D.s the odds drop to a 4 percent chance. As you can see, the burger-flipping probability decreases with degrees earned. For those who are thinking about postponing the inevitable job thing, that's good news.

8   For anyone else eager to get on with a career, including Benjamin, if you're still looking, I've talked to plenty of people who have advice. And they're not talking plastics.

9   But before diving into how to get a job, there's one thing to keep in mind, and it's this: Bosses hate hiring people; in fact, they loathe and generally resent the entire process. Put yourself in a boss's shoes. The person they hired two years, or maybe just six months ago, has quit, and now they have to dig through the résumés on their desks and meet with a bunch of random strangers all over again. Or not. What they usually do is toss those résumés in the old circular file and call their friends and business associates, asking them if they know of anyone who's looking for a job.

10   This is exactly how Lauren Marino, a book editor at Hyperion (a trade-book publishing company owned by Disney), hired her assistant. She called the literary agencies she works with on a daily basis and asked her contacts if they knew anyone who was looking for a job. "Not only do they know the business already," she says, "but if someone I know recommends them, then it's not going to be a complete waste of time meeting with them."

11   So how do you get to be the person who is recommended? Get in the loop. You will never even hear of most of the job openings out there if you're not in the loop. Once you get your first job, however, you're automatically in the loop. In many companies, workers are paid to talk to people at different companies all day. And it will instantly start to make sense how the average worker manages to change jobs 7.5 times between the ages of 18 and 30. As obnoxious as the word sounds, it's all about *networking*.

12   For recent graduates without the benefits of business contacts and associates, instant entry into the loop is through a connection. For a lot of people, the word *connection* is as loathsome as that other word. Friends will snivel, "Hey, man, he only got that job because he knows somebody." Absolutely. It's how the game works. So don't discount anyone as a connection—your neighbor, your

parents' friends, your baby sitter from 10 years ago. Ask them if they know any-one—or know anyone who knows anyone—who works in the industry into which you want to get. Meet with as many people as you can for a five-minute informational interview, and then go in there and pick their brains: Are they hiring? Do they know anyone who is? (But let them think you're there to sim-ply learn what they do. They know why you're really there.)

Don't worry that you'll be bugging them. As Bill Wright-Swadel, direc- 13
tor of career services at Dartmouth College, says, "Most people who have an expertise love to talk about the things that they're knowledgeable about." Contacts aren't just about getting an interview, though. Once you've inter-viewed somewhere, find out if any alumni from your college work there—or any friend of a friend. Call that person, say you've just interviewed and ask him to make a call on your behalf. Basically, it's just someone giving testament that you're *one of them*. It's standard networking procedure—but something often ignored.

"People don't know how to network," says David McNulty, a recruiter 14
for Smith Barney. "If you want to get hired by a Wall Street firm, you should find out who went to your school and who works in the firm and call them."

Melissa Statmore, human-resources manager at J. Walter Thompson 15
advertising, agrees. "Use any connections you have," she says. "We love re-ferrals. They're taken very seriously."

RECRUITING ROULETTE

Say, however, that you've got no connections. You've just crawled out from un- 16
der the rock of your undergraduate studies, your parents live in Tibet, and you have no friends. There's always recruiting, right? Yes and no. Finding a job by interviewing with firms that show up on your campus is like getting a job through the want ads—it's a passive take-what's-being-thrown-in-front-of-you-approach. And considering that employers will visit an average of 7.4 fewer campuses in 1995 than they did in 1994, it's also a somewhat dying approach.

If you're at one of the Ivy League schools, the University of Virginia, 17
Stanford, Michigan or about a dozen select others, and if you want to work for Smith Barney, you're lucky—the company will visit your school. And if you want to work for J. Walter Thompson, and if you're at Amherst, Yale, Colby or Bates, to name a random few, you're also in luck. My senior year at school—not among the chosen few—I remember seeing recruiters from a railroad, a pharmaceutical firm and a company that had something to do with socks and underwear.

Even though it's March, and you haven't scored a job via recruiting with 18
some company you never really wanted to work for in the first place, don't worry about it—you're probably better off. Remember Lauren Marino, the editor who was looking for an assistant? When Marino was about to gradu-ate, she interviewed on campus with a printing company based in Tennessee and was offered a job. The company then had to rescind the offer because of a hiring freeze, and Marino was forced to continue searching. If the offer

hadn't been rescinded, instead of loving her life as a book editor (at only 27) in New York, she would be destined, as she puts it, to be "living in Kingsport, Tenn., a member of the Junior League and would have 10 kids."

INTERN INTO THE LOOP

19   So don't fret that you blew off that recruiter. Truth is, if you're about to graduate, it may not be you they're after. The new trend in recruiting is lassoing sophomores and juniors as interns, giving them a summer or semester of experience and then hiring them as soon as they're done with school. This gives the company a chance to see if they fit in and saves time and money in training.

20   But just because you're about to graduate doesn't mean you can't still intern. In fact, you probably should. In a survey by the College Placement Council, employers say that three out of 10 new hires will be former interns. Christian Breheney is part of that 30 percent. Right before she was about to graduate a semester early from Johns Hopkins and armed with her Spanish major, she saw a flier on a bulletin board and ripped it off the wall. After she was offered the nonpaying internship at *Late Night with David Letterman*, she put the flier back up.

21   Some of her friends thought that Breheney's decision to work for free was questionable. After all, she was about to be a college graduate. Her plan worked, though. After four months of commuting from New Jersey five days a week, working from 10 A.M. to 7 P.M., she got her break. A receptionist quit, and Breheney got the job. How? "If you're well liked and make a good impression, you can get hired right off of your internship," she says. Which is something that happens quite often, apparently, as she lists about a dozen full timers who started as interns.

22   Two years later and now the assistant to the head writer at the *Late Show with David Letterman*, Breheney has yet to send out a single résumé. It's just been a matter of "moving up that ladder," she says gleefully.

TEMP INTO THE LOOP

23   The cost-effective benefits in hiring interns—pretrained, proven commodities—are the same reason that temps (temporary employees who are hired to fill in when needed) are landing full-time jobs at the companies where they're assigned. Thirty-eight percent of all temporary workers are offered full-time employment while on an assignment.

24   Temping has become a recruiting technique in itself, not just a means of replacing somebody when he or she is out sick. It's becoming known as "temping to perm." As Jules Young, president of Friedman Personnel Agency, in West Hollywood, Calif., says: "Temping is like living with someone before you marry them. A lot of placement is based on chemistry between the people you're going to work with. That's why a temp is a good way to go—because it gives the employer a chance to check out whether the chemistry matches."

At many large companies like Nike or Paramount Pictures—as well as   25
most of the faster-growing small companies (200 employees or fewer) that by
the year 2000 will employ 85 percent of all Americans—a great way in, and a
fairly common one, is through temping. The best way to go is to call the company you want to work for and ask which temp agency they use. Then call that
agency, go in and pass its typing test and boom! You're in the door. Get familiar with some of the more popular computer programs (WordPerfect, Mi-
crosoft Word, Excel and Lotus 1-2-3)—the agencies are going to be looking
for them.

THE PERSONNEL MYTH

We're practically programmed to do it. We make a list of the companies we   26
want to work for, write a standard cover letter (changing the name of the company and the person to whom we're sending it, of course) and drop that and a
résumé in the mailbox. A hundred letters sent to 100 personnel departments.
Probability alone suggests that at least one or two interviews will come out of
it, right? Not likely. You know how many résumés Nike got in 1994? More
than 23,000. It hired 511 people. Smith Barney hired around 80 people last
year from a pool of applicants that numbered about 10,000. Do the math: The
odds aren't good.

When Lauren Marino decided to go into publishing, she sent résumés   27
to every publishing house in New York. You know how many interviews she
got? Zero. As she realizes now, "That was a huge waste of my time. Personnel departments don't hire anybody. The only way to get an editorial job
in publishing is by knowing somebody or by sending a letter directly to the
editor."

Although it's not a rule to live by, most people don't use their company's   28
personnel departments for a job search. If you want to work at a company, pin-
point which department you want to work in and then find the person who
can make a hiring decision. Approach that person directly.

If you don't know anybody who knows anybody who knows anybody   29
who knows the person with whom you want to work—or under—at a specific
company, then you're going to have to be a little resourceful. The first tactic
is obvious. Cold-call them. Pick up the phone and try to get the person on the
line. Tell him truthfully how you would really love to work for his company
and would love to meet with him for five minutes. Chances are you're not going to get past this person's assistant, however.

This is exactly what happened to Michael Landau when he called the na-   30
tional sales manager (he got her name from a friend) at Nicole Miller, a New
York fashion-design company. The first four times he called, he got an assistant on the phone who was nice enough but wouldn't put her boss on the
phone. This is what assistants are for.

Figuring that the assistant probably left at around 6 P.M., Landau called   31
at 6:30, thinking the boss might still be there—and if so, would pick up her
own phone. She was, and she did. She was nice to him but said there wasn't

anything available. Standard stuff, but Landau was persistent, and as luck would have it, the CEO of the company walked into the sales manager's office. "Talk to this guy, he sounds good," the sales manager said to her colleague. The exec repeated that the company wasn't hiring but that it was, however, always interested in meeting good people.

32   At that moment, Landau decided to fly to New York, a trip he told them he just happened to be taking. Landau started out in sales and is now happily employed in the public-relations department at Nicole Miller.

SAY YES

33   This is the first thing you should know about interviewing: If someone asks you in an interview if you know a certain computer program (which you don't) or if you know how to drive a car (and you never have), just say yes. As Sheryl Vandermolen, a junior designer at Robert Metzger Interiors, says: "It's all about selling yourself and believing in yourself. Don't say you think you can, say you can—even if you don't know if you can."

RESEARCH

34   "Please do your research," says Cheryl Nickerson, director of employment for Nike. "Be able to ask intelligent questions about the company and what's going on in the industry. [As an employer] you're making a judgment about that person's curiosity, their willingness to learn and grow." And where do you find information about the company? Start by reading the firm's annual report. Not doing this is a "cardinal sin," says David McNulty of Smith Barney. Just call up the company and ask that a report be mailed to you. You don't even have to leave your couch.

GET PSYCHED

35   Employers want someone who's going to come in and kick ass. Interviews are about convincing the employer that you're that person. As Brian Johnson, co-owner of the Dogwater Cafe, a fast-growing restaurant chain in Florida, says, "When I'm interviewing, I'm looking for someone with a lot of energy who wants this job more than anything. I want them to basically beg me not to interview anybody else—that this is their job."

FOLLOW UP

36   When I was in Jules Young's office at the Friedman agency, a young woman who had just had an interview with someone at the William Morris Agency called to report back that it had gone well. Without pausing, Young said, "Drop a note off to her in the morning thanking her and saying you really want the job. Drop it off in person to the reception desk."

"I don't think people [write thank-you notes] as much as they think they   37
should anymore," says Nike's Cheryl Nickerson. "If you're in the running,
that special touch of following up to say thank you may be the edge that you
need." Sometimes, however, a thank-you letter isn't enough to push you over
that edge. You need to do more. You need to . . .

BE PERSISTENT

When Tracy Grandstaff interviewed for her first job, at MTV, she was told   38
that they would let her know quickly since they needed someone right away.
"It took three months of me hounding this woman to get that job," she says.
"I called her constantly. She couldn't make a decision." Finally, the woman
told Grandstaff that it was between her and someone else and that she just
couldn't decide. To which Grandstaff said, "Flat out: What do I have to say to
you to give me the edge? What do you want to hear, and I'll say it. What do
you want me to do? I'll do it." Apparently these questions were what the MTV
executive wanted to hear. Grandstaff got the job.

BE NICE TO THE INTERVIEWER'S SECRETARY

A survey of executives at the country's largest companies found that nearly   39
two-thirds of the interviewers consider the opinion of their administrative assistants with regard to the interviewee who walks past them on their way in
and out of their bosses' offices. So be smart and just say, "I just had some water, I'm fine, thank you," when they ask you if you would like anything to
drink. Asking for a coffee, light, one sugar, isn't going to score you points.

There's no formula to any of this. Some applicants get really lucky and   40
land something quickly. Most, however, collect a few horror stories to tell.
And that's the reality: At best, getting a job has always been an elusive and difficult task. So whatever you do, don't get sucked into that slacker pity party
presently taking place on couches and in bars everywhere, the one that goes
like this: "Man, there's no jobs available. The baby boomers took them all."

As Greg Drebin, vice president of programming at MTV, says, "When   41
people say, 'Well, now is a really hard time for the industry,' and all that . . .
well, it's always a hard time. There's no such thing as 'Oh, it's hiring season;
we've got all these jobs that just became available.' You know what? There's
always jobs, and there's never jobs."

QUESTIONS ON SUBJECT AND PURPOSE

1. Drozdyk's opening example is drawn from a film, *The Graduate*, made
   in 1967. How effective is that example? Why might he use it?
2. Are there ever times in Drozdyk's essay when you disagree or feel
   uncomfortable with the advice that he is giving?
3. What assumptions does Drozdyk make about the reasons why people
   attend college? Do you agree with those assumptions?

QUESTIONS ON STRATEGY AND AUDIENCE

1. Why might Drozdyk title the essay "Into the Loop"?
2. Drozdyk quotes from a number of people throughout the essay. Why might he do so, and how effective is the strategy?
3. To whom is Drozdyk writing? How specifically can you define that audience?

QUESTIONS ON VOCABULARY AND STYLE

1. How would you characterize the tone of Drozdyk's essay? (See the glossary for a definition of *tone*.)
2. Find examples of words or expressions that Drozdyk uses to connect with an audience of late teenagers and "twentysomethings."
3. Be prepared to define the following words and phrases: *barrage* (paragraph 1), *catatonic* (1), *snivel* (12), *rescind* (18), *proven commodities* (23), *cold-call* (29), *cardinal sin* (34).

WRITING SUGGESTIONS

1. **For Your Journal.** Jot down in your journal a list of possible internships or volunteer positions for which you might apply. Remember that such positions might not involve specific job skills but rather particular "people" skills that are transferable to many jobs. Visit your college's placement office for possible suggestions as well. Your major department might also be a source of information.
2. **For a Paragraph.** Using your list, the advice in Drozdyk's essay, and any advice that you can get from your college's placement office, write a paragraph in which you describe the process by which you (or anyone else) would apply for a specific internship or volunteer position.
3. **For an Essay.** Write an essay in which you offer advice on how an undergraduate at your college can locate and apply for internships and volunteer positions. With your instructor's approval, you might consider writing the essay for your school's student newspaper or as a brochure that could be handed out by the placement office.
4. **For Research.** In what ways is electronic communication changing the nature of a job search? For example, increasing numbers of individuals are mounting personal Web pages that advertise their talents and skills in ways somewhat similar to the old printed résumé. How are the new technologies influencing job search strategies? Research the problem and the future directions. Remember that source information will have to be current, so look for very recent books and articles. You might want to use the World Wide Web to find examples, as well, or interview people. In a researched essay, bring Drozdyk's advice up to date for the early 2000s.

FOR FURTHER STUDY

Focusing on Grammar and Writing. Drozdyk uses a large number of quotations from interviewers. Look carefully at how he integrates these quotations into his essay. Try writing a set of guidelines for your classmates on how to integrate quotations into an essay.

Working Together. Working in small groups, brainstorm about how a first-year college student might find a great summer job. What do each of you plan to do this summer? How would you go about finding a great summer job? What would be "great" about that job? Where on campus or on the Web could you go for help in your job search?

Seeing Other Modes at Work. Locate the places in the essay in which Drozdyk uses a cause-and-effect strategy.

Finding Connections. The process example in the introductory section of this chapter, "Getting the Interview Edge 'Apprentice-Style'" is a good pairing.

Exploring the Web. Can the Web help you find a job? What Web resources are available for job seekers? If you post your résumé on the Web, what are your chances of finding a job? Are there any dangers or risks in using the Web to search for a job or to post a résumé? For some tips on where to begin, go to **www.prenhall.com/miller.**

STRIPPED FOR PARTS

Jennifer Kahn

A graduate of Princeton and the University of California, Berkeley, Jennifer Kahn is a writer and a contributing editor to magazines such as Wired *and* National Geographic. *In 2003, she was awarded a journalism fellowship from the American Academy of Neurology; in 2004, the CASE-UCLA media fellowship in neuroscience. "Stripped for Parts" first appeared in* Wired *in 2003.*

On Writing: *Commenting on the essay, Kahn noted: "It was one of those stories that turn out to be dramatically different from the original assignment. Basically, I'd been sent out to find out what was new in the world of transplant surgery: the standard 'hooray for scientific progress' tale. Instead I was struck by how fragile the organ recovery process was. . . . In the end the piece was quite controversial; there were a lot of angry letters from people who accused me of discouraging donation."*

BEFORE READING

Connecting: What do know about organ donations? Are you are organ donor? Many states allow this designation to be placed on a driver's license.

Anticipating: What surprises you the most in the essay?

1   The television in the dead man's room stays on all night. Right now the program is *Shipmates*, a reality-dating drama that's barely audible over the hiss of the ventilator. It's 4 AM, and I've been here for six hours, sitting in the corner while three nurses fuss intermittently over a set of intravenous drips. They're worried about the dead man's health.

2   To me, he looks fine. His face is slack but flush, he breathes steadily, and his heart beats like a clock, despite the fact that his lungs have recently begun to leak fluid. The nurses roll the body from side to side periodically so that the liquid doesn't pool. At one point, a white plastic vest designed to clear the lungs inflates and begins to vibrate violently—as if some invisible person has seized the dead man by the shoulders and is trying to shake him awake. The rest of the time, the nurses consult monitors and watch for signs of cardiac arrest. When someone scratches the bottom of the dead man's foot, it twitches.

3   None of this is what I expected from an organ transplant. When I arrived last night at this Northern California hospital I was prepared to see a fast-paced surgery culminating in renewal: the mortally ill patient restored to glorious health. In all my preliminary research on transplants, the dead man was rarely mentioned. Even doctors I spoke with avoided the subject, and popular accounts I came across ducked the matter of provenance altogether. In the movies, for instance, surgeons tended to say it would take time to "find"

a heart—as though one had been hidden behind a tree or misplaced along with the car keys. Insofar as corpses came up, it was only in anxious reference to the would-be recipient whose time was running out.

In the dead man's room, a different calculus is unfolding. Here the or- 4
gan is the patient, and the patient a mere container, the safest place to store body parts until surgeons are ready to use them. It can be more than a day from the time a donor dies until his organs are harvested—the surgery alone takes hours, not to mention the time needed to do blood tests, match tissue, and fly in special surgical teams for the evisceration. And yet, a heart lasts at most six hours outside the body, even after it has been kneaded, flushed with preservatives, and packed in a cooler. Organs left on ice too long tend to per- form poorly in their new environment, and doctors are picky about which vis- cera they're willing to work with. Even an ailing cadaver is a better container than a cooler.

These conditions create a strange medical specialty. Rather than extract- 5
ing this man's vitals right away, the hospital contacts the California Transplant Donor Network, which dispatches a procurement team to begin "donor main- tenance": the process of artificially supporting a dead body until recipients are ready. When the parathyroid gland stops regulating calcium, key to keeping the heart pumping, the team sends the proper amount down an intravenous drip. When blood pressure drops, they add vasoconstrictors, which contract the blood vessels. Normally the brain would compensate for a decrease in blood pressure, but with it out of commission, the three-nurse procurement team must take over.

In this case, the eroding balance will have to be sustained for almost 24 6
hours. The goal is to fool the body into believing that it's alive and well, even as everything is falling apart. As one crew member concedes, "It's unbelievable that all this stuff is being done to a dead person."

Unbelievable and, to me, somehow barbaric. Sustaining a dead body un- 7
til its organs can be harvested is a tricky process requiring the latest in med- ical technology. But it's also a distinct anachronism in an era when medicine is becoming less and less invasive. Fixing blocked coronary arteries, which not long ago required prying a patient's chest open with a saw and spreader, can now be accomplished with a tiny stent delivered to the heart on a slender wire threaded up the leg. Exploratory surgery has given way to robot cameras and high-resolution imaging. Already, we are eyeing the tantalizing summit of gene therapy, where diseases are cured even before they do damage. Compared with such microscale cures, transplants—which consist of salvaging entire organs from a heart-beating cadaver and sewing them into a different body—seem crudely mechanical, even medieval.

"To let an organ reach a state where the only solution is to cut it out is 8
not progress; it's a failure of medicine," says pathologist Neil Theise of NYU. Theise, who was the first researcher to demonstrate that stem cells can become liver cells in humans, argues that the future of transplantation lies in regener- ation. Within five years, he estimates, we'll be able to instruct the body to send stem cells to the liver from the store that exists in bone marrow, hopefully

countering the effects of a disease like hepatitis A or B and letting the body heal itself. And numerous researchers are forging similar paths. One outspoken surgeon, Richard Satava from the University of Washington, says that medicine is only now catching on to the fundamental lesson of modern industry, which is that when our car alternator breaks, we get a brand new one. Transplantation, he argues, is a dying art.

9   Few researchers predict that human-harvested organs will become obsolete anytime soon, however; one cardiovascular pathologist, Charles Murry, says we'll still be using them a century from now. But it's reasonable to expect—and hope for—an alternative. "I don't think anybody enjoys recovering organs," Murry says frankly. "You tell yourself it's for a good cause, which it is, a very good cause, but you're still butchering a human."

10   Intensive care is not a good place to spend the evening. Tonight, the ward has perhaps 12 patients, including a woman who moans constantly and a deathly pale man who reportedly jumped out the window of a moving Greyhound bus. The absence of clocks and the always-on lights create a casino-like timelessness. In the staff lounge, which smells of stale pizza, a lone nurse corners me and describes watching a man bleed to death ("He was conscious. He knew what was happening"), and announces, sotto voce, that she knows of South American organ brokers who charge $60,000 for a heart, then swap it for a baboon's.

11   Although I don't admit it to the procurement team, I've grown attached to the dead man. There's something vulnerable about his rumpled hair and middle-aged body, naked save a waist-high sheet. Under the hospital lights, everything is exposed: the muscular arms gone flabby above the elbow; the legs, wiry and lean, foreshortened under a powerful torso. It's the body of a man in his fifties, simultaneously bullish and elfin. One foot, the right, peeps out from the sheet, and for a brief moment I want to hold it and rub the toes that must be cold—a hopeless gesture of consolation.

12   Organ support is about staving off entropy. In the moments after death, a cascade of changes sweeps over the body. Potassium diminishes and salt accumulates, drawing fluid into cells. Sugar builds up in the blood. With the pituitary system offline, the heart fills with lactic acid like the muscles of an exhausted runner. Free radicals circulate unchecked and disrupt other cells, in effect causing the body to rust. The process quickly becomes irreversible. As cell membranes grow porous, a "death gene" is activated and damaged cells begin to self-destruct. All this happens in minutes.

13   When transplant activists talk about an organ shortage, it's usually to lament how few people are willing to donate. This is a valid worry, but it eclipses an important point, which is that the window for retrieving a viable organ is staggeringly small. Because of how fast the body degrades once the heart stops, there's no way to recover an organ from someone who dies at home, in a car, in an ambulance, or even while on the operating table. In fact, the only situation that really lends itself to harvest is brain death, which means finding an otherwise healthy patient whose brain activity has ceased but whose heart continues to beat—right up until the moment it's taken out. In short,

victims of stroke or severe head injury. These cases are so rare (approximately 0.5 percent of all deaths in the US) that even if everybody in America were to become a donor, they wouldn't clear the organ wait lists.

This is partly a scientific problem. Cell death remains poorly understood, and for years now, cadaveric transplants have lingered on a research plateau. While immunosuppressants have improved incrementally, transplants proceed much as they did 20 years ago. Compared with a field like psychopharmacology, the procedure has come to a near-standstill.   14

But there are cultural factors as well. Medicine has always reserved its glory for the living. Even among transplant surgeons, a hierarchy exists: Those who put organs into living patients have a higher status than those who extract them from the dead. One anesthesiologist confesses that his peers don't like to work on cadaveric organ recoveries. (Even brain-dead bodies require sedation, since spinal reflexes can make a corpse "buck" in surgery.) "You spend all this time monitoring the heartbeat, the blood pressure," the anesthesiologist explains. "To just turn everything off when you're done and walk out. It's bizarre."   15

Although the procurement team will stay up all night, I break at 4:30 AM for a two-hour nap on an empty bed in the ICU. The nurse removes a wrinkled top sheet but leaves the bottom one. Doctors sleep like this all the time, I know, catnapping on gurneys, but I can't shake the feeling of climbing onto my deathbed. The room is identical to the one I've been sitting in for the past eight hours, and I'd prefer to sleep almost anywhere else—in the nurses lounge or even on the small outside balcony. Instead, I lie down in my clothes and pull the sheet up under my arms.   16

For a while I read a magazine, then finally close my eyes, hoping I won't dream.   17

By morning, little seems to have changed, except that the commotion of chest X-rays and ultrasounds has left the dead man's hair more mussed. On both sides of his bed, vital stats scroll across screens: oxygen ratios, pulse, blood volumes.   18

All of this vigilance is good, of course: After all, transplants save lives. Every year, thousands of people who would otherwise die survive with organs from brain-dead donors; sometimes, doctors say, a patient's color will visibly change on the operating table once a newly attached liver begins to work. Still—and with the possible exception of kidneys—transplants have never quite lived up to their initial promise. In the early 1970s, few who received new organs lasted even a year, and most died within weeks. Even today, 22 percent of heart recipients die in less than four years, and 12 percent reject a new heart within the first few months. Those who survive are usually consigned to a lifetime regime of costly immunosuppressive drugs, some with debilitating side effects. Recipients of artificial hearts traditionally fare the worst, alongside those who receive transplants from animals. Under the circumstances, it took a weird kind of perseverance for doctors operating in 1984 to suggest sewing a walnut-sized baboon heart into a human baby. And there was grief, if not surprise, when the patient died of a morbid immune reaction just 21 days later.   19

***

20   By the time we head into surgery, the patient has been dead for more than 24 hours, but he still looks pink and healthy. In the operating room, all the intravenous drips are still flowing, convincing the body that everything's fine even as it's cleaved in half.

21   Although multiorgan transfer can involve as many as five teams in the OR at once, this time there is only one: a four-man surgical unit from Southern California. They've flown in to retrieve the liver, but because teams sometimes swap favors, they'll also remove the kidneys for a group of doctors elsewhere—saving them a last-minute, late-night flight. One of the doctors has brought a footstool for me to stand on at the head of the operating table, so that I can see over the sheet that hangs between the patient's head and body. I've been warned that the room will smell bad during the "opening," like flesh and burning bone—an odor that has something in common with a dentist's drill. Behind me, the anesthesiologist checks the dead man's mask and confirms that he's sedated. The surgery will take four hours, and the doctors have arranged for the score of Game Five of the World Series to be phoned in at intervals.

22   I've heard that transplant doctors are the endurance athletes of medicine, and the longer I stand on the stool, the better I understand the comparison. Below me, the rib cage has been split, and I can see the heart, strangely yellow, beating inside a cave of red muscle. It doesn't beat forward, as I expect, but knocks anxiously back and forth like a small animal trapped in a cage. Farther down, the doctors rummage under the slough of intestines as though through a poorly organized toolbox. When I tell the anesthesiologist that the heart is beautiful, he says that livers are the transplants to watch. "Hearts are slash and burn," he shrugs, adjusting a dial. "No finesse."

23   Two hours pass, and the surgeons make progress. Despite the procurement team's best efforts, however, most of the organs have already been lost. The pancreas was deemed too old before surgery. One lung was bad at the outset, and the other turned out to be too big for the only matching recipients—a short list given the donor's rare blood type. At 7 this morning, the heart went bust after someone at the receiving hospital suggested a shot of thyroid hormone, shown in some studies to stimulate contractions—but even before then, the surgeon had had second thoughts. A 54-year-old heart can't travel far—and this one was already questionable—but the hospital may have thought this would improve its chances. Instead, the dead man's pulse shot to 140, and his blood began circulating so fast it nearly ruptured his arteries. Now the heart will go to Cryolife, a biosupply company that irradiates and freeze-dries the valves, then packages them for sale to hospitals in screw-top jars. The kidneys have remained healthy enough to be passed on—one to a man who will soon be in line for a pancreas, the other to a 42-year-old woman.

24   Both kidneys have been packed off in quart-sized plastic jars. Originally, the liver was going to a nearby hospital, but an ultrasound suggested it was hyperechoic, or probably fatty. On the second pass, it was accepted by a doctor in Southern California and ensconced in a bag of icy slurry.

25   The liver is enormous—it looks like a polished stone, flat and purplish—and with it gone, the body seems eerily empty, although the heart continues

to beat. Watching this pumping vessel makes me oddly anxious. It's sped up slightly, as though sensing what will happen next. Below me, the man's face is still flushed. He's the one I wish would survive, I realize, even though there was never any chance of that. Meanwhile, the head surgeon has walked away. He's busy examining the liver and relaying a description over the phone to the doctor who will perform the attachment. Almost unnoticed, an aide clamps the arteries above and below the heart, and cuts. The patient's face doesn't move, but its pinkness drains to a waxy yellow. After 24 hours, the dead man finally looks dead.

Once all the organs are out, the tempo picks up in the operating room. 26 The heart is packed in a cardboard box also loaded with the kidneys, which are traveling by Learjet to a city a few hundred miles away. Someday, I'm convinced, transporting organs in coolers will seem as strange and outdated as putting a patient in an iron lung. In the meantime, transplants will survive: a vehicle, like the dead man, to get us to a better place. As an assistant closes, sewing up the body so that it will be ready for its funeral, I get on the plane with the heart and the kidneys. They've become a strange, unhealthy orange in their little jars. But no one else seems worried. "A kidney almost always perks up," someone tells me, "once we get it in a happier environment."

QUESTIONS ON SUBJECT AND PURPOSE

1. What did Kahn expect to see at an organ transplant operation?
2. Why does Kahn get on the airplane with the heart and kidneys at the end of the story?
3. Having read the essay, have you changed your attitude toward organ donation? Do you think that Kahn wants to change your opinion?

QUESTIONS ON STRATEGY AND AUDIENCE

1. Why might Kahn have titled the essay "Stripped for Parts"? What associations do you have with that phrase?
2. How effective is the opening paragraph? Does it make you want to keep reading?
3. What could Kahn assume about her audience?

QUESTIONS ON VOCABULARY AND STYLE

1. How is the story told or narrated to the reader? How else might the story have been told?
2. How would you describe the tone of the essay?
3. Be prepared to define the following words: *culminating* (paragraph 3), *provenance* (3), *evisceration* (4), *viscera* (4), *anachronism* (7), *sotto voce* (10), *elfin* (11), *entropy* (12), *debilitating* (19), *morbid* (19), *slough* (22), *hyperechoic* (24), *ensconced* (24).

WRITING SUGGESTIONS

1. **For Your Journal.** Why is this side of organ donation—that is, the harvesting—ignored? Record your impressions and feelings about the whole process in your journal. You are not constructing an argument; you are just recording your emotions and reactions.

2. **For a Paragraph.** Based on your impressions recorded in your journal, what would you want to happen to you if you had a fatal accident?

3. **For an Essay.** Living wills have been much in the news recently. What is the process through which one makes a living will? What are the options? How is it worded? Consult some print or online sources to gather information. Then, in an essay aimed at an audience of your contemporaries, describe the process of making such a will.

4. **For Research.** In paragraph 8, Kahn quotes a stem-cell researcher who "argues that the future of transplantation lies in regeneration" through instructing the body to "send stem cells" from one part of the body to regenerate other organs in the body. The researcher says that "within five years" we might be able to do that. What is the state of stem-cell research right now, and how close are researchers to being able to regenerate organs rather than transplant them? Research the issue and the technology through online and print sources, and in a research essay, describe the process by which scientists think that this might be possible.

FOR FURTHER STUDY

Focusing on Grammar and Writing. Kahn makes extensive use of the dash in the essay. Identify all the occurrences in the essay and see if you can classify them according to the grammatical situations in which they occur. Can you then write a list of rules under which the dash is used in writing?

Working Together. Divide into groups. Each group should take a couple of paragraphs from the essay and rewrite the paragraphs so that the "I" of the narrator is replaced with an objective third person. What happens to the story when that is done? Can you see why Kahn chose to tell the story from her own point of view—as an observer who watched the whole process?

Seeing Other Modes at Work. The essay is a narrative; it also has elements of description and cause and effect (in the description of why and how the body breaks down so quickly).

Finding Connections. The essay could be linked with Wilfred Owen's "Dulce et Decorum" (Chapter 9) and with Virginia Woolf's "Death of a Moth" (10).

Exploring the Web. Many sites on the Web are devoted to organ donation. For some suggestions, visit **www.prenhall.com/miller.**

CAUSE AND EFFECT

PREPARING TO WRITE

WHAT IS CAUSE AND EFFECT?

It is a rainy morning and you are late for class. Driving to campus in an automobile with faulty brakes, you have an accident. Considering the circumstances, the accident might be attributable to a variety of causes:

> You were driving too fast.
> The visibility was poor.
> The roads were slippery.
> The brakes did not work properly.

Visually, cause and effect can be displayed in diagrams, called "fishbone" diagrams, which are tools used to analyze and display possible causes. If we used a fishbone diagram to analyze your accident, it might look like this:

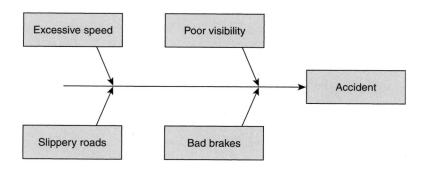

The diagram could also branch out further since the accident, in turn, could produce a series of consequences or effects:

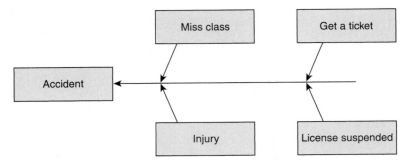

Susan Strasser, for example, uses a cause-and-effect strategy when she suggests that part of the popularity of fast-food restaurants lies in the appeal of "stylized, repetitive, stereotyped events." Notice how Strasser structures the following paragraph to show how this ritualization is one "cause" for such restaurants' popularity:

> People arrive at McDonald's—and to a lesser extent at the other chains—knowing what they will eat, what they will pay, what to say to the counter person and how she or he will respond, what the restaurant will look like—in short, knowing exactly what to expect and how to behave; children learn these expectations and behaviors early in life. For some, the ritual constitutes an attraction of these restaurants; they neither wish to cook nor to chat with a waitress as she intones and delivers the daily specials. The fast-food ritual requires no responsibility other than ordering (with as few words as possible) and paying; nobody has to set or clear the table, wash the dishes, or compliment the cook on her cuisine, the traditional responsibilities of husbands and children at the family dinner.*

Strasser turns her analysis of fast-food restaurants in the other direction—toward effects—when she discusses how "fast food eating" has affected mealtime rituals at home:

> Fast foods have changed eating habits far beyond the food itself; they have invaded the mealtime ritual even at home. The chief executive officer of Kraft, Inc., maintained that eating out accustomed people to "portion control" and therefore to accepting a processor's statement that a package of macaroni and cheese serves four. "Generally speaking," one writer claimed in *Advertising Age*, "the homemaker no longer sets the table with dishes of food from which the family fills their plates—the individual plates are filled and placed before the family, no second helpings." Eating out even accustoms diners at the same table to eating different food, putting home meals of different prepared foods within the realm of possibility and altering the nature of parental discipline; freed from the "shut up—you'll eat what we're eating" rule, children experience the pleasures and also the isolation of individual free choice at earlier ages.

*Susan Strasser, *Never Done: A History of American Housework* (New York: Random House, 1982), pp. 296–97.

Causes and effects can be either immediate or remote with reference to time. The lists regarding the hypothetical car accident suggest only immediate causes and effects, things that could be most directly linked in time to the accident. Another pair of lists of more remote causes and effects could be compiled—for example, your brakes were faulty because you did not have the money to fix them, or because of your accident, your insurance rates will go up.

Causes and effects can be either primary or secondary with reference to their significance or importance. If you had not been in a hurry and driving too fast, it might not have mattered that the visibility was poor, the roads were slippery, or your brakes were faulty. Similarly, if you or someone else had been injured, the other consequences would have seemed insignificant in comparison.

In some instances, causes and effects are linked in a causal chain: if you were driving too fast and tried to stop on slippery roads with inadequate brakes, each of those causes is interlinked in the inevitable accident. Likewise, the accident means that you will get a ticket, that ticket carries points against your license, your license could as a result be suspended, and either way your insurance rates will certainly climb.

WHY DO YOU WRITE A CAUSE-AND-EFFECT ANALYSIS?

Cause-and-effect analyses are intended to reveal the reasons why something happened or the consequences of a particular occurrence. E. M. Forster in "My Wood" examines the consequences of owning property. Joan Jacobs Brumberg in "The Origins of Anorexia Nervosa" examines some of the causes of anorexia nervosa, tracing the disease back to its origins in middle-class families in the nineteenth century. Brent Staples in "Black Men and Public Space" uses his own experiences as an urban night walker to explore the effects that he, as a black male, has on those who share the streets with him. Veronica Chambers in "Dreadlocked" explains both why she wears her hair in dreadlocks and what those "dreads" suggest to people. Andres Martin in "On Teenagers and Tattoos" explores some of the reasons why tattoos and body piercings appeal to adolescents. Finally, Malcolm Gladwell in "The Trouble with Fries" tackles the question of why, when we all know better, we consume so much fast food and resist attempts to make it healthier for us.

Cause-and-effect analyses can also be used to persuade readers to do or believe something. Andres Martin's analysis of body markings and teenagers is written to an audience of clinicans who work with adolescents. His analysis is also persuasive for he suggests that such markings provide a point of contact with patients and offer insights into their perceptions of self and reality. Brent Staples's experiences as an urban night walker challenge all of us when we realize how quickly and easily we form stereotypes—a young, large black man dressed casually on an urban street must be dangerous, must be someone to avoid. Malcolm Gladwell, although he does not ask us to stop eating fast-food fries, does force us to stop and think about our own behavior: Why do we do this even when we are fully aware that it is unhealthy?

How Do You Choose a Subject?

In picking a subject to analyze, first remember the limits of your assignment. The larger the subject, the more difficult it will be to do justice to. Trying to analyze the causes of the Vietnam War or the effects of technology in five hundred words is an invitation to disaster. Second, make sure that the relationships you see between causes and effects are genuine. The fact that a particular event preceded another does not necessarily mean that the first caused the second. In logic this error is labeled *post hoc, ergo propter hoc* ("after this, therefore because of this"). If a black cat crossed the street several blocks before your automobile accident, that does not mean that the cat was a cause of the accident.

How Do You Isolate and Evaluate Causes and Effects?

Before you begin to write, take time to analyze and, if necessary, research your subject thoroughly. It is important that your analysis consider all of the major factors involved in the relationship. Relatively few things are the result of a single cause, and rarely does a cause have a single effect. Owning a piece of property—even if it is something that cannot possibly be stolen—can have a number of effects on you, as E. M. Forster discovers. He becomes far more preoccupied by his property than he ever thought possible. Veronica Chambers discovers that her dreadlocks conjure up in people's minds a whole series of different identities. She is, in the eyes of others, simultaneously a "rebel child, Rasta mama, Nubian princess, drug dealer, unemployed artist, rock star, world-famous comedienne, and nature chick."

Prewriting Suggestions

1. Choose a subject that can be analyzed within the amount of space that you have available.
2. Decide whether you are exploring causes or effects. In a short paper, it is probably not possible to do both.
3. Make a list of possible causes and effects. Test each item on your list to make sure that it is a likely cause or effect—just because something happens before or after your subject does not necessarily mean that it is a cause or an effect.
4. Rank the causes or effects in terms of their significance. Typically, you are not asked to analyze all of the possible causes or effects. You are to focus on the most important ones. In a short paper, you will probably not treat more than three to five causes or effects.
5. Remember your audience. How much do they already know about the subject? Will your analysis be too complex and technical? Will it be too obvious? Either extreme presents problems.

ɔn your subject, your analysis could be based on personal ex-
ful reflection and examination, or research. E. M. Forster's
:cts of owning property is derived completely from studying
. Brent Staples draws on his own personal experiences and
ɔlack journalist. Veronica Chambers's analysis of the effects
is based on the reactions of those around her. Andres Mar-
ɪdolescent psychiatry, and his analysis depends on his expe-
ɪnts and his knowledge of published research. Clearly
l has researched his essay on french fries, for he quotes from
: sources. Joan Jacobs Brumberg's essay is also built on ex-
:specially in sources in history, literature, medicine, and psy-
selections show, sometimes causes and effects are certain and
ɪt other times, the relationships are only probable or even

_____ ɪave gathered a list of possible causes or effects, the next
step is to evaluate each item. Any phenomenon can have many causes or
many effects, so you will have to select the explanations that seem the most
relevant or most convincing. Rarely should you list every cause or every effect you can find. Generally, you choose the causes or effects that are immediate and primary, although the choice is always determined by your
purpose.

WRITING

HOW DO YOU STRUCTURE A CAUSE-AND-EFFECT ANALYSIS?

By definition, causes precede effects, so a cause-and-effect analysis involves a
linear or chronological order. Most commonly, you structure your analysis to
reflect that sequence. If you are analyzing causes, typically you begin by identifying the subject that you are trying to explain and then move to analyze its
causes. Malcolm Gladwell begins by narrating McDonald's founder Ray
Kroc's role in the scientific development of the fast-food french fry. The perfection of the french fry has had, however, serious health consequences. Gladwell points to some possible solutions to the unhealthy french fry, but then
explores why American consumers seem unwilling to demand that fast food
become healthy food. Knowing the health risks, and having alternative answers at hand, why do we persist in eating unhealthy food?

If you are analyzing effects, typically you begin by identifying the subject that produced the effects and then move to enumerate or explain what
those effects were. E. M. Forster begins by describing how he came to purchase his "wood" and then describes four distinct effects that ownership had
on him.

A cause-and-effect analysis can also go in both directions. Veronica Chambers begins by remembering what it was like to have "bad" nappy hair and what
that meant in the black community in the late 20th century. She explains the
causes that led to her decision to wear her hair in dreadlocks. But Chambers also

moves forward, looking then at the effects that her hairstyle had on others. "My hair," she writes, "says a lot of things."

Within these patterns, you face one other choice: If you are listing multiple causes or effects, how do you decide in what order to treat them? That arrangement depends on whether or not the reasons or consequences are linked in a chain. If they happen in a definite sequence, you would arrange them in an order to reflect that sequence—normally a chronological order (this happened, then this, and finally this). This linear arrangement is very similar to what you do in a process narrative except that your purpose is to answer the question *why* rather than *how*. In "Black Men and Public Space," Brent Staples follows a chronological pattern of development. He begins with his first experience as a night walker in Chicago and ends with his most recent experiences in Brooklyn. The essay includes a brief flashback as well, to his childhood days in Chester, Pennsylvania. As he is narrating his experiences, Staples explores the reasons why people react as they do when they encounter him at night on a city street. At the same time, Staples analyzes the impact or effects that their reactions have had on him.

But multiple causes and effects are not always linked. Brumberg's causes do not occur in any inevitable chronological order, nor do Forster's effects. If the causes or effects that you have isolated are not linked in a chain, you must find another way in which to order them. They could be arranged from immediate to remote, for example. When the degree of significance or importance varies, the most obvious structural choice would be to move from the primary to the secondary or from the secondary to the primary. Before you set any sequence, study your list of causes or effects to see whether any principle of order is evident—chronological, spatial, immediate to remote, primary to secondary. If you see a logical order, follow it.

Drafting Suggestions

1. Plan a middle for your essay. How are you going to arrange the causes and effects? Which comes first in the body of your paper; which comes last? Are you moving from the most important to the least? From the chronologically first to last?

2. Place each cause or effect in a separate paragraph. Make sure that the paragraph is more than one sentence long. Explain or develop each cause or effect so that the reader can clearly understand your analysis.

3. Write a purpose statement for your essay as it is developing. What are you trying to explain in the paper? Why might the reader want this knowledge? Identifying a need or interest in your perspective reader always suggests strategies by which you can open your essay.

4. Think about the extent to which your draft is objective and factual and to what extent it is subjective and argumentative. How likely are your readers to agree with what you attribute to cause and what to effect? Have you done research to support your analysis? Cause-and-effect essays are often difficult to write simply from pre-existing knowledge.

5. Draft an introduction and a conclusion to the essay that appeals to your reader's need for this knowledge. Why would the reader want to have this information?

REVISING

HOW DO YOU REVISE A CAUSE-AND-EFFECT ESSAY?

Your success in any paper is always dependent upon your readers. If your readers like it, if they feel that it was worth reading, if it taught them something that they wanted to know or persuaded them to agree with you, then you have succeeded. Unless your readers agree, it does not matter if you think that the paper is clear and interesting. For that reason when you are revising, you should always seek feedback from readers. Perhaps in your writing class you have regular opportunities to read each other's papers and offer advice. Maybe you have a writing center that you can visit or your instructor has the time to read a first draft and suggest possible revisions. If so, take advantage of those readers. Ask them specific questions; ask for their advice. If such situations are not part of the formal structure of the class, ask a roommate or a friend to read your essay and pay attention to what he or she says.

A cause-and-effect essay is primarily explanatory and informative. It explains the reasons or causes for why something happened or the consequences or effects that come from whatever happened. The best cause-and-effect analyses are based on thoughtful analysis and research. The worst cause-and-effect analyses grow only out of subjective, biased, unsubstantiated opinions. If you are sick, you want accurate, objective medical advice. What caused my illness? What are the likely side effects of this course of treatment?

When revising a cause-and-effect essay, play particular attention to the following areas: retesting your subject, concentrating on the important, checking for organization, and beginning and ending appropriately.

Retesting Your Subject   Once you have a draft of your essay, look again at your subject. Ask yourself two questions and answer each honestly. First, were you able to adequately develop your subject in the space that you had available, or were you forced to skim over the surface? Some subjects are simply too large and too complicated to be analyzed within three or four pages. Second, were you objective and accurate in what you identified as causes and effects? The world—and especially the Web—is full of bogus explanations for what caused this or what the effects of that have been. Sometimes people are deliberately misleading, parading their own biases and opinions as objective facts. Readers want accurate and reliable information and analyses. Not every subject needs research—sometimes our personal experience is adequate; sometimes we can thoughtfully analyze a situation. But even then, our response is based on knowledge that we have acquired through experience. Did you adequately research the topic? Is your analysis based on accurate information?

Concentrating on the Important   You will never be given a paper assignment that says to "find all of the causes or all of the effects" of something. In some cases, of course, causes and effects are many. Think about the lists of possible "side effects" that accompany any prescription drug. They often consist of lists that are several paragraphs long. Similarly, many illnesses can result from a complex series of causes, some interacting in causal chains. In a typical writing situation, however, you need to concentrate on the major causes and effects. Once you have identified causes or effects, number them in order of their significance or importance. Depending on the length of your paper—is it a "regular" essay or a term or research paper?—choose to discuss only the most important.

Checking for Logical Organization   Look again at how you have arranged either the causes or the effects in the body of your essay. A typical organizational strategy is to put the main cause or the main effect first and then to move down the list in descending order of importance. You could move in the opposite direction, building to your strongest or most forceful cause or effect, but there would be no logic in placing the most important cause or effect in the middle of the list. Causes and effects can also be listed in a chronological order, especially if there is a causal chain ("this happens, which leads to this, which then leads to this"). Other possible organizational strategies might also be appropriate—for example, from the most visible effect to the least visible. Whatever order you use should be a conscious and thoughtful act on your part, and you should be able to defend your choice to any critic.

Another aspect of logical organization is proportion. You should treat your causes or effects in paragraphs or paragraph blocks of roughly the same length. You do not want to start with a long, detailed paragraph and then have the rest of the essay trail off into a series of ever-shorter, thinner paragraphs.

Logical organization grows out of the careful, intentional arrangement of your analysis, but transitional devices can also play an important role. As you move from one cause or effect to another, make sure you signal that move to your reader. Develop each cause or effect in a separate paragraph, and start each paragraph with an explanatory statement of how this fits into what has gone before. Use parallelism and transitional phrases or markers. Think of such devices as road signs for your reader to tell them what to expect ahead.

Beginning and Ending   Your teacher is the only reader who *has* to read your essay. Your introduction needs to catch your readers' attention and pull them into the paper. Think about why your readers would want to read an essay about this subject. What value does it hold for them? How curious might they be about the subject? What will you help them understand? Your introduction needs to be an inviting bridge between the world of your reader and the essay. Of course, you will explain what your thesis is and why you are writing about this subject, but try to suggest as well what is of particular interest or importance about this subject.

Every paper needs a conclusion. You should never simply stop because you have run out of time. In a short paper, a conclusion does not need to summarize the causes or effects. The reader has just read them. Try instead to end by again stressing the significance of the analysis you have just provided and how it helps the reader to understand the subject. Look at the conclusions that the six writers provided to their essays in this chapter. More concluding strategies for papers can be found in the Glossary and Ready Reference.

Revising Suggestions

1. Have you been able to treat your subject adequately in the space that you have available? Do you need to narrow the subject in any way? Or is the subject too narrow to begin with?

2. Look critically at the body of your essay. Are the paragraphs substantial in length? Are they roughly proportional to one another in length? Your essay should not consist of lots of very short paragraphs or a couple of very long paragraphs and some very short paragraphs.

3. Have you provided clear transitions from one paragraph or section to another? Have you used transitional expressions or time and place markers to indicate that you are moving from one cause or effect to another?

4. Examine the conclusion. Does it just repeat the words of the opening paragraph in a slightly different way? Does it build a bridge between your subject and your reader, pointing out what is interesting or important about the subject?

5. Make a list of the potential problems that you sense in your essay. These may be grammatical or mechanical, or they might be structural. Take your list and a copy of your paper to your school's writing center and ask a tutor for help, or take your list to your instructor—perhaps during office hours—and ask for advice.

SAMPLE STUDENT ESSAY

For a cause-and-effect analysis, Cathy Ferguson chose to examine the effects that television's depiction of violence has on young children.

TV AGGRESSION AND CHILDREN

Let's face it. Television producers are out to make money. Their main concern is with what sells. What does sell? Sensationalism. People like shocking stories. In the effort to sell, the limit of the outrageous on TV has been pushed far beyond what it was, say, ten years ago. Television aggression is one aspect of sensationalism that has been exploited to please a thrill-seeking audience. Television is not showing a greater number of aggressive scenes, but the scenes portray more violent and hostile acts. Psychologists, prompted by concerned parents, have been studying the effects of children viewing increased aggression, since the average program for kids contains twenty acts of violence per hour, while the overall average is only seven acts of violence per hour. Research reveals three outstanding consequences of viewing greater TV hostility. First of all, TV aggression numbs children to real-world violence. One experiment showed that even a brief exposure to a fairly violent show made kids indifferent to the same aggression in real life. Preschoolers are especially affected by TV violence because they are usually unable to distinguish between reality and fantasy. If they see a hostile act, they are liable to believe that it is reality and accept it as the norm.

This leads to the second effect of viewing TV aggression: a distorted perception of the world. Most TV shows do not present real-world consequences of violence; thus children are getting a false picture of their world. Some kids are led to believe that acts of hostility are normal, common, expected even, and may lead a fearfully restricted life. In general, however, most children learn not how to be afraid of violence but how to be violent, which is the third and most drastic effect of viewing television aggression. Almost all studies show that kids are more aggressive after they watch an aggressive show, like "Batman" or "Power Rangers," than after watching a pro-social show like "Barney and Friends" or a neutral show. So although sensationalism, especially violent sensationalism, is making money for TV producers, it is also creating a generation that is numb to real violence, has a distorted picture of the environment, and is itself more hostile. These effects are so palpable, it is now realized that the single best predictor of how aggressive an 18-year-old will be is how much aggressive television he watched when he was 8 years old.

COMMENTS

After Cathy handed in her first draft, she had a conference with her instructor. The instructor commented on her effective use of examples. Because the essay contains specific evidence, the cause and effect analysis seems much more convincing.

Her instructor offered some specific advice about revisions in word choice, sentence structure, and paragraph division. He noted that the essay repeated the phrase "television aggression" or a related variant seven times. Since condensed forms can be confusing, he recommended that she indicate that what she was writing about was aggression, violence, or hostility depicted on television shows. Noting that her first draft begins with five very short sentences and a single-word sentence fragment, he urged her to combine the sentences to reduce the choppy effect. Finally, he recommended that she use paragraph divisions to separate the three effects that she discusses. That division would make it easier for her reader to see the structure of the paper.

Cathy's revision addressed each of the problems that had been discussed in conference. In addition, she made a number of minor changes to tighten the prose and make it clearer.

R E V I S E D　D R A F T

THE INFLUENCE OF TELEVISED VIOLENCE ON CHILDREN

Let's face it. Television producers are in business to make money. Their main concern is what sells, and nothing sells better than sensationalism. In an effort to gain a larger share of the audience, television producers now treat subject matter that would never have been acceptable ten years ago. The depiction of violence on television is one aspect of that sensationalism, exploited to please a thrill-seeking audience. The number of aggressive scenes shown on television has not increased, but those scenes now portray more violent and hostile acts. This is especially true on shows aimed at children.

Psychologists, prompted by concerned parents, have begun studying the effects on children of viewing this increased aggression. The average program for children contains twenty acts of violence per hour, compared to an overall average of seven acts of violence per hour. Research reveals three significant consequences of viewing violence on television.

First, aggressive acts on television numb children to real-world violence. One study showed that even a brief exposure to a fairly violent show made children indifferent to the same aggression in real life. Preschoolers are especially affected by television because they are usually unable to distinguish between reality and fantasy. If they see an aggressive act, they are likely to believe that it is real and so accept it as normal.

This potential confusion leads to the second effect of watching violence on television: a distorted perception of the world. Some children are led to believe that acts of hostility are normal, common, and even expected. As a result, these children may lead a restricted life, afraid of the violence that they imagine lurks everywhere.

In general, however, most children learn not to be afraid of violence but how to be violent—the third and most drastic effect of viewing aggression on television. Almost all studies show that children are more aggressive after they watch a show that includes violence than after watching a show that excludes it.

All three effects are so palpable that it is now realized the single best predictor of how aggressive an 18-year-old will be is how much violence he watched on television when he was 8 years old.

SOME THINGS TO REMEMBER

1. Choose a topic that can be analyzed thoroughly within the limits of the assignment.
2. Decide on a purpose: are you trying to explain or to persuade?
3. Determine an audience. For whom are you writing? What does your audience already know about your subject?
4. Analyze and research your subject. Remember to provide factual support wherever necessary. Not every cause-and-effect analysis can rely on unsupported opinion.
5. Be certain that the relationships you see between causes and effects are genuine.
6. Concentrate your efforts on immediate and primary causes or effects rather than on remote or secondary ones. Do not try to list every cause or every effect that you can.
7. Begin with the cause and then move to effects, or begin with an effect and then move to its causes.
8. Look for a principle of order to organize your list of causes or effects. It might be chronological or spatial, for example, or it might move from immediate to remote or from primary to secondary.
9. Remember that you are explaining why something happens or what will happen. You are not just describing how.

CAUSE AND EFFECT AS A LITERARY STRATEGY

Marge Piercy's poem "Barbie Doll" uses a cause-and-effect structure in order to comment on the physical ideals that society offers to young women. As you read, think about what is the cause and what is the effect and how those two elements are arranged in the poem.

BARBIE DOLL

Marge Piercy

This girlchild was born as usual
and presented dolls that did pee-pee
and miniature GE stoves and irons
and wee lipsticks the color of cherry candy.
Then in the magic of puberty, a classmate said:
You have a great big nose and fat legs.

She was healthy, tested intelligent,
possessed strong arms and back,
abundant sex drive and manual dexterity.
She went to and fro apologizing.
Everyone saw a fat nose on thick legs.

She was advised to play coy,
exhorted to come on hearty,
exercise, diet, smile and wheedle.
Her good nature wore out
like a fan belt.
So she cut off her nose and her legs
and offered them up.
In the casket displayed on satin she lay
with the undertaker's cosmetics painted on,
a turned-up putty nose,
dressed in a pink and white nightie.
Doesn't she look pretty? everyone said.
Consummation at last.
To every woman a happy ending.

DISCUSSION QUESTIONS

1. What happens to the "girlchild" in the story?
2. What is the cause and what is the effect in the poem?
3. What role does "Barbie" play in what happens?
4. In the final stanza, what is the significance of details describing the woman's body?
5. What reaction might Piercy be trying to evoke in her readers? How is cause and effect being used in the poem?

WRITING SUGGESTIONS

It is difficult sometimes even to be aware of the pressures generated by popular culture yet alone to be able to deal with them. How are you influenced by what you see around you—by images in magazines, in advertisements, in films, in music, in television? To what extent are those images a problem? Do they ever make you do things you shouldn't, feel bad about yourself, or feel pressured to change or conform? Explore in an essay one aspect of the influence of popular culture on your life. Possible points of departure might include:

a. Your physical self—size, proportions, appearance
b. Your values or expectations in life—how do you measure success? happiness? fulfillment?
c. Your possessions

READING CAUSE AND EFFECT

When you are sick and visit a doctor, you want to know what has caused the problem and how it can be corrected or alleviated. Sometimes you get fairly precise answers; sometimes you get educated guesses. There might be many possible causes of a disease: often, doctors understand the symptoms and the progression of an illness or disease but cannot pin down a single cause. For example, cigarette smoking and exposure to asbestos can be causes of lung cancer, but there are many others as well.

Many people suffer from migraine headaches and would surely do whatever they could to prevent their reoccurrence if only they knew what it was that caused the migraine. Read the following explanation of "What Causes Migraine Headaches" from **www.emedicinehealth.com.**

As you read, remember what you have learned about how to write using cause and effect and how that knowledge might help you as a reader.

- An analysis of cause explains why something happens or how it came about. An analysis of effect explains the consequences that flow from an event or situation.
- Causes and effects are related to the event by factors other than the time of their occurrence. A rainstorm right after you washed your car was not caused by your action.
- Cause-and-effect analyses tend to concentrate either on causes or on effects rather than attempting to do both.
- Causes and effects vary in importance and in timing. Some are primary and some are secondary; some are immediate and others are remote.
- Causes and effects are logically organized, typically moving from first to last, most important to least, immediate to remote.
- Cause and effect employs transitions and parallelism to signal to the reader the structure of the analysis.

WHAT CAUSES MIGRAINE
HEADACHES?

Description of the physical process by which pain is produced

No one fully understands the exact cause(s) of migraine headaches. Many experts think that a migraine begins with abnormal

	brainstem (a part of the brain) activity that leads to spasms (rapid contraction) of blood vessels in the cerebrum (main part of the
Medical terms defined within parentheses	brain) and dura (the covering of the brain). The first wave of spasm decreases blood supply, which causes the aura that some people
Immediate cause of a migraine	experience. After the first spasm, the same arteries become abnormally relaxed, which increases blood flow and gives rise to migraine headache pain.

Certain chemicals normally found in the brain (namely, dopamine and serotonin) may be involved in causing migraines. These chemicals are called neurotransmitters because they transmit signals within the brain. Neurotransmitters can cause blood vessels to act in unusual ways if they are present in abnormal amounts or if the blood vessels are particularly sensitive to them.

Contributing cause *(margin note)*

"Triggers" set off the physical sequence that produces the pain *(margin note)*

Triggers, however, are not the causes *(margin note)*

Various triggers are thought to bring about migraine in people who have a natural tendency for having migraine headaches. Different people may have different triggers.

- Certain foods, especially chocolate, cheese, nuts, alcohol, and monosodium glutamate (MSG) can trigger migraines. (MSG is a food enhancer used in many foods, including Chinese food.)
- Missing a meal may bring on a headache.
- Stress and tension are also risk factors. People often have migraines during times of increased emotional or physical stress.

Distinguished another type of headache—not a migraine *(margin note)*

- Birth control pills are a common trigger. Women may have migraines at the end of the pill cycle as the estrogen component of the pill is stopped. This is called an estrogen-withdrawal headache.

RESPONDING TO A VISUAL

Photographs and illustrations are static: they show a particular moment in time. A cause-and-effect analysis applied to that visual can extend in opposite directions from that frozen moment. An exploration of causes moves backward to explore how that moment came into being. An exploration of effects moves forward from that moment to see what consequences it had. Consider the following photograph of an older woman.

READING AND WRITING ABOUT IMAGES

You can never know for certain what has brought the woman in the photograph to this point or how her present circumstances will influence her future. However, you can see her as a symbol, a representative of many people in our society who are facing similar circumstances. Using the photograph as a starting point, write an essay in response to one of the following topics:

a. Analyze some of the major causes of homelessness in America (you might want to limit the subject by focusing, for example, on homelessness among older women).
b. Construct a causal chain that interlinks causes to produce a result such as this.
c. Analyze some of the major effects of homelessness on American society.

VISITING THE WEB

The companion Website, **www.prenhall.com/miller**, has additional information about cause and effect and about the writers in this chapter. You will also find a number of links to other sources of information about the subjects of the essays found in this chapter.

EXPLORING ON YOUR OWN

Finding accurate and reliable information on the Web can be a challenge. Anyone can mount a professional-looking Website and present subjective, biased, even inaccurate information. When you are using information from Websites in your research, you should always assess the reliability and objectivity of the site that you are using. Tips on doing this can be found in the appendix, "Finding Using, and Documenting Sources."

LOOKING FOR WRITING SUGGESTIONS

Most of the following topics can be explored in either direction: What are the causes, and what are the effects?

1. Cell phones
2. Clothing (that consumers purchase, that advertises a product)
3. Blogging
4. Credit card debt
5. Rising costs of college
6. Terrorism
7. Instant messaging
8. Inflation
9. Natural disaster (for example, earthquake, volcanic eruption, tornado)
10. Eating disorders
11. Binge drinking
12. AIDS
13. Global warming
14. Extreme sports
15. Medical costs

MY WOOD

E. M. Forster

Edward Morgan Forster (1879–1970) was born in London, England, and earned two undergraduate degrees and a master's degree from King's College, Cambridge University. He is best known as a novelist, but he also wrote short stories, literary criticism, biographies, histories, and essays. His novels, many of which have recently been made into popular films, include A Room with a View *(1908),* Howards End *(1910), and* A Passage to India *(1924). He published two collections of essays,* Abinger Harvest *(1936) and* Two Cheers for Democracy *(1951).*

On Writing: *Once, after having broken his right arm in a fall, Forster contemplated writing with his left hand: "The attempt to write with the left hand raises new hopes in the human heart. For how many years have our thoughts been transmitted by the nerves and muscles of the right hand. How much of their essence might not have been absorbed in the passage. Now when new organs are brought into play new thoughts or new parts of thoughts may find their way on to the page, how many old ones can be absent and fail to reach it. A physiological outcry may be raised at this. But at all events the thought that it may occur is new. . . . [T]he thoughts that have so long struggled for expression may at last find it."*

BEFORE READING

Connecting: What would you regard as the most important "thing" that you own? Why is it most important to you?

Anticipating: Forster observes that owning the wood made him feel "heavy." In what sense does it make him feel "heavy"?

1   A few years ago I wrote a book which dealt in part with the difficulties of the English in India. Feeling that they would have had no difficulties in India themselves, the Americans read the book freely. The more they read it the better it made them feel, and a cheque to the author was the result. I bought a wood with the cheque. It is not a large wood—it contains scarcely any trees, and it is intersected, blast it, by a public footpath. Still, it is the first property that I have owned, so it is right that other people should participate in my shame, and should ask themselves, in accents that will vary in horror, this very important question: What is the effect of property upon the character? Don't let's touch economics; the effect of private ownership upon the community as a whole is another question—a more important question, perhaps, but another one. Let's keep to psychology. If you own things, what's their effect on you? What's the effect on me of my wood?

In the first place, it makes me feel heavy. Property does have this effect. 2
Property produces men of weight, and it was a man of weight who failed to get into the Kingdom of Heaven. He was not wicked, that unfortunate millionaire in the parable, he was only stout; he stuck out in front, not to mention behind, and as he wedged himself this way and that in the crystalline entrance and bruised his well-fed flanks, he saw beneath him a comparatively slim camel passing through the eye of a needle and being woven into the robe of God. The Gospels all through couple stoutness and slowness. They point out what is perfectly obvious, yet seldom realized: that if you have a lot of things you cannot move about a lot, that furniture requires dusting, dusters require servants, servants require insurance stamps, and the whole tangle of them makes you think twice before you accept an invitation to dinner or go for a bathe in the Jordan. Sometimes the Gospels proceed further and say with Tolstoy that property is sinful; they approach the difficult ground of asceticism here, where I cannot follow them. But as to the immediate effects of property on people, they just show straightforward logic. It produces men of weight. Men of weight cannot, by definition, move like the lightning from the East unto the West, and the ascent of a fourteen-stone bishop into a pulpit is thus the exact antithesis of the coming of the Son of Man. My wood makes me feel heavy.

In the second place, it makes me feel it ought to be larger. 3

The other day I heard a twig snap in it. I was annoyed at first, for I 4
thought that someone was blackberrying, and depreciating the value of the undergrowth. On coming nearer, I saw it was not a man who had trodden on the twig and snapped it, but a bird, and I felt pleased. My bird. The bird was not equally pleased. Ignoring the relation between us, it took fright as soon as it saw the shape of my face, and flew straight over the boundary hedge into a field, the property of Mrs. Henessy, where it sat down with a loud squawk. It had become Mrs. Henessy's bird. Something seemed grossly amiss here, something that would not have occurred had the wood been larger. I could not afford to buy Mrs. Henessy out, I dared not murder her, and limitations of this sort beset me on every side. Ahab did not want that vineyard—he only needed it to round off his property, preparatory to plotting a new curve—and all the land around my wood has become necessary to me in order to round off the wood. A boundary protects. But—poor little thing—the boundary ought in its turn to be protected. Noises on the edge of it. Children throw stones. A little more, and then a little more, until we reach the sea. Happy Canute! Happier Alexander! And after all, why should even the world be the limit of possession? A rocket containing a Union Jack, will, it is hoped, be shortly fired at the moon. Mars. Sirius. Beyond which . . . But these immensities ended by saddening me. I could not suppose that my wood was the destined nucleus of universal dominion—it is so very small and contains no mineral wealth beyond the blackberries. Nor was I comforted when Mrs. Henessy's bird took alarm for the second time and flew clean away from us all, under the belief that it belonged to itself.

In the third place, property makes its owner feel that he ought to do 5
something to it. Yet he isn't sure what. A restlessness comes over him, a vague

sense that he has a personality to express—the same sense which, without any vagueness, leads the artist to an act of creation. Sometimes I think I will cut down such trees as remain in the wood, at other times I want to fill up the gaps between them with new trees. But impulses are pretentious and empty. They are not honest movements towards money-making or beauty. They spring from a foolish desire to express myself and from an inability to enjoy what I have got. Creation, property, enjoyment form a sinister trinity in the human mind. Creation and enjoyment are both very, very good, yet they are often unattainable without a material basis, and at such moments property pushes itself in as a substitute, saying, "Accept me instead—I'm good enough for all three." It is not enough. It is, as Shakespeare said of lust, "the expense of spirit in a waste of shame": it is "Before, a joy proposed; behind, a dream." Yet we don't know how to shun it. It is forced on us by our economic system as the alternative to starvation. It is forced on us by an internal defect in the soul, by the feeling that in property may lie the germs of selfdevelopment and of exquisite or heroic deeds. Our life on earth is, and ought to be, material and carnal. But we have not learned to manage our materialism and carnality properly; they are still entangled with the desire for ownership, where (in the words of Dante) "Possession is one with loss."

6

7   And this brings us to our fourth and final point: the blackberries.

Blackberries are not plentiful in the meagre grove, but they are easily seen from the public footpath which traverses it, and all too easily gathered. Foxgloves, too—people will pull up the foxgloves, and ladies of an educational tendency even grub for toadstools to show them on the Monday in class. Other ladies, less educated, roll down the bracken in the arms of their gentlemen friends. There is paper, there are tins. Pray, does my wood belong to me or doesn't it? And, if it does, should I not own it best by allowing no one else to walk there? There is a wood near Lyme Regis, also cursed by a public footpath, where the owner has not hesitated on this point. He has built high stone walls on each side of the path, and has spanned it by bridges, so that the public circulate like termites while he gorges on the blackberries unseen. He really does own his wood, this able chap. Dives in Hell did pretty well, but the gulf dividing him from Lazarus could be traversed by vision, and nothing traverses it here. And perhaps I shall come to this in time. I shall wall in and fence out until I really taste the sweets of property. Enormously stout, endlessly avaricious, pseudocreative, intensely selfish, I shall weave upon my forehead the quadruple crown of possession until those nasty Bolshies come and take it off again and thrust me aside into the outer darkness.

QUESTIONS ON SUBJECT AND PURPOSE

1. According to Forster, what are the consequences of owning property?

2. Is there any irony in buying property from the royalties earned from a book about England's problems in India?

3. What purpose or purposes might Forster have had in writing the essay?

QUESTIONS ON STRATEGY AND AUDIENCE

1. In what way is this a cause-and-effect essay?
2. Look at the conclusion of the essay. Why does Forster end in this way? Why not add a more conventional conclusion?
3. What expectations does Forster seem to have about his audience? How do you know?

QUESTIONS ON VOCABULARY AND STYLE

1. Characterize the tone of Forster's essay. Is it formal? Informal? How is that tone achieved?
2. Forster makes extensive use of allusion in the essay. Some of the names are easily recognizable; others are less so. Identify the following allusions (all but c are to biblical stories). How does each fit into the context of the essay?
   a. The wealthy man in the parable (paragraph 2)
   b. Ahab and the vineyard (4)
   c. Canute and Alexander (4)
   d. Dives and Lazarus (7)
3. Be able to define the following words: *asceticism* (paragraph 2), *stone* (2), *depreciating* (4), *pretentious* (5), *carnal* (5), *foxgloves* (7), *bracken* (7), *avaricious* (7), *Bolshies* (7).

WRITING SUGGESTIONS

1. **For Your Journal.** Commenting on the second effect of owning property, Forster observes: "it makes me feel it ought to be larger" (paragraph 3). To what extent does something you own make you want to own something more? Concentrate on the possession you value most highly. Does owning it ever make you want to own more? Explore the idea.
2. **For a Paragraph.** Select something you own that is important to you—a house, a car, a stereo system, a pet, something you use for recreation. In a paragraph, describe the consequences of owning it. How has it changed your life and behavior? Are there negative as well as positive consequences?
3. **For an Essay.** Extend your paragraph into an essay. Explore each of the consequences you described in a separate paragraph.
4. **For Research.** Property ownership has frequently been used throughout history as a precondition for full participation in the affairs of government (voting, for example). A number of states in this country applied such a restriction until the practice was declared unconstitutional. Using outside sources, write a research essay that

explains and analyzes either the reasons for such practices or their negative consequence. Be sure to document your sources.

FOR FURTHER STUDY

Focusing on Grammar and Writing. Write a new ending for Forster's essay. Try one that follows the advice you have learned from writing the typical five-paragraph essay—that is, write a very conventional, English-class-sounding conclusion. What is the effect of adding this ending to the essay? What does this suggest about writing effective conclusions?

Working Together. Working with classmates in small groups, try to characterize Forster's tone in the essay. You must first define tone (see the glossary for help) and discuss the elements that can create or influence tone in an essay. Then isolate specific effects—things such as word choice and phrasing—that influence our perceptions of tone.

Seeing Other Modes at Work. Although the essay does not seem to reach a conclusion about the effects of property ownership, it could easily be recast with a persuasive purpose. What would it require to make Forster's essay "argue" for or against the ownership of property? In paragraph 4, Forster uses narrative—that is, he tells a story—to illustrate the second consequence of property ownership.

Finding Connections. A good pairing is with Lars Eighner's "My Daily Dives in the Dumpster" (Chapter 6). To what extent do both Forster and Eighner achieve a similar insight about material possessions? Another pairing is with Peter Singer's "The Singer Solution" (Chapter 10).

Exploring the Web. A number of Websites include information about E. M. Forster and his writings, including hypertext and e-text editions of his work. You can also locate information about Merchant/Ivory Productions, the film company responsible for making, among others, film versions of Forster's novels *Howard's End* and *A Room with a View.* Starting points can be found at **www.prenhall.com/miller.**

THE ORIGINS OF ANOREXIA NERVOSA

Joan Jacobs Brumberg

Born in 1944 in Mount Vernon, New York, Joan Jacobs Brumberg earned a Ph.D. in American history at the University of Virginia. She is the Stephen H. Weiss Presidential Fellow and Professor at Cornell University. She has written many articles and several books, including Fasting Girls: The Emergence of Anorexia Nervosa *(1988), which studies the disease from historical, social, and familial perspectives. Her most recent book is* Kansas Charley: The Story of a 19th-Century Boy Murderer *(2003). The following selection is from* Fasting Girls *and was published in* Harper's *magazine.*

On Writing: *In her preface to* The Body Project, *Brumberg praised an editor for helping her achieve "accessibility" and "shed the girdle of academese that shapes so many historical accounts of the past."*

BEFORE READING

Connecting: What attitudes toward food and toward mealtime do the members of your family share? Do you have "family" meals? Are there any rituals connected with mealtime?

Anticipating: Brumberg defines a certain environment in which anorexia nervosa emerged. What are the essential conditions of that environment?

Contrary to the popular assumption that anorexia nervosa is a peculiarly modern disorder, the malady first emerged in the Victorian era—long before the pervasive cultural imperative for a thin female body. The first clinical descriptions of the disorder appeared in England and France almost simultaneously in 1873. They were written by two well-known physicians: Sir William Withey Gull and Charles Lasègue. Lasègue, more than any other nineteenth-century doctor, captured the rhythm of repeated offerings and refusals that signaled the breakdown of reciprocity between parents and their anorexic daughter. By returning to its origins, we can see anorexia nervosa for what it is: a dysfunction in the bourgeois family system.

Family meals assumed enormous importance in the bourgeois milieu, in the United States as well as in England and France. Middle-class parents prided themselves on providing ample food for their children. The abundance of food and the care in its preparation became expressions of social status. The ambience of the meal symbolized the values of the family. A popular domestic manual advised, "Simple, healthy food, exquisitely prepared, and served upon shining dishes and brilliant silverware . . . a gentle blessing, and cheerful conversation, embrace the sweetest communions and the happiest moments of life." Among the middle class it seems that eating correctly was emerging as a new morality, one that set its members apart from the working class.

3   At the same time, food was used to express love in the nineteenth-century bourgeois household. Offering attractive and abundant meals was the particular responsibility and pleasure of middle-class wives and mothers. In America the feeding of middle-class children, from infancy on, had become a maternal concern no longer deemed appropriate to delegate to wet nurses, domestics, or governesses. Family meals were expected to be a time of instructive and engaging conversation. Participation was expected on both a verbal and gustatory level. In this context, refusing to eat was an unabashedly antisocial act. Anorexic behavior was antithetical to the ideal of bourgeois eating. One advice book, *Common Sense for Maid, Wife, and Mother,* stated: "Heated discussion and quarrels, fretfulness and sullen taciturnity while eating, are as unwholesome as they are unchristian."

4   Why would a daughter affront her parents by refusing to eat? Lasègue's 1873 description of anorexia nervosa, along with other nineteenth-century medical reports, suggests that pressure to marry may have precipitated the illness.

5   Ambitious parents surely understood that by marrying well, at an appropriate moment, a daughter, even though she did not carry the family name, could help advance a family's social status—particularly in a burgeoning middle-class society. As a result, the issue of marriage loomed large in the life of a dutiful middle-class daughter. Although marriage did not generally occur until the girl's early twenties, it was an event for which she was continually prepared, and a desirable outcome for all depended on the ability of the parents and the child to work together—that is, to state clearly what each wanted or to read each other's heart and mind. In the context of marital expectations, a daughter's refusal to eat was a provocative rejection of both the family's social aspirations and their goodwill toward her. All of the parents' plans for her future (and their own) could be stymied by her peculiar and unpleasant alimentary nihilism.

6   Beyond the specific anxieties generated by marital pressure, the Victorian family milieu in America and in Western Europe harbored a mélange of other tensions and problems that provided the emotional preconditions for the emergence of anorexia nervosa. As love replaced authority as the cement of family relations, it began to generate its own set of emotional disorders.

7   Possessiveness, for example, became an acute problem in Victorian family life. Where love between parents and children was the prevailing ethic, there was always the risk of excess. When love became suffocating or manipulative, individuation and separation from the family could become extremely painful, if not impossible. In the context of increased intimacy, adolescent privacy was especially problematic: For parents and their sexually maturing daughters, what constituted an appropriate degree of privacy? Middle-class girls, for example, almost always had their own rooms or shared them with sisters, but they had greater difficulty establishing autonomous psychic space. The well-known penchant of adolescent girls for novel-reading was an expression of their need for imaginative freedom. Some parents, recognizing that their daughters needed channels for expressing emotions, encouraged diary-keeping.

But some of the same parents who gave lovely marbled journals as gifts also monitored their content. Since emotional freedom was not an acknowledged prerogative of the Victorian adolescent girl, it seems likely that she would have expressed unhappiness in non-verbal forms of behavior. One such behavior was refusal of food.

When an adolescent daughter became sullen and chronically refused to eat, her parents felt threatened and confused. The daughter was perceived as willfully manipulating her appetite the way a younger child might. Because parents did not want to encourage this behavior, they often refused at first to indulge the favorite tastes or caprices of their daughter. As emaciation became visible and the girl looked ill, many violated the contemporary canon of prudent child-rearing and put aside their moral objections to pampering the appetite. Eventually they would beg their daughter to eat whatever she liked— and eat she must, "as a sovereign proof of affection" for them. From the parents' perspective, a return to eating was a confirmation of filial love.   8

The significance of food refusal as an emotional tactic within the family depended on food's being plentiful, pleasing, and connected to love. Where food was eaten simply to assuage hunger, where it had only minimal aesthetic and symbolic messages, or where the girl had to provide her own nourishment, refusal of food was not particularly noteworthy or defiant. In contrast, the anorexic girl was surrounded by a provident, if not indulgent, family that was bound to be distressed by her rejection of its largess.   9

Anorexia nervosa was an intense form of discourse that honored the emotional guidelines that governed the middle-class Victorian family. Refusing to eat was not as confrontational as yelling, having a tantrum, or throwing things; refusing to eat expressed emotional hostility without being flamboyant. And refusing to eat had the advantage of being ambiguous. If a girl repeatedly claimed lack of appetite she might indeed be ill and therefore entitled to special treatment and favors.   10

In her own way, the anorexic was respectful of what historian Peter Gay called "the great bourgeois compromise between the need for reserve and the capacity for emotion." The rejection of food, while an emotionally charged behavior, was also discreet, quiet, and ladylike. The unhappy adolescent who was in all other ways a dutiful daughter chose food refusal from within the symptom repertoire available to her. Precisely because she was not a lunatic, she selected a behavior that she knew would have some efficacy within her own family.   11

QUESTIONS ON SUBJECT AND PURPOSE

1. According to Brumberg, when did anorexia nervosa emerge as a definable disease? Why did it emerge in that particular time period?

2. On the basis of what Brumberg writes here, who is the most likely candidate for anorexia nervosa?

3. What purpose might Brumberg have in writing about anorexia nervosa?

QUESTIONS ON STRATEGY AND AUDIENCE

1. Why does Brumberg begin by referring to "the popular assumption that anorexia nervosa is a peculiarly modern disorder"?

2. To what extent does isolating the origins of anorexia nervosa help us understand the disorder in young people today?

3. Brumberg uses quite a few words that might be unfamiliar to many readers. What do her vocabulary choices imply about her sense of audience?

QUESTIONS ON VOCABULARY AND STYLE

1. In paragraphs 2 and 3, Brumberg quotes from two popular domestic manuals of the nineteenth century. What do the quotations contribute to her essay?

2. In paragraph 5, Brumberg uses the phrase "alimentary nihilism" with reference to anorexics. What does the phrase mean?

3. Be prepared to define the following words: *malady* (paragraph 1), *imperative* (1), *reciprocity* (1), *dysfunction* (1), *bourgeois* (1), *milieu* (2), *ambience* (2), *wet nurses* (3), *gustatory* (3), *unabashedly* (3), *antithetical* (3), *taciturnity* (3), *burgeoning* (5), *stymied* (5), *alimentary* (5), *nihilism* (5), *mélange* (6), *individuation* (7), *autonomous* (7), *penchant* (7), *prerogative* (7), *caprices* (8), *emaciation* (8), *assuage* (9), *largess* (9), *flamboyant* (10), *efficacy* (11).

WRITING SUGGESTIONS

1. **For Your Journal.** How would you characterize your mealtimes? Do you care about the circumstances in which you eat? Do you have to eat with someone else? Can you just grab something on the run? Explore your attitudes toward mealtime. Do not just accept what you are doing without thinking about it. What do you expect of meals? Why?

2. **For a Paragraph.** Define your "ideal" body. Then in a second paragraph speculate on the reasons why that body type or shape seems "ideal."

3. **For an Essay.** Cultural historians have observed that American society is "obesophobic" (excessively or irrationally fearful of fat and being fat). Certainly weight consciousness permeates American society and the weight-loss industries are multimillion dollar businesses. Why?

4. **For Research.** Anorexia nervosa is only one of a number of diseases that are common today but were previously unknown or undiagnosed. Other examples include Alzheimer's disease, osteoporosis, premenstrual syndrome, and chronic fatigue syndrome. Select a "new" disease or disorder, and research its history. When was it first defined? What might account for its emergence during the past decade or two?

If you are using information from electronic sources, such as the World Wide Web, make sure that the information is authoritative. Be sure to document all of your sources, including electronic ones, wherever appropriate.

FOR FURTHER STUDY

Focusing on Grammar and Writing. Brumberg uses quite a few words that are not part of most people's working vocabularies. Underline every unfamiliar word in the essay. Next to each word, write down what you guess it might mean. Check your guess against a dictionary definition.

Working Together. Working in small groups, discuss the reasons why our culture has a fear of "fatness." Brainstorm about possible reasons for this obsession with thinness. Each group should present its ideas to the class as a whole. As a class, try to construct an analysis of the causes that could be used as the framework for an essay on the topic.

Seeing Other Modes at Work. In tracing the origins of anorexia nervosa, Brumberg uses narration as well as cause-and-effect strategies. How is narrative used in the essay?

Finding Connections. A excellent pairing is with Margaret Atwood's "The Female Body" (Chapter 8). Another, more unusual, pairing is with Tom Haines's "Facing Famine" (Chapter 2).

Exploring the Web. The Web has extensive resources for dealing with anorexia nervosa and related eating disorders. A list of places to start can be found at **www.prenhall.com/miller.**

ON TEENAGERS AND TATTOOS

Andres Martin

Andres Martin received his M.D. from the Universidad Nacional Antonoma de Mexico in 1990. He is currently an associate professor and medical director of the Child Psychiatric Impatient Service at Yale University. He specializes in inpatient child and adolescent psychiatry and psychopharmacology. A widely known authority, he is the author of many professional publications. "On Teenagers and Tattoos" was first published in the Journal of Child and Adolescent Psychiatry *in 1997.*

BEFORE READING

Connecting: Do you have any tattoos or piercings? How many? How old were you when you got each?

Anticipating: Martin suggests reasons why adolescents get tattoos and piercings. Do you recognize any of these reasons as ones that motivated you or a friend to get either a tattoo or a piercing?

> The skeleton dimensions I shall now proceed to set down are copied verbatim from my right arm, where I had them tattooed: as in my wild wanderings at that period, there was no other secure way of preserving such valuable statistics.
>
> —Melville, *Moby Dick*

1   Tattoos and piercing have become a part of our everyday landscape. They are ubiquitous, having entered the circles of glamour and the mainstream of fashion, and they have even become an increasingly common feature of our urban youth. Legislation in most states restricts professional tattooing to adults older than 18 years of age, so "high end" tattooing is rare in children and adolescents, but such tattoos are occasionally seen in older teenagers. Piercings, by comparison, as well as self-made or "jailhouse" type tattoos, are not at all rare among adolescents or even among school-age children. Like hairdo, makeup, or baggy jeans, tattoos and piercings can be subject to fad influence or peer pressure in an effort toward group affiliation. As with any other fashion statement, they can be construed as bodily aids in the inner struggle toward identity consolidation, serving as adjuncts to the defining and sculpting of the self by means of external manipulations. But unlike most other body decorations, tattoos and piercings are set apart by their irreversible and permanent nature, a quality at the core of their magnetic appeal to adolescents.

2   Adolescents and their parents are often at odds over the acquisition of bodily decorations. For the adolescent, piercing or tattoos may be seen as personal and beautifying statements, while parents may construe them as oppositional and enraging affronts to their authority. Distinguishing bodily adornment from self-mutilation may indeed prove challenging, particularly when a family is in disagreement over a teenager's motivations and a clinician

is summoned as the final arbiter. At such times it may be most important to realize jointly that the skin can all too readily become but another battle-ground for the tensions of the age, arguments having less to do with tattoos and piercings than with core issues such as separation from the family matrix. Exploring the motivations and significance [underlying] tattoos (Grumet, 1983) and piercings can go a long way toward resolving such differences and can become a novel and additional way of getting to know teenagers. An interested and nonjudgmental appreciation of teenagers' surface presentations may become a way of making contact not only in their terms but on their turfs: quite literally on the territory of their skins.

The following three sections exemplify some of the complex psychological   3
underpinnings of youth tattooing.

Identity and the Adolescent's Body

Tattoos and piercing can offer a concrete and readily available solution for many   4
of the identity crises and conflicts normative to adolescent development. In us-ing such decorations, and by marking out their bodily territories, adolescents can support their efforts at autonomy, privacy, and insulation. Seeking individ-uation, tattooed adolescents can become unambiguously demarcated from oth-ers and singled out as unique. The intense and often disturbing reactions that are mobilized in viewers can help to effectively keep them at bay, becoming tan-tamount to the proverbial "Keep Out" sign hanging from a teenager's door.

Alternatively, feeling prey to a rapidly evolving body over which they   5
have no say, self-made and openly visible decorations may restore adolescents' sense of normalcy and control, a way of turning a passive experience into an active identity. By indelibly marking their bodies, adolescents can strive to re-claim their bearings within an environment experienced as alien, estranged, or suffocating or to lay claim over their evolving and increasingly unrecognizable bodies. In either case, the net outcome can be a resolution to unwelcome im-positions: external, familial, or societal in one case; internal and hormonal in the other. In the words of a 16-year-old girl with several facial piercings, and who could have been referring to her body just as well as to the position within her family: "If I don't fit in, it is because I say so."

Incorporation and Ownership

Imagery of a religious, deathly, or skeletal nature, the likenesses of fierce ani-   6
mals or imagined creatures, and the simple inscription of names are some of the time-tested favorite contents for tattoos. In all instances, marks become not only memorials or recipients for dearly held persons or concepts: they strive for incorporation, with images and abstract symbols gaining substance on becoming a permanent part of the individual's skin. Thickly embedded in personally meaningful representations and object relations, tattoos can be-come not only the ongoing memento of a relationship, but at times even the only evidence that there ever was such a bond. They can quite literally become the relationship itself. The turbulence and impulsivity of early attachments and infatuations may become grounded, effectively bridging oblivion through the visible reality to tattoos.

7   Case Vignette: "A," a 13-year-old boy, proudly showed me his tattooed deltoid. The coarsely depicted roll of the dice marked the day and month of his birth. Rather disappointed, he then uncovered an immaculate back, going on to draw for me the great "piece" he envisioned for it. A menacing figure held a hand of cards: two aces, two eights, and a card with two sets of dates. "A's" father had belonged to Dead Man's Hand, a motorcycle gang named after the set of cards (aces and eights) that the legendary Wild Bill Hickock had held in the 1890s when shot dead over a poker table in Deadwood, South Dakota. "A" had only the vaguest memory of and sketchiest information about his father, but he knew he had died in a motorcycle accident: The fifth card marked the dates of his birth and death.

8   The case vignette also serves to illustrate how tattoos are often the culmination of a long process of imagination, fantasy, and planning that can start at an early age. Limited markings, or relatively reversible ones such as piercings, can at a later time scaffold toward the more radical commitment of a permanent tattoo.

The Quest of Permanence

9   The popularity of the anchor as a tattoo motif may historically have had to do less with guild identification among sailors than with an intense longing for rootedness and stability. In a similar vein, the recent increase in the popularity and acceptance of tattoos may be understood as an antidote or counterpoint to our urban and nomadic lifestyles. Within an increasingly mobile society, in which relationships are so often transient—as attested by the frequencies of divorce, abandonment, foster placement, and repeated moves, for example—tattoos can be a readily available source of grounding. Tattoos, unlike many relationships, can promise permanence and stability. A sense of constancy can be derived from unchanging marks that can be carried along no matter what the physical, temporal, or geographical vicissitudes at hand. Tattoos stay, while all else may change.

10   Case Vignette: A proud father at 17, "B" had had the smiling face of his 4-month-old baby girl tattooed on his chest. As we talked at a tattoo convention, he proudly introduced her to me, explaining how he would "always know how beautiful she is today" when years from then he saw her semblance etched on himself.

11   The quest for permanence may at other times prove misleading and offer premature closure to unresolved conflicts. At a time of normative uncertainties, adolescents may maladaptively and all too readily commit to a tattoo and its indefinite presence. A wish to hold on to a current certainty may lead the adolescent to lay down in ink what is valued and cherished one day but may not necessarily be in the future. The frequency of self-made tattoos among hospitalized, incarcerated, or gang-affiliated youths suggests such motivations: A sense of stability may be a particularly dire need under temporary, turbulent, or volatile conditions. In addition, through their designs teenagers may assert a sense of bonding and allegiance to a group larger than themselves. Tattoos may attest to powerful experiences, such as adolescence itself, lived and even survived together. As with Moby Dick's protagonist, Ishmael, they may bear witness to the "valuable statistics" of one's "wild wandering(s)": those of adolescent exhilaration and excitement on the one hand; of growing pains, shared misfortune, or even incarceration on the other.

Adolescents' bodily decorations, at times radical and dramatic in their　12
presentation, can be seen in terms of figuration rather than disfigurement, of
the natural body being through them transformed into a personalized body
(Brain, 1979). They can often be understood as self-constructive and adorn-
ing efforts, rather than prematurely subsumed as mutilatory and destructive
acts. If we bear all of this in mind, we may not only arrive at a position to pass
more reasoned clinical judgment, but become sensitized through our patients'
skins to another level of their internal reality.

REFERENCES

Brain, R. (1979). *The decorated body*. New York: Harper & Row.

Grumet, G. W. (1983). Psychodynamic implications of tattoos. *American Journal
of Orthopsychiatry*, 53, 482–92.

QUESTIONS ON SUBJECT AND PURPOSE

1. In what ways are tattoos and piercings different from hair styles or
   clothing fads?
2. According to Martin, what is the typical parental reaction to such
   markings?
3. What purpose might Martin have in the essay? Before you answer this,
   you should define his audience (see question 3 in Strategy and
   Audience just below).

QUESTIONS ON STRATEGY AND AUDIENCE

1. What is the effect on the reader of subdividing the text with additional
   white space and providing headings for the subsections?
2. What is the effect of including the two "case vignettes" (paragraphs 7
   and 10)?
3. Who does Martin imagine as his audience, and what evidence can you
   cite to support your answer?

QUESTIONS ON VOCABULARY AND STYLE

1. What is the significance of the quotation from Melville's *Moby Dick*,
   which prefaces the essay?
2. What does the presence of documented sources in the essay suggest?
3. Be prepared to define the following words: *ubiquitous* (paragraph 1),
   affront (2), *demarcated* (4), *tantamount* (4), *nomadic* (9), *vicissitudes*
   (9), *maladaptively* (11), *volatile* (11).

WRITING SUGGESTIONS

1. **For Your Journal.** How do you react to body markings (tattoos or
   piercings)? In your journal, jot down your thoughts. If you object to

such things, why? If you would never do such things, why not? If you have such markings, what motivated you to have them done?

2. **For a Paragraph.** In a paragraph, perhaps drawing on your own experiences and certainly on your own opinions, analyze two potential effects on the individual of having such permanent body markings.

3. **For an Essay.** Interview a substantial number of friends or classmates who have tattoos and/or body piercings. Ask them why they chose their bodily adornments—what were the reasons or causes? What are the effects of having tattoos and/or piercings? How do people react to them? How does body art affect their sense of self and self-image? Make sure you have a large number of interviewees. Then, in an essay, write about the causes that they reported (whether or not they agree with the causes suggested by Martin) or about the effects that they have experienced since getting tattooed or pierced.

4. **For Research.** Martin identifies some of the reasons adolescents in America choose to make such "surface presentations." An analysis can also be done in the other direction: What are the effects of such markings? Those effects would include physical, psychological, and cultural factors. Using a variety of resources, including both print and online searches, analyze in a research paper the major effects that such markings have on the person who is wearing them.

FOR FURTHER STUDY

Focusing on Grammar and Writing. How does Martin use transitional devices in the essay to move from one cause or reason to another? Do his transitions depend upon words and phrases? Typographical devices? Logical organization? What do such transitional devices do for the essay?

Working Together. Working in small groups, divide the essay into blocks of paragraphs. Each group should look for evidence in the text that indicates Martin's sense of audience. How does what he says and how he says it reveal his understanding of his audience?

Seeing Other Modes at Work. Even though the essay is a cause-and-effect analysis, Martin is also trying to persuade his readers of the value of understanding why young people mark their bodies—that the knowledge is a valuable tool in their professional roles as clinicians. Where do you see persuasive elements at work in the essay?

Finding Connections. An interesting pairing is with Veronica Chambers' "Dreadlocked" (in this chapter).

Exploring the Web. The Web has many sites that are devoted to tattoos and piercings, including personal experience stories, pro/con debates, parental reactions, galleries of photographs, and even suggestions on how to persuade your parents to allow you to be tattooed! For some suggestions of sites to visit, check the listing at **www.prenhall.com/miller**.

BLACK MEN AND PUBLIC SPACE

Brent Staples

Born in Chester, Pennsylvania, Brent Staples graduated from Widener University in 1973 and earned a Ph.D. in psychology from the University of Chicago in 1982. He worked for the Chicago Sun-Times *as a reporter before moving to* The New York Times *in 1985. In 1994 he published a memoir,* Parallel Time: Growing Up in Black and White, *which tells the story of his childhood in Chester, a mixed-race, economically declining town. The book focuses on his younger brother, a drug dealer who died of gunshot wounds at age twenty-two.*

"Black Men and Public Space" was originally published in Ms. *magazine under the title "Just Walk on By: A Black Man Ponders His Power to Alter Public Space." In revised and edited form, it was reprinted in* Harper's *with the current title.*

On Writing: *In* Parallel Time, *Staples describes how, in his early twenties, he began to explore his voice as a writer: "I was carrying a journal with me everywhere. . . . I wrote on buses and on the Jackson Park el—though only at the stops to keep the writing legible. I traveled to distant neighborhoods, sat on the curbs, and sketched what I saw in words. Thursday meant free admission at the Art Institute. All day I attributed motives to people in paintings, especially people in Rembrandts. At closing time, I went to a nightclub in The Loop and spied on the patrons, copied their conversations, and speculated about their lives. The journal was more than 'a record of my inner transactions.' It was a collection of stolen souls from which I would one day construct a book."*

BEFORE READING

Connecting: What precautions do you take if you have to walk at night in public spaces?

Anticipating: Why does Staples whistle melodies from classical music when he walks at night? What effect does that particular "cowbell" have on people?

My first victim was a woman—white, well dressed, probably in her early   1
twenties. I came upon her late one evening on a deserted street in Hyde Park, a relatively affluent neighborhood in an otherwise mean, impoverished section of Chicago. As I swung onto the avenue behind her, there seemed to be a discreet, uninflammatory distance between us. Not so. She cast back a worried glance. To her, the youngish black man—a broad six feet two inches with a beard and billowing hair, both hands shoved into the pockets of a bulky military jacket—seemed menacingly close. After a few more quick glimpses, she picked up her pace and was soon running in earnest. Within seconds she disappeared into a cross street.

2   That was more than a decade ago. I was twenty-two years old, a graduate student newly arrived at the University of Chicago. It was in the echo of
that terrified woman's footfalls that I first began to know the unwieldy inheritance I'd come into—the ability to alter public space in ugly ways. It was clear
that she thought herself the quarry of a mugger, a rapist, or worse. Suffering
a bout of insomnia, however, I was stalking sleep, not defenseless wayfarers.
As a softy who is scarcely able to take a knife to a raw chicken—let alone hold
one to a person's throat—I was surprised, embarrassed, and dismayed all at
once. Her flight made me feel like an accomplice in tyranny. It also made it
clear that I was indistinguishable from the muggers who occasionally seeped
into the area from the surrounding ghetto. That first encounter, and those
that followed, signified that a vast, unnerving gulf lay between nighttime
pedestrians—particularly women—and me. And I soon gathered that being
perceived as dangerous is a hazard in itself. I only needed to turn a corner into
a dicey situation, or crowd some frightened, armed person in a foyer somewhere, or make an errant move after being pulled over by a policeman. Where
fear and weapons meet—and they often do in urban America—there is always
the possibility of death.

3   In that first year, my first away from my hometown, I was to become thoroughly familiar with the language of fear. At dark, shadowy intersections, I could
cross in front of a car stopped at a traffic light and elicit the *thunk, thunk, thunk,
thunk* of the driver—black, white, male, or female—hammering down the door
locks. On less traveled streets after dark, I grew accustomed to but never comfortable with people crossing to the other side of the street rather than pass me.
Then there were the standard unpleasantries with policemen, doormen, bounc-
ers, cabdrivers, and others whose business it is to screen out troublesome individuals *before* there is any nastiness.

4   I moved to New York nearly two years ago and I have remained an avid
night walker. In central Manhattan, the near-constant crowd cover minimizes
tense one-on-one street encounters. Elsewhere—in SoHo, for example, where
sidewalks are narrow and tightly spaced buildings shut out the sky—things can
get very taut indeed.

5   After dark, on the warrenlike streets of Brooklyn where I live, I often see
women who fear the worst from me. They seem to have set their faces on neutral, and with their purse straps strung across their chests bandolier-style, they
forge ahead as though bracing themselves against being tackled. I understand,
of course, that the danger they perceive is not a hallucination. Women are particularly vulnerable to street violence, and young black males are drastically
overrepresented among the perpetrators of that violence. Yet these truths are
no solace against the kind of alienation that comes of being ever the suspect,
a fearsome entity with whom pedestrians avoid making eye contact.

6   It is not altogether clear to me how I reached the ripe old age of twenty-
two without being conscious of the lethality nighttime pedestrians attributed to
me. Perhaps it was because in Chester, Pennsylvania, the small, angry industrial
town where I came of age in the 1960s, I was scarcely noticeable against a back-
drop of gang warfare, street knifings, and murders. I grew up one of the good

boys, had perhaps a half-dozen fistfights. In retrospect, my shyness of combat has clear sources.

As a boy, I saw countless tough guys locked away; I have since buried several, too. They were babies, really—a teenage cousin, a brother of twenty-two, a childhood friend in his mid-twenties—all gone down in episodes of bravado played out in the streets. I came to doubt the virtues of intimidation early on. I chose, perhaps unconsciously, to remain a shadow—timid, but a survivor. 7

The fearsomeness mistakenly attributed to me in public places often has a perilous flavor. The most frightening of these confusions occurred in the late 1970s and early 1980s, when I worked as a journalist in Chicago. One day, rushing into the office of a magazine I was writing for with a dead-line story in hand, I was mistaken for a burglar. The office manager called security and, with an ad hoc posse, pursued me through the labyrinthine halls, nearly to my editor's door. I had no way of proving who I was. I could only move briskly toward the company of someone who knew me. 8

Another time I was on assignment for a local paper and killing time before an interview. I entered a jewelry store on the city's affluent Near North Side. The proprietor excused herself and returned with an enormous red Doberman pinscher straining at the end of a leash. She stood, the dog extended toward me, silent to my questions, her eyes bulging nearly out of her head. I took a cursory look around, nodded, and bade her good night. 9

Relatively speaking, however, I never fared as badly as another black male journalist. He went to nearby Waukegan, Illinois, a couple of sum-mers ago to work on a story about a murderer who was born there. Mis-taking the reporter for the killer, police officers hauled him from his car at gunpoint and but for his press credentials would probably have tried to book him. Such episodes are not uncommon. Black men trade tales like this all the time. 10

Over the years, I learned to smother the rage I felt at so often being taken for a criminal. Not to do so would surely have led to madness. I now take precautions to make myself less threatening. I move about with care, particularly late in the evening. I give a wide berth to nervous people on subway platforms during the wee hours, particularly when I have exchanged business clothes for jeans. If I happen to be entering a building behind some people who appear skittish, I may walk by, letting them clear the lobby be-fore I return, so as not to seem to be following them. I have been calm and extremely congenial on those rare occasions when I've been pulled over by the police. 11

And on late-evening constitutionals I employ what has proved to be an ex-cellent tension-reducing measure: I whistle melodies from Beethoven and Vi-valdi and the more popular classical composers. Even steely New Yorkers hunching toward night-time destinations seem to relax, and occasionally they even join in the tune. Virtually everybody seems to sense that a mugger wouldn't be warbling bright, sunny selections from Vivaldi's *Four Seasons*. It is my equiva-lent of the cowbell that hikers wear when they know they are in bear country. 12

QUESTIONS ON SUBJECT AND PURPOSE

1. What does Staples mean by the phrase "public space"? In what way is he capable of altering it?
2. What types of evidence does Staples provide to illustrate his point—that black men can alter public space?
3. What purpose might Staples have had in writing the essay?

QUESTIONS ON STRATEGY AND AUDIENCE

1. In addition to cause and effect, what other structure is at work in the essay?
2. When the essay was first published, it was entitled "Just Walk on By." When it appeared in a slightly revised form, it was retitled, "Black Men and Public Space." What is the effect of the change in title?
3. The essay first appeared in *Ms.* magazine. What assumptions could Staples have had about his initial audience?

QUESTIONS ON VOCABULARY AND STYLE

1. What is the effect of Staples's opening sentence in the essay? Why does he write "my first victim"?
2. In paragraph 5, Staples writes the phrase "on the warrenlike streets of Brooklyn." What is a *warren?* To what does the term usually refer? Can you think of another word or phrase that Staples could have used instead that might be more vivid to most readers?
3. Be prepared to define the following words: *discreet* (paragraph 1), *dicey* (2), *errant* (2), *taut* (4), *warrenlike* (5), *bandolier* (5), *solace* (5), *entity* (5), *bravado* (7), *ad hoc* (8), *cursory* (9), *skittish* (11), *congenial* (11), *constitutionals* (12).

WRITING SUGGESTIONS

1. **For Your Journal.** Have you ever been frightened in a public space? Explore your memories or your recent experiences, and jot down a few such times. Try to capture a few details about each experience.
2. **For a Paragraph.** Select one of the experiences you entered in your journal for Suggestion 1, and narrate that experience in a paragraph. Why did you react as you did? Was your fear justified? You can also turn the topic around and describe a time when your presence frightened someone else while in a public space.
3. **For an Essay.** Regardless of our age or sex or color, we all provoke reactions from people who do not know us. Sometimes, in fact, we go out of our way to elicit a reaction—dressing in a certain way, driving a particular type of car, engaging in an unusual activity, wearing our hair

in a peculiar style. Describe your image and behavior, and analyze how people react to you and why they react as they do.

4. **For Research.** Who mugs whom? Research the problem of assault or mugging either in the country as a whole or in your own community. What are your chances of being mugged? Who is likely to do it to you? Where is it most likely to happen? If you decide to focus on your own community or college campus, remember to interview the local police.

FOR FURTHER STUDY

Focusing on Grammar and Writing. Staples often uses vivid verbs in telling his story. Go through the essay and make a list of such verbs. What do they suggest about how to create an arresting story or description? Do you use verbs in the same way in your writing?

Working Together. Staples's introduction, though brilliant, seems more appropriate for a magazine targeted for women than for men. Working in small groups, recast the opening of the essay as if it might appear in a magazine aimed at a male audience. Share your new introductions with the rest of the class.

Seeing Other Modes at Work. Staples uses both narration and description in the essay as well.

Finding Connections. An interesting pairing is with Judith Ortiz Cofer's "The Myth of the Latin Woman" (Chapter 4). Both essays deal with people's reactions to skin color or ethnicity.

Exploring the Web. Additional information about Staples and examples of his writing can be found at a number of Websites. Start at **www.prenhall.com/miller.**

DREADLOCKED

Veronica Chambers

Veronica Chambers was born in Brooklyn, the daughter, she writes, of "two black Latinos from Panama." Educated at Simon's Rock College, she has worked as a journalist, editor, and photographer for magazines such as Sassy, Seventeen, Essence, The New York Times Magazine, Newsweek, *and, most recently,* Savoy. *She is the author of children's books as well. Her most recent book is the novel* When Did You Stop Loving Me *(2004).*

On Writing: *In an interview aired on National Public Radio's* Anthem *series, Chambers said of her writing, "I go to poetry a lot. . . . I found, for example, in writing* Mama's Girl *that it was hard for me to read other people's memoirs. . . . So I read almost exclusively a lot of poetry . . . to keep myself with words, but not get myself mired in other stories."*

BEFORE READING

Connecting: What associations do you have with dreadlocks? Are those associations stereotypes?

Anticipating: What do Chambers's dreadlocks mean or symbolize to her?

1   I have two relationships with the outside world: One is with my hair, and the other is with the rest of me. Sure, I have concerns and points of pride with my body. I like the curve of my butt but dislike my powerhouse thighs. My breasts, once considered too small, have been proclaimed perfect so often that not only am I starting to believe the hype, but also am booking my next vacation to a topless resort in Greece. But my hair. Oh, my hair.

2   I have reddish brown dreadlocks that fall just below shoulder length. Eventually, they will cover my aforementioned breasts, at which time I will give serious thought to nude modeling at my local art school. I like my hair—a lot. But over the last eight years my dreadlocks have conferred upon me the following roles: rebel child, Rasta mama, Nubian princess, drug dealer, unemployed artist, rock star, world-famous comedienne, and nature chick. None of which is true. It has occurred to me more than once that my hair is a whole lot more interesting than I am.

3   Because I am a black woman, I have always had a complicated relationship with my hair. Here's a quick primer on the politics of hair and beauty aesthetics in the black community vis-à-vis race and class in the late 20th century: "Good" hair is straight and, preferably, long. Think Naomi Campbell. Diana Ross. For that matter, think RuPaul. "Bad" hair is thick and coarse, aka "nappy," and, often, short. Think Buckwheat in *The Little Rascals*. Not the more recent version, but the old one in which Buckwheat looked like Don King's grandson.

Understand that these are stereotypes: broad and imprecise. Some will 4
say that the idea of "good" hair and "bad" hair is outdated. And it is less prevalent than in the '70s when I was growing up. Sometimes I see little girls with
their hair in braids and Senegalese twists sporting cute little T-shirts that say
HAPPY TO BE NAPPY and I get teary-eyed. I was born between the black
power Afros of the '60s and the blue contact lenses and weaves of the '80s; in
my childhood, no one seemed happy to be nappy at all.

I knew from the age of 4 that I had "bad" hair because my relatives and 5
family friends discussed it as they might discuss a rare blood disease. "Something must be done," they would chick sadly. "I think I know someone," an
aunt would murmur, referring to a hair-dresser as if she were a medical specialist. Some of my earliest memories are of Brooklyn apartments where
women did hair for extra money. These makeshift beauty parlors were lively
and loud, the air thick with the smell of lye from harsh relaxer, the smell of
hair burning as the hot straightening comb did its job.

When did I first begin to desire hair that bounced? Was it because black 6
Barbie wasn't, and still isn't, happy to be nappy? Was it Brenda, the redhead,
my best friend in second grade? Every time she flicked her hair to the side, she
seemed beyond sophistication. My hair bounced the first day back from the
hairdresser's, but not much longer. "Don't sweat out that perm," my mother
would call. But I found it impossible to sit still. Hairdressers despaired like
cowardly lion tamers at the thought of training my kinky hair. "This is some
hard hair," they would say. I knew that I was not beautiful and I blamed it on
my hair.

The night I began to twist my hair into dreads, I was 19 and a junior in 7
college. It was New Year's Eve and the boy I longed for had not called. A few
months before, Alice Walker had appeared on the cover of *Essence*, her locks
flowing with all the majesty of a Southern American Cleopatra. I was inspired.
It was my family's superstition that the hours between New Year's Eve and
New Year's Day were the time to cast spells. "However New Year's catches you
is how you'll spend the year," my mother always reminded me.

I decided to use the hours that remained to transform myself into the 8
vision I'd seen on the magazine. Unsure of how to begin, I washed my hair,
carefully and lovingly. I dried it with a towel, then opened a jar of hair grease.
Using a comb to part the sections, I began to twist each section into baby
dreads. My hair, at the time, couldn't have been longer than an inch. I twisted
for two hours, and in the end was far from smitten with what I saw: My full
cheeks dominated my face now that my hair lay in flat twists around my head.
My already short hair seemed shorter. I did not look like the African goddess
I had imagined. I emerged from the bathroom and ran into my aunt Diana,
whose luxuriously long, straight black hair always reminded me of Diahann
Carroll on *Dynasty*. "Well, Vickie," she said, shaking her head. "Well, well."
I knew that night my life would begin to change. I started my dreadlocks and
began the process of seeing beauty where no one had ever seen beauty before.

There are, of course, those who see my hair and still consider it "bad." 9
A family friend touched my hair recently, then said, "Don't you think it's a

waste? All that lovely hair twisted in those things?" I have been asked by more than one potential suitor if I had any pictures of myself before "you did that to your hair." A failure at small talk and countless other social graces, I sometimes let my hair do the talking for me. At a cocktail party, I stroll through the room, silently, and watch my hair tell white lies. In literary circles, it brands me "interesting, adventurous." In black middle-class circles, I'm "rebellious" or, more charitably. "Afro-centric." In predominantly white circles, my hair doubles my level of exotica. My hair says, "Unlike the black woman who reads you the evening news, I'm not even trying to blend in."

10   For those ignorant enough to think that they can read hair follicles like tea leaves, my hair says a lot of things it doesn't mean. Taken to the extreme, it says that I am a pot-smoking Rastafarian wannabe who in her off-hours strolls through her house in an African dashiki, lighting incense and listening to Bob Marley. I don't smoke pot. In my house, I wear Calvin Klein nightshirts, and light tuberose candles that I buy from Diptyque in Paris. I play tennis in my off-hours and, while I love Bob Marley, I mostly listen to jazz vocalists like Ella Fitzgerald and Diana Krall.

11   Once after a dinner party in Beverly Hills, a white colleague of mine lit up a joint. Everyone at the table passed and when I passed too, the man cajoled me relentlessly. "Come on," he kept saying. "Of all people, I thought you'd indulge." I shrugged and said nothing. As we left the party that night, he kissed me goodbye. "Boy, were you a disappointment," he said, as if I had been a bad lay. But I guess I had denied him a certain sort of pleasure. It must have been his dream to smoke a big, fat spliff with a real live Rastafarian.

12   As much as I hate to admit it, I've been trained to turn my head to any number of names that aren't mine. I will answer to "Whoopi." I will turn when Jamaican men call out "Hey, Rasta" on the street. I am often asked if I am a singer, and I can only hope that I might be confused with the gorgeous Cassandra Wilson, whose dreadlocks inspired me to color my hair a jazzy shade of red. Walking through the streets of Marrakesh, I got used to trails of children who would follow me, trying to guess which country I came from. "Jamaica!" they would shout. "Ghana! Nigeria!" I shook my head no to them all. They did not believe me when I said I was from America: instead, they called me "Mama Africa" all day long. It's one of my favorite memories of the trip.

13   Once, after the end of a great love affair, I watched a man cut all of his dreadlocks off and then burn them in the backyard. This, I suspect, is the reason that might tempt me to change my hair. After all, a broken heart is what started me down this path of twisting hair. Because I do not cut my hair, I carry eight years of history on my head. One day, I may tire of this history and start anew. But one thing is for sure, whatever style I wear my hair in, I will live happily— and nappily—ever after.

QUESTIONS ON SUBJECT AND PURPOSE

   1. What are *dreadlocks?* Do you know where the term came from?
   2. When does Chambers first wear "dreads"?

3. How does wearing "dreads" change the way in which others perceive her? Does it also change the way in which she perceives herself?

QUESTIONS ON STRATEGY AND AUDIENCE

1. In what ways is this a cause and effect analysis?
2. In addition to cause and effect, what other organizational strategy can you find in the essay?.
3. What expectations might Chambers have of her audience? For example, what do the allusions or names mentioned in the essay suggest about Chambers's sense of her readers?

QUESTIONS ON VOCABULARY AND STYLE

1. Are the last two sentences in paragraph 1 really sentences? If not, what are they?
2. In paragraph 6, Chambers writes: "Hairdressers despaired like cowardly lion tamers at the thought of training my kinky hair." What figure of speech is she using?
3. Be prepared to define the following words: *Nubian* (2), *aka* (3), *cajoled* (11).

WRITING SUGGESTIONS

1. **For Your Journal.** Think about yourself, a sibling, or a friend. To what extent do you or that person adopt or affect an appearance? What has influenced how you or that person looks and acts? To what extent is the appearance intended to suggest or evoke something else? Think about the choices that can be made in physical appearances (such as hairstyles, clothing styles, piercings or tattoos, body jewelry) or in behavior (such as mannerisms, language habits, actions). In your journal try to list some possible causes and effects of such decisions.
2. **For a Paragraph.** Using your journal entry as a prewriting activity, expand your cause and effect analysis into a paragraph. Select one element in that appearance and try to explain what brought it about and what results that element has produced.
3. **For an Essay.** Expand your paragraph writing into an essay. Instead of concentrating on a single element in that appearance, expand your analysis to include all of the aspects of both appearance and behavior.
4. **For Research.** Not so long ago, one found tattoos mostly on former soldiers and sailors and on motorcyclists. Today, many young people sport tattoos. Why? What explanation can be given for the popularity of tattoos among young adults? In a research essay, explore the phenomenon and analyze why tattoos are so popular. Another possibility might be body piercings or extreme hairstyles or colors.

FOR FURTHER STUDY

Focusing on Grammar and Writing. What is a topic sentence, and what function does it have in a paragraph? Look critically at Chambers's essay. Does she use topic sentences? If so, what role do they play in organizing the essay? What role do they play in helping you read the essay? What does this suggest about your own writing?

Working Together. Divide into small groups. Each group should take one of the following sections to evaluate:

Paragraphs 3 and 4
Paragraphs 5 and 6
Paragraphs 7 and 8
Paragraphs 10 and 11
Paragraph 12

What do the details in each paragraph add to the story?

Seeing Other Modes at Work. Chambers's essay also uses narration throughout.

Finding Connections. Possible pairings might include Janice Mirikitani's poem "Recipe" (Chapter 6), Robin D. G. Kelley's "The People in Me," and Margaret Atwood's "The Female Body" (both in Chapter 8).

Exploring the Web. Want to know more about dreadlocks, Bob Marley, Rastafarianism, and Veronica Chambers? Start at **www.prenhall.com/miller.**

THE TROUBLE WITH FRIES

Malcolm Gladwell

Malcolm Gladwell (1963–) was born in England and grew up in Canada. A graduate of the University of Toronto with a degree in history, he was a reporter for The Washington Post *before becoming a staff writer for* The New Yorker *magazine. His most recent book is* Blink: The Power of Thinking Without Thinking *(2005). "The Trouble with Fries" originally appeared in* The New Yorker.

On Writing: *Gladwell comments: "The most common question I get from readers is: 'Where do you get your ideas?' And the answer I always give is 'I don't know.' . . . It's just that the question seems to presuppose that there is a place where I find ideas—a system—and there isn't. . . . The process of generating ideas, for me, is entirely unpredictable and serendipitous. . . . The other important piece to the puzzle is that having an idea for a story is actually overrated. The idea is actually the easy part. The execution is the hard part."*

BEFORE READING

Connecting: How often do you eat at fast-food restaurants each week? Do you ever worry about the fat or the calories in that food?

Anticipating: Gladwell suggests that we already have the technology to make fast food more healthy for us. If so, why have changes not been made?

In 1954, a man named Ray Kroc, who made his living selling the five-spindle Multimixer milkshake machine, began hearing about a hamburger stand in San Bernardino, California. This particular restaurant, he was told, had no fewer than eight of his machines in operation, meaning that it could make forty shakes simultaneously. Kroc was astounded. He flew from Chicago to Los Angeles, and drove to San Bernardino, sixty miles away, where he found a small octagonal building on a corner lot. He sat in his car and watched as the workers showed up for the morning shift. They were in starched white shirts and paper hats, and moved with a purposeful discipline. As lunchtime approached, customers began streaming into the parking lot, lining up for bags of hamburgers. Kroc approached a strawberry blonde in a yellow convertible.

"How often do you come here?" he asked.

"Anytime I am in the neighborhood," she replied, and, Kroc would say later, "it was not her sex appeal but the obvious relish with which she devoured the hamburger that made my pulse begin to hammer with excitement." He came back the next morning, and this time set up inside the kitchen, watching the griddle man, the food preparers, and, above all, the French-fry operation, because it was the French fries that truly captured his imagination. They were made from top-quality oblong Idaho russets, eight ounces apiece, deep-fried to a golden brown, and salted with a shaker that, as he put it, kept going like a Salvation Army girl's tambourine. They were crispy on the outside and buttery soft on the inside, and that day Kroc had a vision of a chain of restaurants, just like the one in San Bernardino, selling golden fries from one end of the country to the other. He asked the two brothers who owned the hamburger stand if he could buy their franchise rights. They said yes. Their names were Mac and Dick McDonald.

4   Ray Kroc was the great visionary of American fast food, the one who brought the lessons of the manufacturing world to the restaurant business. Before the fifties, it was impossible, in most American towns, to buy fries of consistent quality. Ray Kroc was the man who changed that. "The french fry," he once wrote, "would become almost sacrosanct for me, its preparation a ritual to be followed religiously." A potato that has too great a percentage of water— and potatoes, even the standard Idaho russet burbank, vary widely in their water content—will come out soggy at the end of the frying process. It was Kroc, back in the fifties, who sent out field men, armed with hydrometers, to make sure that all his suppliers were producing potatoes in the optimal solids range of twenty to twenty-three per cent. Freshly harvested potatoes, furthermore, are rich in sugars, and if you slice them up and deep-fry them the sugars will caramelize and brown the outside of the fry long before the inside is cooked. To make a crisp French fry, a potato has to be stored at a warm temperature for several weeks in order to convert those sugars to starch. Here Kroc led the way as well, mastering the art of "curing" potatoes by storing them under a giant fan in the basement of his first restaurant, outside Chicago.

5   Perhaps his most enduring achievement, though, was the so-called potato computer—developed for McDonald's by a former electrical engineer for Motorola named Louis Martino—which precisely calibrated the optimal cooking time for a batch of fries. (The key: when a batch of cold raw potatoes is dumped into a vat of cooking oil, the temperature of the fat will drop and then slowly rise. Once the oil has risen three degrees, the fries are ready.) Previously, making high-quality French fries had been an art. The potato computer, the hydrometer, and the curing bins made it a science. By the time Kroc was finished, he had figured out how to turn potatoes into an inexpensive snack that would always be hot, salty, flavorful, and crisp, no matter where or when you bought it.

6   This was the first fast-food revolution—the mass production of food that had reliable mass appeal. But today, as the McDonald's franchise approaches its fiftieth anniversary, it is clear that fast food needs a second revolution. As many Americans now die every year from obesity-related illnesses—heart disease and complications of diabetes—as from smoking, and the fast-food toll grows heavier every year. In the fine new book *Fast Food Nation*, the journalist Eric Schlosser writes of McDonald's and Burger King in the tone usually reserved for chemical companies, sweatshops, and arms dealers, and, as shocking as that seems at first, it is perfectly appropriate. Ray Kroc's French fries are killing us. Can fast food be fixed?

7   Fast-food French fries are made from a baking potato like an Idaho russet, or any other variety that is mealy, or starchy, rather than waxy. The potatoes

are harvested, cured, washed, peeled, sliced, and then blanched—cooked enough so that the insides have a fluffy texture but not so much that the fry gets soft and breaks. Blanching is followed by drying, and drying by a thirty-second deep fry, to give the potatoes a crisp shell. Then the fries are frozen until the moment of service, when they are deep-fried again, this time for somewhere around three minutes. Depending on the fast-food chain involved, there are other steps interspersed in this process. McDonald's fries, for example, are briefly dipped in a sugar solution, which gives them their golden-brown color; Burger King fries are dipped in a starch batter, which is what gives those fries their distinctive hard shell and audible crunch. But the result is similar. The potato that is first harvested in the field is roughly eighty per cent water. The process of creating a French fry consists, essentially, of removing as much of that water as possible—through blanching, drying, and deep-frying—and replacing it with fat.

Elisabeth Rozin, in her book *The Primal Cheeseburger*, points out that the   8
idea of enriching carbohydrates with fat is nothing new. It's a standard part of the cuisine of almost every culture. Bread is buttered; macaroni comes with cheese; dumplings are fried; potatoes are scalloped, baked with milk and cheese, cooked in the drippings of roasting meat, mixed with mayonnaise in a salad, or pan-fried in butterfat as latkes. But, as Rozin argues, deep-frying is in many ways the ideal method of adding fat to carbohydrates. If you put butter on a mashed potato, for instance, the result is texturally unexciting: it simply creates a mush. Pan-frying results in uneven browning and crispness. But when a potato is deep-fried the heat of the oil turns the water inside the potato into steam, which causes the hard granules of starch inside the potato to swell and soften: that's why the inside of the fry is fluffy and light. At the same time, the outward migration of the steam limits the amount of oil that seeps into the interior, preventing the fry from getting greasy and concentrating the oil on the surface, where it turns the outer layer of the potato brown and crisp. "What we have with the french fry," Rozin writes, "is a near perfect enactment of the enriching of a starch food with oil or fat."

This is the trouble with the French fry. The fact that it is cooked in fat makes   9
it unhealthy. But the contrast that deep-frying creates between its interior and its exterior—between the golden shell and the pillowy whiteness beneath—is what makes it so irresistible. The average American now eats a staggering thirty pounds of French fries a year, up from four pounds when Ray Kroc was first figuring out how to mass-produce a crisp fry. Meanwhile, fries themselves have become less healthful. Ray Kroc, in the early days of McDonald's, was a fan of a hot-dog stand on the North Side of Chicago called Sam's, which used what was then called the Chicago method of cooking fries. Sam's cooked its fries in animal fat, and Kroc followed suit, prescribing for his franchises a specially formulated beef tallow called Formula 47 (in reference to the forty-seven-cent McDonald's "All-American meal" of the era: fifteen-cent hamburger, twelve-cent fries, twenty-cent shake). Among aficionados, there is general agreement that those early McDonald's fries were the finest mass-market fries ever made: the beef tallow gave them an unsurpassed rich, buttery taste. But in 1990, in the face of public concern about the health risks of cholesterol in animal-based cooking oil,

McDonald's and the other major fast-food houses switched to vegetable oil. That wasn't an improvement, however. In the course of making vegetable oil suitable for deep-frying, it is subjected to a chemical process called hydrogenation, which creates a new substance called a trans unsaturated fat. In the hierarchy of fats, polyunsaturated fats—the kind found in regular vegetable oils—are the good kind; they lower your cholesterol. Saturated fats are the bad kind. But trans fats are worse: they wreak havoc with the body's ability to regulate cholesterol. According to a recent study involving some eighty thousand women, for every five-per-cent increase in the amount of saturated fats that a woman consumes, her risk of heart disease increases by seventeen per cent. But only a two-per-cent increase in trans fats will increase her heart-disease risk by ninety-three per cent. Walter Willett, an epidemiologist at Harvard—who helped design the study—estimates that the consumption of trans fats in the United States probably causes about thirty thousand premature deaths a year.

10   McDonald's and the other fast-food houses aren't the only purveyors of trans fats, of course; trans fats are in crackers and potato chips and cookies and any number of other processed foods. Still, a lot of us get a great deal of our trans fats from French fries, and to read the medical evidence on trans fats is to wonder at the odd selectivity of the outrage that consumers and the legal profession direct at corporate behavior. McDonald's and Burger King and Wendy's have switched to a product, without disclosing its risks, that may cost human lives. What is the difference between this and the kind of thing over which consumers sue companies every day?

11   The French-fry problem ought to have a simple solution: cook fries in oil that isn't so dangerous. Oils that are rich in monounsaturated fats, like canola oil, aren't nearly as bad for you as saturated fats, and are generally stable enough for deep-frying. It's also possible to "fix" animal fats so that they aren't so problematic. For example, K. C. Hayes, a nutritionist at Brandeis University, has helped develop an oil called Appetize. It's largely beef tallow, which gives it a big taste advantage over vegetable shortening, and makes it stable enough for deep-frying. But it has been processed to remove the cholesterol, and has been blended with pure corn oil, in a combination that Hayes says removes much of the heart-disease risk.

12   Perhaps the most elegant solution would be for McDonald's and the other chains to cook their fries in something like Olestra, a fat substitute developed by Procter & Gamble. Ordinary fats are built out of a molecular structure known as a triglyceride: it's a microscopic tree, with a trunk made of glycerol and three branches made of fatty acids. Our bodies can't absorb triglycerides, so in the digestive process each of the branches is broken off by enzymes and absorbed separately. In the production of Olestra, the glycerol trunk of a fat is replaced with a sugar, which has room for not three but eight fatty acids. And our enzymes are unable to break down a fat tree with eight branches—so the Olestra molecule can't be absorbed by the body at all. "Olestra" is as much a process as a compound: you can create an "Olestra" version of any given fat. Potato chips, for instance, tend to be fried in cottonseed oil, because of its distinctively clean taste. Frito-Lay's no-fat Wow! chips are made with an Olestra version of cottonseed oil, which behaves just like regular

cottonseed oil except that it's never digested. A regular serving of potato chips has a hundred and fifty calories, ninety of which are fat calories from the cooking oil. A serving of Wow! chips has seventy-five calories and no fat. If Procter & Gamble were to seek F.D.A. approval for the use of Olestra in commercial deep-frying (which it has not yet done), it could make an Olestra version of the old McDonald's Formula 47, which would deliver every nuance of the old buttery, meaty tallow at a fraction of the calories.

Olestra, it must be said, does have some drawbacks—in particular, a   13
reputation for what is delicately called "gastrointestinal distress." The F.D.A. has required all Olestra products to carry a somewhat daunting label saying that they may cause "cramping and loose stools." Not surprisingly, sales have been disappointing, and Olestra has never won the full acceptance of the nutrition community. Most of this concern, however, appears to be overstated. Procter & Gamble has done randomized, double-blind studies—one of which involved more than three thousand people over six weeks—and found that people eating typical amounts of Olestra-based chips don't have significantly more gastrointestinal problems than people eating normal chips. Diarrhea is such a common problem in America—nearly a third of adults have at least one episode each month—that even F.D.A. regulators now appear to be convinced that in many of the complaints they received Olestra was unfairly blamed for a problem that was probably caused by something else. The agency has promised Procter & Gamble that the warning label will be reviewed.

Perhaps the best way to put the Olestra controversy into perspective is   14
to compare it to fibre. Fibre is vegetable matter that goes right through you: it's not absorbed by the gastrointestinal tract. Nutritionists tell us to eat it because it helps us lose weight and it lowers cholesterol—even though if you eat too many baked beans or too many bowls of oat bran you will suffer the consequences. Do we put warning labels on boxes of oat bran? No, because the benefits of fibre clearly outweigh its drawbacks. Research has suggested that Olestra, like fibre, helps people lose weight and lowers cholesterol; too much Olestra, like too much fibre, may cause problems. (Actually, too much Olestra may not be as troublesome as too much bran. According to Procter & Gamble, eating a large amount of Olestra—forty grams—causes no more problems than eating a small bowl—twenty grams—of wheat bran.) If we had Olestra fries, then, they shouldn't be eaten for breakfast, lunch, and dinner. In fact, fast-food houses probably shouldn't use hundred-per-cent Olestra; they should cook their fries in a blend, using the Olestra to displace the most dangerous trans and saturated fats. But these are minor details. The point is that it is entirely possible, right now, to make a delicious French fry that does not carry with it a death sentence. A French fry can be much more than a delivery vehicle for fat.

Is it really that simple, though? Consider the cautionary tale of the efforts   15
of a group of food scientists at Auburn University, in Alabama, more than a decade ago to come up with a better hamburger. The Auburn team wanted to create a leaner beef that tasted as good as regular ground beef. They couldn't just remove the fat, because that would leave the meat dry and mealy. They

wanted to replace the fat. "If you look at ground beef, it contains moisture, fat, and protein," says Dale Huffman, one of the scientists who spearheaded the Auburn project. "Protein is relatively constant in all beef, at about twenty per cent. The traditional McDonald's ground beef is around twenty per cent fat. The remainder is water. So you have an inverse ratio of water and fat. If you re-duce fat, you need to increase water." The goal of the Auburn scientists was to cut about two-thirds of the fat from normal ground beef, which meant that they needed to find something to add to the beef that would hold an equivalent amount of water—and continue to retain that water even as the beef was being grilled. Their choice? Seaweed, or, more precisely, carrageenan. "It's been in use for centuries," Huffman explains. "It's the stuff that keeps the suspension in chocolate milk—otherwise the chocolate would settle at the bottom. It has tremendous water-holding ability. There's a loose bond between the car-rageenan and the moisture." They also selected some basic flavor enhancers, designed to make up for the lost fat "taste." The result was a beef patty that was roughly three-quarters water, twenty per cent protein, five per cent or so fat, and a quarter of a per cent seaweed. They called it AU Lean.

16   It didn't take the Auburn scientists long to realize that they had created something special. They installed a test kitchen in their laboratory, got hold of a McDonald's grill, and began doing blind taste comparisons of AU Lean burgers and traditional twenty-per-cent-fat burgers. Time after time, the AU Lean burgers won. Next, they took their invention into the field. They re-cruited a hundred families and supplied them with three kinds of ground beef for home cooking over consecutive three-week intervals—regular "market" ground beef with twenty per cent fat, ground beef with five per cent fat, and AU Lean. The families were asked to rate the different kinds of beef, without knowing which was which. Again, the AU Lean won hands down—trumping the other two on "likability," "tenderness," "flavorfulness," and "juiciness."

17   What the Auburn team showed was that, even though people love the taste and feel of fat—and naturally gravitate toward high-fat food—they can be fooled into thinking that there is a lot of fat in something when there isn't. Adam Drewnowski, a nutritionist at the University of Washington, has found a similar effect with cookies. He did blind taste tests of normal and reduced-calorie brownies, biscotti, and chocolate-chip, oatmeal, and peanut-butter cookies. If you cut the sugar content of any of those cookies by twenty-five per cent, he found; people like the cookies much less. But if you cut the fat by twenty-five per cent they barely notice. "People are very finely attuned to how much sugar there is in a liquid or a solid," Drewnowski says. "For fat, there's no sensory break point. Fat comes in so many guises and so many textures it is very difficult to perceive how much is there." This doesn't mean we are obliv-ious of fat levels, of course. Huffman says that when his group tried to lower the fat in AU Lean below five per cent, people didn't like it anymore. But, within the relatively broad range of between five and twenty-five per cent, you can add water and some flavoring and most people can't tell the difference.

18   What's more, people appear to be more sensitive to the volume of food they consume than to its calorie content. Barbara Rolls, a nutritionist at Penn

State, has demonstrated this principle with satiety studies. She feeds one group of people a high-volume snack and another group a low-volume snack. Even though the two snacks have the same calorie count, she finds that people who eat the highvolume snack feel more satisfied. "People tend to eat a constant weight or volume of food in a given day, not a constant portion of calories," she says. Eating AU Lean, in short, isn't going to leave you with a craving for more calories; you'll feel just as full.

For anyone looking to improve the quality of fast food, all this is heart- 19
ening news. It means that you should be able to put low-fat cheese and low-fat mayonnaise in a Big Mac without anyone's complaining. It also means that there's no particular reason to use twenty-per-cent-fat ground beef in a fast-food burger. In 1990, using just this argument, the Auburn team suggested to McDonald's that it make a Big Mac out of AU Lean. Shortly thereafter, Mc-Donald's came out with the McLean Deluxe. Other fast-food houses scrambled to follow suit. Nutritionists were delighted. And fast food appeared on the verge of a revolution.

Only, it wasn't. The McLean was a flop, and four years later it was off 20
the market. What happened? Part of the problem appears to have been that McDonald's rushed the burger to market before many of the production kinks had been worked out. More important, though, was the psychological handicap the burger faced. People liked AU Lean in blind taste tests because they didn't know it was AU Lean; they were fooled into thinking it was regular ground beef. But nobody was fooled when it came to the McLean Deluxe. It was sold as the healthy choice—and who goes to McDonald's for health food?

Leann Birch, a developmental psychologist at Penn State, has looked at 21
the impact of these sorts of expectations on children. In one experiment, she took a large group of kids and fed them a big lunch. Then she turned them loose in a room with lots of junk food. "What we see is that some kids eat almost nothing," she says. "But other kids really chow down, and one of the things that predicts how much they eat is the extent to which parents have restricted their access to high-fat, high-sugar food in the past: the more the kids have been restricted, the more they eat." Birch explains the results two ways. First, restricting food makes kids think not in terms of their own hunger but in terms of the presence and absence of food. As she puts it, "The kid is essentially saying, 'If the food's here I better get it while I can, whether or not I'm hungry.' We see these five-year-old kids eating as much as four hundred calories." Birch's second finding, though, is more important. Because the children on restricted diets had been told that junk food was bad for them, they clearly thought that it had to taste good. When it comes to junk food, we seem to follow an implicit script that powerfully biases the way we feel about food. We like fries not in spite of the fact that they're unhealthy but because of it.

That is sobering news for those interested in improving the American diet. 22
For years, the nutrition movement in this country has made transparency one of its principal goals: it has assumed that the best way to help people improve their diets is to tell them precisely what's in their food, to label certain foods good and certain foods bad. But transparency can back-fire, because sometimes nothing is

more deadly for our taste buds than the knowledge that what we are eating is good for us. McDonald's should never have called its new offering the McLean Deluxe, in other words. They should have called it the Burger Supreme or the Monster Burger, and then buried the news about reduced calories and fat in the tiniest type on the remotest corner of their Web site. And if we were to cook fries in some high-tech, healthful cooking oil—whether Olestrized beef tallow or something else with a minimum of trans and saturated fats—the worst thing we could do would be to market them as healthy fries. They will not taste nearly as good if we do. They have to be marketed as better fries, as Classic Fries, as fries that bring back the rich tallowy taste of the original McDonald's.

23   What, after all, was Ray Kroc's biggest triumph? A case could be made for the field men with their hydrometers, or the potatocuring techniques, or the potato computer, which turned the making of French fries from an art into a science. But we should not forget Ronald McDonald, the clown who made the McDonald's name irresistible to legions of small children. Kroc understood that taste comprises not merely the food on our plate but also the associations and assumptions and prejudices we bring to the table—that half the battle in making kids happy with their meal was calling what they were eating a Happy Meal. The marketing of healthful fast food will require the same degree of subtlety and sophistication. The nutrition movement keeps looking for a crusader—someone who will bring about better public education and tougher government regulations. But we need much more than that. We need another Ray Kroc.

QUESTIONS ON SUBJECT AND PURPOSE

1. What is the "trouble" with French fries? Is the essay just about fries?
2. Why is the problem difficult to solve?
3. What purpose might Gladwell have in the essay?

QUESTIONS ON STRATEGY AND AUDIENCE

1. Why might Gladwell begin his essay with the familiar story of Ray Kroc, the founder of McDonald's?
2. In paragraphs 15 through 22, Gladwell traces the rise and fall of the "lean" hamburger, marketed by McDonald's as the "McLean Deluxe." What does this story have to do with the "trouble with fries"?
3. What assumptions could Gladwell make about his audience?

QUESTIONS ON VOCABULARY AND STYLE

1. What is a rhetorical question? (You can check the glossary.) How many rhetorical questions can you find in Gladwell's essay? Why might he use them?
2. Why does Gladwell return to Ray Kroc in his final paragraph?
3. Be prepared to define the following words: *sacrosanct* (paragraph 4), *calibrated* (5), *latkes* (8), *aficionados* (9), *purveyors* (10), *nuance* (12), *daunting* (13), *satiety* (18).

GESTIONS

Journal. Gladwell suggests that eating fast food is a health
ng it to cigarette smoking. The truth is that many people
dangerous behaviors, even though they supposedly know the
y? In your journal make a list of the risky behaviors that you,
, or a friend has engaged in. Next to each behavior, suggest a
hy you or others knowingly have taken the risk.

aragraph. Expand on your journal by writing a paragraph in
ou examine either the causes or the effects of a specific risky
the paragraph, choose either to write about causes or about
. Doing both would probably be attempting too much for a
paragraph.

3. **For an Essay.** Choose a single risky behavior that is commonly
   engaged in by your peers—things such as cigarette smoking, binge
   drinking, purging, unprotected sex, recreational drug use, criminal
   acts. In an essay, explore through a cause and effect analysis why such
   behavior has an appeal. Knowing that such things are risky or
   dangerous or even life threatening, why do people in your peer group
   engage in them? Remember that interviewing peers might prove to be
   an excellent source of information.

4. **For Research.** Expand the essay topic into a research paper using
   online and printed sources as well as interviews. What explanations
   have been offered by others to explain such decisions and behaviors? Is
   there any hope for changing or modifying such behaviors?

FOR FURTHER STUDY

Focusing on Grammar and Writing. Gladwell uses quite a few
dashes in his essay. What is a dash? Why and when is it used? Make a
list of each use of the dash in the essay. What other marks of
punctuation might have been used instead? Are there any instances in
which you could not substitute another punctuation mark? Do you
ever have to rewrite the sentence in order to remove the dash?

Working Together. Working in small groups, examine one of the
following details. What does each detail add to the story?

1. The opening story of Kroc watching the restaurant
2. The strawberry blond in a yellow convertible (paragraphs 1–3)
3. The examples of carbohydrates enriched with fat (8)
4. The analogy between Olestra and fibre (14)
5. Children and junk food (31)
6. Ronald McDonald (3)

Seeing Other Modes at Work. Gladwell's essay shows process
analysis at work, especially in describing the creation and cooking of
the fast-food French fry, in describing how Olestra works, and in

describing the creation of a leaner beef. Also present are narration and comparison and contrast.

Finding Connections. An interesting pairing is with Martin Espada's poem, "Coca-Cola and Coco-Frio" (Chapter 5).

Exploring the Web. Gladwell has his own Website where you can read some of his recent essays. All of the fast-food restaurants maintain Websites as well. Some starting points can be found at **www.prenhall.com/miller.**

8

DEFINITION

PREPARING TO WRITE

WHAT IS DEFINITION?

def • i • ni • tion (def′ ə nish′ə n) *n.* [ME *diffinicioun* < OR
definition & ML *diffinitio*, both < L *difinitio*] **1** a defining
or being defined **2** a statement of what a thing is **3** a
statement of the meaning of a word, phrase, etc.

On the midterm examination in your introductory economics class, only the essay question remains to be answered: "What is capitalism?" You are tempted to write the one-sentence definition you memorized from the glossary of your textbook and dash from the room. But it is unlikely that your professor will react positively or even charitably to such a skimpy (rote) response. Instead, you realize that what is needed is an extended definition, one that explains what factors were necessary before capitalism could emerge, what elements are most characteristic of a capitalistic economy, how capitalism differs from other economic systems, how a capitalistic economy works, how capitalism is linked to technology and politics. What you need is a narrative, a division, a comparison and contrast, a process, and a cause and effect analysis all working together to provide a full definition of what is finally a very complex term.

When you are asked to define a word, you generally do two things: first, you provide a dictionary-like definition, normally a single sentence; and second, if the occasion demands, you provide a longer, extended definition, analyzing the subject and giving examples or details. If you use technical or specialized words that may be unfamiliar to your reader, you include a parenthetical definition: "Macroeconomics, the portion of economics concerned with large-scale movements such as inflation and deflation, is particularly interested in changes in the GDP, or gross domestic product."

What Is the Difference Between Denotation and Connotation?

Definitions can be denotative, connotative, or a mixture of the two. Dictionary definitions are denotative; that is, they offer a literal and explicit definition of a word. A dictionary, for example, defines the word *prejudice* as "a judgment or opinion formed before the facts are known; preconceived idea." In most cases, however, a single sentence is not enough to give a reader a clear understanding of the word or concept.

Many words have more than just literal meanings; they also carry connotations, either positive or negative, and these connotations may make up part of an extended definition. For example, in 1944, when the United States was at war on two fronts, E. B. White was asked to write about the "meaning of democracy" for the Writers' War Board. White's one-paragraph response goes beyond a literal definition to explore the connotations and associations that surround the word *democracy:*

Show
don't
Tell

> Surely the Board knows what democracy is. It is the line that forms on the right. It is the don't in Don't Shove. It is the hole in the stuffed shirt through which the sawdust trickles; it is the dent in the high hat. Democracy is the recurrent suspicion that more than half of the people are right more than half of the time. It is the feeling of privacy in the voting booths, the feeling of communion in the libraries, the feeling of vitality everywhere. Democracy is the score at the beginning of the ninth. It is an idea which hasn't been disproved yet, a song the words of which have not gone bad. It's the mustard on the hot dog and the cream in the rationed coffee. Democracy is a request from a War Board, in the middle of a morning in the middle of a war, wanting to know what democracy is.

Democracy was, to White, not simply a form of government, but a whole way of life.

Most writing situations, especially those you encounter in college, require extended definitions. The selections in this chapter define a variety of subjects, and they suggest how differently extended definitions can be handled. Ben Stein's definition of a hero consists of a series of examples of selfless people who dedicate their lives to helping others. He contrasts these "real" heroes with the Hollywood celebrities idolized by Americans. Judy Brady defines the word *wife* through the many associations that people have with that word. Robin D. G. Kelley explains how a seemingly simple question, "What are you?", can be very difficult to answer. Amy Tan explores a definition of *mother tongue* based on her own mother's Chinese-inflected English. John Hollander describes the *mess* in his office, offering both a history of the word's meaning and examples of how artists have represented "messes." Finally Margaret Atwood uses multiple examples to define that "capacious" topic, the *female body*.

How Much Do You Include in a Definition?

Every word, whether it refers to a specific physical object or to the most theoretical concept, has a dictionary definition. Whether that one-sentence definition is sufficient depends on why you are defining the word. Complex words and words with many nuances and connotations generally require a fuller definition than a single sentence can provide. Moreover, one-sentence definitions often contain other words and phrases that also need to be defined.

For example, if you were asked, "What is a wife?" you could reply, "A woman married to a man." Although that definition is accurate, it does not convey any sense of what such a relationship might involve. Judy Brady's "I Want a Wife" defines the word by showing what men (or some men) expect in a wife. Brady divides and lists a wife's many responsibilities—things expected of her by an actual or potential husband. Brady's essay, comically overstated as it is, offers a far more meaningful definition of the term *wife* than any one-sentence dictionary entry. Her intention surely was to reveal inequality in marriage, and she makes her point by listing a stereotypical set of male expectations.

Writing a definition is a fairly common activity in college work. In your literature course, you are asked to define the romantic movement; in art history, the baroque period; in psychology, abnormal behavior. Since a single-sentence definition can never do justice to such complicated terms, an extended definition is necessary. In each case, the breadth and depth of your knowledge is being tested; your professor expects you to formulate a definition that accounts for the major subdivisions and characteristics of the subject. Your purpose is to convince your professor that you have read and mastered the assigned materials and can select among them and organize them, often adding some special insight of your own, into a logical and coherent response.

Politicians are not the only people who know how to manipulate meaning by changing the definitions of the words.
www.CartoonStock.com

Prewriting Suggestions

1. Once you have chosen or been assigned a word or phrase to define, first write a short dictionary definition of it. Concentrate on its denotative meaning.

2. Write a purpose statement for your paper: "My purpose in this essay is to. . . ." Use that statement as a way of testing your developing draft.

3. Describe your intended audience. How much do they know about this term? Is it technical? Complicated? Will you need to provide parenthetical definitions of other words or phrases as you are defining?

4. Will visuals—diagrams, photographs, sketches—be helpful? Check with your instructor to see if you can include such devices in your essay.

5. Remember that a definition essay involves an extended definition— that is, you must add appropriate details and examples. What types of details or examples would help fill out your definition? Will they come from observation? From research? Plan a strategy by which you can gain the necessary details for an extended definition. Make a list of those details and examples.

WRITING

HOW DO YOU STRUCTURE A DEFINITION ESSAY?

Sentence definitions are relatively easy to write. You first place the word in a general class ("A wife is a *woman*") and then add any distinguishing features that set it apart from other members of the class ("married to a man"). But the types of definitions you are asked to write for college are generally more detailed than dictionary entries. How, then, do you get from a single sentence to a paragraph or an essay?

Extended definitions do not have a structure peculiar to themselves. That is, when you write a definition, you do not have a predetermined structural pattern as you do with comparison and contrast, division and classification, process, or cause and effect. Instead, definitions are constructed using all of the various strategies in this book. Ben Stein uses examples and contrast to define who the "real" heroes are. Judy Brady's definition of a wife uses division to organize the many types of responsibilities demanded of a wife. Robin D. G. Kelley and Amy Tan use narration as a vital part of their definitions. John Hollander uses description and comparison and contrast. Margaret Atwood gathers a wide range of examples to suggest the complexity involved in the phrase "the female body," ending with an imaginative contrast between the brain of a man and that of a woman.

Drafting Suggestions

1. Look at the list of details and examples that you gathered as preparation for writing this essay. Can you sort them into structural categories as a first step in planning an organization for your essay? For example, do any involve comparison and contrast? Division or classification, cause or effect? Narration or description? Process? Remember that extended definitions make use of other structural patterns.

2. Have you considered all the connotations of the word or concept that you are defining? Readers have associations with terms that are not necessarily a part of their denotative definitions.

3. Think about your audience's prior knowledge about this subject. Does your definition essay involve technical concepts or specialized knowledge? Use your statement of intended audience as a way of judging how much explanation you need to provide.

4. Like every essay, your definition paper needs an introduction, a body or middle, and a conclusion. As you write, jot down an outline of the developing structure of your paper. Middles are the longest and most complicated, but in a definition essay, your middle is likely to use structures derived from the other modes discussed and illustrated in this text.

5. Plan at least two different introductions to your essay: one could be a straightforward explanation of what you are defining; the other ought to be more reader-friendly. Maybe you could begin with an example or a story, maybe a provocative statement.

Once you have chosen a subject for definition, think first about its essential characteristics, steps, or parts. What examples would best define it? Then plan your organization by seeing how those details can be presented most effectively to your reader. If your definition involves breaking a subject into its parts, use division or possibly even process. If you are defining by comparing your subject to another, use a comparison and contrast structure. If your subject is defined as the result of some causal connection, use a cause and effect structure. Definitions can also involve narration, description, and even persuasion. The longer the extended definition, the greater the likelihood that your paper will involve a series of structures.

REVISING

HOW DO YOU REVISE A DEFINITION ESSAY?

You look for a definition of a word in a dictionary or an encyclopedia in order to find out what it means—you need the information to understand the word or concept. You expect to come away with a clear understanding of the word's meaning. If you are confused by other terms used in the definition or if the information presented isn't clear, logical, and easily understood, then your needs have not been met. All definitions, including the extended definition essays that you write in academic courses, must meet those tests of clarity and comprehension. As you are revising your definition essay, enlist the help of other readers, especially peer readers. After they have read your paper, ask them to rephrase the definition in their own words. Have they understood what you are trying to explain? Ask them to identify any words or phrases in your essay that they do not understand or cannot define. Address all of those potential problems as you revise your draft.

When revising a definition essay, play particular attention to audience, organization, and the beginning and ending of your essay.

Paying Attention to Your Audience   Look again at your statement of intended audience and your reader's responses. Have you adequately and clearly defined your subject? Have you used words they will understand? If your definition contains technical words and phrases, make sure they are defined in context for your readers. You can do so in two ways. First, you can insert a parenthetical definition (enclosed either within a pair of commas or within parentheses) after the word or phrase—for example, "hyperactivity (feelings of restlessness, fidgeting, or inappropriate activity when one is expected to be quiet)." Second, you can include a definition or example in the sentence without enclosing it in commas or parentheses—for example, "Hyperactivity refers to feelings of restlessness, fidgeting, or inappropriate activity (running, wandering) when one is expected to be quiet."

Checking Organization   Your essay needs a clear organizational structure. Outline your draft to see if the sections of the essay fit together in a way that is easy to follow. Broadly speaking, definition essays can be either inductively or deductively organized. That is, you could begin with a sentence definition and then expand that definition by using examples, developing contrasts, explaining causes or effects, or by any of a number of other strategies. You could also invert the pattern in some cases so that your sentence definition comes toward the end of your essay.

As you move from section to section, make sure you clearly signal to your reader what follows. You can do so with topic sentences that introduce the subject to be covered in the next paragraph or section, or you can subdivide your text using typographical devices such as centered headings, numbered sections, or extra white space. If your extended definition makes use of any of the other strategies discussed in this text—for example, comparison, contrast, process—review the advice offered in that chapter as your revise what you have written.

Beginning and Ending   Writing the middle of any essay is generally easier than writing either the beginning or the ending, but a good definition essay needs both a strong introduction and a strong conclusion. When

Revising Suggestions

1. Ask a peer or a classmate to read your essay and to comment on how clear your definition is. Does your reader understand all of the words and concepts that you have used in your definition? What might need further explanation or definition?

2. Check again the body of your essay. Have you used a clear organizational pattern? If you have used any of the other strategies discussed in this book, check back for advice on how to structure and develop each one.

3. Have you clearly signaled transitions as you move from section to section in your essay? Have you used topic sentences for these sections? Typographical devices to set them off?

4. Have you provided enough examples or details to support your generalizations? Are your examples and details really helpful in defining your subject? Are they all relevant?

5. Look carefully at your title. A title is part of the appeal in an essay. Things like "Essay #5" or "Definition Essay" are simply not titles.

you consult a dictionary or a textbook for a definition, you expect it to be thesis driven. When you read an extended definition in a magazine or on a Website, you expect it to also be interesting, to reach out and pull you into the piece. In extended definitions that you write for courses, try to find a reader-friendly way to begin. Avoid opening sentences that begin something like "According to a dictionary, ADHD is defined as . . ." or "ADHD is when. . . ." Can you start with an example? With an interesting fact or quotation? Can you begin with a provocative statement? Your reader in a writing class is typically reading not because he or she needs the information but because the subject and the approach are readable and interesting.

Similarly, resist the temptation to end your essay with a simple repetition of the short definition of your subject or with a paraphrase of the opening of your essay. Do not just stop your essay either, providing no sense of closure. Your reader needs to feel that the essay is now over—it has reached its logical and appropriate conclusion. You might study some of the endings that the writers in this chapter use for their essays. You might also look in the Glossary and Ready Reference for some additional suggestions for effective conclusions.

SOME THINGS TO REMEMBER

1. Choose a subject that can be reasonably and fully defined within the limits of your paper. That is, make sure it is neither too limited nor too large.

2. Determine a purpose for your definition.
3. Spend time analyzing your subject to see what its essential characteristics, steps, or parts are.
4. Write a dictionary-type definition for your subject. Do this even if you are writing an extended definition. The features that set your subject apart from others in its general class reveal what must be included in your definition.
5. Choose examples that are clear and appropriate.
6. Decide which of the organizational patterns will best convey the information you have gathered.
7. Be careful about beginning with a direct dictionary definition. There are usually more effective and interesting ways to announce your subject.

SAMPLE STUDENT ESSAY

Sherry Heck's essay started from a simple set of directions: "Write an extended definition of a word of your choice." Sherry's approach to the assignment, however, was very different from everyone else's in the class. In her purpose statement, Sherry wrote, "I wanted to inform a general audience in an amusing way of the connotations and associations that accrue to the word *fall*. I got the idea while thumbing through a dictionary looking for words!" Her first draft reads as follows.

FIRST DRAFT

FALLING

When you were four years old, covered in scrapes and bruises, the word <u>fall</u> was probably too familiar. Perhaps you went exploring, discovering the creek in the woods, and following it to its falls. Summers would end too quickly and fall would arrive, and Mom would send you off to school.

You mastered the art of walking, yet it remained all too easy to fall over yourself in front of your peers. The popular kids would laugh, sending you to fall into the wrong crowd. As you sprayed graffiti triumphantly, you fell into agreement with your friends that this was the best way to slander the principal.

Then one day, you are sitting in school and you feel someone's glance fall on you. You fall silent and stare back. Soon you find yourself falling for that special someone, and you fall in love. Eventually, you have a huge falling out with that person. Your friends have long abandoned you, leaving you no one to fall back on. Your spirits fall, and you feel like the fall guy around your old peers.

Eventually, out of school, you fall into a good job, and you are able to fall out of your trance. Determined not to fall short of your career goals, you fall into line with society. Events seem to fall into place. The pace of the job speeds up, and several people fall out of the rat race. Their jobs fall to you, tripling your workload. It is difficult not to avoid falling from power, and your life's plans begin to fall through.

Alone, rejected, and jobless, you begin to blame your misfortunes on the root of all evil, the fall of Adam and Eve. Life continues, and you ponder this thought until your friends begin to fall off. Your face falls at the thought of your own fall. Your bones are weak, and falling means more than a scraped knee. Your blood pressure falls more easily. These physical worries all disappear when one day, after feeling a free-fall sensation, you fall asleep, peacefully, forever.

COMMENTS

Sherry met with her instructor, Nathan Andrews, to go over her preliminary draft. He encouraged her to watch that she not repeat phrases—for example, in the fourth paragraph, Sherry had repeated *fall out* twice. After they had brainstormed some additional *fall* phrases, he encouraged her to search for more in the dictionaries in her school's library. He also suggested that she italicize each *fall* phrase so that the reader could more easily see the word play. In her revised essay, Sherry was able to add a number of new examples.

REVISED DRAFT

INFALLIBLE

When you were four years old, covered in scrapes and bruises, the word <u>fall</u> was probably too familiar. Perhaps you went exploring, discovering the creek in the woods, and following it to its <u>falls</u>. Summers would end too quickly and <u>fall</u> would arrive, and Mom would send you off to school.

You mastered the art of walking, yet it remained all too easy to <u>fall all over yourself</u> in front of your peers. The popular kids would laugh, sending you to <u>fall in with</u> the wrong crowd. As you sprayed the graffiti triumphantly, you <u>fell in agreement</u> with your friends that this was the best way to slander the principal. Your behavior was leading you to <u>fall afoul</u> of the law.

Then one day, you are sitting in school and you feel someone's glance <u>fall on</u> you. You <u>fall silent</u> and stare back. Soon you find yourself <u>falling for</u> that special someone, and you <u>fall in love</u>. Eventually, you have a huge <u>falling out</u> with that person. The relationship <u>falls apart</u>. Your friends have long abandoned you, leaving you no one to <u>fall back on</u>. Your cries for help <u>fall on deaf ears</u>. Your <u>spirits fall</u>, and you feel like the <u>fall guy</u> around your old peers.

Eventually, out of school, you <u>fall over backwards</u> to get a good job, and you are able to <u>fall out of your trance</u>. Your love life has <u>fallen by the wayside</u>. Determined not to <u>fall short</u> of your career goals, you <u>fall into line</u> with society. Events seem to <u>fall into place</u>. The pace of the job speeds up, and several people <u>fall on their faces</u>. Their jobs <u>fall to you</u>, tripling your workload. You <u>fall behind</u> in your work. It is difficult not to avoid <u>falling from power</u>, and your life's plans begin to <u>fall through</u>.

Alone, rejected and jobless, you begin to blame your misfortunes on the root of all evil, the <u>Fall</u> of Adam and Eve. Life continues, and you ponder this thought until your friends begin to <u>fall off</u>. Your <u>face falls</u> at the thought of your own <u>fall</u>. Your bones are weak, and <u>falling</u> means more than a scraped knee. Your <u>blood pressure falls</u> more easily. These physical worries all disappear when one day, after feeling a <u>free-fall</u> sensation, you <u>fall asleep</u>, peacefully, forever.

DEFINITION AS A LITERARY STRATEGY

How and why might you define a "foot"? Alice Jones in her poem "The Foot" undertakes a definition that mixes anatomical terms with poetic images. As you read, notice how Jones organizes and develops her definition.

THE FOOT

Alice Jones

Our improbable support, erected
on the osseous architecture
of the calcaneus, talus, cuboid,
navicular, cuneiforms, metatarsals,
phalanges, a plethora of hinges,

all strung together by gliding
tendons, covered by the pearly
plantar fascia, then fat-padded
to form the sole, humble surface
of our contact with earth.

Here the body's broadest tendon
anchors the heel's fleshy base,
the finely wrinkled skin stretches
forward across the capillaried arch,
to the ball, a balance point.

A wide web of flexor tendons
and branched veins maps the dorsum,
fades into the stub-laden bone
splay, the stuffed sausage sacks
of toes, each with a tuft

of proximal hairs to introduce
the distal nail, whose useless
curve remembers an ancestor,
the vanished creature's wild
and necessary claw.

DISCUSSION QUESTIONS

1. Is the poem a denotative or a connotative definition? Or a mixture of both? Support your conclusion with specific evidence from the poem.
2. How is the definition (and the poem) organized? Is there a clear organizational plan?
3. Why might Jones have chosen to define the word *foot?* What does the poem do as a definition that a picture and a definition in an anatomy book might not do?
4. Do you sense any change in the poem—in its method of definition, in its diction—in stanzas 4 and 5?
5. What is the effect of the final three and a half lines of the poem?

WRITING SUGGESTIONS

Definitions can do many things. In part, they tell us what something is—we look up a word or a phrase in a dictionary or an encyclopedia so that we understand it. But definitions can also suggest or offer new perspectives on the familiar—they can allow us to see things in a fresh way. Write a definition for something in which you mix technical, precise language with a more creative and suggestive perception. Consider the following suggestions as possibilities:

   a. A part of a face, a hand, teeth, hair
   b. A common, useful object—a hairbrush, a comb, scissors, a pencil, a computer mouse
   c. A term connected with school—dropping or adding a course, auditing, being a "work study" student, staying up all night to study or write a paper

READING DEFINITION

What is it? That is a question you ask—consciously or unconsciously—every time you encounter something new or something you do not understand. You consult a dictionary to understand unfamiliar words you encounter; you expect that textbooks will clearly explain and define technical concepts. Definition can be pretty straightforward for simple subjects but fairly complex and extended for more complicated subjects.

Read the following definition of attention deficit hyperactivity disorder (ADHD) from the online Columbia Electronic Encyclopedia. As you read, remember what you have learned about how to write a definition and how that knowledge might help you as a reader.

- A sentence definition places a word in a general class ("a chronic, neurological-based syndrome") and then adds distinguishing features that set it apart from other members of the class ("characterized by any or all of three types of behaviors").
- A definition essay is an extended definition in which additional information or details are added to clarify or explain further the subject.
- Definitions must take into consideration the prior knowledge of readers. A technical or complicated subject is likely to require parenthetical definitions of other words and phrases. An effective definition is measured by its clarity in explaining the subject to its readers.
- The primary purpose of a definition essay is to provide its readers with information. Clarity and logical organization are essential.
- Definitions make use of a range of possible organizational strategies: they might provide examples; classify or divide the subject; use process, narration, or description; compare or contrast the essay topic with a topic that helps clarify the definition; or separate causes and effects.

Definition has no single structural pattern that is always used; it is a composite of other patterns employed together.

Dictionary definition	Attention deficit hyperactivity disorder
Definition describes behaviors	(ADHD), formely called hyperkinesis or minimal brain dysfunction, a chronic, neurologically based syndrome characterized by any or all of three types of behavior: hyperactivity, distractibility, and impulsivity.
Each behavior is then defined	Hyperactivity refers to feelings of restlessness, fidgeting, or inappropriate activity (running, wandering) when one is expected to be quiet; distractibility to heightened distraction by irrelevant sights and sounds or carelessness and inability to carry simple tasks to completion; and impulsivity to socially inappropriate speech (e.g., blurting out something without thinking) or striking out. Unlike similar behaviors caused by emotional problems or anxiety, ADHD does not fluctuate with emotional states. While the three typical behaviors occur in nearly everyone from time to time, in those with ADHD they are excessive, longterm, and pervasive and create difficulties in school, at home, or at work. ADHD is usually diagnosed before age seven. It is often accompanied by a learning disability.
Although the behaviors can be commonly found, in ADHD they are consistent and do not fluctuate	

RESPONDING TO A VISUAL

Larger dictionaries include illustrations as part of the definitions for many words. When the word being defined is a concrete noun, for example, a picture is often a better way of defining that word than is a sentence-long description. If you want to know what a *quoin* is, the picture that a typical dictionary includes is far more helpful than a definition that reads "the external corner of a building, esp., any of the large squared stones by which the corner of a building is marked." On the other hand, if the word is an abstract noun, such as *economy*, or an adverb such as *slowly*, or a verb such as *seemed*, a picture is either impossible or simply not helpful.

Complex words or subjects often resist being defined by a few words. If someone asks "Who are you?" you might find that you could give a wide range of answers. If you are traveling internationally, the definition of self you must provide is your passport; if you are registering for courses, your definition of self is a Social Security number or your student ID. Consider the photograph on the next page—a collage of credit cards and identity cards.

READING AND WRITING ABOUT IMAGES

What is in your wallet? How do those items serve to define you? Sit down with your wallet or purse and look at what it contains. If someone found it and tried to discover who would were, what would they be able to tell about you from what you carry in your wallet? How many cards? Of what type? Any pictures? Of whom? Any other pieces of information? Using the evidence that you carry around with you every day, write an essay of self-definition.

VISITING THE WEB

The companion Website, **www.prenhall.com/miller**, has additional information about definition and about the writers in this chapter. You will also find a number of links to other sources of information about the subjects of the essays found in this chapter.

EXPLORING ON YOUR OWN

When you are writing with information taken from sources, your instructors typically caution you about plagiarism—using someone else's words or ideas without properly acknowledging that source. Colleges and universities have plagiarism policies, and the penalties for plagiarism can be quite severe. Plagiarism, however, can be a little more complicated than the short definition given above implies. Using the Web as a source of information, explore the meanings of the word *plagiarism.* How does the law define that word? Does it matter if the borrowing is unintentional? How do you know what you need to acknowledge and what you do not? What is common knowledge? Strictly speaking, in a research paper, would you need to footnote almost every sentence?

LOOKING FOR WRITING SUGGESTIONS

Subjects from other academic courses are also good possibilities for definition topics.

1. Terrorist/insurgent/revolutionary/martyr
2. "For Mature Audiences"
3. Love/infatuation
4. "Ideal Body"
5. "A Just War"
6. "American Way of Life"/patriotism
7. Success/independence/adulthood
8. Democracy/socialism/tyranny
9. Global warming/free trade
10. Life/death/courage/fear
11. Cheating
12. Generation X/baby boomers
13. "Right to Bear Arms"
14. Disrespecting
15. Marriage

HOW CAN SOMEONE WHO LIVES IN INSANE LUXURY BE A STAR IN TODAY'S WORLD?

Ben Stein

Ben Stein (1944–) graduated from Columbia University with a degree in econom-ics and from Yale Law School. He has worked as a lawyer and as a law professor for a number of years. In the 1970s he was a speechwriter and lawyer for President Richard Nixon. A columnist and editorial writer for major newspapers and magazines, he is also the author or co-author of sixteen books. In addition, he has written scripts and has acted in film, television, and commercials. "How Can Someone" was the final bi-weekly column in a series titled "Monday Night at Morton's" published by E!Online, a Webzine devoted to entertainment news and celebrity gossip. Morton's is a famous chain of steakhouses. The column originally appeared in December 2003 and has a wide distribution on the Web.

On Writing: *Stein, a widely published, prolific writer, once indicated to an in-terviewer that writing is one of the things he likes the least. Although, he added, he does it nevertheless.*

BEFORE READING

Connecting: Are you ever interested in the celebrity gossip? Do you ever read any of the many publications or watch any of the television shows devoted to the lives of Hollywood stars?

Anticipating: What are the circumstances that seem to have led Stein to writing this particular column?

1   As I begin to write this, I "slug" it, as we writers say, which means I put a heading on top of the document to identify it. This heading is "eonlineFI-NAL," and it gives me a shiver to write it. I have been doing this column for so long that I cannot even recall when I started.

2   I loved writing this column so much for so long I came to believe it would never end. Lew Harris, who founded this great site, asked me to do it maybe seven or eight years ago, and I loved writing this column so much for so long I came to believe it would never end.

3   But again, all things must pass, and my column for E! Online must pass. In a way, it is actually the perfect time for it to pass. Lew, whom I have known forever, was impressed that I knew so many stars at Morton's on Monday nights.

4   He could not get over it, in fact. So, he said I should write a column about the stars I saw at Morton's and what they had to say.

It worked well for a long time, but gradually, my changing as a person 5
and the world's change have overtaken it. On a small scale, Morton's, while
better than ever, no longer attracts as many stars as it used to. It still brings in
the rich people in droves and definitely some stars.

I saw Samuel L. Jackson there a few days ago, and we had a nice visit, 6
and right before that, I saw and had a splendid talk with Warren Beatty in an
elevator, in which we agreed that *Splendor in the Grass* was a super movie.

But Morton's is not the star galaxy it once was, though it probably will 7
be again.

Beyond that, a bigger change has happened. I no longer think Holly- 8
wood stars are terribly important. They are uniformly pleasant, friendly people, and they treat me better than I deserve to be treated. But a man or woman
who makes a huge wage for memorizing lines and reciting them in front of a
camera is no longer my idea of a shining star we should all look up to.

A real star is the soldier of the 4th Infantry Division who poked his head 9
into a hole on a farm near Tikrit, Iraq. How can a man or woman who makes
an eight-figure wage and lives in insane luxury really be a star in today's
world, if by a "star" we mean someone bright and powerful and attractive as
a role model?

Real stars are not riding around in the backs of limousines or in Porsches 10
or getting trained in yoga or Pilates and eating only raw fruit while they have
Vietnamese girls do their nails. They can be interesting, nice people, but they
are not heroes to me any longer.

A real star is the soldier of the 4th Infantry Division who poked his head 11
into a hole on a farm near Tikrit, Iraq. He could have been met by a bomb or
a hall of AK-47 bullets. Instead, he faced an abject Saddam Hussein and the
gratitude of all of the decent people of the world.

A real star is the U.S. soldier who was sent to disarm a bomb next to a road 12
north of Baghdad. He approached it, and the bomb went off and killed him.

A real star, the kind who haunts my memory night and day, is the U.S. 13
soldier in Baghdad who saw a little girl playing with a piece of unexploded ordnance on a street near where he was guarding a station. He pushed her aside
and threw himself on it just as it exploded. He left a family desolate in California and a little girl alive in Baghdad.

I no longer want to perpetuate poor values by pretending that who is 14
eating at Morton's is a big subject. The stars who deserve media attention are
not the ones who have lavish weddings on TV but the ones who patrol the
streets of Mosul even after two of their buddies were murdered and their bodies battered and stripped for the sin of trying to protect Iraqis from terrorists.

We put couples with incomes of $100 million a year on the covers of our 15
magazines. The noncoms and officers who barely scrape by on military pay
but stand on guard in Afghanistan and Iraq and on ships and in submarines
and near the Arctic Circle are anonymous as they live and die.

I am no longer comfortable being a part of the system that has such poor 16
values, and I do not want to perpetuate those values by pretending that who is
eating at Morton's is a big subject.

17   There are plenty of other stars in the American firmament. The policemen and women who go off on patrol in South Central and have no idea if they will return alive. The orderlies and paramedics who bring in people who have been in terrible accidents and prepare them for surgery. The teachers and nurses who throw their whole spirits into caring for autistic children. The kind men and women who work in hospices and in cancer wards.

18   Think of each and every fireman who was running up the stairs at the World Trade Center as the towers began to collapse.

19   Now you have my idea of a real hero.

20   Last column, I told you a few of the rules I had learned to keep my sanity. Well, here is a final one to help you keep your sanity and keep you in the running for stardom: We are puny, insignificant creatures.

21   We are not responsible for the operation of the universe, and what happens to us is not terribly important. God is real, not a fiction, and when we turn over our lives to Him, he takes far better care of us than we could ever do for ourselves.

22   In a word, we make ourselves sane when we fire ourselves as the directors of the movie of our lives and turn the power over to Him.

23   I came to realize that life lived to help others is the only one that matters. This is my highest and best use as a human. I can put it another way. Years ago, I realized I could never be as great an actor as Olivier or as good a comic as Steve Martin—or Martin Mull or Fred Willard—or as good an economist as Samuelson or Friedman or as good a writer as Fitzgerald. Or even remotely close to any of them.

24   But I could be a devoted father to my son, husband to my wife and, above all, a good son to the parents who had done so much for me. This came to be my main task in life.

25   I did it moderately well with my son, pretty well with my wife and well indeed with my parents (with my sister's help). I cared for and paid attention to them in their declining years. I stayed with my father as he got sick, went into extremis and then into a coma and then entered immortality with my sister and me reading him the Psalms.

26   This was the only point at which my life touched the lives of the soldiers in Iraq or the firefighters in New York. I came to realize that life lived to help others is the only one that matters and that it is my duty, in return for the lavish life God has devolved upon me, to help others He has placed in my path. This is my highest and best use as a human.

27   As so many of you know, I am an avid Bush fan and a Republican. But I think the best guidance I ever got was from the inauguration speech of Democrat John F. Kennedy in January of 1961.

28   On a very cold and bright day in D.C., he said, "With a good conscience our only sure reward, with history the final judge of our deeds, let us go forth . . . asking His blessing and His help but knowing that here on Earth, God's work must surely be our own."

29   And then to paraphrase my favorite president, my boss and friend Richard Nixon, when he left the White House in August 1974, with me standing a few

feet away, "This is not goodbye. The French have a word for it—au revoir. We'll see you again."

Au revoir, and thank you for reading me for so long. God bless every one of you. We'll see you again.   30

QUESTIONS ON SUBJECT AND PURPOSE

1. Judging from what Stein writes in his essay (originally a column in an electronic publication), what was his normal subject matter for his column?
2. What is the occasion of this column?
3. What is Stein's stated intention or thesis in the essay?

QUESTIONS ON STRATEGY AND AUDIENCE

1. In paragraphs 1 though 8 Stein reflects on what he has been doing in writing the column. This section is not what we might expect as an "introduction" to the essay that follows. In what way, though, are those introductory paragraphs related to what follows in the essay?
2. How does Stein define a *hero* in the essay? What strategy does he use for his definition?
3. What expectations might Stein have had about his audience?

QUESTIONS ON VOCABULARY AND STYLE

1. How would you describe the tone of Stein's essay?
2. Can you think of another title for the essay? Write one and explain why you think it is as effective or more effective than the one that Stein originally wrote.
3. Be prepared to define the following words: *abject* (paragraph 11), *ordnance* (13), *firmament* (17), *extremis* (25), *devolved* (26).

WRITING SUGGESTIONS

1. **For Your Journal.** Is there a difference between a star and a hero? What associations do you have with each word? In your journal, explore the connotations and denotations that these two words have for you.
2. **For a Paragraph.** Do you agree with Stein's definition of a hero? In a paragraph, define hero and give an example of someone you would regard as hero, explaining what is heroic about this person.
3. **For an Essay.** In the essay, Stein mentions that not only has he changed over the years but the world has changed as well, implying perhaps that in a post-9/11 world, people are rethinking their values. Do you agree with that statement? Do you think that your generation (however that might be defined) has a different sense of heroism than that of your parents' or grandparents' generation? Or is it the same?

Interview some of your peers: Do they agree or disagree? How might you define heroism in the twenty-first century?

4. **For Research.** Are the qualities of heroism universal, or do they vary from one culture to another? Can a hero in one culture be a terrorist or an insurgent in another? Choose a culture that is very different from that of the United States and explore what heroism might mean in that culture. Be sure to use both print and online sources and perhaps even interviews with students from that culture. Remember to acknowledge all of your sources.

FOR FURTHER STUDY

Focusing on Grammar and Writing. In the core section of the essay on "real heroism," Stein uses parallel structures to call attention to his examples. Find those parallel structures and see how they work in the essay.

Working Together. Like columns or articles that appear in a newspaper, Stein's essay consists of many very short paragraphs. Working in small groups, explore one of the following topics:

1. Can you explain why Stein paragraphs as he does? That is, what principle seems to be at work when he ends one paragraph and begins another?

2. Can you re-paragraph the essay simply by removing some of the indentations?

3. Can you combine a group of smaller paragraphs into one larger paragraph? Do you have to add anything to make that new, larger paragraph work?

Seeing Other Modes at Work. To what extent does Stein use elements of persuasion in the essay?

Finding Connections. A controversial pairing, but a provocative one, is with David Brooks's "The Culture of Martyrdom" (Chapter 6). Wouldn't a martyr be seen as a hero in another culture?

Exploring the Web. You might want to visit the E!Online Website to see where Stein's column originally appeared. In addition, Stein maintains a huge personal Website with extensive links to his many articles and books. These links and others can be found at **www.prenhall.com/miller.**

I WANT A WIFE

Judy Brady

Judy Brady was born in 1937 in San Francisco, California, and received a B.F.A. in painting from the University of Iowa. As a freelance writer, Brady has written essays on topics such as union organizing, abortion, and the role of women in society. Currently an activist focusing on issues related to cancer and the environment, she has edited several books on the subject, including One in Three: Women with Cancer Confront an Epidemic *(1991).*

Brady's most frequently reprinted essay is "I Want a Wife," which originally appeared in Ms. *magazine in 1971. After examining the stereotypical male demands in marriage, Brady concludes, "Who wouldn't want a wife?"*

BEFORE READING

Connecting: In a relationship, what separates reasonable needs or desires from unreasonable or selfish ones?

Anticipating: What is the effect of the repetition of the phrase "I want a . . ." in the essay?

I belong to that classification of people known as wives. I am A Wife. And, not altogether incidentally, I am a mother.

Not too long ago a male friend of mine appeared on the scene fresh from a recent divorce. He had one child, who is, of course, with his ex-wife. He is obviously looking for another wife. As I thought about him while I was ironing one evening, it suddenly occurred to me that I, too, would like to have a wife. Why do I want a wife?

I would like to go back to school so that I can become economically independent, support myself, and, if need be, support those dependent upon me. I want a wife who will work and send me to school. And while I am going to school I want a wife to take care of my children. I want a wife to keep track of the children's doctor and dentist appointments. And to keep track of mine, too. I want a wife to make sure my children eat properly and are kept clean. I want a wife who will wash the children's clothes and keep them mended. I want a wife who is a good nurturant attendant to my children, who arranges for their schooling, makes sure that they have an adequate social life with their peers, takes them to the park, the zoo, etc. I want a wife who takes care of the children when they are sick, a wife who arranges to be around when the children need special care, because, of course, I cannot miss classes at school. My wife must arrange to lose time at work, and not lose the job. It may mean a small cut in my wife's income from time to time, but I guess I can tolerate that.

Needless to say, my wife will arrange and pay for the care of the children while my wife is working.

4   I want a wife who will take care of my physical needs. I want a wife who will keep my house clean. A wife who will pick up after me. I want a wife who will keep my clothes clean, ironed, mended, replaced when need be, and who will see to it that my personal things are kept in their proper place so that I can find what I need the minute I need it. I want a wife who cooks the meals, a wife who is a good cook. I want a wife who will plan the meals, do the necessary grocery shopping, prepare the meals, serve them pleasantly, and then do the cleaning up while I do my studying. I want a wife who will care for me when I am sick and sympathize with my pain and loss of time from school. I want a wife to go along when our family takes a vacation so that someone can continue to care for me and my children when I need a rest and change of scene.

5   I want a wife who will not bother me with rambling complaints about a wife's duties. But I want a wife who will listen to me when I feel the need to explain a rather difficult point I have come across in my course of studies. And I want a wife who will type my papers for me when I have written them.

6   I want a wife who will take care of the details of my social life. When my wife and I are invited out by my friends, I want a wife who will take care of the babysitting arrangements. When I meet people at school that I like and want to entertain, I want a wife who will have the house clean, will prepare a special meal, serve it to me and my friends, and not interrupt when I talk about the things that interest me and my friends. I want a wife who will have arranged that the children are fed and ready for bed before my guests arrive so that the children do not bother us. I want a wife who takes care of the needs of my guests so that they feel comfortable, who makes sure that they have an ashtray, that they are passed the hors d'oeuvres, that they are offered a second helping of the food, that their wine glasses are replenished when necessary, that their coffee is served to them as they like it. And I want a wife who knows that sometimes I need a night out by myself.

7   I want a wife who is sensitive to my sexual needs, a wife who makes love passionately and eagerly when I feel like it, a wife who makes sure that I am satisfied. And, of course, I want a wife who will not demand sexual attention when I am not in the mood for it. I want a wife who assumes the complete responsibility for birth control, because I do not want more children. I want a wife who will remain sexually faithful to me so that I do not have to clutter up my intellectual life with jealousies. And I want a wife who understands that *my* sexual needs may entail more than strict adherence to monogamy. I must, after all, be able to relate to people as fully as possible.

8   If, by chance, I find another person more suitable as a wife than the wife I already have, I want the liberty to replace my present wife with another one. Naturally I will expect a fresh, new life; my wife will take the children and be solely responsible for them so that I am left free.

9   When I am through with school and have a job, I want my wife to quit working and remain at home so that my wife can more fully and completely take care of a wife's duties.

10   My God, who *wouldn't* want a wife?

QUESTIONS ON SUBJECT AND PURPOSE

1. In what way is this a definition of a wife? Why does Brady avoid a more conventional definition?
2. Is Brady being fair? Is there anything that she leaves out of her definition that you would have included?
3. What purpose might Brady have been trying to achieve?

QUESTIONS ON STRATEGY AND AUDIENCE

1. How does Brady structure her essay? What is the order of the development? Could the essay have been arranged in any other way?
2. Why does Brady identify herself by her roles—wife and mother—at the beginning of the essay? Is that information relevant in any way?
3. What assumptions does Brady have about her audience (readers of *Ms.* magazine in the early 1970s)? How do you know?

QUESTIONS ON VOCABULARY AND STYLE

1. How does Brady use repetition in the essay? Why? Does it work? What effect does it create?
2. How effective is Brady's final rhetorical question? Where else in the essay does she use a rhetorical question?
3. Be able to define the following words: *nurturant* (paragraph 3), *hors d'oeuvres* (6), *replenished* (6), *monogamy* (7).

WRITING SUGGESTIONS

1. **For Your Journal.** What do you look for in a possible spouse or "significant other"? Make a list of what you expect or want from a relationship with another person. Once you have brainstormed the list, rank each item in order of importance—which is most important, and which is least important? If you are in a relationship right now, try evaluating that relationship in light of your own priorities.
2. **For a Paragraph.** Using the material that you generated in your journal entry, write a paragraph definition of the kind of person you seek for a committed relationship. Be serious. Do not try to imitate Brady's style.
3. **For an Essay.** Define a word naming a central human relationship role, such as *husband, lover, friend, mother, father, child, sister, brother,* or *grandparent.* Define the term indirectly by showing what such a person does or should do.
4. **For Research.** What does it mean to be a wife in another culture? Choose at least two other cultures, and research those societies' expectations of a wife. Try to find cultures that show significant differences. Remember that interviews might be a good source of information—even e-mail interviews with wives in other cultures.

Using your research, write an essay offering a comparative definition of *wife*. Assume that your audience is American. Be certain to document your sources, including any interviews or e-mail conversations.

FOR FURTHER STUDY

Focusing on Grammar and Writing. The most distinctive stylistic feature of Brady's essay is the repetitive sentence opener "I want a wife who. . . ." Normally, no one would ever advise you to repeat the same sentence structure over and over, let alone to repeat the same words again and again. How effective is the strategy in Brady's essay? Why might she have consciously chosen to repeat this structure? How is this structure appropriate for what the narrator is saying?

Working Together. Working with classmates in small groups, brainstorm ideas for an essay titled "I Want a Husband." Each group should compile a list of duties or responsibilities to be included in such an essay. Once the planning is done, each group should share its ideas with the class as a whole.

Seeing Other Modes at Work. Throughout the body of the essay, Brady uses division to organize the "duties" of a wife. How is division crucial to the definition of a wife that Brady offers?

Finding Connections. Related essays include Anna Quindlen's "The Name Is Mine" (Chapter 1) and Margaret Atwood's "The Female Body" (this chapter).

Exploring the Web. Visit a group of Websites devoted to marriage and marital contracts—get a range from the most conservative to the most liberal. What do couples say when they take their wedding vows? Do women still promise to "obey" their husbands? Some places to start can be found at **www.prenhall.com/miller.**

THE PEOPLE IN ME

Robin D. G. Kelley

Robin D. G. Kelley (1962–) was born in New York City and raised in Harlem, Seat-tle, and Pasadena, California. A graduate of California State University, Long Beach, Kelley earned his M.A. and Ph.D. at the University of California, Los Ange-les. Currently a professor of history at Columbia University, Kelley has been called "the preeminent historian of black popular culture writing today." The author and editor of many books, Kelley's most recent collections of essays include Yo' Mama's Dis-Funktional!: Fighting the Culture Wars in Urban America *(1997) and* Freedom Dreams: The Black Radical Imagination *(2002).*

On Writing: *Complimented in an interview on the accessibility of his writ-ing, Kelley replied, "That's the biggest compliment, because that's the one thing I try to achieve, only because I can't understand academic writing myself. I'm just not that smart."*

BEFORE READING

Connecting: Who are the people in you? What do you know about your ancestors?

Anticipating: Kelley prefers the word "polycultural" rather than "multicul-tural." Why? What is the difference?

"**S**o, what are you?" I don't know how many times people have asked me   1
that. "Are you Puerto Rican? Dominican? Indian or something? You must be mixed." My stock answer has rarely changed: "My mom is from Jamaica but grew up in New York, and my father was from North Carolina but grew up in Boston. Both black."

My family has lived with "the question" for as long as I can remember.   2
We're "exotics," all cursed with "good hair" and strange accents—we don't sound like we from da Souf or the Norwth, and don't have that West Coast-by-way-of-Texas Calabama thang going on. The only one with the real West Indian singsong vibe is my grandmother, who looks even more East Indian than my sisters. Whatever Jamaican patois my mom possessed was pummeled out of her by cruel preteens who never had sensitivity seminars in diversity. The result for us was a nondescript way of talking, walking, and being that made us not black enough, not white enough—just a bunch of not-quite-nappy-headed enigmas.

My mother never fit the "black momma" media image. A beautiful, de-   3
mure, light brown woman, she didn't drink, smoke, curse, or say things like "Lawd Jesus" or "hallelujah," nor did she cook chitlins or gumbo. A vegetarian, she played the harmonium (a foot-pumped miniature organ), spoke softly with

textbook diction, meditated, followed the teachings of Paramahansa Yogananda, and had wild hair like Chaka Khan. She burned incense in our tiny Harlem apartment, sometimes walked the streets barefoot, and, when she could afford it, cooked foods from the East.

4   To this day, my big sister gets misidentified for Pakistani or Bengali or Ethiopian. (Of course, changing her name from Sheral Anne Kelley to Makani Themba has not helped.) Not long ago, an Oakland cab driver, apparently a Sikh who had immigrated from India, treated my sister like dirt until he discovered that she was not a "scoundrel from Sri Lanka," but a common black American. Talk about ironic. How often are black women spared indignities *because* they are African American?

5   "What are you?" dogged my little brother more than any of us. He came out looking just like his father, who was white. In the black communities of Los Angeles and Pasadena, my baby bro' had to fight his way into blackness, usually winning only when he invited his friends to the house. When he got tired of this, he became what people thought he was—a cool white boy. Today he lives in Tokyo, speaks fluent Japanese, and is happily married to a Japanese woman (who is actually Korean passing as Japanese!) He stands as the perfect example of our mulattoness: a black boy trapped in a white body who speaks English with a slight Japanese accent and has a son who will spend his life confronting "the question."

6   Although folk had trouble naming us, we were never blanks or aliens in a "black world." We were and are "polycultural," and I'm talking about all peoples in the Western world. It is not skin, hair, walk, or talk that renders black people so diverse. Rather, it is the fact that most of them are products of different "cultures"—living cultures, not dead ones. These cultures live in and through us every day, with almost no self-consciousness about hierarchy or meaning. "Polycultural" works better than "multicultural," which implies that cultures are fixed, discrete entities that exist side by side—a kind of zoological approach to culture. Such a view obscures power relations, but often reifies race and gender differences.

7   Black people were polycultural from the get-go. Most of our ancestors came to these shores not as Africans, but as Ibo, Yoruba, Hausa, Kongo, Bambara, Mende, Mandingo, and so on. Some of our ancestors came as Spanish, Portuguese, French, Dutch, Irish, English, Italian. And more than a few of us, in North America as well as in the Caribbean and Latin America, have Asian and Native American roots.

8   Our lines of biological descent are about as pure as O. J.'s blood sample, and our cultural lines of descent are about as mixed up as a pot of gumbo. What we know as "black culture" has always been fluid and hybrid. In Harlem in the late 1960s and 1970s, Nehru suits were as popular—and as "black"—as dashikis, and martial arts films placed Bruce Lee among a pantheon of black heroes that included Walt Frazier of the New York Knicks and Richard Rountree, who played John Shaft in blaxploitation cinema. How do we understand the zoot suit—or the conk—without the pachuco culture of Mexican American youth, or low riders in black communities without Chicanos? How can we

discuss black visual artists in the interwar years without reference to the Mexican muralists, or the radical graphics tradition dating back to the late 19th century, or the Latin American artists influenced by surrealism?

Vague notions of "Eastern" religion and philosophy, as well as a variety 9 of Orientalist assumptions, were far more important to the formation of the Lost-Found Nation of Islam than anything coming out of Africa. And Rastafarians drew many of their ideas from South Asians, from vegetarianism to marijuana, which was introduced into Jamaica by Indians. Major black movements like Garveyism and the African Blood Brotherhood are also the products of global developments. We won't understand these movements until we see them as part of a dialogue with Irish nationalists from the Easter Rebellion, Russian and Jewish émigrés from the 1905 and 1917 revolutions, and Asian socialists like India's M. N. Roy and Japan's Sen Katayama.

Indeed, I'm not sure we can even limit ourselves to Earth. How do we 10 make sense of musicians Sun Ra, George Clinton, and Lee "Scratch" Perry or, for that matter, the Nation of Islam, when we consider the fact that space travel and notions of intergalactic exchange constitute a key source of their ideas?

So-called "mixed race" children are not the only ones with a claim to mul- 11 tiple heritages. All of us are inheritors of European, African, Native American, and Asian pasts, even if we can't exactly trace our bloodlines to these continents.

To some people that's a dangerous concept. Too many Europeans don't 12 want to acknowledge that Africans helped create so-called Western civilization, that they are both indebted to and descendants of those they enslaved. They don't want to see the world as One—a tiny little globe where people and cultures are always on the move, where nothing stays still no matter how many times we name it. To acknowledge our polycultural heritage and cultural dynamism is not to give up our black identity. It does mean expanding our definition of blackness, taking our history more seriously, and looking at the rich diversity within us with new eyes.

So next time you see me, don't ask where I'm from or what I am, unless 13 you're ready to sit through a long-ass lecture. As singer/songwriter Abbey Lincoln once put it, "I've got some people in me."

QUESTIONS ON SUBJECT AND PURPOSE

1. Why is the question "What are you?" not a simple one?
2. The first section of the essay (through paragraph 5) deals with Kelley's family. What does their story have to do with the rest of the essay?
3. What might be Kelley's purpose in the essay?

QUESTIONS ON STRATEGY AND AUDIENCE

1. Does Kelley's opening paragraph catch your attention? Why or why not?
2. How would you characterize the first five paragraphs in Kelley's essay? What is he doing? What organizational strategy does he use?

3. In what way is the example of his brother's child (paragraph 5) a perfect example of the polyculturalism that Kelley is talking about?

QUESTIONS ON VOCABULARY AND STYLE

1. Can you find examples in the essay of informal, even colloquial word choices?
2. Can you find examples in the essay of formal word choices?
3. Be prepared to define the following words: *patois* (paragraph 2), *pummeled* (2), *nondescript* (2), *enigmas* (2), *demure* (3), *entities* (6), *reifies* (6).

WRITING SUGGESTIONS

1. **For Your Journal.** To what extent can you see in American culture, or perhaps in the things in which you are interested, evidence of polycultural heritage? Think about food, music, clothing or hairstyles, behavior, language habits, popular idols. Think about your friends—in high school, at college. In your journal make a list of things central to your life and your friends' lives that are clearly derived from cultures and heritages other than your own.

2. **For a Paragraph.** Select one example that you recorded in your journal (or a series of related examples) and in a paragraph explore the appeal that such a thing has for you and/or your friends.

3. **For an Essay.** Explore the question that Kelley begins with. If someone asked you, "What are you?", how would you reply? In an essay define yourself (and/or your family).

4. **For Research.** Select a word or phrase such as *race, nationality, ethnic origin, multicultural,* or *polycultural* and research what it means. Drawing upon your research, write an extended definition of that term. Be sure to document your sources fully.

FOR FURTHER STUDY

Focusing on Grammar and Writing. Kelley encloses quite a few words and phrases within quotation marks. When do you use quotation marks in this way? What is the difference between using quotation marks and using italics? After you have examined the essay, try writing some advice to student writers about when to put words and phrases into quotation marks.

Working Together. Working in small groups, focus on the concluding paragraph of the essay. Each group should write a new conclusion for the essay. Perhaps it might be a more conventional "freshman English" ending. Share your new endings with the whole class. What similarities do the new endings have? What do they do that Kelley didn't? Which type of ending is more effective and why?

Seeing Other Modes at Work. In the first half of the essay, Kelley uses narration to discuss his own family.

Finding Connections. Interesting pairings include Denzy Senna's "The Color of Love" (Chapter 5) and Veronica Chambers' "Dreadlocked" (Chapter 7).

Exploring the Web. Interviews with Kelley and some of his other essays can be found on the Web. Places to start are at **www.prenhall.com/miller.**

MOTHER TONGUE

Amy Tan

Born in Oakland, California, in 1952 to Chinese immigrants, Amy Tan graduated from San Jose State University with a double major in English and linguistics and an M.A. in linguistics. Tan did not write fiction until 1985, when she began the stories that would become her first and very successful novel, The Joy Luck Club *(1989), also a popular film. Tan's children's book* The Chinese Siamese Cat *(1994) is the basis for the daily animated television series,* Sagwa, The Chinese Siamese Cat *(PBS). Her most recent novel is* Saving Fish From Drowning *(2005).*

On Writing: *Asked about her writing, Tan responded: "I welcome criticism when I'm writing my books. I want to become better and better as a writer. I go to a writer's group every week. We read our work aloud." In another interview she commented, "I still think of myself, in many ways, as a beginning writer. I'm still learning my craft, learning what makes for a good story, what's an honest voice."*

BEFORE READING

Connecting: How sensitive are you to the language that you use or your family uses? Are you ever conscious of that language? Are you ever embarrassed by it? Are you proud of it?

Anticipating: In what ways does the language of Tan and her mother "define" them in the eyes of others?

1   I am not a scholar of English or literature. I cannot give you much more than personal opinions on the English language and its variations in this country or others.

2   I am a writer. And by that definition, I am someone who has always loved language. I am fascinated by language in daily life. I spend a great deal of my time thinking about the power of language—the way it can evoke an emotion, a visual image, a complex idea, or a simple truth. Language is the tool of my trade. And I use them all—all the Englishes I grew up with.

3   Recently, I was made keenly aware of the different Englishes I do use. I was giving a talk to a large group of people, the same talk I had already given to half a dozen other groups. The nature of the talk was about my writing, my life, and my book, *The Joy Luck Club*. The talk was going along well enough, until I remembered one major difference that made the whole talk sound wrong. My mother was in the room. And it was perhaps the first time she had heard me give a lengthy speech, using the kind of English I have never used with her. I was saying things like, "The intersection of memory upon imagination" and "There is an aspect of my fiction that relates to thus-and-thus"—a speech filled with carefully wrought grammatical phrases, burdened, it suddenly

seemed to me, with nominalized forms, past perfect tenses, conditional phrases, all the forms of standard English that I had learned in school and through books, the forms of English I did not use at home with my mother.

Just last week, I was walking down the street with my mother, and I again found myself conscious of the English I was using, the English I do use with her. We were talking about the price of new and used furniture and I heard myself saying this: "Not waste money that way." My husband was with us as well, and he didn't notice any switch in my English. And then I realized why. It's because over the twenty years we've been together I've often used that same kind of English with him, and sometimes he even uses it with me. It has become our language of intimacy, a different sort of English that relates to family talk, the language I grew up with.

So you'll have some idea of what this family talk I heard sounds like, I'll quote what my mother said during a recent conversation which I videotaped and then transcribed. During this conversation, my mother was talking about a political gangster in Shanghai who had the same last name as her family's, Du, and how the gangster in his early years wanted to be adopted by her family, which was rich by comparison. Later, the gangster became more powerful, far richer than my mother's family, and one day showed up at my mother's wedding to pay his respects. Here's what she said in part:

"Du Yusong having business like fruit stand. Like off the street kind. He is Du like Du Zong—but not Tsung-ming Island people. The local people call putong, the river east side, he belong to that side local people. That man want to ask Du Zong father take him in like become own family. Du Zong father wasn't look down on him, but didn't take seriously, until that man big like become a mafia. Now important person, very hard to inviting him. Chinese way, came only to show respect, don't stay for dinner. Respect for making big celebration, he shows up. Mean gives lots of respect. Chinese custom. Chinese social life that way. If too important won't have to stay too long. He come to my wedding. I didn't see, I heard it. I gone to boy's side, they have YMCA dinner. Chinese age I was nineteen."

You should know that my mother's expressive command of English belies how much she actually understands. She reads the *Forbes* report, listens to *Wall Street Week*, converses daily with her stockbroker, reads all of Shirley MacLaine's books with ease—all kinds of things I can't begin to understand. Yet some of my friends tell me they understand 50 percent of what my mother says. Some say they understand 80 to 90 percent. Some say they understand none of it, as if she were speaking pure Chinese. But to me, my mother's English is perfectly clear, perfectly natural. It's my mother tongue. Her language, as I hear it, is vivid, direct, full of observation and imagery. That was the language that helped shape the way I saw things, expressed things, made sense of the world.

Lately, I've been giving more thought to the kind of English my mother speaks. Like others, I have described it to people as "broken" or "fractured" English. But I wince when I say that. It has always bothered me that I can think of no way to describe it other than "broken," as if it were damaged and needed to be fixed, as if it lacked a certain wholeness and soundness. I've heard other terms used, "limited English," for example. But they seem just as bad, as if everything is limited, including people's perceptions of the limited English speaker.

9   I know this for a fact, because when I was growing up, my mother's "limited" English limited *my* perception of her. I was ashamed of her English. I believed that her English reflected the quality of what she had to say. That is, because she expressed them imperfectly her thoughts were imperfect. And I had plenty of empirical evidence to support me: the fact that people in department stores, at banks, and at restaurants did not take her seriously, did not give her good service, pretended not to understand her, or even acted as if they did not hear her.

10   My mother has long realized the limitations of her English as well. When I was fifteen, she used to have me call people on the phone to pretend I was she. In this guise, I was forced to ask for information or even to complain and yell at people who had been rude to her. One time it was a call to her stockbroker in New York. She had cashed out her small portfolio and it just so happened we were going to go to New York the next week, our very first trip outside California. I had to get on the phone and say in an adolescent voice that was not very convincing, "This is Mrs. Tan."

11   And my mother was standing in the back whispering loudly, "Why he don't send me check, already two weeks late. So mad he lie to me, losing me money."

12   And then I said in perfect English, "Yes, I'm getting rather concerned. You had agreed to send the check two weeks ago, but it hasn't arrived."

13   Then she began to talk more loudly. "What he want, I come to New York tell him front of his boss, you cheating me?" And I was trying to calm her down, make her be quiet, while telling the stockbroker, "I can't tolerate any more excuses. If I don't receive the check immediately, I am going to have to speak to your manager when I'm in New York next week." And sure enough, the following week there we were in front of this astonished stockbroker, and I was sitting there red-faced and quiet, and my mother, the real Mrs. Tan, was shouting at his boss in her impeccable broken English.

14   We used a similar routine just five days ago, for a situation that was far less humorous. My mother had gone to the hospital for an appointment, to find out about a benign brain tumor a CAT scan had revealed a month ago. She said she had spoken very good English, her best English, no mistakes. Still, she said, the hospital did not apologize when they said they had lost the CAT scan and she had come for nothing. She said they did not seem to have any sympathy when she told them she was anxious to know the exact diagnosis, since her husband and son had both died of brain tumors. She said they would not give her any more information until the next time and she would have to make another appointment for that. So she said she would not leave until the doctor called her daughter. She wouldn't budge. And when the doctor finally called her daughter, me, who spoke in perfect English—lo and behind—we had assurances the CAT scan would be found, promises that a conference call on Monday would be held, and apologies for any suffering my mother had gone through for a most regrettable mistake.

I think my mother's English almost had an effect on limiting my possi-   15
bilities in life as well. Sociologists and linguists probably will tell you that a
person's developing language skills are more influenced by peers. But I do
think that the language spoken in the family, especially in immigrant families
which are more insular, plays a large role in shaping the language of the child.
And I believe that it affected my results on achievement tests, IQ tests, and the
SAT. While my English skills were never judged as poor, compared to math,
English could not be considered my strong suit. In grade school I did moderately well, getting perhaps B's, sometimes B-pluses, in English and scoring
perhaps in the sixtieth or seventieth percentile on achievement tests. But those
scores were not good enough to override the opinion that my true abilities lay
in math and science, because in those areas I achieved A's and scored in the
ninetieth percentile or higher.

This was understandable. Math is precise; there is only one correct an-   16
swer. Whereas, for me at least, the answers on English tests were always a
judgment call, a matter of opinion and personal experience. Those tests were
constructed around items like fill-in-the-blank sentence completion, such as,
"Even though Tom was _____, Mary thought he was _____." And the correct
answer always seemed to be the most bland combinations of thoughts, for example, "Even though Tom was shy, Mary thought he was charming," with the
grammatical structure "even though" limiting the correct answer to some sort
of semantic opposites, so you wouldn't get answers like, "Even though Tom
was foolish, Mary thought he was ridiculous." Well, according to my mother,
there were very few limitations as to what Tom could have been and what
Mary might have thought of him. So I never did well on tests like that.

The same was true with word analogies, pairs of words in which you were   17
supposed to find some sort of logical, semantic relationship—for example, "*Sunset
is to nightfall* as _____ is to _____." And here you would be presented with a list
of four possible pairs, one of which showed the same kind of relationship: *red* is
to *stoplight, bus* is to *arrival, chills* is to *fever, yawn* is to *boring*. Well, I could never
think that way. I knew what the tests were asking, but I could not block out of
my mind the images already created by the first pair, "*sunset* is to *nightfall*"—and
I would see a burst of colors against a darkening sky, the moon rising, the lowering of a curtain of stars. And all the other pairs of words—*red, bus, stoplight,
boring*—just threw up a mass of confusing images, making it impossible for me
to sort out something as logical as saying: "A sunset precedes nightfall" is the
same as "a chill precedes a fever." The only way I would have gotten that answer
right would have been to imagine an associative situation, for example, my being disobedient and staying out past sunset, catching a chill at night, which turns
into feverish pneumonia as punishment, which indeed did happen to me.

I have been thinking about all this lately, about my mother's English,   18
about achievement tests. Because lately I've been asked, as a writer, why there
are not more Asian-Americans represented in American literature. Why are
there few Asian Americans enrolled in creative writing programs? Why do so
many Chinese students go into engineering? Well, these are broad sociological

questions I can't begin to answer. But I have noticed in surveys—in fact, just last week—that Asian students, as a whole, always do significantly better on math achievement tests than in English. And this makes me think that there are other Asian-American students whose English spoken in the home might also be described as "broken" or "limited." And perhaps they also have teachers who are steering them away from writing and into math and science, which is what happened to me.

19   Fortunately, I happen to be rebellious in nature and enjoy the challenge of disproving assumptions made about me. I became an English major my first year in college, after being enrolled as pre-med. I started writing nonfiction as a freelancer the week after I was told by my former boss that writing was my worst skill and I should hone my talents toward account management.

20   But it wasn't until 1985 that I finally began to write fiction. And at first I wrote using what I thought to be wittily crafted sentences, sentences that would finally prove I had mastery over the English language. Here's an example from the first draft of a story that later made its way into *The Joy Luck Club*, but without this line: "That was my mental quandary in its nascent state." A terrible line, which I can barely pronounce.

21   Fortunately, for reasons I won't get into today, I later decided I should envision a reader for the stories I would write. And the reader I decided upon was my mother, because these were stories about mothers. So with this reader in mind—and in fact she did read my early drafts—I began to write stories using all the Englishes I grew up with: the English I spoke to my mother, which for lack of a better term might be described as "simple"; the English she used with me, which for lack of a better term might be described as "broken"; my translation of her Chinese, which could certainly be described as "watered down"; and what I imagined to be her translation of her Chinese if she could speak in perfect English, her internal language, and for that I sought to preserve the essence, but neither an English nor a Chinese structure. I wanted to capture what language ability tests can never reveal: her intent, her passion, her imagery, the rhythms of her speech and the nature of her thoughts.

22   Apart from what any critic had to say about my writing, I knew I had succeeded where it counted when my mother finished reading my book and gave me her verdict: "So easy to read."

QUESTIONS ON SUBJECT AND PURPOSE

1. What does the title "Mother Tongue" suggest?
2. How many subjects does Tan explore in the essay?
3. How does Tan feel about her mother's "tongue"?

QUESTIONS ON STRATEGY AND AUDIENCE

1. In paragraph 6, Tan quotes part of one of her mother's conversations. Why?

2. After paragraphs 7 and 17, Tan uses additional space to indicate divisions in her essay. Why does she divide the essay into three parts?

3. Tan notes in paragraph 21 that she thinks of her mother as her audience when she writes stories. Why?

QUESTIONS ON VOCABULARY AND STYLE

1. How would you characterize Tan's tone (see the glossary for a definition) in the essay?

2. In paragraph 20, Tan quotes a "terrible line" she once wrote: "That was my mental quandary in its nascent state." What is so terrible about that line?

3. Be prepared to define the following words: *belies* (7), *empirical* (9), *benign* (14), *insular* (15), *semantic* (16), *hone* (19), *quandary* (20), *nascent* (20).

WRITING SUGGESTIONS

1. **For Your Journal.** What makes up your "mother tongue"? To what extent is your language (such things as word choice, pronunciation, dialect, and second-language skills) influenced by your parents, your education, the part of the country in which you grew up, and your peers? Make a series of notes exploring those influences.

2. **For a Paragraph.** Using the information that you gathered for your journal entry, write a paragraph in which you define your "mother tongue." Try to define the influences that have shaped both how and what you say.

3. **For an Essay.** Tan suggests that a certain type or dialect of English is a language of power, that if you speak and write that English, people in authority will listen to you and respect you. How might that public, powerful English (sometimes referred to as "edited American English") be defined?

4. **For Research.** Linguists have defined a wide range of dialects in the United States. Choose one of the dialects that interests you—a reference librarian or your instructor can help you find a list. You might choose one based on the geographical area in which you live or one defined by your heritage. Using the resources of your library, write a definition of that dialect. What are its distinctive features? Where did those features come from? Where is this dialect spoken in the United States? What are some particularly colorful examples? Be sure to document your sources wherever appropriate.

FOR FURTHER STUDY

Focusing on Grammar and Writing. Tan occasionally writes an extremely long sentence. For example, look at the final sentences in paragraphs 3, 8, 13, 14, and 17, and the next to last sentence in paragraph 21. How can Tan write such a long sentence and still achieve clarity? Choose one or more of these sentences and analyze how it is constructed. What is essential in a very long sentence?

Working Together. Working in small groups, choose one of the following topics and examine its role in the essay as a whole.

1. The introduction, with its emphasis on language (paragraphs 1 and 2).
2. The transcription of her mother's conversation (6)
3. The example of the stockbroker (10–13)
4. The example of the CAT scan (14)
5. The examples from the verbal sections of achievement tests (16–17)

Seeing Other Modes at Work. At several points in the essay, Tan talks about the "different Englishes" that she uses. How does she use classification to help structure the essay?

Finding Connections. Interesting pairings are with Judith Ortiz Cofer's "The Myth of the Latin Woman" (Chapter 4), Robin D. G. Kelley's "The People in Me" (this chapter), and Richard Rodriguez's "None of This Is Fair" (Chapter 9).

Exploring the Web. Read online interviews with Tan, watch video clips of her talking about her books, listen to audio excerpts from her works. Places to start can be found at **www.prenhall.com/miller.**

MESS

John Hollander

Born in 1929, John Hollander is a distinguished and widely published poet, editor, and critic. He is Sterling Professor of English at Yale University and the author of many books of poetry. His most recent books are Figurehead: And Other Poems *(1999) and* Picture Window: Poems *(2003). "Mess" was originally published in the* Yale Review *in 1995.*

On Writing: *Commenting on this essay, Hollander observed: "This brief essay was generated more from within, like a poem, than most other prose of mine—nobody asked me to write it, but I felt impelled to observe something about one aspect of life that tends to get swept under the rug, as it were."*

BEFORE READING

Connecting: Are you "messy"? How do you feel about the messes that you make or about the messes of others?

Anticipating: In the final paragraph, Hollander refers to his essay as a "meditation on mess." What does the word *meditation* suggest to you? In what ways is the essay a meditation?

M ess is a state of mind. Or rather, messiness is a particular relation between   1
the state of arrangement of a collection of things and a state of mind that contemplates it in its containing space. For example, X's mess may be Y's delight—sheer profusion, uncompromised by any apparent structure even in the representation of it. Or there may be some inner order or logic to A's mess that B cannot possibly perceive. Consider: someone—Alpha—rearranges all the books on Beta's library shelf, which have been piled or stacked, sometimes properly, sometimes not, but all in relevant sequence (by author and, within that, by date of publication), and rearranges them neatly, by size and color. Beta surveys the result, and can only feel, if not blurt out, "WHAT A MESS!" This situation often occurs with respect to messes of the workplace generally.

For there are many kinds of mess, both within walls and outside them: 2
neglected gardens and the aftermath of tropical storms, and the indoor kinds of disorder peculiar to specific areas of our life with, and in and among, *things*. There are messes of one's own making, messes not even of one's own person, places, or things. There are personal states of mind about common areas of messiness—those of the kitchen, the bedroom, the bathroom, the salon (of whatever sort, from half of a bed-sitter to some grand public parlor), or those of personal appearance (clothes, hair, etc.). Then, for all those who are in any way self-employed or whose avocations are practiced in some private space—a workshop, a darkroom, a study or a studio—there is the mess of the workplace.

It's not the most common kind of mess, but it's exemplary: the eye surveying it is sickened by the roller-coaster of scanning the scene. And, alas, it's the one I'm most afflicted with.

3   I know that things are really in a mess when—as about ninety seconds ago—I reach for the mouse on my Macintosh and find instead a thick layer of old envelopes, manuscript notes consulted three weeks ago, favorite pens and inoperative ones, folders used hastily and not replaced, and so forth. In order to start working, I brush these accumulated impedimenta aside, thus creating a new mess. But this is, worse yet, absorbed by the general condition of my study: piles of thin books and thick books, green volumes of the Loeb Classical Library and slimy paperbacks of ephemeral spy-thrillers, mostly used notepads, bills paid and unpaid, immortal letters from beloved friends, unopened and un-trashed folders stuffed with things that should be in various other folders, book-mailing envelopes, unanswered mail whose cries for help and attention are muffled by three months' worth of bank statements enshrouding them in the gloom of continued neglect. Even this fairly orderly inventory seems to simplify the confusion: in actuality, searching for a letter or a page of manu-script in this state of things involves crouching down with my head on one side and searching vertically along the outside of a teetering pile for what may be a thin, hidden layer of it.

4   Displacement, and lack of design, are obscured in the origins of our very word *mess.* The famous biblical "mess of red pottage" (lentil mush or dal) for which Esau sold his birthright wasn't "messy" in our sense (unless, of course, in the not very interesting case of Esau having dribbled it on his clothing). The word meant a serving of food, or a course in a meal: something *placed* in front of you (from the Latin *missus,* put or placed), hence "messmates" (dining com-panions) and ultimately "officers' mess" and the like. It also came to mean a dish of prepared mixed food—like an *olla podrida* or a minestrone—then by extension (but only from the early nineteenth century on) any hodge-podge: inedible, and outside the neat confines of a bowl or pot, and thus unpleasant, confusing, and agitating or depressing to contemplate. But for us, the associ-ation with food perhaps remains only in how much the state of mind of being messy is like that of being fat: for example, X says, "God I'm getting gross! I'll have to diet!" Y, *really* fat, cringes on hearing this, and feels that for the slen-der X to talk that way is an obscenity. Similarly, X: "God, this place is a pigsty!" Y: (ditto). For a person prone to messiness, Cyril Connolly's celebrated ob-servation about fat people is projected onto the world itself: inside every neat arrangement is a mess struggling to break out, like some kind of statue of chaos lying implicit in the marble of apparent organization.

5   In Paradise, there was no such thing as messiness. This was partly because unfallen, ideal life needed no supplemental *things*—objects of use and artifice, elements of any sort of technology. Thus there was nothing to leave lying around, messily or even neatly, by Adam and Eve—according to Milton—"at their savory dinner set / Of herbs and other country messes." But it was also because order, hence orderliness, was itself so natural that whatever bit of nature Adam and Eve might have been occupied with, or even using in a momentary

tool-like way, flew or leapt or crept into place in some sort of reasonable arrangement, even as in our unparadised state things *fall* under the joyless tug of grav-
ity. But messiness may seem to be an inevitable state of the condition of having
so many *things*, precious or disposable, in one's life.

As I observed before, even to describe a mess is to impose order on it.   6
The ancient Greek vision of primal chaos, even, was not *messy* in that it was
pre-messy: there weren't any categories by which to define order, so that there
could be no disorder—no nextness or betweenness, no above, below, here,
there, and so forth. *"Let there be light"* meant "Let there be perception of
something," and it was then that order became possible, and mess possibly implied. Now, a list or inventory is in itself an orderly literary form, and even in-
coherent assemblages of items fall too easily into some other kind of order: in
Through the Looking-Glass, the Walrus's "Of shoes, and ships, and sealing-wax, /
Of cabbages, and kings," is given a harmonious structure by the pairs of allit-
erating words, and even by the half-punning association of "ships, [sailing]
sealing-wax." The wonderful catalogue in *Tom Sawyer* of the elements of what
must have been, pocketed or piled on the ground, a mess of splendid proportions, is a poem of its own. The objects of barter for a stint of fence white-
washing (Tom, it will be remembered, turns *having* to do a chore into *getting*
to do it by sheer con-man's insouciance) comprise

> twelve marbles, part of a jewsharp, a piece of blue bottle-glass to look through, a
> spool cannon, a key that wouldn't unlock anything, a fragment of chalk, a glass
> stopper of a decanter, a tin soldier, a couple of tadpoles, six fire-crackers, a
> kitten with only one eye, a brass door-knob, a dog collar—but no dog—the
> handle of a knife, four pieces of orange peel, and a dilapidated old window sash.

Thus such representations of disorder as lists, paintings, photos, etc., all   7
compromise the purity of true messiness by the verbal or visual order they impose on the confusion. To get at the mess in my study, for example, a movie
might serve best, alternately mixing mid-shot and zoom on a particular portion of the disaster, which would, in an almost fractal way, seem to be a mini-
disaster of its own. There are even neatly conventionalized emblems of
messiness that are, after all, all too neat; thus, whenever a movie wants to show
an apartment or office that has been ransacked by Baddies (cop Baddies or
baddy Baddies or whatever) in search of the Thing They Want, the designer
is always careful to show at least one picture on the wall hanging carefully
askew. All this could possibly tell us about a degree of messiness is that the
searchers were so messy (at another level of application of the term) in their
technique that they violated their search agenda to run over to the wall and tilt
the picture (very messy procedure indeed), or that, hastily leaving the scene to
avoid detection, they nonetheless took a final revenge against the Occupant for
not having the Thing on his or her premises, and tilted the picture in a fit of
pique. And yet a tilted picture gives good cueing mileage: it can present a good
bit of disorder at the expense of a minimum of misalignment, after all.

A meditation on mess could be endless. As I struggle to conclude this   8
one, one of my cats regards me from her nest in and among one of the disaster

areas that all surfaces in my study soon become. Cats disdain messes in several ways. First, they are proverbially neat about their shit and about the condition of their fur. Second, they pick their way so elegantly among my piles of books, papers, and ancillary objects (dishes of paper clips, scissors, functional and dried-out pens, crumpled envelopes, outmoded postage stamps, boxes of slides and disks, staplers, glue bottles, tape dispensers—*you* know) that they cannot even be said to acknowledge the mess's existence. The gray familiar creature currently making her own order out of a region of mess on my desk—carefully disposing herself around and over and among piles and bunches and stacks and crazily oblique layers and thereby reinterpreting it as natural landscape—makes me further despair until I realize that what she does with her body, I must do with my perception of this inevitable disorder—shaping its forms to the disorder and thereby shaping the disorder to its forms. She has taught me resignation.

QUESTIONS ON SUBJECT AND PURPOSE

1. In what sense is a mess "a state of mind"?
2. What role do "things" play in creating a mess?
3. Having contemplated the "mess" in which he works, Hollander reaches what conclusion?

QUESTIONS ON STRATEGY AND AUDIENCE

1. In what way does describing a mess "impose order on it" (paragraph 6)?
2. Toward the end of the essay, Hollander notes that he "struggles" to conclude. Why is it a struggle?
3. Hollander makes reference throughout the essay to other writers and works of literature. What do these allusions suggest about Hollander and his sense of his audience?

QUESTIONS ON VOCABULARY AND STYLE

1. Hollander is a poet. Does he ever sound like a poet in the essay? Can you find examples of phrasing or language that sounds like something you would imagine a poet would write?
2. Find the two shortest sentences in the essay (not counting the exchange between X and Y in paragraph 4).
3. Make a list of words in the essay whose meanings are uncertain to you. Bring your list to class.

WRITING SUGGESTIONS

1. **For Your Journal.** In your journal, brainstorm a list of words that you might define. Try for a list of words that are somehow related to or associated with you. They might be words that describe your behavior (for example, *orderly, outgoing, shy, ambitious*), your physical self (*short,*

tall, athletic), or your attitudes toward life or events *(optimistic, cynical)*. Try for a substantial list.

2. **For a Paragraph.** In a paragraph, define one of the words. Do not write a dictionary definition; write an extended definition that includes examples, details, connotations.

3. **For an Essay.** Select one of the words from your journal, and write an essay definition of the word. Remember to get your instructor's approval of the word.

4. **For Research.** To judge from the number of books, videos, and products that are marketed to American consumers, messiness is clearly something that people would like to avoid. Whether it is how to clean up the clutter on your desk or in your closets at home or how to organize your every moment through elaborate daily planners and software programs, we seem to want desperately to be "neat." In a researched essay, define the word *neat.* You can draw examples from advertisements as well as from books, articles, and the electronic media. You will also want to research the history of the word (using, for example, some of the historical dictionaries in your school's library). Be sure to document all of your sources.

FOR FURTHER STUDY

Focusing on Grammar and Writing. Hollander has a fondness for linking sentences together with a colon. Make a list of each instance in which he uses this construction, study those sentences, and then write a rule for the use of a colon as a mark to link sentences together. Do you ever use such a construction in your own writing?

Working Together. Divide into small groups. Each group should evaluate one of the following sections:

1. The etymological history of the word *mess* (paragraph 4)
2. The references to Adam and Eve and John Milton (5)
3. The reference to primal chaos (6)
4. The catalogues from *Through the Looking Glass* and *Tom Sawyer* (6)
5. The "tilted" picture symbol (7)

What does each example or reference add to the essay?

Seeing Other Modes at Work. Hollander makes extensive use of comparison and contrast throughout the essay.

Finding Connections. What might Susan Britt, "Neat People vs. Sloppy People" (Chapter 5) or Lars Eighner, "My Daily Dives in the Dumpster" (Chapter 6), have to say about the "mess" in Hollander's office?

Exploring the Web. A number of Hollander's poems as well as an audio file in which you can hear him read can be found on the Web. Places to start can be found at **www.prenhall.com/miller.**

THE FEMALE BODY

Margaret Atwood

Margaret Atwood was born in Ottawa, Canada, in 1939. She received a B.A. from the University of Toronto in 1961 and earned an M.A. at Radcliffe College in 1962. A poet, essayist, short story writer, and novelist, Atwood has enjoyed critical and popular acclaim throughout her writing career, winning numerous awards and honorary degrees. Her work has explored broad themes of feminism, dystopia, and the opposition of art and nature, but always through the eyes of an individual. Her best known novel is The Handmaid's Tale *(1986), in which a totalitarian state assigns roles to women according to their reproductive abilities.*

On Writing: *At a meeting of the Toronto Council of Teachers of English, Atwood was asked about the importance of punctuation in good writing. She commented on her own use of punctuation: "I've recently taken up a new device, which is the set of dashes. Some people overuse this quite a lot—everything is a set of dashes—but in prose I'm tending to prefer it to parentheses. In prose fiction a lot is associative, one idea suggests another which can lead to an interposition in the middle of a sentence. The question is, how do you set that off? Sometimes you can do it with parenthesis, but sets of dashes are often quite useful."*

BEFORE READING

Connecting: What image is suggested to you by the phrase "the female body"?

Anticipating: Does Atwood's essay fulfill your expectations of an essay on the "female body"? Why or why not?

> . . . entirely devoted to the subject of "The Female Body." Knowing how well you have written on this topic . . . this capacious topic . . .
>
> Letter from *Michigan Quarterly Review*

1

1   I agree, it's a hot topic. But only one? Look around, there's a wide range. Take my own, for instance.

2   I get up in the morning. My topic feels like hell. I sprinkle it with water, brush parts of it, rub it with towels, powder it, add lubricant. I dump in the fuel and away goes my topic, my topical topic, my controversial topic, my capacious topic, my limping topic, my nearsighted topic, my topic with back problems, my badly behaved topic, my vulgar topic, my outrageous topic, my aging topic, my topic that is out of the question and anyway still can't spell, in its oversized coat and worn winter boots, scuttling along the sidewalk as if it were flesh and blood, hunting for what's out there, an avocado, an alderman, an adjective, hungry as ever.

2

The basic Female Body comes with the following accessories: garter belt, 3
panti-girdle, crinoline, camisole, bustle, brassiere, stomacher, chemise, virgin
zone, spike heels, nose ring, veil, kid gloves, fishnet stockings, fichu, bandeau,
Merry Widow, weepers, chokers, barrettes, bangles, beads, lorgnette, feather
boa, basic black, compact, Lycra stretch one-piece with modesty panel, designer peignoir, flannel nightie, lace teddy, bed, head.

3

The Female Body is made of transparent plastic and lights up when you 4
plug it in. You press a button to illuminate the different systems. The circula-
tory system is red, for the heart and arteries, purple for the veins; the respiratory
system is blue; the lymphatic system is yellow; the digestive system is green,
with liver and kidneys in aqua. The nerves are done in orange and the brain is
pink. The skeleton, as you might expect, is white.

The reproductive system is optional, and can be removed. It comes with 5
or without a miniature embryo. Parental judgment can thereby be exercised.
We do not wish to frighten or offend.

4

He said, I won't have one of those things in the house. It gives a young 6
girl a false notion of beauty, not to mention anatomy. If a real woman was built
like that she'd fall on her face.

She said, If we don't let her have one like all the other girls she'll feel sin- 7
gled out. It'll become an issue. She'll long for one and she'll long to turn into
one. Repression breeds sublimation. You know that.

He said, It's not just the pointy plastic tits, it's the wardrobes. The 8
wardrobes and that stupid male doll, what's his name, the one with the underwear glued on.

She said, Better to get it over with when she's young. He said, All right, 9
but don't let me see it.

She came whizzing down the stairs, thrown like a dart. She was stark 10
naked. Her hair had been chopped off, her head was turned back to front, she
was missing some toes and she'd been tattooed all over her body with purple
ink in a scrollwork design. She hit the potted azalea, trembled there for a moment
like a botched angel, and fell.

He said, I guess we're safe. 11

5

The Female Body has many uses. It's been used as a door knocker, a bot- 12
tle opener, as a clock with a ticking belly, as something to hold up lampshades,
as a nutcracker, just squeeze the brass legs together and out comes your nut.
It bears torches, lifts victorious wreaths, grows copper wings and raises aloft a
ring of neon stars; whole buildings rest on its marble heads.

It sells cars, beer, shaving lotion, cigarettes, hard liquor; it sells diet plans 13
and diamonds, and desire in tiny crystal bottles. Is this the face that launched
a thousand products? You bet it is, but don't get any funny big ideas, honey,
that smile is a dime a dozen.

14   It does not merely sell, it is sold. Money flows into this country or that country, flies in, practically crawls in, suitful after suitful, lured by all those hairless pre-teen legs. Listen, you want to reduce the national debt, don't you? Aren't you patriotic? That's the spirit. That's my girl.

15   She's a natural resource, a renewable one luckily, because those things wear out so quickly. They don't make 'em like they used to. Shoddy goods.

6

16   One and one equals another one. Pleasure in the female is not a requirement. Pair-bonding is stronger in geese. We're not talking about love, we're talking about biology. That's how we all got here, daughter.

17   Snails do it differently. They're hermaphrodites, and work in threes.

7

18   Each Female Body contains a female brain. Handy. Makes things work. Stick pins in it and you get amazing results. Old popular songs. Short circuits. Bad dreams.

19   Anyway: each of these brains has two halves. They're joined together by a thick cord; neural pathways flow from one to the other, sparkles of electric information washing to and fro. Like light on waves. Like a conversation. How does a woman know? She listens. She listens in.

20   The male brain, now, that's a different matter. Only a thin connection. Space over here, time over there, music and arithmetic in their own sealed compartments. The right brain doesn't know what the left brain is doing. Good for aiming through, for hitting the target when you pull the trigger. What's the target? Who's the target? Who cares? What matters is hitting it. That's the male brain for you. Objective.

21   This is why men are so sad, why they feel so cut off, why they think of themselves as orphans cast adrift, footloose and stringless in the deep void. What void? she asks. What are you talking about? The void of the universe, he says, and she says Oh and looks out the window and tries to get a handle on it, but it's no use, there's too much going on, too many rustlings in the leaves, too many voices, so she says, Would you like a cheese sandwich, a piece of cake, a cup of tea? And he grinds his teeth because she doesn't understand, and wanders off, not just alone but Alone, lost in the dark, lost in the skull, searching for the other half, the twin who could complete him.

22   Then it comes to him: he's lost the Female Body! Look, it shines in the gloom, far ahead, a vision of wholeness, ripeness, like a giant melon, like an apple, like a metaphor for "breast" in a bad sex novel; it shines like a balloon, like a foggy noon, a watery moon, shimmering in its egg of light.

23   Catch it. Put it in a pumpkin, in a high tower, in a compound, in a chamber, in a house, in a room. Quick, stick a leash on it, a lock, a chain, some pain, settle it down, so it can never get away from you again.

QUESTIONS ON SUBJECT AND PURPOSE

1. What appears to be the occasion for Atwood's essay?
2. In what ways might this be considered a definition of the "female body"?

3. Is it true, as Atwood notes in section 7, that the structure of the brain varies with gender?

QUESTIONS ON STRATEGY AND AUDIENCE

1. Why might Atwood have chosen to divide the essay as she does?
2. Why doesn't Atwood write transitions to bridge from one section of the essay to another instead of dividing it into sections?
3. The letter from the magazine refers to the topic as "capacious." What does that word mean? In what way does that word suggest the shape and nature of Atwood's response?

QUESTIONS ON VOCABULARY AND STYLE

1. How would you characterize Atwood's tone in the essay? (See the glossary for a definition of *tone*.)
2. In what context might you expect to find section 3 of the essay? What does it sound like?
3. Be prepared to define the words *alderman* (paragraph 2) and *sublimation* (7).

WRITING SUGGESTIONS

1. **For Your Journal.** Suppose you had been invited to write something (an essay, a poem, a story) about either the male or the female body. What would you say? In your journal, jot down some possible ideas for your response.
2. **For a Paragraph.** Select one of the ideas that you came up with in your journal writing, and expand that into a developed paragraph. Remember to use example—either a variety of different ones or a single, extended one—to develop your definition.
3. **For an Essay.** In section 5, Atwood makes numerous references to the ways in which the female body has been used to sell products. Similarly, advertisers today also use male bodies. Judging just from the images of women or of men presented in advertisements, write an essay about how the female or male body is defined in our culture.
4. **For Research.** How have society's definitions of *masculinity* and *femininity* changed over time? Choose one of the two terms, and research its shifting definitions over the past two hundred years. What did society expect of a man or a women in 1800? In 1900? In the early 2000s? What is considered masculine or feminine? Remember that no single reference source will provide you with the answers you need. You may need to infer the definitions from the roles that society forced on men and women and the images that represented those roles. Be sure to acknowledge your sources wherever appropriate.

FOR FURTHER STUDY

Focusing on Grammar and Writing. The first three paragraphs in Atwood's essay contain quite a few sentence fragments. How many can you find? What makes each a fragment? Try adding words to each fragment to make it into a sentence. What is gained or lost in the process? Can a sentence fragment be effective? Under what circumstances?

Working Together. Divide into seven small groups. Each group should take one of the numbered sections of the essay and (1) determine the focus of that section, (2) speculate on why Atwood might have chosen to include that perspective, and (3) suggest how that section contributes to the effect that the entire essay creates.

Seeing Other Modes at Work. In section 7, Atwood contrasts the male brain with the female brain. How is that contrast important to the points that she is trying to make?

Finding Connections. Interesting pairings are with Leslie Haywood's "One of the Girls" (Chapter 1), Janice Mirikitani's "Recipe" (Chapter 6), and Marge Piercy's "Barbie Doll" (Chapter 7).

Exploring the Web. Atwood maintains an extensive Website. In addition, information about her and her work can be found on dozens of other Websites. Some good starting points can be found at **www.prenhall.com/miller.**

9

ARGUMENT AND PERSUASION

PREPARING TO WRITE

WHAT IS THE DIFFERENCE BETWEEN ARGUMENT AND PERSUASION?

We live in a world of persuasive messages—billboards, advertisements in newspapers and magazines, commercials on television and radio, electronic advertisements on the Web, signs on storefronts, bumper stickers, T-shirts and caps with messages, and manufacturers' logos prominently displayed on clothing. Advertisements demonstrate a wide range of persuasive strategies. Sometimes they appeal to logic and reason—they ask you to compare the features and price of one car with those of any competitor and judge for yourself. More often, though, they appeal to your emotions and feelings—you will not be stylish unless you wear this particular style and brand of athletic shoe; you are not a "real man" unless you smoke this brand of cigarette; you have not signaled your success in the world unless you drive this particular German automobile.

In the following paragraph, William Junius Wilson appeals to logic when he argues that the "school-to-work transition" confronts many young Americans by citing specific factual evidence to establish the magnitude of the problem:

> The problem of school-to-work transition confronts young people of all ethnic and racial backgrounds, but it is especially serious for black youths. According to a recent report by the U.S. Bureau of Labor Statistics, only 42 percent of black youths who had not enrolled in college had jobs in October after graduating from high school a few months earlier in June, compared with 69 percent of their white counterparts. The figures for black youngsters in inner-city ghetto neighborhoods are obviously even lower. The inadequate system of school-to-work transition has also contributed significantly to the growing wage gap between those with high school diplomas and those with college training. In the 1950s and 1960s, when school-to-work transition was compatible with the mass production system, the average earnings of college graduates was only about 20 percent higher than those of high school graduates. By 1979, it had increased to 49 percent, and then rapidly grew to 83 percent by 1992.

Thus, the school-to-work transition is a major problem in the United States, and it has reached crisis proportions in the inner-city ghetto.

In the face of such evidence, few readers would dispute the need to attack this problem. Later in this chapter, in the debate about the value of college, Katherine Porter cites a body of statistical evidence to support her assertion that graduates of four-year colleges average substantially more income over a working lifetime than graduates of two-year programs or just of high school. On the other hand, factual evidence often can be found to support either side of an argument. In the debate about grade inflation, Vanderslice and Kohn offer opposing arguments, each of which are supported by research studies.

As an example of an argument appealing to readers' emotions, notice how the writer of this editorial from the magazine *The Disability Rag* persuasively argues against the substitution of the phrase "physically challenged" for "physically disabled":

> "Physically challenged" attempts to conceal a crucial fact: that the reason we can't do lots of things is not because we're lazy or because we won't accept a "challenge," but because many things are simply beyond our control—like barriers. Like discrimination. People who favor "physically challenged" are making a statement: Barriers, discrimination, are not problems for us, but challenges. We want those barriers, we almost seem to be saying—because by overcoming them we'll become better persons! Stronger. More courageous. After all, isn't that what challenges are for.
>
> Until you've made it your responsibility to get downtown, and discovered that there are no buses with lifts running on that route, you may not fully comprehend that it isn't a personal "challenge" you're up against, but a system resistant to change.

Similarly, later in this chapter Martin Luther King Jr., in his famous "I Have a Dream" speech, appeals to his listeners' (and readers') emotions. Despite the differences in strategy, though, the objective in both argument and persuasion is the same: to convince readers to believe or act in a certain way.

What Do You Already Know about Arguing and Persuading?

Whether you realize it or not, you have already had extensive experience in constructing arguments and in persuading an audience. Every time you try to convince someone to do or to believe something, you have to argue. Consider a hypothetical example. You are concerned about your father's health. He smokes cigarettes, avoids exercise, is overweight, and works long hours in a stressful job. Even though you are worried, he is completely unconcerned and has always resisted your family's efforts to change his ways. Your task is to persuade him to change or modify his lifestyle, and doing so involves making its dangers clear, offering convincing reasons for change, and urging specific action.

Establishing the dangers is the first step, and you have a wide range of medical evidence from which to draw. That evidence involves statistics,

If we associate argument with reason and factual evidence, we tend to associate persuasion with emotional appeals. Salespeople are persuaders, as are those who use the "soapbox" approach.

testimony or advice from doctors, and case histories of men who have suffered the consequences of years of abusing or ignoring their health. From that body of material, you select the items that are most likely to get through to your obstinate father. He might not be moved by cold statistics citing life-expectancy tables for smokers and nonexercisers, but he might be touched by the story of a friend his age who suffered a heart attack or stroke. The evidence you gather and use becomes a part of the convincing reasons for change that you offer in your argument. If your father persists in ignoring his health, he is likely to suffer some consequences. You might at this point include emotional appeals in your strategy. If he is not concerned about what will happen to him, what about his family? What will they do if he dies?

Having gotten your father to realize and acknowledge the dangers inherent in his lifestyle and to understand the reasons why he should make changes, what remains is to urge specific action. In framing a plan for that action, you again need to consider your audience. If you urge your father to stop smoking immediately, join a daily exercise class at the local YMCA or health club, go on a thousand-calorie-a-day diet, and find a new job, chances are that he will think your proposal too drastic even to try. Instead, you might urge a more moderate plan, phasing in changes over a period of time or offering compromises (for example, that he work fewer hours).

How Do You Analyze Your Audience?

Argument and persuasion, unlike the other types of writing included in this text, have a special purpose—to persuade its audience. Because you want your reader to agree with your position or act as you urge, you need to analyze your audience carefully before you start to write. Try to answer each of the following questions:

- Who are my readers?
- What do they already know about this subject?
- How interested are they likely to be?
- How impartial or prejudiced are they going to be?
- What values do my readers share?
- Is my argument going to challenge any of my readers' beliefs or values?
- What types of evidence are most likely to be effective?
- Is my plan for requested action reasonable?

Your argumentative strategy should always reflect an awareness of your audience. Even in the hypothetical case of the unhealthy father, it is obvious that some types of evidence would be more effective than others and that some solutions or plans for action would be more reasonable and therefore more acceptable than others.

The second important consideration in any argument is to anticipate your audience's objections and be ready to answer them. Debaters study both sides of an argument so that they can effectively counter any opposition. In arguing the abortion issue, the right-to-life speaker has to be prepared to deal with subjects such as abnormal fetuses or pregnancy resulting from rape or incest. The pro-choice speaker must face questions about when life begins and when the rights of the unborn might take precedence over the mother's rights.

What Does It Take to Persuade Your Reader?

In some cases, nothing will persuade your reader. For example, if you are arguing for legalized abortion, you will never convince a reader who believes that an embryo is a human being from the moment of conception. Abortion to that reader will always be murder. It is extremely difficult to argue any position that is counter to your audience's moral or ethical values. It is also difficult to argue a position that is counter to your audience's normal patterns of behavior. For example, you could reasonably argue that your readers ought to stop at all stop signs and to obey the speed limit. However, the likelihood of persuading your audience to always do these two things—even though not doing so breaks the law—is slim.

These cautions are not meant to imply that you should argue only "safe" subjects or that winning is everything. Choose a subject about which you feel strongly; present a fair, logical argument; express honest emotion; but avoid distorted evidence or inflammatory language. Even if no one is finally persuaded, at least you have offered a clear, intelligent explanation of your position.

In most arguments, you have two possible types of support: you can supply factual evidence, and you can appeal to your reader's values. Suppose you are arguing that professional boxing should be prohibited because it is dangerous. The reader may or may not accept your premise but at the very least would expect some support for your assertion. Your first task would be to gather evidence. The strongest evidence is factual—statistics dealing with the number of fighters each year who are fatally injured or mentally impaired. You might quote appropriate authorities—physicians, scientists, former boxers—on the risks connected with professional boxing. You might relate several instances of boxing injuries or even a single example of a particular fighter who was killed or permanently injured while boxing. You might describe in detail how blows affect the body or head; you might trace the process by which a series of punches can cause brain damage. You might catalog the effects that years of physical punishment can produce in the human body. In your argument you might use some or all of this factual evidence. Your job as a writer is to gather the best—the most accurate and the most effective—evidence and present it in a clear and orderly way for your reader.

You can also appeal to your reader's values. You could argue that a sport in which a participant can be killed or permanently injured is not a sport at all. You could argue that the objective of a boxing match—to render one's opponent unconscious or too impaired to continue—is different in kind from any other sport and not one that we, as human beings, should condone, let alone encourage. Appeals to values can be extremely effective.

Effective argumentation generally involves appealing to both reason and emotion. It is often easier to catch your reader's attention by using an emotional appeal. Demonstrators against vivisection, the dissecting of animals for laboratory research, display photographs of the torments suffered by these animals. Organizations that fight famine throughout the world use photographs of starving children. Advertisers use a wide range of persuasive tactics to touch our fears, our anxieties, our desires. But the types of argumentative writing that you are asked to do in college or in your job rarely allow for only emotional evidence.

One final thing is crucially important in persuading your reader. You must sound (and be) fair, reasonable, and credible in order to win the respect and possibly the approval of your reader. Readers distrust arguments that use unfair or inflammatory language, faulty logic, and biased or distorted evidence.

Prewriting Suggestions

1. Consider your choice of subject carefully in light of the proposed length of the paper. How complex is the topic? Can you realistically do justice to it within the space available? Or should you impose some restrictions on the topic? Remember that you are taking a stand or a position on the topic. You are arguing in support of that position.

2. Analyze the audience to whom you are writing. What assumptions or ideas do they already have about this subject? Does the subject involve deeply held beliefs, either moral or ethical? For example, it is easier to persuade an audience to register to vote than it is to persuade an audience to support physician-assisted suicide.

3. Be sure to anticipate what your opponents are likely to feel and think about the subject—regardless of how "right" you think your position is. Make a list of possible objections or counters to each point you are making. The quality of an argument is always improved when you understand both sides of an issue.

4. Remember that in college-level writing, you need specific, accurate information to argue convincingly. Facts, statistics, and quotations from authorities carry weight with your readers. Most arguments in college writing need more than unsubstantiated personal opinions.

5. Write a specific statement of the action or reaction that you want to elicit from your audience. As you write and revise, use that statement as a way of checking your developing argument.

WRITING

How Do You Make Sure That Your Argument Is Logical?

Because logic or reason is so crucial to effective argumentation, you will want to avoid logical fallacies or errors. When you construct your argument, make sure that you have avoided the following common mistakes:

*   **Ad hominem argument** (literally to argue "to the person"): criticizing a person's position by criticizing his or her personal character. If an underworld figure asserts that boxing is the manly art of self-defense, you do not counter his argument by claiming that he makes money by betting on the fights.

*   **Ad populum argument** (literally to argue "to the people"): appealing to the prejudices of your audience instead of offering facts or reasons. You do not defend boxing by asserting that it is part of the American way of life and that anyone who criticizes it is a communist who seeks to undermine our society.

- **Appeal to an unqualified authority:** using testimony from someone who is unqualified to give it. In arguing against boxing, your relevant authorities would be physicians or scientists or former boxers—people who have had some direct experience. You do not quote a professional football player or your dermatologist.

- **Begging the question:** assuming the truth of whatever you are trying to prove. "Boxing is dangerous, and because it is dangerous, it ought to be outlawed." The first statement ("boxing is dangerous") is the premise you set out to prove, but the second statement uses that unproved premise as a basis for drawing a conclusion.

- **Either-or:** stating or implying that there are only two possibilities. Do not assert that the two choices are either to ban boxing or to allow this brutality to continue. Perhaps other changes might make the sport safer and hence less objectionable.

- **Faulty analogy:** using an inappropriate or superficially similar analogy as evidence. "Allowing a fighter to kill another man with his fists is like giving him a gun and permission to shoot to kill." The analogy might be vivid, but the two acts are much more different than they are similar.

- **Hasty generalization:** basing a conclusion on evidence that is atypical or unrepresentative. Do not assert that every boxer has suffered brain damage just because you can cite a few well-known cases.

- **Non sequitur** (literally "it does not follow"): arriving at a conclusion not justified by the premises or evidence. "My father has watched many fights on television; therefore, he is an authority on the physical hazards that boxers face."

- **Oversimplification:** suggesting a simple solution to a complex problem. "If professional boxers were made aware of the risks they take, they would stop boxing."

HOW DO YOU STRUCTURE AN ARGUMENT?

If you are constructing an argument based on a formal, logical progression, you can use either *inductive* or *deductive* reasoning. An *inductive* argument begins with specific evidence and then moves to a generalized conclusion that accounts for the evidence. The writer assumes the role of detective, piecing together the evidence in an investigation and only then arriving at a conclusion. An inductive structure is often effective because it can arouse the reader's interest or even anger by focusing on examples. If your thesis is likely to be rejected immediately by some readers, an inductive strategy can also be effective since it hides the thesis until the readers are involved in reading. Jonathan Swift's narrator in his satire "A Modest Proposal" (Chapter 10) begins his essay by pointing to a conspicuous social problem in Ireland: its large numbers of poor, starving children. His contemporary readers would have likely agreed with his observation: "Whoever could find out a fair, cheap, and easy method of making these children, sound, useful members of the commonwealth would deserve so well of the public as to have his statue set up for a preserver of the nation." Having established the magnitude of the problem and his own disinterested situation (he himself has no children), he delays his outrageous solution until nearly halfway through the essay: a portion of the children should be sold for food! The inductive pattern allows Swift to draw his readers into the essay, winning their initial agreement to the magnitude of the problem and the reasons for it. Had he announced his proposed "solution" first, no one would have bothered to read the essay.

A *deductive* argument moves in the opposite direction: It starts with a general truth or assumption and moves to provide evidence or support. Here the detective announces who the murderer is and then proceeds to show us how she arrived at that conclusion. Linda Lee in "The Case Against College" signals her thesis even in her title. Two paragraphs into the essay, she makes her argumentative, and provocative, assertion: "Not everyone needs a higher education." In the rest of her essay, Lee provides the support that leads to her conclusion, drawing from statistics and from her own experience with her son. Since a deductive pattern immediately announces its thesis, it can run the risk of instantly alienating a reader, especially if it is arguing for something about which many of its readers might disagree. David Gelernter in "What Do Murderers Deserve?" is careful not to announce his point—murderers ought to be executed—until he has invited his readers to think about why we hesitate to exercise this "moral responsibility."

The simplest form of a deductive argument is the *syllogism*, a three-step argument involving a major premise, a minor premise, and a conclusion. Few essays—either those you write or those you read—can be reduced to a syllogism. Our thought patterns are rarely so logical; our reasoning is rarely so precise. Although few essays state a syllogism explicitly, syllogisms do play a role in shaping an argument. For example, a number of essays in this reader begin with the same syllogism, even though it is not directly stated:

Major premise: All people should have equal opportunities.
Minor premise: Minorities are people.
Conclusion: Minorities should have equal opportunities.

Despite the fact that a syllogism is a precise structural form, you should not assume that a written argument will imitate it—that the first paragraph or group of paragraphs will contain a major premise; the next, a minor premise; and the final, a conclusion. Syllogisms can be basic to an argument without being the framework on which it is constructed.

No matter how you structure your argument, one final consideration is important. Since the purpose of argumentation is to get a reader to agree with your position or to act in a particular way, it is always essential to end your paper decisively. Effective endings or conclusions to arguments can take a variety of forms. You might end with a call to action. For example, Martin Luther King's speech rises to an eloquent, rhythmical exhortation to his audience to continue to fight until they are "free at last."

You might end with a thought-provoking question or image. Richard Rodriguez, aware of the poor and the silent who are generally bypassed by opportunity despite affirmative action programs, chooses to end his essay with an arresting image: "They are distant, faraway figures like the boys I have seen peering down from freeway overpasses in some other part of town."

If you have used personal experience as evidence in your argument or injected yourself into the argument in some way, you might end as Linda Lee does in "The Case Against College." Throughout the essay, Lee has used her son as an example of a child not ready for college. After two years in school and two years of working, her son has found a job that he loves. Now, four years later, he has had, she notes, "his own graduation day . . . and he did it, for the most part, in spite of college." Or you might end by reaffirming the point that your argument has been making. David Gelernter in "What Do Murderers Deserve?" concludes: "In executing murderers, we declare that deliberate murder is absolutely evil and absolutely intolerable." Finally, Peter Singer, who in "The Singer Solution to World Poverty" (Chapter 10) has made us increasingly uncomfortable by pointing out our moral obligation to sacrifice to help the needy children of the world, reminds us one final time we are in the same situation as the fictional Bob who could save a child's life by sacrificing his savings.

Drafting Suggestions

1. Look carefully at how you have structured your essay. Did you begin with a position and then provide evidence (deductive order), or did you begin with specific examples and then draw your conclusion (inductive order)? Why did you choose the order that you did? Consider the other order.

2. Rate the points that you are making in terms of their effectiveness or power. Within the deductive or inductive pattern, have you placed your strongest points first or last? Are the points arranged in an effective way? Consider other possible arrangements.

3. Use a color highlighter to mark all of the specific evidence you have included in your essay. Remember that details—accurate, factual, logical—are vital to making an argument effective. Have you included enough? Do they meet the tests of accuracy? Remember that each body paragraph needs specifics, not just generalizations or unsubstantiated opinions.

4. Use a color highlighter to mark all of the emotionally charged words and phrases in your essay. Remember that you are not selling a product or writing a negative "attack ad" for a political campaign! Think about how your audience will react to those charged words and phrases. Avoid distorted or inflammatory language.

5. Document all information and quotations taken from sources. Not to do so is to plagiarize. Moreover, the documentation allows your readers to evaluate the types of sources or informants you have used. You can find more advice on plagiarism and documentation in the appendix, "Finding, Using, and Documenting Sources."

REVISING

How Do You Revise an Argumentative or Persuasive Essay?

Argument and persuasion are particularly reader-oriented. That is, the goal of argument and persuasion is not simply to inform or to entertain readers but to get readers to commit to a certain course of action or to agree with (or at the very least to understand) the writer's stand on the issue or subject. Argument presumes that there is at least one other side, that disagreement can and generally does already exist about the subject. Persuasion suggests that readers can be brought into agreement with the writer's position.

Readers typically approach argument and persuasion with some preformed opinions; they are not generally completely neutral about the subject. In some cases, readers will not actively resist a point of view, even if they do not commit to the desired course of action. For example, surely very few people in the United States believe that smoking tobacco is good for you. They might not disagree with an essay meant to persuade smokers to stop, but that of course does not mean that they will stop. Habit and addiction can be far stronger than logical argument or emotional appeal. On subjects that touch on deeply held religious or ethical beliefs, many readers simply will never be persuaded to accept an argument that runs counter to those beliefs. If your readers believe in intelligent design, they will never accept that evolution is the only answer to the origins of human life.

Because argument and persuasion seek to engage an audience in particular ways, it is especially important that you involve readers in the revising stage of your essay. You want to get a minimum of several readers, ideally readers who do not agree with you or who will not agree just to please or humor you. Get them to react to your argument. Do they agree with you? Why or why not? Is this a subject about which they could be open-minded? What is your strongest argument? What is your weakest? What might it take to convince them that even if you are not "right," you have at least articulated a position that they can understand and respect.

When writing an argumentative or persuasive essay, pay particular attention to the following areas: understanding and respecting your opposition, being honest and fair, and ending forcefully.

Understanding and Respecting Your Opposition　In planning, writing, and revising argument and persuasion, you need to be aware of the "other" sides that can exist to the argument. Debaters prepare by being able to argue either side of an issue; lawyers in a courtroom have to anticipate and be ready to counter moves made by their adversaries. As you write and revise, you must decide which points you have to concede and which points can be refuted. Alfie Kohn's long essay on "The Dangerous Myth of Grade Inflation" is an excellent example of how a writer deals with counterarguments. Although Kohn does not think that grades in college courses are "inflated" or that instructors have become "easy" graders, he must acknowledge, for example, that at some schools the majority of students receive As and Bs and graduate with honors. That is a fact that cannot be denied. However, Kohn argues, there might be other reasons why the grades are so high at that school (for example, exceptionally qualified students, course objectives that stress achievement). Furthermore, just because grades at one school are high does not mean that the same is true elsewhere. Always anticipate those who will disagree with you.

Remembering Where You Are: Being Honest and Fair   Every day of your life you are surrounded by attempts at argument and persuasion. A little child throws a temper tantrum in the store; a television political attack ad denounces the untrustworthiness and seemingly criminal behavior of the opposition; a print commercial implies that the "good" life lies in owning this particular car or watch or drinking this expensive brand of vodka; a salesman and his manager try to close the deal by pressuring you. In much of the argument and persuasion that surrounds us, the goal is winning—winning by any means, no matter how unscrupulous, deceitful, or biased. That is never the goal of argumentative or persuasive writing in college. As you review your draft, look again at the nature of the evidence and the language that you have used in your essay. Is the information accurate and fair? Is your language free from inflammatory words and phrases?

Ending Forcefully   Conclusions to argument and persuasion essays are especially important. Obviously, they bring closure to the stand or position that you have been advocating, and they are what remains in your readers' minds. If you are urging readers to commit to a particular course of action (for example, to register and then vote), you need to end with a specific request or call to action. If you are trying to get readers to agree with your position, you need to remind them again of what that position is and why they should agree with you.

Revising Suggestions

1. Find several classmates or peers to read your draft essay—this is vitally important in writing argument or persuasion. Ask your readers to evaluate honestly your position in the paper. Do they agree with you? Why or why not? If they disagree, what are their reasons? Can you address those reasons?

2. Look back to your list of counterarguments those who disagree with you might use in reply. Have you attempted to anticipate their points? Have you conceded those that simply cannot be disputed? Your argument must acknowledge or confront the positions of the other side.

3. Check the list of logical fallacies or errors in this chapter. Have you avoided each of these in your essay?

4. Have you provided a clear organizational pattern in your essay? Outline it. Does it make sense? Are you following an inductive or deductive order? Have you arranged your points in an effective order? Have you clearly signaled the shift from one point to another?

5. Remember that conclusions are especially important in argument and persuasion. Look at what you have written. What do you want your readers to do at the end of the essay? Are you urging a course of action? Are you just trying to change the way in which they understand the issues?

SAMPLE STUDENT ESSAY

Beth Jaffe decided to tackle a subject on the minds of many career-minded, dollar-conscious college students: why do you have to take so many courses outside of your major? Beth's argument is sure to arouse the attention of every advocate of a liberal arts education, and you might consider exploring the subject in an argument of your own.

FIRST DRAFT

REDUCING COLLEGE REQUIREMENTS

With the high costs of college still on the rise, it is not fair to make college students pay for courses labeled "requirements" which are not part of their major. Although many students want a well-rounded college education, many cannot afford to pay for one. By eliminating all of the requirements that do not pertain to a student's major, college costs could be cut tremendously. At the University of Delaware, for example, a student in the College of Arts and Science is required to take twelve credits of arts and humanities, twelve of culture and institutions of time, twelve of human beings and their environment, and thirteen of natural phenomena or science which include at least one lab. Although some of their major courses may fit into these categories, many others do not. Frequently students do not like and are not interested in the courses which fit into the four categories and feel they are wasting their money by paying for courses they do not enjoy, do not put much work into, and usually do not get much out of. It should be an option to the student to take these extra courses. Why should a humanities or social studies major have to take biology or chemistry? Many of these students thought their struggle with science was over after high school only to come to college and find yet more "requirements" in the sciences. Students are getting degrees in one area of concentration. They should be able to take only courses in their field of study and not have to waste their money on courses they have no desire to take.

COMMENTS

Beth's essay, with her permission, was duplicated and discussed in class. Not surprisingly, it provoked a lively reaction. One student asked Beth whether she was serious and exactly what it was that she was proposing. Beth admitted that she did not advocate turning a college education into career training but that she had a number of friends who were deeply in debt because of their four-year education. "Why not just cut some requirements?" Beth asked. Several other students then suggested that since she did not really advocate an extreme position, maybe she could find a compromise proposal. Her instructor added that she might find a way of rewording her remarks about science classes. Few people, after all, are sympathetic to a position that seems to say, "I don't want to do that. It's too hard. It's too boring."

When Beth revised her paper, she tried to follow the advice the class had offered. In addition, she made the problem vivid by using her roommate as an example and by pointing out what specifically might be saved by her proposal.

REVISED DRAFT

LOWERING THE COST OF A COLLEGE EDUCATION

When my roommate graduates in June, she will be $20,000 in debt. The debt did not come from spring breaks in Fort Lauderdale or a new car. It came from four years of college expenses, expenses that were not covered by the money she earned as a part-time waitress or by the small scholarship she was awarded annually. So now in June at age 21, with her first full-time job (assuming she gets one), Alison can start repaying her student loans.

Alison's case is certainly not unusual. In fact, because she attends a state-assisted university, her debt is less than it might be. We cannot expect education to get cheaper. We cannot expect government scholarship programs to get larger. We cannot ask that students go deeper and deeper into debt. We need a new way of combating this cost problem. We need the Jaffe proposal.

If colleges would eliminate some of the general education course requirements, college costs could be substantially lowered. At the University of Delaware, for example, a student at the College of Arts and Science is required to take twelve credits of arts and humanities, twelve of culture and the institutions of time, twelve of human beings and their environment, and thirteen of natural phenomena or science, including at least one laboratory course. Approximately half of these requirements are fulfilled by courses which are required for particular majors. The others are not, and these are likely to be courses that students are not interested in and so get little out of.

If some of these requirements were eliminated, a student would need approximately twenty-five fewer credits for a bachelor's degree. A student who took a heavier load or went to summer school could graduate either one or two semesters earlier. The result would cut college costs by anywhere from one-eighth to one-fourth.

The Jaffe proposal does decrease the likelihood that a college graduate will receive a well-rounded education. On the other hand, it allows students to concentrate their efforts in courses which they feel are relevant. Perhaps most important, it helps reduce the burden that escalating college costs have placed on all of us.

SOME THINGS TO REMEMBER

1. Choose a subject that allows for the possibility of persuading your reader. Avoid emotionally charged subjects that resist logical examination.
2. Analyze your audience. Who are your readers? What do they already know about your subject? How are they likely to feel about it? How impartial or prejudiced are they going to be?
3. Make a list of the evidence or reasons you will use in your argument. Analyze each piece of evidence to see how effective it might be in achieving your end.
4. Honest emotion is fair, but avoid anything that is distorted, inaccurate, or inflammatory. Argue with solid, reasonable, fair, and relevant evidence.
5. Avoid the common logical fallacies listed in this introduction.
6. Make a list of all the possible counterarguments or objections your audience might have. Think of ways in which you can respond to those objections.
7. Decide how to structure your essay. You can begin with a position and then provide evidence, or you can begin with the evidence and end with a conclusion. Which structure seems to fit your subject and evidence better?
8. End forcefully. Conclusions are what listeners and readers are most likely to remember. Repeat or restate your position. Drive home the importance of your argument.

ARGUMENT AND PERSUASION AS A LITERARY STRATEGY

British poet Wilfred Owen served as a British soldier during World War I. The human death toll in World War I was over 8.5 million soldiers; on a single day, the British lost more than 57,000 soldiers. The third leading cause of death was poison gas, used by both sides during the war. Owen's title is taken from the Latin quotation from Horace, cited at the end of the poem, which translates "It is sweet and fitting to die for one's country." As you read the poem, think about whether or not Owen agreed with Horace.

DULCE ET DECORUM EST
Wilfred Owen

Bent double, like old beggars under sacks,
Knock-kneed, coughing like hags, we cursed through sludge,
Till on the haunting flares we turned our backs,
And towards our distant rest began to trudge.

Men marched asleep. Many had lost their boots,
But limped on, blood-shod. All went lame, all blind;
Drunk with fatigue; deaf even to the hoots
Of gas-shells dropping slowly behind.

Gas! GAS! Quick, boys! An ecstasy of fumbling,
Fitting the clumsy helmets just in time,
But someone still was yelling out and stumbling
And flound'ring like a man in fire or lime.—
Dim through the misty panes and thick green light,
As under a green sea, I saw him drowning.

If in some smothering dreams, you too could pace
Behind the wagon that we flung him in,
And watch the white eyes writhing in his face,
His hanging face, like a devil's sick of sin,
If you could hear, at every jolt, the blood
Come gargling from the froth-corrupted lungs
Bitter as the cud
Obscene as cancer,
Of vile, incurable sores on innocent tongues,—
My friend, you would not tell with such zest
To children ardent for some desperate glory,
The old lie: Dulce et decorum est
        Pro patria mori.

DISCUSSION QUESTIONS

1. How does Owen feel about war? How does he reveal his feelings in the poem?

2. Does the poem depend more on logical argument or on emotional persuasion? How is that strategy effective here?

3. Is describing the death of a single soldier an effective strategy? Why might Owen choose to focus on just one example and not on many? Would more examples make the poem more effective?

4. Do you think that Owen was being unpatriotic in writing this poem? Why or why not?

5. What purpose might Owen have had in writing the poem? Who might he have been trying to persuade? What might he have wanted his reader to see, feel, or understand?

WRITING SUGGESTIONS

Living as we do in a world full of advertisements, we are surrounded by persuasion—buy this, do this. Choose a social or moral issue about which you have strong feelings, and then using a single extended example persuade your audience to agree with you and/or to do something. Some possibilities might be:

a. The plight of the homeless in the United States
b. The dangers of addiction or at-risk behavior
c. Cloning or genetic engineering

READING ARGUMENT AND PERSUASION

The effectiveness of argument or persuasion can be measured by its success in convincing readers or bringing them to action. In our daily world, that success typically means, did consumers buy the product, or did they vote for the candidate or the issue you were promoting? In college writing, however, the goal is not always action but often understanding. Effective argument and persuasion is founded on evidence, on logic and reason, on the integrity and commitment of the writer. In effective college writing, the end does not justify the means.

Read the following selection from a larger article that appears at **www.teenadvice.about.com**, a Website devoted to "teen advice." The essay urges youth to register and vote in elections, offering five reasons why they should.

As you read, remember what you have learned about how to write an argumentative and persuasive essay and how that knowledge might help you as a reader:

- Argument and persuasion essays always have a specific goal, typically to get readers to commit to a course of action (here, it is to register and vote) or to understand more fully (and hopefully to agree with) the writer's position.

- Because it is goal-driven, argument and persuasion involve a thorough understanding of what the audience already knows and feels about the subject. If your position on the subject runs counter to the audience's deeply held beliefs (moral, religious, ethical), your argument is not likely to convince any reader. You can, however, at least make your position known.

- Argument and persuasion must take into consideration objections or counterarguments that the other side would offer. You cannot ignore the opposition. Your essay must concede certain points; it must refute others.

- Argument and persuasion essays in college writing require convincing reasons and evidence. Typically, you need to support your position with facts or quotations or logical reasoning. This is especially true if positions on the subject are debatable.

- Arguments are clearly and logical organized in a deductive (the position or stand is stated first, the reasons or evidence follows) or an inductive pattern (evidence first, then position or stand).

- Argument and persuasion in college writing should not resort to inflammatory, emotional, or biased language or evidence. The goal is never "win at all costs."

Title states the position

TOP 5 REASONS YOUTH SHOULD VOTE

Writer can assume a teen audience given the Website

Concedes reasons why young people might not vote—takes some time and energy

Conversational, appealing to audience

Argument consists of five reasons

First reason

Statistics not provided since readers are not not likely to doubt

Appeal to a motivation for teens

You live in a democracy and that means that you get a say in who runs your country, and by way of this privilege you also get a say about how your country is run. It is very easy to be blasé about your right to vote and take a "whatever, who cares" kind of attitude about it but you shouldn't brush this great honor off so quickly. Sure, registering can be a bit of a chore, and yes, you have to head down to a polling station on voting day to pull your lever, which takes some time out of your day and may cost you a few bucks in gas, but whether you know it or not these are very small prices to pay for the right to vote. In some countries people are literally dying to be able to cast a ballot and make a difference. Here, we list <u>five very good reasons that every eligible young person should get out and vote</u>.

<u>The youth vote is sadly underestimated by party analysts</u>. Yes, it is true, the trend analysts who tell party spindoctors where to target their advertising dollars and public relations efforts traditionally overlook the youth market. Why? Because the sad reality is that election year after election year the percentage of eligible youth who actually register and vote is small when compared with other demographics. This doesn't mean the youth market isn't a force, just that it isn't a main motivator in the drafting of campaign platforms and pre-election advertising. So, like any self-respecting rebellious young person, the natural thing to do is <u>go against the grain and do the unexpected</u>. Keep them on their toes, shock them into the 21st century and get out and vote!

RESPONDING TO A VISUAL

You are surrounded each day by hundreds of examples of visual argumentation and persuasion—advertisements. Sometimes advertisements appeal to reason, citing specific facts, figures, and statistics to buttress their claims. Other times, you are assaulted by subtle persuasive appeals: if you wear this

cologne or perfume, you would be irresistible, if you drove this automobile, you would be a hardy adventurer or an important professional. You might like to think that you see "through" these claims of advertisers, that you are not susceptible to their appeals. The truth, however, is that we do respond to these visual appeals—otherwise, companies would stop advertising their goods and services.

Visuals are also used to persuade you to commit to a certain course of action or to believe in or support a particular cause. Bumper stickers, posters, and placards announce your political and social agendas. In times of national conflict, posters and and advertisements enlist our support and participation. Consider this famous U.S. Army poster created by artist James Montgomery Flagg during World War I and then later revived during World War II.

READING AND WRITING ABOUT IMAGES

Over four million copies of this poster were printed during World War I, and countless Americans found its appeal persuasive. Study the poster and then respond to one of the following topics:

1. What is persuasive about this image? To what does it appeal? To what extent might its "message" have appealed to both young and old, women and men? That is, is it intended simply to encourage enlistment in the U.S. Army, or does it have a larger appeal?
2. How persuasive do you find this image in the twenty-first century? Why?
3. Describe an armed forces poster that might be persuasive in the twenty-first century. What elements would it include and why? For some suggestions about what advertising agencies think will work today, check out the various Websites for the branches of the U.S. military.

VISITING THE WEB

The companion Website, **www.prenhall.com/miller**, has additional information about argumentation and persuasion and about the writers in this chapter. You will also find a number of links to other sources of information about the subjects found in this chapter.

EXPLORING ON YOUR OWN

Large number of Websites are persuasive in nature, and you can find all kinds of opinions and positions represented on the Web. Remember, of course, that anyone can mount a Website and make claims or provide "evidence" that is biased, fragmentary, or even fraudulent. When you are using Websites as sources of information for an argumentative or a persuasive paper, always try to assess the credibility of the site first and scrutinize its information carefully. Information about how to do so can be found in the appendix "Finding, Using, and Documenting Sources."

As a high school and college student, you probably have had a number of minimum wage jobs. But what if your future was limited to minimum wage jobs? Arguments for and against the existence of a minimum wage and possible increases if the minimum wage is retained occur annually in Congress and surface in every presidential election. Not surprisingly, the Web has an abundance of arguments for and against both the existence of a minimum wage and the rate at which that minimum wage should be set. Visit sites devoted to both sides of the argument and sort through the "evidence" and the "arguments" that they present. Then in an essay, take your own position on the issue.

LOOKING FOR WRITING SUGGESTIONS

This listing is just of possible subjects; any subject can be argued from several different positions.

1. Federal scholarship aid/loans for college students
2. Legal age at which alcohol can be consumed

3. Distribution requirements in areas outside of the major
4. Math courses for non-math majors; science courses for non-science majors/foreign language requirements
5. Study abroad/internship or community service/mission trips
6. Draft for military/all-volunteer military
7. Women serving in combat zones
8. Foreign aid/debt relief for foreign nations
9. Stem cell research/cloning/in vitro fertilization
10. Smoking/cell phones in public places
11. Birth control/abstinence
12. Lobbyists/political action groups
13. Energy policies/conservation/oil drilling/fuel efficiency
14. Religion and government (role of, conflict between)
15. Global warming/automobile emissions/fossil fuels

DEBATE: IS A COLLEGE EDUCATION WORTH ITS COST?

College costs (tuition, room and board, fees, books) are increasing substantially every year. Low-cost loan programs have been sharply cut back. Financial realities have forced many students and parents to weigh the benefits of a two- or four-year college education. Schools that provide technical job training are flourishing as a more affordable alternative. These two essays debate the "value" of a college education. Porter's essay is objective and scholarly, citing evidence provided by a number of research studies; Lee's essay is subjective and draws upon her experience with her son. Lee argues, for example, that the benefit or value of a college education depends upon the student's attitude and seriousness. Because of the difference in their approaches, their conclusions can be equally valid.

BEFORE READING

Connecting: Was there ever a debate in your family or in your mind about whether it was worthwhile to attend a college or a university? Are you serious about your education? Or are you just having a good time?

Anticipating: Do you think that any of the evidence that Porter provides would have changed Lee's mind? Her son's motivation? Why or why not?

THE VALUE OF A COLLEGE DEGREE

Katherine Porter

This essay originally appeared in the ERIC Clearinghouse on Higher Education in 2002.

1   The escalating cost of higher education is causing many to question the value of continuing education beyond high school. Many wonder whether the high cost of tuition, the opportunity cost of choosing college over full-time employment, and the accumulation of thousands of dollars of debt is, in the long run, worth the investment. The risk is especially large for low-income families who have a difficult time making ends meet without the additional burden of college tuition and fees.

The Economic Value of Higher Education

2   In order to determine whether higher education is worth the investment, it is useful to examine what is known about the value of higher education and the rates of return on investment to both the individual and to society.

3   There is considerable support for the notion that the rate of return on investment in higher education is high enough to warrant the financial burden associated with pursuing a college degree. Though the earnings differential between college and high school graduates varies over time, college graduates, on average, earn more than high school graduates. According to the Census Bureau, over an adult's working life, high school graduates earn an average of $1.2 million; associate's degree holders earn about $1.6 million; and bachelor's degree holders earn about $2.1 million (Day and Newburger, 2002).

4   These sizeable differences in lifetime earnings put the costs of college study in realistic perspective. Most students today—about 80 percent of all students—enroll either in public 4-year colleges or in public 2-year colleges. According to the U.S. Department of Education report, Think College Early, a full-time student at a public 4-year college pays an average of $8,655 for in-state tuition, room and board (U.S. Dept. of Education, 2002). A full-time student in a public 2-year college pays an average of $1,359 per year in tuition (U.S. Dept. of Education, 2002).

5   These statistics support the contention that, though the cost of higher education is significant, given the earnings disparity that exists between those who earn a bachelor's degree and those who do not, the individual rate of return on investment in higher education is sufficiently high to warrant the cost.

Other Benefits of Higher Education

6   College graduates also enjoy benefits beyond increased income. A 1998 report published by the Institute for Higher Education Policy reviews the individual benefits that college graduates enjoy, including higher levels of saving, increased

personal/professional mobility, improved quality of life for their offspring, better consumer decision making, and more hobbies and leisure activities (Institute for Higher Education Policy, 1998). According to a report published by the Carnegie Foundation, non-monetary individual benefits of higher education include the tendency for postsecondary students to become more open-minded, more cultured, more rational, more consistent and less authoritarian; these benefits are also passed along to succeeding generations (Rowley and Hurtado, 2002). Additionally, college attendance has been shown to "decrease prejudice, enhance knowledge of world affairs and enhance social status" while increasing economic and job security for those who earn bachelor's degrees (Ibid.)

Research has also consistently shown a positive correlation between completion of higher education and good health, not only for oneself, but also for one's children. In fact, "parental schooling levels (after controlling for differences in earnings) are positively correlated with the health status of their children" and "increased schooling (and higher relative income) are correlated with lower mortality rates for given age brackets" (Cohn and Geske, 1992).

The Social Value of Higher Education

A number of studies have shown a high correlation between higher education and cultural and family values, and economic growth. According to Elchanan Cohn and Terry Geske (1992), there is the tendency for more highly educated women to spend more time with their children; these women tend to use this time to better prepare their children for the future. Cohn and Geske (1992) report that "college graduates appear to have a more optimistic view of their past and future personal progress."

Public benefits of attending college include increased tax revenues, greater workplace productivity, increased consumption, increased workforce flexibility, and decreased reliance on government financial support (Institute for Higher Education Policy, 1998).

College Attendance Versus College Completion

In their report, "College for All? Is There Too Much Emphasis on Getting a 4-Year College Degree?" Boesel and Fredland estimate that around 600,000 students leave 4-year colleges annually without graduating. These noncompleters earn less than college graduates because they get fewer years of education. More surprising, they tend to earn less than or the same amount as 2-year college students who have as much education. Furthermore, 2-year college students show about the same gains in tested cognitive skills for each year of attendance as 4-year college students. Students at 4-year colleges also pay more in tuition and are more likely to have student loan debts than 2-year students (Boesel and Fredland, 1999, p. viii). The authors conclude that high school graduates of modest ability or uncertain motivation-factors that increase their chances of leaving college before graduation-would be well-advised to consider attending 2-year, instead of 4-year, colleges. If they did, they would probably realize the same earnings and cognitive skill gains at lower cost and with less debt. In order to maximize the return on their time and monetary investment, students who do choose to enroll in 4-year colleges should do everything in their power to graduate. (Boesel and Fredland, 1999, p. ix).

Conclusion

11 While it is clear that investment in a college degree, especially for those students in the lowest income brackets, is a financial burden, the long-term benefits to individuals as well as to society at large, appear to far outweigh the costs.

REFERENCES

Boesel, D., & Fredland, E. (1999). College for all? Is there too much emphasis on getting a 4-year college degree? Washington, DC: U.S. Department of Education, Office of Educational Research and Improvement, National Library of Education.

Cohn, E., & Geske, T. G. (1992). Private Nonmonetary Returns to Investment in Higher Education. In W. Becker & D. Lewis, *The Economics of American Higher Education*. Boston, MA: Kluwer Academic Publishers.

The College Board. (2001). *Trends in Student Aid 2001*. New York: The College Board.

Day, J. C., & Newburger, E. C. (2002). The Big Payoff: Educational Attainment and Synthetic Estimates of Work-Life Earnings. (Current Population Reports, Special Studies, P23-210). Washington, DC: Commerce Dept., Economics and Statistics Administration, Census Bureau. [On-Line]. Available: http://www.census.gov/prod/2002pubs/p23-210.pdf

Institute for Higher Education Policy (1998). *Reaping the Benefits: Defining the Public and Private Value of Going to College*. The New Millennium Project on Higher Education Costs, Pricing, and Productivity. Washington, DC: Author.

Rowley, L. L., & Hurtado, S. (2002). *The Non-Monetary Benefits of an Undergraduate Education*. University of Michigan: Center for the Study of Higher and Postsecondary Education.

Schultz, T. W. (1961). Investment in Human Capital. *American Economic Review*, 51: 1–17.

U.S. Department of Education (2001). Digest of Education Statistics 2001. [On-Line]. Available: http://nces.ed.gov/pubs2002/digest2001/tables/PDF/table170.pdf

U.S. Department of Education (2000). Think College Early: Average College Costs. [On-Line]. Available: http://www.ed.gov/offices/OPE/thinkcollege/early/parents/college_cos ts.htm

Wolfe, B. L. (1994). External Benefits of Education. *International Encyclopedia of Education*. Oxford; New York: Pergamon Press.

QUESTIONS ON SUBJECT AND PURPOSE

1. Porter does not just limit her argument to the financial benefits of a four-year education. What other benefits does she cite?

2. Are you convinced by her argument? Why or why not?
3. What does the range of benefits to the family and society that Porter cites suggest about her purpose in the essay?

QUESTIONS ON STRATEGY AND AUDIENCE

1. What typographical devices does Porter use in the essay and why?
2. What is the effect on the readers of the parenthetical citations of authorities and the list of references?
3. How might Porter have defined her audience? How can you tell?

QUESTIONS ON VOCABULARY AND STYLE

1. How would you describe the tone of the essay?
2. What difference in point of view do you notice between Porter's essay and Lee's essay?
3. Be prepared to define the following words: *warrant* (paragraph 3), *disparity* (5), *cognitive* (10).

WRITING SUGGESTIONS

1. **For Your Journal.** Why did you come to college? In your journal, reflect on your own reasons—no matter what they were. To what extent were your reasons similar to your parents' reasons for sending you? Make some lists.
2. **For a Paragraph.** In a paragraph, identify and then explain what you see as the primary reason that you attend college. Be specific: develop that reason in some detail. Be honest.
3. **For an Essay.** Assume that a younger sibling, relative, or friend is uncertain about attending college. Write an essay intended for that person in which you either encourage or discourage. Be sure to have persuasive reasons for your position.
4. **For Research.** Although Porter cites much evidence to support the economic benefits of a four-year college education, she does not argue for the value of attending an expensive, prestigious college or university as opposed to a lower-cost one. Is there any evidence to suggest that attending an expensive institution produces a greater economic benefit? Research the question and write an essay arguing either position.

FOR FURTHER STUDY

Focusing on Grammar and Writing. How does Porter document her sources in the essay? How might she change her format if the essay were to appear in a popular magazine?

Working Together. The essay begins and ends with a thesis-driven paragraph. Given the potential audience appeal of such a topic (for example, parents of every college-age student), it could well have appeared in a wide-circulation magazine. Working in small groups, brainstorm about other strategies that could be used to open and close the essay. Each group should share its ideas with the class as a whole.

Seeing Other Modes at Work. In outlining the various categories under which the benefits of a four-year college education can be organized, Porter uses classification.

Finding Connections. The obvious pairing is with Linda Lee's "The Case Against College."

Exploring the Web. The essay cites a substantial amount of research to support its conclusions. Are there, though, any dissenting opinions or evidence to suggest that the case might be exaggerated here? Search the Web to see what else you might find.

THE CASE AGAINST COLLEGE

Linda Lee

This essay first appeared in *Family Circle* magazine in 2001.

Do you, like me, have a child who is smart but never paid attention in class? 1
Now it's high school graduation time. Other parents are talking Stanford this
and State U. that. Your own child has gotten into a pretty good college. The
question is: Is he ready? Should he go at all?

In this country two-thirds of high school graduates go on to college. In 2
some middle-class suburbs, that number reaches 90 percent. So why do so
many feel the need to go?

America is obsessed with college. It has the second-highest number of 3
graduates worldwide, after (not Great Britain, not Japan, not Germany)
Australia. Even so, only 27 percent of Americans have a bachelor's degree
or higher. That leaves an awful lot who succeed without college, or at least
without a degree. Many read books, think seriously about life and have
well-paying jobs. Some want to start businesses. Others want to be electri-
cians or wilderness guides or makeup artists. Not everyone needs a higher
education.

What about the statistics showing that college graduates make more 4
money? First, until the computer industry came along, all the highest-paying
jobs *required* a college degree: doctor, lawyer, engineer. Second, on average,
the brightest and hardest-working kids in school go to college. So is it a surprise that they go on to make more money? And those studies almost always
pit kids with degrees against those with just high school. An awful lot have additional training, but they are not included. Ponder for a moment: Who makes
more, a plumber or a philosophy major?

These are tough words. I certainly wouldn't have listened to them five 5
years ago when my son was graduating from high school. He had been smart
enough to get into the Bronx High School of Science in New York and did
well on his SATs. But I know now that he did not belong in college, at least
not straight out of high school.

But he went, because all his friends were going, because it sounded like 6
fun, because he could drink beer and hang out. He did not go to study philosophy. Nor did he feel it incumbent to go to class or complete courses. Meanwhile I was paying $1,000 a week for this pleasure cruise.

Eventually I asked myself, "Is he getting $1,000 a week's worth of educa- 7
tion?" Heck no. That's when I began wondering why everyone needs to go to college. (My hair colorist makes $300,000 a year without a degree.) What about the
famous people who don't have one, like Bill Gates (dropped out of Harvard) and
Walter Cronkite (who left the University of Texas to begin a career in journalism)?

8   So I told my son (in a kind way) that his college career was over for now, but he could reapply to the Bank of Mom in two years if he wanted to go back. Meanwhile, I said, get a job.

9   If college is so wonderful, how come so many kids "stop out"? (That's the new terminology.) One study showed only 26 percent of those who began four-year colleges had earned a degree in six years. And what about the kids who finish, then can't find work? Of course, education is worth a great deal more than just employment. But most kids today view college as a way to get a good job.

10   I know, I know. What else is there to do? Won't he miss the "college experience?" First off, there are thousands of things for kids to do. And yes, he will miss the college experience, which may include binge drinking, reckless driving and sleeping in on class days. He can have the same experience in the Marine Corps, minus the sleeping in, and be paid good money for it and learn a trade and discipline.

11   If my son had gone straight through college, he would be a graduate by now. A number of his friends are, and those who were savvy enough to go into computers at an Ivy League school walked into $50,000-a-year jobs. But that's not everyone. An awful lot became teachers making half that. And some still don't know what they want to do.

12   They may, like my son, end up taking whatever jobs they can get. Over the last two years, he's done roofing, delivered UPS packages and fixed broken toilets. His phone was turned off a few times, and he began to pay attention to details, like the price of a gallon of gasoline.

13   But a year ago he began working at a telecommunications company. He loves his work, and over the last year, he's gotten a raise and a year-end bonus. He tells me now he plans to stay there and become a manager.

14   So, just about on schedule, my son has had his own graduation day. And although I won't be able to take a picture of him in cap and gown, I couldn't be any more proud. He grew up, as most kids do. And he did it, for the most part, in spite of college.

QUESTIONS ON SUBJECT AND PURPOSE

1. How does Lee feel about a college education? What reservations does she have? Under what circumstances does she have reservations?

2. The essay appeared in a June issue of *Family Circle* magazine, probably on sale by late May. How is that timing reflected in the essay?

3. What purpose might Lee have had in the essay?

QUESTIONS ON STRATEGY AND AUDIENCE

1. Judging just from the first sentence of the essay, to whom do you think Lee is writing?

2. Can you find a thesis statement in the essay? Where is it?

3. The essay originally appeared in *Family Circle* magazine. Have you ever seen *Family Circle*? Who is the audience for the magazine?

QUESTIONS ON VOCABULARY AND STYLE

1. What is the effect of opening the essay with a question and of addressing the reader as "you"?

2. How would you define the "tone" of Lee's essay? Is it formal or informal? Conversational?

3. Be prepared to define the following words: *incumbent* (paragraph 6) and *savvy* (11).

WRITING SUGGESTIONS

1. **For Your Journal.** Why did you come to college? Was it just expected of you? Did you just expect to do so? Did you consider other, noncollege options? Why or why not? In your journal jot down your thoughts, memories, and experiences connected with the decision to go to college.

2. **For a Paragraph.** Do you agree or disagree with Lee's argument? In a paragraph, respond to that argument. Focus on your own experience; probably just one aspect of that experience will be enough.

3. **For an Essay.** Whether you agree with Lee or not, write a rebuttal to her essay—title it something like "The Case for College." Think of your essay as something that might be published in *Family Circle* as the other side of the argument.

4. **For Research.** Lee cites a study that found that only "26 percent of those who began four-year colleges had earned a degree in six years." Is that statistic widely accepted? Locate other studies on the same subject; check with your school's admissions or alumni office. Why is the "stop out" rate so high? What explanations does the research offer for this phenomenon? Using your research, write an essay aimed at the incoming freshman class at your school in which you try to persuade them to make good use of their college experiences.

FOR FURTHER STUDY

Focusing on Grammar and Writing. How effective is Lee's intro duction? Remember the audience for which it was written. What are they likely to find appealing in it? Why might Lee choose to begin with a question rather than with a thesis statement? What is gained by delaying the thesis statement? What does this suggest about introductions for your essays?

Working Together. Divide into small groups. Each group should discuss what they expect their college education will do for them. How will they benefit? Are they "taking advantage" of this experience? Is a college education a "right" or a "privilege"? How would they react if their parents did what Lee did to her son?

Seeing Other Modes at Work. Lee also makes use of cause and effect in her essay, as well as narration in relating the experiences of her son.

Finding Connections. Besides its obvious pairing with Katherine Porter's "The Value of a College Degree," the essay can also be linked with Richard Rodriguez's "None of This Is Fair" (this chapter).

Exploring the Web. Want to check out the statistics on college "stop out" rates or the reasons for these rates? Some starting places for online research can be found at **www.prenhall.com/miller.**

DEBATE: ARE COLLEGE GRADES "INFLATED"?

Do your grades matter to you? Do you think that high grades are important to your future? Do you ever choose a course because you have heard that the instructor is an "easy grader"? The subject of grade inflation is debated on most college and university campuses, and a number of plans are being considered to tighten grading standards. The two essays that follow offer two quite different viewpoints on the subject. Both are scholarly articles that appeared in educational journals. Both are more argumentative than persuasive, choosing to cite evidence to support their assertions and conclusion.

BEFORE READING

Connecting: Do you object to an "easy A"? Do you object if nearly everyone else in the class also earns an A?

Anticipating: Which of the two arguments do you find more convincing? Why?

WHEN I WAS YOUNG AN A WAS AN A

Ronna Vanderslice

This essay originally appeared in *Phi Kappa Phi Forum*, a publication of the Honor Society of Phi Kappa Phi, in 2004.

1   People often criticize elementary and secondary schools for their low standards and elevated grades. Political candidates use higher standards in education as a platform for their campaign; yet institutions of higher education cannot deny the statistics: only 10 to 20 percent of all college students receive grades lower than a B–. This figure means that between 80 and 90 percent of all college students receive grades of either A or B (Farley, cited in Sonner). In 1969, 7 percent of all students received grades of A– or higher. By 1993, this proportion had risen to 26 percent. In contrast, grades of C or less moved from 25 percent in 1969 to 9 percent in 1993. The pattern, which continues today, reveals an issue that concerns academicians and the general public alike.

2   One may wonder why this is a problem. For one, employers seem very concerned that good grades on transcripts have very little meaning. It is extremely difficult to differentiate between competent students and incompetent ones by viewing a transcript from most institutions of higher education today. Also, students may be left with an incorrect picture of their own competence. Most importantly, how grades relate to student learning and understanding is not clear. Variety in grading practices across disciplines and between institutions further complicates the question of what exactly an A means.

3   Universities must initiate reforms that increase standards instead of decreasing them. Even though some educators clearly see the wrong in grade inflation, for others it has become such a routine that universities must be explicit in their plan of remedy for this situation. A head-on approach that has been used lately is to include on student transcripts not only the grade for the class, but also the average grade for all students enrolled in the class. Indiana University, Eastern Kentucky University, and Dartmouth College are institutions that have used some type of indexing system. Harvey Mansfield, a longtime critic of grade inflation, uses a similar approach within his own classroom at Harvard University, giving each student two grades: one for the registrar and the public record, and the other in private. The private grades give students a realistic, useful assessment of how well they did and where they stand in relation to others.

4   Indiana University also proposed a three-year moratorium on the use of student evaluations in personnel decisions as a method to curb the problem of too many high grades. The university believes that removing concerns over student complaints about receiving lower grades might motivate all instructors to reset their standards, free from the pressures to give A's in exchange for high evaluations (McSpirit). Felton also recommends that universities rethink the validity of student-opinion surveys as a measure of teaching effectiveness.

Other institutional practices include requiring schools and departments 5
to review grading practices with the goal of bringing rigor to their programs.
An emphasis in student recruitment on what is expected of students in terms
of academic preparation also may be worthwhile (Wilson). In addition, faculty
should take an active approach in insisting that academic standards are an essential part of the academic ethic and that by rewarding mediocrity, we discourage excellence (Wilson). Simply recognizing that grade inflation devalues
your content to students is a necessary step in the right direction. Wilson
points out that grade inflation reveals a loss of faculty morale. It signifies that
professors care less about their teaching. Anyone who cares a lot about something is very critical in making judgments about it. Far from the opposite of
caring, being critical is the very consequence of caring.

REFERENCES

Felton, J. et al. "Web-based Student Evaluations of Professors: The Relations between Perceived Quality, Easiness, and Sexiness." *Assessment
and Evaluation in Higher Education*, 29.1 (2004): 91–109.

Mansfield, H. C. "Grade Inflation: It's Time to Face the Facts." *Chronicle
of Higher Education*, 47.30 (2001): B24.

McSpirit, S. "Faculty Opinion on Grade Inflation: College and University." *Journal of the American Association of Collegiate Registrars*, 75.3 (2000):
19–26.

Sonner, B. A. "A Is for 'Adjunct': Examining Grade Inflation in Higher
Education." *Journal of Education for Business*, 76.1 (2000): 5–9.

Wilson, B. P. "The Phenomenon of Grade Inflation in Higher Education." *National Forum*, 79.4 (1999): 38–41.

QUESTIONS ON SUBJECT AND PURPOSE

1. To what extent does Vanderslice's title suggest her position on the
   subject?
2. Does it matter to you that only 10 to 20 percent of students earn a
   grade lower than a B– (the statistic that Vanderslice cites)? Do you feel
   that lowers the value of an A?
3. Vanderslice never argues that the problem could be solved simply if
   instructors graded more strictly, gave more demanding assignments, or
   graded on a curve. Why not?

QUESTIONS ON STRATEGY AND AUDIENCE

1. What is the effect of paragraph 1, and how is that effect achieved?
2. In paragraph 2, Vanderslice outlines some reasons why grade inflation
   is a problem. What are her reasons?
3. To whom is Vanderslice writing, and how do you know that?

QUESTIONS ON VOCABULARY AND STYLE

1. Despite the use of the first person ("I") in the title of the essay, Vanderslice does not use personal experience in her essay. Why not?
2. What is the effect of providing a list of sources in an argumentative essay?
3. Be prepared to define the following words: *moratorium* (paragraph 4), *mediocrity* (5), *morale* (5).

WRITING SUGGESTIONS

1. **For Your Journal.** Truthfully, how do you feel about grades? Would you say, "What matters to me is what I learned" rather than "What matters to me is my grade in the course"? In your journal, explore honestly your own feelings.
2. **For a Paragraph.** Suppose a friend who had earned a bad grade in a course complained to you: "I paid a lot of money for this course, so I deserve a passing grade," or "I came to class and did the work, so I deserve at least a B regardless of how I did on the exams and papers," or "I have got to get an A in this class or I will never get into law school." In a paragraph, respond to one of these positions, arguing for or against your friend's assertions.
3. **For an Essay.** In such debates, it is typical to assert that students give "easy graders" higher evaluations than "hard" graders. Whether or not that assertion is true, how students evaluate a course and an instructor varies from student to student. In an essay—perhaps something that might appear in your campus newspaper—define and argue for a set of standards that students should use in evaluating courses and instructors.
4. **For Research.** Are there any discussions on your school's campus about inflated grades? Using campus resources—the newspaper, records of faculty meetings, interviews—see how the argument has been phrased on your campus. Are there any plans to tighten the standards by which grades are assigned? Using the evidence that you have accumulated and other research from online and print sources, write a research paper in which you argue for or against toughening grading standards.

FOR FURTHER STUDY

Focusing on Grammar and Writing. Study the structures that Vanderslice uses in her body paragraphs. Do you see topic sentences? What principles of paragraph organization and development does she use?

Working Together. Working in small groups, discuss what you see as an aspect of this argument for which you would like additional information or evidence. Does anything in the essay seem problematic? You might want to compare Vanderslice's argument to Kohn's. Do they differ in the nature of the evidence that they cite?

Once your group has finished, share your thoughts with the rest of the class.

Seeing Other Modes at Work. In paragraph 2, Vanderslice uses classification to organize some reasons why grade inflation is a problem.

Finding Connections. The obvious pairing is with Alfie Kohn's "The Dangerous Myth of Grade Inflation."

Exploring the Web. You can find an extensive debate on this issue on the Web with sites that present almost every possible position and plenty of conflicting "evidence." Some particularly interesting places to visit can be found at **www.prenhall.com/miller.**

THE DANGEROUS MYTH OF GRADE INFLATION

Alfie Kohn

The essay originally appeared in *The Chronicle of Higher Education* in November 2002.

Grade inflation got started . . . in the late '60s and early '70s. . . . The grades that faculty members now give . . . deserve to be a scandal.
—Professor Harvey Mansfield, Harvard University, 2001

Grades A and B are sometimes given too readily—Grade A for work of no very high merit, and Grade B for work not far above mediocrity. . . . One of the chief obstacles to raising the standards of the degree is the readiness with which insincere students gain passable grades by sham work.
—Report of the Committee on Raising the Standard, Harvard University, 1894

1    $\mathbf{C}$omplaints about grade inflation have been around for a very long time. Every so often a fresh flurry of publicity pushes the issue to the foreground again, the latest example being a series of articles in *The Boston Globe* last year that disclosed—in a tone normally reserved for the discovery of entrenched corruption in state government—that a lot of students at Harvard were receiving A's and being graduated with honors.

2   The fact that people were offering the same complaints more than a century ago puts the latest bout of harrumphing in perspective, not unlike those quotations about the disgraceful values of the younger generation that turn out to be hundreds of years old. The long history of indignation also pretty well derails any attempts to place the blame for higher grades on a residue of bleeding-heart liberal professors hired in the '60s. (Unless, of course, there was a similar countercultural phenomenon in the 1860s.)

3   Yet on campuses across America today, academe's usual requirements for supporting data and reasoned analysis have been suspended for some reason where this issue is concerned. It is largely accepted on faith that grade inflation—an upward shift in students' grade-point averages without a similar rise in achievement—exists, and that it is a bad thing. Meanwhile, the truly substantive issues surrounding grades and motivation have been obscured or ignored.

4   The fact is that it is hard to substantiate even the simple claim that grades have been rising. Depending on the time period we're talking about, that claim may well be false. In their book *When Hope and Fear Collide* (Jossey-Bass, 1998), Arthur Levine and Jeanette Curteon tell us that more undergraduates in 1993 reported receiving A's (and fewer reported receiving grades of C or below) compared with their counterparts in 1969 and 1976 surveys. Unfortunately, self-reports are notoriously unreliable, and the numbers become even more dubious when only a self-selected, and possibly unrepresentative, segment bothers to

return the questionnaires. (One out of three failed to do so in 1993; no information is offered about the return rates in the earlier surveys.)

To get a more accurate picture of whether grades have changed over the years, one needs to look at official student transcripts. Clifford Adelman, a senior research analyst with the U.S. Department of Education, did just that, reviewing transcripts from more than 3,000 institutions and reporting his results in 1995. His finding: "Contrary to the widespread lamentations, grades actually declined slightly in the last two decades." Moreover, a report released just this year by the National Center for Education Statistics revealed that fully 33.5 percent of American undergraduates had a grade-point average of C or below in 1999–2000, a number that ought to quiet "all the furor over grade inflation," according to a spokesperson for the Association of American Colleges and Universities. (A review of other research suggests a comparable lack of support for claims of grade inflation at the high-school level.)

However, even where grades *are* higher now as compared with then—which may well be true in the most selective institutions—that does not constitute proof that they are inflated. The burden rests with critics to demonstrate that those higher grades are undeserved, and one can cite any number of alternative explanations. Maybe students are turning in better assignments. Maybe instructors used to be too stingy with their marks and have become more reasonable. Maybe the concept of assessment itself has evolved, so that today it is more a means for allowing students to demonstrate what they know rather than for sorting them or "catching them out." (The real question, then, is why we spent so many years trying to make good students look bad.) Maybe students aren't forced to take as many courses outside their primary areas of interest in which they didn't fare as well. Maybe struggling students are now able to withdraw from a course before a poor grade appears on their transcripts. (Say what you will about that practice, it challenges the hypothesis that the grades students receive in the courses they complete are inflated.)

The bottom line: No one has ever demonstrated that students today get A's for the same work that used to receive B's or C's. We simply do not have the data to support such a claim.

Consider the most recent, determined effort by a serious source to prove that grades are inflated: "Evaluation and the Academy: Are We Doing the Right Thing?" a report released this year by the American Academy of Arts and Sciences. Its senior author is Henry Rosovsky, formerly Harvard's dean of the faculty. The first argument offered in support of the proposition that students couldn't possibly deserve higher grades is that SAT scores have dropped during the same period that grades are supposed to have risen. But this is a patently inapt comparison, if only because the SAT is deeply flawed. It has never been much good even at predicting grades during the freshman year in college, to say nothing of more-important academic outcomes. A four-year analysis of almost 78,000 University of California students, published last year by the UC president's office, found that the test predicted only 13.3 percent of variation in freshman grades, a figure roughly consistent with hundreds of previous studies. (I outlined numerous other problems with the test in "Two Cheers for an End to the SAT," *The Chronicle*, March 9, 2001.)

9   Even if one believes that the SAT is a valid and valuable exam, however, the claim that scores are dropping is a poor basis for the assertion that grades are too high. First, it is difficult to argue that a standardized test taken in high school and grades for college course work are measuring the same thing. Second, changes in aggregate SAT scores mostly reflect the proportion of the eligible population that has chosen to take the test. The American Academy's report states that average SAT scores dropped slightly from 1969 to 1993. But over that period, the pool of test takers grew from about one-third to more than two-fifths of high-school graduates—an addition of more than 200,000 students.

10   Third, a decline in overall SAT scores is hardly the right benchmark against which to measure the grades earned at Harvard or other elite institutions. Every bit of evidence I could find—including a review of the SAT scores of entering students at Harvard over the past two decades, at the nation's most selective colleges over three and even four decades, and at all private colleges since 1985—uniformly confirms a virtually linear rise in both verbal and math scores, even after correcting for the renorming of the test in the mid-1990s. To cite just one example, the latest edition of "Trends in College Admissions" reports that the average verbal-SAT score of students enrolled in all private colleges rose from 543 in 1985 to 558 in 1999. Thus, those who regard SAT results as a basis for comparison should *expect* to see higher grades now rather than assume that they are inflated.

11   The other two arguments made by the authors of the American Academy's report rely on a similar sleight of hand. They note that more college students are now forced to take remedial courses, but offer no reason to think that this is especially true of the relevant student population—namely, those at the most selective colleges who are now receiving A's instead of B's. Finally, they report that more states are adding high-school graduation tests and even standardized exams for admission to public universities. Yet that trend can be explained by political factors and offers no evidence of an objective decline in students' proficiency. For instance, scores on the National Assessment of Educational Progress, known as "the nation's report card" on elementary and secondary schooling, have shown very little change over the past couple of decades, and most of the change that has occurred has been for the better. As David Berliner and Bruce Biddle put it in their tellingly titled book *The Manufactured Crisis* (Addison-Wesley, 1995), the data demonstrate that "today's students are at least as well informed as students in previous generations." The latest round of public-school bashing—and concomitant reliance on high-stakes testing—began with the Reagan administration's "Nation at Risk" report, featuring claims now widely viewed by researchers as exaggerated and misleading.

12   Beyond the absence of good evidence, the debate over grade inflation brings up knotty epistemological problems. To say that grades are not merely rising but inflated—and that they are consequently "less accurate" now, as the American Academy's report puts it—is to postulate the existence of an objectively

correct evaluation of what a student (or an essay) deserves, the true grade that ought to be uncovered and honestly reported. It would be an understatement to say that this reflects a simplistic and outdated view of knowledge and of learning.

In fact, what is most remarkable is how rarely learning even figures into the discussion. The dominant disciplinary sensibility in commentaries on this topic is not that of education—an exploration of pedagogy or assessment—but rather of economics. That is clear from the very term "grade inflation," which is, of course, just a metaphor. Our understanding is necessarily limited if we confine ourselves to the vocabulary of inputs and outputs, incentives, resource distribution, and compensation.

Suppose, for the sake of the argument, we assumed the very worst—not only that students are getting better grades than did their counterparts of an earlier generation, but that the grades are too high. What does that mean, and why does it upset some people so?

To understand grade inflation in its proper context, we must acknowledge a truth that is rarely named: The crusade against it is led by conservative individuals and organizations who regard it as analogous—or even related—to such favorite whipping boys as multicultural education, the alleged radicalism of academe, "political correctness" (a label that permits the denigration of anything one doesn't like without having to offer a reasoned objection), and too much concern about students' self-esteem. Mainstream media outlets and college administrators have allowed themselves to be put on the defensive by accusations about grade inflation, as can be witnessed when deans at Harvard plead nolo contendere and dutifully tighten their grading policies.

What are the critics assuming about the nature of students' motivation to learn, about the purpose of evaluation and of education itself? (It is surely revealing when someone reserves time and energy to complain bitterly about how many students are getting A's—as opposed to expressing concern about, say, how many students have been trained to think that the point of going to school is to get A's.)

"In a healthy university, it would not be necessary to say what is wrong with grade inflation," Harvey Mansfield asserted in an opinion article last year (*The Chronicle*, April 6, 2001). That, to put it gently, is a novel view of health. It seems reasonable to expect those making an argument to be prepared to defend it, and also valuable to bring their hidden premises to light. Here are the assumptions that seem to underlie the grave warnings about grade inflation:

The professor's job is to sort students for employers or graduate schools. Some are disturbed by grade inflation—or, more accurately, grade compression—because it then becomes harder to spread out students on a continuum, ranking them against one another for the benefit of postcollege constituencies. One professor asks, by way of analogy, "Why would anyone subscribe to *Consumers Digest* if every blender were rated a 'best buy'"?

But how appropriate is such a marketplace analogy? Is the professor's job to rate students like blenders for the convenience of corporations, or to offer feedback that will help students learn more skillfully and enthusiastically? (Notice, moreover, that even consumer magazines don't grade on a curve.

They report the happy news if it turns out that every blender meets a reasonable set of performance criteria.)

20   Furthermore, the student-as-appliance approach assumes that grades provide useful information to those postcollege constituencies. Yet growing evidence—most recently in the fields of medicine and law, as cited in publications like *The Journal of the American Medical Association* and the *American Educational Research Journal*—suggests that grades and test scores do not in fact predict career success, or much of anything beyond subsequent grades and test scores.

21   **Students should be set against one another in a race for artificially scarce rewards.** "The essence of grading is exclusiveness," Mansfield said in one interview. Students "should have to compete with each other," he said in another.

22   In other words, even when no graduate-school admissions committee pushes for students to be sorted, they ought to be sorted anyway, with grades reflecting relative standing rather than absolute accomplishment. In effect, this means that the game should be rigged so that no matter how well students do, only a few can get A's. The question guiding evaluation in such a classroom is not "How well are they learning?" but "Who's beating whom?" The ultimate purpose of good colleges, this view holds, is not to maximize success, but to ensure that there will always be losers.

23   A bell curve may sometimes—but only sometimes—describe the range of knowledge in a roomful of students at the beginning of a course. When it's over, though, any responsible educator hopes that the results would skew drastically to the right, meaning that most students learned what they hadn't known before. Thus, in their important study, *Making Sense of College Grades* (Jossey-Bass, 1986), Ohmer Milton, Howard Pollio, and James Eison write, "It is not a symbol of rigor to have grades fall into a 'normal' distribution; rather, it is a symbol of failure—failure to teach well, failure to test well, and failure to have any influence at all on the intellectual lives of students." Making sure that students are continually re-sorted, with excellence turned into an artificially scarce commodity, is almost perverse.

24   What does relative success signal about student performance in any case? The number of peers that a student has bested tells us little about how much she knows and is able to do. Moreover, such grading policies may create a competitive climate that is counterproductive for winners and losers alike, to the extent that it discourages a free exchange of ideas and a sense of community that's conducive to exploration.

25   **Harder is better (or higher grades mean lower standards).** Compounding the tendency to confuse excellence with victory is a tendency to confuse quality with difficulty—as evidenced in the accountability fad that has elementary and secondary education in its grip just now, with relentless talk of "rigor" and "raising the bar." The same confusion shows up in higher education when professors pride themselves not on the intellectual depth and value of their classes but merely on how much reading they assign, how hard their tests are, how rarely they award good grades, and so on. "You're going to have to *work* in here!" they announce, with more than a hint of machismo and self-congratulation.

Some people might defend that posture on the grounds that students will   26
perform better if A's are harder to come by. In fact, the evidence on this question is decidedly mixed. Stringent grading sometimes has been shown to boost
short-term retention as measured by multiple-choice exams—never to improve understanding or promote interest in learning. The most recent analysis, released in 2000 by Julian R. Betts and Jeff Grogger, professors of
economics at the University of California at San Diego and at Los Angeles,
respectively, found that tougher grading was initially correlated with higher
test scores. But the long-term effects were negligible—with the exception of
minority students, for whom the effects were negative.

It appears that something more than an empirical hypothesis is behind   27
the "harder is better" credo, particularly when it is set up as a painfully false
dichotomy: Those easy-grading professors are too lazy to care, or too worried
about how students will evaluate them, or overly concerned about their students' self-esteem, whereas *we* are the last defenders of what used to matter in
the good old days. High standards! Intellectual honesty! No free lunch!

The American Academy's report laments an absence of "candor" about   28
this issue. Let us be candid, then. Those who grumble about undeserved
grades sometimes exude a cranky impatience with—or even contempt for—
the late adolescents and young adults who sit in their classrooms. Many people teaching in higher education, after all, see themselves primarily as
researchers and regard teaching as an occupational hazard, something
they're not very good at, were never trained for, and would rather avoid. It
would be interesting to examine the correlation between one's view of teaching (or of students) and the intensity of one's feelings about grade inflation.
Someone also might want to examine the personality profiles of those who
become infuriated over the possibility that someone, somewhere, got an A
without having earned it.

Grades motivate. With the exception of orthodox behaviorists, psy-   29
chologists have come to realize that people can exhibit qualitatively different
kinds of motivation: intrinsic, in which the task itself is seen as valuable, and
extrinsic, in which the task is just a means to the end of gaining a reward or escaping a punishment. The two are not only distinct but often inversely related.
Scores of studies have demonstrated, for example, that the more people are
rewarded, the more they come to lose interest in whatever had to be done in
order to get the reward. (That conclusion is essentially reaffirmed by the latest major meta-analysis on the topic: a review of 128 studies, published in 1999
by Edward L. Deci, Richard Koestner, and Richard Ryan.)

Those unfamiliar with that basic distinction, let alone the supporting   30
research, may be forgiven for pondering how to "motivate" students, then
concluding that grades are often a good way of doing so, and consequently
worrying about the impact of inflated grades. But the reality is that it doesn't
matter how motivated students are; what matters is *how* students are motivated. A focus on grades creates, or at least perpetuates, an extrinsic orientation that is likely to undermine the love of learning we are presumably
seeking to promote.

31   Three robust findings emerge from the empirical literature on the subject: Students who are given grades, or for whom grades are made particularly salient, tend to display less interest in what they are doing, fare worse on meaningful measures of learning, and avoid more-challenging tasks when given the opportunity—as compared with those in a nongraded comparison group. College instructors cannot help noticing, and presumably being disturbed by, such consequences, but they may lapse into blaming students ("grade grubbers") rather than understanding the systemic sources of the problem. A focus on whether too many students are getting A's suggests a tacit endorsement of grades that predictably produces just such a mind-set in students.

32   These fundamental questions are almost completely absent from discussions of grade inflation. The American Academy's report takes exactly one sentence—with no citations—to dismiss the argument that "lowering the anxiety over grades leads to better learning," ignoring the fact that much more is involved than anxiety. It is a matter of why a student learns, not only how much stress he feels. Nor is the point just that low grades hurt some students' feelings, but that grades, per se, hurt all students' engagement with learning. The meaningful contrast is not between an A and a B or C, but between an extrinsic and an intrinsic focus.

33   Precisely because that is true, a reconsideration of grade inflation leads us to explore alternatives to our (often unreflective) use of grades. Narrative comments and other ways by which faculty members can communicate their evaluations can be far more informative than letter or number grades, and much less destructive. Indeed, some colleges—for example, Hampshire, Evergreen State, Alverno, and New College of Florida—have eliminated grades entirely, as a critical step toward raising intellectual standards. Even the American Academy's report acknowledges that "relatively undifferentiated course grading has been a traditional practice in many graduate schools for a very long time." Has that policy produced lower-quality teaching and learning? Quite the contrary: Many people say they didn't begin to explore ideas deeply and passionately until graduate school began and the importance of grades diminished significantly.

34   If the continued use of grades rests on nothing more than tradition ("We've always done it that way"), a faulty understanding of motivation, or excessive deference to graduate-school admissions committees, then it may be time to balance those factors against the demonstrated harms of getting students to chase A's. Ohmer Milton and his colleagues discovered—and others have confirmed—that a "grade orientation" and a "learning orientation" on the part of students tend to be inversely related. That raises the disturbing possibility that some colleges are institutions of higher learning in name only, because the paramount question for students is not "What does this mean?" but "Do we have to know this?"

35   A grade-oriented student body is an invitation for the administration and faculty to ask hard questions: What unexamined assumptions keep traditional grading in place? What forms of assessment might be less destructive? How can professors minimize the salience of grades in their classrooms, so long as grades

must still be given? And: If the artificial inducement of grades disappeared, what sort of teaching strategies might elicit authentic interest in a course?

To engage in this sort of inquiry, to observe real classrooms, and to re-   36
view the relevant research is to arrive at one overriding conclusion: The real threat to excellence isn't grade inflation at all; it's grades.

QUESTIONS ON SUBJECT AND PURPOSE

1. Does Kohn agree with the assumption that grade inflation exists today?
2. Does any issue involving grades and students concern Kohn?
3. What purpose does Kohn seem to have?

QUESTIONS ON STRATEGY AND AUDIENCE

1. What is the effect of the two quotations that preface the essay?
2. Why is the myth of grade inflation "dangerous"?
3. To whom is Kohn writing? How do you know?

QUESTIONS ON VOCABULARY AND STYLE

1. Do you see any place in the essay in which Kohn abandons logic and argument and instead launches a personal attack on those who are concerned about grade inflation?
2. How would you characterize the tone of the essay?
3. Be prepared to define the following words: *entrenched* (paragraph 1), *inapt* (8), *aggregate* (9), *concomitant* (12), *epistemological* (13), *postulate* (13), *denigration* (16), *nolo contendere* (16), *skew* (24), *machismo* (26), *dichotomy* (28), *candor* (29), *empirical* (32), *salient* (32), *tacit* (32).

WRITING SUGGESTIONS

1. **For Your Journal.** Think about the courses you have taken in high school and in college. Was there ever a course in which you really worked hard and not because of the grade? What motivated you to work hard? Was it an intrinsic or an extrinsic reward? What kinds of learning most appeal to you? What kind of objectives or forms of evaluation? What could Kohn learn about grades and motivation from talking with you?
2. **For a Paragraph.** How important are grades to you? Does it matter what you earn in a course? What other options would you prefer to letter grades? Or are grades what you really prefer? In a paragraph, either propose a realistic, alternative means of assessment or argue for the value of the letter grade.
3. **For an Essay.** Suppose that your college is planning to abolish grades, that in the future what everyone will get is a written evaluation of his or her work in every course. You have been asked to express your

reaction to this proposed change in an editorial in the school newspaper. Argue for or against such an idea. Be honest about your feelings.

4. **For Research.** Kohn is deeply critical of the conventional practice of grading. He rejects the idea that grades are a good form of motivation, especially because students become more interested in the grade than in learning. Is there widespread agreement among other researchers about this issue? Do grades motivate? Can grades be a positive form of motivation? Using online and print research, see what other scholars say about grades as a source of motivation for learning. Using your evidence, argue for or against Kohn's position.

FOR FURTHER STUDY:

Focusing on Grammar and Writing. Kohn frequently uses parentheses to insert material into the essay. Locate all the instances in which he does so, then see if you can write some rules that govern these uses of parentheses. Why not use dashes to separate the information?

Working Together. Divide the class in half. Each half should prepare material for an in-class debate. Half of the class should argue for Vanderslice's position and half for Kohn's. You are free to use your own personal experience and opinions in the debate. Once the groups have prepared their arguments and counterarguments, choose three people from each group to participate in the debate.

Seeing Other Modes at Work. The essay makes extensive use of classification throughout the body of the essay. Kohn also uses a cause-and-effect analysis, particularly when writing about motivation toward the end of the essay.

Finding Connections. The obvious connection is with the paired essay by Ronna Vanderslice, "When I Was Young an A Was an A."

Exploring the Web. Much more information and disagreement about this subject can be found on the Web. For a list of interesting places to visit, check the material provided at **www.prenhall.com/miller.**

DEBATE: SHOULD MURDERERS BE EXECUTED?

Sister Helen Prejean and David Gelernter hold fundamentally opposed positions on the death penalty, and both appeal to the same argument to support their position: a moral or religious mandate. Sister Prejean observes: "To have a firm moral bedrock for our society we must establish that no one is permitted to kill—and that includes governments" (paragraph 14). Murder, Gelernter counters, is a crime against a whole community and against God. He argues: "By executing murderers, the community affirms the truth that absolute evil exists and must be punished" (paragraph 10). Both writers obviously feel that their position is the right and the moral one. Both writers bring personal experience to their essays and positions as well. Sister Prejean has been the spiritual advisor to three men who have been executed. Gelernter was a victim of Theodore Kaczynski, the so-called Unabomber who mailed anonymous packages containing explosives to a number of people involved in technological research. The injuries that Gelernter suffered required ten operations.

BEFORE READING

Connecting: How do you feel about the death penalty? If you had to vote in a referendum on legalizing or outlawing the death penalty in your state, how would you vote and why?

Anticipating: Which position do you feel is "right"? Would anything be likely to change how you feel? Why or why not?

MEMORIES OF A DEAD MAN WALKING

Sister Helen Prejean

This essay appeared first appeared in the quarterly literary magazine *Oxford American* in 1996.

1   THERE SHE WAS during the filming of *Dead Man Walking*, Susan Sarandon being me, going into the women's room in the death house, putting her head against the tile wall, grabbing the crucifix around her neck, praying, "Please God, don't let him fall apart." It's something to watch a film of yourself happening in front of your eyes, kind of funny to hear somebody saying that she's you, but I don't stay long with this mirror stuff. What happens is that I'm sucked back into the original scene, the white-hot fire of what actually happened.

2   There in the Louisiana death house on April 4, 1984, I was scared out of my mind. I had never watched anybody be killed. I was supposed to be the condemned man's spiritual advisor. I was in over my head. All I had agreed to in the beginning was to be a pen pal to Patrick Sonnier. Sure, I said, I could write letters. But the man was all alone. He had no one to visit him, and it was like a current in a river: I got sucked in, and the next thing I was saying was, Okay, sure, I'll come to visit you, and when I filled out the prison application form to be approved as his visitor, he suggested spiritual advisor, and I said, Sure. He was Catholic, and I'm a Catholic nun, and it seemed right, but I didn't know that at the end, on the evening of the execution, everybody has to leave the death house at 5:45 p.m. Everybody but the spiritual advisor. The spiritual advisor stays to the end. The spiritual advisor witnesses the execution.

3   People ask me all the time, What's a nun doing getting involved with these murderers? You know how people have these stereotypical images of nuns—nuns teach, nuns nurse the sick. I tell people: Look at who Jesus hung out with—lepers, prostitutes, thieves, the throwaways of his day. People don't get it. There's a lot of "biblical quarterbacking" in death penalty debates, with people tossing in quotes from the Bible to back up what they've already decided on, people wanting to practice vengeance and have God agree with them. The same thing happened in this country in the slavery debates and in the debates over women's suffrage. Quote that Bible. God said torture. God said get revenge. Religion is tricky business.

4   But here's the real reason I got involved with death row inmates: I got involved with poor people. And everybody who lives on this planet and has at least one eye open knows that only poor people get selected for death row. On June 1, 1981, I drove a little brown truck into St. Thomas, a black, inner-city housing project in New Orleans, and began to live there with four other sisters (with my scared Catholic Mama kneeling on crushed glass and saying her rosary, praying that her daughter wouldn't be shot). ("Kneeling on crushed glass" is just an expression. Read *fervently*.)

5   Growing up a Southern white girl in Baton Rouge, right on the cusp of the upper class, I had only known black people as my servants. I went to an

all-white high school—this was in the fifties—and black people had to sit in the back of the bus and up in the balcony of the Paramount and Hart theaters.

I got a whole other kind of education in the St. Thomas Projects. I still **6** go there every Monday to keep close to friends I made there and to keep close to the struggle. Living there; it didn't take long to see that there was a greased track to prison and death row. As one Mama put it: "Our boys leave here in a police car or a hearse."

When I began visiting Pat Sonnier in 1982, I couldn't have been more **7** naïve about prisons. The only other experience with prisoners I'd had was in the '60s when Sister Cletus and I—decked in full head-to-toe habits—went to Orleans Parish Prison one time to play our guitars and sing with the prisoners. This was the era of singing nuns, the "Dominica-nica-nica" era, and the guards brought us all into this big room with over one hundred prisoners and I said, "Let's do 'If I Had a Hammer,' " and the song took off like a shot. The men really got into it and started making up their own verses: *"If I had a switchblade . . ."* laughing and singing loud, and the guards were rolling their eyes. Sister Cletus and I weren't invited back to sing there again. And the movie got this scene right, at least the telling of it. Sister Helen/Susan tells this story to the chaplain who has asked her if she's had any experience in prisons. He's not amused.

I wrote Patrick Sonnier about life in St. Thomas, and he wrote me about **8** life in a six-by-eight foot cell. He and forty other men were confined twenty-three out of twenty-four hours a day in cells of this size, and he'd say how glad he was when summer was over because there was no fresh air in their unventilated cells, and he'd sometimes wet the sheet from his bunk and put it on the cement floor to try to cool off, or he'd clean out his toilet bowl and stand in it and use a small plastic container to get water from his lavatory and pour it over his body. Patrick was on death row four years before they killed him.

I made a bad mistake. When I found out about Patrick Sonnier's crime— **9** he and his brother were convicted of killing two teenage kids—I didn't go to see the victims' families. I stayed away because I wasn't sure how to deal with such raw pain. The movie's got this part down pat. It really takes you over to the victims' families and helps you see their pain and my awful tension with them. In real life I was a coward. I stayed away and only met the victims' families at Patrick's pardon board hearing. They were there to demand the execution. I was there to ask the board to show mercy. It was not a good time to meet.

Here were two sets of parents whose children had been ripped from them, **10** condemned in their pain and loss to a kind of death row of their own. I felt terrible. I was powerless to assuage their grief. It would take me a long time to learn how to help victims' families, a long time before I would sit at their support group meetings and hear their unspeakable stories of loss and grief and rage and guilt. I would learn that the divorce rate for couples who lose a child is over seventy percent—a new twist to "until death do us part." I would learn that often after a murder, friends stay away because they don't know how to respond to the pain. I would learn that black families or Hispanic families or poor families who have a loved one murdered not only don't expect the district attorney's office to pursue the death penalty but are surprised when the case is prosecuted at all. In Louisiana, murder victims' families are allowed to sit on the front row in the execution chamber to watch the murderer die. Some families. Not all. But black families almost never witness the execution of someone who has killed their loved one, because in Louisiana, the hangman's noose, then the electric chair, and now the lethal injection gurney, are almost exclusively reserved for those who killed whites. Ask Virginia Smith's African-American family. She was fourteen when three white youths took her into the woods, raped, and stabbed her to death. None of them got the death penalty. They had all-white juries.

11   Patrick tried to protect me from watching him die. He told me he'd be okay, I didn't have to come with him into the execution chamber. "Electric chair's not a pretty sight, it could scare you," he told me, trying to be brave. I said, "No, no, Pat, if they kill you, I'll be there," and I said to him, "You look at me, look at my face, and I will be the face of Christ for you, the face of love." I couldn't bear it that he would die alone. I said, "God will help me." And there in the women's room, just a few hours before the execution, my only place of privacy in that place of death, God and I met, and the strength was there, and it was like a circle of light, and it was just in the present moment. If I tried to think ahead to what would happen at midnight, I started coming unraveled, but there in the present I could hold together, and Patrick was strong and kept asking me, "Sister Helen, are you all right?"

12   Being in the death house was one of the most bizarre, confusing experiences I have ever had because it wasn't like visiting somebody dying in a hospital, where you can see the person getting weaker and fading. Patrick was so fully alive, talking and responding to me and writing letters to people and eating, and I'd look around at the polished tile floors—everything so neat—all the officials following a protocol, the secretary typing up forms for the witnesses to sign, the coffee pot percolating, and I kept feeling that I was in a hospital, and the final act would be to save this man's life. It felt strange and terrifying because everyone was so polite. They kept asking Patrick if he needed anything. The chef came by to ask him if he liked his last meal—the steak (medium rare), the potato salad, the apple pie for dessert.

13   When the warden with the strap-down team came for Patrick at midnight, I walked behind him. In a hoarse, child-like voice he asked the warden, "Can Sister Helen touch my arm?" I put my hand on his shoulder and read to him from Isaiah, Chapter 43; "I have called you by your name . . . if you walk through fire I will be with you." God heard his prayer, "Please, God, hold up my legs." It was the last piece of dignity he could muster. He wanted to walk. I saw this dignity in him, and I have seen it in the other two men I have accompanied to their deaths. I wonder how I would hold up if I were walking across a floor to a room where people were waiting to kill me. The essential torture of the death penalty is not finally the physical method: a bullet or rope or gas or electrical current or injected drugs. The torture happens when conscious human beings are condemned to death and begin to anticipate that death and die a thousand times before they die.

14   I'm not saying that Patrick Sonnier or any of the condemned killers I've accompanied were heroes. I do not glorify them. I do not condone their terrible crimes. But each of these men was a human being, and each had a transcendence, a dignity, which should assure them of two very basic human rights

that the United Nations Universal Declaration of Human Rights calls for: the right not to be tortured, the right not to be killed. To have a firm moral bedrock for our societies we must establish that no one is permitted to kill—and that includes governments.

At the end I was amazed at how ordinary Patrick Sonnier's last moments   15
were. He walked to the dark oak chair and sat in it. As guards were strapping his legs and arms and trunk, he found my face and his voice and his last words of life were words of love to me and I took them in like a lightning rod and I have been telling his story ever since.

When they filmed the execution scene of *Dead Man Walking* on a set in   16
New York City, I was there for the whole last week, watching Sean Penn, as the death row inmate Matthew Poncelet, get executed by lethal injection. It was tense, it was slow, it was hard. They shot each scene ten or more times. It took forever. Sean dying, Susan accompanying him, me remembering. Once, during a break, Sean stayed strapped to the gurney and Susan went to visit with him for a while. He's strapped at his neck, trunk, legs, arms, ankles. The cameras are over him. There's a hushed buzz from other actors and technicians. Susan's standing close and talking softly to him. I notice she's holding his hand. It's just a movie. He's not really dying, but there she is holding his hand. Even playing at dying and killing can be real, real hard on you.

QUESTIONS ON SUBJECT AND PURPOSE

1. How is the film *Dead Man Walking* likely to influence some readers' reactions to the essay?
2. Is your reaction to Sister Prejean's argument influenced by her being a nun? Why or why not?
3. Does Sister Prejean suggest a purpose for writing at any point in the essay?

QUESTIONS ON STRATEGY AND AUDIENCE

1. Sister Prejean does not cite Biblical passages to support her position or to counter the arguments of others. In fact, she writes, "There's a lot of 'biblical quarterbacking' in death penalty debates" (paragraph 3). What does she mean?
2. Sister Prejean's essay depends heavily on narrative. How is that reflected in her title?
3. The essay originally appeared in the *Oxford American*, a small-circulation literary journal published quarterly and devoted primarily to writing from the south. What does that placement suggest about her audience?

QUESTIONS ON VOCABULARY AND STYLE

1. How would you characterize the tone of Sister Prejean's essay?
2. What effect does the first-person narration and the conversational tone of the essay have on you as a reader?
3. Be prepared to define the following words: *cusp* (paragraph 5), *assuage* (10), *condone* (14).

WRITING SUGGESTIONS

1. **For Your Journal.** To what extent do you think that personal experience might influence people's attitude toward the death penalty? Both writers of these essays have had personal experiences connected with convicted murderers.

2. **For a Paragraph.** Are there any circumstances under which a convicted murderer ought or ought not to be executed? In a paragraph, choose one position and then define the relevant criteria that should be applied in the circumstances.

3. **For an Essay.** Using the types of evidence that each writer uses, write an essay in which you attempt to persuade the other writer (either Sister Prejean or David Gelernter) than her or his position is wrong. What would she say to him? What would he say to her? Write as one of the writers to the other writer.

4. **For Research.** Sister Prejean writes: "Only poor people get selected for death row" (paragraph 4). Is that really true? If so, why? Do "poor people" commit more crimes punishable by death? Is our legal system flawed? If that comment is true, how does it affect any argument that justifies or defends the death penalty on moral grounds? For a research essay, persuasively and argumentatively address this issue.

FOR FURTHER STUDY

Focusing on Grammar and Writing. What is a cliché? How do you know when a cliché is a cliché? Can you locate any in the essay? Typically, instructors tell you to avoid clichés. Why then might a professional use them?

Working Together. Divide the class into small groups. Each group should choose one of the following details from the essay and be prepared to discuss what it contributes to the essay as a whole.

1. Sister Prejean's experiences in St. Thomas (paragraphs 4–6)
2. Her "singing nun" experience (7)
3. Sonnier's cell in the summer (8)
4. The parents' grief (9–10)
5. The final scene in which Sean Penn is strapped to the gurney (16)

Seeing Other Modes at Work. The essay uses narration as a fundamental organizational structure.

Finding Connections. In addition to David Gelernter's "What Do Murderers Deserve?" (the paired essay), Evans D. Hopkins's "Lockdown" (Chapter 2) deals with a similar subject.

Exploring the Web. Meet Sister Prejean and find out more about the film *Dead Man Walking* on the Web. Read an essay in which Sister Prejean expands on her religious justification for abolishing the death penalty ("Would Jesus Have Pulled the Switch?"). Places to start can be found at **www.prenhall.com/miller**.

WHAT DO MURDERERS DESERVE?

David Gelernter

This essay first appeared in *Commentary* in 1998, a monthly magazine of opinion published by the American Jewish Committee.

A Texas woman, Karla Faye Tucker, murdered two people with a pickax, was said to have repented in prison, and was put to death. A Montana man, Theodore Kaczynski, murdered three people with mail bombs, did not repent, and struck a bargain with the Justice Department: He pleaded guilty and will not be executed. (He also attempted to murder others and succeeded in wounding some, myself included.) Why did we execute the penitent and spare the impenitent? However we answer this question, we surely have a duty to ask it.   1

And we ask it—I do, anyway—with a sinking feeling, because in modern   2
America, moral upside-downness is a specialty of the house. To eliminate race prejudice we discriminate by race. We promote the cultural assimilation of immigrant children by denying them schooling in English. We throw honest citizens in jail for child abuse, relying on testimony so phony any child could see through it. We make a point of admiring manly women and womanly men. None of which has anything to do with capital punishment directly, but it all obliges us to approach any question about morality in modern America in the larger context of this country's desperate confusion about elementary distinctions.

Why execute murderers? To deter? To avenge? Supporters of the death   3
penalty often give the first answer, opponents the second. But neither can be the whole truth. If our main goal were deterring crime, we would insist on public executions—which are not on the political agenda, and not an item that many Americans are interested in promoting. If our main goal were vengeance, we would allow the grieving parties to decide the murderer's fate; if the victim had no family or friends to feel vengeful on his behalf, we would call the whole thing off.

In fact, we execute murderers in order to make a communal proclama-   4
tion: that murder is intolerable. A deliberate murderer embodies evil so terrible that it defiles the community. Thus the late social philosopher Robert Nisbet wrote: "Until a catharsis has been effected through trial, through the finding of guilt and then punishment, the community is anxious, fearful, apprehensive, and, above all, contaminated."

When a murder takes place, the community is obliged to clear its throat   5
and step up to the microphone. Every murder demands a communal response. Among possible responses, the death penalty is uniquely powerful because it is permanent. An execution forces the community to assume forever the burden of moral certainty; it is a form of absolute speech that allows no waffling or equivocation.

Of course, we could make the same point less emphatically, by locking up   6
murderers for life. The question then becomes: Is the death penalty overdoing it?

7   The answer might be yes if we were a community in which murder was a shocking anomaly. But we are not. "One can guesstimate," writes the criminologist and political scientist John J. DiIulio Jr., "that we are nearing or may already have passed the day when 500,000 murderers, convicted and undetected, are living in American society."

8   DiIulio's statistics show an approach to murder so casual as to be depraved. Our natural bent in the face of murder is not to avenge the crime but to shrug it off, except in those rare cases when our own near and dear are involved.

9   This is an old story. Cain murders Abel, and is brought in for questioning: "Where is Abel, your brother?" The suspect's response: "What am I, my brother's keeper?" It is one of the first human statements in the Bible; voiced here by a deeply interested party, it nonetheless expresses a powerful and universal inclination. Why mess in other people's problems?

10   Murder in primitive societies called for a private settling of scores. The community as a whole stayed out of it. For murder to count, as it does in the Bible, as a crime not merely against one man but against the whole community and against God is a moral triumph still basic to our integrity, and it should never be taken for granted. By executing murderers, the community reaffirms this moral understanding and restates the truth that absolute evil exists and must be punished.

11   On the whole, we are doing a disgracefully bad job of administering the death penalty. We are divided and confused: The community at large strongly favors capital punishment; the cultural elite is strongly against it. Consequently, our attempts to speak with assurance as a community sound like a man fighting off a chokehold as he talks. But a community as cavalier about murder as we are has no right to back down. The fact that we are botching things does not entitle us to give up.

12   Opponents of capital punishment describe it as a surrender to emotions—to grief, rage, fear, blood lust. For most supporters of the death penalty, this is false. Even when we resolve in principle to go ahead, we have to steel ourselves. Many of us would find it hard to kill a dog, much less a man. Endorsing capital punishment means not that we yield to our emotions but that we overcome them. If we favor executing murderers, it is not because we want to but because, however much we do not want to, we consider ourselves obliged to.

13   Many Americans no longer feel that obligation; we have urged one another to switch off our moral faculties: "Don't be judgmental!" Many of us are no longer sure evil even exists. The cultural elite oppose executions not (I think) because they abhor killing more than others do, but because the death penalty represents moral certainty, and doubt is the black-lung disease of the intelligentsia—an occupational hazard now inflicted on the whole culture.

14   Returning then to the penitent woman and the impenitent man: The Karla Faye Tucker case is the harder of the two. We are told that she repented. If that is true, we would still have had no business forgiving her, or forgiving any murderer. As theologian Dennis Prager has written apropos

this case, only the victim is entitled to forgive, and the victim is silent. But showing mercy to penitents is part of our religious tradition, and I cannot imagine renouncing it categorically.

I would consider myself morally obligated to think long and hard before 15 executing a penitent. But a true penitent would have to have renounced (as Karla Faye Tucker did) all legal attempts to overturn the original conviction. If every legal avenue has been tried and has failed, the penitence window is closed.

As for Kaczynski, the prosecutors say they got the best outcome they 16 could, under the circumstances, and I believe them. But I also regard this failure to execute a cold-blooded, impenitent terrorist and murderer as a tragic abdication of moral responsibility. The community was called on to speak unambiguously. It flubbed its lines, shrugged its shoulders, and walked away.

In executing murderers, we declare that deliberate murder is absolutely 17 evil and absolutely intolerable. This is a painfully difficult proclamation for a self-doubting community to make. But we dare not stop trying. Communities in which capital punishment is no longer the necessary response to deliberate murder may exist. America today is not one of them.

QUESTIONS ON SUBJECT AND PURPOSE

1. How does Gelernter feel about the death penalty? Would there ever be circumstances that might affect his attitude?
2. In the first paragraph Gelernter mentions that he was one of the many victims of Theodore Kaczynski (the Unabomber). Does knowing that have any impact on your reading of the essay?
3. What might Gelernter's purpose be in writing?

QUESTIONS ON STRATEGY AND AUDIENCE

1. In paragraph 2, Gelernter cites a number of examples of what he regards as the "moral upside-downness" of American society. Does this strategy strengthen or weaken his argument for you?
2. What expectations does Gelernter's title create in your mind? Can you anticipate his position from his title?
3. Gelernter criticizes the "cultural elite" in this country in part because they lack "moral certainty." Who do you think those "cultural elite" might be? Could you define the characteristics of such a group?

QUESTIONS ON VOCABULARY AND STYLE

1. What does it mean to be "penitent"? "Impenitent"?
2. How would you characterize the tone of Gelernter's essay? (See the glossary for a definition of *tone*.)
3. Be prepared to define the following words: *assimilation* (paragraph 2), *catharsis* (4), *equivocation* (5), *anomaly* (7), *cavalier* (11), *abhor* (13), *apropos* (14), *abdication* (16).

WRITING SUGGESTIONS

1. **For Your Journal.** How do you feel about the death penalty? In your journal, brainstorm about your feelings.

2. **For a Paragraph.** Extend your journal writing into a paragraph. Given the space restrictions, focus on what you regard as your strongest argument about the issue.

3. **For an Essay.** Extend the paragraph writing into an essay. Your essay could be argumentative or persuasive or contain elements of both. That means that you might want to use specific examples, facts, and statistics to buttress your position. If you are going to take a qualified position (under certain circumstances), make sure that you make those circumstances clear.

4. **For Research.** Does your state (either the state in which you live or the state in which you go to school) enforce the death penalty? To what extent should states be allowed to decide independently whether or not murder should be punished by execution? Why should such a decision rest with the states? In an essay, argue either for or against uniform penalties for murder in all fifty states. Be sure to document all of your sources including information you gathered from the Web.

FOR FURTHER STUDY

Focusing on Grammar and Writing. Gelernter uses the colon at a number of places in the essay. Make a list of those instances and then write a set of rules for using colons in writing. Compare those rules with those in a grammar handbook. Do you ever use colons in your own writing?

Working Together. Divide the class in half and then subdivide into smaller working groups. Prepare for an in-class debate. One half of the class must argue in favor of the death penalty, one half in opposition. Each subgroup should propose a list of arguments either for or against the penalty. When the two larger groups reassemble, share the strongest points from each list. The two larger groups should then select three classmates to argue their position in the debate.

Seeing Other Modes at Work. Gelernter uses comparison and contrast in the essay, especially in contrasting Karla Faye Tucker and Theodore Kaczynski.

Finding Connections. In addition to Sister Helen Prejean's "Memories of a Dead Man Walking" (the paired essay), a good comparison can also be made with Evans D. Hopkins's "Lockdown" (Chapter 2).

Exploring the Web. The Death Penalty Information Center is a good place to begin gathering additional information. The Web also has an online interview with Gelernter that took place when he was a victim of the Unabomber. Start at **www.prenhall.com/miller.**

I HAVE A DREAM
Martin Luther King Jr.

Martin Luther King Jr. (1929–1968) was born in Atlanta, the son of a Baptist minister. Ordained in his father's church in 1947, King received a doctorate in theology from Boston University in 1955. That same year he achieved national prominence by leading a boycott protesting the segregation of the Montgomery, Alabama, city bus system, based on ideas of nonviolent civil resistance derived from Thoreau and Gandhi. A central figure in the civil rights movement, King was awarded the Nobel Peace Prize in 1964. He was assassinated in Memphis in 1968. His birthday, January 15, is celebrated as a national holiday.

King's "I Have a Dream" speech was delivered at the Lincoln Memorial to an audience of 250,000 people who assembled in Washington, D.C., on August 28, 1963. That march, commemorating in part the hundredth anniversary of Lincoln's Emancipation Proclamation, was intended as an act of "creative lobbying" to win the support of Congress and the president for pending civil rights legislation. King's speech is one of the most memorable and moving examples of American oratory.

BEFORE READING

Connecting: Probably every American has heard at least a small portion of King's speech. Before you begin to read, jot down what you know about the speech or the phrases that you remember from recordings and television clips.

Anticipating: King's speech is marked by the extensive use of images. As you read, make a note of the most powerful and recurrent images that he uses.

Five score years ago, a great American, in whose symbolic shadow we stand, 1 signed the Emancipation Proclamation. This momentous decree came as a great beacon light of hope to millions of Negro slaves who had been seared in the flames of withering injustice. It came as a joyous daybreak to end the long night of captivity.

But one hundred years later, we must face the tragic fact that the Negro 2 is still not free. One hundred years later, the life of the Negro is still sadly crippled by the manacles of segregation and the chains of discrimination. One hundred years later, the Negro lives on a lonely island of poverty in the midst of a vast ocean of material prosperity. One hundred years later, the Negro is still languishing in the corners of American society and finds himself an exile in his own land. So we have come here today to dramatize an appalling condition.

In a sense we have come to our nation's capital to cash a check. When 3 the architects of our republic wrote the magnificent words of the Constitution and the Declaration of Independence, they were signing a promissory note to which every American was to fall heir. This note was a promise that all men would be guaranteed the unalienable rights of life, liberty, and the pursuit of happiness.

4   It is obvious today that America has defaulted on this promissory note insofar as her citizens of color are concerned. Instead of honoring this sacred obligation, America has given the Negro people a bad check; a check which has come back marked "insufficient funds." But we refuse to believe that the bank of justice is bankrupt. We refuse to believe that there are insufficient funds in the great vaults of opportunity of this nation. So we have come to cash this check—a check that will give us upon demand the riches of freedom and the security of justice. We have also come to this hallowed spot to remind America of the fierce urgency of *now*. This is no time to engage in the luxury of cooling off or to take the tranquilizing drugs of gradualism. *Now* is the time to make real the promises of Democracy. *Now* is the time to rise from the dark and desolate valley of segregation to the sunlit path of racial justice. *Now* is the time to open the doors of opportunity to all of God's children. *Now* is the time to lift our nation from the quicksands of racial injustice to the solid rock of brotherhood.

5   It would be fatal for the nation to overlook the urgency of the moment and to underestimate the determination of the Negro. This sweltering summer of the Negro's legitimate discontent will not pass until there is an invigorating autumn of freedom and equality. 1963 is not an end, but a beginning. Those who hope that the Negro needed to blow off steam and will now be content will have a rude awakening if the nation returns to business as usual. There will be neither rest nor tranquility in America until the Negro is granted his citizenship rights. The whirlwinds of revolt will continue to shake the foundations of our nation until the bright day of justice emerges.

6   But there is something that I must say to my people who stand on the warm threshold which leads into the palace of justice. In the process of gaining our rightful place we must not be guilty of wrongful deeds. Let us not seek to satisfy our thirst for freedom by drinking from the cup of bitterness and hatred. We must forever conduct our struggle on the high plane of dignity and discipline. We must not allow our creative protest to degenerate into physical violence. Again and again we must rise to the majestic heights of meeting physical force with soul force. The marvelous new militancy which has engulfed the Negro community must not lead us to a distrust of all white people, for many of our white brothers, as evidenced by their presence here today, have come to realize that their destiny is tied up with our destiny and their freedom is inextricably bound to our freedom. We cannot walk alone.

7   And as we walk, we must make the pledge that we shall march ahead. We cannot turn back. There are those who are asking the devotees of civil rights, "When will you be satisfied?" We can never be satisfied as long as the Negro is the victim of the unspeakable horrors of police brutality. We can never be satisfied as long as our bodies, heavy with the fatigue of travel, cannot gain lodging in the motels of the highways and the hotels of the cities. We cannot be satisfied as long as the Negro's basic mobility is from a smaller ghetto to a larger one. We can never be satisfied as long as a Negro in Mississippi cannot

vote and a Negro in New York believes he has nothing for which to vote. No, no, we are not satisfied, and we will not be satisfied until justice rolls down like waters and righteousness like a mighty stream.

I am not unmindful that some of you have come here out of great trials and tribulations. Some of you have come fresh from narrow jail cells. Some of you have come from areas where your quest for freedom left you battered by the storms of persecution and staggered by the winds of police brutality. You have been the veterans of creative suffering. Continue to work with the faith that unearned suffering is redemptive.   8

Go back to Mississippi, go back to Alabama, go back to South Carolina, go back to Georgia, go back to Louisiana, go back to the slums and ghettos of our northern cities, knowing that somehow this situation can and will be changed. Let us not wallow in the valley of despair.   9

I say to you today, my friends, that in spite of the difficulties and frustrations of the moment I still have a dream. It is a dream deeply rooted in the American dream.   10

I have a dream that one day this nation will rise up and live out the true meaning of its creed: "We hold these truths to be selfevident: that all men are created equal."   11

I have a dream that one day on the red hills of Georgia the sons of former slaves and the sons of former slave owners will be able to sit down together at the table of brotherhood.   12

I have a dream that one day even the state of Mississippi, a desert state sweltering with the heat of injustice and oppression, will be transformed into an oasis of freedom and justice.   13

I have a dream that my four little children will one day live in a nation where they will not be judged by the color of their skin but by the content of their character.   14

I have a dream today.   15

I have a dream that one day the state of Alabama, whose governor's lips are presently dripping with the words of interposition and nullification, will be transformed into a situation where little black boys and black girls will be able to join hands with little white boys and white girls and walk together as sisters and brothers.   16

I have a dream today.   17

I have a dream that one day every valley shall be exalted, every hill and mountain shall be made low, the rough places will be made plain, and the crooked places will be made straight, and the glory of the Lord shall be revealed, and all flesh shall see it together.   18

This is our hope. This is the faith with which I return to the South. With this faith we will be able to hew out of the mountain of despair a stone of hope. With this faith we will be able to transform the jangling discords of our nation into a beautiful symphony of brotherhood. With this faith we will be able to work together, to pray together, to struggle together, to go to jail together, to stand up for freedom together, knowing that we will be free one day.   19

20   This will be the day when all of God's children will be able to sing with new meaning

> My country, 'tis of thee,
> Sweet land of liberty,
>   Of thee I sing:
> Land where my fathers died,
> Land of the pilgrims' pride,
> From every mountain-side
>   Let freedom ring.

21   And if America is to be a great nation this must become true. So let freedom ring from the prodigious hilltops of New Hampshire. Let freedom ring from the mighty mountains of New York. Let freedom ring from the heightening Alleghenies of Pennsylvania!

22   Let freedom ring from the snowcapped Rockies of Colorado!

23   Let freedom ring from the curvaceous peaks of California!

24   But not only that; let freedom ring from Stone Mountain of Georgia!

25   Let freedom ring from Lookout Mountain of Tennessee!

26   Let freedom ring from every hill and molehill of Mississippi. From every mountainside, let freedom ring.

27   When we let freedom ring, when we let it ring from every village and every hamlet, from every state and every city, we will be able to speed up that day when all of God's children, black men and white men, Jews and Gentiles, Protestants and Catholics, will be able to join hands and sing in the words of the old Negro spiritual, "Free at last! free at last! thank God almighty, we are free at last!"

QUESTIONS ON SUBJECT AND PURPOSE

1. What is King's dream?
2. King's essay was a speech delivered before thousands of marchers and millions of television viewers. How are its oral origins revealed in the written version?
3. In what way is King's speech an attempt at persuasion? Whom was he trying to persuade to do what?

QUESTIONS ON STRATEGY AND AUDIENCE

1. Why does King begin with the words "Five score years ago"? Why does he say at the end of paragraph 6, "We cannot walk alone"? What do such words have to do with the context of King's speech?
2. How does King structure his speech? Is there an inevitable order or movement? How effective is his conclusion?
3. What expectations does King have of his audience? How do you know that?

QUESTIONS ON VOCABULARY AND STYLE

1. How many examples of figurative speech (images, metaphors, similes) can you find in the speech? What effect does such figurative language have?
2. The speech is full of parallel structures. See how many you can find. Why does King use so many?
3. Be able to define the following words: *seared* (paragraph 1), *manacles* (2), *languishing* (2), *promissory note* (3), *unalienable* (3), *invigorating* (5), *inextricably* (6), *tribulations* (8), *nullification* (16), *prodigious* (21).

WRITING SUGGESTIONS

1. **For Your Journal.** It is impossible for most people to read or hear King's speech without being moved. What is it about the speech that makes it so emotionally powerful? In your journal, speculate on the reasons the speech has such an impact. What does it suggest about the power of language?
2. **For a Paragraph.** In a paragraph, argue for equality for a minority group of serious concern on your campus (the disabled; a sexual, racial, or religious minority; returning adults, commuters).
3. **For an Essay.** Expand the argument you explored in Suggestion 2 to essay length.
4. **For Research.** According to the U.S. Census Bureau, 43 million Americans have some type of physical or mental disability. Like members of other minorities, the disabled regularly confront discrimination ranging from prejudice to physical barriers that deny them equal access to facilities. The federal government, with the passage of Title V of the Rehabilitation Act in 1973 and the Americans with Disabilities Act of 1990, has attempted to address these problems. Research the problem on your college's campus. What has been done to eliminate discrimination against the disabled? What remains to be done? Argue for the importance of such changes. Alternatively, you might argue that the regulations are burdensome and should be abandoned. Be sure to document your sources wherever appropriate.

FOR FURTHER STUDY

Focusing on Grammar and Writing. What is a paragraph? Once you have a working definition, look at the 27 paragraphs in this essay. What theoretical and grammatical principles does King seem to use in deciding when to begin a new paragraph? Do his principles change as the essay progresses? When and why? What does the essay suggest about the structure and nature of paragraphs?

Working Together. Working in small groups, divide King's essay into blocks of paragraphs. Locate all the instances of parallelism in your section (check the glossary for a definition and examples of parallelism). How many examples can you find?

Seeing Other Modes at Work. How does King's use of narration early in his speech contribute to his persuasive purpose?

Finding Connections. Aspects of the same subject are explored in Richard Rodriguez's "None of This Is Fair" (this chapter) and in Brent Staples's "Black Men and Public Space" (Chapter 7).

Exploring the Web. Extensive online resources are available for King, including texts of his speeches, video and audio clips, texts of sermons, and photographs. Some key sites, all with extensive hyperlinks, can be found at **www.prenhall.com/miller**.

NONE OF THIS IS FAIR

Richard Rodriguez

Born in 1944 in San Francisco to Spanish-speaking Mexican-American parents, Richard Rodriguez first learned English in grade school. Educated in English litera-ture at Stanford, Columbia, and the University of California at Berkeley, Rodriguez is best known for his conservative opinions on bilingual education and affirmative ac-tion, and in "None of This Is Fair" he uses his personal experience to argue that af-firmative action programs are ineffective in reaching the seriously disadvantaged. Yet he also suggests in his two autobiographical works, Hunger of Memory: The Edu-cation of Richard Rodriguez *(1982) and* Days of Obligation: An Argument with My Mexican Father *(1992), that he harbors deep regret at losing his own His-panic heritage when he became assimilated into the English-speaking world. His most recent book is* Brown: The Last Discovery of America *(2002).*

Basically, the phrase "affirmative action" refers to policies and programs that try to redress past discrimination by increasing opportunities for underrepresented or minority groups. In the United States, the major classifications affected by affirma-tive action are defined by age, race, religion, national origin, and sex. The phrase was coined in 1965 in an executive order issued by President Lyndon Johnson that re-quired any contractor dealing with the federal government to "take affirmative ac-tion to ensure that applicants are employed . . . without regard to their race, creed, color, or national origin." In the decades following, affirmative action, in the form of weighted admissions policies, became a potent tool for colleges and universities seeking increased enrollments of previously underrepresented students. Controversy has always surrounded such policies, and in recent years a number of states have enacted legisla-tion banning race-based admissions selection.

On Writing: *In an interview, Rodriguez noted: "It takes me a very long time to write. What I try to do when I write is break down the line separating the prosaic world from the poetic world. I try to write about everyday concerns—an educational issue, say, or the problems of the unemployed—but to write about them as powerfully, as richly, as well as I can."*

BEFORE READING

Connecting: To what extent has your education—in elementary and second-ary schools—provided you with opportunities that others have not had?

Anticipating: Why did it trouble Rodriguez to be labeled as a "minority student"?

My plan to become a professor of English—my ambition during long years   1
in college at Stanford, then in graduate school at Columbia and Berkeley—
was complicated by feelings of embarrassment and guilt. So many times I

would see other Mexican-Americans and know we were alike only in race. And yet, simply because our race was the same, I was, during the last years of my schooling, the beneficiary of their situation. Affirmative Action programs had made it all possible. The disadvantages of others permitted my promotion; the absence of many Mexican-Americans from academic life allowed my designation as a "minority student."

2   For me opportunities had been extravagant. There were fellowships, summer research grants, and teaching assistantships. After only two years in graduate school, I was offered teaching jobs by several colleges. Invitations to Washington conferences arrived and I had the chance to travel abroad as a "Mexican-American representative." The benefits were often, however, too gaudy to please. In three published essays, in conversations with teachers, in letters to politicians and at conferences, I worried the issue of Affirmative Action. Often I proposed contradictory opinions. Though consistent was the admission that—because of an early, excellent education—I was no longer a principal victim of racism or any other social oppression. I said that but still I continued to indicate on applications for financial aid that I was a Hispanic-American. It didn't really occur to me to say anything else, or to leave the question unanswered.

3   Thus I complied with and encouraged the odd bureaucratic logic of Affirmative Action. I let government officials treat the disadvantaged condition of many Mexican-Americans with my advancement. Each fall my presence was noted by Health, Education, and Welfare department statisticians. As I pursued advanced literary studies and learned the skill of reading Spenser and Wordsworth and Empson, I would hear myself numbered among the culturally disadvantaged. Still, silent, I didn't object.

4   But the irony cut deep. And guilt would not be evaded by averting my glance when I confronted a face like my own in a crowd. By late 1975, nearing the completion of my graduate studies at Berkeley, I was so wary of the benefits of Affirmative Action that I feared my inevitable success as an applicant for a teaching position. The months of fall—traditionally that time of academic job-searching—passed without my applying to a single school. When one of my professors chanced to learn this in late November, he was astonished, then furious. He yelled at me: Did I think that because I was a minority student jobs would just come looking for me? What was I thinking? Did I realize that he and several other faculty members had already written letters on my behalf? Was I going to start acting like some other minority students he had known? They struggled for success and then when it was almost within reach, grew strangely afraid and let it pass. Was that it? Was I determined to fail?

5   I did not respond to his questions. I didn't want to admit to him, and thus to myself, the reason I delayed.

6   I merely agreed to write to several schools. (In my letter I wrote: "I cannot claim to represent disadvantaged Mexican-Americans. The very fact that I am in a position to apply for this job should make that clear.") After two or three days, there were telegrams and phone calls, invitations to interviews, then airplane trips. A blur of faces and the murmur of their soft questions.

And, over someone's shoulder, the sight of campus buildings shadowing pictures I had seen years before when I leafed through Ivy League catalogues with great expectations. At the end of each visit, interviewers would smile and wonder if I had any questions. A few times I quietly wondered what advantage my race had given me over other applicants. But that was an impossible question for them to answer without embarrassing me. Quickly, several persons insisted that my ethnic identity had given me no more than a "foot inside the door"; at most, I had a "slight edge" over other applicants. "We just looked at your dossier with extra care and we liked what we saw. There was never any question of having to alter our standards. You can be certain of that."

In the early part of January, offers arrived on stiffly elegant stationery. 7
Most schools promised terms appropriate for any new assistant professor. A few made matters worse—and almost more tempting—by offering more: the use of university housing; an unusually large starting salary; a reduced teaching schedule. As the stack of letters mounted, my hesitation increased. I started calling department chairmen to ask for another week, then 10 more days—"more time to reach a decision"—to avoid the decision I would need to make.

At school, meantime, some students hadn't received a single job offer. 8
One man, probably the best student in the department, did not even get a request for his dossier. He and I met outside a classroom one day and he asked about my opportunities. He seemed happy for me. Faculty members beamed. They said they had expected it. "After all, not many schools are going to pass up getting a Chicano with a Ph.D. in Renaissance literature," somebody said, laughing. Friends wanted to know which of the offers I was going to accept. But I couldn't make up my mind. February came and I was running out of time and excuses. (One chairman guessed my delay was a bargaining ploy and increased his offer with each of my calls.) I had to promise a decision by the 10th; the 12th at the very latest.

On the 18th of February, late in the afternoon, I was in the office I 9
shared with several other teaching assistants. Another graduate student was sitting across the room at his desk. When I got up to leave, he looked over to say in an uneventful voice that he had some big news. He had finally decided to accept a position at a faraway university. It was not a job he especially wanted, he admitted. But he had to take it because there hadn't been any other offers. He felt trapped, and depressed, since his job would separate him from his young daughter.

I tried to encourage him by remarking that he was lucky at least to have 10
found a job. So many others hadn't been able to get anything. But before I finished speaking I realized that I had said the wrong thing. And I anticipated his next question.

"What are your plans?" he wanted to know. "Is it true you've gotten an 11
offer from Yale?"

I said that it was. "Only, I still haven't made up my mind." 12

He stared at me as I put on my jacket. And smiling, then unsmiling, he 13
asked if I knew that he too had written to Yale. In his case, however, no one had bothered to acknowledge his letter with even a postcard. What did I think of that?

14   He gave me no time to answer.

15   "Damn!" he said sharply and his chair rasped the floor as he pushed himself back. Suddenly, it was to *me* that he was complaining. "It's just not right, Richard. None of this is fair. You've done some good work, but so have I. I'll bet our records are just about equal. But when we look for jobs this year, it's a different story. You get all of the breaks."

16   To evade his criticism, I wanted to side with him. I was about to admit the injustice of Affirmative Action. But he went on, his voice hard with accusation. "It's all very simple this year. You're a Chicano. And I am a Jew. That's the only real difference between us."

17   His words stung me: there was nothing he was telling me that I didn't know. I had admitted everything already. But to hear someone else say these things, and in such an accusing tone, was suddenly hard to take. In a deceptively calm voice, I responded that he had simplified the whole issue. The phrases came like bubbles to the tip of my tongue: "new blood"; "the importance of cultural diversity"; "the goal of racial integration." These were all the arguments I had proposed several years ago—and had long since abandoned. Of course the offers were unjustifiable. I knew that. All I was saying amounted to a frantic self-defense. I tried to find an end to a sentence. My voice faltered to a stop.

18   "Yeah, sure," he said. "I've heard all that before. Nothing you say really changes the fact that Affirmative Action is unfair. You see that, don't you? There isn't any way for me to compete with you. Once there were quotas to keep my parents out of certain schools; now there are quotas to get you in and the effect on me is the same as it was for them."

19   I listened to every word he spoke. But my mind was really on something else. I knew at that moment that I would reject all of the offers. I stood there silently surprised by what an easy conclusion it was. Having prepared for so many years to teach, having trained myself to do nothing else, I had hesitated out of practical fear. But now that it was made, the decision came with relief. I immediately knew I had made the right choice.

20   My colleague continued talking and I realized that he was simply right. Affirmative Action programs *are* unfair to white students. But as I listened to him assert his rights, I thought of the seriously disadvantaged. How different they were from white, middle-class students who come armed with the testimony of their grades and aptitude scores and self-confidence to complain about the unequal treatment they now receive. I listen to them. I do not want to be careless about what they say. Their rights are important to protect. But inevitably when I hear them or their lawyers, I think about the most seriously disadvantaged, not simply Mexican-Americans, but of all those who do not ever imagine themselves going to college or becoming doctors: white, black, brown. Always poor. Silent. They are not plaintiffs before the court or against the misdirection of Affirmative Action. They lack the confidence (my confidence!) to assume their right to a good education. They lack the confidence and skills a good primary and secondary education provides and which are prerequisites for informed public life. They remain silent.

The debate drones on and surrounds them in stillness. They are distant, 21
faraway figures like the boys I have seen peering down from freeway overpasses in some other part of town.

QUESTIONS ON SUBJECT AND PURPOSE

1. In paragraph 4, Rodriguez makes reference to the "irony" of the situation. In what ways was it ironic?
2. Why does Rodriguez decide to reject all of the offers?
3. Is Rodriguez criticizing affirmative action policies? How could such policies reach or change the lives of those who are really seriously disadvantaged?

QUESTIONS ON STRATEGY AND AUDIENCE

1. To what extent does Rodriguez present a formal argument based on an appeal to reason? To what extent does he attempt to persuade through an appeal to emotion? Which element is stronger in the piece?
2. What is the difference between objectively stating an opinion and narrating a personal experience? Do we as readers react any differently to Rodriguez's story as a result?
3. What expectations does Rodriguez have of his audience? How do you know that?

QUESTIONS ON VOCABULARY AND STYLE

1. In paragraphs 11–18, Rodriguez dramatizes a scene with a fellow student. He could have just summarized what was said without using dialogue. What advantage is gained by developing the scene?
2. Be prepared to discuss the significance of the following sentences:
    a. "For me opportunities had been extravagant" (paragraph 2).
    b. "The benefits were often, however, too gaudy to please" (2).
    c. "The phrases came like bubbles to the tip of my tongue" (17).
    d. "Always poor. Silent" (20).
3. What is the effect of the simile ("like the boys I have seen . . .") Rodriguez uses in the final line?

WRITING SUGGESTIONS

1. **For Your Journal.** What made you pursue your education? What are the important motivating factors? Explore the questions in your journal.
2. **For a Paragraph.** Describe a time when you encountered an obstacle because of your age, gender, race, religion, physical ability, physical appearance, or socioeconomic status. Describe the experience briefly, and then argue against the unfairness of such discrimination.

3. **For an Essay.** Are minorities and women fairly represented on the faculty of your college or university? Check the proportion of white males to minority and women faculty members, looking not only at raw numbers but also at rank, tenure, and so forth. Then, in an essay, argue for or against the need to achieve a better balance.

4. **For Research.** Rodriguez feels that as a result of "an early, excellent education" (paragraph 2), he was no longer "a principal victim of racism or any other social oppression." If the key to helping the "seriously disadvantaged" lies in improving the quality of elementary and secondary education, how successful have American schools been? Has the quality of education for the disadvantaged improved in the past twenty years? Research the problem, and then write an essay in which you evaluate some existing programs and make recommendations about continuing, expanding, modifying, or dropping them. Be sure to document your sources wherever appropriate.

FOR FURTHER STUDY

Focusing on Grammar and Writing. Rewrite paragraphs 11 to 18, changing the dialogue into indirect discourse (a model would be paragraphs 4 to 6). What is the difference between the two strategies? What are the advantages and disadvantages of each? What happens to the essay when this change is made? What does Rodriguez gain by dramatizing the situation with the other teaching assistant? What does this activity suggest about using dialogue at appropriate times in your own essays?

Working Together. Rodriguez objects to affirmative action policies because they do not reach the seriously disadvantaged. How, though, might that be done? What changes might a writer argue for? Divide into small groups and brainstorm some possible solutions to the problems that Rodriguez sees.

Seeing Other Modes at Work. Rodriguez uses narration throughout the essay, using his own experiences as part of his persuasive strategy.

Finding Connections. Interesting pairings include Judith Ortiz Cofer's "The Myth of the Latin Woman" (Chapter 4) and Amy Tan's "Mother Tongue" (Chapter 8).

Exploring the Web. Extensive resources for Richard Rodriguez and for affirmative action policies can be found online. Places to start are listed at **www.prenhall.com/miller.**

10

COMBINATIONS AT WORK

The essays in the first nine chapters of this text are grouped according to particular organizational patterns that they show. These organizational patterns are often labeled in a variety of ways: modes, rhetorical structures, ways of knowing, patterns for writers. Regardless of what they are called, each has distinguishing features and distinctive elements and structures. They are the common building blocks of most writing; indeed, most are also the common ways in which we come to know and perceive. They are, in that sense, worth studying and practicing on their own.

As you have seen, however, most of the essays in the earlier chapters of this text involve more than one mode or pattern or strategy. Except in a very short essay, it is rare to find only a single pattern at work. For example, narration rarely occurs without description; process uses narration; definition uses all of the patterns. In fact, for every essay in this book, the section "Seeing Other Modes at Work" identifies at least one other pattern that can be seen in the essay. Still, each essay in the earlier chapters is placed where it is because it predominantly displays one pattern.

What you will find in this chapter is a gathering of classic essays that show a mixture of strategies at work. They offer you the opportunity to see how writers combine the patterns into a whole; they are in that sense extensions of the other chapters in this text. As you read, notice how the patterns interact and combine to make an artistic whole.

A MODEST PROPOSAL

For Preventing the Children of Poor People in Ireland from Being a Burden to Their Parents or Country, and for Making Them Beneficial to the Public

Jonathan Swift

Jonathan Swift (1667–1745) was born in Dublin of an English Tory family and entered Trinity College in 1682, studying for a career in the church. He was ordained in 1695 and was assigned to a small country parish in Kilroot, Ireland. Swift traveled to England several times hoping for advancement, and in 1713 was made dean of St. Patrick's Cathedral in Dublin. A satirist and an active propagandist for the Tory party and the Irish cause, Swift is best known for A Tale of a Tub *(1704),* Gulliver's Travels *(1726), and "A Modest Proposal" (1729).*

Swift's "modest proposal" grew out of a number of factors and conditions that had reduced the Irish people to poverty. First, England had long regarded Ireland, not as a sister kingdom, but as a colony to be exploited. Toward the end of the seventeenth century, the English Parliament had passed a number of restrictive laws to control Irish agriculture and thereby protect English industries. The measures severely reduced Irish revenues and food production. Second, Irish titles, estates, and appointments were part of the English patronage system and were given to Englishmen who had no interest in Ireland's welfare and who did not reside there. Revenue generated in Ireland was spent in England. Swift himself had estimated that absentee landlords drew off as much as two-thirds of all Irish revenues. Third, for three years prior to 1729, Ireland had suffered a near famine occasioned by the failure of grain crops. Irish people were starving to death. Swift's ironic proposal was intended to dramatize Ireland's plight and to rebuke the English for their failure to help.

On Writing: *In his poem "Verses on the Death of Dr. Swift," Swift noted:*

> As with a moral view designed
> To cure the vices of mankind:
> Yet malice never was his aim;
> He lashed the vice but spared the name.
> No individual could resent,
> Where thousands equally were meant.
> His satire points at no defect
> But what all mortals can correct.

BEFORE READING

Connecting: What does the word *modest* suggest to you? In what way is this a "modest proposal"?

Anticipating: How do the verses quoted above in "On Writing" apply to "A Modest Proposal"?

LOOKING FOR COMBINATIONS

Swift's essay is primarily persuasive, but it uses other strategies as well. Fairly obvious are classification and cause and effect. Can you locate those patterns in the essay? Can you find any others at work? What role do these strategies or patterns play in the essay as a whole?

It is a melancholy object to those who walk through this great town,[1] or travel in the country, when they see the streets, the roads, and cabin-doors crowded with beggars of the female sex, followed by three, four, or six children all in rags, and importuning every passenger for an alms.[2] These mothers, instead of being able to work for their honest livelihood, are forced to employ all their time in strolling, to beg sustenance for their helpless infants, who, as they grow up, either turn thieves for want of work, or leave their dear native country to fight for the Pretender in Spain,[3] or sell themselves to the Barbadoes.[4] **1**

I think it is agreed by all parties that this prodigious number of children, in the arms, or on the backs, or at the heels of their mothers, and frequently of their fathers, is in the present deplorable state of the kingdom a very great additional grievance; and therefore whoever could find out a fair, cheap, and easy method of making these children sound and useful members of the commonwealth would deserve so well of the public as to have his statue set up for a preserver of the nation. **2**

But my intention is very far from being confined to provide only for the children of professed beggars; it is of a much greater extent, and shall take in the whole number of infants at a certain age who are born of parents in effect as little able to support them as those who demand our charity in the streets. **3**

As to my own part, having turned my thoughts for many years upon this important subject, and maturely weighed the several schemes of other projectors,[5] I have always found them grossly mistaken in their computation. It is true a child just dropped from its dam may be supported by her milk for a solar year with little other nourishment, at most not above the value of two shillings, which the mother may certainly get, or the value in scraps, by her lawful occupation of begging, and it is exactly at one year old that I propose to provide for them, in such a manner as, instead of being a charge upon their parents, or the parish, or wanting food and raiment for the rest of their lives, they shall, on the contrary, contribute to the feeding and partly to the clothing of many thousands. **4**

There is likewise another great advantage in my scheme, that it will prevent those voluntary abortions, and that horrid practice of women murdering their bastard children, alas, too frequent among us, sacrificing the poor innocent babes, I doubt, more to avoid the expense than the shame, which would move tears and pity in the most savage and inhuman breast. **5**

[1] Dublin.
[2] A contemporary estimate placed the number of itinerent beggars in Ireland at 34,425.
[3] Irish Catholics had been recruited to fight for Spain and France against England. One attempt in 1719 had tried to restore the "Pretender," James Stuart, to the English throne.
[4] Large numbers of Irishmen emigrated to the British West Indies
[5] For Swift, a "projector" was one who proposed foolish plans.

6   The number of souls in Ireland being usually reckoned one million and a half, of these I calculate there may be about two hundred thousand couples whose wives are breeders from which number I subtract thirty thousand couples who are able to maintain their own children, although I apprehend there cannot be so many under the present distresses of the kingdom, but this being granted, there will remain an hundred and seventy thousand breeders. I again subtract fifty thousand for those women who miscarry, or whose children die by accident or disease within the year. There only remain an hundred and twenty thousand children of poor parents annually born: the question therefore is, how this number shall be reared, and provided for, which, as I have already said, under the present situation of affairs is utterly impossible by all the methods hitherto proposed, for we can neither employ them in handicraft or agriculture; we neither build houses (I mean in the country), nor cultivate land: they can very seldom pick up a livelihood by stealing until they arrive at six years old, except where they are of towardly[6]parts, although I confess they learn the rudiments much earlier, during which time they can however be properly looked upon only as probationers, as I have been informed by a principal gentleman in the County of Cavan, who protested to me that he never knew above one or two instances under the age of six, even in a part of the kingdom so renowned for the quickest proficiency in the art.

7   I am assured by our merchants that a boy or a girl before twelve years old, is no saleable commodity, and even when they come to this age, they will not yield above three pounds, or three pounds and half-a-crown at most on the Exchange, which cannot turn to account either to the parents or the kingdom, the charge of nutriment and rags having been at least four times that value.

8   I shall now therefore humbly propose my own thoughts, which I hope will not be liable to the least objection.

9   I have been assured by a very knowing American of my acquaintance in London, that a young healthy child well nursed is at a year old a most delicious, nourishing and wholesome food, whether stewed, roasted, baked, or boiled, and I make no doubt that it will equally serve in a fricassee, or a ragout.

10   I do therefore humbly offer it to public consideration, that of the hundred and twenty thousand children already computed, twenty thousand may be reserved for breed, whereof only one fourth part to be males, which is more than we allow to sheep, black-cattle, or swine, and my reason is that these children are seldom the fruits of marriage, a circumstance not much regarded by our savages, therefore one male will be sufficient to serve four females. That the remaining hundred thousand may at a year old be offered in sale to the persons of quality, and fortune, through the kingdom, always advising the mother to let them suck plentifully in the last month, so as to render them plump, and fat for a good table. A child will make two dishes at an entertainment for friends, and when the family dines alone, the fore or hind quarter will make a reasonable dish, and seasoned with a little pepper or salt will be very good boiled on the fourth day, especially in winter.

[6]Promising.

I have reckoned upon a medium, that a child just born will weigh twelve   11
pounds, and in a solar year if tolerably nursed increaseth to twenty-eight pounds.

I grant this food will be somewhat dear, and therefore very proper for   12
landlords, who, as they have already devoured most of the parents, seem to
have the best title to the children.

Infant's flesh will be in season throughout the year, but more plentiful in   13
March, and a little before and after, for we are told by a grave author,[7] an eminent French physician, that fish being a prolific diet, there are more children
born in Roman Catholic countries about nine months after Lent than at any
other season; therefore reckoning a year after Lent, the markets will be more
glutted than usual, because the number of Popish infants is at least three to
one in this kingdom, and therefore it will have one other collateral advantage
by lessening the number of Papists among us.

I have already computed the charge of nursing a beggar's child (in which   14
list I reckon all cottagers, labourers, and four-fifths of the farmers) to be about
two shillings per annum, rags included, and I believe no gentleman would repine to give ten shillings for the carcass of a good fat child, which, as I have said,
will make four dishes of excellent nutritive meat, when he hath only some particular friend or his own family to dine with him. Thus the Squire will learn to
be a good landlord and grow popular among his tenants, the mother will have
eight shillings net profit, and be fit for work until she produces another child.

Those who are more thrifty (as I must confess the times require) may   15
flay the carcass; the skin of which artificially dressed, will make admirable
gloves for ladies, and summer boots for fine gentlemen.[8]

As to our city of Dublin, shambles[9] may be appointed for this purpose, in   16
the most convenient parts of it, and butchers we may be assured will not be
wanting, although rather recommend buying the children alive, and dressing
them hot from the knife, as we do roasting pigs.

A very worthy person, a true lover of his country, and whose virtues I   17
highly esteem, was lately pleased, in discoursing on this matter to offer a refinement upon my scheme. He said that many gentlemen of this kingdom,
having of late destroyed their deer, he conceived that the want of venison
might be well supplied by the bodies of young lads and maidens, not exceed-
ing fourteen years of age, not under twelve, so great a number of both sexes in
every country being now ready to starve, for want of work and service and
these to be disposed of by their parents if alive, or otherwise by their nearest
relations. But with due deference to so excellent a friend, and so deserving a
patriot, I cannot be altogether in his sentiments. For as to the males, my
American acquaintance assured me from frequent experience that their flesh
was generally tough and lean, like that of our schoolboys, by continual exercise, and their taste disagreeable, and to fatten them would not answer the
charge. There as to the females, it would, I think with humble submission be

---

[7]François Rabelais (1494?–1553), a French satirist.
[8]With art or skill.
[9]A meat market.

a loss to the public, because they soon would become breeders themselves: and besides, it is not improbable that some scrupulous people might be apt to censure such a practice (although indeed very unjustly) as a little bordering upon cruelty, which I confess, hath always been with me the strongest objection against any project, howsoever well intended.

18   But in order to justify my friend, he confessed that this expedient was put into his head by the famous Psalmanazar, [10]a native of the island Formosa, who came from thence to London, above twenty years ago, and in conversation told my friend that in his country when any young person happened to be put to death, the executioner sold the carcass to persons of quality, as a prime dainty, and that, in his time, the body of a plump girl of fifteen, who was crucified for an attempt to poison the emperor, was sold to his Imperial Majesty's Prime Minister of State, and other great Mandarins of the Court, in joints from the gibbet, at four hundred crowns. Neither indeed can I deny that if the same use were made of several plump young girls in this town who, without one single groat to their fortunes, cannot stir abroad without a chair,[11] and appear at the playhouse and assemblies in foreign fineries, which they never will pay for, the kingdom would not be the worse.

19   Some persons of a desponding spirit are in great concern about that vast number of poor people, who are aged, diseased, or maimed, and I have been desired to employ my thoughts what course may be taken to ease the nation of so grievous an encumbrance. But I am not in the least pain upon that matter, because it is very well known that they are every day dying, and rotting, by cold, and famine, and filth, and vermin, as fast as can be reasonably expected. And as to the younger labourers they are now in almost as hopeful a condition. They cannot get work, and consequently pine away from want of nourishment, to a degree that if at any time they are accidentally hired to common labour, they have not strength to perform it; and thus the country and themselves are in a fair way of being soon delivered from the evils to come.

20   I have too long digressed, and therefore shall return to my subject. I think the advantages by the proposal which I have made are obvious and many, as well as of the highest importance.

21   For first, as I have already observed, it would greatly lessen the number of Papists, with whom we are yearly overrun, being the principal breeders of the nation, as well as our most dangerous enemies, and who stay at home on purpose with a design to deliver the kingdom to the Pretender, hoping to take their advantage by the absence of so many good Protestants, who have chosen rather to leave their country than stay at home and pay tithes against their conscience to an idolatrous Episcopal curate.

22   Secondly, the poorer tenants will have something valuable of their own, which by law may be made liable to distress,[12] and help to pay their

---

[10]An imposter who in 1704 published a fictitious account of Formosa.
[11]A sedan chair.
[12]Subject to seizure because debts were not paid.

landlord's rent, their corn and cattle being already seized, and money a thing unknown.

Thirdly, whereas the maintenance of an hundred thousand children, 23 from two years old, and upwards, cannot be computed at less than ten shillings a piece per annum, the nation's stock will be thereby increased fifty thousand pounds per annum, besides the profit of a new dish, introduced to the tables of all gentlemen of fortune in the kingdom, who have any refinement in taste, and the money will circulate among ourselves, the goods being entirely of our own growth and manufacture.

Fourthly, the constant breeders, besides the gain of eight shillings ster- 24 ling per annum, by the sale of their children, will be rid of the charge of maintaining them after the first year.

Fifthly, this food would likewise bring great custom to taverns, where 25 the vintners will certainly be so prudent as to procure the best receipts for dressing it to perfection, and consequently have their houses frequented by all the fine gentlemen, who justly value themselves upon their knowledge in good eating; and a skilful cook, who understands how to oblige his guests, will contrive to make it as expensive as they please.

Sixthly, this would be a great inducement to marriage, which all wise 26 nations have either encouraged by rewards, or enforced by laws and penalties. It would increase the care and tenderness of mothers towards their children, when they were sure of a settlement for life, to the poor babes, provided in some sort by the public to their annual profit instead of expense. We should soon see an honest emulation among the married women, which of them could bring the fattest child to the market. Men would become as fond of their wives, during the time of their pregnancy, as they are now of their mares in foal, their cows in calf, or sows when they are ready to farrow, nor offer to beat or kick them (as it is too frequent a practice) for fear of a miscarriage.

Many other advantages might be enumerated. For instance, the addition 27 of some thousand carcasses in our exportation of barrelled beef; the propagation of swine's flesh, and improvement in the art of making good bacon, so much wanted among us by the great destruction of pigs, too frequent at our tables, and no way comparable in taste or magnificence to a well-grown, fat yearling child, which roasted whole will make a considerable figure at a Lord Mayor's feast, or any other public entertainment. But this and many others I omit, being studious of brevity.

Supposing that one thousand families in this city would be constant cus- 28 tomers for infants' flesh, besides others who might have it at merry meetings, particularly weddings and christenings; I compute that Dublin would take off annually about twenty thousand carcasses, and the rest of the kingdom (where probably they will be sold somewhat cheaper) the remaining eighty thousand.

I can think of no one objection that will possibly be raised against this 29 proposal, unless it should be urged that the number of people will be thereby much lessened in the kingdom. This I freely own, and it was indeed one principal design in offering it to the world. I desire the reader will observe, that I calculate my remedy for this one individual Kingdom of Ireland, and for no other that ever was, is, or, I think, ever can be upon earth. Therefore let no man talk to me of other expedients: Of taxing our absentees at five shillings a pound: Of using neither clothes, nor household furniture, except what is of our own growth and manufacture: Of utterly rejecting the materials and instruments that promote foreign luxury: Of curing the expensiveness of pride, vanity, idleness, and gaming in our women: Of introducing a vein of parsimony, prudence, and temperance: Of learning to love our country, wherein we differ even from Laplanders, and the inhabitants of Topinamboo: Of quitting our animosities and factions, nor act any longer like the Jews, who were murdering one another at the very moment their city was taken: Of being a little cautious not to sell our country and consciences for nothing: Of teaching landlords to have at least one degree of mercy towards their tenants. Lastly, of putting a spirit of honesty, industry, and skill into our shopkeepers, who, if a resolution could now be taken to buy only our native goods, would immediately unite to cheat and exact upon us in the price, the measure and the goodness, nor could ever yet be brought to make one fair proposal of just dealing, though often and earnestly invited to it.

30   Therefore I repeat, let no man talk to me of these and the like expedients, till he hath at least a glimpse of hope that there will ever be some hearty and sincere attempt to put them in practice.

31   But as to myself, having been wearied out for many years with offering vain, idle, visionary thoughts, and at length utterly despairing of success, I fortunately fell upon this proposal, which as it is wholly new, so it hath something solid and real, of no expense and little trouble, full in our own power, and whereby we can incur no danger in disobliging England. For this kind of commodity will not bear exportation, the flesh being of too tender a consistence to admit a long continuance in salt, although perhaps I could name a country which would be glad to eat up our whole nation without it.[13]

32   After all I am not so violently bent upon my own opinion as to reject any offer, proposed by wise men, which shall be found equally innocent, cheap, easy and effectual. But before some thing of that kind shall be advanced in contradiction to my scheme, and offering a better, I desire the author, or authors, will be pleased maturely to consider two points. First, as things now stand, how they will be able to find food and raiment for a hundred thousand useless mouths and backs? And secondly, there being a round million of creatures in human figure, throughout this kingdom, whose whole subsistence put into a common stock would leave them in debt two millions of pounds sterling; adding those who are beggars by profession, to the bulk of farmers, cottagers, and labourers with their wives and children, who are beggars in effect; I desire those politicians who dislike my overture, and may perhaps be so bold to attempt an answer, that they will first ask the parents of these mortals whether they would not at this day think it a great happiness to have been

---

[13]England.

sold for food at a year old, in the manner I prescribe, and thereby have avoided such a perpetual scene of misfortunes as they have since gone through, by the oppression of landlords, the impossibility of paying rent without money or trade, the want of common sustenance, with neither house nor clothes to cover them from the inclemencies of weather, and the most inevitable prospect of entailing the like, or greater miseries upon their breed for ever.

I profess in the sincerity of my heart that I have not the least personal interest in endeavouring to promote this necessary work, having no other motive than the public good of my country, by advancing our trade, providing for infants, relieving the poor, and giving some pleasure to the rich. I have no children by which I can propose to get a single penny; the youngest being nine years old, and my wife past child-bearing. 33

QUESTIONS ON SUBJECT AND PURPOSE

1. What is Swift's thesis? Summarize it in a sentence or two.
2. Swift explains his motive for writing in the final paragraph. Is he being serious? How much of what he says can be taken seriously?
3. What could Swift hope to accomplish by offering such an outrageous proposal?

QUESTIONS ON STRATEGY AND AUDIENCE

1. Is Swift's essay persuasive? Be prepared to explain why you think that Swift's proposal either succeeds or fails.
2. Does Swift direct his criticism toward any specific group or groups?
3. What is the digression that Swift mentions in paragraph 20? What purpose does it serve?

QUESTIONS ON VOCABULARY AND STYLE

1. Characterize the tone of the essay. How is that tone achieved? How does it contribute to the effect of the essay?
2. Trace the following throughout the essay and be prepared to explain the function of each:
   a. animal imagery
   b. monetary, statistical terminology
   c. food imagery
   d. death imagery
3. Be able to define the following words: *importuning* (paragraph 1), *alms* (1), *sustenance* (1), *dam* (4), *raiment* (4), *rudiments* (6), *nutriment* (7), *fricassee* (9), *ragout* (9), *repine* (14), *flay* (15), *maimed* (19), *encumbrance* (19), *vintners* (25), *emulation* (26), *farrow* (26), *yearling* (27), *expedients* (29), *parsimony* (29).

WRITING SUGGESTIONS

1. **For Your Journal.** In your journal, make a list of social problems in the United States that might be the subject of a "modest proposal." They might grow out of economic issues (lack of jobs in certain parts of the country, low-paying jobs, inadequate or unaffordable daycare), medical issues (no health coverage, catastrophic medical costs), or any similar topic. Brainstorm a list of possibilities.

2. **For a Paragraph.** In a paragraph, draw up a modest (and outrageous) proposal for dealing with one of the problems. Swift has already suggested selling children as food, so you cannot use that again. Be imaginative and try to develop your proposal in sufficient detail to make a substantial paragraph.

3. **For an Essay.** Expand your paragraph into an essay. Remember that in addition to your outrageous solution, you must provide a number of more realistic and workable possibilities. It is not enough to be critical; you need to make some solid, reasonable suggestions as well. Although Swift's strategy is to shock, he also offers some sound possible solutions as well. That is an essential part of the assignment.

4. **For Research.** The problems about which Swift writes have not disappeared from the world. Every year, thousands of children starve to death, particularly in Africa. Peter Singer's essay, "The Singer Solution to World Poverty" (this chapter), in addition to many of the world social services organizations, such as Save the Children and CARE, can provide detailed documentation of the problem. The problem is of such magnitude that many people, although they might be sympathetic and wish to help, feel it is simply too large for them to make any difference. In a serious research essay, suggest possible ways in which we as a nation might help combat this problem. First, document the magnitude of the problem, then suggest some possible serious solutions.

FOR FURTHER STUDY

Focusing on Grammar and Writing. Swift uses parallelism extensively in his essay, especially in paragraphs and in sentence structures. How many instances of parallelism can you locate in the essay. How does parallelism work to make the essay clearer and more readable?

Working Together. Swift creates a persona in the essay—a narrator who is not Swift but a fictional creation. Divide into groups and assign each group an equal number of paragraphs from the essay. Each group should study the assigned block of paragraphs and analyze the values, character, and voice of the persona. What does he sound like? What are his distinctive characteristics? How do you know that he is a persona and not Swift himself?

Seeing Other Modes at Work. In addition to persuasion, the essay makes use of classification and cause and effect.

Finding Connections. An interesting pairing is with Peter Singer's "The Singer Solution to World Poverty" (this chapter).

Exploring the Web. The Web has many sites devoted to Swift's writing and "A Modest Proposal," as well as Websites that document the problem of poverty both in the United States and the world. Some places to begin can be found at **www.prenhall.com/miller**.

THE DEATH OF THE MOTH
Virginia Woolf

*Born in London and educated at home, Virginia Woolf (1882–1941) is generally re-
garded as one of the finest writers of the twentieth century. A novelist, essayist, and
critic, she was a member of the Bloomsbury group—a circle of artists and writers, including John Maynard Keynes, Lytton Strachey, Vanessa and Clive Bell, and E. M.
Forster, active in London from about 1906 to the early 1930s. She and her husband
Leonard Woolf founded the Hogarth Press, which published books by her and other
members of the Bloomsbury group. Her novels include* The Voyage Out *(1915),* Ja-
cob's Room *(1922),* Mrs. Dalloway *(1925),* To the Lighthouse *(1927),* Or-
lando *(1928), and* The Waves *(1931). Woolf's essays and reviews have been collected
in works such as* The Common Reader *(1925, 1932) and a four-volume* Collected
Essays *(1967). In "The Death of the Moth," was originally collected posthumously in*
The Death of the Moth and Other Essays *(1942).*

On Writing: *In her novel,* A Room of One's Own, *Woolf commented on the
links between a writer's work and her life: "Imaginative work . . . is like a spider's
web, attached ever so lightly perhaps, but still attached to life at all four corners. . . .
But when the web is pulled askew, hooked up at the edge, torn in the middle, one remembers that these webs are not spun in midair by incorporeal creatures, but are the
work of suffering, human beings, and are attached to the grossly material things, like
health and money and the houses we live in."*

BEFORE READING

Connecting: Everyone has killed an insect or watched one die. Can you recall a time when you thought about that death and what it symbolized?

Anticipating: The moth is at a window, and Woolf links the moth's struggles
inside the window with the activity that is going on outside the window. Why?

LOOKING FOR COMBINATIONS

Woolf's essay is primarily narration—she tells us about the death of the moth
at her window. However, she uses other modes as well. For example, the essay
uses description extensively, comparison and contrast, and cause and effect.
Can you locate those patterns in the essay? Can you find any others at work?
What roles do these strategies or modes play in the essay as a whole?

1   MOTHS THAT FLY BY DAY are not properly to be called moths; they do not
excite that pleasant sense of dark autumn nights and ivy-blossom which the
commonest yellow underwing asleep in the shadow of the curtain never fails
to rouse in us. They are hybrid creatures, neither gay like butterflies nor sombre

like their own species. Nevertheless the present specimen, with his narrow hay-coloured wings, fringed with a tassel of the same colour, seemed to be content with life. It was a pleasant morning, mid-September, mild, benignant, yet with a keener breath than that of the summer months. The plough was already scoring the field opposite the window, and where the share had been, the earth was pressed flat and gleamed with moisture. Such vigour came rolling in from the fields and the down beyond that it was difficult to keep the eyes strictly turned upon the book. The rooks too were keeping one of their annual festivities; soaring round the tree-tops until it looked as if a vast net with thousands of black knots in it has been cast up into the air; which, after a few moments sank slowly down upon the trees until every twig seemed to have a knot at the end of it. Then, suddenly, the net would be thrown into the air again in a wider circle this time, with the utmost clamour and vociferation, as though to be thrown into the air and settle slowly down upon the tree-tops were a tremendously exciting experience.

2   The same energy which inspired the rooks, the ploughmen, the horses, and even, it seemed, the lean bare-backed downs, sent the moth fluttering from side to side of his square of the window-pane. One could not help watching him. One was, indeed, conscious of a queer feeling of pity for him. The possibilities of pleasure seemed that morning so enormous and so various that to have only a moth's part in life, and a day moth's at that, appeared a hard fate, and his zest in enjoying his meagre opportunities to the full, pathetic. He flew vigorously to one corner of his compartment, and, after waiting there a second, flew across to the other. What remained for him but to fly to a third corner and then to a fourth? That was all he could do, in spite of the size of the downs, the width of the sky, the far-off smoke of houses, and the romantic voice, now and then, of a steamer out at sea. What he could do he did. Watching him, it seemed as if a fibre, very thin but pure, of the enormous energy of the world had been thrust into his frail and diminutive body. As often as he crossed the pane, I could fancy that a thread of vital light became visible. He was little or nothing but life.

3   Yet, because he was so small, and so simple a form of the energy that was rolling in at the open window and driving its way through so many narrow and intricate corridors in my own brain and in those of other human beings, there was something marvelous as well as pathetic about him. It was as if someone had taken a tiny bead of pure life and decking it as lightly as possible with down and feathers, had set it dancing and zig-zagging to show us the true nature of life. Thus displayed one could not get over the strangeness of it. One is apt to forget all about life, seeing it humped and bossed and garnished and cumbered so that it has to move with the greatest circumspection and dignity. Again, the thought of all that life might have been had he been born in any other shape caused one to view his simple activities with a kind of pity.

4   After a time, tired by his dancing apparently, he settled on the window ledge in the sun, and the queer spectacle being at an end, I forgot about him. Then, looking up, my eye was caught by him. He was trying to resume his dancing, but seemed either so stiff or so awkward that he could only flutter to

the bottom of the window-pane; and when he tried to fly across it he failed. Being intent on other matters I watched these futile attempts for a time without thinking, unconsciously waiting for him to resume his flight, as one waits for a machine, that has stopped momentarily, to start again without considering the reason for its failure. After perhaps a seventh attempt he slipped from the wooden ledge and fell, fluttering his wings, on to his back on the window-sill. The helplessness of his attitude roused me. It flashed upon me that he was in difficulties; he could no longer raise himself; his legs struggled vainly. But, as I stretched out a pencil, meaning to help him to right himself, it came over me that the failure and awkwardness were the approach of death. I laid the pencil down again.

5   The legs agitated themselves once more. I looked as if for the enemy against which he struggled. I looked out of doors. What had happened there? Presumably it was midday, and work in the fields had stopped. Stillness and quiet had replaced the previous animation. The birds had taken themselves off to feed in the brooks. The horses stood still. Yet the power was there all the same, massed outside indifferent, impersonal, not attending to anything in particular. Somehow it was opposed to the little hay-coloured moth. It was useless to try to do anything. One could only watch the extraordinary efforts made by those tiny legs against an oncoming doom which could, had it chosen, have submerged an entire city, not merely a city, but masses of human beings; nothing, I knew, had any chance against death. Nevertheless after a pause of exhaustion the legs fluttered again. It was superb this last protest, and so frantic that he succeeded at last in righting himself. One's sympathies, of course, were all on the side of life. Also, when there was nobody to care or to know, this gigantic effort on the part of an insignificant little moth, against a power of such magnitude, to retain what no one else valued or desired to keep, moved one strangely. Again, somehow, one saw life, a pure bead. I lifted the pencil again, useless though I knew it to be. But even as I did so, the unmistakable tokens of death showed themselves. The body relaxed, and instantly grew stiff. The struggle was over. The insignificant little creature now knew death. As I looked at the dead moth, this minute wayside triumph of so great a force over so mean an antagonist filled me with wonder. Just as life had been strange a few minutes before, so death was now as strange. The moth having righted himself now lay most decently and uncomplainingly composed. O yes, he seemed to say, death is stronger than I am.

QUESTIONS ON SUBJECT AND PURPOSE

1. What does Woolf see in the moth fluttering at the window?
2. How much time elapses in the narrative? Why is time important?
3. Why should the death of the moth be interesting to a reader?

QUESTIONS ON STRATEGY AND AUDIENCE

1. What does Woolf see outside of the window? How is that scene connected with the moth?

2. What is "superb" about the moth's final struggle to right itself before dying?

3. How, as a reader, do you react to the title "The Death of the Moth"? Does the title seem effective?

QUESTIONS ON VOCABULARY AND STYLE

1. In what sense does the plow "score" the field?

2. Woolf switches pronouns (from "I" to "one") at several points in the essay. Why?

3. Be prepared to define the following words: *benignant* (paragraph 1), *down* (1), *clamour* (1), *vociferation* (1), *cumbered* (2), *antagonist* (5).

WRITING SUGGESTIONS

1. **For Your Journal.** Woolf's essay grows out of an observation of a moth that dies at her window. Set aside an hour or two to pay attention to your environment and its connection with the natural world and living things. Sit on a bench on campus; take a walk in a field or woods; watch an insect. In your journal, record what you see.

2. **For a Paragraph.** Using the journal material, write a paragraph in which you use your observation of the natural world to draw a link between it and your life or to speculate on life and its processes.

3. **For an Essay.** The seemingly insignificant can always contain or reflect a universal truth or principle—about life, about experience, about human motivation and behavior. Make a list of possible subjects, including events in nature and predictable, common events in human life. Use the event in nature to connect with and illuminate the life lesson.

4. **For Research.** Woolf committed suicide in 1941; the essay was published after her death. What links do literary biographers and scholars see between the essay and Woolf's own depression and suicide. Using online and print sources, research the connection (or lack of a connection) and present your findings in a research paper.

FOR FURTHER STUDY

Focusing on Grammar and Writing. How would you define the word *thesis*? Can you find a thesis in Woolf's essay? Is it where you initially thought you might find it?

Working Together. Divide into small groups. Each group should select one of the following passages or events to examine:
1. the rooks
2. the ploughmen (notice that the word is plural)
3. the window
4. the moth
5. the writer's position within the room

What does Woolf tell us about each of these things? What does she omit? Why?

Seeing Other Modes at Work. The essay uses description extensively.

Finding Connections. An interesting pairing is with M. Scott Momaday's "The Way to Rainy Mountain" (Chapter 3).

Exploring the Web. Information about Virginia Woolf's life and writings can be found on many Websites. Some places to start can be found at **www.prenhall.com/miller.**

ONCE MORE TO THE LAKE

E. B. White

Elwyn Brooks White (1899–1985) was born in Mount Vernon, New York, and re-ceived a B.A. from Cornell in 1921. His freshman English teacher was William Strunk, whose Elements of Style *White revised in 1959 and made into a textbook classic. In 1925 White began writing for* The New Yorker *and was one of the main-stays of that magazine, his precise, ironic, nostalgic prose style closely associated with its own. From 1937 to 1943, he also wrote the column "One Man's Meat" for* Harper's. *His books include the children's classic* Charlotte's Web *(1952),* The Second Tree From the Corner *(1954),* The Essays of E. B. White *(1977), and* The Poems and Sketches of E. B. White *(1981).*

White revisited the Belgrade Lakes in Maine in the summer of 1936. The es-say was not written until 1941 and was published in his collection Essays of E. B. White *that same year.*

On Writing: *Commenting on his writing, White observed: "Sometimes I'm asked how old I was when I started to write, and what made me want to write. I started early–as soon as I could spell. In fact, I can't remember any time in my life when I was-n't busy writing. I don't know what caused me to do it, or why I enjoyed it, but I think children often find pleasure and satisfaction in trying to set their thoughts down on pa-per, either in words or in pictures. I was no good at drawing, so I used words instead. As I grew older, I found that writing can be a way of earning a living."*

BEFORE READING

Connecting: Have you ever revisited a place where you and your family va-cationed some years before? Or a neighborhood or town in which you once lived? Was the experience the same as you remembered?

Anticipating: Why does White get so confused about who is the father and who is the son in the essay? What is he suggesting?

LOOKING FOR COMBINATIONS

White's primary structural mode in the essay is narration—he tells us a story. However, he uses other modes as well. For example, the essay uses description extensively and comparison and contrast. Can you locate those patterns in the essay? Can you find any others at work? What roles do these strategies or modes play in the essay as a whole?

ONE SUMMER along about 1904, my father rented a camp on a lake in Maine   1
and took us all there for the month of August. We all got ringworm from some

kittens and had to rub Pond's Extract on our arms and legs night and morning, and my father rolled over in a canoe with all his clothes on; but outside of that the vacation was a success and from then on none of us ever thought there was any place in the world like that lake in Maine. We returned summer after summer—always on August 1st for one month. I have since become a salt-water man, but sometimes in summer there are days when the restlessness of the tides and the fearful cold of the sea water and the incessant wind that blows across the afternoon and into the evening make me wish for the placidity of a lake in the woods. A few weeks ago this feeling got so strong I bought myself a couple of bass hooks and a spinner and returned to the lake where we used to go, for a week's fishing and to revisit old haunts.

2   I took along my son, who had never had any fresh water up his nose and who had seen lily pads only from train windows. On the journey over to the lake I began to wonder what it would be like. I wondered how time would have marred this unique, this holy spot—the coves and streams, the hills that the sun set behind, the camps and the paths behind the camps. I was sure that the tarred road would have found it out and I wondered in what other ways it would be desolated. It is strange how much you can remember about places like that once you allow your mind to return into the grooves that lead back. You remember one thing, and that suddenly reminds you of another thing. I guess I remembered clearest of all the early mornings, when the lake was cool and motionless, remembered how the bedroom smelled of the lumber it was made of and of the wet woods whose scent entered through the screen. The partitions in the camp were thin and did not extend clear to the top of the rooms, and as I was always the first up I would dress softly so as not to wake the others, and sneak out into the sweet outdoors and start out in the canoe, keeping close along the shore in the long shadows of the pines. I remembered being very careful never to rub my paddle against the gunwale for fear of disturbing the stillness of the cathedral.

3   The lake had never been what you would call a wild lake. There were cottages sprinkled around the shores, and it was in farming country although the shores of the lake were quite heavily wooded. Some of the cottages were owned by nearby farmers, and you would live at the shore and eat your meals at the farmhouse. That's what our family did. But although it wasn't wild, it was a fairly large and undisturbed lake and there were places in it which, to a child at least, seemed infinitely remote and primeval.

4   I was right about the tar: it led to within half a mile of the shore. But when I got back there, with my boy, and we settled into a camp near a farmhouse and into the kind of summertime I had known, I could tell that it was going to be pretty much the same as it had been before—I knew it, lying in bed the first morning, smelling the bedroom, and hearing the boy sneak quietly out and go off along the shore in a boat. I began to sustain the illusion that he was I, and therefore, by simple transposition, that I was my father. This sensation persisted, kept cropping up all the time we were there. It was not an entirely new feeling, but in this setting it grew much stronger. I seemed to be living a dual existence. I would be in the middle of some simple act, I would

be picking up a bait box or laying down a table fork, or I would be saying something, and suddenly it would be not I but my father who was saying the words or making the gesture. It gave me a creepy sensation.

We went fishing the first morning. I felt the same damp moss covering   5
the worms in the bait can, and saw the dragonfly alight on the tip of my rod as it hovered a few inches from the surface of the water. It was the arrival of this fly that convinced me beyond any doubt that everything was as it always had been, that the years were a mirage and there had been no years. The small waves were the same, chucking the rowboat under the chin as we fished at anchor, and the boat was the same boat, the same color green and the ribs broken in the same places, and under the floor-boards the same fresh-water leavings and debris—the dead helgramite, the wisps of moss, the rusty discarded fishhook, the dried blood from yesterday's catch. We stared silently at the tips of our rods, at the dragonflies that came and went. I lowered the tip of mine into the water, tentatively, pensively dislodging the fly, which darted two feet away, poised, darted two feet back, and came to rest again a little farther up the rod. There had been no years between the ducking of this dragonfly and the other one—the one that was part of memory. I looked at the boy, who was silently watching his fly, and it was my hands that held his rod, my eyes watching. I felt dizzy and didn't know which rod I was at the end of.

We caught two bass, hauling them in briskly as though they were mack-   6
erel, pulling them over the side of the boat in a businesslike manner without any landing net, and stunning them with a blow on the back of the head. When we got back for a swim before lunch, the lake was exactly where we had left it, the same number of inches from the dock, and there was only the merest suggestion of a breeze. This seemed an utterly enchanted sea, this lake you could leave to its own devices for a few hours and come back to, and find that it had not stirred, this constant and trustworthy body of water. In the shallows, the dark, water-soaked sticks and twigs, smooth and old, were undulating in clusters on the bottom against the clean ribbed sand, and the track of the mussel was plain. A school of minnows swam by, each minnow with its small individual shadow, doubling the attendance, so clear and sharp in the sunlight. Some of the other campers were in swimming, along the shore, one of them with a cake of soap, and the water felt thin and clear and unsubstantial. Over the years there had been this person with the cake of soap, this cultist, and here he was. There had been no years.

Up to the farmhouse to dinner through the teeming, dusty field, the   7
road under our sneakers was only a two-track road. The middle track was missing, the one with the marks of the hooves and splotches of dried, flaky manure. There had always been three tracks to choose from in choosing which track to walk in; now the choice was narrowed down to two. For a moment I missed terribly the middle alternative. But the way led past the tennis court, and something about the way it lay there in the sun reassured me; the tape had loosened along the backline, the alleys were green with plantains and other weeds, and the net (installed in June and removed in September) sagged in the dry noon, and the whole place steamed with midday heat and hunger and

emptiness. There was a choice of pie for dessert, and one was blueberry and one was apple, and the waitresses were the same country girls, there having been no passage of time, only the illusion of it as in a dropped curtain—the waitresses were still fifteen; their hair had been washed, that was the only difference—they had been to the movies and seen the pretty girls with the clean hair.

8   Summertime, oh summertime, pattern of life indelible, the fadeproof lake, the woods unshatterable, the pasture with the sweetfern and the juniper forever and ever, summer without end; this was the background, and the life along the shore was the design, the cottages with their innocent and tranquil design, their tiny docks with the flagpole and the American flag floating against the white clouds in the blue sky, the little paths over the roots of the trees leading from camp to camp and the paths leading back to the outhouses and the can of lime for sprinkling, and at the souvenir counters at the store the miniature birch-bark canoes and the post cards that showed things looking a little better than they looked. This was the American family at play, escaping the city heat, wondering whether the newcomers in the camp at the head of the cove were "common" or "nice," wondering whether it was true that the people who drove up for Sunday dinner at the farmhouse were turned away because there wasn't enough chicken.

9   It seemed to me, as I kept remembering all this, that those times and those summers had been infinitely precious and worth saving. There had been jollity and peace and goodness. The arriving (at the beginning of August) had been so big a business in itself, at the railway station the farm wagon drawn up, the first smell of the pine-laden air, the first glimpse of the smiling farmer, and the great importance of the trunks and your father's enormous authority in such matters, and the feel of the wagon under you for the long ten-mile haul, and at the top of the last long hill catching the first view of the lake after eleven months of not seeing this cherished body of water. The shouts and cries of the other campers when they saw you, and the trunks to be unpacked, to give up their rich burden. (Arriving was less exciting nowadays, when you sneaked up in your car and parked it under a tree near the camp and took out the bags and in five minutes it was all over, no fuss, no loud wonderful fuss about trunks.)

10   Peace and goodness and jollity. The only thing that was wrong now, really, was the sound of the place, an unfamiliar nervous sound of the outboard motors. This was the note that jarred, the one thing that would sometimes break the illusion and set the years moving. In those other summertimes all motors were inboard; and when they were at a little distance, the noise they made was a sedative, an ingredient of summer sleep. They were one-cylinder and two-cylinder engines, and some were make-and-break and some were jump-spark, but they all made a sleepy sound across the lake. The one-lungers throbbed and fluttered, and the twin-cylinder ones purred and purred, and that was a quiet sound too. But now the campers all had outboards. In the daytime, in the hot mornings, these motors made a petulant, irritable sound; at night, in the still evening when the afterglow lit the water, they whined about

one's ears like mosquitoes. My boy loved our rented outboard, and his great desire was to achieve singlehanded mastery over it, and authority, and he soon learned the trick of choking it a little (but not too much), and the adjustment of the needle valve. Watching him I would remember the things you could do with the old one-cylinder engine with the heavy flywheel, how you could have it eating out of your hand if you got really close to it spiritually. Motor boats in those days didn't have clutches, and you would make a landing by shutting off the motor at the proper time and coasting in with a dead rudder. But there was a way of reversing them, if you learned the trick, by cutting the switch and putting it on again exactly on the final dying revolution of the flywheel, so that it would kick back against compression and begin reversing. Approaching a dock in a strong following breeze, it was difficult to slow up sufficiently by the ordinary coasting method, and if a boy felt he had complete mastery over his motor, he was tempted to keep it running beyond its time and then reverse it a few feet from the dock. It took a cool nerve, because if you threw the switch a twentieth of a second too soon you would catch the flywheel when it still has speed enough to go up past center, and the boat would leap ahead, charging bull-fashion at the dock.

We had a good week at the camp. The bass were biting well and the sun shone endlessly, day after day. We would be tired at night and lie down in the accumulated heat of the little bedrooms after the long hot day and the breeze would stir almost imperceptibly outside and the smell of the swamp drift in through the rusty screens. Sleep would come easily and in the morning the red squirrel would be on the roof, tapping out his gay routine. I kept remembering everything, lying in bed in the mornings—the small steamboat that had a long rounded stern like the lip of a Ubangi, and how quietly she ran on the moonlight sails, when the older boys played their mandolins and the girls sang and we ate doughnuts dipped in sugar, and how sweet the music was on the water in the shining night, and what it had felt like to think about girls then. After breakfast we would go up to the store and the things were in the same place—the minnows in a bottle, the plugs and spinners disarranged and pawed over by the youngsters from the boys' camp, the fig newtons and the Beeman's gum. Outside, the road was tarred and cars stood in front of the store. Inside, all was just as it had always been, except that there was more Coca Cola and not so much Moxie and root beer and birch beer and sarsaparilla. We would walk out with a bottle of pop apiece and sometimes the pop would backfire up our noses and hurt. We explored the streams, quietly, where the turtles slid off the sunny logs and dug their way into the soft bottom; and we lay on the town wharf and fed worms to the tame bass. Everywhere we went I had trouble making out which was I, the one walking at my side, the one walking in my pants. 11

One afternoon while we were there at that lake a thunderstorm came up. 12
It was like the revival of an old melodrama that I had seen long ago with childish awe. The second-act climax of the drama of the electrical disturbance over a lake in America had not changed in any important respect. This was the big scene, still the big scene. The whole thing was so familiar, the first feeling of

oppression and heat and a general air around camp of not wanting to go very far away. In midafternoon (it was all the same) a curious darkening of the sky, and a lull in everything that had made life tick; and then the way the boats suddenly swung the other way at their moorings with the coming of a breeze out of the new quarter, and the premonitory rumble. Then the kettle drum, then the snare, then the bass drum and cymbals, then crackling light against the dark, and the gods grinning and licking their chops in the hills. Afterward the calm, the rain steadily rustling in the calm lake, the return of light and hope and spirits, and the campers running out in joy and relief to go swimming in the rain, their bright cries perpetuating the deathless joke about how they were getting simply drenched, and the children screaming with delight at the new sensation of bathing in the rain, and the joke about getting drenched linking the generations in a strong indestructible chain. And the comedian who waded in carrying an umbrella.

13   When the others went swimming my son said he was going in too. He pulled his dripping trunks from the line where they had hung all through the shower, and wrung them out. Languidly, and with no thought of going in, I watched him, his hard little body, skinny and bare, saw him wince slightly as he pulled up around his vitals the small, soggy, icy garment. As he buckled the swollen belt suddenly my groin felt the chill of death.

QUESTIONS ON SUBJECT AND PURPOSE

1. Why does White go "once more" to the lake?
2. In what ways does White's son remind him of himself as a child? Make a list of the similarities he notices.
3. What is the meaning of the final sentence? Why does he feel "the chill of death"?

QUESTIONS ON STRATEGY AND AUDIENCE

1. How does White structure his narrative? What events does he choose to highlight?
2. No narrative can record everything, and this is certainly not an hour-by-hour account of what happened. What does White ignore? Why, for example, does he end his narrative before the end of the actual experience (that is, leaving the lake)?
3. Why is his son never described?

QUESTIONS ON VOCABULARY AND STYLE

1. At several points White has trouble distinguishing between who is the son and who is the father. Select one of those scenes and examine how White describes the moment. How does the prose capture that confusion?
2. Can you find examples of figurative language—similes and metaphors, for example—in White's essay? Make a list.

3. Be able to define the following words: *placidity* (paragraph 1), *gunwale* (2), *primeval* (3), *teeming* (7), *premonitory* (12), *languidly* (13).

WRITING SUGGESTIONS

1. **For Your Journal.** Choose a particular year from your elementary school experience. It would probably be easiest to choose a year like third or fourth grade. In your journal, make a list of what you remember from that year. What was the school's name? Your teacher's name? What did the classroom look like? Where did you sit? What happened that year? Who were your friends? Allow a day or two at least to pass while you try to remember, and you will discover that more and more details will surface. Record as many details as you can in your journal.

2. **For a Paragraph.** In a paragraph, re-create for the reader a moment out of that year in school. Narrate the experience and describe the setting. Do not try to make the moment significant or earthshaking. Remember that you can fill in or add details that are true to the time or that could have happened (see in this chapter Joan Didion's "On Keeping a Notebook" for more explanation).

3. **For an Essay.** You do not have to be middle-aged to have the experience of returning somewhere that you have been some years before and sensing either changelessness or change. More often, things change rather than stay the same. Think about your experiences. Have you ever re-experienced something some years later—a summer vacation to the same place, an encounter with someone who was a good friend some years before, a visit to a house, apartment, or neighborhood in which your family once lived? Find an experience that you have had twice, separated by at least several years. Re-create those experiences for your reader and, like White, speculate on what you have learned or sensed from the two.

4. **For Research.** What is your earliest memory? What factors control memories? Is it possible to remember events that took place before you could talk? To what extent do memories grow out of photographs? Are memories actually stored and retrieved, or are they re-created by the mind? What kinds of memories are most easily recalled? In a research paper, using both online and print sources, try to answer some of these questions.

FOR FURTHER STUDY

Focusing on Grammar and Writing. The essay averages 24 words per sentence. How does White manage to structure his sentences so that they can contain so much information yet remain clear? You might want to focus on a single paragraph, looking carefully at the sentences it contains, or a single sentence, de-combining that sentence into a series of shorter, simpler sentences.

Working Together. Divide into small groups. Each group should choose one descriptive passage in the essay. What does White focus on? How does this description contribute to the essay? Possible passages to analyze include

1. the bedroom in the morning (paragraph 2)
2. the fishing scene (5)
3. the bottom of the lake (6)
4. the road to the farmhouse (7)
5. the tennis court at "dry noon" (7)
6. the arrival (9)
7. the motorboats (10)

Seeing Other Modes at Work. Although the basic pattern in the essay comes from narration, White uses description extensively to create the vivid scenes he experiences.

Finding Connections. Another essay about the identification between a father and a child is Scott Sanders's "The Inheritance of Tools" (Chapter 8). One dealing with a daughter and her mother is Amy Tan's "Mother Tongue" (Chapter 8).

Exploring the Web. Ever wonder what the lake might have looked like? Visit Belgrade Lakes in central Maine on the Web. Check out the many Websites devoted to the life and work of E. B. White, starting from **www.prenhall.com/miller.**

ON KEEPING A NOTEBOOK

Joan Didion

Joan Didion was born in Sacramento in 1934 and received a B.A. from the University of California at Berkeley in 1956. Also a novelist and screen-writer, Didion is probably best-known for her nonfiction reporting and her personal essays. Her most recent book is The Year of Magical Thinking *(2005). In much of her writing she vividly portrays the personal chaos of modern American life through gripping examples and pointed direct quotations. One critic recently observed: "Didion . . . [is] practical, existential, and thoroughly informed about the facts of whatever event or subject she chooses to write about. She is voracious for facts. Her workspace must be crammed with notebooks."*

"On Keeping a Notebook" appeared in her famous collection of personal essays, Slouching towards Bethlehem *(1968).*

On Writing: *Didion is a keeper of notebooks that serve as "seedbeds" for her essays. She explains, "The point of my keeping a notebook has never been, nor is it now, to have an accurate factual record of what I have been doing or thinking. . . .* "How it felt to me: *that is closer to the truth about a notebook."*

LOOKING FOR COMBINATIONS

Didion's essay intricately interweaves a number of strategies or modes. In one sense, the primary pattern is process—how she uses her notebooks in her writing. Along the way, however, she uses others, modes, including, for example, narration and description to re-create the little scenes that her notebook entries record and cause and effect to explain what the scenes mean to her. Can you locate those patterns in the essay? Can you find any others at work? What roles do these strategies or modes play in the essay as a whole?

BEFORE READING

Connecting: What would you expect that a writer would record in her notebook? Would it be the same as what she might record in a diary? To you, do the two words—notebook and diary—imply different types of records?

Anticipating: According to the essay, why does Didion keep notebooks?

" 'That woman Estelle,' " the note reads, " 'is partly the reason why George   1
Sharp and I are separated today.' *Dirty crepe-de-Chine wrapper, hotel bar, Wilmington RR, 9:45* A.M. August Monday morning."

Since the note is in my notebook, it presumably has some meaning to   2
me. I study it for a long while. At first I have only the most general notion of

what I was doing on an August Monday morning in the bar of the hotel across from the Pennsylvania Railroad station in Wilmington, Delaware (waiting for a train? missing one? 1960? 1961? why Wilmington?), but I do remember being there. The woman in the dirty crepe-de-Chine wrapper had come down from her room for a beer, and the bartender had heard before the reason why George Sharp and she were separated today. "Sure," he said, and went on mopping the floor. "You told me." At the other end of the bar is a girl. She is talking, pointedly, not to the man beside her but to a cat lying in the triangle of sunlight cast through the open door. She is wearing a plaid silk dress from Peck & Peck, and the hem is coming down.

3   Here is what it is: the girl has been on the Eastern Shore, and now she is going back to the city, leaving the man beside her, and all she can see ahead are the viscous summer sidewalks and the 3 A.M. long-distance calls that will make her lie awake and then sleep drugged through all the steaming mornings left in August (1960? 1961?). Because she must go directly from the train to lunch in New York, she wishes that she had a safety pin for the hem of the plaid silk dress, and she also wishes that she could forget about the hem and the lunch and stay in the cool bar that smells of disinfectant and malt and make friends with the woman in the crepe-de-Chine wrapper. She is afflicted by a little self-pity, and she wants to compare Estelles. That is what that was all about.

4   Why did I write it down? In order to remember, of course, but exactly what was it I wanted to remember? How much of it actually happened? Did any of it? Why do I keep a notebook at all? It is easy to deceive oneself on all those scores. The impulse to write things down is a peculiarly compulsive one, inexplicable to those who do not share it, useful only accidentally, only secondarily, in the way that any compulsion tries to justify itself. I suppose that it begins or does not begin in the cradle. Although I have felt compelled to write things down since I was five years old, I doubt that my daughter ever will, for she is a singularly blessed and accepting child, delighted with life exactly as life presents itself to her, unafraid to go to sleep and unafraid to wake up. Keepers of private notebooks are a different breed altogether, lonely and resistant rearrangers of things, anxious malcontents, children afflicted apparently at birth with some presentiment of loss.

5   My first notebook was a Big Five tablet, given to me by my mother with the sensible suggestion that I stop whining and learn to amuse myself by writing down my thoughts. She returned the tablet to me a few years ago; the first entry is an account of a woman who believed herself to be freezing to death in the Arctic night, only to find, when day broke, that she had stumbled onto the Sahara Desert, where she would die of the heat before lunch. I have no idea what turn of a five-year-old's mind could have prompted so insistently "ironic" and exotic a story, but it does reveal a certain predilection for the extreme which has dogged me into adult life; perhaps if I were analytically inclined I would find it a truer story than any I might have told about Donald Johnson's birthday party or the day my cousin Brenda put Kitty Litter in the aquarium.

***

So the point of my keeping a notebook has never been, nor is it now, to 6
have an accurate factual record of what I have been doing or thinking. That
would be a different impulse entirely, an instinct for reality which I sometimes
envy but do not possess. At no point have I ever been able successfully to keep
a diary; my approach to daily life ranges from the grossly negligent to the
merely absent, and on those few occasions when I have tried dutifully to
record a day's events, boredom has so overcome me that the results are mysterious at best. What is this business about "shopping, typing piece, dinner
with E, depressed"? Shopping for what? Typing what piece? Who is E? Was
this "E" depressed, or was I depressed? Who cares?

In fact I have abandoned altogether that kind of pointless entry; instead 7
I tell what some would call lies. "That's simply not true," the members of my
family frequently tell me when they come up against my memory of a shared
event. "The party was not for you, the spider was *not* a black widow, *it wasn't
that way at all.*" Very likely they are right, for not only have I always had trouble distinguishing between what happened and what merely might have happened, but I remain unconvinced that the distinction, for my purposes,
matters. The cracked crab that I recall having for lunch the day my father
came home from Detroit in 1945 must certainly be embroidery, worked into
the day's pattern to lend verisimilitude; I was ten years old and would not now
remember the cracked crab. The day's events did not turn on cracked crab.
And yet it is precisely that fictitious crab that makes me see the afternoon all
over again, a home movie run all too often, the father bearing gifts, the child
weeping, an exercise in family love and guilt. Or that is what it was to me. Similarly, perhaps it never did snow that August in Vermont; perhaps there never
were flurries in the night wind, and maybe no one else felt the ground hard-
ening and summer already dead even as we pretended to bask in it, but that
was how it felt to me, and it might as well have snowed, could have snowed,
did snow.

How it felt to me: that is getting closer to the truth about a notebook. I 8
sometimes delude myself about why I keep a notebook, imagine that some
thrifty virtue derives from preserving everything observed. See enough and
write it down, I tell myself and then some morning when the world seems
drained of wonder, some day when I am only going through the motions of
doing what I am supposed to do, which is write—on that bankrupt morning I
will simply open my notebook and there it will be, a forgotten account with
accumulated interest, paid passage back to the world out there: dialogue over-
heard in hotels and elevators and at the hatcheck counter in Pavillon (one
middle-aged man shows his hat check to another and says, "That's my old
football number"); impressions of Bettina Aptheker and Benjamin Sonnen-
berg and Teddy ("Mr. Acapulco") Stauffer; careful *aperçus* about tennis bums
and failed fashion models and Greek shipping heiresses, one of whom taught
me a significant lesson (a lesson I could have learned from F. Scott Fitzgerald,
but perhaps we all must meet the very rich for ourselves) by asking, when I arrived to interview her in her orchid-filled sitting room on the second day of a
paralyzing New York blizzard, whether it was snowing outside.

9   I imagine, in other words, that the notebook is about other people. But of course it is not. I have no real business with what one stranger said to another at the hatcheck counter in Pavillon; in fact I suspect that the line "That's my old football number" touched not my own imagination at all, but merely some memory of something once read, probably "The Eighty-Yard Run." Nor is my concern with a woman in a dirty crepe-de-Chine wrapper in a Wilmington bar. My stake is always, of course, in the unmentioned girl in the plaid silk dress. *Remember what it was to be me: that is always the point.*

10   It is a difficult point to admit. We are brought up in the ethic that others, any others, all others, are by definition more interesting than ourselves; taught to be diffident, just this side of self-effacing. ("You're the least important person in the room and don't forget it," Jessica Mitford's governess would hiss in her ear on the advent of any social occasion; I copied that into my notebook because it is only recently that I have been able to enter a room without hearing some such phrase in my inner ear.) Only the very young and the very old may recount their dreams at breakfast, dwell upon self, interrupt with memories of beach picnics and favorite Liberty lawn dresses and the rainbow trout in a creek near Colorado Springs. The rest of us are expected, rightly, to affect absorption in other people's favorite dresses, other people's trout.

11   And so we do. But our notebooks give us away, for however dutifully we record what we see around us, the common denominator of all we see is always, transparently, shamelessly, the implacable "I". We are not talking here about the kind of notebook that is patently for public consumption, a structural conceit for binding together a series of graceful *pensées;* we are talking about something private, about bits of the mind's string too short to use, an indiscriminate and erratic assemblage with meaning only for its maker.

12   And sometimes even the maker has difficulty with the meaning. There does not seem to be, for example, any point in my knowing for the rest of my life that, during 1964, 720 tons of soot fell on every square mile of New York City, yet there it is in my notebook, labeled "FACT." Nor do I really need to remember that Ambrose Bierce liked to spell Leland Stanford's name "£eland $tanford" or that "smart women almost always wear black in Cuba," a fashion hint without much potential for practical application. And does not the relevance of these notes seem marginal at best?:

13   In the basement museum of the Inyo County Courthouse in Independence, California, sign pinned to a mandarin coat: "This MANDARIN COAT was often worn by Mrs. Minnie S. Brooks when giving lectures on her TEAPOT COLLECTION."

Redhead getting out of car in front of Beverly Wilshire Hotel, chinchilla stole, Vuitton bags with tags reading:

MRS LOU FOX

HOTEL SAHARA

VEGAS

Well, perhaps not entirely marginal. As a matter of fact, Mrs. Minnie S.   14
Brooks and her MANDARIN COAT pull me back into my own childhood,
for although I never knew Mrs. Brooks and did not visit Inyo County until I
was thirty, I grew up in just such a world, in houses cluttered with Indian relics
and bits of gold ore and ambergris and the souvenirs my Aunt Mercy
Farnsworth brought back from the Orient. It is a long way from that world to
Mrs. Lou Fox's world where we all live now, and is it not just as well to remember that? Might not Mrs. Minnie S. Brooks help me to remember what I
am? Might not Mrs. Lou Fox help me to remember what I am not?

But sometimes the point is harder to discern. What exactly did I have in   15
mind when I noted down that it cost the father of someone I know $650 a month
to light the place on the Hudson in which he lived before the Crash? What use
was I planning to make of this line by Jimmy Hoffa: "I may have my faults, but
being wrong ain't one of them"? And although I think it interesting to know
where the girls who travel with the Syndicate have their hair done when they find
themselves on the West Coast, will I ever make suitable use of it? Might I not be
better off just passing it on to John O'Hara? What is a recipe for sauerkraut doing in my notebook? What kind of magpie keeps this notebook? *"He was born the
night the* Titanic *went down."* That seems a nice enough line, and I even recall who
said it, but is it not really a better line in life than it could ever be in fiction?

But of course that is exactly it: not that I should ever use the line, but   16
that I should remember the woman who said it and the afternon I heard it. We
were on her terrace by the sea, and we were finishing the wine left from lunch,
trying to get what sun there was, a California winter sun. The woman whose
husband was born the night the *Titanic* went down wanted to rent her house,
wanted to go back to her children in Paris. I remember wishing that I could
afford the house, which cost $1,000 a month. "Someday you will," she said
lazily. "Someday it all comes." There in the sun on her terrace it seemed easy
to believe in someday but later I had a low-grade afternoon hangover and ran
over a black snake on the way to the supermarket and was flooded with inexplicable fear when I heard the checkout clerk explaining to the man ahead of
me why she was finally divorcing her husband. "He left me no choice," she
said over and over as she punched the register. "He has a little seven-month-
old baby by her, he left me no choice." I would like to believe that my dread
then was for the human condition, but of course it was for me, because I
wanted to own the house that cost $1,000 a month to rent and because I had
a hangover.

It all comes back. Perhaps it is difficult to see the value in having one's   17
self back in that kind of mood, but I do see it; I think we are well advised to
keep on nodding terms with the people we used to be, whether we find them
attractive company or not. Otherwise they turn up unannounced and surprise
us, come hammering on the mind's door at 4 A.M. of a bad night and demand
to know who deserted them, who betrayed them, who is going to make
amends. We forget all too soon the things we thought we could never forget.
We forget the loves and the betrayals alike, forget what we whispered and

what we screamed, forget who we were. I have already lost touch with a couple of people I used to be; one of them, a seventeen-year-old, presents little threat, although it would be of some interest to me to know again what it feels like to sit on a river levee drinking vodka-and-orange-juice and listening to Les Paul and Mary Ford and their echoes sing "How High the Moon" on the car radio. (You see I still have the scenes, but I no longer perceive myself among those present, no longer could even improvise the dialogue.) The other one, a twenty-three-year old, bothers me more. She was always a good deal of trouble, and I suspect she will reappear when I least want to see her, skirts too long, shy to the point of aggravation, always the injured party, full of recriminations and little hurts and stories I do not want to hear again, at once saddening me and angering me with her vulnerability and ignorance, an apparition all the more insistent for being so long banished.

18   It is a good idea, then, to keep in touch and I suppose that keeping in touch is what notebooks are all about. And we are all on our own when it comes to keeping those lines open to ourselves: your notebooks will never help me, nor mine you. *"So what's new in the whiskey business?"* What could that possibly mean to you? To me it means a blonde in a Pucci bathing suit sitting with a couple of fat men by the pool at the Beverly Hills Hotel. Another man approaches, and they all regard one another in silence for a while. "So what's new in the whiskey business?" one of the fat men finally says by way of welcome, and the blonde stands up, arches one foot and dips it in the pool, looking all the while at the cabana where Baby Pignatari is talking on the telephone. That is all there is to that, except that several years later I saw the blonde coming out of Saks Fifth Avenue in New York with her California complexion and a voluminous mink coat. In the harsh wind that day she looked old and irrevocably tired to me, and even the skins in the mink coat were not worked the way they were doing them that year, not the way she would have wanted them done, and there is the point of the story. For a while after that I did not like to look in the mirror, and my eyes would skim the newspapers and pick out only the deaths, the cancer victims, the premature coronaries, the suicides, and I stopped riding the Lexington Avenue IRT because I noticed for the first time that all the strangers I had seen for years—the man with the seeing-eye dog, the spinster who read the classified pages every day, the fat girl who always got off with me at Grand Central—looked older than they once had.

19   It all comes back. Even that recipe for sauerkraut: even that brings it back. I was on Fire Island when I first made that sauerkraut, and it was raining, and we drank a lot of bourbon and ate the sauerkraut and went to bed at ten, and I listened to the rain and the Atlantic and felt safe. I made the sauerkraut again last night and it did not make me feel any safer, but that is, as they say, another story.

QUESTIONS ON SUBJECT AND PURPOSE

1. Why does Didion keep a notebook? What types of things does she record? How does a notebook differ from a diary?

2. In paragraph 7, Didion acknowledges that what she records did not always happen and that, for her purposes, it does not really matter. What does she mean by this? Why would she record "lies"?

3. If the notebook helps Didion remember "what it was to be me" (paragraph 9), why should anyone be interested in her essay? Is the essay as egocentric as the notebook? Is there any purpose to this other than self-discovery—what all this means to *me*, Joan Didion?

QUESTIONS ON STRATEGY AND AUDIENCE

1. The essay follows a pattern of discovery. Didion seems to discover why she keeps a notebook as she writes the essay. But that might also be a fiction. She might have known before she wrote the essay. Either way, what does such a pattern add to the essay? Why might Didion have chosen to explain in such a way?

2. How effective is the introduction? The conclusion?

3. What do the examples in her notebook tell Didion? What common thread links all of the examples she uses?

QUESTIONS ON VOCABULARY AND STYLE

1. Why does Didion use typographical devices in the essay (things like the italics or the parentheses or the indented entries in paragraph 13)?

2. At a number of points in the essay Didion asks a group of questions about a particular entry and then goes on to answer them. What is the effect of this stylistic device? How is it related to the structure of the essay?

3. Be able to define the following: *crepe-de-Chine* (paragraph 1), *malcontent* (4), *presentiment* (4), *predilection* (5), *verisimilitude* (7), *aperçus* (8), *implacable* (11), *pensées* (11), *ambergris* (14), *recriminations* (17).

WRITING SUGGESTIONS

1. **For Your Journal.** After carefully reading Didion's essay, write an entry modeled on the type that Didion records in her notebooks. Remember that she notes, "the point of my keeping a notebook has never been . . . to have an accurate factual record of what I have been doing or thinking." What then is the point of making entries? Answer that question by writing an entry that reveals about you what Didion's entries reveal about her.

2. **For a Paragraph.** Using the advice that Didion provides (often indirectly) write a paragraph in which you explain to a reader how to keep a notebook. Think of your paragraph as something that could be given to writers who are puzzled about the directions for the previous journal writing assignment. Make the process and the advice clear.

3. **For an Essay.** Didion describes by means of process how influences and experiences have shaped her life. Look back on what has brought you here to this present moment. Then select several important events or influences that helped shape your life. Using those examples, write a process analysis on how you have come to be where you are now.

4. **For Research.** Didion remarks, "I think we are well advised to keep on nodding terms with the people we used to be" (paragraph 17). Is it ever possible to remember who we used to be? To what extent do we "rewrite" our lives as we grow older? Is any autobiography true? What goes into an autobiography? Research what writers have said about writing autobiography (the *Library of Congress Subject Headings* in your school's library will give you a good place to start). Then, in an essay, describe the process of writing autobiography. Be sure to document your sources wherever appropriate.

FOR FURTHER STUDY

Focusing on Grammar and Writing. Didion has a fondness for short, simple sentences, particularly as opening sentences in a paragraph (for example, paragraphs 10–12, 14, 15, 17, and 19). Look for similar short sentences in Didion's essay. What is the effect of these sentences? What is the effect of beginning seven paragraphs with them?

Working Together. Divide into small groups. Subdivide the essay into blocks of paragraphs. Mark off each entry in the essay that Didion quotes or alludes to in the essay. What do these entries have in common? What role do they play in the essay?

Seeing Other Modes at Work. Although it is not her primary purpose, Didion does define the term *notebook* during the essay. In what ways does Didion use definition in the essay?

Finding Connections. How does Didion's notebook-keeping fit into the writing process as it would be outlined by the two writers in William Zinsser's "The Transaction" (Chapter 5)?

Exploring the Web. The Web includes an extensive number of sites with information about Didion and her writing. Read other essays written by Didion and check out some of the interviews that she has given. Places to start can be found at **www.prenhall.com/miller**.

THE SINGER SOLUTION TO WORLD POVERTY

Peter Singer

Peter Singer (1946–), born in Australia, is Ira W. DeCamp Professor of Bioethics at the University Center for Human Values at Princeton. A prolific author on a wide range of ethical issues, Singer has been referred to as "maybe the most controversial [ethicist] alive . . . [and] certainly among the most influential." His most recent book is The President of Good and Evil: The Ethics of George W. Bush *(2004). This essay originally appeared in* The New York Times Magazine.

On Writing: *In an interview, Singer had this to say about the effects of argument: "I think we are (mostly) rational beings and rational argument does move people to action particularly when it gets them to see that what they are doing is inconsistent with other beliefs that they have and other values that they have that are important to them. But it is also true that we are self-interested beings to some extent. That's part of our nature and you can't get away from that. . . . If we put a rational argument in front of people, some are moved by it a lot of the way, it moves others a little bit of the way, and some people just shrug it off because it is too much against what they want to do."*

BEFORE READING

Connecting: How much money do you contribute annually to organizations seeking to care for children in need throughout the world?

Anticipating: As you read, think about whether or not Singer's essay has persuaded you to change your own behavior. Why or why not?

LOOKING FOR COMBINATIONS

Singer's purpose is persuasive, but persuasion uses a variety of other strategies to achieve its end. In places, Singer uses narration, comparison and contrast, and classification. Can you locate those patterns in the essay? Can you find any others at work? What roles do these strategies or modes play in the essay as a whole?

I N THE BRAZILIAN FILM *Central Station*, Dora is a retired schoolteacher who   1
makes ends meet by sitting at the station writing letters for illiterate people. Suddenly she has an opportunity to pocket a thousand dollars. All she has to do is persuade a homeless nine-year-old boy to follow her to an address she has been given. (She is told he will be adopted by wealthy foreigners.) She delivers the boy, gets the money, spends some of it on a television set, and settles down to enjoy her new acquisition. Her neighbor spoils the fun, however, by

telling her that the boy was too old to be adopted—he will be killed and his organs sold for transplantation. Perhaps Dora knew this all along, but after her neighbor's plain speaking, she spends a troubled night. In the morning Dora resolves to take the boy back.

2   Suppose Dora had told her neighbor that it is a tough world, other people have nice new TVs too, and if selling the kid is the only way she can get one, well, he was only a street kid. She would then have become, in the eyes of the audience, a monster. She redeems herself only by being prepared to bear considerable risks to save the boy.

3   At the end of the movie, in cinemas in the affluent nations of the world, people who would have been quick to condemn Dora if she had not rescued the boy go home to places far more comfortable than her apartment. In fact, the average family in the United States spends almost one third of its income on things that are no more necessary to them than Dora's new TV was to her. Going out to nice restaurants, buying new clothes because the old ones are no longer stylish, vacationing at beach resorts—so much of our income is spent on things not essential to the preservation of our lives and health. Donated to one of a number of charitable agencies, that money could mean the difference between life and death for children in need.

4   All of which raises a question: in the end, what is the ethical distinction between a Brazilian who sells a homeless child to organ peddlers and an American who already has a TV and upgrades to a better one, knowing that the money could be donated to an organization that would use it to save the lives of kids in need?

5   Of course, there are several differences between the two situations that could support different moral judgments about them. For one thing, to be able to consign a child to death when he is standing right in front of you takes a chilling kind of heartlessness; it is much easier to ignore an appeal for money to help children you will never meet. Yet for a utilitarian philosopher like myself—that is, one who judges whether acts are right or wrong by their consequences—if the upshot of the American's failure to donate the money is that one more kid dies on the streets of a Brazilian city, then it is in some sense just as bad as selling the kid to the organ peddlers. But one doesn't need to embrace my utilitarian ethic to see that at the very least, there is a troubling incongruity in being so quick to condemn Dora for taking the child to the organ peddlers while at the same time not regarding the American consumer's behavior as raising a serious moral issue.

6   In his 1996 book, *Living High and Letting Die*, the New York University philosopher Peter Unger presented an ingenious series of imaginary examples designed to probe our intuitions about whether it is wrong to live well without giving substantial amounts of money to help people who are hungry, malnourished, or dying from easily treatable illnesses like diarrhea. Here's my paraphrase of one of these examples:

7   Bob is close to retirement. He has invested most of his savings in a very rare and valuable old car, a Bugatti, which he has not been able to insure. The Bugatti is his pride and joy. In addition to the pleasure he gets from driving

and caring for his car, Bob knows that its rising market value means that he will always be able to sell it and live comfortably after retirement. One day when Bob is out for a drive, he parks the Bugatti near the end of a railway siding and goes for a walk up the track. As he does so, he sees that a runaway train, with no one aboard, is running down the railway track. Looking farther down the track, he sees the small figure of a child very likely to be killed by the runaway train. He can't stop the train and the child is too far away to warn of the danger, but he can throw a switch that will divert the train down the siding where his Bugatti is parked. Then nobody will be killed—but the train will destroy his Bugatti. Thinking of his joy in owning the car and the financial security it represents, Bob decides not to throw the switch. The child is killed. For many years to come, Bob enjoys owning his Bugatti and the financial security it represents.

Bob's conduct, most of us will immediately respond, was gravely wrong. Unger agrees. But then he reminds us that we too have opportunities to save the lives of children. We can give to organizations like UNICEF or Oxfam America. How much would we have to give one of these organizations to have a high probability of saving the life of a child threatened by easily preventable diseases? (I do not believe that children are more worth saving than adults, but since no one can argue that children have brought their poverty on themselves, focusing on them simplifies the issues.) Unger called up some experts and used the information they provided to offer some plausible estimates that include the cost of raising money, administrative expenses, and the cost of delivering aid where it is most needed. By his calculation, $200 in donations would help a sickly two-year-old transform into a healthy six-year-old—offering safe passage through childhood's most dangerous years. To show how practical philosophical argument can be, Unger even tells his readers that they can easily donate funds by using their credit card and calling one of these toll-free numbers: (800) 367-5437 for UNICEF; (800) 693-2687 for Oxfam America.

Now you too have the information you need to save a child's life. How should you judge yourself if you don't do it? Think again about Bob and his Bugatti. Unlike Dora, Bob did not have to look into the eyes of the child he was sacrificing for his own material comfort. The child was a complete stranger to him and too far away to relate to in an intimate, personal way. Unlike Dora too, he did not mislead the child or initiate the chain of events imperiling him. In all these respects, Bob's situation resembles that of people able but unwilling to donate to overseas aid and differs from Dora's situation.

If you still think that it was very wrong of Bob not to throw the switch that would have diverted the train and saved the child's life, then it is hard to see how you could deny that it is also very wrong not to send money to one of the organizations listed above. Unless, that is, there is some morally important difference between the two situations that I have overlooked.

Is it the practical uncertainties about whether aid will really reach the people who need it? Nobody who knows the world of overseas aid can doubt that such uncertainties exist. But Unger's figure of $200 to save a child's life was reached after he had made conservative assumptions about the proportion of the money donated that will actually reach its target.

12   One genuine difference between Bob and those who can afford to donate to overseas aid organizations but don't is that only Bob can save the child on the tracks, whereas there are hundreds of millions of people who can give $200 to overseas aid organizations. The problem is that most of them aren't doing it. Does this mean that it is all right for you not to do it?

13   Suppose that there were more owners of priceless vintage cars—Carol, Dave, Emma, Fred, and so on, down to Ziggy—all in exactly the same situation as Bob, with their own siding and their own switch, all sacrificing the child in order to preserve their own cherished car. Would that make it all right for Bob to do the same? To answer this question affirmatively is to endorse follow-the-crowd ethics—the kind of ethics that led many Germans to look away when the Nazi atrocities were being committed. We do not excuse them because others were behaving no better.

14   We seem to lack a sound basis for drawing a clear moral line between Bob's situation and that of any reader of this article with $200 to spare who does not donate it to an overseas aid agency. These readers seem to be acting at least as badly as Bob was acting when he chose to let the runaway train hurtle toward the unsuspecting child. In the light of this conclusion, I trust that many readers will reach for the phone and donate that $200. Perhaps you should do it before reading further.

*

15   Now that you have distinguished yourself morally from people who put their vintage cars ahead of a child's life, how about treating yourself and your partner to dinner at your favorite restaurant? But wait. The money you will spend at the restaurant could also help save the lives of children overseas! True, you weren't planning to blow $200 tonight, but if you were to give up dining out just for one month, you would easily save that amount. And what is one month's dining out compared to a child's life? There's the rub. Since there are a lot of desperately needy children in the world, there will always be another child whose life you could save for another $200. Are you therefore obliged to keep giving until you have nothing left? At what point can you stop?

16   Hypothetical examples can easily become farcical. Consider Bob. How far past losing the Bugatti should he go? Imagine that Bob had got his foot stuck in the track of the siding, and if he diverted the train, then before it rammed the car it would also amputate his big toe. Should he still throw the switch? What if it would amputate his foot? His entire leg?

17   As absurd as the Bugatti scenario gets when pushed to extremes, the point it raises is a serious one: only when the sacrifices become very significant indeed would most people be prepared to say that Bob does nothing wrong when he decides not to throw the switch. Of course, most people could be wrong; we can't decide moral issues by taking opinion polls. But consider for yourself the level of sacrifice that you would demand of Bob, and then think about how much money you would have to give away in order to make a sacrifice that is

roughly equal to that. It's almost certainly much, much more than $200. For most middle-class Americans, it could easily be more like $200,000.

Isn't it counterproductive to ask people to do so much? Don't we run the risk that many will shrug their shoulders and say that morality, so conceived, is fine for saints but not for them? I accept that we are unlikely to see, in the near or even medium-term future, a world in which it is normal for wealthy Americans to give the bulk of their wealth to strangers. When it comes to praising or blaming people for what they do, we tend to use a standard that is relative to some conception of normal behavior. Comfortably off Americans who give, say, 10 percent of their income to overseas aid organizations are so far ahead of most of their equally comfortable fellow citizens that I wouldn't go out of my way to chastise them for not doing more. Nevertheless, they should be doing much more, and they are in no position to criticize Bob for failing to make the much greater sacrifice of his Bugatti. 18

At this point various objections may crop up. Someone may say, "If every citizen living in the affluent nations contributed his or her share, I wouldn't have to make such a drastic sacrifice, because long before such levels were reached the resources would have been there to save the lives of all those children dying from lack of food or medical care. So why should I give more than my fair share?" Another, related objection is that the government ought to increase its overseas aid allocations, since that would spread the burden more equitably across all taxpayers. 19

Yet the question of how much we ought to give is a matter to be decided in the real world—and that, sadly, is a world in which we know that most people do not, and in the immediate future will not, give substantial amounts to overseas aid agencies. We know too that at least in the next year, the United States government is not going to meet even the very modest United Nations–recommended target of 0.7 percent of gross national product; at the moment it lags far below that, at 0.09 percent, not even half of Japan's 0.22 percent or a tenth of Denmark's 0.97 percent. Thus, we know that the money we can give beyond that theoretical "fair share" is still going to save lives that would otherwise be lost. While the idea that no one need do more than his or her fair share is a powerful one, should it prevail if we know that others are not doing their fair share and that children will die preventable deaths unless we do more than our fair share? That would be taking fairness too far. 20

Thus, this ground for limiting how much we ought to give also fails. In the world as it is now, I can see no escape from the conclusion that each one of us with wealth surplus to his or her essential needs should be giving most of it to help people suffering from poverty so dire as to be life-threatening. That's right: I'm saying that you shouldn't buy that new car, take that cruise, redecorate the house, or get that pricy new suit. After all, a thousand-dollar suit could save five children's lives. 21

So how does my philosophy break down in dollars and cents? An American household with an income of $50,000 spends around $30,000 annually on necessities, according to the Conference Board, a nonprofit economic research 22 organization. Therefore, for a household bringing in $50,000 a year, donations to help the world's poor should be as close as possible to $20,000. The $30,000 required for necessities holds for higher incomes as well. So a household making $100,000 could cut a yearly check for $70,000. Again, the formula is simple: whatever money you're spending on luxuries, not necessities, should be given away.

23   Now, evolutionary psychologists tell us that human nature just isn't sufficiently altruistic to make it plausible that many people will sacrifice so much for strangers. On the facts of human nature, they might be right, but they would be wrong to draw a moral conclusion from those facts. If it is the case that we ought to do things that, predictably, most of us won't do, then let's face that fact head-on. Then, if we value the life of a child more than going to fancy restaurants, the next time we dine out we will know that we could have done something better with our money. If that makes living a morally decent life extremely arduous, well, then that is the way things are. If we don't do it, then we should at least know that we are failing to live a morally decent life—not because it is good to wallow in guilt but because knowing where we should be going is the first step toward heading in that direction.

24   When Bob first grasped the dilemma that faced him as he stood by that railway switch, he must have thought how extraordinarily unlucky he was to be placed in a situation in which he must choose between the life of an innocent child and the sacrifice of most of his savings. But he was not unlucky at all. We are all in that situation.

QUESTIONS ON SUBJECT AND PURPOSE

1. Singer labels himself a "utilitarian" philosopher. How does he explain what that means?
2. Is there any limit for Singer to how much money one ought to give away for overseas aid?
3. What type of response do you think that Singer hopes from his audience? Expects from his audience?

QUESTIONS ON STRATEGY AND AUDIENCE

1. Why might Singer choose to begin with the example of Dora in the Brazilian film *Central Station*?
2. The text of the essay is separated after paragraph 14 by a centered asterisk (*). What division does this indicate in the essay itself?
3. What assumptions could Singer make about his audience?

QUESTIONS ON VOCABULARY AND STYLE

1. What is an analogy? Does Singer use analogy in his argument?
2. Why is the effect of including the telephone numbers for UNICEF and Oxfam America in the essay?

3. Be prepared to define the following words: *affluent* (paragraph 3), *incongruity* (5), *ingenious* (6), *altruistic* (23), *arduous* (23).

WRITING SUGGESTIONS

1. **For Your Journal.** Over the course of a week, jot down in your journal a detailed list of how you spent your money. Try to record everything. For each expenditure over 50 cents, write an explanation for where and why the money was spent. At the end of the week, make some notes about your spending habits.

2. **For a Paragraph.** What did your journal reveal? In a paragraph, explore your values and either defend or criticize your behavior.

3. **For an Essay.** Singer notes (citing the research of someone else) that a $200 donation would "help a sickly two-year-old transform into a healthy six-year-old." That works out to about 55 cents per day yearly. Could you and your friends, even as college students, find a way to trim 55 cents a day (or less than $4 a week) out of what you already spend? In an essay aimed at undergraduates at your school, argue for a schoolwide campaign to get everyone to contribute to such a cause.

4. **For Research.** Why is it that the richest nation in the world is one of the world's poorest contributors to overseas aid? In an essay research this situation. How much does the United States contribute? What factors have accounted for our current position? Are there good reasons why we as a nation should not contribute more? In an essay arguing either side, take a stand on the United States' overseas aid policy.

FOR FURTHER STUDY

Focusing on Grammar and Writing. Choose one or more of Singer's longer paragraphs and look closely at how it is organized. You might want to outline it. Does the paragraph achieve unity and coherence? How? Does the paragraph have a topic sentence? Does it use transitional devices to link sentences together? What observations could you make about effective body paragraphs based on the example you studied?

Working Together. Singer divides his essay into four parts, each marked by the addition of extra white space between the blocks of paragraphs. Divide the class into small groups; each group should take one of the blocks to examine. Why is this section set off? What unifies it?

1. Paragraphs 1–5
2. Paragraphs 6–14
3. Paragraphs 15–17
4. Paragraphs 18–24

Seeing Other Modes at Work. Singer's essay uses comparison and contrast, especially since he makes extensive use of analogy in establishing links among the decisions facing Dora, Bob, and the reader.

Finding Connections. Interesting pairings are with Tom Haines's "Facing Famine" (Chapter 2) and Lars Eighner's "My Daily Dives in the Dumpster" (Chapter 6).

Exploring the Web. The Web offers a number of sites where you can read more of Singer's work, explore the objections that some critics have to some of his ethical stands, and make a contribution to UNICEF, Oxfam America, or the relief agency of your choice.

A

FINDING, USING,
AND DOCUMENTING SOURCES

FINDING SOURCES

All effective writing involves some form of research. To write a laboratory report in chemistry, you use the information gathered from performing the experiment. To write an article for the student newspaper on your college's latest
tuition increase, you include information gathered in interviews with those involved in making that decision. To answer a midterm examination, you mar-
shal evidence from lecture notes and from required reading.

As these examples demonstrate, you may use a wide variety of sources
when you research any particular topic.

- *Firsthand knowledge.* Your own observations and experiences play a
  major role in much of your writing. Such knowledge can be simple and
  acquired easily (before writing a review of a restaurant, you would
  sample the cuisine and service) or complex and gathered laboriously
  (scientists will study a virus for years, gathering information and testing
  out hypotheses by performing experiments).
- *Printed knowledge.* The bulk of your knowledge for the papers you will
  typically write in college comes from printed sources, including
  reference works such as dictionaries and encyclopedias, books, articles
  in magazines and journals, articles in newspapers, and government
  publications.
- *Electronic documents.* The Internet and the World Wide Web contain
  important sources of information. Many magazines, newspapers, and
  academic journals can be found in electronic form. Some journals,
  in fact, are available only electronically. Organizations and even
  individuals maintain home pages with valuable information. Our
  research in the future increasingly will be done through computers.
- *Interviewing.* On many topics, you can gather information by talking
  with the people involved. A newspaper reporter writing about the
  latest tuition increase, for example, would have to rely on
  information provided by administrators and budget analysts.

Thanks to the increasing use of electronic mail (e-mail), interviewing no longer requires face-to-face contact or a telephone call.

Although all writing uses sources, not all writing meets the special considerations that we associate with a research paper. Not only does a research paper document its sources, but it also exhibits a particular approach to its subject. A research paper is not just a collection of information about a subject. Instead, a research paper poses a particular question or thesis about its subject and then sets out to answer that question or test the validity of that thesis.

In important ways, you should approach the research that you do for a college paper in the same way that a scientist sets about exploring a problem. The idea behind research—all research—is to isolate a particular aspect of a subject, to become an expert in that defined area, and to present an original or new conclusion about that material. Because research papers have a thesis, they differ significantly from the informational overviews that we find in encyclopedia articles. Many writers confuse the two forms of writing. The confusion probably dates back to grade school when a teacher assigned a report on, say, Jupiter. What most of us did was go to the encyclopedia, look up "Jupiter," and copy down the entry. That might have been an appropriate response for a grade school assignment, but such a strategy will never work for a college research paper.

USING REFERENCE BOOKS AS A STARTING POINT: ENCYCLOPEDIAS AND DICTIONARIES

If you do not already have a fairly detailed knowledge about your subject, encyclopedias and dictionaries can be good places to begin your research. Before using such reference works, however, you should remember three important points. First, encyclopedias and dictionaries are only good as *starting points*, providing just a basic overview of a subject. You will never be able to rely solely on such sources for college-level research. Second, encyclopedias and dictionaries range from general works that cover a wide range of subjects (such as the *Encyclopaedia Britannica, Encyclopedia Americana*, and *Collier's Encyclopedia*) to highly specialized works focused around a single area or subject. Third, although some encyclopedias are available in electronic formats (for example, the *Encyclopaedia Britannica* has a version known as *Britannica Online*), many of the most detailed specialized encyclopedias and dictionaries are currently available only in print form.

Because general encyclopedias provide information about a variety of subjects, they can never contain as much information about a single subject as you can find in an encyclopedia that specializes in that subject. For this reason, you might begin any search with a specialized encyclopedia. The word *specialized* in this sense refers primarily to the more focused subject coverage that these works offer; most of the articles are still written in nontechnical language. The word *dictionary*, as it is used in the titles of these works, means essentially the same thing as *encyclopedia*—a collection of articles of varying lengths arranged alphabetically.

Your school is likely to have a wide range of specialized encyclopedias and dictionaries. To locate these reference tools, try the following steps:

1. Consult a guide to reference works. The following guides to reference books are widely available in college and university libraries. Use one or more of them to establish a list of possible works to consult.

   - Robert Kieft (Ed.), *Guide to Reference Sources*, 12th ed. (Forthcoming).
   - Robert Balay, *Guide to Reference Books*, 11th ed. (1996).

2. Check in the library's catalog under the headings "Encyclopedias and Dictionaries—Bibliography," "[Your subject]—Dictionaries," and "[Your subject]—Dictionaries and Encyclopedias."

3. Ask a reference librarian for advice on the specialized sources likely to be relevant to your topic.

4. If your school's library maintains an electronic database, check to see if any dictionaries or encyclopedias are networked into it.

FINDING BOOKS: YOUR LIBRARY'S CATALOG

Every library maintains an index or catalog that lists the material kept in its collections. The record for each item often provides a wide range of information, but it always includes the author's name, the title of the item, and a few of the most important subject headings. Most college and university libraries are now computerized. With all the information about each item contained in one large database, users can access holdings through a computer terminal, searching by keyword(s), by author, by title, by subject, and often by date or place of publication. Most online catalogs not only display call numbers but also tell you whether the item you want has been checked out or is on the shelves. Often you no longer need to visit the library to search its catalog; it is accessible at home or in your dorm room via modem or network cabling.

When you start a search for books in your library's catalog, remember these key points:

- Always read the "help" menu the first time you use an on-line catalog. Do not assume that you know how the search functions work. Knowing *how* to search often makes the difference between disappointment and success.
- All catalogs—whether filed in drawers or stored online—list only material owned by that particular library or other libraries in the area or state. No library owns a copy of every book.
- Library catalogs list books (by author, title, and a few subject headings) and journals (*only* by title). Library catalogs never include the authors or titles of individual articles contained in journals or magazines.
- Much information on any subject—and generally the most current information—is found in journal articles, not in books. Remember as

well that certain subjects may not be treated in books. For example, if a subject is very current or too specialized, no book may have been written about it. Therefore, a search for sources should *never* be limited to the references found in a library catalog.

- In initial searches for information, you are typically looking for subjects—that is, you do not yet have a specific title or author to look up. Searching for subjects in a library catalog can be considerably more complicated than it might initially seem since the subject headings used in library catalogs are often not what you might expect. Unless you use the subject heading or keyword that the catalog uses, you will not find what you are looking for. The next section offers some advice about subject headings.

Choosing the Right Subject Heading

The success of any research paper depends in part on finding reliable and appropriate sources of information. For most college papers, your information will come from *secondary* sources, typically books and articles that report the research done by others. Depending on your subject, you might also be able to use *primary* sources—original documents (historical records, letters, works of literature) or the results of original research (laboratory experiments, interviews, questionnaires).

Finding sources is not hard, no matter what your subject, but it does require knowing *how* and *where* to look. A quick tour of your college or university library, with its rows of shelves, or an hour on the Web will vividly demonstrate that you need a *search strategy*. The first step in that strategy is to find subject headings and keywords that can be used to retrieve information.

The subject headings used in library catalogs and periodical indexes are part of a fixed, interlocking system that is both logically organized and highly structured. The idea is not to list every possible subject heading under which a particular subject might be found but to establish general headings under which related subjects can be grouped. Most libraries use the subject headings suggested by the Library of Congress and published in the *Library of Congress Subject Headings* (LCSH), a five-volume set of books typically found near your library's catalog or in the reference area. In addition, most periodical indexes also use either the same system or one so similar that the LCSH headings will still serve your purpose. As a result, the most efficient way to begin a subject search is to check the LCSH for appropriate subject headings under which books and articles on your subject will be listed.

For example, suppose you were surprised to read that even today, women earn less than 80 percent of what men earn doing the same job. You want to research why that disparity exists and what is being done to remedy that inequity. Exactly what keywords or subject headings would you look under in a catalog, a database, or a periodical index to find appropriate sources: *Women? Work? Job discrimination? Salaries?* Unless you know where to begin, you might waste a considerable amount of time guessing randomly or conclude (quite wrongly) that your library had no information on the topic.

If you consulted the *Library of Congress Subject Headings*, you would find cross-references that would lead you to the following:

Equal pay for work of comparable value
   USE Pay equity
Equal pay for equal work *(May Subd Geog)*
   Here are entered works on equal pay for jobs that require identical skills, responsibilities, and effort. Works on comparable pay for jobs that require comparable skills, responsibilities, effort, and working conditions are entered under Pay equity.
   BT   Discrimination in employment Wages
   RT   Women—Employment
   —Law and registration *(May Subd Geog)*
      BT Labor laws and legislation
Equal pay for work of comparable value
   USE Pay equity

The LCSH use abbreviations to indicate the relationships among subjects. By following the cross-references, you can conduct a more thorough search. The relationships that are signaled include these:

Equivalence:	USE
Hierarchy:	BT (broader term)
	NT (narrower term)
Association:	RT (related term)

Having checked the key to using the headings, you know from these entries not to search under "Equal pay for comparable work" since the heading is not in bold type; instead, you are told to use "Pay equity." The best heading under which to search for books and articles related to your topic is **"Equal pay for equal work."** The abbreviation *May Subd Geog* indicates that the heading might be subdivided geographically, for example, "Equal pay for equal work—Delaware." The LCSH also suggests other possibilities: for a broader term, use "Discrimination in employment" or "Wages"; for a related term, use "Woman—Employment." You will find relevant information under all of these possible headings. In general, no one subject heading will lead you to all of the books your library has on a particular topic.

Here are a few cautions to keep in mind when using subject headings:

1. Always check the *Library of Congress Subject Headings* first to find the best headings to use for your subject. The quickest way to short-circuit your search strategy is to begin with a heading that you think will work, find nothing, and conclude that your library has no information on that topic.

2. Remember that the headings used might not be as specific as you want. You might need to browse through a group of related materials to find the more precise information you are seeking.

Subject headings use a *controlled vocabulary;* that is, all information about a particular subject is grouped under a single heading with appropriate cross-references from other related headings. For example, if your subject was "capital punishment," you would not also need to look under the headings "death penalty," "execution," or "death row." Controlled vocabularies do, however, place some restrictions on your search strategy. As we've mentioned, subject headings aren't always as precise as you would like them to be. Furthermore, timely or very recent subjects might not appear within the classification scheme for several years.

An on-line alternative to subject heading searches is *keyword* searching. A keyword is a significant word, almost always a noun, that is used in the titles (or someplace else in the computerized record) of books, reports, or articles. By combining keywords, you can conduct very precise searches. You will learn how to combine keywords and what "operators" to use (words such as *and, near,* and *or* that indicate the relationships between those keywords) only if you take the time to study the help menu. Keyword searches that do not specify the relationship between the words tend to produce unwieldy strings of "hits"—records that contain those words. The computer just lists every record that contains those words anywhere in it, even if the records themselves are completely unrelated to your topic or to each other. Keyword searches are especially valuable when you cannot find the appropriate subject heading (for example, "glass ceiling," referring to the limited promotion possibilities for someone within a company or organization) or when you want to combine several concepts (for example, "children and violence and television").

FINDING SOURCES ON THE WEB

The Web is expanding at a prodigious rate—in 1997, it contained an estimated 320 million pages; in 1999, it had grown to 800 million pages; by the time you read this, it will probably be several billion pages. Given that growth, it is not surprising that no single search engine (the term applied to software programs that index information on the Web) can retrieve it all. What this means is that for the best results on a research project, you should use at least two different search engines. Unfortunately, every list of relevant sites retrieved is likely to contain some dead links—that is, the information is no longer available at the listed site. It's frustrating to encounter such links, but it's also common.

Retrieving relevant sites of information is only one problem. Anyone can post anything on the Web. Just because it is there, just because the Web pages look professional, there is no guarantee that you can trust every document you retrieve. Evaluating Web sources is covered a little later in this appendix. Don't forget to look at the advice there (and on the *Reader*'s Website at **www.prenhall.com/miller**) before you start using Web sources to write your research paper.

Choosing a Search Engine

In searching the Web, like searching most libraries' computerized catalogs, you have two initial choices: you can search by subject or by keyword. A number of sites offer indexes or catalogs of Web documents arranged by subject. One popular and effective subject organized site is Yahoo!, where human editors have selected the best information available on the Web and presented it in a large, comprehensive, and well-organized directory.

You can also search the Web by keywords or key phrases. Search engines such as Google.com and teoma.com are both highly rated keyword engines. The problem with most keyword searches—like keyword searches in an online library catalog—is that they deliver a huge number of "hits" or references that are listed together only because each one contains—somewhere—the word or phrase you typed in. An initial search for a single word might turn up thousands of documents, the majority of which are irrelevant to the topic you want. Just as in the case of a keyword search in an online library catalog, you need to narrow your search by using precise terms and "operators." If your search turns up 100,000 seemingly relevant sites, don't just walk away from the computer in frustration. You need to learn how to tailor your requests to control the information you get back. For some starting tips, see the box "Web Searching Tips."

Web Searching Tips

A good place to start is to visit the *Reader*'s Website at **www.prenhall.com/ miller**. There you will find:

- A hot-linked list of the major research engines with comments on their strengths and weaknesses.
- Detailed suggestions for defining your Web queries more precisely.
- Advice on how to evaluate the accuracy of Web information, with some helpful hotlinks.
- Some tips on how searching online databases can help you better define your searches on the Web.
- How to find photographs or images on the Web using a search engine.

Some essentials:

1. As you research, develop a list of synonyms or related subjects. Vital resources might be irretrievable, if you don't enter the right key word or the exact subject heading. A good search generally involves searching multiple terms rather than searching a single word or phrase.
2. Use at least two search engines in every Web search. Remember different engines will retrieve different documents.

3. Read the help screens on each search engine to get the most precise advice on tailoring your search and organizing its results.
4. Learn to use *operators*—words or symbols that signal the relationship between words in a search entry. A large list of common ones can be found at the *Reader's* Website. Here are a few examples from that list that are particularly effective in Web searches:

" "	Place a phrase in quotation marks to find occurrences of that particular phrase in exactly that order rather than occurrences of each individual word in a phrase.
	Disadvantage: In finding names, such a query would not retrieve names where a middle name or initial intervened or where the first and last name were inverted.
+ or *and*	Attach the plus as a prefix to a word or the "and" between words to indicate that the word(s) must appear on a page.
– or *and not*	Attach the minus as a prefix to a word or the "and not" between words to indicate the second word cannot also appear on the page.
	Example:
	+ Frankenstein + Dracula (both must appear on the same page, although not necessarily side by side)
	+ Frankenstein – Dracula (only references to Frankenstein without references to Dracula
* or ?	Most search engines have a symbol for truncation, sometimes called a wild card. Truncation symbols are essential when a word might have alternate spellings (theater or theatre) or alternate endings (theater, theaters, theatrical).

USING YOUR SEARCH FOR SUBJECT HEADINGS AND KEYWORDS TO REVISE YOUR TOPIC

Your search for subject headings and keywords is also a valuable tool in helping you sharpen and define your topic. Typically, despite the most diligent efforts to find a specific topic within a larger subject, you will begin your research strategy with a topic that is really still a subject, too large to research effectively or write about within the limits of a freshman English research paper. If the subject headings you use yield a mountain of published research, obviously you need to focus your topic more precisely.

FINDING MAGAZINES, JOURNALS, AND NEWSPAPERS

The greater amount of information on almost any topic will be found not in books but in magazines and journals. (College and university libraries generally do not use the term *magazine;* they refer to *periodicals* or *serials.* These two terms indicate that the publication appears periodically or that it is an install-ment of a larger series.) You'll find that most of the thousands of magazines sold at your local newsstand—whether issued weekly, biweekly, or monthly—cannot be found in your college or university library. Correspondingly, most of the journals found in your college's periodical room cannot be purchased on a newsstand. They are too specialized; they appeal to too limited an audience. Most, if not all, of your research for college papers should be done in the jour-nals that your library holds.

Increasingly, the way in which libraries provide access to journals is changing. More and more libraries are discontinuing their subscriptions to printed copies of journals and are providing electronic access to journals. The switch has some significant advantages. Many electronic databases include not just a bare bibliographical citation, or a short abstract, but also the full text of the essay. Some journals are exclusively available as electronic documents. In general, computer technologies have significantly increased our access to pe-riodical literature, although that access is often through an electronic copy.

Increased access doesn't necessarily mean, however, that it is always eas-ier to find the information that you need. For example, there is no single in-dex to all periodical literature. (Similarly, many newspapers are not indexed at all). Instead, you have to consult a variety of indexes, depending on the par-ticular subject that you are researching. Indexes to periodicals are found in two forms. Some come as printed volumes, with regular supplements, that are typ-ically kept in the reference section of your library. Others are available in elec-tronic formats and you search for information using a computer.

Printed indexes require that you search your subject through a series of separate volumes devoted to particular years. Once you have the citations you need, you then have to find the appropriate bound volume of the journals in your library. Admittedly, it can be a slow process. Electronic databases, on the other hand, allow you instantly to conduct a search of many sources published over a multiyear period. If the database includes full-text formats, you can retrieve on the computer screen the text of the article (sometimes even with illustrations). Electronic databases make the task of retrieving the articles simpler. Not sur-prisingly, printed indexes are gradually being replaced by electronic ones.

When you start your research, first visit your school's library and explore what types of indexes are available. Where are they located? How can you ac-cess them? Visit the reference section of the library. Are there printed indexes available? Check your library's computer network or Web page. Are the elec-tronic databases listed there? How are they organized? What is available varies from school to school; there are no absolute certainties about what you will find.

For example, at my university, the library maintains an extensive listing of databases that are available for searching. This listing includes some that are still only available in print and some that are only available in electronic form. The listing—which can be found on the library's Website—also indi-cates the date at which the databases started indexing and the subjects and pe-riodicals included in it. The indexes are grouped so that you are first directed to general databases that are good places to start in any search. From here, the indexes are arranged in a series of subject areas: arts and humanities, business and economics, engineering, government, law, and politics, health sciences, life science, physical sciences, and social sciences.

The list of indexes that follows is representative. Your library might have all or only some of these. Different publishers market different databases, so the names might change as well, depending upon the service to which your library subscribes.

- *General Indexes: Good Places to Start.* These four sets of indexes are held by many libraries. Check to see if any or all are available at your school's library.

    Expanded Academic ASAP (Covers 1980–). Provides coverage of nearly every discipline. Also indexes national news magazines and newspapers.

    LexisNexis Academic (Coverage varies depending on the section). Composed of five sections—news, business, legal research, medical, and reference. Also has a detailed "Help" on how to use the different sections.

    The Readers' Guide to Periodical Literature (Covers 1900–). Indexes popular periodicals, most of which can be purchased at newsstands. Available in both printed and electronic forms. Likely to be available in almost every library.

    The New York Times Index (Covers 1851–). Indexes news and articles in the newspaper. Since many libraries subscribe to *The Times* and since it is a national newspaper, it can be a useful source of information. The *Index* and a group of other specialized indexes to *The Times* are available in both print and electronic formats.

- *Specialized Periodical Indexes: The Next Step.* About 200 different indexes to the periodical literature in specialized subject areas are available. Any library is likely to have a number of these; most will not have them all. Visit your library and ask what is available. In some cases, similar coverages are provided by indexes that have different names. The listing below includes those most widely held and used:

    Art Abstracts/Art Index (Covers 1929– for indexing; 1994– for abstracts). Indexes periodicals, yearbooks, and museum bulletins in art areas such as archaeology, architecture, art history, city planning, crafts, films, graphic arts, photography.

    Biography and Genealogy Master Index. The place to begin for biographical information about people living or dead. Indexes biographical dictionaries, encyclopedias, and other reference sources. Widely available in print and also in an electronic format.

    Biological and Agricultural Index (Covers 1983–). Indexes articles on biology, agriculture, and related sciences in scholarly and popular periodicals.

Computer Database (Covers 1996–). Indexes journals devoted to computer science, electronic, telecommunications, and microcomputer applications. Full-text format is available for many journals.

ERIC [U.S. Department of Education Resources Information Center] (Covers 1966–). Indexes, with abstracts, articles in professional journals in educations and other educational documents. Most libraries will also have print guides to ERIC materials as well.

General Business File ASAP (Covers 1980–). Indexes and abstracts periodicals on a broad range of business, management, trade, technology, marketing, and advertising issues. Full-text format is provided for many of the periodicals.

Health Reference Center (Covers 1995–). Indexes medical journals and consumer health magazines as well as health-related articles in general interest magazines. Many essays are available as full-text.

MLA International Bibliography (Covers 1922–) in print format; 1963–) in electronic format). Indexes articles and books on modern languages, literature, linguistics, and folklore.

PsycINFO (Covers 1887–). Indexes and abstracts journals in areas such as psychiatry, nursing, sociology, education, pharmacology, and physiology.

Sociological Abstracts (Covers 1963–). Indexes and abstracts journals in sociology and related areas such as anthropology, economics, demography, political science, and social psychology.

FINDING GOVERNMENT DOCUMENTS

The United States government is the world's largest publisher of statistical information. On many research topics, government documents represent an excellent source of information. Most college libraries house collections of such documents, often located in a special area. Government documents are arranged by a Superintendent of Documents call number system that indicates the agency that released the document. Check with your reference or government documents librarian for help in locating relevant documents for your research. Depending on what indexes your library owns, the following are good starting points for research.

- *Marcive Web DOCS* (Covers 1976–). Indexes U.S. government publications cataloged by the Government Printing Office.
- *LexisNexis Statistical* (Covers 1973–). Indexes and abstracts statistical publications produced by the federal and state governments, by international and intergovernmental organizations, and by private publishers. Includes a searchable version of the information contained within the *Statistical Abstract of the United States*.

- *Monthly Catalog of U.S. Government Publications* (Covers 1895–). Printed catalog held by most libraries.

INTERVIEWING

Depending on your topic, you may find that people—and not just books and articles—will be an important source of information. If you decide to interview someone in the course of your research, you must first choose a person who has special credentials or knowledge about the subject. For example, while working on an essay about campus drinking, you might realize that it would be valuable and interesting to include specific information about the incidence of drinking at your school. To get such data, you could talk to the dean of students or the director of health services. You might also talk to students who acknowledge that they have had problems with alcohol.

Once you have drawn up a list of possible people to interview, you need to plan your interviewing strategy. When you first contact someone to request an interview, always explain who you are, what you want to know, and how you will use the information. Whether you are doing the interview in person, on the telephone, or via e-mail, establish first any crucial guidelines for the interview—students who have problems with binge drinking, for instance, would probably not want to have their real names used in an essay. Once you have agreed on a time for an in-person or telephone interview, be on time. If you are using e-mail for the interview, make sure that your source knows when you will need a reply.

No matter what the circumstances of the interview, always be prepared—do some fairly thorough research about the topic ahead of time. Do not impose on your source by stating, "I've just started to research this problem, and I would like you to tell me everything you know about it." Prepare a list of questions in advance, the more specific the better. However, do not be afraid to ask your source to elaborate on a response. Take notes, but expand those notes as soon as you leave the interview, while the conversation is still fresh in your mind. If you plan to use any direct quotations, make sure that your source is willing to be quoted and that your wording of the quotation is accurate. If possible, check the quotations with your source one final time.

Quotations from interviews should be integrated into your text in the same way as quotations from printed texts—make sure they are essential to your paper, keep them short, use ellipses to indicate omissions, and try to position them at the ends of your sentences. When you are quoting someone who is an expert or an authority, it is best to include a reference to his or her position within your text, setting off that description or job title with commas:

> "We've inherited this notion that if it pops up on a screen and looks good, we think of it as fairly credible," said Paul Gilster, author of *Digital Literacy* (Wiley Computer Publishing, 1997).

USING SOURCES

Most researched writing—and virtually every college research paper—needs to be based on a variety of sources, not just one or two. A single source always represents only one point of view and necessarily contains a limited amount of information. In fact, a wide range of sources are available for any subject—encyclopedias and other reference tools; books; articles in specialized journals, popular magazines, and newspapers; pamphlets; government documents; interviews; research experiments or studies; electronic mail postings or documents from Web home pages. Your instructor might specify both the number and the nature of the sources that you are to use, but even if the choice is up to you, make sure that you have a varied set of sources.

EVALUATING SOURCES

Primarily, you want your sources to be accurate, specific, up-to-date, and unbiased. Not every source will meet those criteria. Just because something is in print or posted on a Website doesn't mean that it is true or accurate—just think of the tabloids displayed at any supermarket checkout. In your search for information, you need to evaluate the reliability and accuracy of each source, because you don't want to base your paper on inaccurate, distorted, or biased information.

Obviously, evaluating sources is less difficult if you are already an expert on the subject you are researching. But how can you evaluate sources when you first start to gather information? The problem is not as formidable as it at first seems, for you regularly evaluate written sources when you try to answer day-to-day questions.

For example, if you are interested in information about the best way to lose weight, which of the following sources would you be most likely to trust?

- An article in the *National Enquirer* ("Lose 10 Pounds This Weekend on the Amazing Prune Diet!")
- An article in a popular magazine ("How to Lose a Pound a Week")
- A Web document urging the value of a particular weight reduction program (for example, electrotherapy treatments, a liquid diet plan, or wraps)
- A newspaper article offering advice on weight loss
- A magazine article published in 1930 dealing with diets
- A book written by medical doctors, dietitians, and fitness experts published in 2005
- The Website maintained by the American College of Sports Medicine

You would probably reject the *National Enquirer* article (not necessarily objective, accurate, or reliable), the Web document urging a particular program (potentially biased and likely to exaggerate the value of that particular treatment), and the article published in 1930 (out-of-date). The articles in the popular magazine and the newspaper might have some value but, given the limitations of space and the interests of their audiences, would probably be too general and too sketchy to be of much use. Presumably, the best source of information would be the new book written by obvious experts or the electronic information provided by a recognizable medical authority.

Evaluating printed sources for a research paper is pretty much a comparable activity. A good source must meet the following tests:

1. **Is the source objective?** You can assess objectivity in several ways. For example, does the language used in the work, and even in its title, seem sensational or biased? Is the work published by an organization that might have a special and hence possibly distorted interest in the subject? Does it contain documented facts? Are there bibliographical references, footnotes, and lists of works consulted? How reliable are the "authorities" quoted? Are their titles or credentials cited? The more scholarly and impartial the source seems, the greater the likelihood that the information it contains can be trusted.

2. **Is the source accurate?** Reputable newspapers and magazines make serious efforts to ensure that what they publish is accurate. Similarly, books published by university presses or by large, well-known publishing houses are probably reliable, and journals published by scholarly or professional organizations and the Websites they maintain very likely contain accurate information. For books, you could check reviews to see critical readers' evaluations. The *Book Review Index* and *Book Review Digest* can be found in your library's reference room.

3. **Is the source current?** In general, the more current the source, the greater the likelihood that new discoveries will be considered. Current information might not be crucial in discussing literary works, but it makes a great deal of difference in many other fields.

4. **Is the source authoritative?** What can you find out about the author's or sponsor's credentials? Are they cited anywhere? What does the nature of the source tell you about the author's expertise?

KNOWING HOW MUCH QUOTATION TO USE

Even though much of the information in a research paper—facts, opinions, statistics, and so forth—will be taken from outside sources, a research paper should never be just a cut-and-paste collection of quotations with a few bridge sentences written by you. The major part of your research paper should be in *your* own words. You can achieve this balance by remembering several points:

- Ask yourself if the quotation is really necessary. If something is common knowledge, you do not need to quote an authority for that information; any information that is widely known or that can be found in general reference works may be included in your own words.

- Keep your quotations as short as possible. Use large chunks of indented direct quotations sparingly, if at all.

- Avoid strings of quotations. You should never pile up quotations in a row. Rather, you should interpret and control the material that you are using and provide transitions for the reader that tie the quotations into your text.

- Learn to paraphrase and summarize instead of giving direct quotations. What is generally important is the idea or the facts that you find in your sources, not the exact words. Paraphrasing means putting the source material into your own words; summarizing goes even further in that you try to condense the quotation into the fewest possible words.

- Use ellipses to shorten quotations. An ellipsis consists of three spaced periods. It is used to indicate that a word, part of a sentence, a whole sentence, or a group of sentences has been omitted from the quotation.

WORKING QUOTATIONS INTO YOUR TEXT

Unless the quotation is only a few words long, try to place it at the end of your sentence. Avoid "sandwich" sentences in which a quotation comes between two parts of your own sentence. If you introduce a several-line quotation into the middle of a sentence, by the end of the sentence the reader will probably have forgotten how your sentence began.

When you place a quotation at the end of a sentence, use a colon or a comma to introduce it. The colon signals that the quotation supports, clarifies, or illustrates the point being made.

> One advice book, *Common Sense for Maid, Wife, and Mother,* stated: "Heated discussion and quarrels, fretfulness and sullen taciturnity while eating, are as unwholesome as they are unchristian."
>
> Joan Jacobs Brumberg, "The Origins of Anorexia Nervosa" (Chapter 7)

If the introductory statement is not an independent clause, always use a comma before the quotation. For example, in the following sentence, the introductory clause ("As Brian Johnson . . . says") is not a complete sentence.

> As Brian Johnson, co-owner of the Dogwater Cafe, a fast-growing restaurant chain in Florida, says, "When I'm interviewing, I'm looking for someone with a lot of energy who wants this job more than anything else."
>
> Charlie Drozdyk, "Into the Loop" (Chapter 6)

If a complete sentence follows a colon, the first word after the colon may or may not be capitalized. The choice is yours, as long as you are consistent. However, if the colon introduces a quotation, the first word following that colon is capitalized.

DOCUMENTING YOUR SOURCES

Research papers require documentation—that is, you need to document or acknowledge all information that you have taken from your sources. The documentation serves two purposes. First, it acknowledges your use of someone else's work. Whenever you take something from a published source—statistics, ideas, or opinions, whether quoted or in your own words—you must indicate where it comes from (thereby acknowledging that it is not your original work). Otherwise, you will be guilty of academic dishonesty. Students who borrow material from sources without acknowledgment—that is, who plagiarize— are subject to some form of academic penalty. Writers and people in the business world who do so can be sued. Documentation is necessary for researchers to maintain their integrity. Documentation also serves a second purpose, however: it gives you greater credibility because your readers know they can consult and evaluate the sources that you used.

Different disciplines use different citation systems. In most introductory writing classes, you will be asked to use either the MLA or the APA form of

---

Plagiarism, Academic Dishonesty, and the Misuse of Sources

The Writing Program Administrators (WPA) Website offers the following definition of *plagiarism:* "In an instructional setting, plagiarism occurs when a writer deliberately uses someone else's language, ideas, or other original (not common knowledge) material without acknowledging its source" (**www.wpacouncil.org**). Every college and university has a policy on plagiarism and academic dishonesty and, if a student is found guilty, assesses some form of penalty, typically ranging from a failure on the paper to suspension from school.

Plagiarism and the misuse of sources comes on a variety of levels, all of which are serious. This section offers a quick overview with some examples. Typically, your college will have guidelines on defining and avoiding plagiarism, and your instructor can explain the types and show you how to avoid each.

1. **Submitting a paper obtained from a paper-writing service or from another student. This is intentional dishonesty, exactly like paying someone to take an examination for you.**

Plagiarism does not have to involve copying a whole paper or even a group of paragraphs. It is not defined by the quantity of material that is taken from a source without acknowledgment. More typical forms of plagiarism (sometimes also called a misuse of sources) include the following abuses or mistakes:

> Source:
> "A number of European studies had raised concerns about the increased risk of benign ear tumors and effects on the brain function of long-term cellphone use. If such risks existed, those most likely to be affected were children, said Stewart, and the younger the child,

'the greater the danger.' Children were more vulnerable because their brains were still developing and their skulls thin, making it easier for radiowaves to penetrate."

Kamala Hayman, "Cellphones 'a Risk to Youngsters'"

2. **Using someone else's words (phrase, sentence, paragraph) without enclosing them in quotation marks and providing appropriate acknowledgment of the source (typically with a parenthetical or endnote citation).**

> Young children should probably not be using cellphones since they pose a possible health hazard. A number of European studies had raised concerns about the increased risk of benign ear tumors and effects on the brain function of long-term cellphone users. Also, the study stated that children were more vulnerable because their brains were still developing and their skulls thinner, making it easier for radiowaves to penetrate (Hayman, 72).

3. **Using someone else's ideas and some of the words while simply substituting synonyms and adding words of your own again without using quotation marks around the material taken from the source and without acknowledgment.**

> Young children should probably not be using cellphones since they pose a possible health hazard. Some European research studies posed questions about the dangers of benign ear tumors and the effect on brain ability of long-term cellephone users. These studies also indicated that children were more susceptible because their brains were still growing and their skulls were thinner, making it easier for radiowaves to damage the brain.

documentation. MLA stands for the Modern Language Association, an organization of teachers of modern foreign languages and of English. A full guide to that system can be found in the *MLA Handbook for Writers of Research Papers* (6th edition, 2003). The APA is the American Psychological Association, and its style guide, *Publication Manual of the American Psychological Association* (5th edition, 2001) is widely used in the social sciences.

Documentation systems are standardized; that is, the systems have a fixed format in which the bibliographical information about the source is given. Even the marks of punctuation are specified. No one, however, expects you to memorize a particular citation system. The style guides are intended to serve as models. You should look at each of your sources, noting its particular features (What type of source was it? How many authors did it have? In what type of book or journal did it appear?). You then look for a similar example in the style guide for the citation system that you are using, and use that sample as a model for your own citation. Citation formats for the types of sources most commonly used in a freshman English research paper are given on the next few pages. But because the range of possible sources on any topic is very large, you might have a source that does not match any of these common examples. For a complete guide, consult the *MLA Handbook* or the APA *Publication Manual*. Both can be found in the reference area of your school's library.

ACKNOWLEDGING SOURCES IN YOUR TEXT

Both the MLA and APA systems acknowledge sources with brief parenthetical citations in the text. The reader can then check the "List of Works Cited" (the MLA title) or "References" (the APA title) at the end of the paper for the full bibliographical reference. In the MLA system, the author's last name is given along with the number of the page on which the information appears. In the APA system, the author's last name is given along with the year the source was published and, for direct quotations, the page number. Notice in the following examples that the punctuation within the parentheses varies between the two systems.

Here is how a quotation from an article, "Immuno-Logistics," written by Gary Stix, that appeared in the June 1994 issue of *Scientific American* would be cited in the two systems:

MLA: The major vaccines—those for diphtheria, pertussis, tetanus, polio, measles, and tuberculosis—cost less to make than they do to distribute: "The United Nations Children's Fund, for example, spends a total of $1.50 on the vaccines. . . . A tenth of what a government then has to disburse for labor, transportation, training and refrigeration to get these vaccines to infants and young children" (Stix 102).

APA: The major vaccines—those for diphtheria, pertussis, tetanus, polio, measles, and tuberculosis—cost less to make than they do to distribute: "The United Nations Children's Fund, for example, spends a total of $1.50 on the vaccines. . . . A tenth of what a government then has to disburse for labor, transportation, training and refrigeration to get these vaccines to infants and young children" (Stix, 1994, p. 102).

Note that in both cases, the parenthetical citation comes before any final punctuation.

If you include the author's name in your sentence, you omit that part of the reference within the parentheses.

MLA: According to Gary Stix, the major vaccines—those for diphtheria, pertussis, tetanus, polio, measles, and tuberculosis—cost less to make than they do to distribute: "The United Nations Children's Fund, for example, spends a total of $1.50 on the vaccines. . . . A tenth of what a government then has to disburse for labor, transportation, training and refrigeration to get these vaccines to infants and young children" (102).

APA: According to Gary Stix (1994), the major vaccines—those for diphtheria, pertussis, tetanus, polio, measles, and tuberculosis— cost less to make than they do to distribute: "The United Nations Children's Fund, for example, spends a total of $1.50 on the vaccines. . . . A tenth of what a government then has to disburse for labor, transportation, training and refrigeration to get these vaccines to infants and young children" (p. 102).

Note that in the APA system the date in such cases goes in parentheses after the author's name in the text.

A quotation of more than four lines (MLA) or more than forty words (APA) should be indented or set off from your text. In such cases, the parenthetical citation comes after the indented quotation. Here is how a quotation from "A Weight That Women Carry" by Sallie Tisdale, which appeared in the March 1993 issue of *Harper's* magazine, would be cited in the two systems:

MLA: Sallie Tisdale points out the links between weight "reduction" and the "smallness" that society presses upon women:

> Small is what feminism strives against, the smallness that women confront everywhere. All of women's spaces are smaller than those of men, often inadequate, without privacy. Furniture designers distinguish between a man's and a woman's chair, because women don't spread out like men. (A sprawling woman means only one thing.) Even our voices are kept down. (53)

APA: Sallie Tisdale (1993) points out the links between weight "reduction" and the "smallness" that society presses upon women:

> Small is what feminism strives against, the smallness that women confront everywhere. All of women's spaces are smaller than those of men, often inadequate, without privacy. Furniture designers distinguish between a man's and a woman's chair, because women don't spread out like men. (A sprawling woman means only one thing.) Even our voices are kept down. (p. 53)

Note in both cases that the parenthetical citation comes after the final period.

If you are quoting material that has been quoted by someone else, cite the secondary source from which you took the material. Do not cite the original if you did not consult it directly. Here is how a quotation from an original source—a nuclear strategist writing in 1967—quoted on page 357 in a 1985 book written by Paul Boyer and titled *By the Bomb's Early Light: American Thought and Culture at the Dawn of the Atomic Age* would be cited.

MLA: Explaining how Americans' views of the atom bomb shifted during the 1950's, Albert Wohlstetter, a nuclear strategist, commented in 1967: "Bright hopes for civilian nuclear energy" proved to be "an emotional counterweight to . . . nuclear destruction" (qtd. in Boyer 357).

APA: Explaining how Americans' views of the atom bomb shifted during the 1950's, Albert Wohlstetter, a nuclear strategist, commented in 1967: "Bright hopes for civilian nuclear energy" proved to be "an emotional counterweight to . . . nuclear destruction" (cited in Boyer, 1985, p. 357).

In certain situations, you may need to include additional or slightly different information in your parenthetical citation. For example, when two or more sources on your list of references are by the same author, your citation will need to make clear to which of these you are referring; in the MLA system you do this by including a brief version of the title along with the author and page number: (Tisdale, "Weight," 53). (Note that this is generally not a problem in the APA system because works by the same author will already be distinguished by date.) For works that do not indicate an author, mention the title fully in your text or include a brief version in the parenthetical citation.

THE "LIST OF WORKS CITED" OR "REFERENCES"

At the end of your essay, on a separate sheet of paper, you should list all of those works that you cited in your paper. In the MLA system, this page is titled "List of Works Cited" (with no quotation marks); in the APA system, it is titled "References" (also no quotation marks). The list should be alphabetized by the authors' last names so that readers can easily find full information about particular sources. Both systems provide essentially the same information, although arranged in a slightly different order.

- *For books:* the author's or authors' names, the title, the place of publication, the publisher's name, and the year of publication
- *For articles:* the author's or authors' names, the title, the name of the journal, the volume number and/or the date of that issue, and the pages on which the article appeared
- *For electronic sources:* the author's or authors' names, the title, date of publication, the URL (Uniform Resource Locator, the electronic address) or other information on how the sources can be accessed, and the date on which you accessed the material. Dates are important in citing electronic sources because the source may change its URL or even disappear after a short period of time.

Note in the following sample entries that in MLA style, the first line of each entry is flush with the left margin and subsequent lines are indented five spaces. Ask your instructor which of the APA's two recommended formats you should use: the first line flush left and subsequent lines indented five spaces (as shown here) or the first line indended five spaces and subsequent lines flush left.

Books

   A book by a single author
MLA:
Boyer, Paul. *By the Bomb's Early Light: American Thought and Culture at the Dawn of the Atomic Age.* New York: Random House, 1985.
APA:
Boyer, P. (1985). *By the bomb's early light: American thought and culture at the dawn of the atomic age.* New York: Random House.

   An anthology
MLA:
Ibieta, Gabriella, ed. *Latin American Writers: Thirty Stories.* New York: St. Martin's, 1993.
APA:
Ibieta, G. (Ed.). (1993). *Latin American writers: Thirty stories.* New York: St. Martin's Press.

   A book by more than one author
MLA:
Burns, Ailsa, and Cath Scott. *Mother-Headed Families and Why They Have Increased.* Hillsdale, NJ: Erlbaum, 1994.
APA:
Burns, A., & Scott, C. (1994). *Mother-headed families and why they have increased.* Hillsdale, NJ: Erlbaum.

   A book with no author's name
MLA:
Native American Directory. San Carlos, AZ: National Native American Co-operative, 1982.
APA:
Native American Directory. (1982). San Carlos, AZ: National Native American Co-operative.

   An article or story in an edited anthology
MLA:
Quartermaine, Peter. "Margaret Atwood's Surfacing: Strange Familiarity." *Margaret Atwood: Writing and Subjectivity.* Ed. Colin Nicholson. New York: St. Martin's, 1994. 119–32.
APA:
Quartermaine, P. (1994). Margaret Atwood's Surfacing: Strange familiarity. In C. Nicholson (Ed.), *Margaret Atwood: Writing and subjectivity* (pp. 119–132). New York: St. Martin's Press.

An article in a reference work

MLA:

"Film Noir." *Oxford Companion to Film*. Ed. Liz-Anne Bawden. New York:
    Oxford UP, 1976. 249.

APA:

Film Noir. (1976). In L.-A. Bawden (Ed.), *Oxford companion to film* (p. 249).
    New York: Oxford University Press.

Articles

An article in a journal that is continuously paginated (that is, issues after the first in a year do not start at page 1)

MLA:

Lenz, Nygel. "'Luxuries' in Prison: The Relationship Between Amenity
    Funding and Public Support." *Crime & Delinquency* 48 (2002):
    499–525.

APA:

Lenz, N. (2002). "Luxuries" in prison: The relationship between amenity
    funding and public support. *Crime & Delinquency, 48,* 499–525.

Note: When each issue of a journal does begin with page 1, also indicate
    the issue number after the volume number. For MLA style, separate
    the two with a period: 9.2. For APA style, use parentheses: *9*(2).

An article in a monthly magazine

MLA:

Milgrom, Mordehai. "Does Dark Matter Really Exist?" *Scientific American*
    Aug. 2002: 42–52.

APA:

Milgrom, M. (2002, August). Does dark matter really exist? *Scientific
    American,* 42–52.

An article in a weekly or biweekly magazine

MLA:

Gladwell, Malcolm. "The Moral-Hazard Myth." *New Yorker* 24 August 2005:
    44–49.

APA:

Gladwell, M. (2005, Aug. 24). The Moral-Hazard Myth. *New Yorker,* 44–49.

An article in a daily newspaper

MLA:

Lacey, Marc. "Engineering Food for Africans." *New York Times* 8 Sep. 2002,
    Sunday National Edition, sec. 1:8.

APA:

Lacey, M. (2002, September 8). Engineering food for Africans. *New York
    Times,* Sunday National Edition, sec. 1, p. 8.

An editorial in a newspaper

MLA:

"Stem Cell End Run?" Editorial. *Washington Post* 24 Aug. 2005, sec. A: 14.

APA:

Stem cell end run? (2005, August 24). [Editorial]. *Washington Post,* sec. A,
      p. 14.

A review

MLA:

Hitchens, Christopher. "The Misfortune of Poetry." Rev. of *Byron: Life
      and Legend,* by Fiona MacCarthy. *Atlantic Monthly* Oct. 2002:
      149–56.

APA:

Hitchens, C. (2002, October). The misfortune of poetry. [Review of *Byron:
      Life and legend,* by Fiona MacCarthy]. *Atlantic Monthly,* 149–56.

Other Sources

An interview

MLA:

Quintana, Alvina. Personal interview. 13 June 2002.

Worthington, Joanne. Telephone interview. 12 Dec. 2002.

Note: APA style does not include personal interviews on the Reference
      list, but rather cites pertinent information parenthetically in the
      text.

A film

MLA:

Silkwood. Writ. Nora Ephron and Alice Arden. Dir. Mike Nichols. With Meryl
      Streep. ABC, 1983.

APA:

Ephron, N. (Writer), & Nichols, M. (Director). (1983). *Silkwood* [Motion
      picture]. Hollywood: ABC.

More than one work by the same author

MLA:

Didion, Joan. *Miami.* New York: Simon & Schuster, 1987.

———. "Why I Write." *New York Times Book Review* 9 Dec. 1976: 22.

APA:

Didion, J. (1976, December 9). Why I write. *New York Times Book Review,* p. 22.

Didion, J. (1987). *Miami.* New York: Simon & Schuster.

Note: MLA style lists multiple works by the same author alphabetically by
      title. APA style lists such works chronologically beginning with the
      earliest.

ELECTRONIC SOURCES

Increasingly the sources that we use for writing research papers are electronic—full-text articles taken from electronic databases available through libraries, journals that exist only in electronic form, documents taken from Websites, e-mail from people whom we have interviewed. Even books today are available—and sometimes only available—in an electronic format. The most recent edition of the *MLA Handbook for Writers of Research Papers* (6th edition, 2003) includes a section on citing electronic publications, as does the *Publication of the American Psychological Association* (5th edition, 2001). What follows here is a guide to citing three of the most common types of electronic sources used in Freshman English research papers. For a fuller guide consult the *MLA Handbook*. For additional help, ask your instructor or the reference department in your library for assistance in locating a published style guide in your area of study.

An e-mail message

MLA:

Miller, George. "On revising." E-mail to Eric Gray. 7 March 2005.

APA:

Miller, G. (2005, March 7). On revising.

The crucial pieces of information in citing an e-mail include the name of the writer, the title of the message (taken from the subject line), the recipient, and the date on which the message was sent.

A full-text article from a periodical available through a library database

MLA:

Seligman, Dan. "The Grade-Inflation Swindle." *Forbes* 18 Mar. 2002: 94.
    Online. Expanded Academic ASAP. 27 Sept. 2002.

APA:

Seligman, D. (2002, March 18). The grade-inflation swindle. *Forbes* p. 94.
    Retrieved September 30, 2002, from Expanded Academic ASAP.

Information from a Website

MLA:

Barndt, Richard. *Fiscal Policy Effects on Grade Inflation.* 27 Sept. 2002
    <http://www.newfoundations.com/Policy/Barndt.html>.

APA:

Barndt, R. (2002, September 27). Fiscal policy effects on grade inflation.
    Retrieved October 3, 2002, from
    http://www.newfoundations.com/Policy/Barndt.html.

ANNOTATED SAMPLE STUDENT RESEARCH PAPER:
MLA DOCUMENTATION STYLE

The following paper was written to fulfill the research component of a freshman composition course and is documented according to guidelines of the Modern Language Association, as required by the instructor. Be sure to consult with your instructor to determine which documentation style you should follow.

 This paper has been annotated to point out important conventions of research writing and documentation. Note that it does not begin with a title page. If, however, your instructor requires an introductory outline, your first page should be a title page (ask about the preferred format), and the next page should be headed with only the title of the essay.

Eric Miller
ENG110
Dr. Miller

① Page numbers in upper right-hand corner with author's last name

③ Title centered

The Cell Phone and Its Hold

on Today's Youth

② Double-spaced throughout

④ "Hook" introduction to catch reader's attention

    Imagine the interior a regular American cafe: the patrons are quietly sipping their double-shot mocha lattés and reading. Then, like a siren from the depths below, a cell phone goes off. Every person in the room pounces to their phone to see if it is his or hers going off. The individual whose phone has rung quietly announces, "It's mine." The patrons all sit back in their seats and return to their lattés. This illustration of the cell phone's dominance in our society, while completely normal now, is a relatively new develop-

⑤ Thesis statement

ment. In recent years, the cell phone has morphed from being an expensive occupational necessity used predominately in businesses to a commonplace personal item used predominately by the youth market.

    The mobile phone, with conceptualization beginning in the late 1940s, was first made available in 1983. Initially very bulky and expensive, "the cell phone," as it is now called, has gradually become more compact and less expensive, fostering its enormous growth. Europe and Asia were, and continue to be, the areas of highest concentration for cell phone use,

Miller 2

namely because of compatible airwave technology across Europe and Asia that yields lower
monthly pay rates (Wikipedia). Indeed, in cer-

⑥ Facts
taken from
on-line en-
cyclopedia
without any
direct
quotation

tain areas of Europe and Asia, up to 100 percent of the population owns a cell phone
(Wikipedia). However, the United States is
quickly catching up, with 64 percent of U.S.
households having at least one phone (Flynn).

⑦ Citation
to an article
from an
electronic
database;
such
sources do
not have
page
numbers

And why not? With many carriers offering free
night, weekend, and long-distance calls, having
a land line seems obsolete and imprudent. Moreover, owning a cell phone can save you money.
But it is not the frugal families of the world who
are making the most significant impact on the
cellular phone market—it's their children.

⑧ Source
acknowl-
edged—no
direct
quotation

　　According to the Yankee Group, a Boston-
based research group, about 55 percent of
Americans ages 13 to 17 own a cell phone; 22
percent of those 9 to 11; and 14 percent of
those 10 to 11 (Melendez). No longer a high-
tech item for executives, the cell phone has become an assumed item of the young American
mindset: "Of course I have a cell phone." The
mere shift in the demographic of cell phone
users also developed with the changing purpose of having a cell phone. While ten years
ago, an executive businessman or woman
might have viewed a cell phone as an extension of the professional workplace (something
as mundane as a fax machine), today teenage

Miller 3

users view a cell phone as an accessory and a stamp of their independence. For many teenagers, the rule was that once you get your driver's license, you get a cell phone—again a measure of practicality and precaution. Also, older teenagers justify the need for a cell phone because as students get into high school, the geographical range of their friends grows, thus requiring a cell phone to keep in contact (Ling 94). However, with the age brackets of cell phone users dipping lower and lower every year, the statistics indicate that the cell phone seems to have been stripped of all its allure of adult responsibility.

⑨ Citation to a book—author's last name and page number

As with most technology, the cell phone's impact is gradually touching the youngest of all age groups. When the cell phone companies realized this trend, they made certain maneuvers to ensure that the ever-exploitable youth market was tapped. First, the companies developed the "family plan" that made the cell phone seem like something Donna Reed might have chosen for her tech-savvy family. Ultimately, however, the family plan, wherein all family members can talk to one another for free, is just a cheaper mode of offering all members of the household a phone. It is easy to assume that brother and sister did not want cell phones just to call mom and dad.

Next, the market turned to teenagers. Sprint's television commercial showing a hoard

Miller 4

of young teenage girls in a hyper-dramatic frenzy over the company's extension of free night-time hours epitomizes the market's approach for the American teenager: the cell phone is life. In an interview to the *Seattle Times,* one cell phone executive is quoted as saying, "If you are a teen, you don't want to have your dad's phone" (Duryee). Coming from a grown man, this remark, which could easily slip from the tongue of a squabbling thirteen-year-old bully, capsulates how the cell phone industry seeks to prey on the insecurity of the American teenager who does not own a cell phone.

⑩ Direct quotation attributed to a source

The latest and most unorthodox development in the cell phone industry is the cell phone designed for children ages 8 to 12, the Firefly. This cheap $120 phone has only five buttons, works on a pay-as-you-go system, and does not allow kids to dial out, providing maximum parental control over their young child's cell phone use (MATP). No longer is the PlaySkool pretend phone satisfactory enough for the entertainment of America's young imaginations; now an actual phone is necessary. Though according to the Yankee Group, only 1 percent of U.S. children under the age of 9 own a cell phone, with the relentless growth of cell phone use, the expectation for a device grows as well (Firefly). It is important to note, however, that just like any childhood toy, the

⑪ Statistic taken from source but no direct quotation

novelty of the bubbly Firefly phone will inevitably wear off, opening the door to a normally functioning, adult phone. If a little girl gets a Firefly phone at age 8, at age 10 she will expect a real phone, replete with camera, text-messaging, and ringtones.

Not only are children beginning to depend upon their cell phones but their parents are, too. One article from *Advertising Age* highlights a San Francisco mother who uses her cell phone as a distraction for her kids. As she says, "Everyone I know is letting their kids play with their phones" (Cuneo). Just as the television often doubles as an inanimate babysitter for kids, the cell phone does as well, with streaming video and games readily available on many state-of-the-art phones. Having made the shift into the realm of entertainment media, Hollywood and the music industry are seizing the opportunity. Verizon Wireless now features videos of "Blue's Clues" and "Sesame Street" (Cuneo), while rapper Snoop Dogg has created his own cell phone with T-Mobile—the $200 Sidekick II. Furthermore, popular teenage programs like "Total Request Live" and "American Idol" allow voting through text messaging as well as music updates and pop ringtones via the partnership of Virgin Mobile and MTV (Duryee).

All the bells and whistles now available for cell phones—different faceplates, ringtones, special holders—have fostered the development of the idea of one's cell phone as an expression of individuality. Functioning as an accessory to one's ensemble, any teenage girl could now get the perfect rhinestone encrusted cell phone to compliment her new belly button piercing. Imagine that: all-American, digital individuality inside a cell phone—for the small fee of, on average for someone 12 to 19, $48.50 plus additional fees (Whipp). That's $582 a year plus the $101 a month that the average American teenager is said to spend, according to Teen Research Unlimited (Duryee). That's $1,794 a year of teenage expenses, not to mention the roughly $100 initially paid for the phone. Forget about health insurance—there's a Cingular bill due tomorrow!

What effect can all of this cell phone use have on our world? What does it say that today's 15-year-old girls are the top consumers of computer chips (Jones)? The effects are many and varied. Today, the young American who does not own a cell phone is undoubtedly an abnormality. "How can you *not* own a cell phone?!" They have to be poor or Amish or simply too weird to not own a cell phone! Beyond the mere expectation of many for everyone else to be similarly glued to their phone, surviving in this world without a cell phone is gradually becoming more difficult. With many college dormitory phones only offering local or intra-campus calls, a cell phone is a necessity if a college student wishes to be able to dial anywhere beyond

the local reach. Furthermore, the phone companies are not only dropping the number of pay-
phones installed but raising their fees.

One more frightening effect of excessive
cell phone use is the fear of severe radiation pen-
etration. Britain's National Radiation Protection
Board issued a statement decrying cell phone
use for those under 14. While they have no "hard
evidence," studies do suggest that with a developing brain and a thinner skull, a child is more
prone to the adverse effects of radiation, which
can include benign ear tumors and brain effects
(Hayman). Even so, the "tween" market, that is,
children ages 8 to 11, continues to be seen as the
next consumer group for cell phone companies,
spurring the likes of Mattel to begin developing
cell phones for this seemingly doomed age
bracket.

On another note, one study done at the
University of Oslo in Norway suggested that the
earlier a teenager has a cell phone (and actively
uses it), the earlier he or she is prone to have sex.
The study found that 60 percent of teenagers
who frequently use cell phones have sex, compared with less than 10 percent of teens who seldom or never use cell phones (Harris). One key
factor in the study was the use of text messaging
as an enabler for sex. A text message initiating
sex? It seems silly but the logic is clear. The cell
phone only serves as a means of initiating interaction—for example, one uses his or her phone to

Miller 8

call their friend to hang out. A flirtatious text message is only the gateway to interaction between these precocious Norwegian teenagers, making the idea of the cell phone functioning as a vehicle for sex not so silly after all. Whether or not the specific numbers in this study hold any validity, it is important to note the far-reaching potential consequences of the ubiquitous cell phone.

The cell phone, then, seems to be a myriad of things. It is a toy for young children; an expression of individuality for teenagers; a conduit of adolescent shenanigans; an item supposedly possessed by every young American; and, above all, an enormously lucrative industry. With all its glamorous appeal, the cell phone is to today's generation what the jalopy was to the teenagers of the 1940s and 50s, what the private phone line was to kids in the 80s and 90s: it is a stamp of independence. To have a cell phone is to imply tacitly that your social life is vivacious enough to merit one, your family is rich enough to pay for one, you have enough technical savvy to use one; and you are simply cool and adultlike enough to possess one (Ling 103). It is the age of technology's teenage liberator. Just as the car could lead to car crashes or the private line lead to late night chats to the dreamboat of the junior class, the cell phone carries with it its own set of hazards, ones that the youth of America seem all too

Miller 9

pleased to risk. And why shouldn't they be?

Mom and dad foot the bill, and in our "live-in-

the-now" American mentality, long-term finan-

cial, health, and social consequences are all too

far removed. What matters now? Getting that

person's cell phone number.

LIST OF WORKS CITED

⑫ List of sources used and cited in the paper

Cuneo, Alice. "Mobile Babysitter." *Advertising*

⑬ Sources listed alpha- betically

    Age 6 June 2005: News, 16. Online. Lexis

    Nexis Academic. 7 July 2005.

⑭ Citations to articles accessed through a library's electronic database includes publication information and how and when it was accessed

Duryee, Tricia. "Cheap but Hip: Cellphones for

    Youth." *The Seattle Times* 28 February

    2005: Business, C3. Online. Lexis Nexis

    Academic. 7 July 2005.

"Firefly Lets Parents Control Kids' Cell Phone."

⑮ Sources without authors are filed by listed letter of the title

    The Chicago Sun-Times. 24 March 2005:

    Financial, 60. Online. Lexis Nexis

    Academic. 7 July 2005.

Flynn, Mary Kathleen. "Who Needs a Wired

    Phone Anymore?" Money & Business;

    Sidebar. *U.S. News & World Report* 7

    March 2005: 40. Online. Lexis Nexis

    Academic. 7 July 2005.

Harris, Misty. "Teen Sex Linked to Cellphones."

    Ottawa Citizen. 8 July 2004: News; C16.

    Online. Lexis Nexis Academic. 7 July

    2005.

Hayman, Kamala. "Cellphones a Risk for

    Youngsters." *The Press.* 13 January 2005:

Miller 10

News; International; 3; News; A. Online.

Lexis Nexis Academic. 7 July 2005.

Jones, Terril Yue. "24/7, Teens Get the

Message." *Los Angeles Times*. 23 June

2005: News; Business Desk; Part A, 1.

Online. Lexis Nexis Academic.

7 July 2005.

Ling, Rich. *The Mobile Connection*. San Franciso:

Morgan Kaufmann Publishers, 2004.

MATP. "Special Phones for Kids." *The

Australian*. 12 April 2005: Features, T08.

Online. Lexis Nexis Academic. 7 July

2005.

Melendez, Michele M. "The Young and the

Wireless." *The Times-Pecayune* [New

Orleans] 23 June 2005: Money, 1. Online.

Lexis Nexis Academic. 7 July 2005.

"*Mobile Phone*." Wikipedia.org. 7 July 2005.

http://en.wikipedia.org/wiki/Cellphone.

Whipp, Ted. "Young Consumers View

Cellphones as Badges of Independence."

The Windsor Star. 2 September 2004: Tech

Weeklz, F2. Online. Lexis Nexis

Academic. 7 July 2005.

GLOSSARY AND READY REFERENCE

This Glossary and Ready Reference has two purposes. First, it is a quick and simple guide to the terms used in discussions of writing. Second, it is a quick reference guide to the most common writing and grammar problems. For a fuller analysis of grammar and the mechanics of writing, refer to a grammar handbook.

Abstract words refer to ideas or generalities—words such as *truth*, *beauty*, and *justice*. The opposite of an abstract word is a concrete one. Margaret Atwood in "The Female Body" (Chapter 8) explores the abstract phrase *female body*, offering a series of more concrete examples or perspectives on the topic.

Allusion is a reference to an actual or fictional person, object, or event. The assumption is that the reference will be understood or recognized by the reader. For that reason, allusions work best when they draw on a shared experience or heritage. Allusions to famous literary works or to historically prominent people or events are likely to have meaning for many readers for an extended period of time. Martin Luther King Jr. in "I Have a Dream" (Chapter 9) alludes to biblical verses, spirituals, and patriotic songs. If an allusion is no longer recognized by an audience, it loses its effectiveness in conjuring up a series of significant associations.

agr **Agreement** problems commonly come in three areas. Subjects and verbs must agree in number (both singular or both plural) and person (first, second, third).

> The paper are due. (paper is)
>
> The requirements on the syllabus is not clear. (requirements are)

Pronouns and their antecedents must agree in person, number, and gender.

> A student must preregister to ensure getting their courses. (his or her courses)

Verb tenses need to agree within a paper—that is, if you are writing in past tense (the action happened yesterday), you should not then switch to present tense (the action is happening).

Analogy is an extended comparison in which an unfamiliar or complex object or event is likened to a familiar or simple one in order to make the former more vivid and more easily understood. Inappropriate or superficially similar analogies should not be used, especially as evidence in an argument. See faulty analogy in the list of logical fallacies in Chapter 9.

Argumentation or persuasion seeks to move a reader, to gain support, to advocate a particular type of action. Traditionally, argumentation appeals to logic and reason, while persuasion appeals to emotion and sometimes prejudice. See the introduction to Chapter 9.

Cause-and-effect analyses explain why something happened or what the consequences are or will be from a particular occurrence. See the introduction to Chapter 7.

Classification is a form of division, but instead of starting with a single subject as a division does, classification starts with many items, then groups or sorts them into categories. See the introduction to Chapter 4.

Cliché is an overused common expression. The term is derived from a French word for a stereotype printing block. Just as many identical copies can be made from such a block, so clichés are typically words and phrases used so frequently that they become stale and ineffective. Everyone uses clichés in speech: "in less than no time" they "spring to mind," but "in the last analysis," a writer ought to "avoid them like the plague," even though they always seem "to hit the nail on the head."An exercise on clichés can be found in the "Focusing on Grammar and Writing" activity with the essay by Prejean (Chapter 9) *cliché d*

Coherence is achieved when all parts of a piece of writing work together as a harmonious whole. If a paper has a well-defined thesis that controls its structure, coherence will follow. In addition, relationships between sentences, paragraphs, and ideas can be made clearer for the reader by using pronoun references, parallel structures (see **Parallelism**), and transitional words and phrases (see **Transitions**). *coh*

Colloquial expressions are informal words and phrases used in conversation but inappropriate for more formal writing situations. Occasionally, professional writers use colloquial expressions to create intentional informality. David Bodanis in "What's in Your Toothpaste?" (Chapter 4) mixes colloquial words (*gob, stuff, goodies, glop*) with formal words (*abrading, gustatory, intrudant*). *coll d*

Comparison involves finding similarities between two or more things, people, or ideas. See the introduction to Chapter 5.

Conclusions should always leave the reader feeling that a paper has come to a logical and inevitable end, that the communication is now complete. As a result, an essay that simply stops, weakly trails off, moves into a previously unexplored area, or raises new or distracting problems lacks that necessary sense of closure. Endings often cause problems because they are written last and hence are often rushed. With proper planning, you can always write an effective and appropriate ending. Keep the following points in mind:

1. An effective conclusion grows out of a paper—it must be logically related to what has been said. It might restate the thesis, summarize the exposition or argument, apply or reflect on the subject under discussion, tell a related story, call for a course of action, or state the significance of the subject.

2. The extent to which a conclusion can repeat or summarize is determined in large part by the length of the paper. A short paper should not have a conclusion that repeats the introduction in slightly varied words. A long essay, however, often needs a conclusion that conveniently summarizes the significant facts or points discussed in the paper.

3. The appropriateness of a particular type of ending is related to a paper's purpose. An argumentative or persuasive essay—one that asks the reader to do or believe something—can always conclude with a statement of the desired action—vote for, do this, do not support. A narrative essay can end at the climactic moment in the action. An expository essay in which points are arranged according to significance can end with the major point.

4. The introduction and conclusion can be used as a related pair to frame the body of an essay. Often in a conclusion you can return to or allude to an idea, an expression, or an illustration used at the beginning of the paper and so enclose the body.

An exercise in writing conclusions can be found in the "Focusing on Grammar and Writing" activity with the essay by Forster (Chapter 7).

Concrete words describe things that exist and can be experienced through the senses. Abstractions are rendered understandable and specific through concrete examples. See **Abstract.**

Connotation and denotation refer to two different types of definition of words. A dictionary definition is denotative—it offers a literal and explicit definition of a word. But words often have more than just literal meanings, for they can carry positive or negative associations or connotations. The denotative definition of wife is "a woman married to a man," but as Judy Brady shows in "I Want a Wife" (Chapter 8), the word *wife* carries a series of connotative associations as well.

Contrast involves finding differences between two or more things, people, or ideas. See the introduction to Chapter 5.

Deduction is the form of argument that starts with a general truth and then moves to a specific application of that truth. See the introduction to Chapter 9.

Definition involves placing a word first in a general class and then adding distinguishing features that set it apart from other members of that class: "A dalmatian is a breed of dog (general class) with a white, short-haired coat and dark spots (distinguishing feature)." Most college writing assignments in definition require extended definitions in which a subject is analyzed with appropriate examples and details. See the introduction to Chapter 8.

Denotation. See **Connotation.**

Dependent clauses are also called subordinate clauses. As the words *dependent* and *subordinate* imply, they are not sentences and cannot stand alone. A clause is made dependent by a subordinating word that comes at the beginning of the clause, reducing it to something that modifies another word in the sentence. Common subordinating words are either conjunctions (such as *although, because, if, since, when, where*) or relative pronouns (such as *which, that, what, who*). Dependent clauses are set off from the rest of the sentence with a comma:

> Although you have a test on Friday , your paper is due on Friday.

> Your paper , which must be at least ten pages in length , is due on Friday.

Description is the re-creation of sense impressions in words. See the introduction to Chapter 3.

Dialect. See **Diction.**

Diction is the choice of words used in speaking or writing. It is frequently divided into four levels: formal, informal, colloquial, and slang. Formal diction is found in traditional academic writing, such as books and scholarly articles; informal diction, generally characterized by words common in conversation contexts, by contractions, and by the use of the first person (I), is found in articles in popular magazines. Bernard R. Berelson's essay "The Value of Children" (Chapter 4) uses formal diction; Judy Brady's "I Want a Wife" (Chapter 8) is informal. See **Colloquial expressions** and **Slang.**   *d*

Two other commonly used labels are also applied to diction:

- **Nonstandard** words or expressions are not normally used by educated speakers. An example would be *ain't.*

- **Dialect** reflects regional or social differences with respect to word choice, grammatical usage, and pronunciation. Dialects are primarily spoken rather than written but are often reproduced or imitated in narratives. William Least Heat Moon in "Nameless, Tennessee" (Chapter 3) captures the dialect of his speakers.

Division breaks a subject into parts. It starts with a single subject and then subdivides that whole into smaller units. See the introduction to Chapter 4.

Documentation involves acknowledging the use of direct quotations and facts taken from someone's else writing. If you do not document your sources, you are guilty of plagiarism (see appendix, "Finding, Using, and Documenting Sources"). Documentation involves enclosing direct quotations within quotation marks ("), providing a parenthetical citation in your text, and listing the source on a list of sources or references at the end of your paper. Detailed advice and helpful models can be found in the appendix. Exercises in   *doc* integrating quotations into your text can be found in the "Focusing on Grammar and Writing" activities for the essays by Drozdyk (Chapter 6), Kelley (Chapter 8), and Porter (Chapter 9).

Essay literally means "attempt," and in writing courses the word is used to refer to brief papers, generally five hundred to one thousand words long, on tightly delimited subjects. Essays can be formal and academic, like Bernard Berelson's "The Value of Children" (Chapter 4), or informal and humorous, like Judy Brady's "I Want a Wife" (Chapter 8).

Example is a specific instance used to illustrate a general idea or statement. Effective writing requires examples to make generalizations clear and vivid to a reader. See the introduction to Chapter 1.

Exposition comes from a Latin word meaning "to expound or explain." It is one of the four modes into which writing is subdivided, the other three being narration, description, and argumentation. Expository writing is information-conveying; its purpose is to inform its reader. This purpose is achieved through a variety of organizational patterns, including division and classification, comparison and contrast, process analysis, cause and effect, and definition.

Figures of speech are deliberate departures from the ordinary and literal meanings of words in order to provide fresh, insightful perspectives or emphasis. Figures of speech are most commonly used in descriptive passages and include the following:

- **Simile** is a comparison of two dissimilar things, introduced by the word *as* or *like*. Maya Angelou in "Sister Monroe" (Chapter 2) describes Sister Monroe as standing before the altar "shaking like a freshly caught trout."

- **Metaphor** is an analogy that directly identifies one thing with another. After Scott Russell Sanders in "The Inheritance of Tools" (Chapter 3) accidentally strikes his thumb with a hammer, he describes the resulting scar using a metaphor: "A white scar in the shape of a crescent moon began to show above the cuticle, and month by month it rose across the pink sky of my thumbnail."

- **Personification** is an attribution of human qualities to an animal, idea, abstraction, or inanimate object. Gordon Grice in "The Black Widow" (How to Revise an Essay) refers to male and female spiders as "lovers."

- **Hyperbole** is a deliberate exaggeration, often done to provide emphasis or humor. Margaret Atwood in comparing the female brain with the male brain (Chapter 8) resorts to hyperbole: "[Female brains are] joined together by a thick cord; neural pathways flow from one to the other, sparkles of electronic information washing to and fro. The male brain, now, that's a different matter. Only a thin connection. Space over here, time over here, music and arithmetic in their sealed compartments. The right brain doesn't know what the left brain is doing."

- **Understatement** is the opposite of hyperbole; it is a deliberate minimizing done to provide emphasis or humor. In William Least Heat Moon's "Nameless, Tennessee" (Chapter 3), Miss Ginny Watts explains how she asked her husband to call the doctor unless he wanted to be "shut of" (rid of) her. Her husband, Thurmond, humorously uses understatement in his reply: "I studied on it."

- **Rhetorical questions** are questions not meant to be answered but instead to provoke thought. Barbara Ehrenreich in "In Defense of Talk Shows" (Chapter 4) poses a series of rhetorical questions toward the end of her essay: "This is class exploitation, pure and simple. What next— 'homeless people so hungry they eat their own scabs'? Or would the next step be to pay people outright to submit to public humiliation? For $50 would you confess to adultery in your wife's presence? For $500 would you reveal your thirteen-year-old's girlish secrets on Ricki Lake?"

- **Paradox** is a seeming contradiction used to catch a reader's attention. An element of truth or rightness often lurks beneath the contradiction. John Hollander in "Mess" (Chapter 8) observes that "to describe a mess is to impose order on it," making it paradoxically not a mess.

An exercise in using figurative language can be found in the "Focusing on Grammar and Writing" activity with the essay by Angelou (Chapter 2).

Fragment (sentence) is anything that is not a complete sentence but is punc- *frag* tuated as if it were. Fragments can be intentionally written—advertisements, for example, make extensive use of fragments ("The latest discovery! Totally redesigned!"). Fragments are common in written dialogue. In most college writing situations, though, make sure that you write only complete sentences. Fragments can be either long or short—their length has nothing to do with whether or not they are fragments. Since every sentence must contain a subject and a verb, fragments are lacking one or the other, typically the verb. The presence of a word at the beginning of the fragment can subordinate a clause, changing what would have been a sentence into a fragment.

> Rain fell. (subject + verb) = sentence
>
> Despite the high winds and rains. (no verb) = fragment
>
> Although it was windy and rainy ("although" subordinates what follows) = fragment

Most fragments occur when a long subordinate clause comes at the end of a sentence and it is then separated and punctuated as if it were a sentence:

> Our class decided to walk to the library to see the video. Although it was very windy and raining heavily. ("although" clause is separated from the sentence to which it belongs).

Exercises in recognizing fragments can be found in the "Focusing on Grammar and Writing" activities with the essays by Heywood (Chapter 1), Haines (Chapter 2), Davis (Chapter 3), Hollander (Chapter 8), and Atwood (Chapter 8).

Generalizations are assertions or conclusions based on some specific instances. The value of a generalization is determined by the quality and quantity of examples on which it is based. Bob Greene in "Cut" (Chapter 1) formulates a generalization—being cut from an athletic team makes men super-achievers later in life—on the basis of five examples. For such a generalization to have validity, however, a proper statistical sample would be essential.

Hyperbole. See **Figures of speech.**

Illustration is providing specific examples for general words or ideas. A writer illustrates by using examples.

Independent clauses are complete sentences. As the word independent suggests, they are capable of standing alone.

Induction is the form of argument that begins with specific evidence and then moves to a generalized conclusion that accounts for the evidence. See the introduction to Chapter 9.

Introductions need to do two essential things: first, catch or arouse a reader's interest, and second, state the thesis of the paper. In achieving both objectives, an introduction can occupy a single paragraph or several. The length of an introduction should always be proportional to the length of the essay— short papers should not have long introductions. Because an introduction lays out what is to follow, it is always easier to write after a draft of the body of the paper has been completed. When writing an introduction, keep the following strategies in mind:

1. Look for an interesting aspect of the subject that might arouse the reader's curiosity. It could be a quotation, an unusual statistic, a narrative, or a provocative question or statement. It should be something that will make the reader want to continue reading, and it should be appropriate to the subject at hand.

2. Provide a clear statement of purpose and thesis, explaining what you are writing about and why.

3. Remember that an introduction establishes a tone or point of view for what follows, so be consistent—an informal personal essay can have a casual, anecdotal beginning, but a serious academic essay needs a serious, formal introduction.

4. Suggest to the reader the structure of the essay that follows. Knowing what to expect makes it easier for the audience to read actively.

An exercise in writing introductions can be found in the "Focusing on Grammar and Writing" activities with the essay by Lee (Chapter 9).

Irony occurs when a writer says one thing but means another. E. M. Forster ends "My Wood" (Chapter 7) ironically by imagining a time when he will "wall in and fence out until I really taste the sweets of property"—which is actually the opposite of the point he is making.

Metaphor. See **Figures of speech.**

Misplaced and dangling modifiers occur when a modifying or limiting element *dang mod* in a sentence cannot be clearly connected with what it modifies. A misplaced modifier creates a sentence that is awkward and confusing for the reader:

> The instructor returned the papers to the students with grades. (Did only the students who had grades receive their papers?)
>
> The instructor returned the graded papers to the students.

A dangling modifier has no element to modify, so it "dangles" unattached to the sentence.

> Returning the papers, the students were relieved.
>
> After the instructor returned the papers, the students were relieved.

Narration involves telling a story, and all stories—whether they are personal-experience essays, imaginative fiction, or historical narratives—have the same essential ingredients: a series of events arranged in an order and told by a narrator for some particular purpose. See the introduction to Chapter 2.

Nonstandard diction. See **Diction.**

Objective writing takes an impersonal, factual approach to a particular subject. Bernard Berelson's "The Value of Children" (Chapter 4) is primarily objective in its approach. Writing frequently blends the objective and subjective together. See **Subjective.**

Paradox. See **Figures of speech.**

Paragraph is both a noun and a verb. A paragraph (noun) is a block of text set ¶ off by white space and indented. To paragraph (verb) means to construct those blocks. The length of paragraphs varies considerably in printed texts. Newspaper articles, because they appear in narrow columns, often put each sentence in a separate paragraph. Articles in magazines or books generally have longer paragraphs. Paragraphing, then, does depend on the format of the printed page. Paragraphing can also achieve emphasis by setting something apart. In a composition class where papers are word-processed on full sheets of paper, you should avoid extremes—no one-page or two-page long paragraphs (allow your reader to rest!), no large clumps of tiny paragraphs (unless you are writing dialogue!).

Even though paragraphing can vary because of print format and emphasis, most paragraphs in college essays are constructed using a model such as

> Topic sentence (which states the controlling idea in what follows)
>
> Body sentences (which provide the details that support that idea)
>
> Concluding or transition sentence (which summarizes, extends, or provides a transition into the next paragraph).

Typical problems with paragraphs include

> Not enough paragraphs—not marking for the reader the structure of the paper, making it difficult to read
>
> Too many paragraphs—paragraphs not developed with enough details or skipping quickly from one idea to another, creating a choppy disconnected effect
>
> Paragraphs not logically organized—ideas out of sequence, lacking topic sentences

Exercises in paragraphing can be found in the "Focusing on Grammar and Writing" activities with the essays by Williams (Chapter 3), King (Chapter 9), Vanderslice (Chapter 9), and Singer (Chapter 10).

// **Parallelism** places words, phrases, clauses, sentences, or even paragraphs equal of importance in equivalent grammatical form. The similar forms make it easier for the reader to see the relationships that exist among the parts; they add force to the expression. Martin Luther King Jr.'s "I Have a Dream" speech (Chapter 9) exhibits each level of parallelism: words ("When all God's children, black and white men, Jews and Gentiles, Protestants and Catholics"), phrases ("With this faith, we will be able to work together, to pray together, to struggle together, to go to jail together, to stand up for freedom together"), clauses ("Go back to Mississippi, go back to Alabama, go back to South Carolina, go back to Georgia, go back to Louisiana, go back to the slums and ghettos of our northern cities"), sentences (the "one hundred years later" pattern in paragraph 2), and paragraphs (the "I have a dream" pattern in paragraphs 11–18). Exercises in paragraphing can be found in the "Focusing on Grammar and Writing" activities with the essays by Pipher (Chapter 5), Stein (Chapter 8), and Swift (Chapter 10).

Person is a grammatical term used to refer to a speaker, the individual being addressed, or an individual being referred to. English has three persons: first (*I* or *we*), second (*you*), and third (*he, she, it,* or *they*).

Personification. See **Figures of speech.**

Persuasion. See **Argumentation.**

Point of view is the perspective the writer adopts toward a subject. In narratives, point of view is either first person (I) or third person (he, she, it). First-person narration implies a subjective approach to a subject; third-person narration promotes an objective approach. Point of view can be limited (revealing only what the narrator knows) or omniscient (revealing what anyone else in the narrative thinks or feels). Sometimes the phrase "point of view" is used simply to describe the writer's attitude toward the subject.

Premise in logic is a proposition—a statement of a truth—that is used to support or help support a conclusion. For an illustration, see Chapter 9.

Process analysis takes one of two forms: either a set of directions intended to allow a reader to duplicate a particular action or a description intended to tell a reader how something happens. See the introduction to Chapter 6.

Pronouns are words used in place of nouns. For a full discussion of the eight *prn* types of pronouns, consult a grammar handbook. In writing, two types of problems are extremely common. First, always use *who* when you are referring to people—never *that* or *which*. Second, pronouns must agree with their antecedent (that is, the word to which it refers) in person, number, and gender. Typical pronoun problems:

> A student <u>that</u> was late missed the assignment. (who)
>
> <u>A student</u> must hand in <u>their</u> paper on Friday. (student is singular; *their* is plural)

Proofreading is the systematic checking of a piece of writing for grammatical and mechanical errors. Proofreading is quite different from revision; see **Revision.**

Punctuation marks are a set of standardized marks used in writing to separate *pn* sentences or parts of sentences or to make the meaning of the sentence clear. Punctuation marks exist only in writing; they have no oral equivalent. Punctuation marks are used to signal the boundaries or parts of a sentence; they reveal the sentence's meaning. It is very difficult to read a passage in which the punctuation marks have been removed. The choice of when to use what mark is determined by how the sentence is structured. The most common problems with punctuation in writing come in a limited range of situations:

a. **Periods (.)** come at the end of complete sentences. Before you use a period at the end of what you think is a sentence, make sure that it is a **sentence** and not a **sentence fragment.**

b. **Colons (:)** are used in only two situations in writing: first, to introduce a quotation, a list, or a series (just as it is used in this sentence); second, to signal a link between two parts of a sentence. In this second instance, a colon works as an equals *(=)* sign, signaling that what comes after the colon is an example or restatement of what comes in the first half of the sentence.

> Jose had one goal this semester: to write an "A" paper.

c. **Semicolons (;)** are "half" colons and are used primarily in two writing constructions. First, they are used to link together two sentences either without a connecting word or with a certain group of connecting words:

> Your research paper is due on Friday; it cannot be late.
>
> Your research paper is due on Friday; moreover, it cannot be late.

Second, a semicolon is used to separate items (phrases, clauses) in a series that already has internal commas. The semicolon helps the reader to see what belongs with what.

An effective research paper shows several characteristics: the use of accurate, appropriate, and varied source materials; careful and accurate documentation of those sources; and clear, effective prose.

d. **Commas (,)** have the widest range of uses of all of the punctuation marks. Commas are used to link, to separate, and to enclose. They link when they are used with a coordinating conjunction (such as *and, but, for*) to link two sentences together.

> Your research paper is due on Friday, and it cannot be late.

They separate items in a series (Bring a bluebook, a pencil, and a dictionary to class), or two or more adjectives that could be linked with *and* (Revising can be a slow, painful process), or introductory elements at the start of a sentence

> If you are uncertain of the spelling of a word, always look it up.
> Finally, do not forget to bring your dictionaries to class.

They enclose elements that are interjected or inserted into a sentence—things like nonessential phrases and clauses (the meaning of the sentence is not changed if the interrupter is omitted).

> All students who miss three or more classes will fail the course. (The words "who miss three or more classes" cannot be omitted from the sentence without changing its meaning)
> Mr. Rodriguez, the instructor of the course, has a very strict attendance policy. (the interrupter could be omitted without changing the meaning, and so it is set off with commas.)
> Your exam, unfortunately, falls just before spring break.

poss   e. **Apostrophes (')** are used in three situations in writing: first, to mark the omission of letters in a contraction (can't = cannot); second, to signal ownership or possession ("It was Tanya's paper"); and third, to mark plurals of letters and numbers (Tanya got all A's on her essays).

f. **Dashes (—)** are two unspaced hyphens with no spaces between the dash and the letter that precedes and follows it and no space between the two hyphens. Dashes are used either alone to add something to the end of a sentence or in pairs to surround or enclose something that is interjected into a sentence.

> The paper is due on Friday—don't forget!
> The paper—and it must be typed—is due on Friday.

g. **Parentheses ( )** always occur in pairs. Like commas and dashes, they are used to insert something into a sentence. Typically, parentheses minimize the importance of the insertion, while dashes emphasize it.

> The paper (it must be at least ten pages long) is due Friday.
> The paper—it must be at least ten pages long—is due Friday.

h. **Quotation marks ("")** are used to enclose dialogue—words that characters or people speak—and to enclose direct quotations taken from print sources.

Exercises in using punctuation can be found in the following "Focusing on Grammar and Writing" activities: parentheses—Cofer (Chapter 4), Ephron (Chapter 6), Kohn (Chapter 9); colons—Cofer (Chapter 2), Senna (Chapter 5), Eighner (Chapter 6), Gelernter (Chapter 9); semicolons—Senna (Chapter 5), Eighner (Chapter 6); commas—Danticat (Chapter 1), Senna (Chapter 5), Santiago (Chapter 5), Ephron (Chapter 6); dashes—Orwell (Chapter 1), Hopkins (Chapter 2), Sanders (Chapter 3), Senna (Chapter 5), Kahn (Chapter 6), Ephron (Chapter 6), Gladwell (Chapter 7); quotation marks—Least Heat Moon (Chapter 3), Rodriguez (Chapter 9).

Purpose involves intent, the reason why a writer writes. Three purposes are fundamental: to entertain, to inform, and to persuade. These are not necessarily separate or discrete; they can be combined. An effective piece of writing has a well-defined purpose.

Revision means "to see again." Revision involves the careful, active scrutiny of every aspect of a paper—subject, audience, thesis, paragraph structures, sentence constructions, and word choice. Revising is more complicated and more wide-ranging than proofreading; see **Proofreading.**

Rhetorical questions. See **Figures of speech.**

Run-on sentences are also called "fused" sentences and occur when two independent clauses (sentences) are fused or run together because a mark of punctuation or a connecting word has been omitted. The independent clauses in such a sentence (compound) must be separated. *run-on f sent*

> Your paper is due Friday it cannot be late (run-on sentence)
>
> Your paper is due Friday, and it cannot be late.
>
> Your paper is due Friday; it cannot be late.

Satire pokes fun at human behavior or institutions in an attempt to correct them. Judy Brady in "I Want a Wife" (Chapter 8) satirizes the stereotypical male demands of a wife, implying that marriage should be a more understanding partnership.

Sentence variety is achieved by mixing up structural sentence types (simple, compound, complex, compound-complex). No essay should contain only one sentence type. Exercises in sentence construction and variety can be found in the "Focusing on Grammar and Writing" activities with the essays by Greene (Chapter 1), Momaday (Chapter 3), Bodanis (Chapter 4), Daum (Chapter 5), Coles (Chapter 6), Brady (Chapter 8), Tan (Chapter 8), and White (Chapter 10). Exercises on simple sentences can be found in "Focusing on Grammar and Writing" activities with the essays by Zinsser (Chapter 5) and Didion (Chapter 10). *sent vary*

Sentences are traditionally defined in English as groups of words that express a complete thought, beginning with a capital letter and ending with a final mark of punctuation such as a period, question mark, or exclamation mark. Grammatically, a sentence must contain a subject and a predicate (verb). Sentences are not defined by length; anything that is punctuated as if it were a sentence but does not express a complete thought and does not have both a subject and predicate is called a **sentence fragment.** Sentences can also be called **independent clauses** or main clauses. Sentences are classified in a variety of ways, but the traditional classification by structure is most helpful to the writer.

> **Simple** sentences contain one independent clause, that is, one subject and one predicate. A simple sentence is a stripped-down sentence that contains no other clauses (either independent or dependent). Typically, simple sentences are short and easy to read and understand. They are not necessarily only a few words in length since they can contain modifying words such as adjectives and adverbs. The danger of using too many simple sentences is that it makes your paper sound like something written for grade-school students.
>
> > Your paper is due on Friday. (complete thought, one subject, one predicate)
> >
> > Your research paper with photocopies of your sources is due on Friday. (complete thought, one subject, one predicate, modifying words and prepositional phrases)
>
> **Compound** sentences contain two independent clauses (sentences) linked by a coordinating word and a mark of punctuation (typically a comma or semicolon).
>
> > Your paper is due on Friday, and it cannot be late.
> >
> > Your paper is due on Friday; it cannot be late.
>
> **Complex** sentences contain one independent clause and one or more dependent clauses (not sentences on their own).
>
> > Although we also have a test that day, your paper is due on Friday. ("Although . . . day" is not a sentence; it is a dependent clause)
> >
> > Although we also have a test that day, your paper, which must be at least ten pages in length, is due on Friday. ("which . . . length" is another dependent clause)
>
> **Compound-complex** sentences contain two independent clauses and at least one dependent clause
>
> > Although we also have a test that day, your paper is due on Friday, and it cannot be late. (dependent, independent, independent)

Simile. See **Figures of speech.**

Slang is common, casual, conversational language that is inappropriate in for- *d*
mal speaking or writing. Slang often serves to define social groups by virtue *ww*
of being a private, shared language not understood by outsiders. Slang changes
constantly and is therefore always dated. For that reason alone, it is wise to
avoid using slang in serious writing.

Spelling errors are common—every writer misspells words occasionally. Ad- *sp*
vice on being aware of your tendency to misspell and on coping with the *ww*
problem can be found in "How to Revise an Essay." Many misspelled words
are simply typographical errors that can be caught by carefully proofreading
your paper. Always allow time to do so; always use a dictionary if you are unsure of the spelling. Automatic spell-checkers on word-processing programs
will eliminate many misspellings, but they will not signal when you have
written the wrong word in the context. For example, be aware of the differences among these commonly mis-used words:

1. affect—verb, "to influence"
   effect—typically a noun meaning the "result"; as a verb, "to bring about"
2. than—signals comparison, as in "faster than"
   then—signals time sequence, as in "and then the race began"
3. its—the possessive form (think of *her* and *his*, which do not have
   apostrophes)
   it's—the contraction for "it is"
4. there—a pronoun that "points out," as in "there are the books"
   their—a plural possessive pronoun signaling belonging to, as in "their
   apartment"
   they're—the contraction for "they are"

Frequently, words do not mean what we think that they do. Do not use a
word in a paper unless you are confident of its meaning. If you are unsure,
always check a dictionary first.

Style is the arrangement of words that a writer uses to express meaning. The
study of an author's style would include an examination of diction or word
choice, figures of speech, sentence constructions, and paragraph divisions.

Subject is what a piece of writing is about. See also **Thesis.** Linda Lee's thesis
in "The Case Against College" (Chapter 9) is "not everyone needs a higher
education."

Subjective writing expresses an author's feelings or opinions about a particular subject. Editorials or columns in newspapers and personal essays tend to
rely on subjective judgments. Writing frequently blends the subjective and
the objective; see **Objective.**

Syllogism is a three-step deductive argument involving a major premise, a
minor premise, and a conclusion. For an illustration, see Chapter 9.

Thesis is a particular idea or assertion about a subject. Effective writing will always have an explicit or implicit statement of thesis; it is the central and controlling idea, the thread that holds the essay together. Frequently, a thesis is stated in a thesis or topic sentence. See **Subject.** An exercise in writing and recognizing thesis statements can be found in the "Focusing on Grammar and Writing" activities with the essay by Copeland (Chapter 4) and Woolf (Chapter 10).

Titles are essential to every paper and "Essay 1" or "Paper 1" or "Cause and Effect Essay" do not qualify as titles. No company would call its product "Automobile" or "Breakfast Cereal." A title creates reader interest; it indicates what will be found in the essay. Consider some of the strategies that writers use for their essays in this *Reader:*

1. Place or personal names (typically in narrative or descriptive essays): for example, "Nameless, Tennessee," "Marina," "The Way to Rainy Mountain"
2. The promise of practical or informational value: "What's in Your Toothpaste?" "The Origins of Anorexia Nervosa," "Why We Travel"
3. An indication of subject and approach (especially in argument essays): "In Defense of Talk Shows," "The Case Against College"
4. A play on words relevant to the subject of the essay: "Virtual Love" (about Internet dating) and "Mother Tongue" (about how the writer communicates with her mother in English)
5. A provocative word or phrase used in the essay: "Salvation," "The Village Watchman," "The Inheritance of Tools," " I Want a Wife"

Writers often use a **colon** in a title, separating a title from what is called a subtitle. A colon (:) is like an equals (=) sign. It signals that what is on one side is roughly equivalent to what is one the other. Typically, the title (to the left of the colon) is a catchy or a general phrase; the subtitle (to the right of the colon) is a more specific statement of what is to be found in the essay; for example, "The Value of Children: A Taxonomical Essay," "Revision and Life: 'Take It from the Top—Again'," "Into the Loop: How to Get the Job You Want after Graduation."

Tone refers to a writer's or speaker's attitude toward both subject and audience. Tone reflects human emotions and so can be characterized or described in a wide variety of ways, including serious, sincere, concerned, humorous, sympathetic, ironic, indignant, and sarcastic.

Topic sentence is a single sentence in a paragraph that contains a statement of subject or thesis. The topic sentence is to the paragraph what the thesis statement is to an essay—the thread that holds the whole together, a device to provide clarity and unity. Because paragraphs have various purposes, not every paragraph will have a topic sentence. The topic sentence is often the first or last sentence in the paragraph. Exercises in writing and recognizing topic sentences can be found in the "Focusing on Grammar and Writing" activities with the essays by Epstein (Chapter 4), Britt (Chapter 5), Brooks (Chapter 6), and Chambers (Chapter 7).

Transitions are links or connections made between sentences, paragraphs, or groups of paragraphs. By using transitions, a writer achieves coherence and unity. Transitional devices include the following:

1. Repeated words, phrases, or clauses
2. Transitional sentences or paragraphs that act as bridges from one section or idea to the next
3. Transition-making words and phrases

Transitional words and phrases can express relationships of various types:

- Addition: again, next, furthermore, last
- Time: soon, after, then, later, meanwhile
- Comparison: but, still, nonetheless, on the other hand
- Example: for instance, for example
- Conclusion: in conclusion, finally, as a result
- Concession: granted, of course

An exercise in using transitions can be found in the "Focusing on Grammar and Writing" activity with the essay by Martin (Chapter 7).

Typographical devices are used to indicate subdivisions, sections, or steps within an essay and to call the reader's attention to a particular section or even word. As the word *typographical* implies, these are devices that have to do with typesetting (or word processing) and include such things as **bold face**, *italics*, <u>underlining</u>, subheadings, numbers, letters, and bullets (•, +) used to mark off sections of a text, as well as extra white space to separate blocks of paragraphs or sentences. Newspapers, magazines, Web pages, and business documents all make extensive use of typographical devices. An exercise in using typographical devices can be found in the "Focusing on Grammar and Writing" activity with the essay by Berelson (Chapter 4).

Understatement. See **Figures of speech.**

Unity is a oneness in which all of the individual parts of a piece of writing work together to form a cohesive and complete whole. It is best achieved by having a clearly stated purpose and thesis against which every sentence and paragraph can be tested for relevance.

Wrong word is simply a word that is not used appropriately. Typically, the *ww* writer has chosen a word that does not mean what the writer thinks it does. Sometimes it is used to refer to a word that is too formal or too learned for the context and audience. Other inappropriate words include **cliches, slang,** and **colloquial expressions.** Exercises in word choice can be found in the "Focusing on Grammar and Writing" activities with the essays by Quindlen (Chapter 1), Ehrenreich (Chapter 4), and Brumberg (Chapter 7).

CREDITS

David Gelernter, "What Do Murderers Deserve?" Reprinted from Commentary, April 1998, by permission. All rights reserved.

Porter, Kathleen. "The Value of a College Degree." ERIC Digest. ERIC identifier ED470038. (US Dept. of Education)

Linda Lee, "The Case Against College." Family Circle, June 6, 2001, p. 172. Reprinted by permission of the author.

Martin Luther King, Jr., "I Have A Dream." Reprinted by arrangement with the Estate of Martin Luther King, Jr. c/o Writers House as agent for the proprietor New York NY. Copyright © 1963 Dr. Martin Luther King, Jr.; copyright renewed 1991 Coretta Scott King.

Richard Rodriguez, "None of this is Fair," from Politicks and Other Human Interests. Copyright © 1977 by Richard Rodriguez. Reprinted by permission of Georges Borchardt, Inc. for the author.

Vanderslice, Ronna. "When I Was Young, an A was an A," Reprinted from Phi Kappa Forum, Volume 84, Number 4 (Fall 2004). Copyright by Ronna Vanderslice. By permission of the publishers.

Prejean, Sister Helen. "Memories of a Dead Man Walking." From Dead Man Walking. Copyright © 1994 Vintage Books. Reprinted by permission of Random House, Inc.

"Dulce et Decorum Est," by Wilfred Owen, from The Collected Poems of Wilfred Owen, copyright © 1963 by Chatto & Windus, Ltd. Reprinted by permission of New Directions Publishing Corporation.

White, E.B. "Once More to the Lake," from "One Man's Meat," text copyright © 1941 by E.B. White. Copyright renewed. Reprinted by permission of Tilbury House Publishers, Gardiner, ME.

"On Keeping a Notebook," from Slouching Towards Bethlehem by Joan Didion. Copyright © 1966, 1968, renewed 1996 by Joan Didion. Reprinted by permission of Farrar, Straus & Giroux, LLC.

Swift, Jonathon. "A Modest Proposal."

Peter Singer, "The Singer Solution to World Poverty," New York Times Magazine, September 5, 1999. Copyright © 1999 by The New York Times Co. Reprinted by permission.

Woolf, Virginia. "The Death of a Moth," from The Death of the Moth and Other Essays. Copyright © 1942 by Harcourt, Inc. Renewed 1970 by Marjorie T. Parsons, Executrix. Reprinted by permission of the publisher.

Woolf, Virginia. "The Death of a Moth," from The Death of the Moth and Other Essays. Copyright © 1942 by Harcourt, Inc. Renewed 1970 by Marjorie T. Parsons, Executrix. Reprinted by permission of the publisher.

PHOTOS

Page 76: a) Laima Druskis; b) Stockbyte; c) Eddie Lawrence, Dorling Kindersley Media Library; d) Laimute Druskis.

Page 114: © The New Yorker Collection 1996 Charles Barsotti from cartoonbank.com. All rights reserved.

Page 125: a) Leanne Temme, Photo library.Com; b) Vincent Besnault, Getty Images, Inc. – Taxi

Page 162: Nebraska State Historical Society

Page 175: Library of Congress

Page 225: Garry Gay, Creative Eye/MIRA.com

Page 268: Andy Singer,

Page 284: a) Joseph Sohm; Visions of America, Corbis/Bettmann; b) Sean Adair, Corbis/Reuters America LLC

Page 322: CartoonStock Ltd. CSL

Page 332: Custom Medical Stock Photo, Inc.

Page 390: Ann Marie Rousseau, The Image Works

Page 429: CartoonStock Ltd. CSL

Page 440: AP Wide World Photos

Page 475: Getty Images Inc. - Hulton Archive Photos

Page 490: Library of Congress

INDEX